A NEXTEXT ANTHOLOGY

American SHORT STORIES

nextext

Cover: *Untitled (First Avenue)* (about 1945), Fairfield Porter. Oil on canvas, 32" x 26 1/4". The Parrish Art Museum, Southhampton, New York. Gift of the Estate of Fairfield Porter (1980.10.16).

Printed in China

ISBN-13: 978-0-618-10725-4
ISBN-10: 0-618-10725-8

8 9 NPC 09 08 07

American Short Stories

PART ONE: ROMANTICISM AND REALISM

PART FOUR: NEW VOICES AND IDENTITIES

Throughout the anthology, vocabulary words appear in boldface type and are footnoted. Specialized or technical words and phrases appear in lightface type and are footnoted.

Part One

Romanticism and Realism

In the 1800s, American writers created a new national literature under the influence of two very different cultural movements—romanticism and realism. From the 1820s to the 1850s, romanticism expressed an optimistic belief in an unlimited human potential, but was also haunted by fear of death and the dark side of human nature. Arriving after the Civil War, realism in America first took the form of local color, the attempt to capture in fiction the authentic speech, customs, and setting of a particular region.

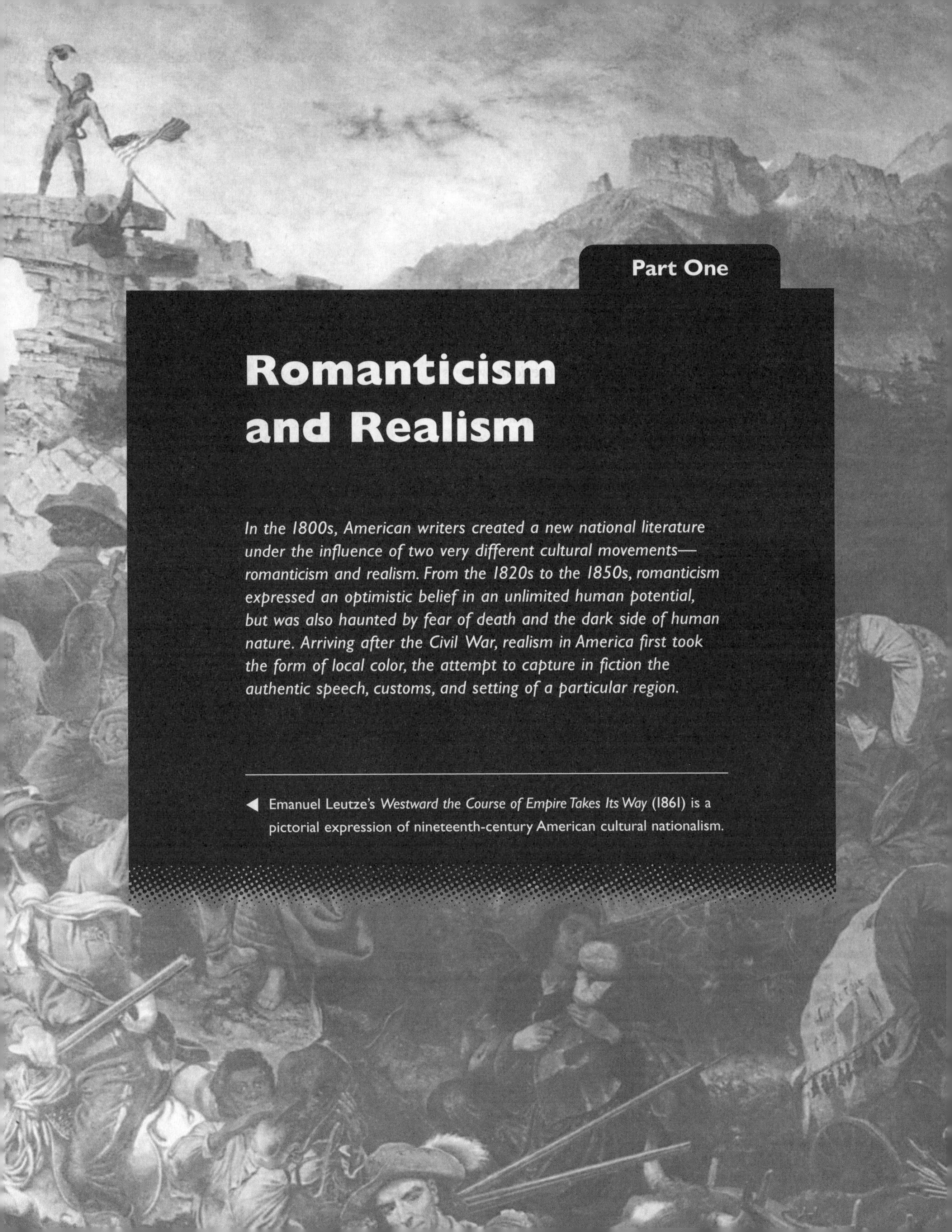

◀ Emanuel Leutze's *Westward the Course of Empire Takes Its Way* (1861) is a pictorial expression of nineteenth-century American cultural nationalism.

1820–1900

Romanticism and Realism

Romanticism *In the 1820s, the work of American writers began to reflect the influence of the European romantic movement. Among the aspects of romanticism that these writers exhibited were an interest in the past, a fascination with death and abnormal states of mind, and a sympathy for outsiders, individuals isolated from society.*

▲ Washington Irving adapted European folklore in "Rip Van Winkle" to create a romantic legendary past for America. The American actor Joseph Jefferson (shown here) delighted audiences for many years in a dramatized version of Irving's story.

◀ Like Irving, Nathaniel Hawthorne explored the past in his work, but he transformed his romantic legends into dark, brooding morality tales.

- **1820** Missouri Compromise passed; Irving's *Sketch Book* published.
- Cooper publishes first Leatherstocking novel.
- **1825** Erie Canal completed.

- American Temperance Society established.
- Jackson elected president.
- **1830**
- Nat Turner's rebellion.
- Morse invents the telegraph.
- American Anti-Slavery Society founded.
- American missionaries settle in Oregon country.
- **1835**
- Texas becomes a republic.

- Hawthorne's *Twice-Told Tales* published.

▲ Edgar Allan Poe also reflected the darker side of romanticism in his fascination with crime, obsession, disease, and death, as in his detective story "The Mystery of Marie Rogêt."

The romantic movement's sympathy with the outsider is evident in Herman Melville's creation of such characters as Bartleby the Scrivener, whose final hours take place in New York City's prison, "The Tombs" (shown here). ▶

1840

Poe's *Tales of the Grotesque and Arabesque* published.

1845

Mexican-American War fought.

Woman's Rights Convention held at Seneca Falls.

Gold rush begins in California.

1850

Compromise of 1850 passed; *Harper's Monthly Magazine* established.

Uncle Tom's Cabin published.

1855

Leaves of Grass first published.

Melville's *Piazza Tales* published.

Atlantic Monthly and *Harper's Weekly* established.

John Brown seizes arsenal at Harpers Ferry.

1860

Lincoln elected president.

Realism *Developing in the mid-1800s, realism was concerned not with the remote past, but with the present. The realists' goal was to convincingly present ordinary people experiencing everyday problems.*

One of the finest of the local colorists, Sarah Orne Jewett presented affectionate but realistic accounts of the lives of the farmers, fishermen, and villagers of the Maine coast, where she lived all her life.

▼

Civil War begins.

1860

Emancipation Proclamation issued; battle of Gettysburg fought.

Slavery is abolished; Civil War ends; Lincoln is assassinated.

1865

Ku Klux Klan founded.

Era of Radical Reconstruction begins; Alaska purchased.

The first baseball team established; Transcontinental railroad completed.

1870

1875

The Battle of Little Bighorn fought; Bell invents telephone.

Reconstruction ends; Great Railroad strike occurs.

◀ In such fiction as *Huckleberry Finn,* Mark Twain took great care to render regional American speech accurately, one of the characteristics of the local-color school of realism.

Stephen Crane's *The Red Badge of Courage* presented as starkly realistic a view of war as this Alexander Gardner photograph of the Confederate dead at Antietam. ▶

◀ In her writing, Mary Wilkins Freeman realistically depicted the decline of New England farming communities after the Civil War.

1880

Edison invents incandescent light bulb.

Rockefeller forms Standard Oil Trust.

First steel-frame skyscraper built.

1885

Twain's *Adventures of Huckleberry Finn* published.

Jewett's *A White Heron* published.

1890

The Battle of Wounded Knee fought; National American Woman Suffrage Association formed.

Basketball is invented; Freeman's *A New England Nun* published.

1895

Crane's *The Red Badge of Courage* published.

Plessy v. *Ferguson* decided.

Spanish-American War.

Chopin's *The Awakening* published; Chesnutt's *The Wife of His Youth* published.

1900

Washington Irving ▶

Rip Van Winkle

BY WASHINGTON IRVING

Washington Irving (1783–1859) was arguably the first serious creative writer in American history. Born in New York, Irving was from an early age fascinated by the theatrical and the literary worlds. He studied law, but thanks to family money never had to practice. This was the period when the new country was still finding and making itself. European, and especially British, models were rejected and the citizens of the new republic were finding out what it meant to be American. Irving had been born the year the United States finally made peace with Great Britain, the Constitution was adopted in 1787, and Washington was chosen as the nation's new capital in 1790. It was a new era and called for a new kind of writer. In 1807, Irving and some friends began to put out an occasional paper called Salmagundi, *full of satirical stories about New York, politics, and fashionable society, all written under outrageous pseudonyms. Irving also brought out a humorous history of New York, purportedly written by a Diedrich Knickerbocker. However it was not success that turned Irving into a full-time author, rather the collapse of his family's importing business in 1818. Irving had gone to Europe the year before to try to save it, and ended up staying for seventeen years. His stories and essays began to appear regularly in magazines. In 1826, Irving took a post at the U.S. embassy in Madrid, Spain, and produced a series of books about the country. Back home in the 1830s, he produced travel works, more stories, and works of history and biography. Irving was a complete author: the first in American history to use his talents to create works of every type and establishing a literary reputation for America abroad. "Rip Van Winkle" is a story about New York's history: Dutch, British, and American, and in it Irving is making implicit comparisons between the European colony and the independent country. Irving's story combines elements of both romanticism and realism.*

A posthumous writing of Diedrich Knickerbocker[1]

> By Woden, God of Saxons,
> From whence comes Wensday, that is
> Wodensday.
> Truth is a thing that ever I will keep
> Unto thylke day in which I creep into
> My sepulchre—
> *Cartwright*[2]

[The following Tale was found among the papers of the late Diedrich Knickerbocker, an old gentleman of New York, who was very curious in the Dutch history of the province, and the manners of the descendants from its primitive settlers.

[1] Diedrich Knickerbocker—pseudonym under which Washington Irving wrote his history of New York.

[2] Cartwright, William (1611–1643)—English poet and dramatist.

His historical researches, however, did not lie so much among books as among men; for the former are lamentably scanty[3] on his favorite topics; whereas he found the old burghers,[4] and still more their wives, rich in that legendary lore, so invaluable to true history. Whenever, therefore, he happened upon a genuine Dutch family, snugly shut up in its low-roofed farmhouse, under a spreading sycamore, he looked upon it as a little clasped volume of black-letter,[5] and studied it with the zeal of a book-worm.

The result of all these researches was a history of the province during the reign of the Dutch governors, which he published some years since. There have been various opinions as to the literary character of his work, and, to tell the truth, it is not a whit better than it should be. Its chief merit is its **scrupulous**[6] accuracy, which indeed was a little questioned on its first appearance, but has since been completely established; and it is now admitted into all historical collections, as a book of unquestionable authority.

The old gentleman died shortly after the publication of his work, and now that he is dead and gone, it cannot do much harm to his memory to say that his time might have been much better employed in weightier labors. He, however, was apt to ride his hobby his own way; and though it did now and then kick up the dust a little in the eyes of his neighbors, and grieve the spirit of some friends, for whom he felt the truest deference[7] and affection; yet his errors and follies are remembered "more in sorrow than in anger," and it begins to be suspected, that he never intended to injure or offend. But however his memory may be appreciated by critics, it is still held dear by many folk, whose good opinion is well worth having; particularly by certain biscuit-bakers, who have gone so far as to imprint his likeness on their new-year cakes; and have thus given him a chance for immortality, almost equal to the being stamped on a Waterloo Medal, or a Queen Anne's Farthing.]

Whoever has made a voyage up the Hudson must remember the Kaatskill[8] mountains. They are a dismembered branch of the great Appalachian family, and are seen away to the west of the river, swelling up to a noble height, and lording it over the surrounding country. Every change of season, every change of weather, indeed, every hour of the day, produces some change in the magical hues and shapes of these mountains, and they are regarded by all the good wives, far and near, as perfect barometers. When the weather is fair and settled, they are clothed

Whoever has made a voyage up the Hudson must remember the Kaatskill mountains.

[3] lamentably scanty—regrettably insufficient.

[4] burghers—citizens.

[5] clasped volume of black-letter—old book printed in an early typeface and with covers that can be kept closed with a fastening.

[6] **scrupulous**—conscientious and exact.

[7] deference—submission.

[8] Kaatskill—more commonly Catskill, a chain of mountains in southeastern New York. They are part of the Appalachian range.

in blue and purple, and print their bold outlines on the clear evening sky; but, sometimes, when the rest of the landscape is cloudless, they will gather a hood of gray vapors about their summits, which, in the last rays of the setting sun, will glow and light up like a crown of glory.

At the foot of these fairy mountains, the voyager may have descried[9] the light smoke curling up from a village, whose shingle roofs gleam among the trees, just where the blue tints of the upland melt away into the fresh green of the nearer landscape. It is a little village, of great antiquity, having been founded by some of the Dutch colonists, in the early times of the province, just about the beginning of the government of the good Peter Stuyvesant,[10] (may he rest in peace!) and there were some of the houses of the original settlers standing within a few years, built of small yellow bricks brought from Holland, having latticed windows and gable fronts, surmounted with weather-cocks.

In that same village, and in one of these very houses (which, to tell the precise truth, was sadly time-worn and weather-beaten), there lived many years since, while the country was yet a province of Great Britain, a simple good-natured fellow, of the name of Rip Van Winkle. He was a descendant of the Van Winkles who figured so gallantly in the chivalrous days of Peter Stuyvesant, and accompanied him to the siege of Fort Christina.[11] He inherited, however, but little of the martial[12] character of his ancestors. I have observed that he was a simple good-natured man; he was, moreover, a kind neighbor, and an obedient hen-pecked husband. Indeed, to the latter circumstance might be owing that meekness of spirit which gained him such universal popularity; for those men are most apt to be **obsequious**[13] and conciliating abroad, who are under the discipline of shrews at home. Their tempers, doubtless, are rendered pliant[14] and malleable[15] in the fiery furnace of domestic tribulation; and a curtain lecture[16] is worth all the sermons in the world for teaching the virtues of patience and long-suffering. A termagant[17] wife may, therefore, in some respects, be considered a tolerable blessing; and if so, Rip Van Winkle was thrice blessed.

Certain it is, that he was a great favorite among all the good wives of the village, who, as usual, with the amiable sex, took his part in all family squabbles; and never failed, whenever they talked those matters over in their evening gossipings, to lay all the blame on Dame Van Winkle. The children of the village, too, would shout with joy whenever he approached. He assisted at their sports, made their playthings, taught them to fly kites and shoot marbles,

---

[9] descried—caught sight of.

[10] Peter Stuyvesant (1592–1672)—Dutch governor of the colony in New Netherlands from 1646 to 1664. The colony became New York when it passed to British control.

[11] Fort Christina—Swedish settlement established on the Delaware River in 1638. It was occupied by the Dutch under Stuyvesant in 1655.

[12] martial—warlike.

[13] **obsequious**—yielding.

[14] pliant—yielding readily to influence or domination.

[15] malleable—easily controlled or influenced.

[16] curtain lecture—private scolding of a husband by a wife; from the time when beds had curtains.

[17] termagant—quarrelsome, scolding.

and told them long stories of ghosts, witches, and Indians. Whenever he went dodging about the village, he was surrounded by a troop of them, hanging on his skirts, clambering on his back, and playing a thousand tricks on him with impunity; and not a dog would bark at him throughout the neighborhood.

The great error in Rip's composition was an insuperable aversion to all kinds of profitable labor. It could not be from the want of **assiduity**[18] or perseverance; for he would sit on a wet rock, with a rod as long and heavy as a Tartar's lance, and fish all day without a murmur, even though he should not be encouraged by a single nibble. He would carry a fowling-piece on his shoulder for hours together, trudging through woods and swamps, and up hill and down dale, to shoot a few squirrels or wild pigeons. He would never refuse to assist a neighbor even in the roughest toil, and was a foremost man at all country frolics for husking Indian corn, or building stone-fences; the women of the village, too, used to employ him to run their errands, and to do such little odd jobs as their less obliging husbands would not do for them. In a word Rip was ready to attend to anybody's business but his own; but as to doing family duty, and keeping his farm in order, he found it impossible.

In fact, he declared it was of no use to work on his farm; it was the most pestilent little piece of ground in the whole country; every thing about it went wrong, and would go wrong, in spite of him. His fences were continually falling to pieces; his cow would either go astray, or get among the cabbages; weeds were sure to grow quicker in his fields than anywhere else; the rain always made a point of setting in just as he had some out-door work to do; so that though his patrimonial estate had dwindled away under his management, acre by acre, until there was little more left than a mere patch of Indian corn and potatoes, yet it was the worst conditioned farm in the neighborhood.

His children, too, were as ragged and wild as if they belonged to nobody. His son Rip, an urchin begotten in his own likeness, promised to inherit the habits, with the old clothes of his father. He was generally seen trooping like a colt at his mother's heels, equipped in a pair of his father's cast-off galligaskins,[19] which he had much ado to hold up with one hand, as a fine lady does her train in bad weather.

Rip Van Winkle, however, was one of those happy mortals, of foolish, well-oiled dispositions, who take the world easy, eat white bread or brown, whichever can be got with least thought or trouble, and would rather starve on a penny than work for a pound. If left to himself, he would have whistled life away in perfect contentment: but his wife kept continually dinning in his ears about his idleness, his carelessness, and the ruin he was bringing on his family. Morning, noon, and night, her tongue was incessantly going, and every thing he said or did was sure to produce a torrent of household eloquence. Rip had but one way

---

[18] **assiduity**—diligence.

[19] galligaskins—also known as breeches. Short loose trousers, fastened at the knee, which were popular in the 1600s.

of replying to all lectures of the kind, and that, by frequent use, had grown into a habit. He shrugged his shoulders, shook his head, cast up his eyes, but said nothing. This, however, always provoked a fresh volley from his wife; so that he was fain to draw off his forces, and take to the outside of the house—the only side which, in truth, belongs to a hen-pecked husband.

Rip's sole domestic adherent was his dog Wolf, who was as much hen-pecked as his master; for Dame Van Winkle regarded them as companions in idleness, and even looked upon Wolf with an evil eye, as the cause of his master's going so often astray. True it is, in all points of spirit befitting an honorable dog, he was as courageous an animal as ever scoured the woods—but what courage can withstand the ever-during, and all-besetting terrors of a woman's tongue? The moment Wolf entered the house his crest fell, his tail drooped to the ground, or curled between his legs, he sneaked about with a gallows air, casting many a sidelong glance at Dame Van Winkle, and at the least flourish of a broomstick or ladle, he would fly to the door with yelping precipitation.

Times grew worse and worse with Rip Van Winkle as years of matrimony rolled on; a tart temper never mellows with age, and a sharp tongue is the only edged tool that grows keener with constant use. For a long while he used to console himself, when driven from home, by frequenting a kind of perpetual club of the sages, philosophers, and other idle personages of the village; which held its sessions on a bench before a small inn, designated by a rubicund portrait of His Majesty George the Third.[20] Here they used to sit in the shade through a long lazy summer's day, talking listlessly over village gossip, or telling endless sleepy stories about nothing. But it would have been worth any statesman's money to have heard the profound discussions that sometimes took place, when by chance an old newspaper fell into their hands from some passing traveler. How solemnly they would listen to the contents, as drawled out by Derrick Van Bummel, the schoolmaster, a dapper learned little man, who was not to be daunted by the most gigantic word in the dictionary; and how sagely they would deliberate upon public events some months after they had taken place.

The opinions of this junto[21] were completely controlled by Nicholas Vedder, a patriarch of the village, and landlord of the inn, at the door of which he took his seat from morning till night, just moving sufficiently to avoid the sun and keep in the shade of a large tree; so that the neighbors could tell the hour by his movements as accurately as by a sun-dial. It is true he was rarely heard to speak, but smoked his pipe incessantly. His adherents, however (for every great man has his adherents), perfectly understood him, and knew how to gather his opinions. When any thing that was read or related displeased him, he was observed to smoke his pipe vehemently, and to send forth short, frequent and angry

[20] George the Third (1738–1820)—King of England from 1760 until his death.

[21] junto—small group united for a common interest.

puffs; but when pleased, he would inhale the smoke slowly and tranquilly, and emit it in light and placid clouds; and sometimes, taking the pipe from his mouth, and letting the fragrant vapor curl about his nose, would gravely nod his head in token of perfect approbation.

From even this stronghold the unlucky Rip was at length routed by his termagant wife, who would suddenly break in upon the tranquillity of the assemblage and call the members all to naught; nor was that august personage, Nicholas Vedder himself, sacred from the daring tongue of this terrible virago,[22] who charged him outright with encouraging her husband in habits of idleness.

Poor Rip was at last reduced almost to despair; and his only alternative, to escape from the labor of the farm and clamor of his wife, was to take gun in hand and stroll away into the woods. Here he would sometimes seat himself at the foot of a tree, and share the contents of his wallet[23] with Wolf, with whom he sympathized as a fellow-sufferer in persecution. "Poor Wolf," he would say, "thy mistress leads thee a dog's life of it; but never mind, my lad, whilst I live thou shalt never want a friend to stand by thee!" Wolf would wag his tail, look wistfully in his master's face, and if dogs can feel pity I verily believe he reciprocated the sentiment with all his heart.

In a long ramble of the kind on a fine autumnal day, Rip had unconsciously scrambled to one of the highest parts of the Kaatskill mountains. He was after his favorite sport of squirrel shooting, and the still solitudes had echoed and reechoed with the reports of his gun. Panting and fatigued, he threw himself, late in the afternoon, on a green knoll, covered with mountain herbage, that crowned the brow of a precipice. From an opening between the trees he could overlook all the lower country for many a mile of rich woodland. He saw at a distance the lordly Hudson, far, far, below him, moving on its silent but majestic course, with the reflection of a purple cloud, or the sail of a lagging bark,[24] here and there sleeping on its glassy bosom, and at last losing itself in the blue highlands.

On the other side he looked down into a deep mountain glen, wild, lonely, and shagged, the bottom filled with fragments from the impending cliffs, and scarcely lighted by the reflected rays of the setting sun. For some time Rip lay musing on this scene; evening was gradually advancing; the mountains began to throw their long blue shadows over the valleys; he saw that it would be dark long before he could reach the village, and he heaved a heavy sigh when he thought of encountering the terrors of Dame Van Winkle.

As he was about to descend, he heard a voice from a distance, hallooing, "Rip Van Winkle! Rip Van Winkle!" He looked round, but could see nothing but a crow winging its solitary flight across the mountain. He thought his fancy must have deceived him, and turned again to descend, when he heard the same cry ring through the still evening air; "Rip Van

[22] virago—noisy, scolding, domineering woman.

[23] wallet—knapsack.

[24] bark—sailing ship.

Winkle! Rip Van Winkle!"—at the same time Wolf bristled up his back, and giving a low growl, skulked to his master's side, looking fearfully down into the glen. Rip now felt a vague apprehension stealing over him; he looked anxiously in the same direction, and perceived a strange figure slowly toiling up the rocks, and bending under the weight of something he carried on his back. He was surprised to see any human being in this lonely and unfrequented place, but supposing it to be some one of the neighborhood in need of his assistance, he hastened down to yield it.

On a level spot in the center was a company of odd-looking personages playing at nine-pins.

On nearer approach he was still more surprised at the singularity of the stranger's appearance. He was a short square-built old fellow, with thick bushy hair, and a grizzled beard. His dress was of the antique Dutch fashion—a cloth jerkin[25] strapped round the waist—several pair of breeches, the outer one of ample volume, decorated with rows of buttons down the sides, and bunches at the knees. He bore on his shoulder a stout keg, that seemed full of liquor, and made signs for Rip to approach and assist him with the load. Though rather shy and distrustful of this new acquaintance, Rip complied with his usual alacrity; and mutually relieving one another, they clambered up a narrow gully, apparently the dry bed of a mountain torrent. As they ascended, Rip every now and then heard long rolling peals, like distant thunder, that seemed to issue out of a deep ravine, or rather cleft, between lofty rocks, toward which their rugged path conducted. He paused for an instant, but supposing it to be the muttering of one of those transient thunder-showers which often take place in mountain heights, he proceeded. Passing through the ravine, they came to a hollow, like a small amphitheater, surrounded by perpendicular precipices, over the brinks of which pending trees shot their branches, so that you only caught glimpses of the azure and the bright evening cloud. During the whole time Rip and his companion had labored on in silence; for though the former marveled greatly what could be the object of carrying a keg of liquor up this wild mountain, yet there was something strange and incomprehensible about the unknown, that inspired awe and checked familiarity.

On entering the amphitheater, new objects of wonder presented themselves. On a level spot in the center was a company of odd-looking personages playing at nine-pins.[26] They were dressed in a quaint outlandish fashion; some wore short doublets,[27] others jerkins, with long knives in their belts, and most of them had enormous breeches, of similar style with that of the guide's. Their visages, too, were peculiar: one had a large beard, broad face,

---

[25] jerkin—short, close-fitting, sleeveless jacket. It was popular in the 1600s.

[26] nine-pins—game in which nine wooden pins are set up and knocked over with a rolled ball; a forerunner of modern bowling.

[27] doublets—close-fitting jackets, popular in the seventeenth century.

and small piggish eyes: the face of another seemed to consist entirely of nose, and was surmounted by a white sugar-loaf hat, set off with a little red cock's tail. They all had beards, of various shapes and colors. There was one who seemed to be the commander. He was a stout old gentleman, with a weather-beaten countenance; he wore a laced doublet, broad belt and hanger,[28] high crowned hat and feather, red stockings, and high-heeled shoes, with roses in them. The whole group reminded Rip of the figures in an old Flemish painting, in the parlor of Dominie Van Shaick, the village parson, and which had been brought over from Holland at the time of the settlement.

What seemed particularly odd to Rip was, that though these folks were evidently amusing themselves, yet they maintained the gravest faces, the most mysterious silence, and were, withal, the most melancholy party of pleasure he had ever witnessed. Nothing interrupted the stillness of the scene but the noise of the balls, which, whenever they were rolled, echoed along the mountains like rumbling peals of thunder.

As Rip and his companion approached them, they suddenly desisted from their play, and stared at him with such fixed statue-like gaze, and such strange, uncouth, lackluster countenances, that his heart turned within him, and his knees smote together. His companion now emptied the contents of the keg into large flagons,[29] and made signs to him to wait upon the company. He obeyed with fear and trembling; they quaffed the liquor in profound silence, and then returned to their game.

By degrees Rip's awe and apprehension subsided. He even ventured, when no eye was fixed upon him, to taste the beverage, which he found had much of the flavor of excellent Hollands.[30] He was naturally a thirsty soul, and was soon tempted to repeat the draught. One taste provoked another; and he reiterated his visits to the flagon so often that at length his senses were overpowered, his eyes swam in his head, his head gradually declined, and he fell into a deep sleep.

On waking, he found himself on the green knoll whence he had first seen the old man of the glen. He rubbed his eyes—it was a bright sunny morning. The birds were hopping and twittering among the bushes, and the eagle was wheeling aloft, and breasting the pure mountain breeze. "Surely," thought Rip, "I have not slept here all night." He recalled the occurrences before he fell asleep. The strange man with a keg of liquor—the mountain ravine—the wild retreat among the rocks—the wobegone party at nine-pins—the flagon—"Oh! that flagon! that wicked flagon!" thought Rip—"what excuse shall I make to Dame Van Winkle!"

He looked round for his gun, but in place of the clean well-oiled fowling-piece, he found an old firelock lying by him, the barrel incrusted with rust, the lock falling off, and the stock worm-eaten. He now suspected that the grave roysters of the mountain had put a trick upon him, and,

---

[28] hanger—short sword.

[29] flagons—large drinking vessels.

[30] Hollands—type of gin.

having dosed him with liquor, had robbed him of his gun. Wolf, too, had disappeared, but he might have strayed away after a squirrel or partridge. He whistled after him and shouted his name, but all in vain; the echoes repeated his whistle and shout, but no dog was to be seen.

He determined to revisit the scene of the last evening's gambol, and if he met with any of the party, to demand his dog and gun. As he rose to walk, he found himself stiff in the joints, and wanting in his usual activity. "These mountain beds do not agree with me," thought Rip, and if this frolic should lay me up with a fit of the rheumatism,[31] I shall have a blessed time with Dame Van Winkle." With some difficulty he got down into the glen: he found the gully up which he and his companion had ascended the preceding evening; but to his astonishment a mountain stream was now foaming down it, leaping from rock to rock, and filling the glen with babbling murmurs. He, however, made shift to scramble up its sides, working his toilsome way through thickets of birch, sassafras, and witch-hazel, and sometimes tripped up or entangled by the wild grapevines that twisted their coils or tendrils from tree to tree, and spread a kind of network in his path.

At length he reached to where the ravine had opened through the cliffs to the amphitheater; but no traces of such opening remained. The rocks presented a high impenetrable wall over which the torrent came tumbling in a sheet of feathery foam, and fell into a broad deep basin, black from the shadows of the surrounding forest. Here, then, poor Rip was brought to a stand. He again called and whistled after his dog; he was only answered by the cawing of a flock of idle crows, sporting high in air about a dry tree that overhung a sunny precipice; and who, secure in their elevation, seemed to look down and scoff at the poor man's perplexities. What was to be done? the morning was passing away, and Rip felt famished for want of his breakfast. He grieved to give up his dog and gun: he dreaded to meet his wife; but it would not do to starve among the mountains. He shook his head, shouldered the rusty firelock, and, with a heart full of trouble and anxiety, turned his steps homeward.

As he approached the village he met a number of people, but none whom he knew, which somewhat surprised him, for he had thought himself acquainted with everyone in the country round. Their dress, too, was of a different fashion from that to which he was accustomed. They all stared at him with equal marks of surprise, and whenever they cast their eyes upon him, invariably stroked their chins. The constant recurrence of this gesture induced Rip, involuntarily, to do the same, when, to his astonishment, he found his beard had grown a foot long!

He had now entered the skirts of the village. A troop of strange children ran at his heels, hooting after him, and pointing at his gray beard. The dogs, too, not one of which he recognized for an old acquaintance, barked at him as he passed. The

[31] rheumatism—disease characterized by the inflammation, swelling, and stiffness of the joints.

very village was altered; it was larger and more populous. There were rows of houses which he had never seen before, and those which had been his familiar haunts had disappeared. Strange names were over the doors—strange faces at the windows—everything was strange. His mind now misgave[32] him; he began to doubt whether both he and the world around him were not bewitched. Surely this was his native village, which he had left but the day before. There stood the Kaatskill mountains—there ran the silver Hudson at a distance—there was every hill and dale precisely as it had always been—Rip was sorely perplexed—"That flagon last night," thought he, "has addled my poor head sadly!"

It was with some difficulty that he found the way to his own house, which he approached with silent awe, expecting every moment to hear the shrill voice of Dame Van Winkle. He found the house gone to decay—the roof fallen in, the windows shattered, and the doors off the hinges. A half-starved dog that looked like Wolf was sulking about it. Rip called him by name, but the cur snarled, showed his teeth, and passed on. This was an unkind cut indeed—"My very dog," sighed poor Rip, "has forgotten me!"

He entered the house, which, to tell the truth, Dame Van Winkle had always kept in neat order. It was empty, forlorn, and apparently abandoned. This desolateness overcame all his **connubial**[33] fears—he called loudly for his wife and children—the lonely chambers rang for a moment with his voice, and then all again was silence.

He now hurried forth, and hastened to his old resort, the village inn—but it too was gone. A large rickety wooden building stood in its place, with great gaping windows, some of them broken and mended with old hats and petticoats, and over the door was painted, "the Union Hotel, by Jonathan Doolittle." Instead of the great tree that used to shelter the quiet little Dutch inn of yore, there now was reared a tall naked pole, with something on the top that looked like a red night-cap, and from it was fluttering a flag, on which was a singular assemblage of stars and stripes—all this was strange and incomprehensible. He recognized on the sign, however, the ruby face of King George, under which he had smoked so many a peaceful pipe; but even this was singularly metamorphosed. The red coat was changed for one of blue and buff, a sword was held in the hand instead of a scepter, the head was decorated with a cocked hat, and underneath was painted in large characters, GENERAL WASHINGTON.

There was, as usual, a crowd of folk about the door, but none that Rip recollected. The very character of the people seemed changed. There was a busy, bustling, disputatious tone about it, instead of the accustomed phlegm[34] and drowsy tranquillity. He looked in vain for the sage Nicholas Vedder, with his broad face, double chin, and fair long pipe, uttering clouds of tobacco-smoke instead of idle speeches; or Van Bummel, the schoolmaster, doling forth the contents of an ancient newspaper.

---

[32] misgave—became suspicious or fearful.

[33] **connubial**—relating to marriage.

[34] phlegm—calm.

In place of these, a lean, bilious-looking fellow, with his pockets full of handbills, was **haranguing**[35] vehemently about rights of citizens—elections—members of congress—liberty—Bunker's Hill[36]—heroes of seventy-six[37]—and other words, which were a perfect Babylonish jargon to the bewildered Van Winkle.

The appearance of Rip, with his long grizzled beard, his rusty fowling-piece, his uncouth dress, and an army of women and children at his heels, soon attracted the attention of the tavern politicians. They crowded around him, eyeing him from head to foot with great curiosity. The orator bustled up to him, and, drawing him partly aside, inquired "on which side he voted?" Rip stared in vacant stupidity. Another short but busy little fellow pulled him by the arm, and, rising on tiptoe, inquired in his ear, "Whether he was Federal or Democrat?" Rip was equally at a loss to comprehend the question; when a knowing, self-important old gentleman, in a sharp cocked hat, made his way through the crowd, putting them to the right and left with his elbows as he passed, and planting himself before Van Winkle, with one arm akimbo,[38] the other resting on his cane, his keen eyes and sharp hat penetrating, as it were, into his very soul, demanded in an austere tone, "what brought him to the election with a gun on his shoulder, and a mob at his heels, and whether he meant to breed a riot in the village?"—"Alas! gentlemen," cried Rip, somewhat dismayed, "I am a poor quiet man, a native of the place, and a loyal subject of the king, God bless him!"

Here a general shout burst from the by-standers—"A tory![39] a tory! a spy! a refugee! hustle him! away with him!" It was with great difficulty that the self-important man in the cocked hat restored order; and, having assumed a tenfold austerity of brow, demanded again of the unknown culprit, what he came there for, and whom he was seeking? The poor man humbly assured him that he meant no harm, but merely came there in search of some of his neighbors, who used to keep about the tavern.

"Well—who are they?—name them."

Rip bethought himself a moment, and inquired, "Where's Nicholas Vedder?"

There was a silence for a little while, when an old man replied, in a thin piping voice, "Nicholas Vedder! why, he is dead and gone these eighteen years! There was a wooden tombstone in the churchyard that used to tell all about him, but that's rotten and gone too."

"Where's Brom Dutcher?"

"Oh, he went off to the army in the beginning of the war; some say he was killed at the storming of Stony Point—others say he was drowned in a squall at the foot of Antony's Nose. I don't know—he never came back again."

"Where's Van Bummel, the schoolmaster?"

---

35 **haranguing**—lecturing noisily.

36 Bunker's Hill—one of the earliest battles of the American Revolutionary War.

37 heroes of seventy-six—reference to the leaders of the American Revolution, which began in 1776.

38 akimbo—bent at the elbow.

39 tory—American loyal to England during the Revolution.

"He went off to the wars too, was a great militia general, and is now in congress."

Rip's heart died away at hearing of these sad changes in his home and friends, and finding himself thus alone in the world. Every answer puzzled him too, by treating of such enormous lapses of time, and of matters which he could not understand: war—congress—Stony Point;—he had no courage to ask after any more friends, but cried out in despair, "Does nobody here know Rip Van Winkle?"

"O, Rip Van Winkle!" exclaimed two or three, "Oh, to be sure! that's Rip Van Winkle yonder, leaning against the tree."

Rip looked, and beheld a precise counterpart of himself, as he went up to the mountain: apparently as lazy, and certainly as ragged. The poor fellow was now completely confounded. He doubted his own identity, and whether he was himself or another man. In the midst of his bewilderment, the man in the cocked hat demanded who he was, and what was his name?

"God knows," exclaimed he, at his wit's end; "I'm not myself—I'm somebody else—that's me yonder—no—that's somebody else got into my shoes—I was myself last night, but I fell asleep on the mountain, and they've changed my gun, and every thing's changed, and I'm changed, and I can't tell what's my name, or who I am!"

The by-standers began now to look at each other, nod, wink significantly, and tap their fingers against their foreheads. There was a whisper, also, about securing the gun, and keeping the old fellow from doing mischief, at the very suggestion of which the self-important man in the cocked hat retired with some precipitation. At this critical moment a fresh comely woman pressed through the throng to get a peep at the gray-bearded man. She had a chubby child in her arms, which, frightened at his looks, began to cry. "Hush, Rip," cried she, "hush, you little fool; the old man won't hurt you." The name of the child, the air of the mother, the tone of her voice, all awakened a train of recollections in his mind. "What is your name, my good woman?" asked he.

"Judith Gardenier."

"And your father's name?"

"Ah, poor man, Rip Van Winkle was his name, but it's twenty years since he went away from home with his gun, and never has been heard of since—his dog came home without him; but whether he shot himself, or was carried away by the Indians, nobody can tell. I was then but a little girl."

Rip had but one question more to ask; but he put it with a faltering voice:

"Where's your mother?"

"Oh, she too had died but a short time since; she broke a blood-vessel in a fit of passion at a New-England peddler."[40]

There was a drop of comfort, at least, in this intelligence. The honest man could contain himself no longer. He caught his daughter and her child in his arms. "I am your father!" cried he—"Young Rip Van Winkle once—old Rip Van Winkle now!—Does nobody know poor Rip Van Winkle?"

All stood amazed, until an old woman, tottering out from among the crowd, put

---

[40] **peddler**—one who sells goods.

her hand to her brow, and peering under it in his face for a moment, exclaimed, "Sure enough! it is Rip Van Winkle—it is himself! Welcome home again, old neighbor—Why, where have you been these twenty long years?"

Rip's story was soon told, for the whole twenty years had been to him but as one night.

Rip's story was soon told, for the whole twenty years had been to him but as one night. The neighbors stared when they heard it; some were seen to wink at each other, and put their tongues in their cheeks: and the self-important man in the cocked hat, who, when the alarm was over, had returned to the field, screwed down the corners of his mouth, and shook his head—upon which there was a general shaking of the head throughout the assemblage.

It was determined, however, to take the opinion of old Peter Vanderdonk, who was seen slowly advancing up the road. He was a descendant of the historian of that name, who wrote one of the earliest accounts of the province. Peter was the most ancient inhabitant of the village, and well versed in all the wonderful events and traditions of the neighborhood. He recollected Rip at once, and corroborated his story in the most satisfactory manner. He assured the company that it was a fact, handed down from his ancestor the historian, that the Kaatskill mountains had always been haunted by strange beings. That it was affirmed that the great Hendrick Hudson, the first discoverer of the river and country, kept a kind of vigil there every twenty years, with his crew of the Half-moon;[41] being permitted in this way to revisit the scenes of his enterprise, and keep a guardian eye upon the river, and the great city called by his name. That his father had once seen them in their old Dutch dresses playing at nine-pins in a hollow of the mountain; and that he himself had heard, one summer afternoon, the sound of their balls, like distant peals of thunder.

To make a long story short, the company broke up, and returned to the more important concerns of the election. Rip's daughter took him home to live with her; she had a snug, well-furnished house, and a stout cheery farmer for a husband, whom Rip recollected for one of the urchins that used to climb upon his back. As to Rip's son and heir, who was the ditto of himself, seen leaning against the tree, he was employed to work on the farm; but **evinced**[42] an hereditary disposition to attend to any thing else but his business.

Rip now resumed his old walks and habits; he soon found many of his former cronies, though all rather the worse for the wear and tear of time, and preferred making friends among the rising generation, with whom he soon grew into great favor.

Having nothing to do at home, and being arrived at that happy age when a man can be idle with **impunity,**[43] he took his place once more on the bench at the

[41] Hendrick Hudson . . . Half-moon—The English explorer Henry Hudson (died 1611) sailed to America in 1609 in the *Half Moon*, a Dutch ship, discovering the river that now bears his name.

[42] **evinced**—to show or demonstrate clearly.

[43] **impunity**—exemption from punishment.

inn door, and was reverenced as one of the patriarchs of the village, and a chronicle of the old times "before the war." It was some time before he could get into the regular track of gossip, or could be made to comprehend the strange events that had taken place during his torpor.[44] How that there had been a revolutionary war—that the country had thrown off the yoke of old England—and that, instead of being a subject of his Majesty George the Third, he was now a free citizen of the United States. Rip, in fact, was no politician; the changes of states and empires made but little impression on him; but there was one species of **despotism**[45] under which he had long groaned, and that was petticoat government.[46] Happily that was at an end; he had got his neck out of the yoke of matrimony, and could go in and out whenever he pleased, without dreading the tyranny of Dame Van Winkle. Whenever her name was mentioned, however, he shook his head, shrugged his shoulders, and cast up his eyes; which might pass either for an expression of resignation to his fate, or joy at his deliverance.

He used to tell his story to every stranger that arrived at Mr. Doolittle's hotel. He was observed, at first, to vary on some points every time he told it, which was, doubtless, owing to his having so recently awaked. It at last settled down precisely to the tale I have related, and not a man, woman, or child in the neighborhood, but knew it by heart. Some always pretended to doubt the reality of it, and insisted that Rip had been out of his head, and that this was one point on which he always remained flighty. The old Dutch inhabitants, however, almost universally gave it full credit. Even to this day they never hear a thunderstorm of a summer afternoon about the Kaatskill, but they say Hendrick Hudson and his crew are at their game of nine-pins; and it is a common wish of all henpecked[47] husbands in the neighborhood, when life hangs heavy on their hands, that they might have a quieting draught out of Rip Van Winkle's flagon.

Note

The foregoing Tale, one would suspect, had been suggested to Mr. Knickerbocker by a little German superstition about the Emperor Frederick *der Rothbart*,[48] and the Kypphaüser mountain: the subjoined note, however, which he had appended to the tale, shows that it is an absolute fact, narrated with his usual fidelity:

"The story of Rip Van Winkle may seem incredible to many, but nevertheless I give it my full belief, for I know the vicinity of our old Dutch settlements to have been very subject to marvellous events and appearances. Indeed, I have heard many stranger stories than this, in the villages along the Hudson; all of which were too well authenticated to admit of a doubt. I

[44] torpor—sleep.

[45] **despotism**—tyranny.

[46] petticoat government—reference to being under the thumb of a wife.

[47] henpecked—dominated, nagged by one's wife.

[48] Emperor Frederick der Rothbart—Holy Roman Emperor Frederick I (1123–1190), called *der Rothbart* or *Barbarossa* ("Red Beard").

have even talked with Rip Van Winkle myself, who, when last I saw him, was a very venerable old man, and so perfectly rational and consistent on every other point, that I think no conscientious person could refuse to take this into the bargain; may, I have seen a certificate on the subject taken before a country justice and signed with a cross, in the justice's own handwriting. The story, therefore, is beyond the possibility of doubt."

D.K.

QUESTIONS TO CONSIDER

1. How would you describe Rip Van Winkle? What does he enjoy? What does he dislike?
2. What is the first indication that this story is not wholly realistic?
3. What is Irving attempting to compare and contrast in this story? What is the message of this comparison?
4. Which elements in this story are romantic? Which elements are realistic?

Nathaniel Hawthorne ▶

The Birthmark

BY NATHANIEL HAWTHORNE

Nathaniel Hawthorne (1804–1864) was born in Salem, Massachusetts, into an old American family. One of his ancestors had been a judge in the Salem witch trials, a fact that would directly inspire Hawthorne's most famous work, The Scarlet Letter *(1850). From the 1820s to the 1850s, New England was the cultural center of the new country. Led by writers like Hawthorne, Ralph Waldo Emerson, Henry David Thoreau, and Henry Wadsworth Longfellow, Americans decided that, in Emerson's words, "We will walk on our own feet; we will work with our own hands; we will speak our own minds." Hawthorne had decided to be a writer from the first, and after graduating from Bowdoin College in Maine, spent more than a decade living as a near-recluse in his mother's house, spending all his time reading and writing. His first published work was a novel,* Fanshawe *(1828), which Hawthorne later did his best to suppress. In 1837,* Twice-Told Tales, *a collection of his stories, was published and brought him some fame and led him to reenter the world. Hawthorne married in 1842 and began to write with greater assurance. Another collection of his tales,* Mosses from an Old Manse, *was published in 1846, and the 1850s saw three major novels:* The Scarlet Letter *(1850),* The House of Seven Gables *(1851), and* The Blithedale Romance *(1852). Hawthorne's view of human nature is not bright, but it is acute. His fiction is dominated by guilt and its consequences, and it is full of allegory and symbolism that are characteristic of a puritan strain in American fiction that can be followed from Hawthorne and Herman Melville through Thomas Wolfe and William Faulkner to Flannery O'Connor and Bernard Malamud. "The Birthmark" is typical of Hawthorne's work: beautifully written, humorous, yet tragic and dark. It is also a typical romantic story.*

In the latter part of the last century there lived a man of science, an eminent proficient in every branch of natural philosophy, who not long before our story opens had made experience of a spiritual affinity[1] more attractive than any chemical one. He had left his laboratory to the care of an assistant, cleared his fine countenance from the furnace smoke, washed the stain of acids from his fingers, and persuaded a beautiful woman to become his wife. In those days when the comparatively recent discovery of electricity and other kindred mysteries of Nature seemed to open paths into the region of miracle, it was not unusual for the love of science to rival the love of woman in its depth and absorbing energy. The higher intellect, the imagination,

[1] affinity—natural attraction or feeling of kinship.

the spirit, and even the heart might all find their congenial aliment[2] in pursuits which, as some of their ardent votaries[3] believed, would ascend from one step of powerful intelligence to another, until the philosopher should lay his hand on the secret of creative force and perhaps make new worlds for himself. We know not whether Aylmer possessed this degree of faith in man's ultimate control over Nature. He had devoted himself, however, too unreservedly to scientific studies ever to be weaned from them by any second passion. His love for his young wife might prove the stronger of the two; but, it could only be by intertwining itself with his love of science, and uniting the strength of the latter to his own.

Such a union accordingly took place, and was attended with truly remarkable consequences and a deeply impressive moral. One day, very soon after their marriage, Aylmer sat gazing at his wife with a trouble in his countenance[4] that grew stronger until he spoke.

"Georgiana," said he, "has it never occurred to you that the mark upon your cheek might be removed?"

"No, indeed," said she, smiling; but perceiving the seriousness of his manner, she blushed deeply. "To tell you the truth it has been so often called a charm that I was simple enough to imagine it might be so."

"Ah, upon another face perhaps it might," replied her husband; "but never on yours. No, dearest Georgiana, you came so nearly perfect from the hand of Nature that this slightest possible defect, which we hesitate whether to term a defect or a beauty, shocks me, as being the visible mark of earthly imperfection."

"Shocks you, my husband!" cried Georgiana, deeply hurt; at first reddening with momentary anger, but then bursting into tears. "Then why did you take me from my mother's side? You cannot love what shocks you!"

To explain this conversation it must be mentioned that in the center of Georgiana's left cheek there was a singular mark, deeply interwoven, as it were, with the texture and substance of her face. In the usual state of her complexion—a healthy though delicate bloom—the mark wore a tint of deeper crimson, which imperfectly defined its shape amid the surrounding rosiness. When she blushed it gradually became more indistinct, and finally vanished amid the triumphant rush of blood that bathed the whole cheek with its brilliant glow. But if any shifting motion caused her to turn pale, there was the mark again, a crimson stain upon the snow, in what Aylmer sometimes deemed an almost fearful distinctness. Its shape bore not a little similarity to the human hand, though of the smallest pygmy size. Georgiana's lovers were wont to say that some fairy, at her birth hour had laid her tiny hand upon the infant's cheek, and left this impress there in token of the magic endowments that were to give her such sway over all hearts. Many a desperate swain[5] would have risked life for the privilege of pressing

---

[2] congenial aliment—suitable food.

[3] votaries—enthusiasts.

[4] countenance—facial expression.

[5] swain—young man.

his lips to the mysterious hand. It must not be concealed, however, that the impression wrought by this fairy sign manual[6] varied exceedingly, according to the difference of temperament in the beholders. Some fastidious persons—but they were exclusively of her own sex—affirmed that the bloody hand, as they chose to call it, quite destroyed the effect of Georgiana's beauty, and rendered her countenance even hideous. But it would be as reasonable to say that one of those small blue stains which sometimes occur in the purest statuary marble would convert the Eve of Powers[7] to a monster. Masculine observers, if the birthmark did not heighten their admiration, contented themselves with wishing it away, that the world might possess one living specimen of ideal loveliness without the semblance of a flaw. After his marriage,—for he thought little or nothing of the matter before,—Aylmer discovered that this was the case with himself.

Had she been less beautiful,—if Envy's self could have found aught else to sneer at,—he might have felt his affection heightened by the prettiness of this mimic hand, now vaguely portrayed, now lost, now stealing forth again and glimmering to and fro with every pulse of emotion that throbbed within her heart; but seeing her otherwise so perfect, he found this one defect grow more and more intolerable with every moment of their united lives. It was the fatal flaw of humanity which Nature, in one shape or another, stamps ineffaceably on all her productions, either to imply that they are temporary and finite, or that their perfection must be wrought by toil and pain. The crimson hand expressed the ineludible gripe[8] in which mortality clutches the highest and purest of earthly mold, degrading them into kindred with the lowest, and even with the very brutes, like whom their visible frames return to dust. In this manner, selecting it as the symbol of his wife's liability to sin, sorrow, decay, and death, Aylmer's somber imagination was not long in rendering the birthmark a frightful object, causing him more trouble and horror than ever Georgiana's beauty, whether of soul or sense, had given him delight.

Aylmer opened his eyes upon his wife's face and recognized the symbol of imperfection.

At all the seasons which should have been their happiest, he invariably and without intending it, nay, in spite of a purpose to the contrary, reverted to this one disastrous topic. Trifling as it at first appeared, it so connected itself with innumerable trains of thought and modes of feeling that it became the central point of all. With the morning twilight Aylmer opened his eyes upon his wife's face and recognized the symbol of imperfection; and when they sat together at the evening hearth his eyes wandered stealthily to her cheek, and beheld, flickering with the blaze of the wood fire, the spectral hand that wrote mortality where he would fain have

[6] sign manual—handprint.

[7] Eve of Powers—sculpture of the first woman by Hiram Powers (1805–1873), the most popular American sculptor of the period.

[8] ineludible gripe—unavoidable grasp.

worshiped. Georgiana soon learned to shudder at his gaze. It needed but a glance with the peculiar expression that his face often wore to change the roses of her cheek into a deathlike paleness, amid which the crimson hand was brought strongly out, like a bas-relief[9] of ruby on the whitest marble.

Late one night when the lights were growing dim, so as hardly to betray the stain on the poor wife's cheek, she herself, for the first time, voluntarily took up the subject.

"Do you remember, my dear Aylmer," said she, with a feeble attempt at a smile, "have you any recollection of a dream last night about this **odious**[10] hand?"

"None! none whatever!" replied Aylmer, starting; but then he added, in a dry, cold tone, affected for the sake of concealing the real depth of his emotion, "I might well dream of it; for before I fell asleep it had taken a pretty firm hold of my fancy."

"And you did dream of it?" continued Georgiana hastily, for she dreaded lest a gush of tears should interrupt what she had to say. "A terrible dream! I wonder that you can forget it. Is it possible to forget this one expression?—'It is in her heart now; we must have it out!' Reflect, my husband, for by all means I would have you recall that dream."

The mind is in a sad state when Sleep, the all-involving, cannot confine her specters within the dim region of her sway, but suffers them to break forth, affrighting this actual life with secrets that perchance[11] belong to a deeper one. Aylmer now remembered his dream. He had fancied himself with his servant Aminadab, attempting an operation for the removal of the birthmark; but the deeper went the knife, the deeper sank the hand, until at length its tiny grasp appeared to have caught hold of Georgiana's heart; whence, however, her husband was **inexorably**[12] resolved to cut or wrench it away.

When the dream had shaped itself perfectly in his memory, Aylmer sat in his wife's presence with a guilty feeling. Truth often finds its way to the mind close muffled in robes of sleep, and then speaks with uncompromising directness of matters in regard to which we practice an unconscious self-deception during our waking moments. Until now he had not been aware of the tyrannizing influence acquired by one idea over his mind, and of the lengths which he might find in his heart to go for the sake of giving himself peace.

"Aylmer," resumed Georgiana solemnly, "I know not what may be the cost to both of us to rid me of this fatal birthmark. Perhaps its removal may cause cureless deformity; or it may be the stain goes as deep as life itself. Again: do we know that there is a possibility, on any terms, of unclasping the firm grip of this little hand which was laid upon me before I came into the world?"

"Dearest Georgiana, I have spent much thought upon the subject," hastily interrupted Aylmer. "I am convinced of the perfect practicability of its removal."

---

9 bas-relief—carving or sculpture in which the figures stand out only slightly from the background.

10 **odious**—hateful.

11 perchance—perhaps.

12 **inexorably**—relentlessly.

"If there be the remotest possibility of it," continued Georgiana, "let the attempt be made at whatever risk. Danger is nothing to me; for life, while this hateful mark makes me the object of your horror and disgust,—life is a burden which I would fling down with joy. Either remove this dreadful hand, or take my wretched life! You have deep science. All the world bears witness of it. You have achieved great wonders. Cannot you remove this little, little mark, which I cover with the tips of two small fingers? Is this beyond your power, for the sake of your own peace, and to save your poor wife from madness?"

"Noblest, dearest, tenderest wife," cried Aylmer rapturously, "doubt not my power. I have already given this matter the deepest thought—thought which might almost have enlightened me to create a being less perfect than yourself. Georgiana, you have led me deeper than ever into the heart of science. I feel myself fully competent to render this dear cheek as faultless as its fellow; and then, most beloved, what will be my triumph when I shall have corrected what Nature left imperfect in her fairest work! Even Pygmalion,[13] when his sculptured woman assumed life, felt not greater ecstasy than mine will be."

"It is resolved, then," said Georgiana, faintly smiling. "And, Aylmer, spare me not, though you should find the birthmark take refuge in my heart at last."

Her husband tenderly kissed her cheek—her right cheek—not that which bore the impress of the crimson hand.

The next day Aylmer **apprised**[14] his wife of a plan that he had formed whereby he might have opportunity for the intense thought and constant watchfulness which the proposed operation would require; while Georgiana, likewise, would enjoy the perfect repose essential to its success. They were to seclude themselves in the extensive apartments occupied by Aylmer as a laboratory, and where, during his toilsome youth, he had made discoveries in the elemental powers of Nature that had roused the admiration of all the learned societies in Europe. Seated calmly in this laboratory, the pale philosopher had investigated the secrets of the highest cloud region and of the profoundest mines; he had satisfied himself of the causes that kindled and kept alive the fires of the volcano; and had explained the mystery of fountains, and how it is that they gush forth, some so bright and pure, and others with such rich medicinal virtues, from the dark bosom of the earth. Here, too, at an earlier period, he had studied the wonders of the human frame, and attempted to fathom the very process by which Nature assimilates all her precious influences from earth and air, and from the spiritual world, to create and foster man, her masterpiece. The latter pursuit, however, Aylmer had long laid aside in unwilling recognition of the truth—against which all seekers sooner or later stumble—that our great creative Mother, while she amuses us with apparently working in the broadest sunshine, is yet severely careful to keep her own secrets, and, in spite of her pretended openness,

[13] Pygmalion—sculptor in ancient Greek myth who fell in love with one of his creations.

[14] **apprised**—informed.

shows us nothing but results. She permits us, indeed, to mar, but seldom to mend, and, like a jealous patentee, on no account to make. Now, however, Aylmer resumed these half-forgotten investigations,—not, of course, with such hopes or wishes as first suggested them, but because they involved much physiological truth and lay in the path of his proposed scheme for the treatment of Georgiana.

He muttered to himself, "If she were my wife, I'd never part with that birthmark."

As he led her over the threshold of the laboratory, Georgiana was cold and **tremulous**.[15] Aylmer looked cheerfully into her face, with intent to reassure her, but was so startled with the intense glow of the birthmark upon the whiteness of her cheek that he could not restrain a strong convulsive shudder. His wife fainted.

"Aminadab! Aminadab!" shouted Aylmer, stamping violently on the floor.

Forthwith there issued from an inner apartment a man of low stature, but bulky frame, with shaggy hair hanging about his visage,[16] which was grimed with the vapors of the furnace. This personage had been Aylmer's underworker during his whole scientific career, and was admirably fitted for that office by his great mechanical readiness, and the skill with which, while incapable of comprehending a single principle, he executed all the details of his master's experiments. With his vast strength, his shaggy hair, his smoky aspect, and the indescribable earthiness that encrusted him, he seemed to represent man's physical nature; while Aylmer's slender figure, and pale, intellectual face, were no less apt a type of the spiritual element.

"Throw open the door of the boudoir, Aminadab," said Aylmer, "and burn a pastille."[17]

"Yes, master," answered Aminadab, looking intently at the lifeless form of Georgiana; and then he muttered to himself, "If she were my wife, I'd never part with that birthmark."

When Georgiana recovered consciousness she found herself breathing an atmosphere of penetrating fragrance, the gentle potency of which had recalled her from her deathlike faintness. The scene around her looked like enchantment. Aylmer had converted those smoky, dingy, somber rooms, where he had spent his brightest years in recondite[18] pursuits, into a series of beautiful apartments not unfit to be the secluded abode of a lovely woman. The walls were hung with gorgeous curtains, which imparted the combination of grandeur and grace that no other species of adornment can achieve; and as they fell from the ceiling to the floor, their rich and ponderous folds, concealing all angles and straight lines, appeared to shut in the scene from infinite space. For aught Georgiana knew, it might be a pavilion among the clouds. And Aylmer, excluding the sunshine, which would have interfered with his chemical processes, had supplied its

---

[15] **tremulous**—trembling, shaking.

[16] visage—face.

[17] pastille—tablet containing aromatic substances, burned to deodorize the air.

[18] recondite—not easily understood.

place with perfumed lamps, emitting flames of various hue, but all uniting in a soft, empurpled radiance. He now knelt by his wife's side, watching her earnestly, but without alarm; for he was confident in his science, and felt that he could draw a magic circle round her within which no evil might intrude.

"Where am I? Ah, I remember," said Georgiana faintly; and she placed her hand over her cheek to hide the terrible mark from her husband's eyes.

"Fear not, dearest!" exclaimed he. "Do not shrink from me! Believe me, Georgiana, I even rejoice in this single imperfection, since it will be such a rapture to remove it."

"Oh, spare me!" sadly replied his wife. "Pray do not look at it again. I never can forget that convulsive shudder."

In order to soothe Georgiana, and, as it were, to release her mind from the burden of actual things, Aylmer now put in practice some of the light and playful secrets which science had taught him among its lore. Airy figures, absolutely bodiless ideas, and forms of unsubstantial beauty came and danced before her, imprinting their momentary footsteps on beams of light. Though she had some indistinct idea of the method of these optical phenomena, still the illusion was almost perfect enough to warrant the belief that her husband possessed sway[19] over the spiritual world. Then again, when she felt a wish to look forth from her seclusion, immediately, as if her thoughts were answered, the procession of external existence flitted across a screen. The scenery and the figures of actual life were perfectly represented, but with that bewitching, yet indescribable difference which always makes a picture, an image, or a shadow so much more attractive than the original. When wearied of this, Aylmer bade her cast her eyes upon a vessel containing a quantity of earth. She did so, with little interest at first; but was soon startled to perceive the germ of a plant shooting upward from the soil. Then came the slender stalk; the leaves gradually unfolded themselves; and amid them was a perfect and lovely flower.

"It is magical!" cried Georgiana. "I dare not touch it."

"Nay, pluck it," answered Aylmer, "pluck it, and inhale its brief perfume while you may. The flower will wither in a few moments and leave nothing save its brown seed vessels; but thence may be perpetuated a race as **ephemeral**[20] as itself."

But Georgiana had no sooner touched the flower than the whole plant suffered a blight, its leaves turning coal-black as if by the agency of fire.

"There was too powerful a stimulus," said Aylmer thoughtfully.

To make up for this abortive experiment, he proposed to take her portrait by a scientific process of his own invention. It was to be effected by rays of light striking upon a polished plate of metal. Georgiana assented; but, on looking at the result, was affrighted to find the features of the portrait blurred and indefinable; while the minute figure of a hand appeared where the cheek should have been. Aylmer

---

[19] sway—influence.

[20] **ephemeral**—very short-lived.

snatched the metallic plate and threw it into a jar of corrosive acid.

Soon, however, he forgot these mortifying failures. In the intervals of study and chemical experiment he came to her flushed and exhausted, but seemed invigorated by her presence, and spoke in glowing language of the resources of his art. He gave a history of the long dynasty of the alchemists,[21] who spent so many ages in quest of the universal solvent[22] by which the golden principle might be elicited from all things vile and base. Aylmer appeared to believe that, by the plainest scientific logic, it was altogether within the limits of possibility to discover this long-sought medium; "but," he added, "a philosopher who should go deep enough to acquire the power would attain too lofty a wisdom to stoop to the exercise of it." Not less singular were his opinions in regard to the elixir vitae.[23] He more than intimated that it was at his option to concoct a liquid that should prolong life for years, perhaps interminably; but that it would produce a discord in Nature which all the world, and chiefly the quaffer[24] of the immortal nostrum,[25] would find cause to curse.

"Aylmer, are you in earnest?" asked Georgiana, looking at him with amazement and fear. "It is terrible to possess such power, or even to dream of possessing it."

"Oh, do not tremble, my love," said her husband. "I would not wrong either you or myself by working such inharmonious effects upon our lives; but I would have you consider how trifling, in comparison, is the skill requisite to remove this little hand."

At the mention of the birthmark, Georgiana, as usual, shrank as if a red-hot iron had touched her cheek.

Again Aylmer applied himself to his labors. She could hear his voice in the distant furnace-room giving directions to Aminadab, whose harsh, uncouth, misshapen tones were audible in response, more like the grunt or growl of a brute than human speech. After hours of absence, Aylmer reappeared and proposed that she should now examine his cabinet of chemical products and natural treasures of the earth. Among the former he showed her a small vial, in which, he remarked, was contained a gentle yet most powerful fragrance, capable of impregnating[26] all the breezes that blow across a kingdom. They were of inestimable value, the contents of that little vial; and, as he said so, he threw some of the perfume into the air and filled the room with piercing and invigorating delight.

"And what is this?" asked Georgiana, pointing to a small crystal globe containing a gold-colored liquid. "It is so beautiful to the eye that I could imagine it the elixir of life."

"In one sense it is," replied Aylmer; "or rather, the elixir of immortality. It is the

---

[21] alchemists—practitioners of the chemistry of the Middle Ages, which combined science, philosophy, and magic.

[22] solvent—substance in which another substance is dissolved, forming a solution.

[23] elixir vitae—medicine capable of prolonging life; cure-all. *Vitae* is a Latin word meaning "of life."

[24] quaffer—drinker.

[25] nostrum—medicine or cure-all.

[26] impregnating—spreading throughout.

most precious poison that ever was concocted in this world. By its aid I could apportion the lifetime of any mortal at whom you might point your finger. The strength of the dose would determine whether he were to linger out years, or drop dead in the midst of a breath. No king on his guarded throne could keep his life if I, in my private station, should deem that the welfare of millions justified me in depriving him of it."

"Why do you keep such a terrific drug?" inquired Georgiana in horror.

"Do not mistrust me, dearest," said her husband, smiling; "its virtuous potency is yet greater than its harmful one. But see! here is a powerful cosmetic. With a few drops of this in a vase of water, freckles may be washed away as easily as the hands are cleansed. A stronger infusion would take the blood out of the cheek, and leave the rosiest beauty a pale ghost."

"Is it with this lotion that you intend to bathe my cheek?" asked Georgiana, anxiously.

"Oh, no," hastily replied her husband; "this is merely superficial. Your case demands a remedy that shall go deeper."

In his interviews with Georgiana, Aylmer generally made minute inquiries as to her sensations and whether the confinement of the rooms and the temperature of the atmosphere agreed with her. These questions had such a particular drift that Georgiana began to conjecture that she was already subjected to certain physical influences, either breathed in with the fragrant air or taken with her food. She fancied likewise, but it might be altogether fancy, that there was a stirring up of her system—a strange, indefinite sensation creeping through her veins, and tingling, half painfully, half pleasurably, at her heart. Still, whenever she dared to look into the mirror, there she beheld herself pale as a white rose and with the crimson birthmark stamped upon her cheek. Not even Aylmer now hated it so much as she.

"It is the most precious poison that ever was concocted in this world."

To dispel the **tedium**[27] of the hours which her husband found it necessary to devote to the processes of combination and analysis, Georgiana turned over the volumes of his scientific library. In many dark old tomes[28] she met with chapters full of romance and poetry. They were the works of the philosophers of the middle ages, such as Albertus Magnus, Cornelius Agrippa, Paracelsus,[29] and the famous friar who created the prophetic Brazen Head.[30] All these antique naturalists stood in advantage of their centuries, yet were imbued[31] with some of their credulity, and therefore were believed, and perhaps imagined themselves to have acquired from the investigation of Nature a power above

[27] **tedium**—boredom.

[28] tomes—books.

[29] Albertus Magnus (c. 1206–1280), Cornelius Agrippa (c. 1486–1535), and Paracelsus (c. 1493–1541) were famous alchemists.

[30] Brazen Head—mythical sculpture of brass, which was said to talk and to be all-wise. Legend credits the great scholar Roger Bacon (c. 1214–1292) with its creation.

[31] imbued—inspired.

Nature, and from physics a sway over the spiritual world. Hardly less curious and imaginative were the early volumes of the Transactions of the Royal Society,[32] in which the members, knowing little of the limits of natural possibility, were continually recording wonders or proposing methods whereby wonders might be wrought.

But to Georgiana the most engrossing volume was a large folio from her husband's own hand, in which he had recorded every experiment of his scientific career, its original aim, the methods adopted for its development, and its final success or failure, with the circumstances to which either event was attributable. The book, in truth, was both the history and emblem of his ardent, ambitious, imaginative, yet practical and laborious life. He handled physical details as if there were nothing beyond them; yet spiritualized them all, and redeemed himself from materialism by his strong and eager aspiration towards the infinite. In his grasp the veriest[33] clod of earth assumed a soul. Georgiana, as she read, reverenced Aylmer and loved him more profoundly than ever, but with a less entire dependence on his judgment than heretofore. Much as he had accomplished, she could not but observe that his most splendid successes were almost invariably failures, if compared with the ideal at which he aimed. His brightest diamonds were the merest pebbles, and felt to be so by himself, in comparison with the inestimable gems which lay hidden beyond his reach. The volume, rich with achievements that had won renown for its author, was yet as melancholy a record as ever mortal hand had penned. It was the sad confession and continual exemplification[34] of the shortcomings of the composite man, the spirit burdened with clay and working in matter, and of the despair that assails the higher nature at finding itself so miserably thwarted by the earthly part. Perhaps every man of genius in whatever sphere might recognize the image of his own experience in Aylmer's journal.

So deeply did these reflections affect Georgiana that she laid her face upon the open volume and burst into tears. In this situation she was found by her husband.

"It is dangerous to read in a sorcerer's books," said he with a smile, though his countenance was uneasy and displeased. "Georgiana, there are pages in that volume which I can scarcely glance over and keep my senses. Take heed lest it prove as detrimental to you."

"It has made me worship you more than ever," said she.

"Ah, wait for this one success," rejoined he, "then worship me if you will. I shall deem myself hardly unworthy of it. But come, I have sought you for the luxury of your voice. Sing to me, dearest."

So she poured out the liquid music of her voice to quench the thirst of his spirit. He then took his leave with a boyish exuberance of gaiety, assuring her that her

[32] Royal Society—most important scientific association in England. It was founded in 1660 and becoming a member is one of the highest honors awarded to English scientists.

[33] veriest—merest.

[34] exemplification—illustration.

seclusion would endure but a little longer, and that the result was already certain. Scarcely had he departed when Georgiana felt irresistibly impelled to follow him. She had forgotten to inform Aylmer of a symptom which for two or three hours past had begun to excite her attention. It was a sensation in the fatal birthmark, not painful, but which induced a restlessness throughout her system. Hastening after her husband, she intruded for the first time into the laboratory.

The first thing that struck her eye was the furnace, that hot and feverish worker, with the intense glow of its fire, which by the quantities of soot clustered above it seemed to have been burning for ages. There was a distilling apparatus in full operation. Around the room were retorts, tubes, cylinders, crucibles, and other apparatus of chemical research. An electrical machine stood ready for immediate use. The atmosphere felt oppressively close, and was tainted with gaseous odors which had been tormented forth by the processes of science. The severe and homely simplicity of the apartment, with its naked walls and brick pavement, looked strange, accustomed as Georgiana had become to the fantastic elegance of her boudoir. But what chiefly, indeed almost solely, drew her attention, was the aspect of Aylmer himself.

He was pale as death, anxious and absorbed, and hung over the furnace as if it depended upon his utmost watchfulness whether the liquid which it was distilling should be the draught[35] of immortal happiness or misery. How different from the sanguine[36] and joyous mien[37] that he had assumed for Georgiana's encouragement!

"Carefully now, Aminadab; carefully, thou human machine—carefully, thou man of clay!" muttered Aylmer, more to himself than his assistant. "Now, if there be a thought too much or too little, it is all over."

"Ho! ho!" mumbled Aminadab. "Look, master! look!"

Aylmer raised his eyes hastily, and at first reddened, then grew paler than ever, on beholding Georgiana. He rushed towards her and seized her arm with a grip that left the print of his fingers upon it.

"Why do you come hither? Have you no trust in your husband?" cried he impetuously. "Would you throw the blight of that fatal birthmark over my labors? It is not well done. Go, prying woman, go!"

"Nay, Aylmer," said Georgiana with the firmness of which she possessed no stinted endowment, "it is not you that have a right to complain. You mistrust your wife; you have concealed the anxiety with which you watch the development of this experiment. Think not so unworthily of me, my husband. Tell me all the risk we run, and fear not that I shall shrink; for my share in it is far less than your own."

"No, no, Georgiana!" said Aylmer impatiently; "it must not be."

"I submit," replied she calmly. "And, Aylmer, I shall quaff whatever draught you

[35] draught—drink.

[36] sanguine—cheerful, confident.

[37] mien—expression.

bring me; but it will be on the same principle that would induce me to take a dose of poison if offered by your hand."

"My noble wife," said Aylmer, deeply moved, "I knew not the height and depth of your nature until now. Nothing shall be concealed. Know, then, that this crimson hand, superficial as it seems, has clutched its grasp into your being with a strength of which I had no previous conception. I have already administered agents powerful enough to do aught except to change your entire physical system. Only one thing remains to be tried. If that fail us we are ruined."

"Why did you hesitate to tell me this?" asked she.

"Because, Georgiana," said Aylmer in a low voice, "there is danger."

"Danger? There is but one danger—that this horrible stigma shall be left upon my cheek!" cried Georgiana. "Remove it, remove it, whatever be the cost, or we shall both go mad!"

"Heaven knows your words are too true," said Aylmer sadly. "And now, dearest, return to your boudoir. In a little while all will be tested."

He conducted her back and took leave of her with a solemn tenderness which spoke far more than his words how much was now at stake. After his departure Georgiana became rapt in musings. She considered the character of Aylmer, and did it completer justice than at any previous moment. Her heart exulted, while it trembled, at his honorable love—so pure and lofty that it would accept nothing less than perfection nor miserably make itself contented with an earthlier nature than he had dreamed of. She felt how much more precious was such a sentiment than that meaner kind which would have borne with the imperfection for her sake, and have been guilty of treason to holy love by degrading its perfect idea to the level of the actual; and with her whole spirit she prayed that, for a single moment, she might satisfy his highest and deepest conception. Longer than one moment she well knew it could not be; for his spirit was ever on the march, ever ascending, and each instant required something that was beyond the scope of the instant before.

The sound of her husband's footsteps aroused her. He bore a crystal goblet containing a liquor colorless as water, but bright enough to be the draught of immortality. Aylmer was pale; but it seemed rather the consequence of a highly wrought state of mind and tension of spirit than of fear or doubt.

"The concoction of the draught has been perfect," said he, in answer to Georgiana's look. "Unless all my science have deceived me, it cannot fail."

"Save on your account, my dearest Aylmer," observed his wife, "I might wish to put off this birthmark of mortality by relinquishing mortality itself in preference to any other mode. Life is but a sad possession to those who have attained precisely the degree of moral advancement at which I stand. Were I weaker and blinder it might be happiness. Were I stronger, it might be endured hopefully. But, being what I find myself, methinks I am of all mortals the most fit to die."

"You are fit for heaven without lasting death!" replied her husband. "But why do we speak of dying? The draught cannot fail. Behold its effect upon this plant."

On the window seat there stood a geranium diseased with yellow blotches, which had overspread all its leaves. Aylmer poured a small quantity of the liquid upon the soil in which it grew. In a little time, when the roots of the plant had taken up the moisture, the unsightly blotches began to be extinguished in a living verdure.[38]

"There needed no proof," said Georgiana quietly. "Give me the goblet. I joyfully stake all upon your word."

"Drink, then, thou lofty creature!" exclaimed Aylmer, with **fervid**[39] admiration. "There is no taint of imperfection on thy spirit. Thy sensible frame, too, shall soon be all perfect."

She quaffed the liquid and returned the goblet to his hand.

"It is grateful," said she, with a **placid**[40] smile. "Methinks it is like water from a heavenly fountain; for it contains I know not what of unobtrusive fragrance and deliciousness. It allays a feverish thirst that had parched me for many days. Now, dearest, let me sleep. My earthly senses are closing over my spirit like the leaves around the heart of a rose at sunset."

She spoke the last words with a gentle reluctance, as if it required almost more energy than she could command to pronounce the faint and lingering syllables. Scarcely had they loitered through her lips ere she was lost in slumber. Aylmer sat by her side, watching her aspect with the emotions proper to a man the whole value of whose existence was involved in the process now to be tested. Mingled with this mood, however, was the philosophic investigation characteristic of the man of science. Not the minutest symptom escaped him. A heightened flush of the cheek, a slight irregularity of breath, a quiver of the eyelid, a hardly perceptible tremor through the frame,—such were the details which, as the moments passed, he wrote down in his folio volume. Intense thought had set its stamp upon every previous page of that volume, but the thoughts of years were all concentrated upon the last.

While thus employed, he failed not to gaze often at the fatal hand, and not without a shudder. Yet once, by a strange and unaccountable impulse, he pressed it with his lips. His spirit recoiled, however, in the very act; and Georgiana, out of the midst of her deep sleep, moved uneasily and murmured as if in remonstrance.[41] Again Aylmer resumed his watch. Nor was it without avail. The crimson hand, which at first had been strongly visible upon the marble paleness of Georgiana's cheek, now grew more faintly outlined. She remained not less pale than ever; but the birthmark, with every breath that came and went, lost somewhat of its former distinctness. Its presence had been

---

[38] verdure—lush greenness of flourishing vegetation.

[39] **fervid**—passionate.

[40] **placid**—calm, quiet.

[41] remonstrance—reasoning or pleading in protest.

awful; its departure was more awful still. Watch the stain of the rainbow fading out of the sky, and you will know how that mysterious symbol passed away.

> **_Do not repent that with so high and pure a feeling, you have rejected the best the earth could offer._**

"By Heaven! it is well-nigh gone!" said Aylmer to himself, in almost irrepressible ecstasy. "I can scarcely trace it now. Success! success! And now it is like the faintest rose color. The lightest flush of blood across her cheek would overcome it. But she is so pale!"

He drew aside the window curtain and suffered the light of natural day to fall into the room and rest upon her cheek. At the same time he heard a gross, hoarse chuckle, which he had long known as his servant Aminadab's expression of delight.

"Ah, clod! ah, earthy mass!" cried Aylmer, laughing in a sort of frenzy, "you have served me well! Matter and spirit—earth and heaven—have both done their part in this! Laugh, thing of the senses! You have earned the right to laugh."

These exclamations broke Georgiana's sleep. She slowly unclosed her eyes and gazed into the mirror which her husband had arranged for that purpose. A faint smile flitted over her lips when she recognized how barely perceptible was now that crimson hand which had once blazed forth with such disastrous brilliancy as to scare away all their happiness. But then her eyes sought Aylmer's face with a trouble and anxiety that he could by no means account for.

"My poor Aylmer!" murmured she.

"Poor? Nay, richest, happiest, most favored!" exclaimed he. "My peerless bride, it is successful! You are perfect!"

"My poor Aylmer," she repeated, with a more than human tenderness, "you have aimed loftily; you have done nobly. Do not repent that with so high and pure a feeling, you have rejected the best the earth could offer. Aylmer, dearest Aylmer, I am dying!"

Alas! it was too true! The fatal hand had grappled with the mystery of life, and was the bond by which an angelic spirit kept itself in union with a mortal frame. As the last crimson tint of the birthmark—that sole token of human imperfection—faded from her cheek, the parting breath of the now perfect woman passed into the atmosphere, and her soul, lingering a moment near her husband, took its heavenward flight. Then a hoarse, chuckling laugh was heard again! Thus ever does the gross fatality of earth exult in its invariable triumph over the immortal essence which, in this dim sphere of half development, demands the completeness of a higher state. Yet, had Aylmer reached a wisdom, he need not thus have flung away the happiness which would have woven his mortal life of the selfsame texture with the celestial. The momentary circumstance was too strong for him; he failed to look beyond the shadowy scope of time, and, living once for all in eternity to find the perfect future in the present.

QUESTIONS TO CONSIDER

1. Why does Aylmer hate his wife's birthmark? Why does Georgiana grow to hate the birthmark?
2. Why does Georgiana praise Aylmer as she is dying?
3. What does Aminadab's second laugh represent?
4. What do you think the birthmark represents?
5. What is the moral of Hawthorne's story?

Edgar Allan Poe ▶

The Tell-Tale Heart

BY EDGAR ALLAN POE

The life of Edgar Allan Poe (1809–1849) was as fantastic as his writings. Born into a theatrical family, he was orphaned at an early age. Taken into the wealthy Allan family, Poe was educated in England and at the University of Virginia, where he lived recklessly and incurred gambling debts, causing his estrangement from his foster father. Stints at West Point and in the army ended poorly, increasing Poe's alienation from his family. To support himself, Poe began to write for newspapers and magazines. Throughout his youth he had written extraordinarily accomplished poems—he had published books in 1827 and 1829—but now he began to turn out stories and critical articles at a fast rate. The pattern of Poe's life was also set: he would work prodigiously for a magazine for a time, then his drinking and temper would bring it all to a tragic close, and he would begin again. In 1836, Poe married his cousin Virginia Clemm, and supporting her and her mother added to Poe's troubles with money. His poem "The Raven" made him nationally famous in 1845, but he was not able to reap the benefits. His wife died in 1847, and Poe's depression drove him to harder drinking. On October 3, 1849, he was found unconscious on a Baltimore street; he died four days later. Poe's poetry, stories, and critical essays are landmarks of American literature. He invented the detective story, introduced the Gothic and the romantic impulses to Americans, and was the first American writer to have an influence on literature in Europe. Poe's posthumous reputation has remained high, and his tales and poetry have entered the popular consciousness in a way few writers have ever achieved. Poe's fictional studies of obsession helped shape modern psychological literature. "The Tell-Tale Heart" exhibits his absolute mastery of using tone to suggest a state of mind: in this case a mood of terror and madness.

True!—nervous—very, very dreadfully nervous I had been and am; but why *will* you say that I am mad? The disease had sharpened my senses—not destroyed—not dulled them. Above all was the sense of hearing acute. I heard all things in the heaven and in the earth. I heard many things in hell. How, then, am I mad? Hearken! and observe how healthily—how calmly I can tell you the whole story.

It is impossible to say how first the idea entered my brain; but, once conceived, it haunted me day and night. Object there was none. Passion there was none. I loved the old man. He had never wronged me. He had never given me insult. For his gold I had no desire. I think it was his eye! yes, it was this! One of his eyes resembled that of a vulture—a pale blue eye, with a film over it. Whenever it fell upon me, my blood ran cold; and so by degrees—very gradually—I made up my mind to take the life of the old man, and thus rid myself of the eye forever.

Now this is the point. You fancy me mad. Madmen know nothing. But you should have seen *me*. You should have seen how wisely I proceeded—with what caution—with what foresight—with what dissimulation[1] I went to work! I was never kinder to the old man than during the whole week before I killed him. And every night, about midnight, I turned the latch of his door and opened it—oh, so gently! And then, when I had made an opening sufficient for my head, I put in a dark lantern, all closed, closed, so that no light shone out, and then I thrust in my head. Oh, you would have laughed to see how cunningly I thrust it in! I moved it slowly—very, very slowly, so that I might not disturb the old man's sleep. It took me an hour to place my whole head within the opening so far that I could see him as he lay upon his bed. Ha!—would a madman have been so wise as this? And then, when my head was well in the room, I undid the lantern cautiously—oh, so cautiously—cautiously (for the hinges creaked)—I undid it just so much that a single thin ray fell upon the vulture eye. And this I did for seven long nights—every night just at midnight—but I found the eye always closed; and so it was impossible to do the work; for it was not the old man who vexed me, but his Evil Eye. And every morning, when the day broke, I went boldly into the chamber and spoke courageously to him, calling him by name in a hearty tone, and inquiring how he had passed the night. So you see he would have been a very profound old man, indeed, to suspect that every night, just at twelve, I looked in upon him while he slept.

Upon the eighth night I was more than usually cautious in opening the door. A watch's minute hand moves more quickly than did mine. Never, before that night, had I *felt* the extent of my own powers—of my **sagacity**.[2] I could scarcely contain my feelings of triumph. To think that there I was, opening the door, little by little, and he not even to dream of my secret deeds or thoughts. I fairly chuckled at the idea; and perhaps he heard me; for he moved on the bed suddenly, as if startled. Now you may think that I drew back—but no. His room was as black as pitch with the thick darkness, (for the shutters were close fastened, through fear of robbers,) and so I knew that he could not see the opening of the door, and I kept pushing it on steadily, steadily.

I had my head in, and was about to open the lantern, when my thumb slipped upon the tin fastening, and the old man sprang up in the bed, crying out—"Who's there?"

I kept quite still and said nothing. For a whole hour I did not move a muscle, and in the meantime I did not hear him lie down. He was still sitting up in the bed, listening;—Just as I have done, night after night, hearkening to the death-watches[3] in the wall.

---

[1] dissimulation—disguise, concealment.

[2] **sagacity**—wisdom.

[3] death-watches—beetles whose heads make a clicking sound that was superstitiously regarded as a portent of death.

Presently I heard a slight groan, and I knew it was the groan of mortal terror. It was not a groan of pain or of grief—oh, no!—It was the low stifled sound that arises from the bottom of the soul when overcharged with awe. I knew the sound well. Many a night, just at midnight, when all the world slept, it has welled up from my own bosom, deepening, with its dreadful echo, the terrors that distracted me. I say I knew it well. I knew what the old man felt, and pitied him, although I chuckled at heart. I knew that he had been lying awake ever since the first slight noise, when he had turned in the bed. His fears had been ever since growing upon him. He had been trying to fancy them causeless, but could not. He had been saying to himself—"It is nothing but the wind in the chimney—it is only a mouse crossing the floor," or "It is merely a cricket which has made a single chirp." Yes, he has been trying to comfort himself with these suppositions: but he had found all in vain. *All in vain;* because Death, in approaching him, had stalked with his black shadow before him, and enveloped[4] the victim. And it was the mournful influence of the unperceived shadow that caused him to feel—although he neither saw nor heard—to *feel* the presence of my head within the room.

Meantime the hellish tattoo of the heart increased.

When I had waited a long time, very patiently, without hearing him lie down, I resolved to open a little—a very, very little crevice in the lantern. So I opened it—you cannot imagine how stealthily, stealthily—until, at length, a single dim ray, like the thread of the spider, shot from out the crevice and fell upon the vulture eye.

It was open—wide, wide open—and I grew furious as I gazed upon it. I saw it with perfect distinctness—all a dull blue, with a hideous veil over it that chilled the very marrow in my bones; but I could see nothing else of the old man's face or person: for I had directed the ray as if by instinct, precisely upon the damned spot.

And now—have I not told you that what you mistake for madness is but over acuteness of the senses?—now, I say there came to my ears a low, dull, quick sound, such as a watch makes when enveloped in cotton. I knew *that* sound well, too. It was the beating of the old man's heart. It increased my fury, as the beating of a drum stimulates the soldier into courage.

But even yet I refrained and kept still. I scarcely breathed. I held the lantern motionless. I tried how steadily I could maintain the ray upon the eye. Meantime the hellish tattoo[5] of the heart increased. It grew quicker and quicker, and louder and louder every instant. The old man's terror *must* have been extreme! It grew louder, I say, louder every moment!—do you mark me well? I have told you that I am nervous: so I am. And now at the dead hour of the night, amid the dreadful silence of that old house, so strange a noise as this excited me to uncontrollable terror. Yet, for some minutes longer I refrained and stood

[4] enveloped—surrounded.

[5] tattoo—beating of a drum.

still. But the beating grew louder, louder! I thought the heart must burst. And now a new anxiety seized me—the sound would be heard by a neighbor! The old man's hour had come! With a loud yell, I threw open the lantern and leaped into the room. He shrieked once—once only. In an instant I dragged him to the floor, and pulled the heavy bed over him. I then smiled gaily, to find the deed so far done. But, for many minutes, the heart beat on with a muffled sound. This, however, did not vex me; it would not be heard through the wall. At length it ceased. The old man was dead. I removed the bed and examined the corpse. Yes, he was stone, stone dead. I placed my hand upon the heart and held it there many minutes. There was no pulsation. He was stone dead. His eye would trouble me no more.

If still you think me mad, you will think so no longer when I describe the wise precautions I took for the concealment of the body. The night waned,[6] and I worked hastily, but in silence. First of all I dismembered the corpse. I cut off the head and the arms and the legs.

I then took up three planks from the flooring of the chamber, and deposited all between the scantlings.[7] I then replaced the boards so cleverly, so cunningly, that no human eye—not even *his*—could have detected anything wrong. There was nothing to wash out—no stain of any kind—no blood-spot whatever. I had been too wary for that. A tub had caught all—ha! ha!

When I had made an end of these labors it was four o'clock—still dark as midnight. As the bell sounded the hour, there came a knocking at the street door. I went down to open it with a light heart,—for what had I *now* to fear? There entered three men, who introduced themselves, with perfect suavity,[8] as officers of the police. A shriek had been heard by a neighbor during the night; suspicion of foul play had been aroused; information had been lodged at the police office, and they (the officers) had been deputed[9] to search the premises.

I smiled,—for *what* had I to fear? I bade the gentlemen welcome. The shriek, I said, was my own in a dream. The old man, I mentioned, was absent in the country. I took my visiters all over the house. I bade them search—search *well*. I led them, at length, to *his* chamber. I showed them his treasures, secure, undisturbed. In the enthusiasm of my confidence, I brought chairs into the room and desired them *here* to rest from their fatigues, while I myself, in the wild **audacity**[10] of my perfect triumph, placed my own seat upon the very spot beneath which reposed the corpse of the victim.

The officers were satisfied. My *manner* had convinced them. I was singularly at ease. They sat, and while I answered cheerily, they chatted of familiar things. But, ere long, I felt myself getting pale and wished them gone. My head ached, and I fancied a

---

6 waned—approached an end.

7 scantlings—pieces of lumber that form a frame for a wall or floor, and onto which the wall or flooring is secured. Also known as a *stud*.

8 suavity—smooth agreeability and courtesy.

9 deputed—appointed; authorized.

10 **audacity**—boldness.

ringing in my ears: but still they sat and still chatted. The ringing became more distinct;—it continued and became more distinct: I talked more freely to get rid of the feeling: but it continued and gained definitiveness—until, at length, I found that the noise was *not* within my ears.

No doubt I now grew *very* pale;—but I talked more fluently, and with a heightened voice. Yet the sound increased—and what could I do? it was a low, dull, quick sound—much such a sound as a watch makes when enveloped in cotton. I gasped for breath—and yet the officers heard it not. I talked more quickly—more vehemently; but the noise steadily increased. I arose and argued about trifles, in a high key and with violent **gesticulations**;[11] but the noise steadily increased. Why *would* they not be gone? I paced the floor to and fro with heavy strides, as if excited to fury by the observations of the men—but the noise steadily increased. Oh God! what *could* I do? I foamed—I raved—I swore! I swung the chair upon which I had been sitting, and grated it upon the boards, but the noise arose over all and continually increased. It grew louder—louder—*louder!* And still the men chatted pleasantly, and smiled. Was it possible they heard not? Almighty God!—no, no! They heard!—they suspected!—they *knew!*—they were making a mockery of my horror!—this I thought, and this I think. But anything was better than this agony! Anything was more tolerable than this **derision**![12] I could bear those hypocritical smiles no longer! I felt that I must scream or die!—and now—again!—hark! louder! louder! louder! *louder!*

"Villains!" I shrieked, "dissemble[13] no more! I admit the deed!—tear up the planks!—here, here!—It is the beating of his hideous heart!"

---

[11] **gesticulations**—vigorous motions or gestures.

[12] **derision**—ridicule.

[13] dissemble—disguise or conceal behind a false appearance.

QUESTIONS TO CONSIDER

1. How would you summarize the plot of "The Tell-Tale Heart" in one sentence?
2. Why does the narrator admit his deed to the police?
3. Why does the narrator want to kill the old man? How would you describe the narrator's state of mind?
4. What form does the story take? Whom do you think the narrator is talking to?
5. Poe is generally considered America's first romantic writer. How is "The Tell-Tale Heart" a good example of romantic literature?

Herman Melville ▶

Bartleby, the Scrivener

BY HERMAN MELVILLE

Herman Melville (1819–1891) was almost wholly misunderstood in his lifetime. To his contemporaries, he was a teller of sea tales—and had been largely forgotten by the time he died. Today, he is known as a key figure in the development of American literature, and the author of Moby Dick, *one of the most innovative novels of the era. Melville was born in New York City, into a once prominent family that had fallen on hard times. At twenty-one, Melville went to sea, sailing across the Atlantic and throughout the Pacific. These adventures became the basis of many of his novels. Upon his return to New York in 1844, Melville wrote* Typee, *an autobiographical account of being captured by cannibals. It was a success and led to a sequel,* Omoo. *Melville seriously embarked on a literary career, studying the great English authors and attempting to write novels that had more meaning and power. He became friends with Hawthorne—the only American author he valued—and they both discussed how stories could express meaning and philosophical messages. Melville still wrote about his adventures, but he combined adventure plots with symbolism, reflections on the nature of reality, and keen psychological understanding. However, as Melville's novels grew more sophisticated, they grew less popular. This culminated in 1851 with the publication of* Moby Dick, *a complete financial failure. Melville supported himself by farming, but after many unsuccessful attempts to lecture and write for a living, in 1857 he took a job as a customs inspector, which he kept until his death. He continued to write, taking up poetry and producing a series of stories that were not published until after his death. His obituaries remembered him as a sailor who was captured by cannibals in the South Seas. "Bartleby the Scrivener" is a complex story with Gothic undertones that can also be read as an allegory of the plight of the artist.*

I am a rather elderly man. The nature of my avocations,[1] for the last thirty years, has brought me into more than ordinary contact with what would seem an interesting and somewhat singular set of men, of whom, as yet, nothing, that I know of, has ever been written—I mean, the law-copyists, or scriveners.[2] I have known very many of them, professionally and privately, and, if I pleased, could relate divers[3] histories, at which good-natured gentlemen might smile, and sentimental souls might weep. But I waive the biographies of all other scriveners, for a few passages in the life of Bartleby, who was a

---

[1] avocations—professional activities.

[2] scriveners—clerks who write letters or documents.

[3] divers—diverse. various, several.

scrivener, the strangest I ever saw, or heard of. While, of other law-copyists, I might write the complete life, of Bartleby nothing of that sort can be done. I believe that no materials exist, for a full and satisfactory biography of this man. It is an irreparable loss to literature. Bartleby was one of those beings of whom nothing is ascertainable, except from the original sources, and, in his case, those are very small. What my own astonished eyes saw of Bartleby, *that* is all I know of him, except, indeed, one vague report, which will appear in the sequel.

All who know me, consider me an eminently safe man.

Ere introducing the scrivener, as he first appeared to me, it is fit I make some mention of myself, my *employés*, my business, my chambers, and general surroundings; because some such description is indispensable to an adequate understanding of the chief character about to be presented. Imprimis:[4] I am a man who, from his youth upwards, has been filled with a profound conviction that the easiest way of life is the best. Hence, though I belong to a profession proverbially energetic and nervous, even to turbulence, at times, yet nothing of that sort have I ever suffered to invade my peace. I am one of those unambitious lawyers who never address a jury, or in any way draws down public applause; but, in the cool tranquillity of a snug retreat, do a snug business among rich men's bonds, and mortgages, and title-deeds. All who know me, consider me an eminently *safe* man. The late John Jacob Astor,[5] a personage little given to poetic enthusiasm, had no hesitation in pronouncing my first grand point to be prudence; my next, method. I do not speak it in vanity, but simply record the fact, that I was not unemployed in my profession by the late John Jacob Astor; a name which, I admit, I love to repeat; for it hath a rounded and orbicular[6] sound to it, and rings like unto bullion.[7] I will freely add, that I was not insensible to the late John Jacob Astor's good opinion.

Some time prior to the period at which this little history begins, my avocations had been largely increased. The good old office, now extinct in the State of New York, of a Master in Chancery,[8] had been conferred upon me. It was not a very **arduous**[9] office, but very pleasantly **remunerative**.[10] I seldom lose my temper; much more seldom indulge in dangerous indignation at wrongs and outrages; but, I must be permitted to be rash here, and declare, that I consider the sudden and violent **abrogation**[11] of the office of Master in Chancery, by the new Constitution, as a—premature act; inasmuch as I had counted upon a life-lease of the profits, whereas I only received those of a few short years. But this is by the way.

---

[4] Imprimis—in the first place.

[5] John Jacob Astor (1763–1848)—American financier of vast wealth.

[6] orbicular—circular or spherical.

[7] bullion—gold or silver in the form of bars, ingots, or plates.

[8] Master in Chancery—officer in a court of equity appointed to assist the court.

[9] **arduous**—difficult.

[10] **remunerative**—profitable.

[11] **abrogation**—abolishing.

My chambers were up stairs, at No. —— Wall Street. At one end, they looked upon the white wall of the interior of a spacious sky-light shaft, penetrating the building from top to bottom.

This view might have been considered rather tame than otherwise, deficient in what landscape painters call "life." But, if so, the view from the other end of my chambers offered, at least, a contrast, if nothing more. In that direction, my windows commanded an unobstructed view of a lofty brick wall, black by age and everlasting shade; which wall required no spy-glass to bring out its lurking beauties, but, for the benefit of all near-sighted spectators, was pushed up to within ten feet of my window panes. Owing to the great height of the surrounding buildings, and my chambers being on the second floor, the interval between this wall and mine not a little resembled a huge square cistern.[12]

At the period just preceding the advent[13] of Bartleby, I had two persons as copyists in my employment, and a promising lad as an office-boy. First, Turkey; second, Nippers; third, Ginger Nut. These may seem names, the like of which are not usually found in the Directory. In truth, they were nicknames, mutually conferred upon each other by my three clerks, and were deemed expressive of their respective persons or characters. Turkey was a short, pursy Englishman, of about my own age—that is, somewhere not far from sixty. In the morning, one might say, his face was of a fine florid hue, but after twelve o'clock, meridian[14]—his dinner hour—it blazed like a grate full of Christmas coals; and continued blazing—but, as it were, with a gradual wane—till six o'clock, P.M., or thereabouts; after which, I saw no more of the proprietor of the face, which, gaining its meridian with the sun, seemed to set with it, to rise, culminate, and decline the following day, with the like regularity and undiminished glory. There are many singular coincidences I have known in the course of my life, not the least among which was the fact, that, exactly when Turkey displayed his fullest beams from his red and radiant countenance, just then, too, at that critical moment, began the daily period when I considered his business capacities as seriously disturbed for the remainder of the twenty-four hours. Not that he was absolutely idle, or averse to business, then; far from it. The difficulty was, he was apt to be altogether too energetic. There was a strange, inflamed, flurried, flighty recklessness of activity about him. He would be incautious in dipping his pen into his inkstand. All his blots upon my documents were dropped there after twelve o'clock, meridian. Indeed, not only would he be reckless, and sadly given to making blots in the afternoon, but, some days, he went further, and was rather noisy. At such times, too, his face flamed with augmented blazonry,[15] as if cannel coal had been heaped on anthracite.[16] He made an unpleasant racket with his chair; spilled his

---

[12] cistern—tank for catching and storing rainwater.

[13] advent—coming or arrival.

[14] meridian—noon.

[15] augmented blazonry—additional ostentatious display.

[16] cannel . . . anthracite—Cannel coal burns brightly with much smoke; anthracite coal burns with very little smoke or flame.

sand-box;[17] in mending his pens, impatiently split them all to pieces, and threw them on the floor in a sudden passion; stood up, and leaned over his table, boxing his papers about in a most indecorous manner, very sad to behold in an elderly man like him. Nevertheless, as he was in many ways a most valuable person to me, and all the time before twelve o'clock, meridian, was the quickest, steadiest creature, too, accomplishing a great deal of work in a style not easily to be matched—for these reasons, I was willing to overlook his eccentricities, though, indeed, occasionally, I remonstrated[18] with him. I did this very gently, however, because, though the civilest, nay, the blandest and most reverential of men in the morning, yet, in the afternoon, he was disposed, upon provocation, to be slightly rash with his tongue—in fact, insolent. Now, valuing his morning services as I did, and resolved not to lose them—yet, at the same time, made uncomfortable by his inflamed ways after twelve o'clock—and being a man of peace, unwilling by my admonitions to call forth unseemly retorts from him, I took upon me, one Saturday noon (he was always worse on Saturdays) to hint to him, very kindly, that, perhaps, now that he was growing old, it might be well to abridge his labors; in short, he need not come to my chambers after twelve o'clock, but, dinner over, had best go home to his lodgings, and rest himself till tea-time. But no; he insisted upon his afternoon devotions. His countenance became intolerably fervid,[19] as he oratorically assured me—**gesticulating**[20] with a long ruler at the other end of the room—that if his services in the morning were useful, how indispensable, then, in the afternoon?

"With submission, sir," said Turkey, on this occasion, "I consider myself your right-hand man. In the morning I but marshal and deploy my columns; but in the afternoon I put myself at their head, and gallantly charge the foe, thus"—and he made a violent thrust with the ruler.

"But the blots, Turkey," **intimated**[21] I.

"True; but, with submission, sir, behold these hairs! I am getting old. Surely, sir, a blot or two of a warm afternoon is not to be severely urged against gray hairs. Old age—even if it blot the page—is honorable. With submission, sir, we *both* are getting old."

This appeal to my fellow-feeling was hardly to be resisted. At all events, I saw that go he would not. So, I made up my mind to let him stay, resolving, nevertheless, to see to it that, during the afternoon, he had to do with my less important papers.

Nippers, the second on my list, was a whiskered, sallow, and, upon the whole, rather piratical-looking young man, of about five and twenty. I always deemed him the victim of two evil powers—ambition and indigestion. The ambition was evinced by a certain impatience of the duties of a mere copyist, an unwarrantable usurpation of strictly professional affairs, such as the original drawing up of legal documents. The indigestion seemed betokened in an occasional nervous testiness and grinning

---

17 sand-box—used for drying ink.

18 remonstrated—protested.

19 fervid—marked by great passion, burning.

20 **gesticulating**—vigorously gesturing.

21 **intimated**—hinted.

irritability, causing the teeth to audibly grind together over mistakes committed in copying; unnecessary maledictions,[22] hissed, rather than spoken, in the heat of business; and especially by a continual discontent with the height of the table where he worked. Though of a very ingenious mechanical turn, Nippers could never get this table to suit him. He put chips under it, blocks of various sorts, bits of pasteboard, and at last went so far as to attempt an exquisite adjustment, by final pieces of folded blotting-paper. But no invention would answer. If, for the sake of easing his back, he brought the table lid at a sharp angle well up towards his chin, and wrote there like a man using the steep roof of a Dutch house for his desk, then he declared that it stopped the circulation in his arms. If now he lowered the table to his waistbands, and stooped over it in writing, then there was a sore aching in his back. In short, the truth of the matter was, Nippers knew not what he wanted. Or, if he wanted anything, it was to be rid of a scrivener's table altogether. Among the manifestations of his diseased ambition was a fondness he had for receiving visits from certain ambiguous-looking fellows in seedy coats, whom he called his clients. Indeed, I was aware that not only was he, at times, considerable of[23] a ward-politician, but he occasionally did a little business at the Justices' courts, and was not unknown on the steps of the Tombs.[24] I have good reason to believe, however, that one individual who called upon him at my chambers, and who, with a grand air, he insisted was his client, was no other than a dun,[25] and the alleged title-deed, a bill. But, with all his failings, and the annoyances he caused me, Nippers, like his compatriot Turkey, was a very useful man to me; wrote a neat, swift hand; and, when he chose, was not deficient in a gentlemanly sort of deportment.[26] Added to this, he always dressed in a gentlemanly sort of way; and so, incidentally, reflected credit upon my chambers. Whereas, with respect to Turkey, I had much ado to keep him from being a reproach to me. His clothes were apt to look oily, and smell of eating-houses. He wore his pantaloons very loose and baggy in summer. His coats were execrable;[27] his hat not to be handled. But while the hat was a thing of indifference to me, inasmuch as his natural civility and deference, as a dependent Englishman, always led him to doff it the moment he entered the room, yet his coat was another matter. Concerning his coats, I reasoned with him; but with no effect. The truth was, I suppose, that a man with so small an income could not afford to sport such a lustrous face and a lustrous coat at one and the same time. As Nippers once observed, Turkey's money went chiefly for red ink. One winter day, I presented Turkey with a highly respectable-looking coat of my own—a padded gray coat, of a most comfortable warmth, and which buttoned straight up from the knee to the neck. I

22 maledictions—curses.
23 considerable of—to some degree, in some measure.
24 the Tombs—city prison in New York.
25 dun—person who collects debts.
26 deportment—personal conduct, behavior.
27 execrable—very bad.

thought Turkey would appreciate the favor, and abate his rashness and **obstreperousness**[28] of afternoons. But no; I verily believe that buttoning himself up in so downy and blanket-like a coat had a **pernicious**[29] effect upon him—upon the same principle that too much oats are bad for horses. In fact, precisely as a rash, restive horse is said to feel his oats, so Turkey felt his coat. It made him insolent. He was a man whom prosperity harmed.

Their fits relieved each other, like guards. When Nippers's was on, Turkey's was off; and vice versa.

Though, concerning the self-indulgent habits of Turkey, I had my own private surmises, yet, touching Nippers, I was well persuaded that, whatever might be his faults in other respects, he was, at least, a **temperate**[30] young man. But, indeed, nature herself seemed to have been his vintner,[31] and, at his birth, charged him so thoroughly with an irritable, brandy-like disposition, that all subsequent potations[32] were needless. When I consider how, amid the stillness of my chambers, Nippers would sometimes impatiently rise from his seat, and stooping over his table, spread his arms wide apart, seize the whole desk, and move it, and jerk it, with a grim, grinding motion on the floor, as if the table were a perverse voluntary agent, intent on thwarting and vexing him, I plainly perceive that, for Nippers, brandy-and-water were altogether superfluous.

It was fortunate for me that, owing to its peculiar cause—indigestion—the irritability and consequent nervousness of Nippers were mainly observable in the morning, while in the afternoon he was comparatively mild. So that, Turkey's paroxysms only coming on about twelve o'clock, I never had to do with their eccentricities at one time. Their fits relieved each other, like guards. When Nippers's was on, Turkey's was off; and *vice versa*. This was a good natural arrangement, under the circumstances.

Ginger Nut, the third on my list, was a lad, some twelve years old. His father was a car-man,[33] ambitious of seeing his son on the bench instead of a cart, before he died. So he sent him to my office, as student at law, errand-boy, cleaner and sweeper, at the rate of one dollar a week. He had a little desk to himself, but he did not use it much. Upon inspection, the drawer exhibited a great array of the shells of various sorts of nuts. Indeed, to this quick-witted youth, the whole noble science of the law was contained in a nutshell. Not the least among the employments of Ginger Nut, as well as one which he discharged with the most **alacrity**,[34] was his duty as cake and apple purveyor for Turkey and Nippers. Copying law-papers being proverbially a dry, husky sort of business, my two

[28] **obstreperousness**—noisy misbehavior.
[29] **pernicious**—destructive.
[30] **temperate**—moderate, restrained.
[31] vintner—wine merchant.
[32] potations—drinks.
[33] car-man—wagon driver.
[34] **alacrity**—eagerness.

scriveners were fain to moisten their mouths very often with Spitzenbergs,[35] to be had at the numerous stalls nigh the Custom House and Post Office. Also, they sent Ginger Nut very frequently for that peculiar cake—small, flat, round, and very spicy—after which he had been named by them. Of a cold morning, when business was but dull, Turkey would gobble up scores of these cakes, as if they were mere wafers—indeed, they sell them at the rate of six or eight for a penny—the scrape of his pen blending with the crunching of the crisp particles in his mouth. Of all the fiery afternoon blunders and flurried rashnesses of Turkey, was his once moistening a ginger-cake between his lips, and clapping it on to a mortgage, for a seal. I came within an ace of dismissing him then. But he mollified me by making an oriental bow, and saying—

"With submission, sir, it was generous of me to find you in stationery on my own account."

Now my original business—that of a conveyancer[36] and title hunter, and drawer-up of recondite[37] documents of all sorts—was considerably increased by receiving the master's office. There was now great work for scriveners. Not only must I push the clerks already with me, but I must have additional help.

In answer to my advertisement, a motionless young man one morning stood upon my office threshold, the door being open, for it was summer. I can see that figure now—pallidly[38] neat, pitiably respectable, incurably forlorn! It was Bartleby.

After a few words touching his qualifications, I engaged him, glad to have among my corps of copyists a man of so singularly **sedate**[39] an aspect, which I thought might operate beneficially upon the flighty temper of Turkey, and the fiery one of Nippers.

I should have stated before that ground glass folding-doors divided my premises into two parts, one of which was occupied by my scriveners, the other by myself. According to my humor, I threw open these doors, or closed them. I resolved to assign Bartleby a corner by the folding-doors, but on my side of them, so as to have this quiet man within easy call, in case any trifling thing was to be done. I placed his desk close up to a small side-window in that part of the room, a window which originally had afforded a lateral view of certain grimy back-yards and bricks, but which, owing to subsequent erections, commanded at present no view at all, though it gave some light. Within three feet of the panes was a wall, and the light came down from far above, between two lofty buildings, as from a very small opening in a dome. Still further to a satisfactory arrangement, I procured a high green folding screen, which might entirely isolate Bartleby from my sight, though not

I can see that figure now—pallidly neat, pitiably respectable, incurably forlorn! It was Bartleby.

---

[35] Spitzenbergs—apples.

[36] conveyancer—lawyer who investigates the ownership of property to prepare its transfer.

[37] recondite—not easily understood.

[38] pallidly—dully.

[39] **sedate**—calm, dignified.

remove him from my voice. And thus, in a manner, privacy and society were conjoined.[40]

At first, Bartleby did an extraordinary quantity of writing. As if long famishing for something to copy, he seemed to gorge himself on my documents. There was no pause for digestion. He ran a day and night line, copying by sun-light and by candle-light. I should have been quite delighted with his application, had he been cheerfully industrious. But he wrote on silently, palely, mechanically.

It is, of course, an indispensable part of a scrivener's business to verify the accuracy of his copy, word by word. Where there are two or more scriveners in an office, they assist each other in this examination, one reading from the copy, the other holding the original. It is a very dull, wearisome, and **lethargic**[41] affair. I can readily imagine that, to some **sanguine**[42] temperaments, it would be altogether intolerable. For example, I cannot credit that the mettlesome[43] poet, Byron,[44] would have contentedly sat down with Bartleby to examine a law document of, say five hundred pages, closely written in a crimpy hand.

Now and then, in the haste of business, it had been my habit to assist in comparing some brief document myself, calling Turkey or Nippers for this purpose. One object I had, in placing Bartleby so handy to me behind the screen, was, to avail myself of his services on such trivial occasions. It was on the third day, I think, of his being with me, and before any necessity had arisen for having his own writing examined, that, being much hurried to complete a small affair I had in hand, I abruptly called to Bartleby. In my haste and natural expectancy of instant compliance, I sat with my head bent over the original on my desk, and my right hand sideways, and somewhat nervously extended with the copy, so that, immediately upon emerging from his retreat, Bartleby might snatch it and proceed to business without the least delay.

In this very attitude did I sit when I called to him, rapidly stating what it was I wanted him to do—namely, to examine a small paper with me. Imagine my surprise, nay, my consternation, when, without moving from his privacy, Bartleby, in a singularly mild, firm voice, replied, "I would prefer not to."

I sat awhile in perfect silence, rallying my stunned faculties. Immediately it occurred to me that my ears had deceived me, or Bartleby had entirely misunderstood my meaning. I repeated my request in the clearest tone I could assume; but in quite as clear a one came the previous reply, "I would prefer not to."

"Prefer not to," echoed I, rising in high excitement, and crossing the room with a stride. "What do you mean? Are you moon-struck? I want you to help me compare this sheet here—take it," and I thrust it towards him.

"I would prefer not to," said he.

I looked at him steadfastly. His face was leanly composed; his gray eye dimly

---

[40] conjoined—united.

[41] **lethargic**—sluggish, inactive.

[42] **sanguine**—cheerfully confident, optimistic.

[43] mettlesome—spirited.

[44] Byron—George Gordon, Lord Byron (1788–1824), English poet.

calm. Not a wrinkle of agitation rippled him. Had there been the least uneasiness, anger, impatience or impertinence in his manner; in other words, had there been any thing ordinarily human about him, doubtless I should have violently dismissed him from the premises. But as it was, I should have as soon thought of turning my pale plaster-of-paris bust of Cicero[45] out of doors. I stood gazing at him awhile, as he went on with his own writing, and then reseated myself at my desk. This is very strange, thought I. What had one best do? But my business hurried me. I concluded to forget the matter for the present, reserving it for my future leisure. So calling Nippers from the other room, the paper was speedily examined.

A few days after this, Bartleby concluded four lengthy documents, being quadruplicates of a week's testimony taken before me in my High Court of Chancery. It became necessary to examine them. It was an important suit, and great accuracy was imperative. Having all things arranged, I called Turkey, Nippers, and Ginger Nut, from the next room, meaning to place the four copies in the hands of my four clerks, while I should read from the original. Accordingly, Turkey, Nippers, and Ginger Nut had taken their seats in a row, each with his document in his hand, when I called to Bartleby to join this interesting group.

"Bartleby! quick, I am waiting."

I heard a slow scrape of his chair legs on the uncarpeted floor, and soon he appeared standing at the entrance of his hermitage.

"What is wanted?" said he, mildly.

"The copies, the copies," said I, hurriedly. "We are going to examine them. There"—and I held towards him the fourth quadruplicate.

"I would prefer not to," he said, and gently disappeared behind the screen.

"I would prefer not to," he said, and gently disappeared behind the screen.

For a few moments I was turned into a pillar of salt, standing at the head of my seated column of clerks. Recovering myself, I advanced towards the screen, and demanded the reason for such extraordinary conduct.

"*Why* do you refuse?"

"I would prefer not to."

With any other man I should have flown outright into a dreadful passion, scorned all further words, and thrust him ignominiously from my presence. But there was something about Bartleby that not only strangely disarmed me, but, in a wonderful manner, touched and disconcerted me. I began to reason with him.

"These are your own copies we are about to examine. It is labor saving to you, because one examination will answer for your four papers. It is common usage. Every copyist is bound to help examine his copy. Is it not so? Will you not speak? Answer!"

"I prefer not to," he replied in a flute-like tone. It seemed to me that, while I had been addressing him, he carefully revolved every statement that I made; fully comprehended the meaning; could not gainsay the irresistible conclusion; but, at the same

---

45 Cicero—Marcus Tullius Cicero (106–43 B.C.), Roman statesman and philosopher.

time, some paramount consideration prevailed with him to reply as he did.

"You are decided, then, not to comply with my request—a request made according to common usage and common sense?"

He briefly gave me to understand, that on that point my judgment was sound. Yes: his decision was irreversible.

It is not seldom the case that, when a man is browbeaten in some unprecedented and violently unreasonable way, he begins to stagger in his own plainest faith. He begins, as it were, vaguely to surmise that, wonderful as it may be, all the justice and all the reason is on the other side. Accordingly, if any disinterested persons are present, he turns to them for some reinforcement of his own faltering mind.

"Turkey," said I, "what do you think of this? Am I not right?"

"With submission, sir," said Turkey, in his blandest tone, "I think that you are."

"Nippers," said I, "what do *you* think of it?"

"I think I should kick him out of the office."

(The reader, of nice perceptions, will here perceive that, it being morning, Turkey's answer is couched in polite and tranquil terms, but Nippers replies in ill-tempered ones. Or, to repeat a previous sentence, Nippers's ugly mood was on duty, and Turkey's off.)

"Ginger Nut," said I, willing to enlist the smallest suffrage in my behalf, "what do *you* think of it?"

"I think, Sir, he's a little *luny*," replied Ginger Nut, with a grin.

"You hear what they say," said I, turning towards the screen, "come forth and do your duty."

But he vouchsafed[46] no reply. I pondered a moment in sore perplexity. But once more business hurried me. I determined again to postpone the consideration of this dilemma to my future leisure. With a little trouble we made out to examine the papers without Bartleby, though at every page or two Turkey deferentially dropped his opinion, that this proceeding was quite out of the common; while Nippers, twitching in his chair with a dyspeptic[47] nervousness, ground out, between his set teeth, occasional hissing maledictions against the stubborn oaf behind the screen. And for his (Nippers's) part, this was the first and the last time he would do another man's business without pay.

Meanwhile Bartleby sat in his hermitage, oblivious to everything but his own peculiar business there.

Some days passed, the scrivener being employed upon another lengthy work. His late remarkable conduct led me to regard his ways narrowly. I observed that he never went to dinner; indeed, that he never went anywhere. As yet I had never, of my personal knowledge, known him to be outside of my office. He was a perpetual sentry in the corner. At about eleven o'clock though, in the morning, I noticed that Ginger Nut would advance toward the opening in Bartleby's screen, as if silently beckoned thither by a gesture

[46] vouchsafed—granted.

[47] dyspeptic—relating to indigestion.

invisible to me where I sat. The boy would then leave the office, jingling a few pence,[48] and reappear with a handful of ginger-nuts, which he delivered in the hermitage, receiving two of the cakes for his trouble.

He lives, then, on ginger-nuts, thought I; never eats a dinner, properly speaking; he must be a vegetarian, then; but no; he never eats even vegetables, he eats nothing but ginger-nuts. My mind then ran on in reveries concerning the probable effects upon the human constitution of living entirely on ginger-nuts. Ginger-nuts are so called, because they contain ginger as one of their peculiar constituents, and the final flavoring one. Now, what was ginger? A hot, spicy thing. Was Bartleby hot and spicy? Not at all. Ginger, then, had no effect upon Bartleby. Probably he preferred it should have none.

Nothing so aggravates an earnest person as a passive resistance. If the individual so resisted be of a not inhumane temper, and the resisting one perfectly harmless in his passivity, then, in the better moods of the former, he will endeavor charitably to construe to his imagination what proves impossible to be solved by his judgment. Even so, for the most part, I regarded Bartleby and his ways. Poor fellow! thought I, he means no mischief; it is plain he intends no insolence; his aspect sufficiently evinces that his eccentricities are involuntary. He is useful to me. I can get along with him. If I turn him away, the chances are he will fall in with some less-indulgent employer, and then he will be rudely treated, and perhaps driven forth miserably to starve. Yes. Here I can cheaply purchase a delicious self-approval. To befriend Bartleby; to humor him in his strange willfulness, will cost me little or nothing, while I lay up in my soul what will eventually prove a sweet morsel for my conscience. But this mood was not invariable with me. The passiveness of Bartleby sometimes irritated me. I felt strangely goaded on to encounter him in new opposition—to elicit some angry spark from him answerable to my own. But, indeed, I might as well have essayed to strike fire with my knuckles against a bit of Windsor soap. But one afternoon the evil impulse in me mastered me, and the following little scene ensued:

"Bartleby," said I, "when those papers are all copied, I will compare them with you."

"I would prefer not to."

"How? Surely you do not mean to persist in that mulish vagary?"[49]

No answer.

I threw open the folding-doors near by, and, turning upon Turkey and Nippers, exclaimed:

"Bartleby a second time says, he won't examine his papers. What do you think of it, Turkey?"

It was afternoon, be it remembered. Turkey sat glowing like a brass boiler; his bald head steaming; his hands reeling among his blotted papers.

"Think of it?" roared Turkey; "I think I'll just step behind his screen, and black his eyes for him!"

---

48 pence—old style plural of the word *penny*.

49 mulish vagary—stubborn whim.

So saying, Turkey rose to his feet and threw his arms into a pugilistic[50] position. He was hurrying away to make good his promise, when I detained him, alarmed at the effect of incautiously rousing Turkey's combativeness after dinner.

"Sit down, Turkey," said I, "and hear what Nippers has to say. What do you think of it, Nippers? Would I not be justified in immediately dismissing Bartleby?"

"Excuse me, that is for you to decide, sir. I think his conduct quite unusual, and, indeed, unjust, as regards Turkey and myself. But it may only be a passing whim."

"Ah," exclaimed I, "you have strangely changed your mind, then—you speak very gently of him now."

"All beer," cried Turkey; "gentleness is effects of beer—Nippers and I dined together today. You see how gentle *I* am, sir. Shall I go and black his eyes?"

"You refer to Bartleby, I suppose. No, not today, Turkey," I replied; "pray, put up your fists."

I closed the doors, and again advanced towards Bartleby. I felt additional incentives tempting me to my fate. I burned to be rebelled against again. I remembered that Bartleby never left the office.

"Bartleby," said I, "Ginger Nut is away; just step around to the Post Office, won't you? (it was but a three minutes' walk), and see if there is anything for me."

"I would prefer not to."

"You *will* not?"

"I *prefer* not."

I staggered to my desk, and sat there in a deep study. My blind inveteracy[51] returned. Was there any other thing in which I could procure myself to be ignominiously repulsed by this lean, penniless wight?[52]—my hired clerk? What added thing is there, perfectly reasonable, that he will be sure to refuse to do?

"Bartleby!"

No answer.

"Bartleby," in a louder tone.

No answer.

"Bartleby," I roared.

Like a very ghost, agreeably to the laws of magical invocation, at the third summons, he appeared at the entrance of his hermitage.

"Go to the next room, and tell Nippers to come to me."

"I prefer not to," he respectfully and slowly said, and mildly disappeared.

"Very good, Bartleby," said I, in a quiet sort of serenely-severe self-possessed tone, intimating the unalterable purpose of some terrible retribution very close at hand. At the moment I half intended something of the kind. But upon the whole, as it was drawing towards my dinner-hour, I thought it best to put on my hat and walk home for the day, suffering much from perplexity and distress of mind.

Shall I acknowledge it? The conclusion of this whole business was, that it soon became a fixed fact of my chambers, that a pale young scrivener, by the name of Bartleby, had a desk there; that he copied for me at the usual rate of four cents a folio (one hundred words); but he was permanently exempt from examining the work

---

50 pugilistic—of boxing.

51 inveteracy—habit.

52 wight—being.

done by him, that duty being transferred to Turkey and Nippers, out of compliment, doubtless, to their superior acuteness; moreover, said Bartleby was never, on any account, to be dispatched on the most trivial errand of any sort; and that even if entreated to take upon him such a matter, it was generally understood that he would "prefer not to"—in other words, that he would refuse point-blank.

As days passed on, I became considerably reconciled to Bartleby. His steadiness, his freedom from all dissipation,[53] his incessant industry (except when he chose to throw himself into a standing revery behind his screen), his great stillness, his unalterableness of demeanor under all circumstances, made him a valuable acquisition. One prime thing was this—*he was always there*—first in the morning, continually through the day, and the last at night. I had a singular confidence in his honesty. I felt my most precious papers perfectly safe in his hands. Sometimes, to be sure, I could not, for the very soul of me, avoid falling into sudden spasmodic passions with him. For it was exceeding difficult to bear in mind all the time those strange peculiarities, privileges, and unheard of exemptions, forming the tacit stipulations[54] on Bartleby's part under which he remained in my office. Now and then, in the eagerness of dispatching pressing business, I would inadvertently summon Bartleby, in a short, rapid tone, to put his finger, say, on the incipient tie of a bit of red tape with which I was about compressing some papers. Of course, from behind the screen the usual answer, "I prefer not to," was sure to come; and then, how could a human creature, with the common infirmities of our nature, refrain from bitterly exclaiming upon such perverseness—such unreasonableness. However, every added repulse of this sort which I received only tended to lessen the probability of my repeating the inadvertence.[55]

As days passed on, I became considerably reconciled to Bartleby.

Here it must be said, that according to the custom of most legal gentlemen occupying chambers in densely-populated law buildings, there were several keys to my door. One was kept by a woman residing in the attic, which person weekly scrubbed and daily swept and dusted my apartments. Another was kept by Turkey for convenience sake. The third I sometimes carried in my own pocket. The fourth I knew not who had.

Now, one Sunday morning I happened to go to Trinity Church, to hear a celebrated preacher, and finding myself rather early on the ground I thought I would walk around to my chambers for a while. Luckily I had my key with me; but upon applying it to the lock, I found it resisted by something inserted from the inside. Quite surprised, I called out; when to my consternation a key was turned from within; and thrusting his lean visage at me, and holding the door ajar, the apparition of Bartleby appeared, in his shirt sleeves, and otherwise

[53] dissipation—amusement, indulgence.

[54] tacit stipulations—unspoken conditions.

[55] inadvertence—unintentional lack of care.

in a strangely tattered deshabille,[56] saying quietly that he was sorry, but he was deeply engaged just then, and—preferred not admitting me at present. In a brief word or two, he moreover added, that perhaps I had better walk around the block two or three times, and by that time he would probably have concluded his affairs.

Now, the utterly unsurmised[57] appearance of Bartleby, tenanting my law-chambers of a Sunday morning, with his cadaverously[58] gentlemanly *nonchalance*,[59] yet withal firm and self-possessed, had such a strange effect upon me, that incontinently[60] I slunk away from my own door, and did as desired. But not without sundry twinges of impotent rebellion against the mild effrontery of this unaccountable scrivener. Indeed, it was his wonderful mildness chiefly, which not only disarmed me, but unmanned me as it were. For I consider that one, for the time, is a sort of unmanned when he tranquilly permits his hired clerk to dictate to him, and order him away from his own premises. Furthermore, I was full of uneasiness as to what Bartleby could possibly be doing in my office in his shirt sleeves, and in an otherwise dismantled condition of a Sunday morning. Was anything amiss going on? Nay, that was out of the question. It was not to be thought of for a moment that Bartleby was an immoral person. But what could he be doing there?—copying? Nay again, whatever might be his eccentricities, Bartleby was an eminently decorous person. He would be the last man to sit down to his desk in any state approaching to nudity. Besides, it was Sunday; and there was something about Bartleby that forbade the supposition that he would by any secular occupation violate the proprieties of the day.

Nevertheless, my mind was not pacified; and full of a restless curiosity, at last I returned to the door. Without hindrance I inserted my key, opened it, and entered. Bartleby was not to be seen. I looked round anxiously, peeped behind his screen; but it was very plain that he was gone. Upon more closely examining the place, I surmised that for an indefinite period Bartleby must have ate, dressed, and slept in my office, and that, too without plate, mirror, or bed. The cushioned seat of a ricketty old sofa in one corner bore the faint impress of a lean, reclining form. Rolled away under his desk, I found a blanket; under the empty grate, a blacking box and brush; on a chair, a tin basin, with soap and a ragged towel; in a newspaper a few crumbs of ginger-nuts and a morsel of cheese. Yes, thought I, it is evident enough that Bartleby has been making his home here, keeping bachelor's hall all by himself. Immediately then the thought came sweeping across me, what miserable friendlessness and loneliness are here revealed! His poverty is great; but his solitude, how horrible! Think of it. Of a Sunday, Wall Street is deserted as Petra;[61] and every night of every day it is an

---

56 deshabille—casual dress.

57 unsurmised—unexpected.

58 cadaverously—emaciatedly, gauntly.

59 *nonchalance*—casual lack of concern.

60 incontinently—immediately.

61 Petra—ancient ruined city in present-day Jordan. Petra was the capital of the Nabatean Empire.

emptiness. This building, too, which of week-days hums with industry and life, at nightfall echoes with sheer vacancy, and all through Sunday is forlorn. And here Bartleby makes his home; sole spectator of a solitude which he has seen all populous—a sort of innocent and transformed Marius[62] brooding among the ruins of Carthage![63]

For the first time in my life a feeling of over-powering stinging melancholy seized me. Before, I had never experienced aught but a not unpleasing sadness. The bond of a common humanity now drew me irresistibly to gloom. A fraternal melancholy! For both I and Bartleby were sons of Adam. I remembered the bright silks and sparkling faces I had seen that day, in gala trim, swan-like sailing down the Mississippi of Broadway;[64] and I contrasted them with the pallid copyist, and thought to myself, Ah, happiness courts the light, so we deem the world is gay; but misery hides aloof, so we deem that misery there is none. These sad fancyings—chimeras,[65] doubtless, of a sick and silly brain—led on to other and more special thoughts, concerning the eccentricities of Bartleby. Presentiments of strange discoveries hovered round me. The scrivener's pale form appeared to me laid out, among uncaring strangers, in its shivering winding sheet.

Suddenly I was attracted by Bartleby's closed desk, the key in open sight left in the lock.

I mean no mischief, seek the gratification of no heartless curiosity, thought I; besides, the desk is mine, and its contents, too, so I will make bold to look within. Everything was methodically arranged, the papers smoothly placed. The pigeon holes were deep, and removing the files of documents, I groped into their recesses. Presently I felt something there, and dragged it out. It was an old bandanna handkerchief, heavy and knotted. I opened it, and saw it was a savings bank.

The bond of a common humanity now drew me irresistibly to gloom.

I now recalled all the quiet mysteries which I had noted in the man. I remembered that he never spoke but to answer; that, though at intervals he had considerable time to himself, yet I had never seen him reading—no, not even a newspaper; that for long periods he would stand looking out, at his pale window behind the screen, upon the dead brick wall; I was quite sure he never visited any refectory or eating house; while his pale face clearly indicated that he never drank beer like Turkey, or tea and coffee even, like other men; that he never went anywhere in particular that I could learn; never went out for a walk, unless, indeed, that was the case at present; that he had declined telling who he was, or whence he came, or whether he had any relatives in the world; that though so thin and pale, he never complained of ill health. And more than all, I remembered a certain unconscious air of pallid—how shall I call

---

[62] Marius (157–86 B.C.)—Roman general and consul who dominated Rome for many years.

[63] Carthage—city in North Africa that was destroyed by the Romans in 146 B.C.

[64] Broadway—one of the main thoroughfares of New York City.

[65] chimeras—illusions.

it?—of pallid haughtiness, say, or rather an austere reserve about him, which had positively awed me into my tame compliance with his eccentricities, when I had feared to ask him to do the slightest incidental thing for me, even though I might know, from his long-continued motionlessness, that behind his screen he must be standing in one of those dead-wall reveries of his.

Revolving all these things, and coupling them with the recently discovered fact, that he made my office his constant abiding place and home, and not forgetful of his morbid moodiness; revolving all these things, a prudential feeling began to steal over me. My first emotions had been those of pure melancholy and sincerest pity; but just in proportion as the forlornness of Bartleby grew and grew to my imagination, did that same melancholy merge into fear, that pity into repulsion. So true it is, and so terrible, took that up to a certain point the thought or sight of misery enlists our best affections; but, in certain special cases, beyond that point it does not. They err who would assert that invariably this is owing to the inherent selfishness of the human heart. It rather proceeds from a certain hopelessness of remedying excessive and organic ill. To a sensitive being, pity is not seldom pain. And when at last it is perceived that such pity cannot lead to effectual **succor**,[66] common sense bids the soul be rid of it. What I saw that morning persuaded me that the scrivener was the victim of innate and incurable disorder. I might give alms to his body; but his body did not pain him; it was his soul that suffered, and his soul I could not reach.

I did not accomplish the purpose of going to Trinity Church that morning. Somehow, the things I had seen disqualified me for the time from church-going. I walked homeward, thinking what I would do with Bartleby. Finally, I resolved upon this—I would put certain calm questions to him the next morning, touching his history, etc., and if he declined to answer them openly and unreservedly (and I supposed he would prefer not), then to give him a twenty dollar bill over and above whatever I might owe him, and tell him his services were no longer required; but that if in any other way I could assist him, I would be happy to do so, especially if he desired to return to his native place, wherever that might be, I would willingly help to defray the expenses. Moreover, if, after reaching home, he found himself at any time in want of aid, a letter from him would be sure of a reply.

The next morning came.

"Bartleby," said I, gently calling to him behind his screen.

No reply.

"Bartleby," said I, in a still gentler tone, "come here; I am not going to ask you to do anything you would prefer not to do—I simply wish to speak to you."

Upon this he noiselessly slid into view.

"Will you tell me, Bartleby, where you were born?"

"I would prefer not to."

"Will you tell me *anything* about yourself?"

"I would prefer not to."

---

[66] **succor**—assistance, relief.

"But what reasonable objection can you have to speak to me—I feel friendly towards you."

He did not look at me while I spoke, but kept his glance fixed upon my bust of Cicero, which, as I then sat, was directly behind me, some six inches above my head.

"What is your answer, Bartleby?" said I, after waiting a considerable time for a reply, during which his countenance remained immovable, only there was the faintest conceivable tremor of the white **attenuated**[67] mouth.

"At present I prefer to give no answer," he said, and retired into his hermitage.

It was rather weak in me I confess, but his manner, on this occasion, nettled me. Not only did there seem to lurk in it a certain calm disdain, but his perverseness seemed ungrateful, considering the undeniable good usage and indulgence he had received from me.

Again I sat ruminating[68] what I should do. Mortified as I was at his behavior, and resolved as I had been to dismiss him when I entered my office, nevertheless I strangely felt something superstitious knocking at my heart, and forbidding me to carry out my purpose, and denouncing me for a villain if I dared to breathe one bitter word against this forlornest of mankind. At last, familiarly drawing my chair behind his screen, I sat down and said: "Bartleby, never mind, then, about revealing your history; but let me entreat you, as a friend, to comply as far as may be with the usages of this office. Say now, you will help to examine papers tomorrow or next day: in short, say now, that in a day or two you will begin to be a little reasonable:—say so, Bartleby."

"At present I would prefer not to be a little reasonable," was his mildly cadaverous reply.

Just then the folding-doors opened, and Nippers approached. He seemed suffering from an unusually bad night's rest, induced by severer indigestion than common. He overheard those final words of Bartleby.

"*Prefer not*, eh?" gritted Nippers—"I'd *prefer* him, if I were you, sir," addressing me—"I'd *prefer* him; I'd give him preferences, the stubborn mule! What is it, sir, pray, that he *prefers* not to do now?"

Bartleby moved not a limb.

"Mr. Nippers," said I, "I'd prefer that you would withdraw for the present."

Somehow, of late, I had got into the way of involuntarily using this word "prefer" upon all sorts of not exactly suitable occasions. And I trembled to think that my contact with the scrivener had already and seriously affected me in a mental way. And what further and deeper aberration might it not yet produce? This apprehension had not been without efficacy in determining me to summary measures.

As Nippers, looking very sour and sulky, was departing, Turkey blandly and deferentially approached.

"With submission, sir," said he, "yesterday I was thinking about Bartleby here, and I think that if he would but prefer to

---

[67] **attenuated**—reduced or weakened in strength.
[68] ruminating—reflecting on.

take a quart of good ale every day, it would do much towards mending him, and enabling him to assist in examining his papers."

"So you have got the word, too," said I, slightly excited.

"With submission, what word, sir," asked Turkey, respectfully crowding himself into the contracted space behind the screen, and by so doing, making me jostle the scrivener. "What word, Sir?"

I looked steadfastly at him, and perceived that his eyes looked dull and glazed.

"I would prefer to be left alone here," said Bartleby, as if offended at being mobbed in his privacy.

"*That's* the word, Turkey," said I—"*that's* it."

"Oh, *prefer?* oh yes—queer word. I never use it myself. But, sir, as I was saying, if he would but prefer—"

"Turkey," interrupted I, "you will please withdraw."

"Oh, certainly, sir, if you prefer that I should."

As he opened the folding-door to retire, Nippers at his desk caught a glimpse of me, and asked whether I would prefer to have a certain paper copied on blue paper or white. He did not in the least roguishly accent the word *prefer*. It was plain that it involuntarily rolled from his tongue. I thought to myself, surely I must get rid of a demented man, who already has in some degree turned the tongues, if not the heads of myself and clerks. But I thought it prudent not to break the dismission at once.

The next day I noticed that Bartleby did nothing but stand at his window in his dead-wall revery. Upon asking him why he did not write, he said that he had decided upon doing no more writing.

"Why, how now? what next?" exclaimed I, "do no more writing?"

"No more."

"And what is the reason?"

"Do you not see the reason for yourself," he indifferently replied.

I looked steadfastly at him, and perceived that his eyes looked dull and glazed. Instantly it occurred to me, that his unexampled diligence in copying by his dim window for the first few weeks of his stay with me might have temporarily impaired his vision.

I was touched. I said something in condolence with him. I hinted that of course he did wisely in abstaining from writing for a while; and urged him to embrace that opportunity of taking wholesome exercise in the open air. This, however, he did not do. A few days after this, my other clerks being absent, and being in a great hurry to dispatch certain letters by the mail, I thought that, having nothing else earthly to do, Bartleby would surely be less inflexible than usual, and carry these letters to the post-office. But he blankly declined. So, much to my inconvenience, I went myself.

Still added days went by. Whether Bartleby's eyes improved or not, I could not say. To all appearance, I thought they did. But when I asked him if they did, he vouchsafed no answer. At all events, he would do no copying. At last, in reply to my urgings, he informed me that he had permanently given up copying.

"What!" exclaimed I; "suppose your eyes should get entirely well—better than ever before—would you not copy then?"

"I have given up copying," he answered, and slid aside.

He remained as ever, a fixture in my chamber. Nay—if that were possible—he became still more of a fixture than before. What was to be done? He would do nothing in the office; why should he stay there? In plain fact, he had now become a millstone to me, not only useless as a necklace, but afflictive[69] to bear. Yet I was sorry for him. I speak less than truth when I say that, on his own account, he occasioned me uneasiness. If he would but have named a single relative or friend, I would instantly have written, and urged their taking the poor fellow away to some convenient retreat. But he seemed alone, absolutely alone in the universe. A bit of wreck in the mid-Atlantic. At length, necessities connected with my business tyrannized over all other considerations. Decently as I could, I told Bartleby that in six days time he must unconditionally leave the office. I warned him to take measures, in the interval, for procuring some other abode. I offered to assist him in this endeavor, if he himself would but take the first step towards a removal. "And when you finally quit me, Bartleby," added I, "I shall see that you go not away entirely unprovided. Six days from this hour, remember."

At the expiration of that period, I peeped behind the screen, and lo! Bartleby was there.

I buttoned up my coat, balanced myself; advanced slowly towards him, touched his shoulder, and said, "The time has come; you must quit this place; I am sorry for you; here is money; but you must go."

"I would prefer not," he replied, with his back still towards me.

"You *must*."

He remained silent.

Now I had an unbounded confidence in this man's common honesty. He had frequently restored to me sixpences and shillings carelessly dropped upon the floor, for I am apt to be very reckless in such shirt-button affairs. The proceeding, then, which followed will not be deemed extraordinary.

"Bartleby," said I, "I owe you twelve dollars on account; here are thirty-two; the odd twenty are yours—Will you take it?" and I handed the bills towards him.

But he made no motion.

"I will leave them here, then," putting them under a weight on the table. Then taking my hat and cane and going to the door, I tranquilly turned and added—"After you have removed your things from these offices, Bartleby, you will of course lock the door—since every one is now gone for the day but you—and if you please, slip your key underneath the mat, so that I may have it in the morning. I shall not see you again; so good-by to you. If, hereafter, in your new place of abode, I can be of any service to you, do

---

69 afflictive—causing pain and distress.

not fail to advise me by letter. Good-by, Bartleby, and fare you well."

But he answered not a word; like the last column of some ruined temple, he remained standing mute and solitary in the middle of the otherwise deserted room.

As I walked home in a pensive mood, my vanity got the better of my pity. I could not but highly plume myself on my masterly management in getting rid of Bartleby. Masterly I call it, and such it must appear to any dispassionate thinker. The beauty of my procedure seemed to consist in its perfect quietness. There was no vulgar bullying, no bravado of any sort, no choleric hectoring,[70] and striding to and fro across the apartment, jerking out vehement commands for Bartleby to bundle himself off with his beggarly traps. Nothing of the kind. Without loudly bidding Bartleby depart—as an inferior genius might have done—I *assumed* the ground that depart he must; and upon that assumption built all I had to say. The more I thought over my procedure, the more I was charmed with it. Nevertheless, next morning, upon awakening, I had my doubts—I had somehow slept off the fumes of vanity. One of the coolest and wisest hours a man has, is just after he awakes in the morning. My procedure seemed as **sagacious**[71] as ever—but only in theory. How it would prove in practice—there was the rub. It was truly a beautiful thought to have assumed Bartleby's departure; but, after all, that assumption was simply my own, and none of Bartleby's. The great point was, not whether I had assumed that he would quit me, but whether he would prefer so to do. He was more a man of preferences than assumptions.

After breakfast, I walked down town, arguing the probabilities *pro* and *con*. One moment I thought it would prove a miserable failure, and Bartleby would be found all alive at my office as usual; the next moment it seemed certain that I should find his chair empty. And so I kept veering about. At the corner of Broadway and Canal Street, I saw quite an excited group of people standing in earnest conversation.

"I'll take odds he doesn't," said a voice as I passed.

"Doesn't go?—done!" said I, "put up your money."

I was instinctively putting my hand in my pocket to produce my own, when I remembered that this was an election day. The words I had overheard bore no reference to Bartleby, but to the success or non-success of some candidate for the mayoralty. In my intent frame of mind, I had, as it were, imagined that all Broadway shared in my excitement, and were debating the same question with me. I passed on, very thankful that the uproar of the street screened my momentary absent-mindedness.

As I had intended, I was earlier than usual at my office door. I stood listening for a moment. All was still. He must be gone. I tried the knob. The door was locked. Yes, my procedure had worked to a charm; he indeed must be vanished. Yet a

---

70 choleric hectoring—angry bullying.

71 **sagacious**—having keen discernment and sound judgment.

certain melancholy mixed with this: I was almost sorry for my brilliant success. I was fumbling under the door mat for the key, which Bartleby was to have left there for me, when accidentally my knee knocked against a panel, producing a summoning sound, and in response a voice came to me from within—"Not yet; I am occupied."

It was Bartleby.

I was thunderstruck. For an instant I stood like the man who, pipe in mouth, was killed one cloudless afternoon long ago in Virginia, by summer lightning; at his own warm open window he was killed, and remained leaning out there upon the dreamy afternoon, till some one touched him, when he fell.

"Not gone!" I murmured at last. But again obeying that wondrous ascendancy which the inscrutable scrivener had over me, and from which ascendancy, for all my chafing, I could not completely escape, I slowly went down stairs and out into the street, and while walking round the block, considered what I should next do in this unheard-of perplexity. Turn the man out by an actual thrusting I could not; to drive him away by calling him hard names would not do; calling in the police was an unpleasant idea; and yet, permit him to enjoy his cadaverous triumph over me—this, too, I could not think of. What was to be done? or, if nothing could be done, was there anything further that I could *assume* in the matter? Yes, as before I had prospectively assumed that Bartleby would depart, so now I might retrospectively assume that departed he was. In the legitimate carrying out of this assumption, I might enter my office in a great hurry, and pretending not to see Bartleby at all, walk straight against him as if he were air. Such a proceeding would in a singular degree have the appearance of a home-thrust. It was hardly possible that Bartleby could withstand such an application of the doctrine of assumptions. But upon second thoughts the success of the plan seemed rather dubious. I resolved to argue the matter over with him again.

"Bartleby," said I, entering the office, with a quietly severe expression, "I am seriously displeased. I am pained, Bartleby. I had thought better of you. I had imagined you of such a gentlemanly organization, that in any delicate dilemma a slight hint would suffice—in short, an assumption. But it appears I am deceived. Why," I added, unaffectedly starting, "you have not even touched that money yet," pointing to it, just where I had left it the evening previous.

He answered nothing.

"Will you, or will you not, quit me?" I now demanded in a sudden passion, advancing close to him.

"I would prefer *not* to quit you" he replied, gently emphasizing the *not*.

"What eathly right have you to stay here? Do you pay any rent? Do you pay my taxes? Or is this property yours?"

He answered nothing.

"Are you ready to go on and write now? Are your eyes recovered? Could you copy a small paper for me this morning? or help examine a few lines? or step round to the Post Office? In a word, will you do anything at all, to give a coloring to your refusal to depart the premises?"

He silently retired into his hermitage.

I was now in such a state of nervous resentment that I thought it but prudent to check myself at present from further demonstrations. Bartleby and I were alone. I remembered the tragedy of the unfortunate Adams and the still more unfortunate Colt in the solitary office of the latter; and how poor Colt, being dreadfully incensed by Adams, and imprudently permitting himself to get wildly excited, was at unawares hurried into his fatal act—an act which certainly no man could possibly **deplore**[72] more than the actor himself. Often it had occurred to me in my ponderings upon the subject, that had that altercation taken place in the public street, or at a private residence, it would not have terminated as it did. It was the circumstance of being alone in a solitary office, up stairs, of a building entirely unhallowed by humanizing domestic associations—an uncarpeted office, doubtless, of a dusty, haggard sort of appearance—this it must have been, which greatly helped to enhance the irritable desperation of the hapless Colt.

But when this old Adam of resentment rose in me and tempted me concerning Bartleby, I grappled him and threw him. How? Why, simply by recalling the divine injunction: "A new commandment give I unto you, that ye love one another." Yes, this it was that saved me. Aside from higher considerations, charity often operates as a vastly wise and prudent principle—a great safeguard to its possessor. Men have committed murder for jealousy's sake, and anger's sake, and hatred's sake, and selfishness' sake, and spiritual pride's sake; but no man, that ever I heard of, ever committed a diabolical murder for sweet charity's sake. Mere self-interest, then, if no better motive can be enlisted, should, especially with high-tempered men, prompt all beings to charity and philanthropy. At any rate, upon the occasion in question, I strove to drown my exasperated feelings towards the scrivener by benevolently construing his conduct. Poor fellow, poor fellow! thought I, he don't mean anything; and besides, he has seen hard times, and ought to be indulged.

I endeavored, also, immediately to occupy myself, and at the same time to comfort my despondency. I tried to fancy, that in the course of the morning, at such time as might prove agreeable to him, Bartleby, of his own free accord, would emerge from his hermitage and take up some decided line of march in the direction of the door. But no. Half-past twelve o'clock came; Turkey began to glow in the face, overturn his inkstand, and become generally obstreperous; Nippers abated down into quietude and courtesy; Ginger Nut munched his noon apple; and Bartleby remained standing at his window in one of his profoundest dead-wall reveries. Will it be credited? Ought I to acknowledge it? That afternoon I left the office without saying one further word to him.

Some days now passed, during which, at leisure intervals I looked a little into "Edwards on the Will," and "Priestly on

[72] **deplore**—regret.

Necessity."[73] Under the circumstances, those books induced a salutary feeling. Gradually I slid into the persuasion that these troubles of mine, touching the scrivener, had been all predestinated from eternity, and Bartleby was billeted upon me for some mysterious purpose of an allwise Providence, which it was not for a mere mortal like me to fathom. Yes, Bartleby, stay there behind your screen, thought I; I shall persecute you no more; you are harmless and noiseless as any of these old chairs; in short, I never feel so private as when I know you are here. At last I see it, I feel it; I penetrate to the predestinated purpose of my life. I am content. Others may have loftier parts to enact; but my mission in this world, Bartleby, is to furnish you with office-room for such period as you may see fit to remain.

I believe that this wise and blessed frame of mind would have continued with me, had it not been for the unsolicited and uncharitable remarks obtruded upon me by my professional friends who visited the rooms. But thus it often is, that the constant friction of illiberal minds wears out at last the best resolves of the more generous. Though to be sure, when I reflected upon it, it was not strange that people entering my office should be struck by the peculiar aspect of the unaccountable Bartleby, and so be tempted to throw out some sinister observations concerning him. Sometimes an attorney, having business with me, and calling at my office, and finding no one but the scrivener there, would undertake to obtain some sort of precise information from him touching my whereabouts; but without heeding his idle talk, Bartleby would remain standing immovable in the middle of the room. So after contemplating him in that position for a time, the attorney would depart, no wiser than he came.

Also, when a reference[74] was going on, and the room full of lawyers and witnesses, and business driving fast, some deeply-occupied legal gentleman present, seeing Bartleby wholly unemployed, would request him to run round to his (the legal gentleman's) office and fetch some papers for him. Thereupon, Bartleby would tranquilly decline, and yet remain idle as before. Then the lawyer would give a great stare, and turn to me. And what could I say? At last I was made aware that all through the circle of my professional acquaintance, a whisper of wonder was running round, having reference to the strange creature I kept at my office. This worried me very much. And as the idea came upon me of his possibly turning out a long-lived man, and keep occupying my chambers, and denying my authority; and perplexing my visitors; and scandalizing my professional reputation; and casting a general gloom over the premises; keeping soul and body together to the last upon his savings (for doubtless he spent but half a dime a day), and in the end perhaps outlive me, and claim possession of my office by right of his perpetual occupancy: as all these dark anticipations crowded upon me more and more, and my friends continually

[73] "Edwards . . . Necessity"—The narrator refers to the American theologian Jonathan Edwards (1703–1758) and the English chemist Joseph Priestly (1733–1804), both of whom concluded that there is no such thing as free will.

[74] reference—referring of legal disputes to arbitrators.

intruded their relentless remarks upon the apparition in my room; a great change was wrought in me. I resolved to gather all my faculties together, and forever rid me of this intolerable incubus.[75] Ere revolving any complicated project, however, adapted to this end, I first simply suggested to Bartleby the propriety of his permanent departure. In a calm and serious tone, I commended the idea to his careful and mature consideration. But, having taken three days to meditate upon it, he apprised me, that his original determination remained the same; in short, that he still preferred to abide with me.

What, then, will you do? For all your coaxing, he will not budge.

What shall I do? I now said to myself, buttoning up my coat to the last button. What shall I do? what ought I to do? what does conscience say I *should* do with this man, or, rather, ghost. Rid myself of him, I must; go, he shall. But how? You will not thrust him, the poor, pale, passive mortal—you will not thrust such a helpless creature out of your door? you will not dishonor yourself by such cruelty? No, I will not, I cannot do that. Rather would I let him live and die here, and then mason up his remains in the wall. What, then, will you do? For all your coaxing, he will not budge. Bribes he leaves under your own paper-weight on your table; in short, it is quite plain that he prefers to cling to you.

Then something severe, something unusual must be done. What! surely you will not have him collared by a constable, and commit his innocent pallor to the common jail? And upon what ground could you procure such a thing to be done?—a vagrant, is he? What! he a vagrant, a wanderer, who refuses to budge? It is because he will *not* be a vagrant, then, that you seek to count him *as* a vagrant. That is too absurd. No visible means of support: there I have him. Wrong again: for indubitably he *does* support himself, and that is the only unanswerable proof that any man can show of his possessing the means so to do. No more, then. Since he will not quit me, I must quit him. I will change my offices; I will move elsewhere, and give him fair notice, that if I find him on my new premises I will then proceed against him as a common trespasser.

Acting accordingly, next day I thus addressed him: "I find these chambers too far from the City Hall; the air is unwholesome. In a word, I propose to remove my offices next week, and shall no longer require your services. I tell you this now, in order that you may seek another place."

He made no reply, and nothing more was said.

On the appointed day I engaged carts and men, proceeded to my chambers, and, having but little furniture, everything was removed in a few hours. Throughout, the scrivener remained standing behind the screen, which I directed to be removed the last thing. It was withdrawn; and, being folded up like a huge folio, left him the motionless occupant of a naked room. I

[75] incubus—evil spirit.

stood in the entry watching him a moment, while something from within me upbraided me.

I re-entered, with my hand in my pocket—and—and my heart in my mouth.

"Good-by, Bartleby; I am going—good-by, and God some way bless you; and take that," slipping something in his hand. But it dropped upon the floor, and then—strange to say—I tore myself from him whom I had so longed to be rid of.

Established in my new quarters, for a day or two I kept the door locked, and started at every footfall in the passages. When I returned to my rooms, after any little absence, I would pause at the threshold for an instant, and attentively listen, ere applying my key. But these fears were needless. Bartleby never came nigh me.

I thought all was going well, when a perturbed-looking stranger visited me, inquiring whether I was the person who had recently occupied rooms at No. — Wall Street.

Full of forebodings, I replied that I was.

"Then, sir," said the stranger, who proved a lawyer, "you are responsible for the man you left there. He refuses to do any copying; he refuses to do anything; he says he prefers not to; and he refuses to quit the premises."

"I am very sorry, sir," said I, with assumed tranquillity, but an inward tremor, "but, really, the man you allude to is nothing to me—he is no relation or apprentice of mine, that you should hold me responsible for him."

"In mercy's name, who is he?"

"I certainly cannot inform you. I know nothing about him. Formerly I employed him as a copyist; but he has done nothing for me now for some time past."

"I shall settle him, then—good morning, sir."

Several days passed, and I heard nothing more; and, though I often felt a charitable prompting to call at the place and see poor Bartleby, yet a certain squeamishness, of I know not what, withheld me.

All is over with him, by this time, thought I, at last, when, through another week, no further intelligence reached me. But, coming to my room the day after, I found several persons waiting at my door in a high state of nervous excitement.

"That's the man—here he comes," cried the foremost one, whom I recognized as the lawyer who had previously called upon me alone.

"You must take him away, sir, at once," cried a portly person among them, advancing upon me, and whom I knew to be the landlord of No. — Wall Street. "These gentlemen, my tenants, cannot stand it any longer; Mr. B —," pointing to the lawyer, "has turned him out of his room, and he now persists in haunting the building generally, sitting upon the banisters of the stairs by day, and sleeping in the entry by night. Everybody is concerned; clients are leaving the offices; some fears are entertained of a mob; something you must do, and that without delay."

Aghast at this torrent, I fell back before it, and would fain have locked myself in my new quarters. In vain I persisted that Bartleby was nothing to me—no more than to any one else. In vain—I was the last person known to have anything to do with him, and they held me to the terrible account. Fearful, then, of being exposed in the papers (as one person present obscurely threatened), I considered the matter, and, at length, said, that if the lawyer would give me a confidential interview with the scrivener, in his (the lawyer's) own room, I would, that afternoon, strive my best to rid them of the nuisance they complained of.

Going up stairs to my old haunt, there was Bartleby silently sitting upon the banister at the landing.

"What are you doing here, Bartleby?" said I.

"Sitting upon the banister," he mildly replied.

I motioned him into the lawyer's room, who then left us.

"Bartleby," said I, "are you aware that you are the cause of great **tribulation**[76] to me, by persisting in occupying the entry after being dismissed from the office?"

No answer.

"Now one of two things must take place. Either you must do something, or something must be done to you. Now what sort of business would you like to engage in? Would you like to re-engage in copying for some one?"

"No; I would prefer not to make any change."

"Would you like a clerkship in a dry-goods store?"

"There is too much confinement about that. No, I would not like a clerkship; but I am not particular."

"Too much confinement," I cried, "why you keep yourself confined all the time!"

"I would prefer not to take a clerkship," he rejoined, as if to settle that little item at once.

"How would a bar-tender's business suit you? There is no trying of the eye-sight in that."

"I would not like it at all; though, as I said before, I am not particular."

His unwonted wordiness inspirited me. I returned to the charge.

"Well, then, would you like to travel through the country collecting bills for the merchants? That would improve your health."

"No, I would prefer to be doing something else."

"How, then, would going as a companion to Europe, to entertain some young gentleman with your conversation—how would that suit you?"

"Not at all. It does not strike me that there is anything definite about that. I like to be stationary. But I am not particular."

"Stationary you shall be, then," I cried, now losing all patience, and, for the first time in all my exasperating connection with him, fairly flying into a passion. "If you do not go away from these premises before night, I shall feel bound—indeed, I *am* bound—to—to—to quit the premises myself!" I rather absurdly concluded, knowing not with what possible threat to try to frighten his immobility into compliance. Despairing of all further efforts, I was **precipitately**[77] leaving him, when a final thought occurred to me—one which had not been wholly unindulged before.

---

[76] **tribulation**—great affliction, distress.

[77] **precipitately**—occurring suddenly and rapidly.

"Bartleby," said I, in the kindest tone I could assume under such exciting circumstances, "will you go home with me now—not to my office, but my dwelling—and remain there till we can conclude upon some convenient arrangement for you at our leisure? Come, let us start now, right away."

"No; at present I would prefer not to make any change at all."

I answered nothing; but, effectually dodging every one by the suddenness and rapidity of my flight, rushed from the building, ran up Wall Street towards Broadway, and, jumping into the first omnibus, was soon removed from pursuit. As soon as tranquillity returned, I distinctly perceived that I had now done all that I possibly could, both in respect to the demands of the landlord and his tenants, and with regard to my own desire and sense of duty, to benefit Bartleby, and shield him from rude persecution. I now strove to be entirely care-free and quiescent;[78] and my conscience justified me in the attempt; though, indeed, it was not so successful as I could have wished. So fearful was I of being again hunted out by the incensed[79] landlord and his exasperated tenants, that, surrendering my business to Nippers, for a few days, I drove about the upper part of the town and through the suburbs, in my rockaway;[80] crossed over to Jersey City and Hoboken, and paid fugitive visits to Manhattanville and Astoria. In fact, I almost lived in my rockaway for the time.

When again I entered my office, lo, a note from the landlord lay upon the desk. I opened it with trembling hands. It informed me that the writer had sent to the police, and had Bartleby removed to the Tombs as a vagrant. Moreover, since I knew more about him than any one else, he wished me to appear at that place, and make a suitable statement of the facts. These tidings had a conflicting effect upon me. At first I was indignant; but, at last, almost approved. The landlord's energetic, summary disposition, had led him to adopt a procedure which I do not think I would have decided upon myself; and yet, as a last resort, under such peculiar circumstances, it seemed the only plan.

As I afterwards learned, the poor scrivener, when told that he must be conducted to the Tombs, offered not the slightest obstacle; but, in his pale, unmoving way, silently **acquiesced**.[81]

Some of the compassionate and curious bystanders joined the party; and headed by one of the constables arm in arm with Bartleby, the silent procession filed its way through all the noise, and heat, and joy of the roaring thoroughfares at noon.

The same day I received the note, I went to the Tombs, or, to speak more properly, the Halls of Justice. Seeking the right officer, I stated the purpose of my call, and was informed that the individual I described was, indeed, within. I then assured the functionary that Bartleby was a perfectly honest man, and greatly to be compassionated, however unaccountably

---

78 quiescent—quiet, still, inactive.

79 incensed—angry.

80 rockaway—light, low four-wheeled carriage.

81 **acquiesced**—consented passively.

eccentric. I narrated all I knew, and closed by suggesting the idea of letting him remain in as indulgent confinement as possible, till something less harsh might be done—though, indeed, I hardly knew what. At all events, if nothing else could be decided upon, the alms-house must receive him. I then begged to have an interview.

"I know you," he said, without looking around—"and I want nothing to say to you."

Being under no disgraceful charge, and quite serene and harmless in all his ways, they had permitted him freely to wander about the prison, and, especially, in the enclosed grass-platted yards thereof. And so I found him there, standing all alone in the quietest of the yards, his face towards a high wall, while all around, from the narrow slits of the jail windows, I thought I saw peering out upon him the eyes of murderers and thieves.

"Bartleby!"

"I know you," he said, without looking around—"and I want nothing to say to you."

"It was not I that brought you here, Bartleby," said I, keenly pained at his implied suspicion. "And to you, this should not be so vile a place. Nothing reproachful attaches to you by being here. And see, it is not so sad a place as one might think. Look, there is the sky, and here is the grass."

"I know where I am," he replied, but would say nothing more, and so I left him.

As I entered the corridor again, a broad meat-like man, in an apron, accosted me, and, jerking his thumb over his shoulder, said—"Is that your friend?"

"Yes."

"Does he want to starve? If he does, let him live on the prison fare, that's all."

"Who are you?" asked I, not knowing what to make of such an unofficially speaking person in such a place.

"I am the grub-man. Such gentlemen as have friends here, hire me to provide them with something good to eat."

"Is this so?" said I, turning to the turnkey.

He said it was.

"Well, then," said I, slipping some silver into the grub-man's hands (for so they called him), "I want you to give particular attention to my friend there; let him have the best dinner you can get. And you must be as polite to him as possible."

"Introduce me, will you?" said the grub-man, looking at me with an expression which seemed to say he was all impatience for an opportunity to give a specimen of his breeding.

Thinking it would prove of benefit to the scrivener, I acquiesced; and, asking the grub-man his name, went up with him to Bartleby.

"Bartleby, this is a friend; you will find him very useful to you."

"Your servant, sir, your servant," said the grub-man, making a low salutation behind his apron. "Hope you find it pleasant here, sir; nice grounds—cool apartments—hope you'll stay with us sometime—try to make it agreeable. What will you have for dinner today?"

"I prefer not to dine today," said Bartleby, turning away. "It would disagree with me; I am unused to dinners." So saying, he slowly moved to the other side of the enclosure, and took up a position fronting the dead-wall.

"How's this?" said the grub-man, addressing me with a stare of astonishment. "He's odd, ain't he?"

"I think he is a little deranged," said I, sadly.

"Deranged? deranged is it? Well, now, upon my word, I thought that friend of yourn was a gentleman forger; they are always pale and genteel-like, them forgers. I can't help pity 'em—can't help it, sir. Did you know Monroe Edwards?" he added, touchingly, and paused. Then, laying his hand piteously on my shoulder, sighed, "he died of consumption at Sing-Sing.[82] So you weren't acquainted with Monroe?"

"No, I was never socially acquainted with any forgers. But I cannot stop longer. Look to my friend yonder. You will not lose by it. I will see you again."

Some few days after this, I again obtained admission to the Tombs, and went through the corridors in quest of Bartleby; but without finding him.

"I saw him coming from his cell not long ago," said a turnkey, "maybe he's gone to loiter in the yards."

So I went in that direction.

"Are you looking for the silent man?" said another turnkey, passing me. "Yonder he lies—sleeping in the yard there. 'Tis not twenty minutes since I saw him lie down."

The yard was entirely quiet. It was not accessible to the common prisoners. The surrounding walls, of amazing thickness, kept off all sounds behind them. The Egyptian character of the masonry weighed upon me with its gloom. But a soft imprisoned turf grew under foot. The heart of the eternal pyramids, it seemed, wherein, by some strange magic, through the clefts, grass-seed, dropped by birds, had sprung.

Strangely huddled at the base of the wall, his knees drawn up, and lying on his side, his head touching the cold stones, I saw the wasted Bartleby. But nothing stirred. I paused; then went close up to him; stooped over, and saw that his dim eyes were open; otherwise he seemed profoundly sleeping. Something prompted me to touch him. I felt his hand, when a tingling shiver ran up my arm and down my spine to my feet.

The round face of the grub-man peered upon me now. "His dinner is ready. Won't he dine today, either? Or does he live without dining?"

"Lives without dining," said I, and closed the eyes.

"Eh!—He's asleep, ain't he?"

"With kings and counselors," murmured I.

There would seem little need for proceeding further in this history. Imagination will readily supply the meager recital of

[82] Sing-Sing—prison in upstate New York.

poor Bartleby's interment. But, ere parting with the reader, let me say, that if this little narrative has sufficiently interested him, to awaken curiosity as to who Bartleby was, and what manner of life he led prior to the present narrator's making his acquaintance, I can only reply, that in such curiosity I fully share, but am wholly unable to gratify it. Yet here I hardly know whether I should divulge one little item of rumor, which came to my ear a few months after the scrivener's decease. Upon what basis it rested, I could never ascertain; and hence, how true it is I cannot now tell. But, inasmuch as this vague report has not been without a certain suggestive interest to me, however sad, it may prove the same with some others; and so I will briefly mention it. The report was this: that Bartleby had been a subordinate clerk in the Dead Letter Office[83] at Washington, from which he had been suddenly removed by a change in the administration. When I think over this rumor, hardly can I express the emotions which seize me. Dead letters! does it not sound like dead men? Conceive a man by nature and misfortune prone to a pallid hopelessness, can any business seem more fitted to heighten it than that of continually handling these dead letters, and assorting them for the flames? For by the cart-load they are annually burned. Sometimes from out the folded paper the pale clerk takes a ring—the finger it was meant for, perhaps, moulders in the grave; a bank-note sent in swiftest charity—he whom it would relieve, nor eats nor hungers any more; pardon for those who died despairing; hope for those who died unhoping; good tidings for those who died stifled by unrelieved calamities. On errands of life, these letters speed to death.

Dead letters! does it not sound like dead men?

Ah, Bartleby! Ah, humanity!

[83] Dead Letter Office—government office which deals with destroying undeliverable mail.

QUESTIONS TO CONSIDER

1. Describe the narrator's three employees. What is peculiar about each of them?
2. Why does the narrator not fire Bartleby when he refuses to do any work? List all of the reasons you can think of. Which seems the most important?
3. Describe the character of the narrator. Do you think he is a good man? Why or why not?
4. What is notable about what Bartleby says to the lawyer at the prison?
5. How does the rumor about the Dead Letter Office help to explain Bartleby's character?
6. What view of society is reflected in this story?
7. In what ways is "Bartleby, the Scrivener" a romantic story? In what ways is it a realistic story?

Sarah Orne Jewett ▶

A White Heron

BY SARAH ORNE JEWETT

Sarah Orne Jewett (1849–1909) will always be associated with rural Maine. She was born in South Berwick and lived almost her entire life within a few miles of the town. Jewett's fiction documents the lives and people of Maine in the late nineteenth century. Because of her subject matter, Jewett is often classed with the local colorists, writers who in the nineteenth century tried to realistically depict the regions of the United States. They concentrated on the landscape, dialect, and traditions that make each part of the nation unique. Jewett was the daughter of a doctor and, in her youth, helped him make his rounds. By her twenties she was regularly selling stories, and in 1877 published her first book, Deephaven, *a series of interlocking tales about her town. Her masterpiece,* The Country of the Pointed Firs, *was published in 1896, by which time local-color writing was being dismissed by critics and readers because America was becoming urban and industrialized. What critics failed to understand was that local-color writing only stresses the past when the setting and details are the main interest in the story, rather than the background to it. In Jewett's best work—as in the work of Mark Twain and Willa Cather, and many other local colorists sometimes dismissed for writing such fiction—the motivations and actions of the characters are universal, as is true of all the best fiction. From Jewett's stories the reader takes away an idea of how she thinks people should live, what is good and what is bad. From "The White Heron," the reader can understand that Jewett favored living in harmony with nature, rejecting the squalor and dislocation resulting from industrialization and progress. Jewett's fiction, like Melville's, is an obvious parent to the greatest works of American modernism.*

I

The woods were already filled with shadows one June evening, just before eight o'clock, though a bright sunset still glimmered faintly among the trunks of the trees. A little girl was driving home her cow, a plodding, dilatory,[1] provoking creature in her behavior, but a valued companion for all that. They were going away from whatever light there was, and striking deep into the woods, but their feet were familiar with the path, and it was no matter whether their eyes could see it or not.

There was hardly a night the summer through when the old cow could be found waiting at the pasture bars; on the contrary, it was her greatest pleasure to hide herself away among the high huckleberry bushes, and though she wore a loud bell she had made the discovery that if one stood

---

[1] dilatory—tending to postpone or delay.

perfectly still it would not ring. So Sylvia had to hunt for her until she found her, and call Co'! Co'! with never an answering Moo, until her childish patience was quite spent. If the creature had not given good milk and plenty of it, the case would have seemed very different to her owners. Besides, Sylvia had all the time there was, and very little use to make of it. Sometimes in pleasant weather it was a consolation to look upon the cow's pranks as an intelligent attempt to play hide and seek, and as the child had no playmates she lent herself to this amusement with a good deal of zest. Though this chase had been so long that the wary animal herself had given an unusual signal of her whereabouts, Sylvia had only laughed when she came upon Mistress Moolly at the swamp-side, and urged her affectionately homeward with a twig of birch leaves. The old cow was not inclined to wander farther, she even turned in the right direction for once as they left the pasture, and stepped along the road at a good pace. She was quite ready to be milked now, and seldom stopped to browse. Sylvia wondered what her grandmother would say because they were so late. It was a great while since she had left home at half past five o'clock, but everybody knew the difficulty of making this errand a short one. Mrs. Tilley had chased the hornèd torment too many summer evenings herself to blame any one else for lingering, and was only thankful as she waited that she had Sylvia, nowadays, to give such valuable assistance. The good woman suspected that Sylvia loitered occasionally on her own account; there never was such a child for straying about out-of-doors since the world was made! Everybody said that it was a good change for a little maid who had tried to grow for eight years in a crowded manufacturing town, but, as for Sylvia herself, it seemed as if she never had been alive at all before she came to live at the farm. She thought often with wistful compassion of a wretched geranium that belonged to a town neighbor.

"'Afraid of folks,'" old Mrs. Tilley said to herself, with a smile, after she had made the unlikely choice of Sylvia from her daughter's houseful of children, and was returning to the farm. "'Afraid of folks,' they said! I guess she won't be troubled no great with 'em up to the old place!" When they reached the door of the lonely house and stopped to unlock it, and the cat came to purr loudly, and rub against them, a deserted pussy, indeed, but fat with young robins, Sylvia whispered that this was a beautiful place to live in, and she never should wish to go home.

The companions followed the shady woodroad, the cow taking slow steps, and the child very fast ones. The cow stopped long at the brook to drink, as if the pasture were not half a swamp, and Sylvia stood still and waited, letting her bare feet cool themselves in the shoal[2] water, while the great twilight moths struck softly against her. She waded on through the brook as the cow moved away, and listened to the thrushes with a heart that beat fast with pleasure. There was a stirring in the great

[2] shoal—shallow.

boughs overhead. They were full of little birds and beasts that seemed to be wide awake, and going about their world, or else saying good-night to each other in sleepy twitters. Sylvia herself felt sleepy as she walked along. However, it was not much farther to the house, and the air was soft and sweet. She was not often in the woods so late as this, and it made her feel as if she were a part of the gray shadows and the moving leaves. She was just thinking how long it seemed since she first came to the farm a year ago, and wondering if everything went on in the noisy town just the same as when she was there; the thought of the great red-faced boy who used to chase and frighten her made her hurry along the path to escape from the shadow of the trees.

Suddenly this little woods-girl is horror-stricken to hear a clear whistle not very far away. Not a bird's whistle, which would have a sort of friendliness, but a boy's whistle, determined, and somewhat aggressive. Sylvia left the cow to whatever sad fate might await her, and stepped discreetly aside into the bushes, but she was just too late. The enemy had discovered her, and called out in a very cheerful and persuasive tone, "Halloa, little girl, how far is it to the road?" and trembling Sylvia answered almost **inaudibly**,[3] "A good ways."

She did not dare to look boldly at the tall young man, who carried a gun over his shoulder, but she came out of her bush and again followed the cow, while he walked alongside.

"I have been hunting for some birds," the stranger said kindly, "and I have lost my way, and need a friend very much. Don't be afraid," he added gallantly. "Speak up and tell me what your name is, and whether you think I can spend the night at your house, and go out gunning early in the morning."

Sylvia was more alarmed than before. Would not her grandmother consider her much to blame?

Sylvia was more alarmed than before. Would not her grandmother consider her much to blame? But who could have foreseen such an accident as this? It did not seem to be her fault, and she hung her head as if the stem of it were broken, but managed to answer "Sylvy," with much effort when her companion again asked her name.

Mrs. Tilley was standing in the doorway when the trio came into view. The cow gave a loud moo by way of explanation.

"Yes, you'd better speak up for yourself, you old trial! Where'd she tuck herself away this time, Sylvy?" But Sylvia kept an awed silence; she knew by instinct that her grandmother did not comprehend the gravity of the situation. She must be mistaking the stranger for one of the farmer-lads of the region.

The young man stood his gun beside the door, and dropped a lumpy game-bag beside it; then he bade Mrs. Tilley good-evening, and repeated his wayfarer's story, and asked if he could have a night's lodging.

[3] **inaudibly**—too quietly to be heard.

"Put me anywhere you like," he said. "I must be off early in the morning, before day; but I am very hungry, indeed. You can give me some milk at any rate, that's plain."

"Dear sakes, yes," responded the hostess, whose long slumbering hospitality seemed to be easily awakened. "You might fare better if you went out to the main road a mile or so, but you're welcome to what we've got. I'll milk right off, and you make yourself at home. You can sleep on husks or feathers,"[4] she proffered[5] graciously. "I raised them all myself. There's good pasturing for geese just below here towards the ma'sh. Now step round and set a plate for the gentleman, Sylvy!" And Sylvia promptly stepped. She was glad to have something to do, and she was hungry herself.

It was a surprise to find so clean and comfortable a little dwelling in this New England wilderness. The young man had known the horrors of its most primitive housekeeping, and the dreary squalor[6] of that level of society which does not rebel at the companionship of hens. This was the best thrift of an old-fashioned farmstead, though on such a small scale that it seemed like a hermitage.[7] He listened eagerly to the old woman's quaint talk, he watched Sylvia's pale face and shining gray eyes with ever growing enthusiasm, and insisted that this was the best supper he had eaten for a month, and afterward the new-made friends sat down in the doorway together while the moon came up.

Soon it would be berry-time, and Sylvia was a great help at picking. The cow was a good milker, though a plaguy[8] thing to keep track of, the hostess gossiped frankly, adding presently that she had buried four children, so Sylvia's mother, and a son (who might be dead) in California were all the children she had left. "Dan, my boy, was a great hand to go gunning," she explained sadly. "I never wanted for pa'tridges or gray squer'ls while he was to home. He's been a great wand'rer, I expect, and he's no hand to write letters. There, I don't blame him, I'd ha' seen the world myself if it had been so I could."

"Sylvia takes after him," the grandmother continued affectionately, after a minute's pause. "There ain't a foot o' ground she don't know her way over, and the wild creaturs counts her one o' themselves. Squer'ls she'll tame to come an' feed right out o' her hands, and all sorts o' birds. Last winter she got the jay-birds to bangeing[9] here, and I believe she'd 'a' scanted herself of her own meals to have plenty to throw out amongst 'em, if I hadn't kep' watch. Anything but crows, I tell her, I'm willin' to help support—though Dan he had a tamed one o' them that did seem to have reason same as folks. It was round here good spell after he went away. Dan an' his father they didn't hitch,—but he never held up his head ag'in after Dan had dared him an' gone off."

---

[4] husks or feathers—reference to mattresses, filled with either goose feathers or with the dry outer coverings of corn.

[5] proffered—offered.

[6] squalor—filthy and wretched condition.

[7] hermitage—place of seclusion.

[8] plaguy—annoying.

[9] bangeing—gathering in groups.

The guest did not notice this hint of family sorrows in his eager interest in something else.

"So Sylvy knows all about birds, does she?" he exclaimed, as he looked round at the little girl who sat, very demure but increasingly sleepy, in the moonlight. "I am making a collection of birds myself. I have been at it ever since I was a boy." (Mrs. Tilley smiled.) "There are two or three very rare ones I have been hunting for these five years. I mean to get them on my own ground if they can be found."

"Do you cage 'em up?" asked Mrs. Tilley doubtfully, in response to this enthusiastic announcement.

"Oh, no, they're stuffed and preserved, dozens and dozens of them," said the ornithologist,[10] "and I have shot or snared every one myself. I caught a glimpse of a white heron[11] three miles from here on Saturday, and I have followed it in this direction. They have never been found in this district at all. The little white heron, it is," and he turned again to look at Sylvia with the hope of discovering that the rare bird was one of her acquaintances.

But Sylvia was watching a hop-toad in the narrow footpath.

"You would know the heron if you saw it," the stranger continued eagerly. "A queer tall white bird with soft feathers and long thin legs. And it would have a nest perhaps in the top of a high tree, made of sticks, something like a hawk's nest."

Sylvia's heart gave a wild beat; she knew that strange white bird, and had once stolen softly near where it stood in some bright green swamp grass, away over at the other side of the woods. There was an open place where the sunshine always seemed strangely yellow and hot, where tall, nodding rushes grew, and her grandmother had warned her that she might sink in the soft black mud underneath and never be heard of more. Not far beyond were the salt marshes just this side the sea itself, which Sylvia wondered and dreamed about, but never had seen, whose great voice could sometimes be heard above the noise of the woods on stormy nights.

Sylvia's heart gave a wild beat; she knew that strange white bird.

"I can't think of anything I should like so much as to find that heron's nest," the handsome stranger was saying. "I would give ten dollars to anybody who could show it to me," he added desperately, "and I mean to spend my whole vacation hunting for it if need be. Perhaps it was only migrating, or had been chased out of its own region by some bird of prey."

Mrs. Tilley gave amazed attention to all this, but Sylvia still watched the toad, not divining,[12] as she might have done at some calmer time, that the creature wished to get to its hole under the door-step, and was much hindered by the unusual spectators at that hour of the evening. No amount of thought, that night, could decide how

---

[10] ornithologist—scientist who studies birds.

[11] white heron—bird generally found in the South, which explains the young man's intense interest.

[12] divining—knowing by intuition.

many wished-for treasures the ten dollars, so lightly spoken of, would buy.

The next day the young sportsman hovered about the woods, and Sylvia kept him company, having lost her first fear of the friendly lad, who proved to be most kind and sympathetic. He told her many things about the birds and what they knew and where they lived and what they did with themselves. And he gave her a jack-knife, which she thought as great a treasure as if she were a desert-islander. All day long he did not once make her troubled or afraid except when he brought down some unsuspecting singing creature from its bough. Sylvia would have liked him vastly better without his gun; she could not understand why he killed the very birds he seemed to like so much. But as the day waned,[13] Sylvia still watched the young man with loving admiration. She had never seen anybody so charming and delightful; the woman's heart, asleep in the child, was vaguely thrilled by a dream of love. Some premonition[14] of that great power stirred and swayed these young creatures who traversed the solemn woodlands with soft-footed silent care. They stopped to listen to a bird's song; they pressed forward again eagerly, parting the branches,—speaking to each other rarely and in whispers; the young man going first and Sylvia following, fascinated, a few steps behind, with her gray eyes dark with excitement.

She grieved because the longed-for white heron was **elusive**,[15] but she did not lead the guest, she only followed, and there was no such thing as speaking first. The sound of her own unquestioned voice would have terrified her,—it was hard enough to answer yes or no when there was need of that. At last evening began to fall, and they drove the cow home together, and Sylvia smiled with pleasure when they came to the place where she heard the whistle and was afraid only the night before.

II

Half a mile from home, at the farther edge of the woods, where the land was highest, a great pine-tree stood, the last of its generation. Whether it was left for a boundary mark, or for what reason, no one could say; the woodchoppers who had felled its mates were dead and gone long ago, and a whole forest of sturdy trees, pines and oaks and maples, had grown again. But the stately head of this old pine towered above them all and made a land-mark for sea and shore miles and miles away. Sylvia knew it well. She had always believed that whoever climbed to the top of it could see the ocean; and the little girl had often laid her hand on the great rough trunk and looked up wistfully at those dark boughs that the wind always stirred, no matter how hot and still the air might be below. Now she thought of the tree with a new excitement, for why, if one climbed it at break of day, could not one see all the world, and easily discover from whence

[13] waned—came to an end.

[14] premonition—sense of what is to come.

[15] **elusive**—hard to find.

the white heron flew, and mark the place, and find the hidden nest?

What a spirit of adventure, what wild ambition! What fancied triumph and delight and glory for the later morning when she could make known the secret! It was almost too real and too great for the childish heart to bear.

All night the door of the little house stood open and the whippoorwills[16] came and sang upon the very step. The young sportsman and his old hostess were sound asleep, but Sylvia's great design kept her broad awake and watching. She forgot to think of sleep. The short summer night seemed as long as the winter darkness, and at last when the whippoorwills ceased, and she was afraid the morning would after all come too soon, she stole out of the house and followed the pasture path through the woods, hastening toward the open ground beyond, listening with a sense of comfort and companionship to the drowsy twitter of a half-awakened bird, whose perch she had jarred in passing. Alas, if the great wave of human interest which flooded for the first time this dull little life should sweep away the satisfactions of an existence heart to heart with nature and the dumb life of the forest!

There was the huge tree asleep yet in the paling moonlight, and small and silly Sylvia began with utmost bravery to mount to the top of it, with tingling, eager blood coursing the channels of her whole frame, with her bare feet and fingers, that pinched and held like bird's claws to the monstrous ladder reaching up, up, almost to the sky itself. First she must mount the white oak tree that grew alongside, where she was almost lost among the dark branches and the green leaves heavy and wet with dew; a bird fluttered off its nest, and a red squirrel ran to and fro and scolded pettishly[17] at the harmless housebreaker. Sylvia felt her way easily. She had often climbed there, and knew that higher still one of the oak's upper branches **chafed**[18] against the pine trunk, just where its lower boughs were set close together. There, when she made the dangerous pass from one tree to the other, the great enterprise would really begin.

She crept out along the swaying oak limb at last, and took the daring step across into the old pine-tree. The way was harder than she thought; she must reach far and hold fast, the sharp dry twigs caught and held her and scratched her like angry talons,[19] the pitch[20] made her thin little fingers clumsy and stiff as she went round and round the tree's great stem, higher and higher upward. The sparrows and robins in the woods below were beginning to wake and twitter to the dawn, yet it seemed much lighter there aloft in the pine-tree, and the child knew that she must hurry if her project were to be of any use.

The tree seemed to lengthen itself out as she went up, and to reach farther and farther upward. It was like a great main-mast[21] to the voyaging earth; it must

---

[16] whippoorwills—spotted brown and black birds that are active at night. The whippoorwill's long, monotonous cry gave it its name.

[17] pettishly—with ill temper.

[18] **chafed**—rubbed.

[19] talons—claws.

[20] pitch—sticky substance that flows from evergreen trees.

[21] main-mast—principal mast of a vessel.

truly have been amazed that morning through all its **ponderous**[22] frame as it felt this determined spark of human spirit winding its way from higher branch to branch. Who knows how steadily the least twigs held themselves to advantage this light, weak creature on her way! The old pine must have loved his new dependent. More than all the hawks, and bats, and moths, and even the sweet voiced thrushes, was the brave, beating heart of the solitary gray-eyed child. And the tree stood still and frowned away the winds that June morning while the dawn grew bright in the east.

Sylvia's face was like a pale star, if one had seen it from the ground, when the last thorny bough was past, and she stood trembling and tired but wholly triumphant, high in the tree-top. Yes, there was the sea with the dawning sun making a golden dazzle over it, and toward that glorious east flew two hawks with slow-moving pinions.[23] How low they looked in the air from that height when one had only seen them before far up, and dark against the blue sky. Their gray feathers were as soft as moths; they seemed only a little way from the tree, and Sylvia felt as if she too could go flying away among the clouds. Westward, the woodlands and farms reached miles and miles into the distance; here and there were church steeples, and white villages; truly it was a vast and awesome world!

The birds sang louder and louder. At last the sun came up bewilderingly bright. Sylvia could see the white sails of ships out at sea, and the clouds that were purple and rose-colored and yellow at first began to fade away. Where was the white heron's nest in the sea of green branches, and was this wonderful sight and pageant of the world the only reward for having climbed to such a giddy height? Now look down again, Sylvia, where the green marsh is set among the shining birches and dark hemlocks; there where you saw the white heron once you will see him again; look, look! a white spot of him like a single floating feather comes up from the dead hemlock and grows larger, and rises, and comes close at last, and goes by the landmark pine with steady sweep of wing and outstretched slender neck and crested head. And wait! wait! do not move a foot or a finger, little girl, do not send an arrow of light and consciousness from your two eager eyes, for the heron has perched on a pine bough not far beyond yours, and cries back to his mate on the nest, and plumes his feathers for the new day!

The child gives a long sigh a minute later when a company of shouting catbirds comes also to the tree, and vexed by their fluttering and lawlessness the solemn heron goes away. She knows his secret now, the wild, light, slender bird that floats and wavers, and goes back like an arrow presently to his home in the green world beneath. Then Sylvia, well satisfied, makes her **perilous**[24] way down again, not daring to look far below the branch she stands on, ready to cry sometimes because her fingers ache and her lamed feet slip. Wondering over and over again what the stranger would say to her, and what he would think

[22] **ponderous**—having great weight.

[23] pinions—birds' wings.

[24] **perilous**—dangerous.

when she told him how to find his way straight to the heron's nest.

"Sylvy, Sylvy!" called the busy old grandmother again and again, but nobody answered, and the small husk bed was empty and Sylvia had disappeared.

The guest waked from a dream, and remembering his day's pleasure hurried to dress himself that might it sooner begin. He was sure from the way the shy little girl looked once or twice yesterday that she had at least seen the white heron, and now she must really be made to tell. Here she comes now, paler than ever, and her worn old frock is torn and tattered, and smeared with pine pitch. The grandmother and the sportsman stand in the door together and question her, and the splendid moment has come to speak of the dead hemlock-tree by the green marsh.

But Sylvia does not speak after all, though the old grandmother fretfully rebukes[25] her, and the young man's kind, appealing eyes are looking straight in her own. He can make them rich with money; he has promised it, and they are poor now. He is so well worth making happy, and he waits to hear the story she can tell.

No, she must keep silence! What is it that suddenly forbids her and makes her dumb? Has she been nine years growing and now, when the great world for the first time puts out a hand to her, must she thrust it aside for a bird's sake? The murmur of the pine's green branches is in her ears, she remembers how the white heron came flying through the golden air and how they watched the sea and the morning together, and Sylvia cannot speak; she cannot tell the heron's secret and give its life away.

Dear loyalty, that suffered a sharp pang as the guest went away disappointed later in the day, that could have served and followed him and loved him as a dog loves! Many a night Sylvia heard the echo of his whistle haunting the pasture path as she came home with the loitering cow. She forgot even her sorrow at the sharp report of his gun and the sight of thrushes and sparrows dropping silent to the ground, their songs hushed and their pretty feathers stained and wet with blood. Were the birds better friends than their hunter might have been,—who can tell? Whatever treasures were lost to her, woodlands and summer-time, remember! Bring your gifts and graces and tell your secrets to this lonely country child!

---

[25] fretfully rebukes—peevishly scolds.

Grandmother buried 4 children
Sylvia takes after her son.

QUESTIONS TO CONSIDER

1. Why has Sylvia come to live with her grandmother?
2. Why is she afraid of the young man when she first sees him?
3. What relationship does Sylvia have with the natural world around her?
4. What do you think motivates Sylvia to make the dangerous climb up the tree?
5. Why does Sylvia not tell her grandmother and the young man about the heron?
6. How does Jewett's realism affect the impact of this story?

5) Sylvia remembers having a connection with the White Heron

Mary E. Wilkins Freeman ▶

The Revolt of "Mother"

BY MARY E. WILKINS FREEMAN

Mary E. Wilkins Freeman (1852–1930) began to write stories when writing was one of the few professions available to a woman in America. Born in Massachusetts, she was a frail, sickly child who spent most of her time reading. Her adult life until she was thirty was devoted to caring for her invalid father. After his death, Freeman was confronted with the necessity of earning a living and took to writing stories—she had written and published poems before. Freeman's stories found immediate success in the popular magazines and her first collection, A Humble Romance and Other Stories, *was published in 1887, followed by* A New England Nun and Other Stories *in 1891. Freeman's stories are all set in the small New England towns where she had grown up. Her great skill was depicting the inner life of ordinary people: most often women whose opportunities were circumscribed by society. Freeman endows even the poorest New Englanders with courage and nobility. Her stories often capture the difficult moments when people have to chose between love and duty. Freeman can be classified as a local colorist, but like the very best of them her settings are merely backgrounds to stories that express universal emotions. Freeman was an early feminist who wrote about female characters trying to expand their lives in a constricting society and about the inner intellectual life of women in America, topics hardly touched by any other writers until the twentieth century. Freeman published twelve novels, as well as plays and poems, but she remains known for her extraordinary stories, almost 250 compressed depictions of the inhabitants of New England.*

"Father!"

"What is it?"

"What are them men diggin' over there in the field for?"

There was a sudden dropping and enlarging of the lower part of the old man's face, as if some heavy weight had settled therein; he shut his mouth tight, and went on harnessing the great bay mare. He hustled the collar on to her neck with a jerk.

"Father!"

The old man slapped the saddle upon the mare's back.

"Look here, father, I want to know what them men are diggin' over in the field for, an' I'm goin' to know."

"I wish you'd go into the house, mother, an' 'tend to your own affairs," the old man said then. He ran his words together, and his speech was almost as **inarticulate**[1] as a growl.

---

[1] **inarticulate**—incomprehensible.

But the woman understood; it was her most native tongue. "I ain't goin' into the house till you tell me what them men are doin' over there in the field," said she.

Then she stood waiting. She was a small woman, short and straight-waisted like a child in her brown cotton gown. Her forehead was mild and benevolent between the smooth curves of gray hair; there were **meek**[2] downward lines about her nose and mouth; but her eyes, fixed upon the old man, looked as if the meekness had been the result of her own will, never of the will of another.

They were in the barn, standing before the wide open doors. The spring air, full of the smell of growing grass and unseen blossoms, came in their faces. The deep yard in front was littered with farm wagons and piles of wood; on the edges, close to the fence and the house, the grass was a vivid green, and there were some dandelions.

The old man glanced doggedly[3] at his wife as he tightened the last buckles on the harness. She looked as immovable to him as one of the rocks in his pasture-land, bound to the earth with generations of blackberry vines. He slapped the reins over the horse, and started forth from the barn.

"Father!" said she.

The old man pulled up. "What is it?"

"I want to know what them men are diggin' over there in that field for."

"They're diggin' a cellar, I s'pose, if you've got to know."

"A cellar for what?"

"A barn."

"A barn? You ain't goin' to build a barn over there where we was goin' to have a house, father?"

"A barn? You ain't goin' to build a barn over there where we was goin' to have a house, father?"

The old man said not another word. He hurried the horse into the farm wagon, and clattered[4] out of the yard, jouncing[5] as sturdily on his seat as a boy.

The woman stood a moment looking after him, then she went out of the barn across a corner of the yard to the house. The house, standing at right angles with the great barn and a long reach of sheds and out-buildings, was infinitesimal[6] compared with them. It was scarcely as **commodious**[7] for people as the little boxes under the barn **eaves**[8] were for doves.

A pretty girl's face, pink and delicate as a flower, was looking out of one of the house windows. She was watching three men who were digging over in the field which bounded the yard near the road line. She turned quietly when the woman entered.

"What are they digging for, mother?" said she. "Did he tell you?"

---

[2] **meek**—timid.

[3] doggedly—stubbornly, perseveringly, tenaciously.

[4] clattered—moved with a rattling sound.

[5] jouncing—bouncing, jolting.

[6] infinitesimal—very small.

[7] **commodious**—spacious, roomy.

[8] **eaves**—projecting overhang at the lower edge of a roof.

"They're diggin' for—a cellar for a new barn."

"Oh, mother, he ain't going to build another barn?"

"That's what he says."

A boy stood before the kitchen glass combing his hair. He combed slowly and painstakingly, arranging his brown hair in a smooth hillock over his forehead. He did not seem to pay any attention to the conversation.

"Sammy, did you know father was going to build a new barn?" asked the girl.

The boy combed assiduously.[9]

"Sammy!"

He turned, and showed a face like his father's under his smooth crest of hair. "Yes, I s'pose I did," he said, reluctantly.

"How long have you known it?" asked his mother.

"'Bout three months, I guess."

"Why didn't you tell of it?"

"Didn't think 'twould do no good."

"I don't see what father wants another barn for," said the girl, in her sweet, slow voice. She turned again to the window, and stared out at the digging men in the field. Her tender, sweet face was full of a gentle distress. Her forehead was as bald and innocent as a baby's, with the light hair strained back from it in a row of curl-papers. She was quite large, but her soft curves did not look as if they covered muscles.

Her mother looked sternly at the boy. "Is he goin' to buy more cows?" said she.

The boy did not reply; he was tying his shoes.

"Sammy, I want you to tell me if he's goin' to buy more cows."

"I s'pose he is."

"How many?"

"Four, I guess."

His mother said nothing more. She went up into the pantry, and there was a clatter of dishes. The boy got his cap from a nail behind the door, took an old arithmetic from the shelf, and started for school. He was lightly built, but clumsy. He went out of the yard with a curious spring in his hips, that made his loose home-made jacket tilt up in the rear.

The girl went to the sink, and began to wash the dishes that were piled up there. Her mother came promptly out of the pantry, and shoved her aside. "You wipe 'em," said she; "I'll wash. There's a good many this mornin'."

The mother plunged her hands vigorously into the water, the girl wiped the plates slowly and dreamily. "Mother," said she, "don't you think it's too bad father's going to build that new barn, much as we need a decent house to live in?"

Her mother scrubbed a dish fiercely. "You ain't found out yet we're women-folks, Nanny Penn," said she. "You ain't seen enough of men-folks yet to. One of these days you'll find it out, an' then you'll know that we know only what men-folks think we do, so far as any use of it goes, an' how we'd ought to reckon men-folks in with Providence,[10] an' not complain of what they do any more than we do of the weather."

---

[9] assiduously—diligently.

[10] Providence—divine care.

"I don't care; I don't believe George is anything like that, anyhow," said Nanny. Her delicate face flushed pink, her lips pouted softly, as if she were going to cry.

"You wait an' see. I guess George Eastman ain't no better than other men. You hadn't ought to judge father, though. He can't help it, 'cause he don't look at things jest the way we do. An' we've been pretty comfortable here, after all. The roof don't leak—ain't never but once—that's one thing. Father's kept it shingled right up."

"I do wish we had a parlor."

"I guess it won't hurt George Eastman any to come to see you in a nice clean kitchen. I guess a good many girls don't have as good a place as this. Nobody's ever heard me complain."

"I ain't complained either, mother."

"Well, I don't think you'd better, a good father an' a good home as you've got. S'pose your father made you go out an' work for your livin'? Lots of girls have to that ain't no stronger an' better able to than you be."

Sarah Penn washed the frying-pan with a conclusive air. She scrubbed the outside of it as faithfully as the inside. She was a masterly keeper of her box of a house. Her one living-room never seemed to have in it any of the dust which the friction of life with inanimate matter produces. She swept, and there seemed to be no dirt to go before the broom; she cleaned, and one could see no difference. She was like an artist so perfect that he has apparently no art. Today she got out a mixing bowl and a board, and rolled some pies, and there was no more flour upon her than upon her daughter who was doing finer work. Nanny was to be married in the fall, and she was sewing on some white cambric[11] and embroidery. She sewed industriously while her mother cooked, her soft milk-white hands and wrists showed whiter than her delicate work.

"We must have the stove moved out in the shed before long," said Mrs. Penn. "Talk about not havin' things, it's been a real blessin' to be able to put a stove up in that shed in hot weather. Father did one good thing when he fixed that stove-pipe out there."

Sarah Penn's face as she rolled her pies had that expression of meek vigor which might have characterized one of the New Testament saints. She was making mince-pies. Her husband, Adoniram Penn, liked them better than any other kind. She baked twice a week. Adoniram often liked a piece of pie between meals. She hurried this morning. It had been later than usual when she began, and she wanted to have a pie baked for dinner. However deep a resentment she might be forced to hold against her husband, she would never fail in sedulous[12] attention to his wants.

Nobility of character manifests itself at loop-holes when it is not provided with large doors. Sarah Penn's showed itself today in flaky dishes of pastry. So she made the pies faithfully, while across the table she could see, when she glanced up from her work, the sight that rankled in her patient and steadfast soul—the digging

[11] cambric—fine thin linen or cotton cloth.

[12] sedulous—persevering and constant in effort or application.

of the cellar of the new barn in the place where Adoniram forty years ago had promised her their new house should stand.

The pies were done for dinner. Adoniram and Sammy were home a few minutes after twelve o'clock. The dinner was eaten with serious haste. There was never much conversation at the table in the Penn family. Adoniram asked a blessing, and they ate promptly, then rose up and went about their work.

"I'm goin' to talk real plain to you; I never have sence I married you, but I'm goin' to now."

Sammy went back to school, taking soft sly lopes out of the yard like a rabbit. He wanted a game of marbles before school, and feared his father would give him some chores to do. Adoniram hastened to the door and called after him, but he was out of sight.

"I don't see what you let him go for, mother," said he. "I wanted him to help me unload that wood."

Adoniram went to work out in the yard unloading wood from the wagon. Sarah put away the dinner dishes, while Nanny took down her curl-papers and changed her dress. She was going down to the store to buy some more embroidery and thread.

When Nanny was gone, Mrs. Penn went to the door. "Father!" she called.

"Well, what is it!"

"I want to see you jest a minute, father."

"I can't leave this wood nohow. I've got to git it unloaded an' go for a load of gravel afore two o'clock. Sammy had ought to helped me. You hadn't ought to let him go to school so early."

"I want to see you jest a minute."

"I tell ye I can't, nohow, mother."

"Father, you come here." Sarah Penn stood in the door like a queen; she held her head as if it bore a crown; there was that patience which makes authority royal in her voice. Adoniram went.

Mrs. Penn led the way into the kitchen, and pointed to a chair. "Sit down, father," said she; "I've got somethin' I want to say to you."

He sat down heavily; his face was quite **stolid**,[13] but he looked at her with restive eyes. "Well, what is it, mother?"

"I want to know what you're buildin' that new barn for, father?"

"I ain't got nothin' to say about it."

"It can't be you think you need another barn?"

"I tell ye I ain't got nothin' to say about it, mother; an' I ain't goin' to say nothin'."

"Be you goin' to buy more cows?"

Adoniram did not reply; he shut his mouth tight.

"I know you be, as well as I want to. Now, father, look here"—Sarah Penn had not sat down; she stood before her husband in the humble fashion of a Scripture woman—"I'm goin' to talk real plain to you; I never have sence I married you, but I'm goin' to now. I ain't never complained, an' I ain't goin' to complain now, but I'm

[13] **stolid**—revealing little emotion; impassive.

goin' to talk plain. You see this room here, father; you look at it well. You see there ain't no carpet on the floor, an' you see the paper is all dirty, an' droppin' off the walls. We ain't had no new paper on it for ten year, an' then I put it on myself, an' it didn't cost but ninepence a roll. You see this room, father; it's all the one I've had to work in an' eat in an' sit in sence we was married. There ain't another woman in the whole town whose husband ain't got half the means you have but what's got better. It's all the room Nanny's got to have her company in; an' there ain't one of her mates but what's got better, an' their fathers not so able as hers is. It's all the room she'll have to be married in. What would you have thought, father, if we had had our weddin' in a room no better than this? I was married in my mother's parlor, with a carpet on the floor, an' stuffed furniture, an' a mahogany cardtable. An' this is all the room my daughter will have to be married in. Look here, father!"

Sarah Penn went across the room as though it were a tragic stage. She flung open a door and disclosed a tiny bedroom, only large enough for a bed and bureau, with a path between. "There, father," said she—"there's all the room I've had to sleep in forty year. All my children were born there—the two that died, an' the two that's livin'. I was sick with a fever there."

She stepped to another door and opened it. It led into the small, ill-lighted pantry. "Here," said she, "is all the buttery' I've got—every place I've got for my dishes, to set away my victuals in, an' to keep my milk-pans in. Father, I've been takin' care of the milk of six cows in this place, an' now you're goin' to build a new barn, an' keep more cows, an' give me more to do in it."

She threw open another door. A narrow crooked flight of stairs wound upward from it. "There, father," said she, "I want you to look at the stairs that go up to them two unfinished chambers that are all the places our son an' daughter have had to sleep in all their lives. There ain't a prettier girl in town nor a more ladylike one than Nanny, an' that's the place she has to sleep in. It ain't so good as your horse's stall; it ain't so warm an' tight."

Sarah Penn went back and stood before her husband. "Now, father," said she, "I want to know if you think you're doin' right an' accordin' to what you profess. Here, when we was married, forty year ago, you promised me faithful that we should have a new house built in that lot over in the field before the year was out. You said you had money enough, an' you wouldn't ask me to live in no such place as this. It is forty year now, an' you've been makin' more money, an' I've been savin of it for you ever since, an' you ain't built no house yet. You've built sheds an' cow-houses an' one new barn, an' now you're goin' to build another. Father, I want to know if you think it's right. You're lodgin' your dumb beasts better than you are your own flesh an' blood. I want to know if you think it's right."

"I ain't got nothin' to say."

"You can't say nothin' without ownin' it ain't right, father. An' there's another thing—I ain't complained; I've got along forty year, an' I s'pose I should forty more, if it wa'n't for that—if we don't have another house. Nanny she can't live with us after she's married. She'll have to go somewheres else to live away from us, an' it don't seem as if I could have it so, noways, father. She wa'n't ever strong. She's got considerable color, but there wa'n't never any backbone to her. I've always took the heft[14] of everything off her, an' she ain't fit to keep house an' do everything herself. She'll be all worn out inside a year. Think of her doin' all the washin' an' ironin' an' bakin' with them soft white hands an' arms, an' sweepin'! I can't have it so, noways, father."

Mrs. Penn's face was burning; her mild eyes gleamed. She had pleaded her little cause like a Webster;[15] she had ranged from severity to **pathos**;[16] but her opponent employed that **obstinate**[17] silence which makes eloquence futile with mocking echoes. Adoniram arose clumsily.

"Father, ain't you got nothin' to say?" said Mrs. Penn.

"I've got to go off after that load of gravel. I can't stan' here talkin' all day."

"Father, won't you think it over, an' have a house built there instead of a barn?"

"I ain't got nothin' to say."

Adoniram shuffled out. Mrs. Penn went into her bedroom. When she came out, her eyes were red. She had a roll of unbleached cotton cloth. She spread it out on the kitchen table, and began cutting out some shirts for her husband. The men over in the field had a team to help them this afternoon; she could hear their halloos. She had a scanty pattern for the shirts; she had to plan and piece the sleeves.

Nanny came home with her embroidery, and sat down with her needlework. She had taken down her curl-papers, and there was a soft roll of fair hair like an aureole[18] over her forehead; her face was as delicately fine and clear as porcelain. Suddenly she looked up, and the tender red flamed all over her face and neck. "Mother," said she.

"What say?"

"I've been thinking—I don't see how we're goin' to have any—wedding in this room. I'd be ashamed to have his folks come if we didn't have anybody else."

"Mebbe we can have some new paper before then; I can put it on. I guess you won't have no call to be ashamed of your belongin's."

"We might have the wedding in the new barn," said Nanny, with gentle pettishness. "Why, mother, what makes you look so?"

Mrs. Penn had started, and was staring at her with a curious expression. She turned again to her work, and spread out a pattern carefully on the cloth. "Nothin'," said she.

Presently Adoniram clattered out of the yard in his two-wheeled dump cart, standing as proudly upright as a Roman charioteer. Mrs. Penn opened the door and stood there a minute looking out; the halloos of the men sounded louder.

---

[14] heft—weight.

[15] Webster—Daniel Webster (1782–1852), American statesman who was renowned as a persuasive orator.

[16] **pathos**—sympathy or pity.

[17] **obstinate**—stubborn.

[18] aureole—circle of light.

It seemed to her all through the spring months that she heard nothing but the halloos and the noises of the saws and hammers. The new barn grew fast. It was a fine **edifice**[19] for this little village. Men came on pleasant Sundays, in their meeting suits and clean shirt bosoms, and stood around it admiringly. Mrs. Penn did not speak of it, and Adoniram did not mention it to her, although sometimes, upon a return from inspecting it, he bore himself with injured dignity.

"It's a strange thing how your mother feels about the new barn," he said, confidentially, to Sammy one day.

Sammy only grunted after an odd fashion for a boy; he had learned it from his father.

The barn was all completed ready for use by the third week in July. Adoniram had planned to move his stock in on Wednesday; on Tuesday he received a letter which changed his plans. He came in with it early in the morning. "Sammy's been to the post-office," said he, "an' I've got a letter from Hiram." Hiram was Mrs. Penn's brother, who lived in Vermont.

"Well," said Mrs. Penn, "what does he say about the folks?"

"I guess they're all right. He says he thinks if I come up country right off there's a chance to buy jest the kind of horse I want." He stared reflectively out of the window at the new barn.

Mrs. Penn was making pies. She went on clapping the rolling-pin into the crust, although she was very pale, and her heart beat loudly.

"I dun' know but what I'd better go," said Adoniram. "I hate to go off jest now, right in the midst of hayin', but the ten-acre lot's cut, an' I guess Rufus an' the others can git along without me three or four days. I can't get a horse round here to suit me, nohow, an' I've got to have another for all the wood-haulin' in the fall. I told Hiram to watch out, an' if he got wind of a good horse to let me know. I guess I'd better go."

The new barn grew fast. It was a fine edifice for this little village.

"I'll get out your clean shirt an' collar," said Mrs. Penn calmly.

She laid out Adoniram's Sunday suit and his clean clothes on the bed in the little bedroom. She got his shaving-water and razor ready. At last she buttoned on his collar and fastened his black cravat.

Adoniram never wore his collar and cravat except on extra occasions. He held his head high, with a rasped dignity. When he was all ready, with his coat and hat brushed, and a lunch of pie and cheese in a paper bag, he hesitated on the threshold of the door. He looked at his wife, and his manner was defiantly apologetic. "*If* them cows come today, Sammy can drive 'em into the new barn," said he; "an' when they bring the hay up, they can pitch it in there."

"Well," replied Mrs. Penn.

Adoniram set his shaven face ahead and started. When he had cleared the doorstep, he turned and looked back with a

[19] **edifice**—building.

kind of nervous solemnity. "I shall be back by Saturday if nothin' happens," said he.

"Do be careful, father," returned his wife.

She stood in the door with Nanny at her elbow and watched him out of sight. Her eyes had a strange, doubtful expression in them; her peaceful forehead was contracted. She went in, and about her baking again. Nanny sat sewing. Her wedding-day was drawing nearer, and she was getting pale and thin with her steady sewing. Her mother kept glancing at her.

"Have you got that pain in your side this mornin'?" she asked.

"A little."

Mrs. Penn's face, as she worked, changed, her perplexed forehead smoothed, her eyes were steady, her lips firmly set. She formed a **maxim**[20] for herself, although incoherently with her unlettered[21] thoughts. "Unsolicited opportunities are the guide-posts of the Lord to the new roads of life," she repeated in effect, and she made up her mind to her course of action.

"S'posin' I *had* wrote to Hiram," she muttered once, when she was in the pantry—"s'posin' I had wrote, an' asked him if he knew of any horse? But I didn't, an' father's goin' wa'n't none of my doin'. It looks like a providence." Her voice rang out quite loud at the last.

"What you talkin' about, mother?" called Nanny.

"Nothin'."

Mrs. Penn hurried her baking; at eleven o'clock it was all done. The load of hay from the west field came slowly down the cart track, and drew up at the new barn. Mrs. Penn ran out. "Stop!" she screamed—"stop!"

The men stopped and looked; Sammy upreared from the top of the load, and stared at his mother.

"Stop!" she cried out again. "Don't you put the hay in that barn; put it in the old one."

"Why, he said to put it in here," returned one of the haymakers, wonderingly. He was a young man, a neighbor's son, whom Adoniram hired by the year to help on the farm.

"Don't you put the hay in the new barn; there's room enough in the old one, ain't there?" said Mrs. Penn.

"Room enough," returned the hired man, in his thick, rustic tones. "Didn't need the new barn, nohow, far as room's concerned. Well, I s'pose he changed his mind." He took hold of the horses' bridles.

Mrs. Penn went back to the house. Soon the kitchen windows were darkened, and a fragrance like warm honey came into the room.

Nanny laid down her work. "I thought father wanted them to put the hay into the new barn?" she said, wonderingly.

"It's all right," replied her mother.

Sammy slid down from the load of hay, and came in to see if dinner was ready.

"I ain't goin' to get a regular dinner today, as long as father's gone," said his mother. "I've let the fire go out. You can have some bread an' milk an' pie. I thought we could get along." She set out some

---

[20] **maxim**—concise form of a principle or general truth.

[21] unlettered—poorly educated.

bowls of milk, some bread, and a pie on the kitchen table. "You'd better eat your dinner now," said she. "You might jest as well get through with it. I want you to help me afterward."

Nanny and Sammy stared at each other. There was something strange in their mother's manner. Mrs. Penn did not eat anything herself. She went into the pantry, and they heard her moving dishes while they ate. Presently she came out with a pile of plates. She got the clothes-basket out of the shed, and packed them in it. Nanny and Sammy watched. She brought out cups and saucers, and put them in with the plates.

"What you goin' to do, mother?" inquired Nanny, in a timid voice. A sense of something unusual made her tremble, as if it were a ghost. Sammy rolled his eyes over his pie.

"You'll see what I'm goin' to do," replied Mrs. Penn. "If you're through, Nanny, I want you to go up-stairs an' pack up your things; an' I want you, Sammy, to help me take down the bed in the bedroom."

"Oh, mother, what for?" gasped Nanny.

"You'll see."

During the next few hours a feat was performed by this simple, pious New England mother which was equal in its way to Wolfe's storming of the Heights of Abraham.[22] It took no more genius and **audacity**[23] of bravery for Wolfe to cheer his wondering soldiers up those steep precipices, under the sleeping eyes of the enemy, than for Sarah Penn, at the head of her children, to move all their little household goods into the new barn while her husband was away.

Nanny and Sammy followed their mother's instructions without a murmur; indeed, they were overawed. There is a certain **uncanny**[24] and superhuman quality about all such purely original undertakings as their mother's was to them. Nanny went back and forth with her light loads, and Sammy tugged with sober energy.

At five o'clock in the afternoon the little house in which the Penns had lived for forty years had emptied itself into the new barn.

Every builder builds somewhat for unknown purposes, and is in a measure a prophet. The architect of Adoniram Penn's barn, while he designed it for the comfort of four-footed animals, had planned better than he knew for the comfort of humans. Sarah Penn saw at a glance its possibilities. Those great box-stalls, with quilts hung before them, would make better bedrooms than the one she had occupied for forty years, and there was a tight carriage-room. The harness room, with its chimney and shelves, would make a kitchen of her dreams. The great middle space would make a parlor, by-and-by, fit for a palace. Up stairs there was as much room as down. With partitions and windows, what a house would

---

[22] Wolfe's storming of the Heights of Abraham—reference to the Battle of Quebec in 1759 where the British, under General James Wolfe, defeated the French. Quebec is located on the heights of the Plains of Abraham.

[23] **audacity**—daring.

[24] **uncanny**—weird, eerie.

there be! Sarah looked at the row of stanchions[25] before the allotted space for cows, and reflected that she would have her front entry there.

At six o'clock the stove was up in the harness-room, the kettle was boiling, and the table set for tea. It looked almost as homelike as the abandoned house across the yard had ever done. The young hired man milked, and Sarah directed him calmly to bring the milk to the new barn. He came gaping, dropping little blots of foam from the brimming pails on the grass. Before the next morning he had spread the story of Adoniram Penn's wife moving into the new barn all over the little village. Men assembled in the store and talked it over, women with shawls over their heads scuttled[26] into each other's houses before their work was done. Any deviation from the ordinary course of life in this quiet town was enough to stop all progress in it. Everybody paused to look at the staid,[27] independent figure on the side track. There was a difference of opinion with regard to her. Some held her to be insane; some, of lawless and rebellious spirit.

It looked almost as homelike as the abandoned house across the yard had ever done.

Friday the minister went to see her. It was in the forenoon, and she was at the barn door shelling peas for dinner. She looked up and returned his salutation with dignity, then she went on with her work. She did not invite him in. The saintly expression of her face remained fixed, but there was an angry flush over it.

The minister stood awkwardly before her, and talked. She handled the peas as if they were bullets. At last she looked up, and her eyes showed the spirit that her meek front had covered for a lifetime.

"There ain't no use talkin', Mr. Hersey," said she. "I've thought it all over an' over, an' I believe I'm doin' what's right. I've made it the subject of prayer, an' it's betwixt me an' the Lord an' Adoniram. There ain't no call for nobody else to worry about it."

"Well, of course, if you have brought it to the Lord in prayer, and feel satisfied that you are doing right, Mrs. Penn," said the minister, helplessly. His thin gray-bearded face was pathetic. He was a sickly man; his youthful confidence had cooled; he had to scourge himself up to some of his pastoral duties as relentlessly as a Catholic ascetic,[28] and then he was prostrated by the smart.[29]

"I think it's right jest as much as I think it was right for our forefathers to come over from the old country 'cause they didn't have what belonged to 'em," said Mrs. Penn. She arose. The barn threshold might have been Plymouth Rock[30] from her bearing. "I don't doubt you mean well, Mr. Hersey," said she, "but there are things

[25] stanchions—framework of two vertical bars which fasten around a cow's neck while it is being milked.

[26] scuttled—ran or moved with short hurried movements, scurried.

[27] staid—dignified, sober.

[28] ascetic—individual who leads a life of self-denial and self-discipline.

[29] prostrated by the smart—overcome by the pain.

[30] Plymouth Rock—site where the Pilgrims landed in 1620.

people hadn't ought to interfere with. I've been a member of the church for over forty year. I've got my own mind an' my own feet, an' I'm goin' to think my own thoughts an' go my own ways, an' nobody but the Lord is goin' to dictate to me unless I've a mind to have him. Won't you come in an' set down? How is Mis' Hersey?"

"She is well, I thank you," replied the minister. He added some more perplexed apologetic remarks; then he retreated.

He could expound the intricacies of every character study in the Scriptures, he was competent to grasp the Pilgrim Fathers and all historical innovators, but Sarah Penn was beyond him. He could deal with primal cases, but parallel[31] ones worsted him. But, after all, although it was aside from his province, he wondered more how Adoniram Penn would deal with his wife than how the Lord would. Everybody shared the wonder. When Adoniram's four new cows arrived, Sarah ordered three to be put in the old barn, the other in the house shed where the cooking-stove had stood. That added to the excitement. It was whispered that all four cows were domiciled in the house.

Towards sunset on Saturday, when Adoniram was expected home, there was a knot of men in the road near the new barn. The hired man had milked, but he still hung around the premises. Sarah Penn had supper all ready. There was brown-bread and baked beans and a custard pie; it was the supper that Adoniram loved on a Saturday night. She had on a clean calico,[32] and she bore herself **imperturbably**.[33] Nanny and Sammy kept close at her heels. Their eyes were large, and Nanny was full of nervous tremors. Still there was to them more pleasant excitement than anything else. An inborn confidence in their mother over their father asserted itself.

Sammy looked out of the harness-room window. "There he is," he announced, in an awed whisper. He and Nanny peeped around the casing.[34] Mrs. Penn kept on about her work. The children watched Adoniram leave the new horse standing in the drive while he went to the house door. It was fastened. Then he went around to the shed. That door was seldom locked, even when the family was away. The thought how her father would be confronted by the cow flashed upon Nanny. There was a hysterical sob in her throat. Adoniram emerged from the shed and stood looking about in a dazed fashion. His lips moved; he was saying something, but they could not hear what it was. The hired man was peeping around a corner of the old barn, but nobody saw him.

Adoniram took the new horse by the bridle and led him across the yard to the new barn. Nanny and Sammy slunk close to their mother. The barn doors rolled back, and there stood Adoniram, with the long mild face of the great Canadian farm horse looking over his shoulder.

Nanny kept behind her mother, but Sammy stepped suddenly forward, and stood in front of her.

---

[31] primal . . . parallel—The minister could understand situations in earlier times but not those of his own day.

[32] calico—coarse, brightly printed cloth.

[33] **imperturbably**—calmly.

[34] casing—window frame.

Adoniram stared at the group. "What on airth you all down here for?" said he. "What's the matter over to the house?"

"We've come here to live, father," said Sammy. His shrill voice quavered out bravely.

"What"—Adoniram sniffed—"what is it smells like cookin?" said he. He stepped forward and looked in the open door of the harness-room. Then he turned to his wife. His old bristling face was pale and frightened. "What on airth does this mean, mother?" he gasped.

"There ain't nothin' to be upset over. But we've come here to live, an' we're goin' to live here."

"You come in here, father," said Sarah. She led the way into the harness-room and shut the door. "Now, father," said she, "you needn't be scared. I ain't crazy. There ain't nothin' to be upset over. But we've come here to live, an' we're goin' to live here. We've got jest as good a right here as new horses an' cows. The house wa'n't fit for us to live in any longer, an' I made up my mind I wa'n't goin' to stay there. I've done my duty by you forty year, an' I'm goin' to do it now; but I'm goin' to live here. You've got to put in some windows and partitions; an' you'll have to buy some furniture."

"Why, mother!" the old man gasped.

"You'd better take your coat off an' get washed—there's the wash-basin—an' then we'll have supper."

"Why, mother!"

Sammy went past the window, leading the new horse to the old barn. The old man saw him, and shook his head speechlessly. He tried to take off his coat, but his arms seemed to lack the power. His wife helped him. She poured some water into the tin basin, and put in a piece of soap. She got the comb and brush, and smoothed his thin gray hair after he had washed. Then she put the beans, the hot bread, and tea on the table. Sammy came in, and the family drew up. Adoniram sat looking dazedly at his plate, and they waited.

"Ain't you goin' to ask a blessin', father?" said Sarah.

And the old man bent his head and mumbled.

All through the meal he stopped eating at intervals, and stared furtively at his wife; but he ate well. The home food tasted good to him, and his old frame was too sturdily healthy to be affected by his mind. But after supper he went out, and sat down on the step of the smaller door at the right of the barn, through which he had meant his jerseys[35] to pass in stately file, but which Sarah designed for her front house door, and he leaned his head on his hands.

After the supper dishes were cleared away and the milk-pans washed, Sarah went out to him. The twilight was deepening. There was a clear green glow in the sky. Before them stretched the smooth level of field; in the distance was a cluster of hay-stacks like the huts of a village; the air was very cool and calm and sweet. The landscape might have been an ideal one of peace.

[35] jerseys—Jersey cows.

Sarah bent over and touched her husband on one of this thin, sinewy shoulders. "Father!"

The old man's shoulders heaved: he was weeping.

"Why, don't do so, father," said Sarah.

"I'll—put up the—partitions, an'—everything you—want, mother."

Sarah put her apron up to her face; she was overcome by her own triumph.

Adoniram was like a fortress whose walls had no active resistance, and went down the instant the right besieging tools were used. "Why, mother," he said, hoarsely, "I hadn't no idee you was so set on't as all this comes to."

QUESTIONS TO CONSIDER

1. Why is Sarah so upset that Adoniram is building another barn? Why does she then tell Nanny not to criticize her father?
2. What drives Sarah to her bold choice?
3. What is Freeman's attitude toward the people in the Penns' town?
4. Why does Adoniram break down at the end of the story?
5. What is Freeman's ultimate message about the relations between men and women?
6. How does Freeman's realism affect the way in which Sarah's thoughts and emotions are expressed?

Charlotte Perkins Gilman ▶

The Yellow Wallpaper

BY CHARLOTTE PERKINS GILMAN

Charlotte Perkins Gilman (1860–1935) was a prominent feminist whose life and multiple careers were much condemned in her lifetime. Gilman was born into a prominent New England family and began writing to amuse herself at an early age. In 1884, after much hesitation, Gilman married the artist Charles Stetson, and they had a child in 1885. Her famous story, "The Yellow Wallpaper," was directly inspired by the three years of depression she suffered after the birth of their child. The cure prescribed for her depression—enforced passivity and a denial of intellectual stimulation—Gilman later wrote had put her "so near the borderline of utter mental ruin that I could see over." She divorced Stetson and left their daughter in his care, feeling that the constraints of marriage and motherhood were driving her mad. Gilman became involved in radical politics, publishing utopian stories and political tracts. She also published her own magazine, The Forerunner, *from 1909 to 1916. Gilman advocated socialism, women's rights, environmental protection, and workers' rights. Her* Women and Economics *(1898), an examination of the economic oppression of women and how society's idealization of women made it impossible for her to fully enter the work force, was known as the "Bible of the Women's Movement." Gilman's other works include* Herland *(1915), a novel about a feminist utopia, and* His Religion and Hers *(1923). She committed suicide in 1935, preferring to die with dignity than to live with the ravages of inoperable cancer. Gilman is principally remembered now for "The Yellow Wallpaper," a masterful story that is one of America's earliest cries for equality between the sexes.*

It is very seldom that mere ordinary people like John and myself secure ancestral halls for the summer.

A colonial mansion, a hereditary estate, I would say a haunted house and reach the height of romantic **felicity**[1]—but that would be asking too much of fate!

Still I will proudly declare that there is something queer about it.

Else, why should it be let so cheaply? And why have stood so long untenanted?[2]

John laughs at me, of course, but one expects that.

John is practical in the extreme. He has no patience with faith, an intense horror of superstition, and he scoffs[3] openly at any talk of things not to be felt and seen and put down in figures.

John is a physician, and *perhaps*—(I would not say it to a living soul, of

---

[1] **felicity**—happiness.

[2] untenanted—without residents.

[3] scoffs—expresses derision or scorn.

course, but this is dead paper and a great relief to my mind)—*perhaps* that is one reason I do not get well faster.

You see, he does not believe I am sick! And what can one do?

If a physician of high standing, and one's own husband, assures friends and relatives that there is really nothing the matter with one but temporary nervous depression—a slight hysterical tendency—what is one to do?

My brother is also a physician, and also of high standing, and he says the same thing.

So I take phosphates or phosphites—whichever it is—and tonics, and air and exercise, and journeys, and am absolutely forbidden to "work" until I am well again.

Personally, I disagree with their ideas.

Personally, I believe that **congenial**[4] work, with excitement and change, would do me good.

But what is one to do?

I did write for a while in spite of them; but it *does* exhaust me a good deal—having to be so sly about it, or else meet with heavy opposition.

I sometimes fancy that in my condition, if I had less opposition and more society and stimulus—but John says the very worst thing I can do is to think about my condition, and I confess it always makes me feel bad.

So I will let it alone and talk about the house.

The most beautiful place! It is quite alone, standing well back from the road, quite three miles from the village. It makes me think of English places that you read about, for there are hedges and walls and gates that lock, and lots of separate little houses for the gardeners and people.

There is a *delicious* garden! I never saw such a garden—large and shady, full of box-bordered[5] paths, and lined with long grape-covered arbors[6] with seats under them.

There were greenhouses, but they are all broken now.

There was some legal trouble, I believe, something about the heirs and co-heirs; anyhow, the place has been empty for years.

That spoils my ghostliness, I am afraid, but I don't care—there is something strange about the house—I can feel it.

I even said so to John one moonlight evening, but he said what I felt was a draught,[7] and shut the window.

I get unreasonably angry with John sometimes. I'm sure I never used to be so sensitive. I think it is due to this nervous condition.

But John says if I feel so, I shall neglect proper self-control; so I take pains to control myself—before him, at least, and that makes me very tired.

I don't like our room a bit. I wanted one downstairs that opened on the piazza and had roses all over the window, and such pretty old-fashioned chintz[8] hangings! But John would not hear of it.

---

[4] **congenial**—suited to one's needs or nature.

[5] box-bordered—lined on both sides by evergreen hedges.

[6] arbors—shady places in a garden or park, often made of latticework on which plants are grown.

[7] draught—draft.

[8] chintz—printed and glazed cotton fabric.

He said there was only one window and not room for two beds, and no near room for him if he took another.

He is very careful and loving, and hardly lets me stir without special direction.

The color is repellant, almost revolting; a smouldering unclean yellow.

I have a schedule prescription for each hour in the day; he takes all care from me, and so I feel basely ungrateful not to value it more.

He said we came here solely on my account, that I was to have perfect rest and all the air I could get. "Your exercise depends on your strength, my dear," said he, "and your food somewhat on your appetite; but air you can absorb all the time." So we took the nursery at the top of the house.

It is a big, airy room, the whole floor nearly, with windows that look all ways, and air and sunshine galore. It was nursery first and then playroom and gymnasium, I should judge; for the windows are barred for little children, and there are rings and things in the walls.

The paint and paper look as if a boys' school had used it. It is stripped off the paper—in great patches all around the head of my bed, about as far as I can reach, and in a great place on the other side of the room low down. I never saw a worse paper in my life. One of those sprawling flamboyant patterns committing every artistic sin.

It is dull enough to confuse the eye in following, pronounced enough to constantly irritate and provoke study, and when you follow the lame uncertain curves for a little distance they suddenly commit suicide—plunge off at outrageous angles, destroy themselves in unheard-of contradictions.

The color is repellant, almost revolting; a smouldering unclean yellow, strangely faded by the slow-turning sunlight. It is a dull yet lurid orange in some places, a sickly sulphur tint in others.

No wonder the children hated it! I should hate it myself if I had to live in this room long.

There comes John, and I must put this away—he hates to have me write a word.

We have been here two weeks, and I haven't felt like writing before, since that first day.

I am sitting by the window now, up in this **atrocious**[9] nursery, and there is nothing to hinder my writing as much as I please, save lack of strength.

John is away all day, and even some nights when his cases are serious.

I am glad my case is not serious!

But these nervous troubles are dreadfully depressing.

John does not know how much I really suffer. He knows there is no reason to suffer, and that satisfies him.

Of course it is only nervousness. It does weigh on me so not to do my duty in any way!

---

[9] **atrocious**—evil, monstrous.

I mean to be such a help to John, such a real rest and comfort, and here I am a comparative burden already!

Nobody would believe what an effort it is to do what little I am able—to dress and entertain, and order things.

It is fortunate Mary is so good with the baby. Such a dear baby!

And yet I *cannot* be with him, it makes me so nervous.

I suppose John never was nervous in his life. He laughs at me so about this wallpaper!

At first he meant to repaper the room, but afterwards he said that I was letting it get the better of me, and that nothing was worse for a nervous patient than to give way to such fancies.

He said that after the wallpaper was changed it would be the heavy bedstead, and then the barred windows, and then that gate at the head of the stairs, and so on.

"You know the place is doing you good," he said, "and really, dear, I don't care to renovate the house just for a three months' rental."

"Then do let us go downstairs," I said. "There are such pretty rooms there."

Then he took me in his arms and called me a blessed little goose, and said he would go down cellar, if I wished, and have it whitewashed into the bargain.

But he is right enough about the beds and windows and things.

It is as airy and comfortable a room as anyone need wish, and, of course, I would not be so silly as to make him uncomfortable just for a whim.

I'm really getting quite fond of the big room, all but that horrid paper.

Out of one window I can see the garden—those mysterious deep-shaded arbors, the riotous[10] old-fashioned flowers, and bushes and gnarly trees.

Out of another I get a lovely view of the bay and a little private wharf belonging to the estate. There is a beautiful shaded lane that runs down there from the house. I always fancy I see people walking in these numerous paths and arbors, but John has cautioned me not to give way to fancy in the least. He says that with my imaginative power and habit of story-making, a nervous weakness like mine is sure to lead to all manner of excited fancies, and that I ought to use my will and good sense to check the tendency. So I try.

I think sometimes that if I were only well enough to write a little it would relieve the press of ideas and rest me.

But I find I get pretty tired when I try.

It is so discouraging not to have any advice and companionship about my work. When I get really well, John says we will ask Cousin Henry and Julia down for a long visit; but he says he would as soon put fireworks in my pillowcase as to let me have those stimulating people about now.

I wish I could get well faster.

But I must not think about that. This paper looks to me as if it *knew* what a vicious influence it had!

There is a recurrent spot where the pattern lolls like a broken neck and two bulbous eyes stare at you upside down.

---

[10] riotous—abundant or luxuriant.

I get positively angry with the impertinence of it and the everlastingness. Up and down and sideways they crawl, and those absurd unblinking eyes are everywhere. There is one place where two breadths didn't match, and the eyes go all up and down the line, one a little higher than the other.

I never saw so much expression in an inanimate thing before, and we all know how much expression they have! I used to lie awake as a child and get more entertainment and terror out of blank walls and plain furniture than most children could find in a toy-store.

I remember what a kindly wink the knobs of our big old bureau used to have, and there was one chair that always seemed like a strong friend.

I used to feel that if any of the other things looked too fierce I could always hop into that chair and be safe.

The furniture in this room is no worse than inharmonious,[11] however, for we had to bring it all from downstairs. I suppose when this was used as a playroom they had to take the nursery things out, and no wonder! I never saw such ravages as the children have made here.

The wallpaper, as I said before, is torn off in spots, and it sticketh closer than a brother—they must have had perseverance as well as hatred.

Then the floor is scratched and gouged and splintered, the plaster itself is dug out here and there, and this great heavy bed which is all we found in the room, looks as if it had been through the wars.

But I don't mind it a bit—only the paper.

There comes John's sister. Such a dear girl as she is, and so careful of me! I must not let her find me writing.

She is a perfect and enthusiastic housekeeper, and hopes for no better profession. I verily[12] believe she thinks it is the writing which made me sick!

But I can write when she is out, and see her a long way off from these windows.

There is one that commands the road, a lovely shaded winding road, and one that just looks off over the country. A lovely country, too, full of great elms and velvet meadows.

This wallpaper has a kind of sub-pattern in a different shade, a particularly irritating one, for you can only see it in certain lights, and not clearly then.

But in the places where it isn't faded and where the sun is just so—I can see a strange, provoking, formless sort of figure that seems to skulk about behind that silly and conspicuous front design.

There's sister on the stairs!

Well, the Fourth of July is over! The people are all gone, and I am tired out. John thought it might do me good to see a little company, so we just had Mother and Nellie and the children down for a week.

Of course I didn't do a thing. Jennie sees to everything now.

But it tired me all the same.

John says if I don't pick up faster he shall send me to Weir Mitchell in the fall.

---

[11] inharmonious—discordant, not pleasing.

[12] verily—truly.

But I don't want to go there at all. I had a friend who was in his hands once, and she says he is just like John and my brother, only more so!

Besides, it is such an undertaking to go so far.

I don't feel as if it was worthwhile to turn my hand over for anything, and I'm getting dreadfully fretful and querulous.[13]

I cry at nothing, and cry most of the time.

Of course I don't when John is here, or anybody else, but when I am alone.

And I am alone a good deal just now. John is kept in town very often by serious cases, and Jennie is good and lets me alone when I want her to.

So I walk a little in the garden or down that lovely lane, sit on the porch under the roses, and lie down up here a good deal.

I'm getting really fond of the room in spite of the wallpaper. Perhaps *because* of the wallpaper.

It dwells in my mind so!

I lie here on this great immovable bed—it is nailed down, I believe—and follow that pattern about by the hour. It is as good as gymnastics, I assure you. I start, we'll say, at the bottom, down in the corner over there where it has not been touched, and I determine for the thousandth time that I *will* follow that pointless pattern to some sort of conclusion.

I know a little of the principle of design, and I know this thing was not arranged on any laws of radiation, or alternation, or repetition, or symmetry, or anything else that I ever heard of.

It is repeated, of course, by the breadths, but not otherwise.

Looked at in one way, each breadth stands alone; the bloated curves and flourishes—a kind of "debased Romanesque"[14] with delirium tremens[15]—go waddling up and down in isolated columns of fatuity.[16]

I cry at nothing, and cry most of the time.

But, on the other hand, they connect diagonally, and the sprawling outlines run off in great slanting waves of optic horror, like a lot of wallowing sea-weeds in full chase.

The whole thing goes horizontally, too, at least it seems so, and I exhaust myself trying to distinguish the order of its going in that direction.

They have used a horizontal breadth for a frieze[17] and that adds wonderfully to the confusion.

There is one end of the room where it is almost intact, and there, when the crosslights fade and the low sun shines directly upon it, I can almost fancy radiation after all—the interminable grotesque seems to form around a common center and rush off in headlong plunges of equal distraction. It makes me tired to follow it. I will take a nap, I guess.

---

13 querulous—quarrelsome.

14 Romanesque—medieval style of art characterized by elaborate ornamentation and religious symbolism.

15 delirium tremens—violent trembling and terrifying hallucinations caused by the prolonged and excessive drinking of alcohol.

16 fatuity—utter foolishness.

17 frieze—horizontal band of decoration around a room or building.

I don't know why I should write this.

I don't want to.

I don't feel able.

And I know John would think it absurd. But I *must* say what I feel and think in some way—it is such a relief!

But the effort is getting to be greater than the relief.

Half the time now I am awfully lazy, and lie down ever so much.

John says I mustn't lose my strength, and has me take cod liver oil and lots of tonics and things, to say nothing of ale and wine and rare meat.

Dear John! He loves me very dearly, and hates to have me sick. I tried to have a real earnest reasonable talk with him the other day, and tell him how I wish he would let me go and make a visit to Cousin Henry and Julia.

But he said I wasn't able to go, nor able to stand it after I got there; and I did not make out a very good case for myself, for I was crying before I had finished.

It is getting to be a great effort for me to think straight. Just this nervous weakness, I suppose.

And dear John gathered me up in his arms, and just carried me upstairs and laid me on the bed, and sat by me and read to me till it tired my head.

He said I was his darling and his comfort and all he had, and that I must take care of myself for his sake, and keep well.

He says no one but myself can help me out of it, that I must use my will and self-control and not let any silly fancies run away with me.

There's one comfort—the baby is well and happy, and does not have to occupy this nursery with the horrid wallpaper.

If we had not used it, that blessed child would have! What a fortunate escape! Why, I wouldn't have a child of mine, an impressionable little thing, live in such a room for worlds.

I never thought of it before, but it is lucky that John kept me here after all, I can stand it so much easier than a baby, you see.

Of course I never mention it to them any more—I am too wise—but I keep watch for it all the same.

There are things in that paper that nobody knows about but me, or ever will.

Behind that outside pattern the dim shapes get clearer every day.

It is always the same shape, only very numerous.

And it is like a woman stooping down and creeping about behind that pattern. I don't like it a bit. I wonder—I begin to think—I wish John would take me away from here!

It is so hard to talk with John about my case, because he is so wise, and because he loves me so.

But I tried it last night.

It was moonlight. The moon shines in all around just as the sun does.

I hate to see it sometimes, it creeps so slowly, and always comes in by one window or another.

John was asleep and I hated to waken him, so I kept still and watched the moonlight on that **undulating**[18] wallpaper till I felt creepy.

The faint figure behind seemed to shake the pattern, just as if she wanted to get out.

I got up softly and went to feel and see if the paper *did* move, and when I came back John was awake.

"What is it, little girl?" he said. "Don't go walking about like that—you'll get cold."

I thought it was a good time to talk, so I told him that I really was not gaining here, and that I wished he would take me away.

"Why, darling!" said he. "Our lease will be up in three weeks, and I can't see how to leave before.

"The repairs are not done at home, and I cannot possibly leave town just now. Of course if you were in any danger, I could and would, but you really are better, dear, whether you can see it or not. I am a doctor, dear, and I know. You are gaining flesh and color, your appetite is better, I feel really much easier about you."

"I don't weigh a bit more," said I, "nor as much; and my appetite may be better in the evening when you are here but it is worse in the morning when you are away!"

"Bless her little heart!" said he with a big hug. "She shall be as sick as she pleases! But now let's improve the shining hours by going to sleep, and talk about it in the morning!"

"And you won't go away?" I asked gloomily.

"Why, how can I, dear? It is only three weeks more and then we will take a nice little trip of a few days while Jennie is getting the house ready. Really, dear, you are better!"

"Better in body perhaps—" I began, and stopped short, for he sat up straight and looked at me with such a stern, reproachful look that I could not say another word.

"My darling," said he, "I beg of you, for my sake and for our child's sake, as well as for your own, that you will never for one instant let that idea enter your mind! There is nothing so dangerous, so fascinating, to a temperament like yours. It is a false and foolish fancy. Can you not trust me as a physician when I tell you so?"

So of course I said no more on that score, and we went to sleep before long. He thought I was asleep first, but I wasn't, and lay there for hours trying to decide whether that front pattern and the back pattern really did move together or separately.

On a pattern like this, by daylight, there is a lack of sequence, a defiance of law, that is a constant irritant to a normal mind.

The color is hideous enough, and unreliable enough, and infuriating enough, but the pattern is torturing.

You think you have mastered it, but just as you get well under way in following, it turns a back-somersault and there you are. It slaps you in the face, it knocks you down, and tramples upon you. It is like a bad dream.

The outside pattern is a florid arabesque,[19] reminding one of a fungus.

---

[18] **undulating**—moving in waves.

[19] florid arabesque—ornate intertwined design.

If you can imagine a toadstool in joints, an interminable string of toadstools, budding and sprouting in endless convolutions—why, that is something like it.

That is, sometimes!

There is one marked peculiarity about this paper, a thing nobody seems to notice but myself, and that is that it changes as the light changes.

When the sun shoots in through the east window—I always watch for that first long, straight ray—it changes so quickly that I never can quite believe it.

That is why I watch it always.

By moonlight—the moon shines in all night when there is a moon—I wouldn't know it was the same paper.

At night in any kind of light, in twilight, candlelight, lamplight, and worst of all by moonlight, it becomes bars! The outside pattern, I mean, and the woman behind it is as plain as can be.

I didn't realize for a long time what the thing was that showed behind, that dim sub-pattern, but now I am quite sure it is a woman.

By daylight she is subdued, quiet. I fancy it is the pattern that keeps her so still. It is so puzzling. It keeps me quiet by the hour.

I lie down ever so much now. John says it is good for me, and to sleep all I can.

Indeed he started the habit by making me lie down for an hour after each meal.

It is a very bad habit I am convinced, for you see, I don't sleep.

And that cultivates deceit, for I don't tell them I'm awake—O no!

The fact is I am getting a little afraid of John.

He seems very queer sometimes, and even Jennie has an **inexplicable**[20] look.

It strikes me occasionally, just as a scientific hypothesis, that perhaps it is the paper!

I have watched John when he did not know I was looking, and come into the room suddenly on the most innocent excuses, and I've caught him several times *looking at the paper!* And Jennie too. I caught Jennie with her hand on it once.

She didn't know I was in the room, and when I asked her in a quiet, a very quiet voice, with the most restrained manner possible, what she was doing with the paper—she turned around as if she had been caught stealing, and looked quite angry—asked me why I should frighten her so!

Then she said that the paper stained everything it touched, that she had found yellow smooches on all my clothes and John's, and she wished we would be more careful!

Did not that sound innocent? But I know she was studying that pattern, and I am determined that nobody shall find it out but myself!

Life is very much more exciting now than it used to be. You see I have something more to expect, to look forward to, to watch. I really do eat better, and am more quiet than I was.

---

[20] **inexplicable**—difficult to explain.

John is so pleased to see me improve! He laughed a little the other day, and said I seemed to be flourishing in spite of my wallpaper.

I turned it off with a laugh. I had no intention of telling him it was *because* of the wallpaper—he would make fun of me. He might even want to take me away.

I don't want to leave now until I have found it out. There is a week more, and I think that will be enough.

I'm feeling so much better!

I don't sleep much at night, for it is so interesting to watch developments; but I sleep a good deal during the daytime.

In the daytime it is tiresome and perplexing.

There are always new shoots on the fungus, and new shades of yellow all over it. I cannot keep count of them, though I have tried conscientiously.

It is the strangest yellow, that wallpaper! It makes me think of all the yellow things I ever saw—not beautiful ones like buttercups, but old, foul, bad yellow things.

But there is something else about that paper—the smell! I noticed it the moment we came into the room, but with so much air and sun it was not bad. Now we have had a week of fog and rain, and whether the windows are open or not, the smell is here.

It creeps all over the house.

I find it hovering in the dining-room, skulking in the parlor, hiding in the hall, lying in wait for me on the stairs.

It gets into my hair.

Even when I go to ride, if I turn my head suddenly and surprise it—there is that smell!

It is the strangest yellow, that wallpaper!

Such a peculiar odor, too! I have spent hours in trying to analyze it, to find what it smelled like.

It is not bad—at first—and very gentle, but quite the subtlest, most enduring odor I ever met.

In this damp weather it is awful. I wake up in the night and find it hanging over me.

It used to disturb me at first. I thought seriously of burning the house—to reach the smell.

But now I am used to it. The only thing I can think of that it is like is the *color* of the paper! A yellow smell.

There is a very funny mark on this wall, low down, near the mopboard.[21] A streak that runs round the room. It goes behind every piece of furniture, except the bed, a long, straight, even *smooch*, as if it had been rubbed over and over.

I wonder how it was done and who did it, and what they did it for. Round and round and round—round and round and round—it makes me dizzy!

I really have discovered something at last.

Through watching so much at night, when it changes so, I have finally found out.

[21] mopboard—line of boards around the base of a wall near the floor, also known as a baseboard.

The front pattern *does* move—and no wonder! The woman behind shakes it!

Sometimes I think there are a great many women behind, and sometimes only one, and she crawls around fast, and her crawling shakes it all over.

Then in the very bright spots she keeps still, and in the very shady spots she just takes hold of the bars and shakes them hard.

And she is all the time trying to climb through. But nobody could climb through that pattern—it strangles so; I think that is why it has so many heads.

They get through, and then the pattern strangles them off and turns them upside down, and makes their eyes white!

If those heads were covered or taken off it would not be half so bad.

I think that woman gets out in the daytime!

And I'll tell you why—privately—I've seen her!

I can see her out of every one of my windows!

It is the same woman, I know, for she is always creeping, and most women do not creep by daylight.

I see her in that long shaded lane, creeping up and down. I see her in those dark grape arbors, creeping all around the garden.

I see her on that long road under the trees, creeping along, and when a carriage comes she hides under the blackberry vines.

I don't blame her a bit. It must be very humiliating to be caught creeping by daylight!

I always lock the door when I creep by daylight. I can't do it at night, for I know John would suspect something at once.

And John is so queer now that I don't want to irritate him. I wish he could take another room! Besides, I don't want anybody to get that woman out at night but myself.

I often wonder if I could see her out of all the windows at once.

But, turn as fast as I can, I can only see out of one at one time.

And though I always see her, she *may* be able to creep faster than I can turn! I have watched her sometimes away off in the open country, creeping as fast as a cloud shadow in a wind.

If only that top pattern could be gotten off from the under one! I mean to try it, little by little.

I have found out another funny thing, but I shan't tell it this time! It does not do to trust people too much.

There are only two more days to get this paper off, and I believe John is beginning to notice. I don't like the look in his eyes.

And I heard him ask Jennie a lot of professional questions about me. She had a very good report to give.

She said I slept a good deal in the daytime.

John knows I don't sleep very well at night, for all I'm so quiet!

He asked me all sorts of questions, too, and pretended to be very loving and kind.

As if I couldn't see through him!

Still, I don't wonder he acts so, sleeping under this paper for three months.

It only interests me, but I feel sure John and Jennie are affected by it.

Hurrah! This is the last day, but it is enough. John is to stay in town over night, and won't be out until this evening.

Jennie wanted to sleep with me—the sly thing; but I told her I should undoubtedly rest better for a night all alone.

That was clever, for really I wasn't alone a bit! As soon as it was moonlight and that poor thing began to crawl and shake the pattern, I got up and ran to help her.

I pulled and she shook, I shook and she pulled, and before morning we had peeled off yards of that paper.

A strip about as high as my head and half around the room.

And then when the sun came and that awful pattern began to laugh at me, I declared I would finish it today!

We go away tomorrow, and they are moving all my furniture down again to leave things as they were before.

Jennie looked at the wall in amazement, but I told her merrily that I did it out of spite at the vicious thing.

She laughed and said she wouldn't mind doing it herself, but I must not get tired.

How she betrayed herself that time!

But I am here, and no person touches this paper but Me—not *alive*!

She tried to get me out of the room—it was too patent![22] But I said it was so quiet and empty and clean now that I believed I would lie down again and sleep all I could; and not to wake me even for dinner—I would call when I woke.

So now she is gone, and the servants are gone, and the things are gone, and there is nothing left but that great bedstead nailed down, with the canvas mattress we found on it.

We shall sleep downstairs tonight, and take the boat home tomorrow.

I quite enjoy the room, now it is bare again.

How those children did tear about here!

This bedstead is fairly gnawed!

But I must get to work.

I have locked the door and thrown the key down into the front path.

I don't want to go out, and I don't want to have anybody come in, till John comes.

I want to astonish him.

I've got a rope up here that even Jennie did not find. If that woman does get out, and tries to get away, I can tie her!

But I forgot I could not reach far without anything to stand on!

This bed will *not* move!

I tried to lift and push it until I was lame, and then I got so angry I bit off a little piece at one corner—but it hurt my teeth.

Then I peeled off all the paper I could reach standing on the floor. It sticks horribly and the pattern just enjoys it! All those strangled heads and bulbous eyes and waddling fungus growths just shriek with **derision**![23]

I am getting angry enough to do something desperate. To jump out of the window would be admirable exercise, but the bars are too strong even to try.

---

[22] patent—obvious.

[23] **derision**—ridicule.

Besides I wouldn't do it. Of course not. I know well enough that a step like that is improper and might be misconstrued.[24]

I don't like to *look* out of the windows even—there are so many of those creeping women, and they creep so fast.

I wonder if they all come out of that wallpaper as I did?

But I am securely fastened now by my well-hidden rope—you don't get *me* out in the road there!

I suppose I shall have to get back behind the pattern when it comes night, and that is hard!

It is so pleasant to be out in this great room and creep around as I please!

I don't want to go outside. I won't, even if Jennie asks me to.

For outside you have to creep on the ground, and everything is green instead of yellow.

But here I can creep smoothly on the floor, and my shoulder just fits in that long smooch around the wall, so I cannot lose my way.

Why there's John at the door!

It is no use, young man, you can't open it!

How he does call and pound!

Now he's crying to Jennie for an axe.

It would be a shame to break down that beautiful door!

"John dear!" said I in the gentlest voice. "The key is down by the front steps, under a plantain leaf!"

That silenced him for a few moments.

Then he said—very quietly indeed, "Open the door, my darling!"

"I can't," said I. "The key is down by the front door under a plantain leaf!"

And then I said it again, several times, very gently and slowly, and said it so often that he had to go and see, and he got it of course, and came in. He stopped short by the door.

"What is the matter?" he cried. "For God's sake, what are you doing!"

I kept on creeping just the same, but I looked at him over my shoulder.

"I've got out at last," said I, "in spite of you and Jane. And I've pulled off most of the paper, so you can't put me back!"

Now why should that man have fainted? But he did, and right across my path by the wall, so that I had to creep over him every time!

---

[24] misconstrued—misinterpreted.

QUESTIONS TO CONSIDER

1. Why have John and the narrator rented the big house?
2. What do you think their bedroom had once been used for?
3. Describe the husband John. What do you think of him? What do you think Gilman thought of him?
4. How would you summarize the plot of "The Yellow Wallpaper"?
5. What is the message Gilman wants to get across? Whom does she want to blame?
6. What elements in "The Yellow Wallpaper" are romantic? What elements are realistic?

Kate Chopin ▶

A Respectable Woman

BY KATE CHOPIN

Kate Chopin (1851–1904) is a writer who in her lifetime was considered by most readers and critics as a local colorist. Born in St. Louis, she married a Louisianan who took her to New Orleans, eventually to live on a large cotton plantation which was later the setting for much of Chopin's fiction. She started to write late, in her thirties, after the death of her husband and her return to St. Louis with their six children. Her stories about life on the plantation quickly earned her success and a reputation as a local colorist. Her only novel, The Awakening *(1899), was considered scandalous for its frank depictions of adultery and mixed marriage. The scandal caused Chopin to all but give up writing in the years that remained before her early death of a brain hemorrhage. Six decades later, Chopin was rediscovered, and* The Awakening *was recognized as a brilliant portrait of a woman finding herself. "A Respectable Woman" is a brief story, but Chopin says all that she needs to fully define a trio of characters in her readers' minds.*

Mrs. Baroda was a little provoked to learn that her husband expected his friend, Gouvernail, up to spend a week or two on the plantation.

They had entertained a good deal during the winter; much of the time had also been passed in New Orleans in various forms of mild dissipation.[1] She was looking forward to a period of unbroken rest, now, and undisturbed tête-à-tête[2] with her husband, when he informed her that Gouvernail was coming up to stay a week or two.

This was a man she had heard much of but never seen. He had been her husband's college friend; was now a journalist, and in no sense a society man or "a man about town," which were, perhaps, some of the reasons she had never met him. But she had unconsciously formed an image of him in her mind. She pictured him tall, slim, cynical; with eye-glasses, and his hands in his pockets; and she did not like him. Gouvernail was slim enough, but he wasn't very tall nor very cynical; neither did he wear eye-glasses nor carry his hands in his pockets. And she rather liked him when he first presented himself.

But why she liked him she could not explain satisfactorily to herself when she partly attempted to do so. She could discover in him none of those brilliant and

---

[1] dissipation—amusement, indulgence.

[2] tête-à-tête—French for "head to head," meaning "alone together."

promising traits which Gaston, her husband, had often assured her that he possessed. On the contrary, he sat rather mute and receptive before her chatty eagerness to make him feel at home and in face of Gaston's frank and wordy hospitality. His manner was as courteous toward her as the most exacting woman could require; but he made no direct appeal to her approval or even esteem.

Gouvernail's personality puzzled Mrs. Baroda, but she liked him.

Once settled at the plantation he seemed to like to sit upon the wide portico in the shade of one of the big Corinthian pillars, smoking his cigar lazily and listening attentively to Gaston's experience as a sugar planter.

"This is what I call living," he would utter with deep satisfaction, as the air that swept across the sugar field caressed him with its warm and scented velvety touch. It pleased him also to get on familiar terms with the big dogs that came about him, rubbing themselves sociably against his legs. He did not care to fish, and displayed no eagerness to go out and kill grosbecs[3] when Gaston proposed doing so.

Gouvernail's personality puzzled Mrs. Baroda, but she liked him. Indeed, he was a lovable, inoffensive fellow. After a few days, when she could understand him no better than at first, she gave over being puzzled and remained piqued.[4] In this mood she left her husband and her guest, for the most part, alone together. Then finding that Gouvernail took no manner of exception to her action, she imposed her society upon him, accompanying him in his idle strolls to the mill and walks along the batture.[5] She persistently sought to penetrate the reserve in which he had unconsciously enveloped himself.

"When is he going—your friend?" she one day asked her husband. "For my part, he tires me frightfully."

"Not for a week yet, dear. I can't understand; he gives you no trouble."

"No. I should like him better if he did; if he were more like others, and I had to plan somewhat for his comfort and enjoyment."

Gaston took his wife's pretty face between his hands and looked tenderly and laughingly into her troubled eyes. They were making a bit of toilet[6] sociably together in Mrs. Baroda's dressing-room.

"You are full of surprises, ma belle,"[7] he said to her. "Even I can never count upon how you are going to act under given conditions." He kissed her and turned to fasten his cravat[8] before the mirror.

"Here you are," he went on, "taking poor Gouvernail seriously and making a commotion over him, the last thing he would desire or expect."

"Commotion!" she hotly resented. "Nonsense! How can you say such a thing? Commotion, indeed! But, you know, you said he was clever."

---

[3] grosbecs—any of several types of colorful finches.

[4] piqued—intrigued.

[5] batture—riverbank.

[6] toilet—dressing or grooming oneself.

[7] ma belle—French for "my pretty."

[8] cravat—scarf or band of fabric worn around the neck as a tie.

"So he is. But the poor fellow is run down by overwork now. That's why I asked him here to take a rest."

"You used to say he was a man of ideas," she retorted, unconciliated. "I expected him to be interesting, at least. I'm going to the city in the morning to have my spring gowns fitted. Let me know when Mr. Gouvernail is gone; I shall be at my Aunt Octavie's."

That night she went and sat alone upon a bench that stood beneath a live oak tree at the edge of the gravel walk.

She had never known her thoughts or her intentions to be so confused. She could gather nothing from them but the feeling of a distinct necessity to quit her home in the morning.

Mrs. Baroda heard footsteps crunching the gravel; but could discern in the darkness only the approaching red point of a lighted cigar. She knew it was Gouvernail, for her husband did not smoke. She hoped to remain unnoticed, but her white gown revealed her to him. He threw away his cigar and seated himself upon the bench beside her; without a suspicion that she might object to his presence.

"Your husband told me to bring this to you, Mrs. Baroda," he said, handing her a filmy, white scarf with which she sometimes enveloped her head and shoulders. She accepted the scarf from him with a murmur of thanks, and let it lie in her lap.

He made some commonplace observation upon the baneful[9] effect of the night air at that season. Then as his gaze reached out into the darkness, he murmured, half to himself:

"'Night of south winds—night of
the large few stars!
Still nodding night—'"

She made no reply to this apostrophe[10] to the night, which indeed, was not addressed to her.

Gouvernail was in no sense a **diffident**[11] man, for he was not a self-conscious one. His periods of reserve were not constitutional, but the result of moods. Sitting there beside Mrs. Baroda, his silence melted for the time.

He talked freely and intimately in a low, hesitating drawl that was not unpleasant to hear. He talked of the old college days when he and Gaston had been a good deal to each other; of the days of keen and blind ambitions and large intentions. Now there was left with him, at least, a philosophic **acquiescence**[12] to the existing order—only a desire to be permitted to exist, with now and then a little whiff of genuine life, such as he was breathing now.

Her mind only vaguely grasped what he was saying. Her physical being was for the moment predominant. She was not thinking of his words, only drinking in the tones of his voice. She wanted to reach out her hand in the darkness and touch him with the sensitive tips of her fingers upon the face or the lips. She wanted to draw close to him and whisper against his

---

[9] baneful—harmful.

[10] apostrophe—words addressed to a thing or idea, as though it were able to hear and answer back.

[11] **diffident**—shy and timid.

[12] **acquiescence**—passive assent or agreement.

cheek—she did not care what—as she might have done if she had not been a respectable woman.

The stronger the impulse grew to bring herself near him, the further, in fact, did she draw away from him. As soon as she could do so without an appearance of too great rudeness, she rose and left him there alone.

Before she reached the house, Gouvernail had lighted a fresh cigar and ended his apostrophe to the night.

Mrs. Baroda was greatly tempted that night to tell her husband—who was also her friend—of this folly that had seized her. But she did not yield to the temptation. Beside being a respectable woman she was a very sensible one; and she knew there are some battles in life which a human being must fight alone.

When Gaston arose in the morning, his wife had already departed. She had taken an early morning train to the city. She did not return till Gouvernail was gone from under her roof.

There was some talk of having him back during the summer that followed. That is, Gaston greatly desired it; but this desire yielded to his wife's strenuous opposition.

However, before the year ended, she proposed, wholly from herself, to have Gouvernail visit them again. Her husband was surprised and delighted with the suggestion coming from her.

"I am glad, chère amie,[13] to know that you have finally overcome your dislike for him; truly he did not deserve it."

"Oh," she told him, laughingly, after pressing a long, tender kiss upon his lips, "I have overcome everything! you will see. This time I shall be very nice to him."

[13] chère amie—French for "dear friend."

QUESTIONS TO CONSIDER

1. Why is Mrs. Baroda annoyed about Gouvernail? Why is he so subdued around her?
2. What is the tone of the story? How is this tone reflected in the story's title?
3. What do you think happens when Mrs. Baroda and Gouvernail meet again? What details did you use to infer the later events?
4. What is Chopin saying about the characters of men and women in this story?
5. In what ways is Chopin a romantic writer? In what ways is she a realist?

Stephen Crane ▶

The Bride Comes to Yellow Sky

BY STEPHEN CRANE

Stephen Crane (1871–1900) lived a very short life, yet his body of work is as impressive as it is varied. He was born in New Jersey and after college became a reporter in New York. He published his first novel, Maggie: A Girl of the Streets, *in 1893, and this account of the brutality of slum life is the prototype of American naturalist fiction. Two years later, Crane brought out the book that made him famous, his impressionistic study of war,* The Red Badge of Courage. *He also published his first volume of poetry that year. Meanwhile Crane was also turning out stories and journalism at a fast rate. He went overseas as a war correspondent and then to live in England when his health began to fail. Crane died of tuberculosis in 1900, having achieved much, but leaving his literary contemporaries wondering what masterpieces died with him.*

Many of Crane's stories document how America was changing in the 1890s. The building of the transcontinental railroad had speeded up the exploitation and settlement of the West by miners, ranchers, and farmers. Following the Civil War, many former soldiers joined this westward movement, particularly Confederates who saw little future in a war-ravaged South. The difficulty of enforcing laws in frontier towns inhabited by many ex-soldiers contributed to the so-called "Wild West," a time well-documented in American popular culture. By the 1890s, the Wild West era was largely over: law, business, and domesticity were the new order. "The Bride Comes to Yellow Sky" shows this change in America at the end of the nineteenth century. The Wild West was growing cultivated, manufacturing was moving in, and the old ways were dying off.

I

The great Pullman[1] was whirling onward with such dignity of motion that a glance from the window seemed simply to prove that the plains of Texas were pouring eastward. Vast flats of green grass, dull-hued spaces of mesquite and cactus, little groups of frame houses, woods of light and tender trees, all were sweeping into the east, sweeping over the horizon, a **precipice**.[2]

A newly married pair had boarded this coach at San Antonio. The man's face was reddened from many days in the wind and sun, and a direct result of his new black clothes was that his brick-colored hands

---

[1] Pullman—sleeping car on a train.

[2] **precipice**—cliff.

were constantly performing in a most conscious fashion. From time to time he looked down respectfully at his attire. He sat with a hand on each knee, like a man waiting in a barber's shop. The glances he devoted to other passengers were **furtive**[3] and shy.

The bride was not pretty, nor was she very young. She wore a dress of blue cashmere, with small reservations[4] of velvet here and there and with steel buttons abounding. She continually twisted her head to regard her puff sleeves, very stiff, straight, and high. They embarrassed her. It was quite apparent that she had cooked, and that she expected to cook, dutifully. The blushes caused by the careless scrutiny of some passengers as she had entered the car were strange to see upon this plain, under-class countenance, which was drawn in **placid**,[5] almost emotionless lines.

They were evidently very happy. "Ever been in a parlor-car before?" he asked, smiling with delight.

"No," she answered. "I never was. It's fine, ain't it?"

"Great! And then after a while we'll go forward to the diner and get a big lay-out. Finest meal in the world. Charge a dollar."

"Oh, do they?" cried the bride. "Charge a dollar? Why, that's too much—for us —ain't it, Jack?"

"Not this trip, anyhow," he answered bravely. "We're going to go the whole thing."

Later, he explained to her about the trains. "You see, it's a thousand miles from one end of Texas to the other, and this train runs right across it and never stops but four times." He had the pride of an owner. He pointed out to her the dazzling fittings of the coach, and in truth her eyes opened wider as she contemplated the sea-green figured velvet, the shining brass, silver, and glass, the wood that gleamed as darkly brilliant as the surface of a pool of oil. At one end a bronze figure sturdily held a support for a separated chamber, and at convenient places on the ceiling were frescoes[6] in olive and silver.

To the minds of the pair, their surroundings reflected the glory of their marriage that morning in San Antonio. This was the environment of their new estate, and the man's face in particular beamed with an elation that made him appear ridiculous to the negro porter. This individual at times surveyed them from afar with an amused and superior grin. On other occasions he bullied them with skill in ways that did not make it exactly plain to them that they were being bullied. He subtly used all the manners of the most unconquerable kind of snobbery. He oppressed them, but of this oppression they had small knowledge, and they speedily forgot that infrequently a number of travelers covered them with stares of **derisive**[7] enjoyment. Historically there was supposed to be something infinitely humorous in their situation.

"We are due in Yellow Sky at 3:42," he said, looking tenderly into her eyes.

---

[3] **furtive**—secretive.

[4] reservations—patches.

[5] **placid**—calm.

[6] frescoes—paintings made with watercolors on damp plaster.

[7] **derisive**—mocking, jeering.

"Oh, are we?" she said, as if she had not been aware of it. To evince[8] surprise at her husband's statement was part of her wifely amiability. She took from a pocket a little silver watch, and as she held it before her and stared at it with a frown of attention, the new husband's face shone.

"I bought it in San Anton' from a friend of mine," he told her gleefully.

"It's seventeen minutes past twelve," she said, looking up at him with a kind of shy and clumsy coquetry.[9] A passenger, noting this play, grew excessively **sardonic**,[10] and winked at himself in one of the numerous mirrors.

At last they went to the dining-car. Two rows of negro waiters in glowing white suits surveyed their entrance with the interest and also the **equanimity**[11] of men who had been forewarned. The pair fell to the lot of a waiter who happened to feel pleasure in steering them through their meal. He viewed them with the manner of a fatherly pilot, his countenance radiant with benevolence. The patronage[12] entwined with the ordinary deference was not plain to them. And yet as they returned to their coach they showed in their faces a sense of escape.

To the left, miles down a long purple slope, was a little ribbon of mist where moved the keening[13] Rio Grande. The train was approaching it at an angle, and the apex was Yellow Sky. Presently it was apparent that as the distance from Yellow Sky grew shorter, the husband became commensurately restless. His brick-red hands were more insistent in their prominence. Occasionally he was even rather absent-minded and far-away when the bride leaned forward and addressed him.

As a matter of truth, Jack Potter was beginning to find the shadow of a deed weigh upon him like a leaden slab. He, the town marshal of Yellow Sky, a man known, liked, and feared in his corner, a prominent person, had gone to San Antonio to meet a girl he believed he loved, and there, after the usual prayers, had actually induced[14] her to marry him, without consulting Yellow Sky for any part of the transaction. He was now bringing his bride before an innocent and unsuspecting community.

He was now bringing his bride before an innocent and unsuspecting community.

Of course, people in Yellow Sky married as it pleased them in accordance with a general custom; but such was Potter's thought of his duty to his friends, or of their idea of his duty, or of an unspoken form which does not control men in these matters, that he felt he was **heinous**.[15] He had committed an extraordinary crime. Face to face with this girl in San Antonio, and spurred by his sharp impulse, he had

---

[8] evince—show or demonstrate clearly.

[9] coquetry—flirtatiousness.

[10] **sardonic**—mocking.

[11] **equanimity**—calmness.

[12] patronage—support, encouragement.

[13] keening—lamenting and wailing.

[14] induced—brought about, influence.

[15] **heinous**—grossly wicked.

gone headlong over all the social hedges. At San Antonio he was like a man hidden in the dark. A knife to sever any friendly duty, any form, was easy to his hand in that remote city. But the hour of Yellow Sky, the hour of daylight, was approaching.

He knew full well that his marriage was an important thing to his town. It could only be exceeded by the burning of the new hotel. His friends would not forgive him. Frequently he had reflected on the advisability of telling them by telegraph, but a new cowardice had been upon him. He feared to do it. And now the train was hurrying him toward a scene of amazement, glee, reproach. He glanced out of the window at the line of haze swinging slowly in toward the train.

Yellow Sky had a kind of brass band which played painfully to the delight of the populace. He laughed without heart as he thought of it. If the citizens could dream of his prospective arrival with his bride, they would parade the band at the station and escort them, amid cheers and laughing congratulations, to his adobe[16] home.

He resolved that he would use all the devices of speed and plains-craft in making the journey from the station to his house. Once within that safe citadel, he could issue some sort of a vocal bulletin, and then not go among the citizens until they had time to wear off a little of their enthusiasm.

The bride looked anxiously at him. "What's worrying you, Jack?"

He laughed again. "I'm not worrying, girl. I'm only thinking of Yellow Sky."

She flushed in comprehension.

A sense of mutual guilt invaded their minds and developed a finer tenderness. They looked at each other with eyes softly aglow. But Potter often laughed the same nervous laugh. The flush upon the bride's face seemed quite permanent.

The traitor to the feelings of Yellow Sky narrowly watched the speeding landscape. "We're nearly there," he said.

Presently the porter came and announced the proximity of Potter's home. He held a brush in his hand and, with all his airy superiority gone, he brushed Potter's new clothes as the latter slowly turned this way and that way. Potter fumbled out a coin and gave it to the porter as he had seen others do. It was a heavy and muscle-bound business, as that of a man shoeing his first horse.

The porter took their bag, and as the train began to slow they moved forward to the hooded platform of the car. Presently the two engines and their long string of coaches rushed into the station of Yellow Sky.

"They have to take water here," said Potter, from a constricted throat and in mournful **cadence**[17] as one announcing death. Before the train stopped his eye had swept the length of the platform, and he was glad and astonished to see there was none upon it but the station-agent, who, with a slightly hurried and anxious air, was walking toward the water-tanks. When the train had halted, the porter alighted first and placed in position a little temporary step.

---

[16] adobe—made of sun-dried clay bricks.

[17] **cadence**—rhythm.

"Come on, girl," said Potter hoarsely. As he helped her down they each laughed on a false note. He took the bag from the negro, and bade his wife cling to his arm. As they slunk rapidly away, his hang-dog glance perceived that they were unloading the two trunks, and also that the station-agent far ahead near the baggage-car had turned and was running toward him, making gestures. He laughed, and groaned as he laughed, when he noted the first effect of his marital bliss upon Yellow Sky. He gripped his wife's arm firmly to his side, and they fled. Behind them the porter stood chuckling **fatuously**.[18] smugly

II

The California Express on the Southern Railway was due at Yellow Sky in twenty-one minutes. There were six men at the bar of the Weary Gentleman saloon. One was a drummer[19] who talked a great deal and rapidly; three were Texans who did not care to talk at that time; and two were Mexican sheep-herders who did not talk as a general practice in the Weary Gentleman saloon. The bar-keeper's dog lay on the board-walk that crossed in front of the door. His head was on his paws, and he glanced drowsily here and there with the constant vigilance of a dog that is kicked on occasion. Across the sandy street were some vivid green grass plots, so wonderful in appearance amid the sands that burned near them in a blazing sun that they caused a doubt in the mind. They exactly resembled the grass mats used to represent lawns on the stage. At the cooler end of the railway station a man without a coat sat in a tilted chair and smoked his pipe. The fresh-cut bank of the Rio Grande circled near the town, and there could be seen beyond it a great plum-colored plain of mesquite.

traveling salesman

"Scratchy Wilson's drunk, and has turned loose with both hands."

Save for the busy drummer and his companions in the saloon, Yellow Sky was dozing. The new-comer leaned gracefully upon the bar, and recited many tales with the confidence of a bard who has come upon a new field.

"—and at the moment that the old man fell down stairs with the bureau in his arms, the old woman was coming up with two scuttles of coal, and, of course—"

The drummer's tale was interrupted by a young man who suddenly appeared in the open door. He cried: "Scratchy Wilson's drunk, and has turned loose with both hands." The two Mexicans at once set down their glasses and faded out of the rear entrance of the saloon.

The drummer, innocent and jocular, answered: "All right, old man. S'pose he has. Come in and have a drink, anyhow."

But the information had made such an obvious cleft in every skull in the room that the drummer was obliged to see its importance. All had become instantly **morose**.[20] "Say," said he, mystified,

gloomy

[18] **fatuously**—smugly, but unconsciously foolishly.

[19] drummer—traveling salesman who sells goods wholesale to other businesses.

[20] **morose**—gloomy.

"what is this?" His three companions made the introductory gesture of eloquent speech, but the young man at the door forestalled them.

"It means, my friend," he answered, as he came into the saloon, "that for the next two hours this town won't be a health resort."

The bar-keeper went to the door and locked and barred it. Reaching out of the window, he pulled in heavy wooden shutters and barred them. Immediately a solemn, chapel-like gloom was upon the place. The drummer was looking from one to another.

"But say," he cried, "what is this, anyhow? You don't mean there is going to be a gun-fight?"

"Don't know whether there'll be a fight or not," answered one man grimly. "But there'll be some shootin'—some good shootin'."

The young man who had warned them waved his hand. "Oh, there'll be a fight fast enough, if anyone wants it. Anybody can get a fight out there in the street. There's a fight just waiting."

The drummer seemed to be swayed between the interest of a foreigner and a perception of personal danger.

"What did you say his name was?" he asked.

"Scratchy Wilson," they answered in chorus.

"And will he kill anybody? What are you going to do? Does this happen often? Does he rampage around like this once a week or so? Can he break in that door?"

"No, he can't break down that door," replied the bar-keeper. "He's tried it three times. But when he comes you'd better lay down on the floor, stranger. He's dead sure to shoot at it, and a bullet may come through."

Thereafter the drummer kept a strict eye upon the door. The time had not yet been called for him to hug the floor, but as a minor precaution he sidled near to the wall. "Will he kill anybody?" he said again.

The men laughed low and scornfully at the question.

"He's out to shoot, and he's out for trouble. Don't see any good in experimentin' with him."

"But what do you do in a case like this? What do you do?"

A man responded: "Why, he and Jack Potter—"

But, in chorus, the other men interrupted: "Jack Potter's in San Anton'."

"Well, who is he? What's he got to do with it?"

"Oh, he's the town marshal. He goes out and fights Scratchy when he gets on one of these tears."

"Wow," said the drummer, mopping his brow. "Nice job he's got."

The voices had toned away to mere whisperings. The drummer wished to ask further questions which were born of an increasing anxiety and bewilderment; but when he attempted them, the men merely looked at him in irritation and motioned him to remain silent. A tense waiting hush was upon them. In the deep shadows of the room their eyes shone as they listened for sounds from the street. One man made three gestures at the bar-keeper, and the latter, moving like a ghost, handed him a glass and a bottle. The man poured a full glass of whisky, and set down the bottle noiselessly. He gulped the whisky in a swallow, and turned again toward the door in immovable silence. The drummer saw that the bar-keeper, without a sound, had taken a Winchester from beneath the bar. Later he saw this individual beckoning to him, so he tiptoed across the room.

"You better come with me back of the bar."

"No, thanks," said the drummer, perspiring. "I'd rather be where I can make a break for the back door."

Whereupon the man of bottles made a kindly but peremptory[21] gesture. The drummer obeyed it, and finding himself seated on a box with his head below the level of the bar, balm was laid upon his soul at sight of various zinc and copper fittings that bore a resemblance to armor-plate. The bar-keeper took a seat comfortably upon an adjacent box.

"You see," he whispered, "this here Scratchy Wilson is a wonder with a gun—a perfect wonder—and when he goes on the war trail, we hunt our holes—naturally. He's about the last one of the old gang that used to hang out along the river here. He's a terror when he's drunk. When he's sober he's all right—kind of simple—wouldn't hurt a fly—nicest fellow in town. But when he's drunk—whoo!"

There were periods of stillness. "I wish Jack Potter was back from San Anton'," said the bar-keeper. "He shot Wilson up once—in his leg—and he would sail in and pull out the kinks in this thing."

Presently they heard from a distance the sound of a shot, followed by three wild yowls. It instantly removed a bond from the men in the darkened saloon. There was a shuffling of feet. They looked at each other. "Here he comes," they said.

III

A man in a maroon-colored shirt, which had been purchased for purposes of decoration and made, principally, by some Jewish women on the East Side of New York, rounded a corner and walked into the middle of the main street of Yellow Sky. In either hand the man held a long, blue-black revolver. Often he yelled, and these cries rang through a semblance of a deserted village, shrilly flying over the roofs in a volume that seemed to have no relation to the arch of a tomb over him. These cries of ferocious challenge rang against walls of silence. And his boots had red tops with gilded imprints, of the kind beloved in winter by little sledding boys on the hillsides of New England.

The man's face flamed in a rage begot of whisky. His eyes, rolling and yet keen for ambush, hunted the still door-ways and windows. He walked with the creeping movement of the midnight cat. As it occurred to him, he roared menacing information. The long revolvers in his hands were as easy as straws; they were moved with an electric swiftness. The little fingers of each hand played sometimes in a

[21] peremptory—expressing a command.

musician's way. Plain from the low collar of the shirt, the cords of his neck straightened and sank, straightened and sank, as passion moved him. The only sounds were his terrible invitations. The calm abodes preserved their demeanor at the passing of this small thing in the middle of the street.

There was no offer of fight; no offer of fight. The man called to the sky. There were no attractions. He bellowed and fumed and swayed his revolvers here and everywhere.

The dog of the bar-keeper of the Weary Gentleman saloon had not appreciated the advance of events. He yet lay dozing in front of his master's door. At sight of the dog, the man paused and raised his revolver humorously. At sight of the man, the dog sprang up and walked diagonally away, with a sullen head and growling. The man yelled, and the dog broke into a gallop. As it was about to enter an alley, there was a loud noise, a whistling, and something spat the ground directly before it. The dog screamed, and, wheeling in terror, galloped headlong in a new direction. Again there was a noise, a whistling, and sand was kicked viciously before it. Fear-stricken, the dog turned and flurried like an animal in a pen. The man stood laughing, his weapons at his hips.

Ultimately the man was attracted by the closed door of the Weary Gentleman saloon. He went to it, and hammering with a revolver, demanded drink.

The door remaining imperturbable,[22] he picked a bit of paper from the walk and nailed it to the framework with a knife. He then turned his back contemptuously upon this popular resort, and walking to the opposite side of the street, and spinning there on his heel quickly and lithely, fired at the bit of paper. He missed it by a half inch. He swore at himself, and went away. Later, he comfortably fusilladed[23] the windows of his most intimate friend. The man was playing with this town. It was a toy for him.

But still there was no offer of fight. The name of Jack Potter, his ancient antagonist, entered his mind, and he concluded that it would be a glad thing if he should go to Potter's house and by bombardment induce him to come out and fight. He moved in the direction of his desire, chanting Apache scalp-music.

When he arrived at it, Potter's house presented the same still, calm front as had the other adobes. Taking up a strategic position, the man howled a challenge. But this house regarded him as might a great stone god. It gave no sign. After a decent wait, the man howled further challenges, mingling with them wonderful epithets.[24]

Presently there came the spectacle of a man churning himself into deepest rage over the immobility of a house. He fumed at it as the winter wind attacks a prairie cabin in the North. To the distance there should have gone the sound of a tumult like the fighting of two hundred Mexicans. As necessity bade him, he paused for breath or to reload his revolvers.

---

[22] imperturbable—unresponsive.

[23] fusilladed—fired many gunshots at.

[24] epithets—abusive or contemptuous phrases.

IV

Potter and his bride walked sheepishly and with speed. Sometimes they laughed together shamefacedly and low.

"Next corner, dear," he said finally.

They put forth the efforts of a pair walking bowed against a strong wind. Potter was about to raise a finger to point the first appearance of the new home when, as they circled the corner, they came face to face with a man in a maroon-colored shirt who was feverishly pushing cartridges into a large revolver. Upon the instant the man dropped this revolver to the ground, and, like lightning, whipped another from its holster. The second weapon was aimed at the bridegroom's chest.

There was a silence. Potter's mouth seemed to be merely a grave for his tongue. He exhibited an instinct to at once loosen his arm from the woman's grip, and he dropped the bag to the sand. As for the bride, her face had gone as yellow as old cloth. She was a slave to hideous rites gazing at the apparitional snake.

The two men faced each other at a distance of three paces. He of the revolver smiled with a new and quiet ferocity. "Tried to sneak up on me," he said. "Tried to sneak up on me!" His eyes grew more baleful.[25] As Potter made a slight movement, the man thrust his revolver venomously forward. "No, don't you do it, Jack Potter. Don't you move a finger toward a gun just yet. Don't you move an eyelash. The time has come for me to settle with you, and I'm goin' to do it my own way and loaf[26] along with no interferin'. So if you don't want a gun bent on you, just mind what I tell you."

Potter looked at his enemy. "I ain't got a gun on me, Scratchy," he said. "Honest, I ain't." He was stiffening and steadying, but yet somewhere at the back of his mind a vision of the Pullman floated, the sea-green figured velvet, the shining brass, silver, and glass, the wood that gleamed as darkly brilliant as the surface of a pool of oil—all the glory of the marriage, the environment of the new estate. "You know I fight when it comes to fighting, Scratchy Wilson, but I ain't got a gun on me. You'll have to do all the shootin' yourself."

"I ain't got a gun on me, Scratchy," he said. "Honest, I ain't."

His enemy's face went livid. He stepped forward and lashed his weapon to and fro before Potter's chest. "Don't you tell me you ain't got no gun on you, you whelp. Don't tell me no lie like that. There ain't a man in Texas ever seen you without no gun. Don't take me for no kid." His eyes blazed with light, and his throat worked like a pump.

"I ain't takin' you for no kid," answered Potter. His heels had not moved an inch backward. "I'm takin' you for a —— fool. I tell you I ain't got a gun, and I ain't. If you're goin' to shoot me up, you better begin now. You'll never get a chance like this again."

---

[25] baleful—ominous.

[26] loaf—pass time at leisure, idle.

So much enforced reasoning had told on Wilson's rage. He was calmer. "If you ain't got a gun, why ain't you got a gun?" he sneered. "Been to Sunday-school?"

"I ain't got a gun because I've just come from San Anton' with my wife. I'm married," said Potter. "And if I'd thought there was going to be any galoots like you prowling around when I brought my wife home, I'd had a gun, and don't you forget it."

"Married!" said Scratchy, not at all comprehending.

"Yes, married. I'm married," said Potter distinctly.

"Married?" said Scratchy. Seemingly for the first time he saw the drooping drowning woman at the other man's side. "No!" he said. He was like a creature allowed a glimpse of another world. He moved a pace backward, and his arm with the revolver dropped to his side. "Is this—is this the lady?" he asked.

"Yes, this is the lady," answered Potter.

There was another period of silence.

"Well," said Wilson at last, slowly, "I s'pose it's all off now."

"It's all off if you say so, Scratchy. You know I didn't make the trouble." Potter lifted his valise.

"Well, I 'low it's off, Jack," said Wilson. He was looking at the ground. "Married!" He was not a student of chivalry; it was merely that in the presence of this foreign condition he was a simple child of the earlier plains. He picked up his starboard revolver, and placing both weapons in their holsters, he went away. His feet made funnel-shaped tracks in the heavy sand.

QUESTIONS TO CONSIDER

1. What does the railroad represent to Yellow Sky?
2. How does Jack Potter think of himself? Do you think he is justified?
3. Why does Jack feel that he has betrayed Yellow Sky?
4. What does Scratchy represent? Why does he give up the fight?
5. Does Crane's story seem basically realistic or romantic? What contributes to this effect?

Charles W. Chesnutt ▶

The Wife of His Youth

BY CHARLES W. CHESNUTT

Charles Chesnutt (1858–1932) was the first African-American author to find a readership in the United States. He was born free in Cleveland, Ohio, but his family moved to the South after the Civil War (1861–1865). He left school at fourteen to go to work as a teacher, eventually rising to be principal of a segregated school in Lafayette, North Carolina. In 1883, Chesnutt left the South, discouraged by the lack of opportunity for African Americans. In New York and Cleveland, he studied law and became a successful lawyer. Chesnutt also began to write. He had continually devoted himself to his education and to reading and wanted to show that African Americans could make a cultural impact. He published in the country's major magazines and brought out three novels and collections of his stories before he inexplicably gave up writing in 1905. Chesnutt's great theme was the state of race relations in the United States. Though the Civil War had ended slavery, African Americans in the South were still kept from exercising their rights by laws and violence. Even in the North, they were typically treated as second-class citizens. Chesnutt was one of the very first writers to depict this aspect of American society. He exposed the cruel treatment African Americans received, and forcefully showed how this degraded all Americans, black or white. He said, "The object of my writings would not be so much the elevation of the colored people as the elevation of the whites—for I consider the unjust spirit of caste which is so insidious as to pervade a whole nation . . . as a barrier to the moral progress of the American people." In "The Wife of His Youth," Chesnutt uses a melodramatic situation to explore the uncertainties of racial loyalty and the color-blind nature of virtue.

I

Mr. Ryder was going to give a ball. There were several reasons why this was an opportune time for such an event.

Mr. Ryder might aptly be called the dean of the Blue Veins. The original Blue Veins were a little society of colored persons organized in a certain Northern city shortly after the war. Its purpose was to establish and maintain correct social standards among a people whose social condition presented almost unlimited room for improvement. By accident, combined perhaps with some natural **affinity**,[1] the society consisted of individuals who were, generally speaking, more white than black. Some envious outsider made the suggestion that no one was eligible for membership who was not white enough to show blue veins. The suggestion was readily

[1] **affinity**—feeling of kinship.

adopted by those who were not of the favored few, and since that time the society, though possessing a longer and more **pretentious**[2] name, had been known far and wide as the "Blue Vein Society," and its members as the "Blue Veins."

The Blue Veins did not allow that any such requirement existed for admission to their circle, but, on the contrary, declared that character and culture were the only things considered; and that if most of their members were light-colored, it was because such persons, as a rule, had had better opportunities to qualify themselves for membership. Opinions differed, too, as to the usefulness of the society. There were those who had been known to assail it violently as a glaring example of the very prejudice from which the colored race had suffered most; and later, when such critics had succeeded in getting on the inside, they had been heard to maintain with zeal and earnestness that the society was a lifeboat, an anchor, a bulwark[3] and a shield,—a pillar of cloud by day and of fire by night,[4] to guide their people through the social wilderness. Another alleged prerequisite for Blue Vein membership was that of free birth;[5] and while there was really no such requirement, it is doubtless true that very few of the members would have been unable to meet it if there had been. If there were one or two of the older members who had come up from the South and from slavery, their history presented enough romantic circumstances to rob their servile origin of its grosser aspects.

While there were no such tests of eligibility, it is true that the Blue Veins had their notions on these subjects, and that not all of them were equally liberal in regard to the things they collectively disclaimed. Mr. Ryder was one of the most conservative. Though he had not been among the founders of the society, but had come in some years later, his genius for social leadership was such that he had speedily become its recognized adviser and head, the custodian of its standards, and the preserver of its traditions. He shaped its social policy, was active in providing for its entertainments, and when the interest fell off, as it sometimes did, he fanned the embers until they burst again into a cheerful flame.

There were still other reasons for his popularity. While he was not as white as some of the Blue Veins, his appearance was such as to confer distinction upon them. His features were of a refined type, his hair was almost straight; he was always neatly dressed; his manners were irreproachable, and his morals above suspicion. He had come to Groveland a young man, and obtaining employment in the office of a railroad company as messenger had in time worked himself up to the position of stationery clerk, having charge of the distribution of the office supplies for the whole company. Although the lack of early

2 **pretentious**—claiming a position of distinction or merit, especially when unjustified.

3 bulwark—defense.

4 pillar of cloud . . . fire by night—allusion to the signs by which God guided the Israelites during their wanderings in the desert.

5 free birth—birth as a free person.

training had hindered the orderly development of a naturally fine mind, it had not prevented him from doing a great deal of reading or from forming decidedly literary tastes. Poetry was his passion. He could repeat whole pages of the great English poets; and if his pronunciation was sometimes faulty, his eye, his voice, his gestures, would respond to the changing sentiment with a precision that revealed a poetic soul and disarmed criticism. He was economical, and had saved money; he owned and occupied a very comfortable house on a respectable street. His residence was handsomely furnished, containing among other things a good library, especially rich in poetry, a piano, and some choice engravings. He generally shared his house with some young couple, who looked after his wants and were company for him; for Mr. Ryder was a single male. In the early days of his connection with the Blue Veins he had been regarded as quite a catch, and young ladies and their mothers had maneuvered with much ingenuity to capture him. Not, however, until Mrs. Molly Dixon visited Groveland had any woman ever made him wish to change his condition to that of a married man.

Mrs. Dixon had come to Groveland from Washington in the spring, and before the summer was over she had won Mr. Ryder's heart. She possessed many attractive qualities. She was much younger than he; in fact, he was old enough to have been her father, though no one knew exactly how old he was. She was whiter than he, and better educated. She had moved in the best colored society of the country, at Washington, and had taught in the schools of that city. Such a superior person had been eagerly welcomed to the Blue Vein Society, and had taken a leading part in its activities. Mr. Ryder had at first been attracted by her charms of person, for she was very good looking and not over twenty-five; then by her refined manners and the **vivacity**[6] of her wit. Her husband had been a government clerk, and at his death had left a considerable life insurance. She was visiting friends in Groveland, and, finding the town and the people to her liking, had prolonged her stay indefinitely. She had not seemed displeased at Mr. Ryder's attentions, but on the contrary had given him every proper encouragement; indeed, a younger and less cautious male would long since have spoken. But he had made up his mind, and had only to determine the time when he would ask her to be his wife. He decided to give a ball in her honor, and at some time during the evening of the ball to offer her his heart and hand. He had no special fears about the outcome, but, with a little touch of romance, he wanted the surroundings to be in harmony with his own feelings when he should have received the answer he expected.

Poetry was his passion. He could repeat whole pages of the great English poets.

Mr. Ryder resolved that this ball should mark an epoch in the social history

[6] **vivacity**—liveliness.

of Groveland. He knew, of course,—no one could know better,—the entertainment's that had taken place in past years, and what must be done to surpass them. His ball must be worthy of the lady in whose honor it was to be given, and must, by the quality of its guests, set an example for the future. He had observed of late a growing liberality, almost a laxity, in social matters, even among members of his own set, and had several times been forced to meet in a social way persons whose complexions and callings in life were hardly up to the standard which he considered proper for the society to maintain. He had a theory of his own.

"I have no race prejudice," he would say, "but we people of mixed blood are ground between the upper and the nether millstone. Our fate lies between absorption by the white race and extinction in the black. The one doesn't want us yet, but may take us in time. The other would welcome us, but it would be for us a backward step. 'With malice towards none, with charity for all,'[7] we must do the best we can for ourselves and those who are to follow us. Self-preservation is the first law of nature."

His ball would serve by its exclusiveness to counteract leveling tendencies, and his marriage with Mrs. Dixon would help to further the upward process of absorption he had been wishing and waiting for.

II

The ball was to take place on Friday night. The house had been put in order, the carpets covered with canvas, the halls and stairs decorated with palms and potted plants; and in the afternoon Mr. Ryder sat on his front porch, which the shade of a vine running up over a wire netting made a cool and pleasant lounging place. He expected to respond to the toast "The Ladies" at the supper, and from a volume of Tennyson[8]—his favorite poet—was fortifying himself with apt quotations. The volume was open at "A Dream of Fair Women." His eyes fell on these lines, and he read them aloud to judge better of their effect:

"At length I saw a lady within call,
Stiller than chisell'd marble standing there;
A daughter of the gods, divinely tall,
And most divinely fair."

He marked the verse, and turning the page read the stanza beginning,—

"O sweet pale Margaret,
O rare pale Margaret."

He weighed the passage a moment, and decided that it would not do. Mrs. Dixon was the palest lady he expected at the ball, and she was of a rather ruddy complexion, and of lively disposition and buxom build. So he ran over the leaves until his eye rested on the description of Queen Guinevere:[9]—

---

[7] 'With malice . . . all'—quotation from Abraham Lincoln's Second Inaugural Address.

[8] Tennyson—Alfred, Lord Tennyson (1809–1892), English poet.

[9] Queen Guinevere—wife of King Arthur.

"She seem'd a part of joyous Spring:
A gown of grass-green silk she wore,
Buckled with golden clasps before;
A light-green tuft of plumes she bore
Closed in a golden ring.

"She look'd so lovely, as she sway'd
The rein with dainty finger-tips,
A man had given all other bliss,
And all his worldly worth for this,
To waste his whole heart in one kiss
Upon her perfect lips."

As Mr. Ryder murmured these words audibly, with an appreciative thrill, he heard the latch of his gate click, and a light footfall sounding on the steps. He turned his head, and saw a woman standing before his door.

She was a little woman, not five feet tall, and proportioned to her height. Although she stood erect, and looked around her with very bright and restless eyes, she seemed quite old; for her face was crossed and recrossed with a hundred wrinkles, and around the edges of her bonnet could be seen protruding here and there a tuft of short gray wool. She wore a blue calico gown of ancient cut, a little red shawl fastened around her shoulders with an old-fashioned brass brooch, and a large bonnet profusely ornamented with faded red and yellow artificial flowers. And she was very black,—so black that her toothless gums, revealed when she opened her mouth to speak, were not red, but blue. She looked like a bit of the old plantation life, summoned up from the past by the wave of a magician's wand, as the poet's fancy had called into being the gracious shapes of which Mr. Ryder had just been reading.

He rose from his chair and came over to where she stood.

She looked like a bit of the old plantation life, summoned up from the past by the wave of a magician's wand.

"Good-afternoon, madam," he said.

"Good-evenin', suh," she answered, ducking suddenly with a quaint curtsy. Her voice was shrill and piping, but softened somewhat by age. "Is dis yere whar Mistuh Ryduh lib, sub?" she asked, looking around her doubtfully, and glancing into the open windows, through which some of the preparations for the evening were visible.

"Yes," he replied, with an air of kindly patronage, unconsciously flattered by her manner, "I am Mr. Ryder. Did you want to see me?"

"Yas, suh, ef I ain't 'sturbin'of you too inuch."

"Not at all. Have a seat over here behind the vine, where it is cool. What can I do for you?"

"'Scuse me, suh," she continued, when she had sat down on the edge of a chair, "'scuse me, suh, I's lookin' for my husban'. I heerd you wuz a big man an' had libbed heah a long time, an' I 'lowed you woud n't min'ef I'd come roun' an' ax you ef you 'd ever heerd of a merlatter[10] man by de name er Sam Taylor 'quirin' roun' in de chu'ches ermongs' de people fer his wife

[10] merlatter—mulatto, that is, person having one white and one black parent.

'Liza Jane? Mr. Ryder seemed to think for a moment.

"There used to be many such cases right after the war," he said, "but it has been so long that I have forgotten them. There are very few now. But tell me your story, and it may refresh my memory."

She sat back farther in her chair so as to be more comfortable, and folded her withered hands in her lap.

"My name's Liza," she began, " 'Liza Jane. W'en I wuz young I us'ter b'long ter Marse[11] Bog Smif, down in ole Missoura. I wuz bawn down dere. W'en I wuz a gal I wuz married ter a man named Jim. But Jim died, an' after dat I married a merlatter man named Sam Taylor. Sam wuz free-bawn, but his mammy and daddy died, an' de w'ite folks 'prenticed him ter my marster fer ter work fer 'im 'tel he wuz growed up. Sam worked in de fiel', an' I wuz de cook. One day Ma'y Ann, ole miss's maid, came rushin' out ter de kitchen, an' says she, 'Liz Jane, ole marse gwine sell yo' Sam down de ribber.'

" 'Go way f'm yere,' says I; 'my hus-ban' 's free!'

" 'Don' make no diff'ence. I heerd ole marse tell ole miss he wuz gwine take yo' Sam 'way wid 'im ter-morrow, fer he needed money, an' he knowed whar he could git a t'ousan' dollars fer Sam an' no questions axed.'

"W'en Sam come home f'm de fiel' dat night, I tole him 'bout ole marse gwine steal 'im, an' Sam run erway. His time wuz mos' up, an' he swo' dat w'en he wuz twenty-one he would come gback an' he'p me run erway, er else save up de money ter buy my freedom. An' I know he's 'a' done it, fer he thought a heap er me, Sam did. But w'en he come back he did n' fin' me, fer I wuz n' dere. Ole marse had heerd dat I warned Sam, so he had me whip' an' sol' down de ribber.

"Den de wah broke out, an' w'en it wuz ober de cullud folks wuz scattered. I went back ter de ole home; but Sam wuz n' dere, an' I could n'l'arn nuffin' 'bout 'im. But I knowed he 'd be'n dere to look fer me an' had n' foun' me, an' had gone erway ter hunt fer me.

"I's be'n lookin' fer 'im eber sence," she added simply, as though twenty-five years were but a couple of weeks, "an' I knows he 's be'n lookin' fer me. Fer he sot a heap er sto' by me, Sam did, an' I know he 's be'n huntin' fer me al dese years,—'less'n he 's be'n sick er sump'n, so he could n' work, er out'n his head, so he could n' 'member his promise. I went back down de ribber, fer I 'lowed he'd gone down dere lookin' fer me. I's be'n ter Noo Orleens, an' Atlanty, an' Charleston, an' Richmon'; an' w'en I'd be'n all ober de Souf I come ter de Norf. Fer I knows I'll fin' 'im some er dese days," she added softly, "er he 'll fin' me, an' den we'll bofe be as happy in freedom as we wuz in de ole days befo' de wah." A smile stole over her withered countenance as she paused a moment, and her bright eyes softened into a faraway look.

This was the substance of the old woman's story. She had wandered a little

---

[11] Marse—master.

here and there. Mr. Ryder was looking at her curiously when she finished.

"How have you lived all these years?" he asked.

"Cookin', suh. I's a good cook. Does you know anybody w'at needs a good cook, suh? I's stoppin' wid a cullud fam'ly roun' de corner yonder 'tel I kin git a place."

"Do you really expect to find your husband? He may be dead long ago."

She shook her head emphatically. "Oh no, he ain' dead. De signs an' de tokens tell me. I dremp three nights runnin' on'y dis las' week dat I foun' him."

"He may have married another woman. Your slave marriage would not have prevented him, for you never lived with him after the war, and without that your marriage doesn't count."

"Would n' make no diff'ence wid Sam. He would n' marry no yuther 'ooman 'tel he foun' out 'bout me. I knows it," she added. "Sum'n 's be'n tellin' me all dese years dat I's gwein fin' Sam 'fo' I dies."

"Perhaps he's outgrown you, and climbed up in the world where he wouldn't care to have you find him."

"No indeed, suh," she replied, "Sam ain' dat kin' er man. He wuz good ter me, Sam wuz, but he wuz n' much good ter nobody e'se, fer he wuz one er de triflin'es' han on de plantation. I 'spec's ter haf ter suppo't 'im w'en I fin' 'im, fer he nebber would work 'less'n he had ter. But den he wuz free, an' he did n' git no pay fer his work, an' I don' blame 'im much. Mebbe he 's done better sence he ran erway, but I ain' 'spectin' much."

"You may have passed him on the street a hundred times during the twenty-five years, and not have known him; time works great changes."

She smiled **incredulously**.[12] "I'd know 'im 'mongs a hund'ed men. Fer dey wuz n' no yuther merlatter like my man Sam, an' I could n' be mistook. I's toted his picture roun' wid me twenty-five years."

"May I see it?" asked Mr. Ryder. "It might help me to remember whether I have seen the original."

As she draw a small parcel from her bosom he saw that it was fastened to a string that went around her neck. Removing several wrappers, she brought to light an old-fashioned daguerreotype[13] in a black case. He looked long and intently at the portrait. It was faded with time, but the features were still distinct, and it was easy to see what manner of man it had represented.

He closed the case, and with a slow movement handed it back to her.

"I don't know of any man in town who goes by that name," he said, "nor have I heard of any one making such inquiries. But if you will leave me your address, I will give the matter some attention, and if I find out anything I will let you know."

She gave him the number of a house in the neighborhood, and went away, after thanking him warmly.

He wrote the address on the fly-leaf of the volume of Tennyson, and, when she had gone, rose to his feet and stood looking

[12] **incredulously**—disbelievingly.

[13] daguerreotype—early form of photograph.

after her curiously. As she walked down the street with mincing step, he saw several persons whom she passed turn and look back at her with a smile of kindly amusement. When she had turned the corner, he went upstairs to his bedroom, and stood for a long time before the mirror of his dressing-case, gazing thoughtfully at the reflection of his own face.

III

At eight o'clock the ballroom was a blaze of light and the guests had begun to assemble; for there was a literary programme and some routine business of the society to be gone through with before the dancing. A black servant in evening dress waited at the door and directed the guests to the dressing-rooms.

The occasion was long memorable among the colored people of the city; not alone for the dress and display, but for the high average of intelligence and culture that distinguished the gathering as a whole. There were a number of school-teachers, several young doctors, three or four lawyers, some professional singers, an editor, a lieutenant in the United States army spending his furlough in the city, and others in various polite callings; these were colored, though most of them would not have attracted even a casual glance because of any marked difference from white people. Most of the ladies were in evening costume, and dress coats and dancing pumps were the rule among the men. A band of string music, stationed in an alcove behind a row of palms, played popular airs where the guests were gathering.

The dancing began at half past nine. At eleven o'clock supper was served. Mr. Ryder had left the ballroom some little time before the intermission, but reappeared at the supper-table. The spread was worthy of the occasion, and the guests did full justice to it. When the coffee had been served, the toastmaster, Mr. Solomon Sadler, rapped for order. He made a brief introductory speech, complimenting host and guests, and then presented in their order the toasts of the evening. They were responded to with a very fair display of after-dinner wit.

"The last toast," said the toast-master, when he reached the end of the list, "is one which must appeal to us all. There is no one of us of the sterner sex who is not at some time dependent upon woman,—in infancy for protection, in manhood for companionship, in old age for care and comforting. Our good host has been trying to live alone, but the fair faces I see around me tonight prove that he too is largely dependent upon the gentler sex for most that makes life worth living,—the society and love of friends, and rumor is at fault if he does not soon yield entire subjection to one of them. Mr. Ryder will now respond to the toast,—The Ladies."

There was a **pensive**[14] look in Mr. Ryder's eyes as he took the floor and adjusted his eyeglasses. He began by speaking of woman as the gift of Heaven to man, and after some general observations on the relations of the sexes he said: "But perhaps the quality which most

---

[14] **pensive**—thoughtful.

distinguishes woman is her fidelity and devotion to those she loves. History is full of examples, but has recorded none more striking than one which only today came under my notice."

He then related, simply but effectively, the story told by his visitor of the afternoon. He gave it in the same soft dialect, which came readily to his lips, while the company listened attentively and sympathetically. For the story had awakened a responsive thrill in many hearts. There were some present who had seen, and others who had heard their fathers and grandfathers tell, the wrongs and sufferings of this past generation, and all of them still felt, in their darker moments, the shadow hanging over them. Mr. Ryder went on:—"Such devotion and confidence are rare even among women. There are many who would have searched a year, some who would have waited five years, a few who might have hoped ten years; but for twenty-five years this woman has retained her affection for and her faith in a man she has not seen or heard of in all that time.

"She came to me today in the hope that I might be able to help her find this long-lost husband. And when she was gone I gave my fancy rein, and imagined a case I will put to you.

"Suppose that this husband, soon after his escape, had learned that his wife had been sold away, and that such inquiries as he could make brought no information of her whereabouts. Suppose that he was young, and she much older than he; that he was light, and she was black; that their marriage was a slave marriage, and legally binding only if they chose to make it so after the war. Suppose, too, that he made his way to the North, as some of us have done, and there, where he had larger opportunities, had improved them, and had in the course of all these years grown to be as different from the ignorant boy who ran away from fear of slavery as the day is from the night. Suppose, even, that he had qualified himself, by industry, by thrift, and by study, to win the friendship and be considered worthy the society of such people as these I see around me tonight, gracing my board[15] and filling my heart with gladness; for I am old enough to remember the day when such a gathering would not have been possible in this land. Suppose, too, that, as the years went by, this man's memory of the past grew more and more indistinct, until at last it was rarely, except in his dreams, that any image of this bygone period rose before his mind. And then suppose that accident should bring to his knowledge the fact that the wife of his youth, the wife he had left behind him,—not one who had walked by his side and kept pace with him in his upward struggle, but one upon whom advancing years and a laborious life had set their mark,—was alive and seeking him, but that he was absolutely safe from recognition or discovery, unless he chose to reveal himself. My friends, what would the man do? I will presume that he was one who loved honor, and tried to deal justly with all men. I will even carry the case further, and suppose that perhaps he had

[15] gracing my board—honoring my table.

set his heart upon another, whom he had hoped to call his own. What would he do, or rather what ought he to do, in such a crisis of a lifetime?

"It seemed to me that he might hesitate, and I imagined that I was an old friend, a near friend, and that he had come to me for advice; and I argued the case with him. I tried to discuss it impartially. After we had looked upon the matter from every point of view, I said to him, in words that we all know:—

'This above all: to thine own self
be true,
And it must follow, as the night
the day,
Thou canst not then be false to
any man.'

"Then, finally, I put the question to him, 'Shall you acknowledge her?'

"And now, ladies and gentlemen, friends and companions, I ask you, what should he have done?"

There was something in Mr. Ryder's voice that stirred the hearts of those who sat around him. It suggested more than mere sympathy with all imaginary situation; it seemed rather in the nature of a personal appeal. It was observed, too, that his look rested more especially upon Mrs. Dixon, with a mingled expression of renunciation and inquiry.

She had listened, with parted lips and streaming[16] eyes. She was the first to speak: "He should have acknowledged her."

"Yes," they all echoed, "he should have acknowledged her."

"My friends and companions," responded Mr. Ryder, "I thank you, one and all. It is the answer I expected, for I knew your hearts."

He turned and walked toward the closed door of an adjoining room, while every eye followed him in wondering curiosity. He came back in a moment, leading by the hand his visitor of the afternoon, who stood startled and trembling at the sudden plunge into this scene of brilliant gayety. She was neatly dressed in gray, and wore the white cap of an elderly woman.

"Ladies and gentlemen," he said, "this is the woman, and I am the man, whose story I have told you. Permit me to introduce to you the wife of my youth."

[16] streaming—full of tears.

QUESTIONS TO CONSIDER

1. What do Mr. Ryder's lifestyle and interests suggest about him?
2. When the poor, elderly, African-American woman arrives at his home, how does he behave toward her?
3. What attitude do you think Chesnutt had toward the Blue Veins? What point do you think he was making here?
4. In what ways does Chesnutt seem to have been a romantic writer? In what ways does he seem to have been a realist?

Mark Twain ▶

The Man That Corrupted Hadleyburg

BY MARK TWAIN

Mark Twain (1835–1910) was almost a metaphor for America in the second half of the 1800s. Raised in Missouri, he worked as a newspaperman and a steamboat pilot before the Civil War. He had a short-lived career as a soldier before heading west, where the mining camps and frontier towns gave him the material for the humorous stories he was already crafting. These stories, particularly "The Celebrated Jumping Frog of Calaveras County," made his name, and he began to lecture and to travel, writing humorous travel pieces and books. Twain was the leading writer of the new school of humorists. Yet financial success and marriage to an Eastern woman injected seriousness into Twain's writing. His novels, such as Tom Sawyer *(1876) and* The Adventures of Huckleberry Finn *(1884), and his autobiographical* Life on the Mississippi *(1883), still have humor but it is part of a larger picture of American life, full of understanding and pathos. Twain had come full circle to become part of the Eastern establishment. As the West settled and grew up, so did Twain. In his last years, Twain's work developed a bitter strain, brought on by the death of his beloved wife and two of his daughters. "The Man That Corrupted Hadleyburg" is from this period and shows a darker view of human nature than Twain's early works. Still, the rich vein of humor is evident, as is the mastery of style and rhythm that made Twain one of America's most famous and beloved writers.*

I

It was many years ago. Hadleyburg was the most honest and upright town in all the region around about. It had kept that reputation unsmirched[1] during three generations, and was prouder of it than of any other of its possessions. It was so proud of it, and so anxious to insure its **perpetuation**,[2] that it began to teach the principles of honest dealing to its babies in the cradle, and made the like teachings the staple of their culture thenceforward through all the years devoted to their education. Also, throughout the formative years temptations were kept out of the way of the young people, so that their honesty could have every chance to harden and solidify, and become a part of their very bone. The neighboring towns were jealous of this honorable supremacy, and affected to

[1] unsmirched—untainted, pure.

[2] **perpetuation**—continuation.

sneer at Hadleyburg's pride in it and call it vanity; but all the same they were obliged to acknowledge that Hadleyburg was in reality an incorruptible town; and if pressed they would also acknowledge that the mere fact that a young man hailed from Hadleyburg was all the recommendation he needed when he went forth from his natal[3] town to seek for responsible employment.

"That is the thing to do—I will corrupt the town."

But at last, in the drift of time, Hadleyburg had the ill luck to offend a passing stranger—possibly without knowing it, certainly without caring, for Hadleyburg was sufficient unto itself, and cared not a rap for strangers or their opinions. Still, it would have been well to make an exception in this one's case, for he was a bitter man and revengeful. All through his wanderings during a whole year he kept his injury in mind, and gave all his leisure moments to trying to invent a compensating satisfaction for it. He contrived many plans, and all of them were good, but none of them was quite sweeping enough; the poorest of them would hurt a great many individuals, but what he wanted was a plan which would comprehend[4] the entire town, and not let so much as one person escape unhurt. At last he had a fortunate idea, and when it fell into his brain it lit up his whole head with an evil joy. He began to form a plan at once, saying to himself, "That is the thing to do—I will corrupt the town."

Six months later he went to Hadleyburg, and arrived in a buggy at the house of the old cashier of the bank about ten at night. He got a sack out of the buggy, shouldered it, and staggered with it through the cottage yard, and knocked at the door. A woman's voice said "Come in," and he entered, and set his sack behind the stove in the parlor, saying politely to the old lady who sat reading the *Missionary Herald* by the lamp:

"Pray keep your seat, madam, I will not disturb you. There—now it is pretty well concealed; one would hardly know it was there. Can I see your husband a moment, madam?"

No, he was gone to Brixton, and might not return before morning.

"Very well, madam, it is no matter. I merely wanted to leave that sack in his care, to be delivered to the rightful owner when he shall be found. I am a stranger; he does not know me; I am merely passing through the town tonight to discharge a matter which has been long in my mind. My errand is now completed, and I go pleased and a little proud, and you will never see me again. There is a paper attached to the sack which will explain everything. Good night, madam."

The old lady was afraid of the mysterious big stranger, and was glad to see him go. But her curiosity was roused, and she went straight to the sack and brought away the paper. It began as follows:

---

[3] **natal—birth.**

[4] **comprehend—include.**

TO BE PUBLISHED: *or, the right man sought out by private inquiry—either will answer. This sack contains gold coin weighing a hundred and sixty pounds four ounces—*

"Mercy on us, and the door not locked!"

Mrs. Richards flew to it all in a tremble and locked it, then pulled down the window-shades and stood frightened, worried, and wondering if there was anything else she could do toward making herself and the money more safe. She listened awhile for burglars, then surrendered to curiosity and went back to the lamp and finished reading the paper:

I am a foreigner, and am presently going back to my own country, to remain there permanently. I am grateful to America for what I have received at her hands during my long stay under her flag; and to one of her citizens—a citizen of Hadleyburg—I am especially grateful for a great kindness done me a year or two ago. Two great kindnesses, in fact. I will explain. I was a gambler. I say I WAS. *I was a ruined gambler. I arrived in this village at night, hungry and without a penny. I asked for help—in the dark; I was ashamed to beg in the light. I begged of the right man. He gave me twenty dollars—that is to say, he gave me life, as I considered it. He also gave me fortune; for out of that money I have made myself rich at the gaming-table. And finally, a remark which he made to me has remained with me to this day, and has at last conquered me; and in conquering has saved the remnant of my morals; I shall gamble no more. Now I have no idea who that man was, but I want him found, and I want him to have this money, to give away, throw away, or keep, as he pleases. It is merely my way of testifying my gratitude to him. If I could stay, I would find him myself; but no matter, he will be found. This is an honest town, an incorruptible town, and I know I can trust it without fear. This man can be identified by the remark which he made to me; I feel persuaded that he will remember it.*

And now my plan is this: if you prefer to conduct the inquiry privately, do so. Tell the contents of this present writing to any one who is likely to be the right man. If he shall answer, "I am the man; the remark I made was so-and-so," apply the test—to wit: open the sack, and in it you will find a sealed envelope containing that remark. If the remark mentioned by the candidate tallies with it, give him the money, and ask no further questions, for he is certainly the right man.

But if you shall prefer a public inquiry, then publish this present writing in the local paper—with these instructions added, to wit: Thirty days from now, let the candidate appear at the town-hall at eight in the evening (Friday), and hand his remark, in a sealed envelope, to the Rev. Mr. Burgess (if he will be kind enough to act); and let Mr. Burgess there and then destroy the seals of the sack, open it, and see if the remark is correct; if correct, let the money be delivered, with my sincere gratitude, to my benefactor thus identified.

Mrs. Richards sat down, gently quivering with excitement, and was soon lost in thinkings—after this pattern: "What a strange thing it is! . . . And what a fortune for that kind man who set his bread afloat upon the waters! . . . If it had only been my husband that did it!—for we are so poor, so old and poor! . . ." Then, with a sigh—"But it was not my Edward; no, it was not he that gave a stranger twenty dollars. It is a pity, too; I see it now. . . ." Then, with a shudder—"But it is *gambler's* money! the wages of sin: we couldn't take it; we couldn't touch it. I don't like to be near it; it seems a defilement."[5] She moved to a farther chair. . . . "I wish Edward would come and take it to the bank; a burglar might come at any moment; it is dreadful to be here all alone with it."

At eleven Mr. Richards arrived, and while his wife was saying, "I am *so* glad you've come!" he was saying, "I'm so tired—tired clear out; it is dreadful to be poor, and have to make these dismal journeys at my time of life. Always at the grind, grind, grind, on a salary—another man's slave, and he sitting at home in his slippers, rich and comfortable."

"I am so sorry for you, Edward, you know that; but be comforted: we have our livelihood; we have our good name—"

"Yes, Mary, and that is everything. Don't mind my talk—it's just a moment's irritation and doesn't mean anything. Kiss me—there, it's all gone now, and I am not complaining any more. What have you been getting? What's in the sack?"

Then his wife told him the great secret. It dazed him for a moment; then he said:

"It weighs a hundred and sixty pounds? Why, Mary, it's for-ty thousand dollars—think of it—a whole fortune! Not ten men in this village are worth that much. Give me the paper."

He skimmed through it and said:

"Isn't it an adventure! Why, it's a romance; it's like the impossible things one reads about in books, and never sees in life." He was well stirred up now; cheerful, even gleeful. He tapped his old wife on the cheek, and said, humorously, "Why, we're rich, Mary, rich; all we've got to do is to bury the money and burn the papers. If the gambler ever comes to inquire, we'll merely look coldly upon him and say: 'What is this nonsense you are talking? We have never heard of you and your sack of gold before'; and then he would look foolish, and—"

"And in the mean time, while you are running on with your jokes, the money is still here, and it is fast getting along toward burglar-time."

"True. Very well, what shall we do—make the inquiry private? No, not that: it would spoil the romance. The public method is better. Think what a noise it will make! And it will make all the other towns jealous; for no stranger would trust such a thing to any town but Hadleyburg, and they know it. It's a great card for us. I must get to the printing-office now, or I shall be too late."

"But stop—stop—don't leave me here alone with it, Edward!"

But he was gone. For only a little while, however. Not far from his own house he met the editor-proprietor of the paper, and gave him the document, and said, "Here is a good thing for you, Cox—put it in."

"It may be too late, Mr. Richards, but I'll see."

At home again he and his wife sat down to talk the charming mystery over;

5 **defilement—corruption.**

they were in no condition for sleep. The first question was, Who could the citizen have been who gave the stranger the twenty dollars? It seemed a simple one; both answered it in the same breath:

"Barclay Goodson."

"Yes," said Richards, "he could have done it, and it would have been like him, but there's not another in the town."

"Everybody will grant that, Edward—grant it privately, anyway. For six months, now, the village has been its own proper self once more—honest, narrow, self-righteous and stingy."

"It is what he always called it, to the day of his death—said it right out publicly, too."

"Yes, and he was hated for it."

"Oh, of course; but he didn't care. I reckon he was the best-hated man among us, except the Reverend Burgess."

"Well, Burgess deserves it—he will never get another congregation here. Mean as the town is, it knows how to estimate *him*. Edward, doesn't it seem odd that the stranger should appoint Burgess to deliver the money?"

"Well, yes—it does. That is—that is—"

"Why so much that-*is*-ing? Would *you* select him?"

"Mary, maybe the stranger knows him better than this village does."

"Much *that* would help Burgess!"

The husband seemed perplexed for an answer; the wife kept a steady eye upon him, and waited. Finally Richards said, with the hesitancy of one who is making a statement which is likely to encounter doubt:

"Mary, Burgess is not a bad man."

His wife was certainly surprised.

"Nonsense!" she exclaimed.

"He is not a bad man. I know. The whole of his unpopularity had its foundation in that one thing—the thing that made so much noise."

The first question was, Who could the citizen have been who gave the stranger the twenty dollars?

"That 'one thing,' indeed! As if that 'one thing' wasn't enough, all by itself."

"Plenty. Plenty. Only he wasn't guilty of it."

"How you talk! Not guilty of it! Everybody knows he *was* guilty."

"Mary, I give you my word—he was innocent."

"I can't believe it, and I don't. How do you know?"

"It is a confession. I am ashamed, but I will make it. I was the only man who knew he was innocent. I could have saved him, and—and—well, you know how the town was wrought up—I hadn't the pluck to do it. It would have turned everybody against me. I felt mean, ever so mean; but I didn't dare; I hadn't the manliness to face that."

Mary looked troubled, and for a while was silent. Then she said, stammeringly:

"I—I don't think it would have done for you to—to— One mustn't —er—public opinion—one has to be so careful—so—" It was a difficult road, and she got mired; but after a little she got started again. "It was a great pity, but— Why, we couldn't afford it, Edward—we couldn't indeed. Oh, I wouldn't have had you do it for anything!"

"It would have lost us the good will of so many people, Mary; and then—and then—"

"What troubles me now is, what *he* thinks of us, Edward."

"He? *He* doesn't suspect that I could have saved him."

"Oh," exclaimed the wife, in a tone of relief, "I am glad of that! As long as he doesn't know that you could have saved him, he—he—well, that makes it a great deal better. Why, I might have known he didn't know, because he is always trying to be friendly with us, as little encouragement as we give him. More than once people have twitted[6] me with it. There's the Wilsons, and the Wilcoxes, and the Harknesses, they take a mean pleasure in saying, '*Your friend* Burgess,' because they know it pesters me. I wish he wouldn't persist in liking us so; I can't think why he keeps it up."

"I can explain it. It's another confession. When the thing was new and hot, and the town made a plan to ride him on a rail,[7] my conscience hurt me so that I couldn't stand it, and I went privately and gave him notice, and he got out of the town and stayed out till it was safe to come back."

"Edward! If the town had found it out—"

"Don't! It scares me yet, to think of it. I repented of it the minute it was done; and I was even afraid to tell you, lest your face might betray it to somebody. I didn't sleep any that night, for worrying. But after a few days I saw that no one was going to suspect me, and after that I got to feeling glad I did it, And I feel glad yet, Mary—glad through and through."

"So do I, now, for it would have been a dreadful way to treat him. Yes, I'm glad; for really you did owe him that, you know. But, Edward, suppose it should come out yet, some day!"

"It won't."

"Why?"

"Because everybody thinks it was Goodson."

"Of course they would!"

"Certainly. And of course *he* didn't care. They persuaded poor old Sawlsberry to go and charge it on him, and he went blustering over there and did it. Goodson looked him over, like as if he was hunting for a place on him that he could despise the most, then he says, 'So you are the Committee of Inquiry, are you?' Sawlsberry said that was about what he was. 'Hm. Do they require particulars, or do you reckon a kind of a *general* answer will do?' 'If they require particulars, I will come back, Mr. Goodson; I will take the general answer first.' 'Very well, then, tell them to go to hell—I reckon that's general enough. And I'll give you some advice, Sawlsberry; when you come back for the particulars, fetch a basket to carry the relics of yourself home in.'"

"Just like Goodson; it's got all the marks. He had only one vanity: he thought he could give advice better than any other person."

"It settled the business, and saved us, Mary. The subject was dropped."

---

[6] **twitted**—taunted, ridiculed, teased.

[7] **ride him on a rail**—put him astride a bar and carry him out of town.

"Bless you, I'm not doubting *that*."

Then they took up the gold-sack mystery again, with strong interest. Soon the conversation began to suffer breaks—interruptions caused by absorbed thinkings. The breaks grew more and more frequent. At last Richards lost himself wholly in thought. He sat long, gazing vacantly at the floor, and by and by he began to punctuate his thoughts with little nervous movements of his hands that seemed to indicate vexation. Meantime his wife too had relapsed into a thoughtful silence, and her movements were beginning to show a troubled discomfort. Finally Richards got up and strode aimlessly about the room, plowing his hands through his hair, much as a somnambulist[8] might do who was having a bad dream. Then he seemed to arrive at a definite purpose; and without a word he put on his hat and passed quickly out of the house. His wife sat brooding, with a drawn face, and did not seem to be aware that she was alone. Now and then she murmured, "Lead us not into t— . . . but—but—we are so poor, so poor! . . . Lead us not into . . . Ah, who would be hurt by it?—and no one would ever know. . . . Lead us . . ." The voice died out in mumblings. After a little she glanced up and muttered in a half-frightened, half-glad way:

"He is gone! But, oh dear, he may be too late—too late. . . . Maybe not—maybe there is still time." She rose and stood thinking, nervously clasping and unclasping her hands. A slight shudder shook her frame, and she said, out of a dry throat, "God forgive me—it's awful to think such things—but . . . Lord, how we are made—how strangely we are made!"

She turned the light low, and slipped stealthily over and kneeled down by the sack and felt of its ridgy sides with her bands, and fondled them lovingly; and there was a gloating light in her poor old eyes. She fell into fits of absence; and came half out of them at times to mutter, "If we had only waited!—oh, if we had only waited a little, and not been in such a hurry!"

Meantime Cox had gone home from his office and told his wife all about the strange thing that had happened, and they had talked it over eagerly, and guessed that the late Goodson was the only man in the town who could have helped a suffering stranger with so noble a sum as twenty dollars. Then there was a pause, and the two became thoughtful and silent. And by and by nervous and fidgety. At last the wife said, as if to herself:

"Nobody knows this secret but the Richardses . . . and us . . . nobody."

The husband came out of his thinkings with a slight start, and gazed wistfully at his wife, whose face was become very pale; then he hesitatingly rose, and glanced **furtively**[9] at his hat, then at his wife—a sort of mute inquiry. Mrs. Cox swallowed once or twice, with her hand at her throat, then in place of speech she nodded her head. In a moment she was alone, and mumbling to herself.

And now Richards and Cox were hurrying through the deserted streets, from opposite directions. They met, panting, at

[8] somnambulist—sleepwalker.

[9] **furtively**—secretly.

the foot of the printing-office stairs; by the night light there they read each other's face. Cox whispered:

"Nobody knows about this but us?"

The whispered answer was,

"Not a soul—on honor, not a soul!"

"If it isn't too late to—"

The men were starting up-stairs; at this moment they were overtaken by a boy, and Cox asked:

"Is that you, Johnny?"

"Yes, sir."

"You needn't ship the early mail—nor *any* mail; wait till I tell you."

"It's already gone, sir."

"Gone?" It had the sound of an unspeakable disappointment in it.

"Yes, sir. Time-table for Brixton and all the towns beyond changed today, sir—had to get the papers in twenty minutes earlier than common. I had to rush; if I had been two minutes later—"

The men turned and walked slowly away, not waiting to hear the rest. Neither of them spoke during ten minutes; then Cox said, in a vexed tone:

"What possessed you to be in such a hurry, *I* can't make out."

The answer was humble enough:

"I see it now, but somehow I never thought, you know, until it was too late. But the next time—"

"Next time be hanged! It won't come in a thousand years."

Then the friends separated without a good night, and dragged themselves home with the gait of mortally stricken men. At their homes their wives sprang up with an eager "Well?"—then saw the answer with their eyes and sank down sorrowing, without waiting for it to come in words. In both houses a discussion followed of a heated sort—a new thing; there had been discussions before, but not heated ones, not ungentle ones. The discussions tonight were a sort of seeming **plagiarisms**[10] of each other. Mrs. Richards said,

"If you had only waited, Edward—if you had only stopped to think; but no, you must run straight to the printing-office and spread it all over the world."

"It *said* publish it."

"That is nothing; it also said do it privately, if you liked. There, now—is that true, or not?"

"Why, yes—yes, it is true; but when I thought what a stir it would make, and what a compliment it was to Hadleyburg that a stranger should trust it so—"

"Oh, certainly, I know all that; but if you had only stopped to think, you would have seen that you *couldn't* find the right man, because he is in his grave, and hasn't left chick nor child nor relation behind him; and as long as the money went to somebody that awfully needed it, and nobody would be hurt by it, and—and—"

She broke down, crying. Her husband tried to think of some comforting thing to say, and presently came out with this:

"But after all, Mary, it must be for the best—it *must* be; we know that. And we must remember that it was so ordered—"

"Ordered! Oh, everything's *ordered*, when a person has to find some way out

---

[10] **plagiarisms**—copies.

when he has been stupid. Just the same, it was *ordered* that the money should come to us in this special way, and it was you that must take it on yourself to go meddling with the designs of Providence[11] —and who gave you the right? It was wicked, that is what it was—just **blasphemous**[12] presumption, and no more becoming to a meek and humble professor of—"

"But, Mary, you know how we have been trained all our lives long, like the whole village, till it is absolutely second nature to us to stop not a single moment to think when there's an honest thing to be done—"

"Oh, I know it, I know it—it's been one everlasting training and training and training in honesty—honesty shielded, from the very cradle, against every possible temptation, and so it's *artificial* honesty, and weak as water when temptation comes, as we have seen this night. God knows I never had shade nor shadow of a doubt of my petrified and indestructible honesty until now—and now, under the very first big and real temptation, I—Edward, it is my belief that this town's honesty is as rotten as mine is; as rotten as yours is. It is a mean town, a hard, stingy town, and hasn't a virtue in the world but this honesty it is so celebrated for and so conceited about; and so help me, I do believe that if ever the day comes that its honesty falls under great temptation, its grand reputation will go to ruin like a house of cards. There, now, I've made confession, and I feel better; I am a humbug, and I've been one all my life, without knowing it. Let no man call me honest again—I will not have it."

"I—well, Mary, I feel a good deal as you do; I certainly do. It seems strange, too, so strange. I never could have believed it—never."

A long silence followed; both were sunk in thought. At last the wife looked up and said:

"Edward, it is my belief that this town's honesty is as rotten as mine is; as rotten as yours is."

"I know what you are thinking, Edward."

Richards had the embarrassed look of a person who is caught.

"I am ashamed to confess it, Mary, but—"

"It's no matter, Edward, I was thinking the same question myself."

"I hope so. State it."

"You were thinking, if a body could only guess out *what the remark was* that Goodson made to the stranger."

"It's perfectly true. I feel guilty and ashamed. And you?"

"I'm past it. Let us make a pallet[13] here; we've got to stand watch till the bank vault opens in the morning and admits the sack. . . . Oh dear, oh dear—if we hadn't made the mistake!"

The pallet was made, and Mary said:

"The open sesame[14]—what could it have been? I do wonder what that remark

[11] Providence—God.

[12] **blasphemous**—irreverent, disrespectful.

[13] pallet—cot.

[14] open sesame—magic phrase that permits access to treasure, a reference to the story of Ali Baba in the Arabian Nights.

could have been? But come; we will get to bed now."

"And sleep?"

"No; think."

"Yes, think."

By this time the Coxes too had completed their spat and their reconciliation, and were turning in—to think, to think, and toss, and fret, and worry over what the remark could possibly have been which Goodson made to the stranded **derelict**;[15] that golden remark; that remark worth forty thousand dollars, cash.

The reason that the village telegraph-office was open later than usual that night was this: The foreman of Cox's paper was the local representative of the Associated Press.[16] One might say its honorary representative, for it wasn't four times a year that he could furnish thirty words that would be accepted. But this time it was different. His dispatch stating what he had caught got an instant answer:

Send the whole thing—all the details—twelve hundred words.

A colossal order! The foreman filled the bill; and he was the proudest man in the State. By breakfast-time the next morning the name of Hadleyburg the Incorruptible was on every lip in America, from Montreal to the Gulf, from the glaciers of Alaska to the orange-groves of Florida; and millions and millions of people were discussing the stranger and his money-sack, and wondering if the right man would be found, hoping some more news about the matter would come soon—right away.

II

Hadleyburg village woke up world-celebrated—astonished—happy—vain. Vain beyond imagination. Its nineteen principal citizens and their wives went about shaking hands with each other, and beaming, and smiling, and congratulating, and saying *this* thing adds a new word to the dictionary—*Hadleyburg*, synonym for *incorruptible*—destined to live in dictionaries forever! And the minor and unimportant citizens and their wives went around acting in much the same way. Everybody ran to the bank to see the gold-sack; and before noon grieved and envious crowds began to flock in from Brixton and all neighboring towns; and that afternoon and next day reporters began to arrive from everywhere to verify the sack and its history and write the whole thing up anew, and make dashing free-hand pictures of the sack, and of Richards's house, and the bank, and the Presbyterian church, and the Baptist church, and the public square, and the town-hall where the test would be applied and the money delivered; and damnable portraits of the Richardses, and Pinkerton the banker, and Cox, and the foreman, and Reverend Burgess, and the postmaster—and even of Jack Halliday, who was the loafing, good-natured, no-account, irreverent fisherman, hunter, boys' friend, stray-dogs' friend, typical "Sam Lawson"[17] of the town. The

---

[15] **derelict**—homeless person.

[16] Associated Press—cooperative news agency that sells copy to regional newspapers. It also employs people to collect the copy.

[17] Sam Lawson—humorous character in Harriet Beecher Stowe's *Oldtown Folks* (1869).

little mean, smirking, oily Pinkerton showed the sack to all comers, and rubbed his sleek palms together pleasantly, and enlarged upon the town's fine old reputation for honesty and upon this wonderful endorsement of it, and hoped and believed that the example would now spread far and wide over the American world, and be epoch-making[18] in the matter of moral regeneration. And so on, and so on.

By the end of a week things had quieted down again; the wild intoxication of pride and joy had sobered to a soft, sweet, silent delight—a sort of deep, nameless, unutterable content. All faces bore a look of peaceful, holy happiness.

Then a change came. It was a gradual change: so gradual that its beginnings were hardly noticed; maybe were not noticed at all, except by Jack Halliday, who always noticed everything; and always made fun of it, too, no matter what it was. He began to throw out chaffing remarks about people not looking quite so happy as they did a day two ago; and next he claimed that the new aspect was deepening to positive sadness; next, that it was taking on a sick look; and finally he said that everybody was become so moody, thoughtful, and absent-minded that he could rob the meanest man in town of a cent out of the bottom of his breeches pocket and not disturb his revery.

At this stage—or at about this stage —a saying like this was dropped at bedtime—with a sigh, usually—by the head of each of the nineteen principal households: "Ah, what *could* have been the remark that Goodson made?"

And straightway—with a shudder—came this, from the man's wife:

"Oh, *don't*! What horrible thing are you mulling in your mind? Put it away from you, for God's sake!"

But that question was wrung from those men again the next night—and got the same retort. But weaker.

And the third night the men uttered the question yet again—with anguish, and absently. This time—and the following night—the wives fidgeted feebly, and tried to say something. But didn't.

And the night after that they found their tongues and responded—longingly:

"Oh, if we *could* only guess!"

Halliday's comments grew daily more and more sparklingly disagreeable and disparaging. He went diligently about, laughing at the town, individually and in mass. But his laugh was the only one left in the village: it fell upon a hollow and mournful vacancy and emptiness. Not even a smile was findable anywhere. Halliday carried a cigar-box around on a tripod, playing that it was a camera, and halted all passers and aimed the thing and said, "Ready!—now look pleasant, please," but not even this capital joke could surprise the dreary faces into any softening.

So three weeks passed—one week was left. It was Saturday evening—after supper. Instead of the aforetime[19] Saturday-evening flutter and bustle and shopping and larking, the streets were empty and desolate. Richards and his old wife sat apart in their

---

[18] epoch-making—highly significant or important.

[19] aforetime—previous.

little parlor—miserable and thinking. This was become their evening habit now: the lifelong habit which had preceded it, of reading, knitting, and contented chat, or receiving or paying neighborly calls, was dead and gone and forgotten, ages ago—two or three weeks ago; nobody talked now, nobody read, nobody visited—the whole village sat at home, sighing, worrying, silent. Trying to guess out that remark.

The postman left a letter. Richards glanced listlessly at the superscription and the postmark—unfamiliar, both—and tossed the letter on the table and resumed his might-have-beens and his hopeless dull miseries where he had left them off. Two or three hours later his wife got wearily up and was going away to bed without a good night—custom now—but she stopped near the letter and eyed it awhile with a dead interest, then broke it open, and began to skim it over. Richards, sitting there with his chair tilted back against the wall and his chin between his knees, heard something fall. It was his wife. He sprang to her side, but she cried out:

"Leave me alone, I am too happy. Read the letter—read it!"

He did. He devoured it, his brain reeling. The letter was from a distant state, and it said:

I am a stranger to you, but no matter: I have something to tell. I have just arrived home from Mexico, and learned about that episode. Of course you do not know who made that remark, but I know, and I am the only person living who does know. It was GOODSON. *I knew him well, many years ago. I passed through your village that very night, and was his guest till the midnight train came along. I overheard him make that remark to the stranger in the dark—it was in Hale Alley. He and I talked of it the rest of the way home, and while smoking in his house. He mentioned many of your villagers in the course of his talk—most of them in a very uncomplimentary way, but two or three favorably; among these latter yourself. I say "favorably"—nothing stronger. I remember his saying he did not actually* LIKE *any person in the town—not one; but that you—I* THINK *he said you—am almost sure—had done him a very great service once, possibly without knowing the full value of it, and he wished he had a fortune, he would leave it to you when he died, and a curse apiece for the rest of the citizens. Now, then, if it was you that did him that service, you are his legitimate heir, and entitled to the sack of gold. I know that I can trust to your honor and honesty, for in a citizen of Hadleyburg these virtues are an unfailing inheritance, and so I am going to reveal to you the remark, well satisfied that if you are not the right man you will seek and find the right one and see that poor Goodson's debt of gratitude for the service referred to is paid. This is the remark:* "YOU ARE FAR FROM BEING A BAD MAN: GO, AND REFORM."

HOWARD L. STEPHENSON

"Oh, Edward, the money is ours, and I am so grateful, *oh*, so grateful—kiss me, dear, it's forever since we kissed—and we needed it so—the money—and now you are free of Pinkerton and his bank, and nobody's slave any more; it seems to me I could fly for joy."

It was a happy half-hour that the couple spent there on the settee caressing each other; it was the old days come again—days that had begun with their courtship and lasted without a break till the stranger brought the deadly money. By and by the wife said:

"Oh, Edward, how lucky it was you did him that grand service, poor Goodson! I never liked him, but I love him now. And it was fine and beautiful of you never to mention it or brag about it." Then, with a touch of reproach, "But you ought to have told *me,* Edward, you ought to have told your wife, you know."

"Well, I—er—well, Mary, you see—"

"Now stop hemming and hawing, and tell me about it, Edward. I always loved you, and now I'm proud of you. Everybody believes there was only one good generous soul in this village, and now it turns out that you—Edward, why don't you tell me?"

"Well—er—er—Why, Mary, I can't!"

"You *can't? Why* can't you?"

"You see, he—well, he—he made me promise I wouldn't."

The wife looked him over, and said, very slowly:

"Made—you—promise? Edward, what do you tell me that for?"

"Mary, do you think I would lie?"

She was troubled and silent for a moment, then she laid her hand within his and said:

"No . . . no. We have wandered far enough from our bearings—God spare us that! In all your life you have never uttered a lie. But now—now that the foundations of things seem to be crumbling from under us, we—we—" She lost her voice for a moment, then said, brokenly, "Lead us not into temptation. . . . I think you made the promise, Edward. Let it rest so. Let us keep away from that ground. Now—that is all gone by; let us be happy again; it is no time for clouds."

Edward found it something of an effort to comply, for his mind kept wandering—trying to remember what the service was that he had done Goodson.

The couple lay awake the most of the night, Mary happy and busy, Edward busy but not so happy. Mary was planning what she would do with the money. Edward was trying to recall that service. At first his conscience was sore on account of the lie he had told Mary—if it was a lie. After much reflection—suppose it *was* a lie? What then? Was it such a great matter? Aren't we always *acting* lies? Then why not *tell* them? Look at Mary—look what she had done. While he was hurrying off on his honest errand, what was she doing? Lamenting because the papers hadn't been destroyed and the money kept! Is theft better than lying?

"That point lost its sting—the lie dropped into the background and left comfort behind it. The next point came to the front: *Had* he rendered that service? Well, here was Goodson's own evidence as reported in Stephenson's letter; there could be no better evidence than that—it was even *proof* that he had rendered it. Of course. So that point was settled. . . . No, not quite. He recalled with a wince that this unknown Mr. Stephenson was just a trifle unsure as to whether the performer

of it was Richards or some other—and, oh dear, he had put Richards on his honor! He must himself decide whither that money must go—and Mr. Stephenson was not doubting that if he was the wrong man he would go honorably and find the right one. Oh, it was **odious**[20] to put a man in such a situation—ah, why couldn't Stephenson have left out that doubt! What did he want to intrude that for?

Further reflection. How did it happen that *Richards's* name remained in Stephenson's mind as indicating the right man, and not some other man's name? That looked good. Yes, that looked very good. In fact, it went on looking better and better, straight along—until by and by it grew into positive *proof.* And then Richards put the matter at once out of his mind, for he had a private instinct that a proof once established is better left so.

He was feeling reasonably comfortable now, but there was still one other detail that kept pushing itself on his notice: of course he had done that service—that was settled; but what *was* that service? He must recall it—he would not go to sleep till he had recalled it; it would make his peace of mind perfect. And so he thought and thought. He thought of a dozen things—possible services, even probable services—but none of them seemed adequate, none of them seemed large enough, none of them seemed worth the money—worth the fortune Goodson had wished he could leave in his will. And besides, he couldn't remember having done them, anyway. Now, then—now, then—what *kind* of a service would it be that would make a man so inordinately grateful? Ah—the saving of his soul! That must be it. Yes, he could remember, now, how he once set himself the task of converting Goodson, and labored at it as much as—he was going to say three months; but upon closer examination it shrunk to a month, then to a week, then to a day, then to nothing: Yes, he remembered now, and with unwelcome vividness, that Goodson had told him to go to thunder and mind his own business—*he* wasn't hankering[21] to follow Hadleyburg to heaven!

So that solution was a failure—he hadn't saved Goodson's soul. Richards was discouraged. Then after a little came another idea: had he saved Goodson's property? No, that wouldn't do—he hadn't any. His life? That is it! Of course. Why, he might have thought of it before. This time he was on the right track, sure. This imagination was hard at work in a minute, now.

Thereafter during a stretch of two exhausting hours he was busy saving Goodson's life. He saved it in all kinds of difficult and perilous ways. In every case he got it saved satisfactorily up to a certain point; then, just as he was beginning to get well persuaded that it had really happened, a troublesome detail would turn up which made the whole thing impossible. As in the matter of drowning, for instance. In that case he had swum out and tugged Goodson ashore in an unconscious state with a great crowd looking on and applauding, but when he had got it all thought out and

---

[20] **odious**—hateful, despicable.

[21] hankering—having a desire to.

was just beginning to remember all about it, a whole swarm of disqualifying details arrived on the ground: the town would have known of the circumstance, Mary would have known of it, it would glare like a limelight[22] in his own memory instead of being an inconspicuous service which he had possibly rendered "without knowing its full value." And at this point he remembered that he couldn't swim, anyway.

Ah—*there* was a point which he had been overlooking from the start: it had to be a service which he had rendered "possibly without knowing the full value of it." Why, really, that ought to be an easy hunt—much easier than those others. And sure enough, by and by he found it. Goodson, years and years ago, came near marrying a very sweet and pretty girl, named Nancy Hewitt, but in some way or other the match had been broken off; the girl died, Goodson remained a bachelor, and by and by became a soured one and a frank despiser of the human species. Soon after the girl's death the village found out, or thought it had found out, that she carried a spoonful of negro blood in her veins. Richards worked at these details a good while, and in the end he thought he remembered things concerning them which must have gotten mislaid in his memory through long neglect. He seemed to dimly remember that it was *he* that found out about the negro blood; that it was he that told the village; that the village told Goodson where they got it; that he thus saved Goodson from marrying the tainted girl; that he had done him this great service "without knowing the full value of it," in fact without knowing that he *was* doing it; but that Goodson knew the value of it, and what a narrow escape he had had, and so went to his grave grateful to his benefactor and wishing he had a fortune to leave him. It was all clear and simple now, and the more he went over it the more luminous and certain it grew; and at last, he nestled to sleep satisfied and happy, he remembered the whole thing just as if it had been yesterday. In fact, he dimly remembered Goodson's *telling* him his gratitude once. Meantime Mary had spent six thousand dollars on a new house for herself and a pair of slippers for her pastor, and then had fallen peacefully to rest.

That same Saturday evening the postman had delivered a letter to each of the other principal citizens—nineteen letters in all. No two of the envelopes were alike, and no two of the superscriptions were in the same hand, but the letters inside were just like each other in every detail but one. They were exact copies of the letter received by Richards—handwriting and all—and were all signed by Stephenson, but in place of Richards's name each receiver's own name appeared.

All night long eighteen principal citizens did what their caste-brother Richards was doing at the same time—they put in their energies trying to remember what notable service it was that they had unconsciously done Barclay Goodson. In no case was it a holiday job; still they succeeded.

---

22 limelight—brilliant white light used as early stage lighting.

And while they were at this work, which was difficult, their wives put in the night spending the money, which was easy. During that one night the nineteen wives spent an average of seven thousand dollars each out of the forty thousand in the sack—a hundred and thirty-three thousand altogether.

Next day there was a surprise for Jack Halliday. He noticed that the faces of the nineteen chief citizens and their wives bore that expression of peaceful and holy happiness again. He could not understand it, neither was he able to invent any remarks about it that could damage it or disturb it. And so it was his turn to be dissatisfied with life. His private guesses at the reasons for the happiness failed in all instances, upon examination. When he met Mrs. Wilcox and noticed the placid ecstasy in her face, he said to himself, "Her cat has had kittens"—and went and asked the cook: it was not so; the cook had detected the happiness, but did not know the cause. When Halliday found the duplicate ecstasy in the face of "Shadbelly" Billson (village nickname), he was sure some neighbor of Billson's had broken his leg, but inquiry showed that this had not happened. The subdued ecstasy in Gregory Yates's face could mean but one thing—he was a mother-in-law short: it was another mistake. "And Pinkerton—Pinkerton—he has collected ten cents that he thought he was going to lose." And so on, and so on. In some cases the guesses had to remain in doubt, in others they proved distinct errors. In the end Halliday said to himself, "Anyway it foots up that there's nineteen Hadleyburg families temporarily in heaven: I don't know how it happened; I only know Providence is off duty today."

An architect and builder from the next state had lately ventured to set up a small business in this unpromising village, and his sign had now been hanging out a week. Not a customer yet; he was a discouraged man, and sorry he had come. But his weather changed suddenly now. First one and then another chief citizen's wife said to him privately:

"Come to my house Monday week—but say nothing about it for the present. We think of building."

He got eleven invitations that day. That night he wrote his daughter and broke off her match with her student. He said she could marry a mile higher than that.

Pinkerton the banker and two or three other well-to-do men planned country-seats—but waited. That kind don't count their chickens until they are hatched.

The Wilsons devised a grand new thing—a fancy-dress ball. They made no actual promises, but told all their acquaintanceship in confidence that they were thinking the matter over and thought they should give it—"and if we do, you will be invited, of course." People were surprised, and said, one to another, "Why, they are crazy, those poor Wilsons, they can't afford it." Several among the nineteen said privately to their husbands, "It is a good idea: we will keep still till their cheap thing is over, then *we* will give one that will make it sick."

The days drifted along, and the bill of future squanderings rose higher and higher, wilder and wilder, more and more foolish and reckless. It began to look as if every member of the nineteen would not only spend his whole forty thousand dollars before receiving-day, but be actually in debt by the time he got the money. In some cases lightheaded people did not stop with planning to spend, they really spent—on credit. They bought land, mortgages, farms, speculative stocks, fine clothes, horses, and various other things, paid down the bonus, and made themselves liable for the rest—at ten days. Presently the sober second thought came, and Halliday noticed that a ghastly anxiety was beginning to show up in a good many faces. Again he was puzzled, and didn't know what to make of it. "The Wilcox kittens aren't dead, they weren't born; nobody's broken a leg; there's no shrinkage in mother-in-laws; *nothing* has happened—it is an unsolvable mystery."

There was another puzzled man, too—the Rev. Mr. Burgess. For days, wherever he went, people seemed to follow him or to be watching for him; and if he ever found himself in a retired spot, a member of the nineteen would be sure to appear, thrust an envelope privately into his hand, whisper "To be opened at the town-hall Friday evening," then vanish away like a guilty thing. He was expecting that there might be one claimant for the sack—doubtful, however, Goodson being dead—but it never occurred to him that all this crowd might be claimants. When the great Friday came at last, he found that he had nineteen envelopes.

III

The town-hall had never looked finer. The platform at the end of it was backed by a showy draping of flags; at intervals along the walls were **festoons**[23] of flags; the gallery fronts were clothed in flags; the supporting columns were swathed in flags; all this was to impress the stranger, for he would be there in considerable force, and in a large degree he would be connected with the press. The house was full. The 412 fixed seats were occupied; also the 68 extra chairs which had been packed into the aisles; the steps of the platform were occupied; some distinguished strangers were given seats on the platform; at the horseshoe of tables which fenced the front and sides of the platform sat a strong force of special correspondents who had come from everywhere. It was the best-dressed house the town had ever produced. There were some tolerably expensive toilets[24] there, and in several cases the ladies who wore them had the look of being unfamiliar with that kind of clothes. At least the town thought they had that look, but the notion could have arisen from the town's knowledge of the fact that these ladies had never inhabited such clothes before.

The gold-sack stood on a little table at the front of the platform where all the house could see it.

The gold-sack stood on a little table at the front of the platform where all the house could see it. The bulk of the house gazed at

[23] **festoons**—decorations.

[24] toilets—clothing.

it with a burning interest, a mouth-watering interest, a wistful[25] and pathetic interest; a minority of nineteen couples gazed at it tenderly, lovingly, proprietarily,[26] and the male half of this minority kept saying over to themselves the moving little **impromptu**[27] speeches of thankfulness for the audience's applause and congratulations which they were presently going to get up and deliver. Every now and then one of these got a piece of paper out of his vest pocket and privately glanced at it to refresh his memory.

Of course there was a buzz of conversation going on—there always is; but at last when the Rev. Mr. Burgess rose and laid his hand on the sack he could hear his microbes gnaw, the place was so still. He related the curious history of the sack, then went on to speak in warm terms of Hadleyburg's old and well-earned reputation for spotless honesty, and of the town's just pride in this reputation. He said that this reputation was a treasure of priceless value; that under Providence its value had now become inestimably enhanced, for the recent episode had spread this fame far and wide, and thus had focused the eyes of the American world upon this village, and made its name for all time, as he hoped and believed, a synonym for commercial incorruptibility. [*Applause*] "And who is to be the guardian of this noble treasure—the community as a whole? No! The responsibility is individual, not communal. From this day forth each and every one of you is in his own person its special guardian, and individually responsible that no harm shall come to it. Do you—does each of you— accept this great trust? [*Tumultuous assent.*[28]] Then all is well. Transmit it to your children and to your children's children. Today your purity is beyond reproach—see to it that it shall remain so. Today there is not a person in your community who could be beguiled[29] to touch a penny not his own—see to it that you abide in this grace. [*"We will! we will!"*] This is not the place to make comparisons between ourselves and other communities—some of them ungracious toward us; they have their ways, we have ours; let us be content. [*Applause.*] I am done. Under my hand, my friends, rests a stranger's eloquent recognition of what we are; through him the world will always henceforth know what we are. We do not know who he is, but in your name I utter your gratitude, and ask you to raise your voices in endorsement."

The house rose in a body and made the walls quake with the thunders of its thankfulness for the space of a long minute. Then it sat down, and Mr. Burgess took an envelope out of his pocket. The house held its breath while he slit the envelope open and took from it a slip of paper. He read its contents—slowly and impressively—the audience listening with tranced attention to this magic document, each of whose words stood for an ingot of gold:

"'The remark which I made to the distressed stranger was *this: "You are very far from being*

---

[25] wistful—thoughtfully sad; melancholy.

[26] proprietarily—possessively.

[27] **impromptu**—unrehearsed.

[28] *Tumultuous assent*—noisy agreement.

[29] beguiled—tempted.

a bad man: go, and reform.'"" Then he continued: "We shall know in a moment now whether the remark here quoted corresponds with the one concealed in the sack; and if that shall prove to be so—and it undoubtedly will—this sack of gold belongs to a fellow-citizen who will henceforth stand before the nation as the symbol of the special virtue which has made our town famous through out the land—Mr. Billson!"

The house had gotten itself all ready to burst into the proper tornado of applause; but instead of doing it, it seemed stricken with a paralysis; there was a deep hush for a moment or two, then a wave of whispered murmurs swept the place—of about this tenor: "*Billson!* oh, come, this is *too* thin! Twenty dollars to a stranger—or *anybody*—*Billson!* tell it to the marines!" And now at this point the house caught its breath all of a sudden in a new access of astonishment, for it discovered that whereas in one part of the hall Deacon Billson was standing up with his head meekly bowed, in another part of it Lawyer Wilson was doing the same. There was a wondering silence now for a while. Everybody was puzzled, and nineteen couples were surprised and **indignant**.[30]

Billson and Wilson turned and stared at each other. Billson asked, bitingly:

"Why do *you* rise, Mr. Wilson?"

"Because I have a right to. Perhaps you will be good enough to explain to the house why *you* rise?"

"With great pleasure. Because I wrote that paper."

"It is an impudent falsity! I wrote it myself."

It was Burgess's turn to be paralyzed. He stood looking vacantly at first one of the men and then the other, and did not seem to know what to do. The house was **stupefied**.[31] Lawyer Wilson spoke up, now, and said,

"Twenty dollars to a stranger—or anybody—Billson! tell it to the marines!"

"I ask the Chair to read the name signed to that paper."

That brought the Chair to itself, and it read out the name:

"'John Wharton *Billson*.'"

"There!" shouted Billson, "what have you got to say for yourself, now? And what kind of apology are you going to make to me and to this insulted house for the imposture which you have attempted to play here?"

"No apologies are due, sir; and as for the rest of it, I publicly charge you with **pilfering**[32] my note from Mr. Burgess and substituting a copy of it signed with your own name. There is no other way by which you could have gotten hold of the test-remark; I alone, of living men, possessed the secret of its wording."

There was likely to be a scandalous state of things if this went on; everybody noticed with distress that the short-hand scribes were scribbling like mad; many

---

[30] **indignant**—angry, offended.

[31] **stupefied**—dumbfounded, surprised.

[32] **pilfering**—stealing.

people were crying "Chair, Chair! Order! order!" Burgess rapped with his gavel, and said:

"Let us not forget the proprieties due. There has evidently been a mistake somewhere, but surely that is all. If Mr. Wilson gave me an envelope—and I remember now that he did—I still have it."

He took one out of his pocket, opened it, glanced at it, looked surprised and worried, and stood silent a few moments. Then he waved his hand in a wandering and mechanical way, and made an effort or two to say something, then gave it up, despondently. Several voices cried out:

"Read it! read it! What is it?"

So he began in a dazed and sleep-walker fashion:

"'*The remark which I made to the unhappy stranger was this: "You are far from being a bad man.* [The house gazed at him, marveling.] *Go, and reform."'* [*Murmurs:* "Amazing! what can this mean?"] This one," said the Chair, "is signed Thurlow G. Wilson."

"There!" cried Wilson. "I reckon that settles it! I knew perfectly well my note was **purloined**."[33]

"Purloined!" retorted Billson. "I'll let you know that neither you nor any man of your kidney[34] must venture to—"

THE CHAIR "Order, gentlemen, order! Take your seats, both of you, please."

They obeyed, shaking their heads and grumbling angrily. The house was profoundly puzzled; it did not know what to do with this curious emergency. Presently Thompson got up. Thompson was the hatter. He would have liked to be a Nineteener; but such was not for him: his stock of hats was not considerable enough for the position. He said:

"Mr. Chairman, if I may be permitted to make a suggestion, can both of these gentlemen be right? I put it to you, sir, can both have happened to say the very same words to the stranger? It seems to me—"

The tanner[35] got up and interrupted him. The tanner was a **disgruntled**[36] man; he believed himself entitled to be a Nineteener, but he couldn't get recognition. It made him a little unpleasant in his ways and speech. Said he:

"Sho, *that's* not the point! *That* could happen—twice in a hundred years—but not the other thing. *Neither* of them gave the twenty dollars!"

[*A ripple of applause.*]

BILLSON "*I* did!"

WILSON "*I* did!"

Then each accused the other of pilfering.

THE CHAIR "Order! Sit down, if you please—both of you. Neither of the notes has been out of my possession at any moment."

A VOICE "Good—that settles *that*!"

THE TANNER "Mr. Chairman, one thing is now plain: one of these men has been eavesdropping under the other one's bed, and filching family secrets. If it is not unparliamentary to suggest it, I will remark both are equal to it. [*The Chair.* "Order! order!"] I withdraw the remark, sir, and will confine myself to suggesting

---

33 **purloined**—stolen.

34 kidney—temperament or disposition.

35 tanner—person who turns hides into leather by soaking them in tannin.

36 **disgruntled**—discontented.

that *if* one of them overheard the other reveal the test-remark to his wife, we shall catch him now."

A VOICE "How?"

THE TANNER "Easily. The two have not quoted the remark in exactly the same words. You would have noticed that, if there hadn't been a considerable stretch of time and an exciting quarrel inserted between the two readings."

A VOICE "Name the difference."

THE TANNER "The word *very* is in Billson's note, and not in the other."

MANY VOICES "That's so—he's right!"

THE TANNER "And so, if the Chair will examine the test-remark in the sack, we shall know which of these two frauds—[*The Chair.* "Order!"]—which of these two adventurers—[*The Chair.* "Order! order!"]—which of these two gentlemen—[*laughter and applause*]—is entitled to wear the belt as being the first dishonest blatherskite[37] ever bred in this town—which he has dishonored, and which will be a sultry place for him from now out!" [*Vigorous applause.*]

MANY VOICES "Open it!—open the sack!"

Mr. Burgess made a slit in the sack, slid his hand in and brought out an envelope. In it were a couple of folded notes. He said:

"One of these is marked, 'Not to be examined until all written communications which have been addressed to the Chair—if any—shall have been read! The other is marked *'The Test.'* Allow me. It is worded—to wit:

"'I do not require that the first half of the remark which was made to me by my benefactor shall be quoted with exactness, for it was not striking, and could be forgotten; but its closing fifteen words are quite striking, and I think easily rememberable; unless *these* shall be accurately reproduced, let the applicant be regarded as an impostor. My benefactor began by saying he seldom gave advice to any one, but that, it always bore the hall-mark[38] of high value when he did give it. Then, he said this—and it has never faded from my memory—"*You are far from being a bad man—*"'"

FIFTY VOICES "That settles it—the money's Wilson's! Wilson! Wilson! Speech! Speech!"

People jumped up and crowded around Wilson, wringing his hand and congratulating **fervently**[39]—meantime the Chair was hammering with the gavel and shouting:

"Order, gentlemen! Order! Order! Let me finish reading, please." When quiet was restored, the reading was resumed—as follows:

*"'"Go, and reform—or, mark my words—some day, for your sins, you will die and go to hell or Hadleyburg—*TRY AND MAKE IT THE FORMER."'"

A ghastly silence followed. First an angry cloud began to settle darkly upon the faces of the citizenship; after a pause the cloud began to rise, and a tickled expression tried to take its place; tried so hard that it was only kept under with great and painful difficulty; the reporters, the

---

37 blatherskite—noisy or talkative fellow.

38 hall-mark—mark guaranteeing the quality of an object.

39 **fervently**—excitedly.

Brixtonites, and other strangers bent their beads down and shielded their faces with their hands, and managed to hold in by main strength and heroic courtesy. At this most inopportune time burst upon the stillness the roar of a solitary voice—Jack Halliday's:

"*That's* got the hall-mark on it!"

Then the house let go, strangers and all. Even Mr. Burgess's gravity broke down presently, then the audience considered itself officially absolved from all restraint, and it made the most of its privilege. It was a good long laugh, and a tempestuously whole-hearted one, but it ceased at last—long enough for Mr. Burgess to try to resume, and for the people to get their eyes partially wiped; then it broke out again; and afterward yet again; then at last Burgess was able to get out these serious words:

"It is useless to try to disguise the fact—we find ourselves in the presence of a matter of grave import. It involves the honor of your town, it strikes at the town's good name. The difference of a single word between the test-remarks offered by Mr. Wilson and Mr. Billson was itself a serious thing, since it indicated that one or the other of these gentlemen had committed a theft—"

The two men were sitting limp, nerveless, crushed; but at these words both were electrified into movement, and started to get up—

"Sit down!" said the Chair, sharply, and they obeyed. "That, as I have said, was a serious thing. And it was—but for only one of them. But the matter has become graver; for the honor of *both* is now in formidable peril. Shall I go even further, and say in inextricable peril? *Both* left out the crucial fifteen words." He paused. During several moments he allowed the pervading stillness to gather and deepen its impressive effects, then added: "There would seem to be but one way whereby this could happen. I ask these gentlemen—Was there *collusion*? —*agreement*?"

A low murmur sifted through the house; its import was, "He's got them both."

Billson was not used to emergencies; he sat in a helpless collapse. But Wilson was a lawyer. He struggled to his feet, pale and worried, and said:

"I ask the indulgence of the house while I explain this most painful matter. I am sorry to say what I am about to say, since it must inflict irreparable injury upon Mr. Billson, whom I have always esteemed and respected until now, and in whose invulnerability to temptation I entirely believed—as did you all. But for the preservation of my own honor I must speak—and with frankness. I confess with shame—and I now beseech your pardon for it—that I said to the ruined stranger all of the words contained in the test-remark, including the disparaging fifteen. [*Sensation.*] When the late publication was made I recalled them, and I resolved to claim the sack of coin, for by every right I was entitled to it. Now I will ask you to consider this point, and weigh it well: that stranger's gratitude to me that night knew no bounds; he said himself that he could find no words for it that were adequate, and that if he should ever be able he would repay me a thousandfold. Now, then, I ask you this: Could I expect—could I believe—could I even remotely imagine—that, feeling as he did, he would do so ungrateful a thing as to add those quite unnecessary fifteen words to his test? —set a trap for me? —expose me as a slanderer of my own town before my own people assembled in a public hall? It was **preposterous**;[40] it was impossible. His test would contain only the kindly opening clause of my remark. Of that I had no shadow of doubt. You would have thought as I did. You would not have expected a base betrayal from one whom you had befriended and against whom you had committed no offense. And so, with perfect confidence, perfect trust, I wrote on a piece of paper the opening words—ending with 'Go, and reform,' —and signed it. When I was about to put it in an envelope I was called into my back office, and without thinking I left the paper lying open on my desk." He stopped, turned his head slowly toward Billson, waited a moment, then added: "I ask you to note this: when I returned, a little later, Mr. Billson was retiring by my street door." [*Sensation.*]

In a moment Billson was on his feet and shouting:

"It's a lie! It's an infamous lie!"

THE CHAIR "Be seated, sir! Mr. Wilson has the floor."

Billson's friends pulled him into his seat and quieted him, and Wilson went on:

"Those are the simple facts. My note was now lying in a different place on the table from where I had left it. I noticed that, but attached no importance to it, thinking a draught had blown it there. That Mr. Billson would read a private paper was a thing which could not occur to me; he was an honorable man, and he would be above that. If you will allow me to say it, I think his extra word *'very'* stands explained; it is attributable to a defect of memory. I was the only man in the world who could furnish here any detail of the test-remark—by *honorable* means. I have finished."

There is nothing in the world like a persuasive speech to fuddle the mental apparatus and upset the convictions and debauch[41] the emotions of an audience not practiced in the tricks and delusions of oratory. Wilson sat down victorious. The house submerged him in tides of approving applause; friends swarmed to him and shook him by the hand and congratulated him, and Billson was shouted down and not allowed to say a word. The Chair hammered and hammered with its gavel, and kept shouting:

"But let us proceed, gentlemen, let us proceed!"

At last there was a measurable degree of quiet, and the hatter said:

"But what is there to proceed with, sir, but to deliver the money?"

VOICES "That's it! That's it! Come forward, Wilson!"

THE HATTER "I move three cheers for Mr. Wilson, Symbol of the special virtue which—"

The cheers burst forth before he could finish; and in the midst of them—and in the midst of the clamor of the gavel also—

[40] **preposterous**—absurd.

[41] debauch—corrupt.

some enthusiasts mounted Wilson on a big friend's shoulder and were going to fetch him in triumph to the platform. The Chair's voice now rose above the noise—

"Order! To your places! You forget that there is still a document to be read." When quiet had been restored he took up the document, and was going to read it, but laid it down again, saying, "I forgot; this is not to be read until all written communications received by me have first been read." He took an envelope out of his pocket, removed its inclosure, glanced at it—seemed astonished—held it out and gazed at it—stared at it.

Twenty or thirty voices cried out:

"What is it? Read it! read it!"

And he did—slowly, and wondering:

"'*The remark which I made to the stranger*—[*Voices*. "Hello! how's this?"] —*was this: "You are far from being a bad man.* [*Voices*. "Great Scott!"] *Go, and reform,"*' [*Voices* "Oh, saw my leg off!"] Signed by Mr. Pinkerton, the banker."

The **pandemonium**[42] of delight which turned itself loose now was of a sort to make the judicious weep. Those whose withers were unwrung[43] laughed till the tears ran down; the reporters, in throes of laughter, set down disordered pot-hooks which would never in the world be decipherable; and a sleeping dog jumped up, scared out of its wits, and barked itself crazy at the turmoil. All manner of cries were scattered through the din: "We're getting rich—*two* Symbols of Incorruptibility!—without counting Billson!" "*Three!*—count Shadbelly in—we can't have too many!" "All right—Billson's elected!" "Alas, poor Wilson—victim of *two* thieves!"

A POWERFUL VOICE "Silence! The Chair's fished up something more out of its pocket."

VOICES "Hurrah! Is it something fresh? Read it! read! read!"

THE CHAIR [*reading*] "'*The remark which I made,*' etc.: '"*You are far from being a bad man. Go,*"' etc. Signed, 'Gregory Yates.'"

TORNADO OF VOICES "Four Symbols!" "'Rah for Yates!" "Fish again!"

The house was in a roaring humor now, and ready to get all the fun out of the occasion that might be in it. Several Nineteeners, looking pale and distressed, got up and began to work their way toward the aisles, but a score of shouts went up:

"The doors, the doors—close the doors; no Incorruptible shall leave this place! Sit down, everybody!"

The mandate was obeyed.

"Fish again! Read! read!"

The Chair fished again, and once more the familiar words began to fall from its lips— "'*You are far from being a bad man.*'"

"Name! name! What's his name?"

"'L. Ingoldsby Sargent.'"

"Five elected! Pile up the Symbols! Go on, go on!"

"'*You are far from being a bad—*'"

"Name! name!"

"'Nicholas Whitworth.'"

---

[42] **pandemonium**—wild uproar or noise.

[43] whose withers were unwrung—who were unhurt. The expression refers to an injury to the withers, or shoulders, of a horse.

"Hooray! hooray! it's a symbolical day!"

Somebody wailed in, and began to sing this rhyme (leaving out "it's") to the lovely "Mikado"[44] tune of "When a man's afraid, a beautiful maid—"; the audience joined in, with joy; then, just in time, somebody contributed another line—

And don't you this forget—

The house roared it out. A third line was at once furnished—

Corruptibles far from Hadleyburg are—

The house roared that one too. As the last note died, Jack Halliday's voice rose high and clear, freighted with a final line—

But the Symbols are here, you bet!

That was sung, with booming enthusiasm. Then the happy house started in at the beginning and sang the four lines through twice, with immense swing and dash, and finished up with a crashing three-times-three and a tiger for "Hadleyburg the Incorruptible and all Symbols of it which we shall find worthy to receive the hall-mark tonight."

Then the shoutings at the Chair began again, all over the place:

"Go on! go on! Read! read some more! Read all you've got!"

"That's it—go on! We are winning eternal celebrity!"

A dozen men got up now and began to protest. They said that this farce was the work of some abandoned joker, and was an insult to the whole community. Without a doubt these signatures were all forgeries—

"Sit down! sit down! Shut up! You are confessing. We'll find *your* names in the lot."

"Mr. Chairman, how many of those envelopes have you got?"

The Chair counted.

"Together with those that have been already examined, there are nineteen."

A storm of derisive applause broke out.

"Perhaps they all contain the secret. I move that you open them all and read every signature that is attached to a note of that sort—and read also the first eight words of the note."

"Second the motion!"

It was put and carried—uproariously. Then poor old Richards got up, and his wife rose and stood at his side. Her head was bent down, so that none might see that she was crying. Her husband gave her his arm, and so supporting her, he began to speak in a quavering[45] voice:

"My friends, you have known us two—Mary and me—all our lives, and I think you have liked us and respected us—"

The Chair interrupted him:

"Allow me. It is quite true—that which you are saying, Mr. Richards: this town *does* know you two; it *does* like you; it *does* respect you; more—it honors you and *loves you*—"

Halliday's voice rang out:

"That's the hall-marked truth, too! If the Chair is right, let the house speak up and say it. Rise! Now, then—hip! hip! hip!—all together!"

The house rose in mass, faced toward the old couple eagerly, filled the air with a snow-storm of waving handkerchiefs, and delivered the cheers with all its affectionate heart.

---

44 "Mikado"—operetta by Gilbert and Sullivan which included the verse "When a man's afraid/A beautiful maid/Is a cheering sight to see."

45 quavering—shaking, unsteady.

The Chair then continued:

"What I was going to say is this: We know your good heart, Mr. Richards, but this is not a time for the exercise of charity toward offenders. [*Shouts of "Right! right!"*] I see your generous purpose in your face, and I cannot allow you to plead for these men—"

"But I was going to—"

"Please take your seat, Mr. Richards. We must examine the rest of these notes—simple fairness to the men who have already been exposed requires this. As soon as that has been done—I give you my word for this—you shall be heard."

MANY VOICES "Right!—the Chair is right—no interruption can be permitted at this stage! Go on!—the names! the names!—according to the terms of the motion!"

The old couple sat reluctantly down, and the husband whispered to the wife, "It is pitifully hard to have to wait; the shame will be greater than ever when they find we were only going to plead for *ourselves*."

Straightway the jollity broke loose again with the reading of the names.

"'You are far from being a bad man—' Signature, 'Robert J. Titmarsh.'

"'You are far from being a bad man—' Signature, 'Eliphalet Weeks.'

"'You are far from being a bad man—' Signature, 'Oscar B. Wilder.'"

At this point the house lit upon the idea of taking the eight words out of the Chairman's hands. He was not unthankful for that. Thenceforward he held up each note in its turn, and waited. The house droned out the eight words in a massed and measured and musical deep volume of sound (with a daringly close resemblance to a well-known church chant) — "'You are f-a-r from being a b-a-a-a-d man."' Then the Chair said, "Signature, 'Archibald Wilcox.'" And so on, and so on, name after name, and everybody had an increasingly and gloriously good time except the wretched Nineteen. Now and then, when a particularly shining name was called, the house made the Chair wait while it chanted the whole of the test-remark from the beginning to the closing words, "And go to hell or Hadleyburg—try and make it the for-or-m-e-r!" and in these special cases they added a grand and agonized and imposing "A-a-a-a-*men!*"

The list dwindled, dwindled, dwindled, poor old Richards keeping tally of the count, wincing when a name resembling his own was pronounced, and waiting in miserable suspense for the time to come when it would be his humiliating privilege to rise with Mary and finish his plea, which he was intending to word thus: ". . . for until now we have never done any wrong thing, but have gone our humble way unreproached. We are very poor, we are old, and have no chick nor child to help us; we were sorely tempted, and we fell. It was my purpose when I got up before to make confession and beg that my name might not be read out in this public place, for it seemed to us that we could not bear it; but I was prevented. It was just; it was our place to suffer with the rest. It has been hard for us. It is the first time we have ever heard our name fall from any one's lips—sullied. Be merciful—for the sake of the better days; make out shame as light to bear as in your charity you can." At this point in his revery Mary nudged him, perceiving that his mind was absent. The house was chanting, "You are f-a-r," etc.

"Be ready," Mary whispered. "Your name comes now; he has read eighteen."

The chant ended.

"Next! next! next!" came volleying from all over the house.

Burgess put his hand into his pocket. The old couple, trembling, began to rise. Burgess fumbled a moment, then said,

"I find I have read them all."

Faint with joy and surprise, the couple sank into their seats, and Mary whispered: "Oh, bless God, we are saved—he has lost ours—I wouldn't give this for a hundred of those sacks!"

The house burst out with its "Mikado" travesty, and sang it three times with ever-increasing enthusiasm, rising to its feet when it reached for the third time the closing line—

But the Symbols are here, you bet!

and finishing up with cheers and a tiger for "Hadleyburg purity and our eighteen immortal representatives of it."

Then Wingate, the saddler, got up and proposed cheers "for the cleanest man in town, the one solitary important citizen in it who didn't try to steal that money—Edward Richards."

They were given with great and moving heartiness; then somebody proposed that Richards be elected sole guardian and Symbol of the Sacred Hadleyburg Tradition, with power and right to stand up and look the whole sarcastic world in the face.

Passed, by acclamation; then they sang the "Mikado" again, and it with:

And there's one *Symbol left, you bet!*

There was a pause; then—

A VOICE "Now, then, who's to get the sack?"

"Oh, bless God, we are saved—he has lost ours—I wouldn't give this for a hundred of those sacks!"

THE TANNER *(with bitter sarcasm)* "That's easy. The money has to be divided among the eighteen Incorruptibles. They gave the suffering stranger twenty dollars apiece—and that remark—each in his turn—it took twenty-two minutes for the procession to move past. Staked the stranger—total contribution, $360. All they want is just the loan back—and interest—forty thousand dollars altogether."

MANY VOICES [*derisively*] "That's it! Divvy! divvy! Be kind to the poor—don't keep them waiting!"

THE CHAIR "Order! I now offer the stranger's remaining document. It says: 'If no claimant shall appear [*grand chorus of groans*] I desire that you open the sack and count out the money to the principal citizens of your town, they to take it in trust [*cries of "Oh! Oh! Oh!"*], and use it in such ways as to them shall seem best for the propagation and preservation of your community's noble reputation for incorruptible honesty [*more cries*] —a reputation to which their names and their efforts will add a new and far-reaching luster.' [*Enthusiastic outburst of sarcastic applause.*] That seems to be all. No—here is a postscript:

'P.S. — CITIZENS OF HADLEYBURG: *There is no test-remark—nobody made one.* [Great sensation.] *There wasn't any pauper stranger, nor any twenty-dollar contribution, nor any accompanying benediction and compliment—these are all inventions.* [General buzz and hum of astonishment and delight.] *Allow me to tell my story—it will take but a word or two. I passed through your town at a certain time, and received a deep offense which I had not earned. Any other man would have been content to kill one or two of you and call it square, but to me that would have been a trivial revenge, and inadequate; for the dead do not* suffer. *Besides, I could not kill you all—and, anyway, made as I am, even that would not have satisfied me. I wanted to damage every man in the place, and every woman—and not in their bodies or in their estate, but in their vanity—the place where feeble and foolish people are most vulnerable. So I disguised myself and came back and studied you. You were easy game. You had an old and lofty reputation for honesty, and naturally you were proud of it—it was your treasure of treasures, the very apple of your eye. As soon as I found out that you carefully and vigilantly kept yourselves and your children out of* temptation, *I knew how to proceed. Why, you simple creatures, the weakest of all weak things is a virtue which has not been tested in the fire. I laid a plan, and gathered a list of names. My project was to corrupt Hadleyburg the Incorruptible. My idea was to make liars and thieves of nearly half a hundred smirchless men and women who had never in their lives uttered a lie or stolen a penny. I was afraid of Goodson. He was neither born nor reared in Hadleyburg. I was afraid that if I started to operate my scheme by getting my letter laid before you, you would say to yourselves, "Goodson is the only man among us who would give away twenty dollars to a poor devil"—and then you might not bite at my bait. But Heaven took Goodson; then I knew I was safe, and I set my trap and baited it. It may be that I shall not catch all the men to whom I mailed the pretended test secret, but I shall catch the most of them, if I know Hadleyburg nature.* [Voices. "*Right—he got every last one of them.*"] *I believe they will even steal ostensible*[46] gamble-money, *rather than miss, poor, tempted, and mistrained fellows. I am hoping to eternally and everlastingly squelch your vanity and give Hadleyburg a new renown—one that will* stick—*and spread far. If I have succeeded, open the sack and summon the Committee on Propagation and Preservation of the Hadleyburg Reputation.*'

A CYCLONE OF VOICES "Open it! Open it! The Eighteen to the front! Committee on Propagation of the Tradition! Forward—the Incorruptibles!"

The Chair ripped the sack wide, and gathered up a handful of bright, broad, yellow coins, shook them together, then examined them—

"Friends, they are only gilded disks of lead!"

There was a crashing outbreak of delight over this news, and when the noise had subsided, the tanner called out:

"By right of apparent seniority in this business, Mr. Wilson is Chairman of the Committee on Propagation of the Tradition. I suggest that he step forward on behalf of his pals, and receive in trust the money."

---

46 *ostensible*—represented or appearing as such.

A HUNDRED VOICES "Wilson! Wilson! Wilson! Speech! Speech!"

WILSON [*in a voice trembling with anger*] "You will allow me to say, and without apologies for my language, *damn* the money!"

A VOICE "Oh, and him a Baptist!"

A VOICE "Seventeen Symbols left! Step up, gentlemen, and assume your trust!"

There was a pause—no response.

THE SADDLER "Mr. Chairman, we've got *one* clean man left, anyway, out of the late aristocracy; and he needs money, and deserves it. I move that you appoint Jack Halliday to get up there and auction off that sack of gilt twenty-dollar pieces, and give the result to the right man—the man whom Hadleyburg delights to honor—Edward Richards."

This was received with great enthusiasm, the dog taking a hand again; the saddler started the bids at a dollar, the Brixton folk and Barnum's representative fought hard for it, the people cheered every jump that the bids made, the excitement climbed moment by moment higher and higher, the bidders got on their mettle and grew steadily more and more daring, more and more determined, the jumps went from a dollar up to five, then to ten, then to twenty, then fifty, then to a hundred, then—

At the beginning of the auction Richards whispered in distress to his wife: "O Mary, can we allow it? It—it—you see, it is an honor-reward, a testimonial to purity of character, and—and—can we allow it? Hadn't I better get up and—O Mary, what ought we to do? —what do you think we— [*Halliday's voice. "Fifteen I'm bid! —fifteen for the sack!—twenty!—ah, thanks!—thirty—thanks again! Thirty, thirty, thirty!—do I hear forty?—forty it is! Keep the ball rolling, gentlemen, keep it rolling!—fifty! thanks, noble Roman! going at fifty, fifty, fifty!—seventy! —ninety! splendid!—a hundred!—pile it up, pile it up!—hundred and twenty—forty!—just in time!—hundred and fifty!—*TWO *hundred!—superb! Do I hear two h— thanks!—two hundred and fifty!—"*]

"It is another temptation, Edward—I'm all in a tremble—but, oh, we've escaped *one* temptation, and that ought to warn us to— [*Six did I hear?—thanks! —six-fifty, six-f—*SEVEN *hundred!"*] And yet, Edward, when you think—nobody susp—— [*"Eight hundred dollars!—hurrah!—make it nine!—Mr. Parsons, did I hear you say—thanks—nine!—this noble sack of virgin lead going at only nine hundred dollars, gilding and all—come! do I hear—a thousand!—gratefully yours!—did some one say eleven?—a sack which is going to be the most celebrated in the whole Uni—"*] "O Edward" (beginning to sob), "we are *so* poor!—but—but—do as you think best—do as you think best."

Edward fell—that is, he sat still; sat with a conscience which was not satisfied, but which was overpowered by circumstances.

Meantime a stranger, who looked like an amateur detective gotten up as an impossible English earl, had been watching the evening's proceedings with manifest interest, and with a contented expression in his face; and he had been privately commenting to himself. He was now soliloquizing somewhat like this: "None of the

Eighteen are bidding; that is not satisfactory; I must change that—the dramatic unities[47] require it; they must buy the sack they tried to steal; they must pay a heavy price, too—some of them are rich. And another thing, when I make a mistake in Hadleyburg nature the man that puts that error upon me is entitled to a high honorarium,[48] and some one must pay it. This poor old Richards has brought my judgment to shame; he is an honest man—I don't understand it, but I acknowledge it. Yes, he saw my deuces *and* with a straight flush, and by rights the pot is his. And it shall be a jack-pot, too, if I can manage it. He disappointed me, but let that pass."

He was watching the bidding. At a thousand, the market broke; the prices tumbled swiftly. He waited—and still watched. One competitor dropped out; then another, and another. He put in a bid or two, now. When the bids had sunk to ten dollars, he added a five; some one raised him a three; he waited a moment, then flung in a fifty-dollar jump, and the sack was his—at $1,828. The house broke out in cheers—then stopped; for he was on his feet, and had lifted his hand. He began to speak.

"I desire to say a word, and ask a favor. I am a speculator in rarities, and I have dealings with persons interested in numismatics[49] all over the world. I can make a profit on this purchase, just as it stands; but there is a way, if I can get your approval, whereby I can make every one of these leaden twenty-dollar pieces worth its face in gold, and perhaps more. Grant me that approval, and I will give part of my gains to your Mr. Richards, whose invulnerable probity[50] you have so justly and so cordially recognized tonight; his share shall be ten thousand dollars, and I will hand him the money tomorrow. [*Great applause from the house.* But the "invulnerable probity" made the Richardses blush prettily; however, it went for modesty, and did no harm.] If you will pass my proposition by a good majority—I would like a two-thirds vote—I will regard that as the town's consent, and that is all I ask. Rarities are always helped by any device which will rouse curiosity and compel remark. Now if I may have your permission to stamp upon the faces of each of these ostensible coins the names of the eighteen gentlemen who—"

Nine-tenths of the audience were on their feet in a moment—dog and all—and the proposition was carried with a whirlwind of approving applause and laughter.

They sat down, and all the Symbols except "Dr." Clay Harkness got up, violently protesting against the proposed outrage, and threatening to—

"I beg you not to threaten me," said the stranger, calmly. "I know my legal rights, and am not accustomed to being frightened at bluster." [*Applause.*] He sat down. "Dr." Harkness saw an opportunity here. He was one of the two very rich men of the place, and Pinkerton was the other. Harkness was proprietor of a

47 dramatic unities—rules established for classical drama.

48 honorarium—fee.

49 numismatics—study and collecting of coins.

50 probity—integrity, honesty.

mint; that is to say, a popular patent medicine. He was running for the legislature on one ticket, and Pinkerton on the other. It was a close race and a hot one, and getting hotter every day. Both had strong appetites for money; each had bought a great tract of land, with a purpose; there was going to be a new railway, and each wanted to be in the legislature and help locate the route to his own advantage; a single vote might make the decision, and with it two or three fortunes. The stake was large, and Harkness was a daring speculator. He was sitting close to the stranger. He leaned over while one or another of the other Symbols was entertaining the house with protests and appeals, and asked, in a whisper.

"What is your price for the sack?"

"Forty thousand dollars."

"I'll give you twenty."

"No."

"Twenty-five"

"No."

"Say thirty."

"The price is forty thousand dollars; not a penny less."

"All right, I'll give it. I will come to the hotel at ten in the morning. I don't want it known: will see you privately."

"Very good." Then the stranger got up and said to the house:

"I find it late. The speeches of these gentlemen are not without merit, not without interest, not without grace; yet if I may be excused I will take my leave. I thank you for the great favor which you have shown me in granting my petition. I ask the Chair to keep the sack for me until tomorrow, and to hand these three five-hundred-dollar notes to Mr. Richards." They were passed up to the Chair. "At nine I will call for the sack, and at eleven will deliver the rest of the ten thousand to Mr. Richards in person, at his home. Good night."

Then he slipped out, and left the audience making a vast noise, which was composed of a mixture of cheers, the "Mikado" song, dog-disapproval, and the chant, "You are f-a-r from being a b-a-a-d man—a-a-a-a-men!"

IV

At home the Richardses had to endure congratulations and compliments until midnight. Then they were left to themselves. They looked a little sad, and they sat silent and thinking. Finally Mary sighed and said,

"Do you think we are to blame, Edward—*much* to blame?" and her eyes wandered to the accusing triplet of big bank-notes lying on the table, where the congratulators had been gloating over them and reverently fingering them. Edward did not answer at once; then he brought out a sigh and said, hesitatingly:

"We—we couldn't help it, Mary. It—well, it was ordered. *All* things are."

Mary glanced up and looked at him steadily, but he didn't return the look. Presently she said:

"I thought congratulations and praises always tasted good. But—it seems to me, now—Edward?"

"Well?"

"Are you going to stay in the bank?"

"N-no."

"Resign?"

"In the morning—by note."

"It does seem best."

Richards bowed his bead in his hands and muttered:

"Before, I was not afraid to let oceans of people's money pour through my hands, but—Mary, I am so tired, so tired—"

"We will go to bed."

At nine in the morning the stranger called for the sack and took it to the hotel in a cab. At ten Harkness had a talk with him privately. The stranger asked for and got five checks on a metropolitan bank—drawn to "Bearer"—four for $1,500 each, and one for $34,000. He put one of the former in his pocketbook, and the remainder, representing $38,500, he put in an envelope, and with these he added a note, which he wrote after Harkness was gone. At eleven he called at the Richards house and knocked. Mrs. Richards peeped through the shutters, then went and received the envelope, and the stranger disappeared without a word. She came back flushed and a little unsteady on her legs, and gasped out:

"I am sure I recognized him!" Last night it seemed to me that maybe I had seen him somewhere before."

"He is the man that brought the sack here?"

"I am almost sure of it."

"Then he is the ostensible Stephenson, too, and sold every important citizen in this town with his bogus secret. Now if he has sent checks instead of money, we are sold, too, after we thought we had escaped. I was beginning to feel fairly comfortable once more, after my night's rest, but the look of that envelope makes me sick. It isn't fat enough; $8,500 in even the largest bank-notes makes more bulk than that."

"Edward, why do you object to checks?"

"Checks signed by Stephenson! I am resigned to take the $8,500 if it could come in bank-notes—for it does seem that it was so ordered, Mary—but I have never had much courage, and I have not the pluck to try to market a check signed with that disastrous name. It would be a trap. That man tried to catch me; we escaped somehow or other; and now he is trying a new way. If it is checks—"

"Oh, Edward, it is *too* bad!" and she held up the checks and began to cry.

"Put them in the fire! quick! we mustn't be tempted. It is a trick to make the world laugh at us, along with the rest, and—Give them to *me*, since you can't do it!" He snatched them and tried to hold his grip till he could get to the stove; but he was human, he was a cashier, and he stopped a moment to make sure of the signature. Then he came near to fainting.

"Fan me, Mary, fan me! They are the same as gold!"

"Oh, how lovely, Edward! Why?"

"Signed by Harkness. What can the mystery of that be, Mary?"

"Edward, do you think"—

"Look here—look at this! Fifteen—fifteen—fifteen—thirty-four. Thirty-eight thousand five hundred! Mary, the sack isn't worth twelve dollars, and Harkness—apparently—has paid about par for it."

"And does it all come to us, do you think—instead of the ten thousand?"

"Why, it looks like it. And the checks are made to 'Bearer,' too."

"Is that good, Edward? What is it for?"

"A hint to collect them at some distant bank, I reckon. Perhaps Harkness doesn't want the matter known. What is that—a note?"

"Yes. It was with the checks."

It was in the "Stephenson" handwriting, but there was no signature. It said:

"I am a disappointed man. Your honesty is beyond the reach of temptation. I had a different idea about it, but I wronged you in that, and I beg pardon, and do it sincerely. I honor you—and that is sincere too. This town is not worthy to kiss the hem of your garment. Dear sir, I made a square bet with myself that there were nineteen debauchable men in your self-righteous community. I have lost. Take the whole pot, you are entitled to it."

Richards drew a deep sigh, and said: "It seems written with fire—it burns so. Mary—I am miserable again."

"I too. Ah, dear, I wish—"

"To think, Mary—he *believes* in me."

"Oh, don't, Edward—I can't bear it."

"If those beautiful words were deserved, Mary—and God knows I believed I deserved them once—I think I could give the forty thousand dollars for them. And I would put that paper away, as representing more than gold and jewels, and keep it always. But now— We could not live in the shadow of its accusing presence, Mary."

He put it in the fire.

A messenger arrived and delivered an envelope.

Richards took from it a note and read it; it was from Burgess.

"You saved me, in a difficult time. I saved you last night. It was at cost of a lie, but I made the sacrifice freely, and out of a grateful heart. None in this village knows so well as I know how brave and good and noble you are. At bottom you cannot respect me, knowing as you do of that matter of which I am accused, and by the general voice condemned; but I beg that you will at least believe that I am a grateful man; it will help me to bear my burden."

[*Signed*] BURGESS

"Saved, once more. And on such terms!" He put the note in the fire.

"I—I wish I were dead, Mary, I wish I were out of it all."

"Oh, these are bitter, bitter days, Edward. The stabs, through their very generosity, are so deep—and they come so fast!"

Three days before the election each of two thousand voters suddenly found himself in possession of a prized memento—one of the renowned bogus double-eagles.[51] Around one of its faces was stamped these words: "THE REMARK I MADE TO THE POOR STRANGER WAS—" Around the other face was stamped these: "GO, AND REFORM. [SIGNED] PINKERTON." Thus the entire remaining refuse of the

[51] double-eagles—nickname for U.S. twenty-dollar coins.

renowned joke was emptied upon a single head, and with calamitous effect. It revived the recent vast laugh and concentrated it upon Pinkerton; and Harkness's election was a walkover.

Within twenty-four hours after the Richardses had received their checks their consciences were quieting down, discouraged; the old couple were learning to reconcile themselves to the sin which they had committed. But they were to learn, now, that a sin takes on new and real terrors when there seems a chance that it is going to be found out. This gives it a fresh and most substantial and important aspect. At church the morning sermon was of the usual pattern; it was the same old things said in the same old way; they had heard them a thousand times and found them **innocuous**,[52] next to meaningless, and easy to sleep under; but now it was different: the sermon seemed to bristle with accusations; it seemed aimed straight and specially at people who were concealing deadly sins. After church they got away from the mob of congratulators as soon as they could, and hurried homeward, chilled to the bone at they did not know what—vague, shadowy, indefinite fears. And by chance they caught a glimpse of Mr. Burgess as he turned a corner. He paid no attention to their nod of recognition! He hadn't seen it; but they did not know that. What could his conduct mean? It might mean—it might mean—oh, a dozen dreadful things. Was it possible that he knew that Richards could have cleared him of guilt in that bygone time, and had been silently waiting for a chance to even up accounts? At home, in their distress they got to imagining that their servant might have been in the next room listening when Richards revealed the secret to his wife that he knew of Burgess's innocence; next Richards began to imagine that he had heard the swish of a gown in there at that time; next, he was sure he *had* heard it. They would call Sarah in, on a pretext, and watch her face: if she had been betraying them to Mr. Burgess, it would show in her manner. They asked her some questions—questions which were so random and incoherent and seemingly purposeless that the girl felt sure that the old people's minds had been affected by their sudden good fortune; the sharp and watchful gaze which they bent upon her frightened her, and that completed the business. She blushed, she became nervous and confused, and to the old people these were plain signs of guilt—guilt of some fearful sort or other—without doubt she was a spy and a traitor. When they were alone again they began to piece many unrelated things together and get horrible results out of the combination. When things had got about to the worst, Richards was delivered of a sudden gasp, and his wife asked:

"Oh, what is it?—what is it?"

"The note—Burgess's note! Its language was sarcastic, I see it now." He quoted: "'At bottom you cannot respect me, *knowing*, as you do, of *that matter* of which I am accused'—oh it is perfectly

[52] **innocuous**—harmless.

plain, now, God help me! He knows that I know! You see the ingenuity of the phrasing. It was a trap—and like a fool, I walked into it. And Mary—?"

"Oh, it is dreadful—I know what you are going to say—he didn't return your transcript of the pretended test-remark."

"No—kept it to destroy us with. Mary, he has exposed us to some already. I know it—I know it well. I saw it in a dozen faces after church. Ah, he wouldn't answer our nod of recognition—*he* knew what he had been doing!"

In the night the doctor was called. The news went around in the morning that the old couple were rather seriously ill—prostrated by the exhausting excitement growing out of their great windfall, the congratulations, and the late hours, the doctor said. The town was sincerely distressed; for these old people were about all it had left to be proud of, now.

Two days later the news was worse. The old couple were delirious, and were doing strange things. By witness of the nurses, Richards had exhibited checks—for $8,500? No—for an amazing sum—$38,500! What could be the explanation of this gigantic piece of luck?

The following day the nurses had more news—and wonderful. They had concluded to hide the checks, lest harm come to them; but when they searched they were gone from under the patient's pillow—vanished away. The patient said:

"Let the pillow alone; what do you want?"

"We thought it best that the checks—"

"You will never see them again—they are destroyed. They came from Satan. I saw the hell-brand on them, and I knew they were sent to betray me to sin." Then he fell to gabbling strange and dreadful things which were not clearly understandable, and which the doctor admonished them to keep to themselves.

Richards was right; the checks were never seen again.

A nurse must have talked in her sleep, for within two days the forbidden gabblings were the property of the town; and they were of a surprising sort. They seemed to indicate that Richards had been a claimant for the sack himself, and that Burgess had concealed that fact and then maliciously betrayed it.

Burgess was taxed with this and stoutly denied it. And he said it was not fair to attach weight to the chatter of a sick old man who was out of his mind. Still, suspicion was in the air, and there was much talk.

After a day or two it was reported that Mrs. Richards's delirious deliveries were getting to be duplicates of her husband's. Suspicion flamed up into conviction, now, and the town's pride in the purity of its one undiscredited important citizen began to dim down and flicker toward extinction.

Six days passed, then came more news. The old couple were dying. Richards's mind cleared in his latest hour, and he sent for Burgess. Burgess said:

"Let the room be cleared, I think he wishes to say something in privacy."

"No!" said Richards: "I want witnesses. I want you all to hear my confession, so that I may die a man, and not a dog. I was clean—artifically—like the rest; and like the rest I fell when temptation came. I signed a lie, and claimed the miserable sack. Mr. Burgess remembered that I had done him a service, and in gratitude (and ignorance) he suppressed my claim and saved me. You know the thing that was charged against Burgess years ago. My testimony, and mine alone, could have cleared him, and I was a coward, and left him to suffer disgrace—"

"No—no—Mr. Richards, you—"

"My servant betrayed my secret to him—"

"No one has betrayed anything to me—"

—"and then he did a natural and justifiable thing, he repented of the saving kindness which he had done me, and he *exposed* me—as I deserved—"

"Never!—I make oath—"

"Out of my heart I forgive him."

Burgess's impassioned protestations fell upon deaf ears; the dying man passed away without knowing that once more he had done poor Burgess a wrong. The old wife died that night.

The last of the sacred Nineteen had fallen a prey to the fiendish sack; the town was stripped of the last rag of its ancient glory. Its mourning was not showy, but it was deep.

By act of the Legislature—upon prayer and petition—Hadleyburg was allowed to change its name to (never mind what—I will not give it away), and leave one word out of the motto that for many generations had graced the town's official seal.

It is an honest town once more, and the man will have to rise early that catches it napping again.

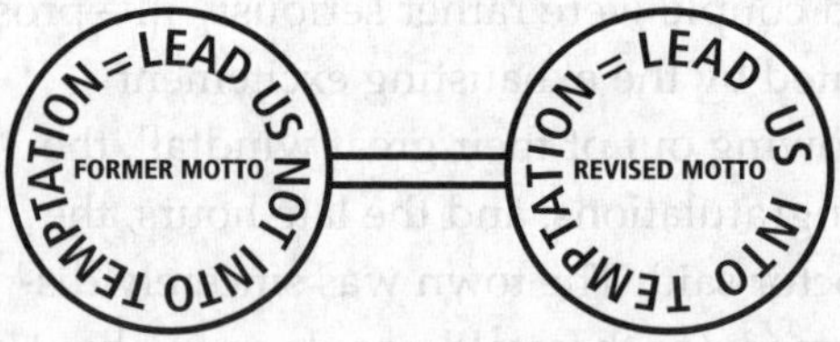

QUESTIONS TO CONSIDER

1. What sort of people are the Richardses? What is their motivation in trying to get the money?
2. Why is Hadleyburg's reputation for honesty artificial?
3. What is the tone of this story? What do you think was Twain's opinion of small-town America?
4. From reading "The Man That Corrupted Hadleyburg," how would you describe Mark Twain's view of mankind?

Writers at Home

The places in which writers live and work often suggest a great deal about how they view themselves and what they do. Sometimes, of course, such surroundings merely indicate what they can afford. The following images show the homes and working spaces of a number of American writers.

▲
Washington Irving's taste for a picturesque past is reflected in his home, Sunnyside, an old stone cottage on the Hudson River.

▲
In July 1842, newlyweds Nathaniel and Sophia Hawthorne moved into the Old Manse in Concord, Massachusetts, where he enjoyed the happiest years of his life.

The poverty and obscurity of Edgar Allan Poe's final years are reflected in the little cottage where he lived at Fordham, New York. ▶

Mark Twain immortalized his boyhood home in Hannibal, Missouri, through his fiction.

▲
Mark Twain did much of his reading and writing in the billiard room at his home in Hartford, Connecticut.

This is the library at Lamb House, Henry James's home in England from 1898 until his death in 1916. ▶

Stephen Crane, shown here at his desk, lived the last year of his short life in a medieval manor house in England, where he entertained a constant stream of guests. ▶

▲
Willa Cather shown here at her desk around 1900.

▲
In the 1930s, Dorothy Parker (shown here in her California home) moved from New York to Hollywood, where she worked as a screenwriter.

▲
One of Ernest Hemingway's several homes was this one in Key West, Florida.

Hemingway is shown working at his desk in his Key West home. ▶

Richard Wright is shown here at work in his home. ►

Except for a brief period spent in Hollywood as a screenwriter, William Faulkner (whose home is shown here) lived all his life in Oxford, Mississippi. ▼

▲
Suffering from lupus, Flannery O'Connor lived the last years of her life on her family's farm in Georgia.

▲
Isaac Bashevis Singer is shown at his desk.

Julia Alvarez periodically returns to the Dominican Republic, where she grew up.

▲
Louise Erdrich is shown in the kitchen of her home with her late husband, Michael Dorris, and their children.

Everywhere
BLUE VALLEY BUTTER is good butter
Pasteurized
VICTOR TYPEWRITER COMPANY

Part Two

The Birth of the Modern

Modernism in American literature developed at the end of the 1800s during a period of enormous change in the United States, which was evolving into an urban, industrialized society with a cosmopolitan culture.

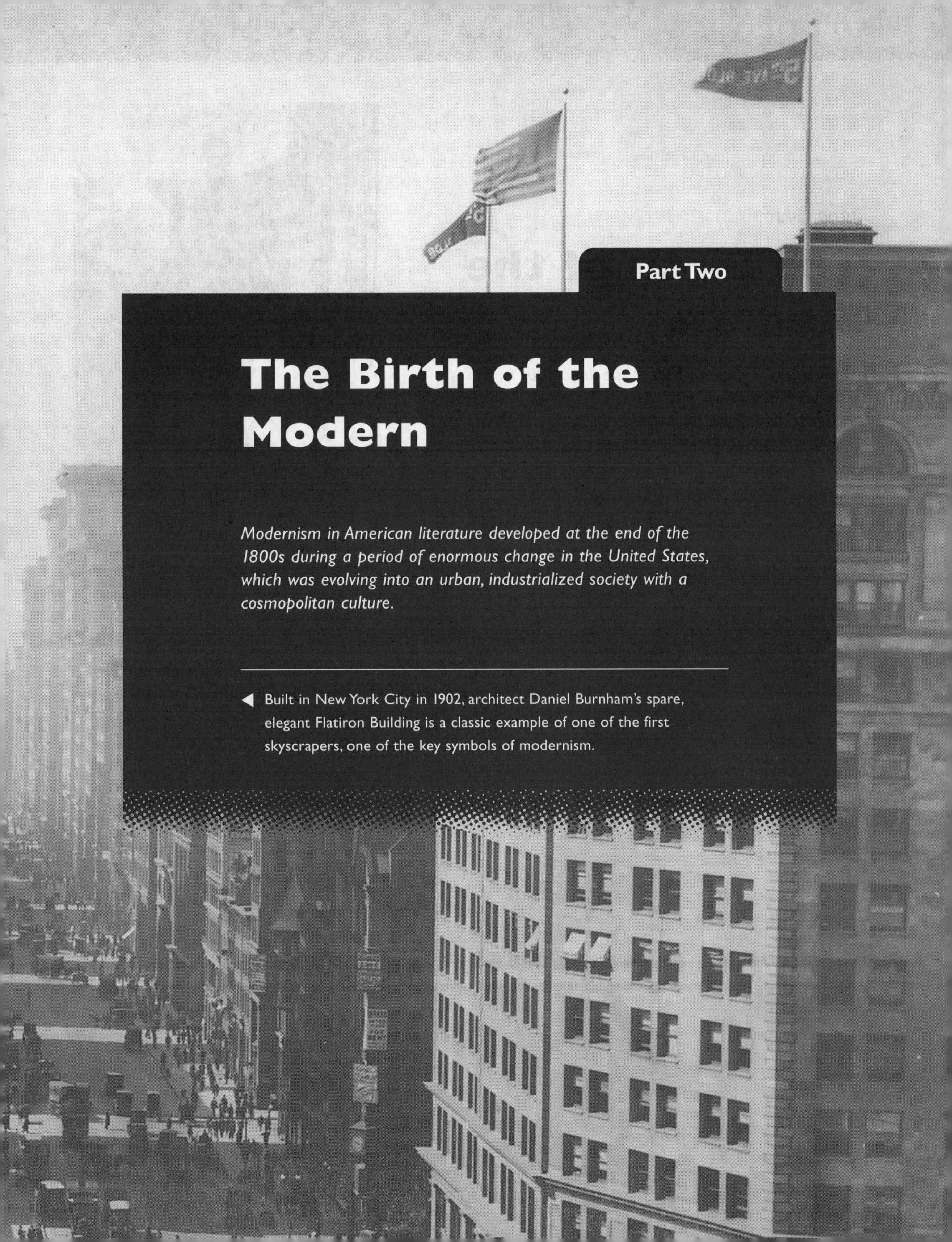

◀ Built in New York City in 1902, architect Daniel Burnham's spare, elegant Flatiron Building is a classic example of one of the first skyscrapers, one of the key symbols of modernism.

1900–1940

The Birth of the Modern

Modernism *First appearing in the late 1880s in the works of Henry James, modernism in American literature emerged fully following World War I in such writers as Sherwood Anderson, Ernest Hemingway, and F. Scott Fitzgerald.*

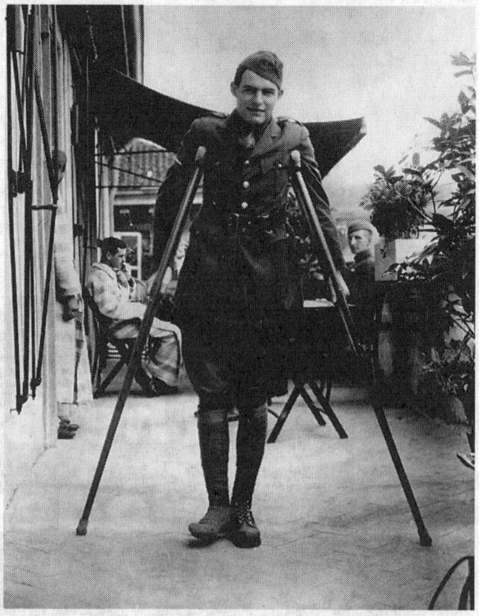

▲ Wounded in World War I, Ernest Hemingway produced sparely written accounts of the "lost generation," disillusioned with wartime idealism, that became modern American classics.

◀ The degree of psychological awareness in the mature works of Henry James, beginning with *The Portrait of a Lady* (1881), marks them as the first masterpieces of modernism in American literature.

1900 — Decade of peak immigration begins.

Wright brothers fly the first airplane.

1905 — San Francisco earthquake.

NAACP founded.

1910

Titanic sinks on its maiden voyage.

World War I begins.

1915

U.S. enters World War I.

World War I ends.

◀ The simple, straightforward language employed by Sherwood Anderson in *Winesburg, Ohio* (1919) was a new departure in modern American realism.

F. Scott Fitzgerald recorded in his modernist fictions the lives of the flappers, liberated young women of the 1920s. ▼

- Anderson's *Winesburg, Ohio* published.
- **1920** — Prohibition begins; Panama Canal opens; women get right to vote.
- **1925** — *The New Yorker* established; *The Great Gatsby* published; Scopes trial held.
- Hemingway's *The Sun Also Rises* published.
- Lindbergh makes first solo flight across Atlantic.
- Stock market crashes.
- **1930**
- FDR elected.

- Prohibition repealed.
- **1935**
- Jesse Owens wins four gold medals at Berlin Olympics.

- World War II begins; Steinbeck's *The Grapes of Wrath* published.
- **1940**

Henry James ▶

The Middle Years

BY HENRY JAMES

Henry James (1843–1916) is a writer who sits uneasily between the cultures of the United States and England. Born in New York, he spent parts of his youth on both sides of the Atlantic, and in the 1870s he settled permanently in England. Much of James's early fiction deals with the impact of Europe on Americans, of an ancient culture on a young country. As James wrote in a letter, "It's a complex fate, being an American, and one of the responsibilities it entails is fighting against a superstitious valuation of Europe." From the 1860s, James was a regular contributor of stories and criticism to the magazines of England and America. His first novel was published in 1871, but he really came into his own with the publication of Portrait of a Lady *in 1881. In many ways, James can be viewed as the first modern novelist. He was a dedicated realist, presenting the people and the world around him, but using his superior critical faculties to shape stories that examine the subtleties of human motivation and emotion. James's admonition to would-be writers perfectly describes his method: "Try to be one of the people on whom nothing is lost." In the 1890s, James's fiction grew more complex, as he developed a style that can be viewed, depending on taste, as overwritten or beautiful. What he did not find was success. His works were less and less successful, and his depression over their failure drove him to work harder, but also to a lonely, despairing view of the artist. "The Middle Years" is a perfect example of the despairing James with the hero vainly trying to overcome his mortal life for immortal art. As he wrote to H. G. Wells in 1915, "It is art that makes life, makes interest, makes importance, for our consideration and application of these things, and I know of no substitute whatever for the force and beauty of its process." James is certainly one of the most acute and persuasive novelists who ever wrote: he requires great efforts from his readers, but realism reaches no greater heights. He was one of the first exponents of what became known as modernism. In his wake first followed writers like Edith Wharton and Willa Cather, and then the great generation of American modernists, including Sherwood Anderson, Ernest Hemingway, F. Scott Fitzgerald, Thomas Wolfe, and William Faulkner.*

The April day was soft and bright, and poor Dencombe, happy in the conceit[1] of reasserted strength, stood in the garden of the hotel, comparing, with a deliberation in which, however, there was still something of **languor,**[2] the attractions of easy strolls. He liked the feeling of the south, so far as you could have it in the north, he liked the sandy cliffs and the clustered pines, he liked even the colorless sea. "Bournemouth[3] as a health-resort" had sounded like a mere

[1] conceit—opinion.

[2] **languor**—dreamy, lazy mood.

[3] Bournemouth—city on the coast of southern England.

advertisement, but now he was reconciled to the **prosaic**.[4] The sociable country postman, passing through the garden, had just given him a small parcel, which he took out with him, leaving the hotel to the right and creeping to a convenient bench that he knew of, a safe recess in the cliff. It looked to the south, to the tinted walls of the Island,[5] and was protected behind by the sloping shoulder of the down.[6] He was tired enough when he reached it, and for a moment he was disappointed; he was better, of course, but better, after all, than what? He should never again, as at one or two great moments of the past, be better than himself. The infinite of life had gone, and what was left of the dose was a small glass engraved like a thermometer by the apothecary.[7] He sat and stared at the sea, which appeared all surface and twinkle, far shallower than the spirit of man. It was the abyss of human illusion that was the real, the tideless deep. He held his packet, which had come by book-post, unopened on his knee, liking, in the lapse of so many joys (his illness had made him feel his age), to know that it was there, but taking for granted there could be no complete renewal of the pleasure, dear to young experience, of seeing one's self "just out." Dencombe, who had a reputation, had come out too often and knew too well in advance how he should look.

His postponement associated itself vaguely, after a little, with a group of three persons, two ladies and a young man, whom, beneath him, straggling and seemingly silent, he could see move slowly together along the sands. The gentleman had his head bent over a book and was occasionally brought to a stop by the charm of this volume, which, as Dencombe could perceive even at a distance, had a cover alluringly red. Then his companions, going a little further, waited for him to come up, poking their parasols into the beach, looking around them at the sea and sky and clearly sensible of the beauty of the day. To these things the young man with the book was still more clearly indifferent; lingering, **credulous**,[8] absorbed, he was an object of envy to an observer from whose connection with literature all such artlessness had faded. One of the ladies was large and mature; the other had the spareness of comparative youth and of a social situation possibly inferior. The large lady carried back Dencombe's imagination to the age of crinoline;[9] she wore a hat of the shape of a mushroom, decorated with a blue veil, and had the air, in her aggressive **amplitude**,[10] of clinging to a vanished fashion or even a lost cause. Presently her companion produced from under the folds of a mantle a limp, portable chair which she stiffened out and of which the large lady took possession. This act, and something in the movement of either party, instantly characterized the performers—

[4] **prosaic**—dull.

[5] Island—reference to the Isle of Wight, just off the coast of England.

[6] down—upland.

[7] apothecary—druggist.

[8] **credulous**—inclined to believe too easily.

[9] crinoline—stiff cloth used as a lining to make a skirt stick out. James is referring to the fashions of about twenty years earlier.

[10] **amplitude**—largeness.

they performed for Dencombe's recreation—as **opulent**[11] matron and humble dependant. What, moreover, was the use of being an approved novelist if one couldn't establish a relation between such figures; the clever theory, for instance, that the young man was the son of the opulent matron, and that the humble dependant, the daughter of a clergyman or an officer, nourished a secret passion for him? Was that not visible from the way she stole behind her protectress to look back at him?—back to where he had let himself come to a full stop when his mother sat down to rest. His book was a novel; it had the catchpenny[12] cover, and while the romance of life stood neglected at his side he lost himself in that of the circulating library. He moved mechanically to where the sand was softer, and ended by plumping down in it to finish his chapter at his ease. The humble dependant, discouraged by his remoteness, wandered, with a martyred droop of the head, in another direction, and the exorbitant[13] lady, watching the waves, offered a confused resemblance to a flying-machine that had broken down.

When his drama began to fail Dencombe remembered that he had, after all, another pastime. Though such promptitude on the part of the publisher was rare, he was already able to draw from its wrapper his "latest," perhaps his last. The cover of "The Middle Years" was duly meretricious,[14] the smell of the fresh pages the very odor of sanctity; but for the moment he went no further—he had become conscious of a strange alienation. He had forgotten what his book was about. Had the assault of his old ailment, which he had so fallaciously[15] come to Bournemouth to ward off, interposed utter blankness as to what had preceded it? He had finished the revision of proof before quitting London, but his subsequent fortnight[16] in bed had passed the sponge over color.[17] He couldn't have chanted to himself a single sentence, couldn't have turned with curiosity or confidence to any particular page. His subject had already gone from him, leaving scarcely a superstition behind. He uttered a low moan as he breathed the chill of this dark void, so desperately it seemed to represent the completion of a sinister process. The tears filled his mild eyes; something precious had passed away. This was the pang that had been sharpest during the last few years—the sense of ebbing time, of shrinking opportunity; and now he felt not so much that his last chance was going as that it was gone indeed. He had done all that he should ever do, and yet he had not done what he wanted. This was the **laceration**[18]—that practically his career was over: it was as violent as a rough hand at his throat. He rose from his seat nervously, like a creature hunted by a dread; then he fell back in his weakness and nervously opened his book.

---

[11] **opulent**—wealthy.
[12] catchpenny—cheap, colorful.
[13] exorbitant—excessive, extreme.
[14] meretricious—attracting attention in a vulgar manner.
[15] fallaciously—deceptively.
[16] fortnight—two weeks.
[17] sponge over color—reference to painters' practice of lightening colors.
[18] **laceration**—wound, cut.

It was a single volume; he preferred single volumes and aimed at a rare compression. He began to read, and little by little, in this occupation, he was pacified and reassured. Everything came back to him, but came back with a wonder, came back, above all, with a high and magnificent beauty. He read his own prose, he turned his own leaves, and had, as he sat there with the spring sunshine on the page, an emotion peculiar and intense. His career was over, no doubt, but it was over, after all, with *that*.

He had forgotten during his illness the work of the previous year; but what he had chiefly forgotten was that it was extraordinarily good. He lived once more into his story and was drawn down, as by a siren's[19] hand, to where, in the dim underworld of fiction, the great glazed tank[20] of art, strange silent subjects float. He recognized his motive and surrendered to his talent. Never, probably, had that talent, such as it was, been so fine. His difficulties were still there, but what was also there, to his perception, though probably, alas! to nobody's else, was the art that in most cases had surmounted them. In his surprised enjoyment of this ability he had a glimpse of a possible reprieve.[21] Surely its force was not spent—there was life and service in it yet. It had not come to him easily, it had been backward and roundabout. It was the child of time, the nursling of delay; he had struggled and suffered for it, making sacrifices not to be counted, and now that it was really mature was it to cease to yield, to confess itself brutally beaten? There was an infinite charm for Dencombe in feeling as he had never felt before that diligence *vincit omnia*.[22] The result produced in his little book was somehow a result beyond his conscious intention: it was as if he had planted his genius, had trusted his method, and they had grown up and flowered with this sweetness. If the achievement had been real, however, the process had been manful enough. What he saw so intensely today, what he felt as a nail driven in, was that only now, at the very last, had he come into possession. His development had been abnormally slow, almost grotesquely gradual. He had been hindered and retarded by experience, and for long periods had only groped[23] his way. It had taken too much of his life to produce too little of his art. The art had come, but it had come after everything else. At such a rate a first existence was too short—long enough only to collect material; so that to fructify, to use the material, one must have a second age, an extension. This extension was what poor Dencombe sighed for. As he turned the last leaves of his volume he murmured: "Ah for another go!—ah for a better chance!"

His development had been abnormally slow, almost grotesquely gradual.

[19] siren's—reference to one of a group of sea nymphs in Greek mythology whose sweet singing lured mariners to destruction on the rocks around their island.

[20] glazed tank—aquarium.

[21] reprieve—temporary relief.

[22] *vincit omnia*—Latin for "conquers all."

[23] groped—reached uncertainly.

The three persons he had observed on the sands had vanished and then reappeared; they had now wandered up a path, an artificial and easy ascent, which led to the top of the cliff. Dencombe's bench was half-way down, on a sheltered ledge, and the large lady, a massive, heterogeneous[24] person, with bold black eyes and kind red cheeks, now took a few moments to rest. She wore dirty gauntlets[25] and immense diamond ear-rings; at first she looked vulgar, but she contradicted this announcement in an agreeable off-hand tone. While her companions stood waiting for her she spread her skirts on the end of Dencombe's seat. The young man had gold spectacles, through which, with his finger still in his red-covered book, he glanced at the volume, bound in the same shade of the same color, lying on the lap of the original occupant of the bench. After an instant Dencombe understood that he was struck with a resemblance, had recognized the gilt stamp on the crimson cloth, was reading "The Middle Years," and now perceived that somebody else had kept pace with him. The stranger was startled, possibly even a little ruffled, to find that he was not the only person who had been favoured with an early copy. The eyes of the two proprietors met for a moment, and Dencombe borrowed amusement from the expression of those of his competitor, those, it might even be inferred, of his admirer. They confessed to some resentment—they seemed to say: "Hang it, has he got it *already?*—Of course he's a brute of a reviewer!" Dencombe shuffled his copy out of sight while the opulent matron, rising from her repose, broke out: "I feel already the good of this air!"

"I can't say I do," said the angular lady. "I find myself quite let down."

"I find myself horribly hungry. At what time did you order lunch?" her protectress pursued.

The young person put the question by. "Doctor Hugh always orders it."

"I ordered nothing today—I'm going to make you diet," said their comrade.

"Then I shall go home and sleep. *Qui dort dine!*"[26]

"Can I trust you to Miss Vernham?" asked Doctor Hugh of his elder companion.

"Don't I trust *you?*" she archly inquired.

"Not too much!" Miss Vernham, with her eyes on the ground, permitted herself to declare. "You must come with us at least to the house," she went on, while the personage on whom they appeared to be in attendance began to mount higher. She had got a little out of ear-shot; nevertheless Miss Vernham became, so far as Dencombe was concerned, less distinctly audible to murmur to the young man: "I don't think you realize all you owe the Countess!"

Absently, a moment, Doctor Hugh caused his gold-rimmed spectacles to shine at her.

"Is that the way I strike you? I see—I see!"

"She's awfully good to us," continued Miss Vernham, compelled by her interlocutor's immovability to stand there in spite of his discussion of private matters. Of

[24] heterogeneous—completely different; incongruous.

[25] gauntlets—gloves.

[26] *Qui dort dine*—"Who sleeps, dines," a French proverb.

what use would it have been that Dencombe should be sensitive to shades had he not declared in that immovability a strange influence from the quiet old **convalescent**[27] in the great tweed cape? Miss Vernham appeared suddenly to become aware of some such connection, for she added in a moment: "If you want to sun yourself here you can come back after you've seen us home."

Doctor Hugh, at this, hesitated, and Dencombe, in spite of a desire to pass for unconscious, risked a covert glance at him. What his eyes met this time, as it happened, was on the part of the young lady a queer stare, naturally vitreous,[28] which made her aspect remind him of some figure (he couldn't name it) in a play or a novel, some sinister governess or tragic old maid. She seemed to scrutinize him, to challenge him, to say, from general spite: "What have you got to do with us?" At the same instant the rich humor of the Countess reached them from above: "Come, come, my little lambs, you should follow your old *bergère*!"[29] Miss Vernham turned away at this, pursuing the ascent, and Doctor Hugh, after another mute appeal to Dencombe and a moment's evident demur, deposited his book on the bench, as if to keep his place or even as a sign that he would return, and bounded without difficulty up the rougher part of the cliff.

Equally innocent and infinite are the pleasures of observation and the resources engendered by the habit of analyzing life. It amused poor Dencombe, as he dawdled in his **tepid**[30] air-bath, to think that he was waiting for a revelation of something at the back of a fine young mind. He looked hard at the book on the end of the bench, but he wouldn't have touched it for the world. It served his purpose to have a theory which should not be exposed to refutation. He already felt better of his melancholy; he had, according to his old formula, put his head at the window. A passing Countess could draw off the fancy when, like the elder of the ladies who had just retreated, she was as obvious as the giantess of a caravan.[31] It was indeed general views that were terrible; short ones, contrary to an opinion sometimes expressed, were the refuge, were the remedy. Doctor Hugh couldn't possibly be anything but a reviewer who had understandings for early copies with publishers or with newspapers. He reappeared in a quarter of an hour, with visible relief at finding Dencombe on the spot, and the gleam of white teeth in an embarrassed but generous smile. He was perceptibly disappointed at the eclipse of the other copy of the book; it was a pretext the less for speaking to the stranger. But he spoke notwithstanding; he held up his own copy and broke out pleadingly:

Equally innocent and infinite are the pleasures of observation and the resources engendered by the habit of analyzing life.

[27] **convalescent**—person who is recovering from an illness.

[28] vitreous—resembling glass.

[29] *bergère*—French for "shepherdess."

[30] **tepid**—moderately warm; lukewarm.

[31] giantess of a caravan—circus freak.

"*Do* say, if you have occasion to speak of it, that it's the best thing he has done yet!"

Dencombe responded with a laugh: "Done yet" was so amusing to him, made such a grand avenue of the future. Better still, the young man took him for a reviewer. He pulled out "The Middle Years" from under his cape, but instinctively concealed any tell-tale look of fatherhood. This was partly because a person was always a fool for calling attention to his work. "Is that what you're going to say yourself?" he inquired of his visitor.

"I'm not quite sure I shall write anything. I don't, as a regular thing—I enjoy in peace. But it's awfully fine."

Dencombe debated a moment. If his interlocutor had begun to abuse him he would have confessed on the spot to his identity, but there was no harm in drawing him on a little to praise. He drew him on with such success that in a few moments his new acquaintance, seated by his side, was confessing candidly that Dencombe's novels were the only ones he could read a second time. He had come the day before from London, where a friend of his, a journalist, had lent him his copy of the last—the copy sent to the office of the journal and already the subject of a "notice" which, as was pretended there (but one had to allow for "swagger") it had taken a full quarter of an hour to prepare. He intimated that he was ashamed for his friend, and in the case of a work demanding and repaying study, of such inferior manners; and, with his fresh appreciation and inexplicable wish to express it, he speedily became for poor Dencombe a remarkable, a delightful apparition. Chance had brought the weary man of letters face to face with the greatest admirer in the new generation whom it was supposable he possessed. The admirer, in truth, was mystifying, so rare a case was it to find a bristling young doctor—he looked like a German physiologist—enamored of literary form. It was an accident, but happier than most accidents, so that Dencombe, exhilarated as well as confounded, spent half an hour in making his visitor talk while he kept himself quiet. He explained his premature possession of "The Middle Years" by an allusion to the friendship of the publisher, who, knowing he was at Bournemouth for his health, had paid him this graceful attention. He admitted that he had been ill, for Doctor Hugh would infallibly have guessed it; he even went so far as to wonder whether he mightn't look for some hygenic "tip" from a personage combining so bright an enthusiasm with a presumable knowledge of the remedies now in vogue.[32] It would shake his faith a little perhaps to have to take a doctor seriously who could take him so seriously, but he enjoyed this gushing modern youth and he felt with an acute pang that there would still be work to do in a world in which such odd combinations were presented. It was not true, what he had tried for renunciation's sake to believe, that all the combinations were exhausted. They were not, they were not—they were infinite: the exhaustion was in the miserable artist.

Doctor Hugh was an ardent physiologist, saturated with the spirit of the age—in

[32] vogue—fashion.

other words he had just taken his degree; but he was independent and various, he talked like a man who would have preferred to love literature best. He would fain[33] have made fine phrases, but nature had denied him the trick. Some of the finest in "The Middle Years" had struck him inordinately, and he took the liberty of reading them to Dencombe in support of his plea. He grew vivid, in the balmy air, to his companion, for whose deep refreshment he seemed to have been sent; and was particularly ingenuous in describing how recently he had become acquainted, and how instantly infatuated, with the only man who had put flesh between the ribs of an art that was starving on superstitions. He had not yet written to him—he was deterred by a sentiment of respect. Dencombe at this moment **felicitated**[34] himself more than ever on having never answered the photographers. His visitor's attitude promised him a luxury of intercourse, but he surmised that a certain security in it, for Doctor Hugh, would depend not a little on the Countess. He learned without delay with what variety of Countess they were concerned, as well as the nature of the tie that united the curious trio. The large lady, an Englishwoman by birth and the daughter of a celebrated baritone, whose taste, without his talent, she had inherited, was the widow of a French nobleman and mistress of all that remained of the handsome fortune, the fruit of her father's earnings, that had constituted her dower.[35] Miss Vernham, an odd creature but an accomplished pianist, was attached to her person at a salary. The Countess was generous, independent, eccentric; she traveled with her minstrel[36] and her medical man. Ignorant and passionate, she had nevertheless moments in which she was almost irresistible. Dencombe saw her sit for her portrait in Doctor Hugh's free sketch, and felt the picture of his young friend's relation to her frame itself in his mind. This young friend, for a representative of the new psychology, was himself easily hypnotized, and if he became abnormally communicative it was only a sign of his real subjection. Dencombe did accordingly what he wanted with him, even without being known as Dencombe.

Taken ill on a journey in Switzerland the Countess had picked him up at an hotel, and the accident of his happening to please her had made her offer him, with her imperious liberality,[37] terms that couldn't fail to dazzle a practitioner without patients and whose resources had been drained dry by his studies. It was not the way he would have elected to spend his time, but it was time that would pass quickly, and meanwhile she was wonderfully kind. She exacted **perpetual**[38] attention, but it was impossible not to like her. He gave details about his queer patient, a "type" if there ever was one, who had in connection with her flushed obesity and in addition to the morbid

[33] fain—happily.

[34] **felicitated**—congratulated.

[35] dower—dowry; money or property brought to a marriage by a woman.

[36] minstrel—musician.

[37] imperious liberality—domineering generosity.

[38] **perpetual**—continual, constant.

strain of a violent and aimless will a grave organic disorder; but he came back to his loved novelist, whom he was so good as to pronounce more essentially a poet than many of those who went in for verse, with a zeal excited, as all his indiscretion had been excited, by the happy chance of Dencombe's sympathy and the coincidence of their occupation. Dencombe had confessed to a slight personal acquaintance with the author of "The Middle Years," but had not felt himself as ready as he could have wished when his companion, who had never yet encountered a being so privileged, began to be eager for particulars. He even thought that Doctor Hugh's eye at that moment emitted a glimmer of suspicion. But the young man was too inflamed to be shrewd and repeatedly caught up the book to exclaim: "Did you notice this?" or "Weren't you immensely struck with that?" "There's a beautiful passage toward the end," he broke out; and again he laid his hand upon the volume. As he turned the pages he came upon something else, while Dencombe saw him suddenly change color. He had taken up, as it lay on the bench, Dencombe's copy instead of his own, and his neighbor immediately guessed the reason of his start. Doctor Hugh looked grave an instant; then he said: "I see you've been altering the text!" Dencombe was a passionate corrector, a fingerer of style; the last thing he ever arrived at was a form final for himself. His ideal would have been to publish secretly, and then, on the published text, treat himself to the terrified revise, sacrificing always a first edition and beginning for posterity and even for the collectors, poor dears, with a second. This morning, in "The Middle Years," his pencil had pricked a dozen lights.[39] He was amused at the effect of the young man's reproach; for an instant it made him change color. He **stammered**,[40] at any rate, **ambiguously**;[41] then, through a blur of ebbing consciousness, saw Doctor Hugh's mystified eyes. He only had time to feel he was about to be ill again—that emotion, excitement, fatigue, the heat of the sun, the solicitation of the air, had combined to play him a trick, before, stretching out a hand to his visitor with a plaintive cry, he lost his senses altogether.

Later he knew that he had fainted and that Doctor Hugh had got him home in a bath-chair, the conductor of which, prowling within hail for custom, had happened to remember seeing him in the garden of the hotel. He had recovered his perception in the transit, and had, in bed, that afternoon, a vague recollection of Doctor Hugh's young face, as they went together, bent over him in a comforting laugh and expressive of something more than a suspicion of his identity. That identity was ineffaceable now, and all the more that he was disappointed, disgusted. He had been rash, been stupid, had gone out too soon, stayed out too long. He oughtn't to have exposed himself to strangers, he ought to have taken his servant. He felt as if he had fallen into a hole too deep to descry any little patch of heaven. He was confused

[39] pricked a dozen lights—made a dozen marks.

[40] **stammered**—spoke with involuntary phrases or repetitions.

[41] **ambiguously**—uncertainly.

about the time that had elapsed—he pieced the fragments together. He had seen his doctor, the real one, the one who had treated him from the first and who had again been very kind. His servant was in and out on tiptoe, looking very wise after the fact. He said more than once something about the sharp young gentleman. The rest was vagueness, in so far as it wasn't despair. The vagueness, however, justified itself by dreams, dozing anxieties from which he finally emerged to the consciousness of a dark room and a shaded candle.

"You'll be all right again—I know all about you now," said a voice near him that he knew to be young. Then his meeting with Doctor Hugh came back. He was too discouraged to joke about it yet, but he was able to perceive, after a little, that the interest of it was intense for his visitor. "Of course I can't attend you professionally—you've got your own man, with whom I've talked and who's excellent," Doctor Hugh went on. "But you must let me come to see you as a good friend. I've just looked in before going to bed. You're doing beautifully, but it's a good job I was with you on the cliff. I shall come in early tomorrow. I want to do something for you. I want to do everything. You've done a tremendous lot for me." The young man held his hand, hanging over him, and poor Dencombe, weakly aware of this living pressure, simply lay there and accepted his devotion. He couldn't do anything less—he needed help too much.

The idea of the help he needed was very present to him that night, which he spent in a lucid stillness, an intensity of thought that constituted a reaction from his hours of **stupor**.[42] He was lost, he was lost—he was lost if he couldn't be saved. He was not afraid of suffering, of death; he was not even in love with life; but he had had a deep demonstration of desire. It came over him in the long, quiet hours that only with "The Middle Years" had he taken his flight; only on that day, visited by soundless processions, had he recognized his kingdom. He had had a revelation of his range. What he dreaded was the idea that his reputation should stand on the unfinished. It was not with his past but with his future that it should properly be concerned. Illness and age rose before him like specters with pitiless eyes: how was he to bribe such fates to give him the second chance? He had had the one chance that all men have—he had had the chance of life. He went to sleep again very late, and when he awoke Doctor Hugh was sitting by his head. There was already, by this time, something beautifully familiar in him.

"Don't think I've turned out your physician," he said; "I'm acting with his consent. He has been here and seen you. Somehow he seems to trust me. I told him how we happened to come together yesterday, and he recognizes that I've a peculiar right."

Dencombe looked at him with a calculating earnestness. "How have you squared the Countess?"

The young man blushed a little, but he laughed. "Oh, never mind the Countess!"

"You told me she was very exacting."

[42] **stupor**—unconsciousness.

Doctor Hugh was silent a moment. "So she is."

"And Miss Vernham's an *intrigante*.[43]"

"How do you know that?"

"I know everything. One *has* to, to write decently!"

"I think she's mad," said limpid[44] Doctor Hugh.

"Well, don't quarrel with the Countess—she's a present help to you."

"I don't quarrel," Doctor Hugh replied. "But I don't get on with silly women." Presently he added: "You seem very much alone."

"That often happens at my age. I've outlived, I've lost by the way."

Doctor Hugh hesitated; then surmounting a soft scruple: "Whom have you lost?"

"Every one."

"Ah, no," the young man murmured, laying a hand on his arm.

"I once had a wife—I once had a son. My wife died when my child was born, and my boy, at school, was carried off by typhoid."

"I wish I'd been there!" said Doctor Hugh simply.

"Well—if you're here!" Dencombe answered, with a smile that, in spite of dimness, showed how much he liked to be sure of his companion's whereabouts.

"You talk strangely of your age. You're not old."

"Hypocrite—so early!"

"I speak physiologically."

"That's the way I've been speaking for the last five years, and it's exactly what I've been saying to myself. It isn't till we are old that we begin to tell ourselves we're not!"

"Yet I know I myself am young," Doctor Hugh declared.

"Not so well as I!" laughed his patient, whose visitor indeed would have established the truth in question by the honesty with which he changed the point of view, remarking that it must be one of the charms of age—at any rate in the case of high distinction—to feel that one has labored and achieved. Doctor Hugh employed the common phrase about earning one's rest, and it made poor Dencombe, for an instant, almost angry. He recovered himself, however, to explain, lucidly enough, that if he, ungraciously, knew nothing of such a balm, it was doubtless because he had wasted inestimable years. He had followed literature from the first, but he had taken a lifetime to get alongside of her. Only today, at last, had he begun to *see,* so that what he had hitherto done was a movement without a direction. He had ripened too late and was so clumsily constituted that he had had to teach himself by mistakes.

"I prefer your flowers, then, to other people's fruit, and your mistakes to other people's successes," said gallant Doctor Hugh. "It's for your mistakes I admire you."

"You're happy—you don't know," Dencombe answered.

Looking at his watch the young man had got up; he named the hour of the afternoon at which he would return. Dencombe

---

43 *intrigante*—French for "schemer."

44 limpid—calm.

warned him against committing himself too deeply, and expressed again all his dread of making him neglect the Countess—perhaps incur her displeasure.

"I want to be like you—I want to learn by mistakes!" Doctor Hugh laughed.

"Take care you don't make too grave a one! But do come back," Dencombe added, with the glimmer of a new idea.

"You should have had more vanity!" Doctor Hugh spoke as if he knew the exact amount required to make a man of letters normal.

"No, no—I only should have had more time. I want another go."

"Another go?"

"I want an extension."

"An extension?" Again Doctor Hugh repeated Dencombe's words, with which he seemed to have been struck.

"Don't you know?—I want to what they call 'live.'"

The young man, for good-bye, had taken his hand, which closed with a certain force. They looked at each other hard a moment. "You *will* live," said Doctor Hugh.

"Don't be superficial. It's too serious!"

"You *shall* live!" Dencombe's visitor declared, turning pale.

"Ah, that's better!" And as he retired the invalid, with a troubled laugh, sank gratefully back.

All that day and all the following night he wondered if it mightn't be arranged. His doctor came again, his servant was attentive, but it was to his confident young friend that he found himself mentally appealing. His collapse on the cliff was plausibly explained, and his liberation, on a better basis, promised for the morrow; meanwhile, however, the intensity of his meditations kept him tranquil and made him indifferent. The idea that occupied him was none the less absorbing because it was a morbid fancy. Here was a clever son of the age, ingenious and ardent, who happened to have set him up for connoisseurs to worship. This servant of his altar had all the new learning in science and all the old reverence in faith; wouldn't he therefore put his knowledge at the disposal of his sympathy, his craft at the disposal of his love? Couldn't he be trusted to invent a remedy for a poor artist to whose art he had paid a tribute? If he couldn't, the alternative was hard: Dencombe would have to surrender to silence, unvindicated and undivined.[45] The rest of the day and all the next he toyed in secret with this sweet **futility**.[46] Who would work the miracle for him but the young man who could combine such lucidity with such passion? He thought of the fairy-tales of science and charmed himself into forgetting that he looked for a magic that was not of this world. Doctor Hugh was an apparition, and that placed him above the law. He came and went while his patient, who sat up, followed him with supplicating eyes. The interest of knowing the great author

"I want to be like you—I want to learn by mistakes!" Doctor Hugh laughed.

[45] undivined—unknown.

[46] **futility**—uselessness.

had made the young man begin "The Middle Years" afresh, and would help him to find a deeper meaning in its pages. Dencombe had told him what he "tried for;" with all his intelligence, on a first perusal, Doctor Hugh had failed to guess it. The baffled celebrity wondered then who in the world *would* guess it: he was amused once more at the fine, full way with which an intention could be missed. Yet he wouldn't rail[47] at the general mind today—consoling as that ever had been: the revelation of his own slowness had seemed to make all stupidity sacred.

Doctor Hugh, after a little, was visibly worried, confessing, on inquiry, to a source of embarrassment at home. "Stick to the Countess—don't mind me," Dencombe said, repeatedly; for his companion was frank enough about the large lady's attitude. She was so jealous that she had fallen ill—she resented such a breach of allegiance. She paid so much for his fidelity that she must have it all: she refused him the right to other sympathies, charged him with scheming to make her die alone, for it was needless to point out how little Miss Vernham was a resource in trouble. When Doctor Hugh mentioned that the Countess would already have left Bournemouth if he hadn't kept her in bed, poor Dencombe held his arm tighter and said with decision: "Take her straight away." They had gone out together, walking back to the sheltered nook in which, the other day, they had met. The young man, who had given his companion a personal support, declared with emphasis that his conscience was clear—he could ride two horses at once. Didn't he dream, for his future, of a time when he should have to ride five hundred? Longing equally for virtue, Dencombe replied that in that golden age no patient would pretend to have contracted with him for his whole attention. On the part of the Countess was not such an avidity[48] lawful? Doctor Hugh denied it, said there was no contract but only a free understanding, and that a **sordid**[49] servitude was impossible to a generous spirit; he liked moreover to talk about art, and that was the subject on which, this time, as they sat together on the sunny bench, he tried most to engage the author of "The Middle Years." Dencombe, soaring again a little on the weak wings of convalescence and still haunted by that happy notion of an organized rescue, found another strain of eloquence to plead the cause of a certain splendid "last manner," the very citadel, as it would prove, of his reputation, the stronghold into which his real treasure would be gathered. While his listener gave up the morning and the great still sea appeared to wait, he had a wonderful explanatory hour. Even for himself he was inspired as he told of what his treasure would consist—the precious metals he would dig from the mine, the jewels rare, strings of pearls, he would hang between the columns of his temple. He was wonderful for himself, so thick his convictions crowded; but he was still more wonderful for Doctor Hugh, who assured him, none the less, that the very pages he had just

[47] rail—criticize harshly.

[48] avidity—ardent desire or craving.

[49] **sordid**—wretched.

published were already encrusted with gems. The young man, however, panted for the combinations to come, and, before the face of the beautiful day, renewed to Dencombe his guarantee that his profession would hold itself responsible for such a life. Then he suddenly clapped his hand upon his watch-pocket and asked leave to absent himself for half an hour. Dencombe waited there for his return, but was at last recalled to the actual by the fall of a shadow across the ground. The shadow darkened into that of Miss Vernham, the young lady in attendance on the Countess; whom Dencombe, recognizing her, perceived so clearly to have come to speak to him that he rose from his bench to acknowledge the civility. Miss Vernham indeed proved not particularly civil; she looked strangely agitated, and her type was now unmistakable.

"Excuse me if I inquire," she said, "whether it's too much to hope that you may be induced to leave Doctor Hugh alone." Then, before Dencombe, greatly disconcerted, could protest: "You ought to be informed that you stand in his light; that you may do him a terrible injury."

"Do you mean by causing the Countess to dispense with his services?"

"By causing her to disinherit him." Dencombe stared at this, and Miss Vernham pursued, in the gratification of seeing she could produce an impression: "It has depended on himself to come into something very handsome. He has had a magnificent prospect, but I think you've succeeded in spoiling it."

"Not intentionally, I assure you. Is there no hope the accident may be repaired?" Dencombe asked.

"She was ready to do anything for him. She takes great fancies, she lets herself go—it's her way. She has no relations, she's free to dispose of her money, and she's very ill."

"I'm very sorry to hear it," Dencombe stammered.

"Wouldn't it be possible for you to leave Bournemouth? That's what I've come to ask you."

Poor Dencombe sank down on his bench. "I'm very ill myself, but I'll try!"

Miss Vernham still stood there with her colorless eyes and the brutality of her good conscience. "Before it's too late, please!" she said; and with this she turned her back, in order, quickly, as if it had been a business to which she could spare but a precious moment, to pass out of his sight.

Oh, yes, after this Dencombe was certainly very ill. Miss Vernham had upset him with her rough, fierce news; it was the sharpest shock to him to discover what was at stake for a penniless young man of fine parts. He sat trembling on his bench, staring at the waste of waters, feeling sick with the directness of the blow. He was indeed too weak, too unsteady, too alarmed; but he would make the effort to get away, for he couldn't accept the guilt of interference, and his honor was really involved. He would hobble home, at any rate, and then he would think what was to be done. He made his way back to the hotel and, as he went, had a characteristic vision of Miss Vernham's great motive. The

Countess hated women, of course; Dencombe was lucid about that; so the hungry pianist had no personal hopes and could only console herself with the bold conception of helping Doctor Hugh in order either to marry him after he should get his money or to induce him to recognize her title to compensation and buy her off. If she had befriended him at a fruitful crisis he would really, as a man of delicacy, and she knew what to think of that point, have to reckon with her.

At the hotel Dencombe's servant insisted on his going back to bed. The invalid had talked about catching a train and had begun with orders to pack; after which his humming nerves had yielded to a sense of sickness. He consented to see his physician, who immediately was sent for, but he wished it to be understood that his door was irrevocably closed to Doctor Hugh. He had his plan, which was so fine that he rejoiced in it after getting back to bed. Doctor Hugh, suddenly finding himself snubbed without mercy, would, in natural disgust and to the joy of Miss Vernham, renew his allegiance to the Countess. When his physician arrived Dencombe learned that he was feverish and that this was very wrong: he was to cultivate calmness and try, if possible, not to think. For the rest of the day he wooed stupidity; but there was an ache that kept him sentient,[50] the probable sacrifice of his "extension," the limit of his course. His medical adviser was anything but pleased; his successive relapses were ominous. He charged this personage to put out a strong hand and take Doctor Hugh off his mind—it would contribute so much to his being quiet. The agitating name, in his room, was not mentioned again, but his security was a smothered fear, and it was not confirmed by the receipt, at ten o'clock that evening, of a telegram which his servant opened and read for him and to which, with an address in London, the signature of Miss Vernham was attached. "Beseech you to use all influence to make our friend join us here in the morning. Countess much the worse for dreadful journey, but everything may still be saved." The two ladies had gathered themselves up and had been capable in the afternoon of a spiteful revolution. They had started for the capital, and if the elder one, as Miss Vernham had announced, was very ill, she had wished to make it clear that she was proportionately reckless. Poor Dencombe, who was not reckless and who only desired that everything should indeed be "saved," sent this missive straight off to the young man's lodging and had on the morrow the pleasure of knowing that he had quitted Bournemouth by an early train.

Two days later he pressed in with a copy of a literary journal in his hand. He had returned because he was anxious and for the pleasure of flourishing the great review of "The Middle Years." Here at least was something adequate—it rose to the occasion; it was an acclamation,[51] a reparation, a critical attempt to place the author in the niche he had fairly won. Dencombe accepted and submitted; he made neither

[50] sentient—conscious.

[51] acclamation—enthusiastic approval.

objection nor inquiry, for old complications had returned and he had had two **atrocious**[52] days. He was convinced not only that he should never again leave his bed, so that his young friend might pardonably remain, but that the demand he should make on the patience of beholders would be very moderate indeed. Doctor Hugh had been to town, and he tried to find in his eyes some confession that the Countess was pacified and his legacy clinched; but all he could see there was the light of his juvenile joy in two or three of the phrases of the newspaper. Dencombe couldn't read them, but when his visitor had insisted on repeating them more than once he was able to shake an unintoxicated head. "Ah, no; but they would have been true of what I *could* have done!"

"What people 'could have done' is mainly what they've in fact done," Doctor Hugh contended.

"Mainly, yes; but I've been an idiot!" said Dencombe.

Doctor Hugh did remain; the end was coming fast. Two days later Dencombe observed to him, by way of the feeblest of jokes, that there would now be no question whatever of a second chance. At this the young man stared; then he exclaimed: "Why, it has come to pass—it has come to pass! The second chance has been the public's—the chance to find the point of view, to pick up the pearl!"

"Oh, the pearl!" poor Dencombe uneasily sighed. A smile as cold as a winter sunset flickered on his drawn lips as he added: "The pearl is the unwritten—the pearl is the unalloyed,[53] the *rest*, the lost!"

From that moment he was less and less present, heedless to all appearance of what went on around him. His disease was definitely mortal, of an action as relentless, after the short arrest that had enabled him to fall in with Doctor Hugh, as a leak in a great ship. Sinking steadily, though this visitor, a man of rare resources, now cordially approved by his physician, showed endless art in guarding him from pain, poor Dencombe kept no reckoning of favor or neglect, betrayed no symptom of regret or speculation. Yet toward the last he gave a sign of having noticed that for two days Doctor Hugh had not been in his room, a sign that consisted of his suddenly opening his eyes to ask of him if he had spent the interval with the Countess.

"The Countess is dead," said Doctor Hugh. "I knew that in a particular contingency she wouldn't resist. I went to her grave."

Dencombe's eyes opened wider. "She left you 'something handsome'?"

The young man gave a laugh almost too light for a chamber of woe. "Never a penny. She roundly cursed me."

"Cursed you?" Dencombe murmured.

"For giving her up. I gave her up for *you*. I had to choose," his companion explained.

"You chose to let a fortune go?"

"I chose to accept, whatever they might be, the consequences of my infatuation," smiled Doctor Hugh. Then, as a larger pleasantry: "A fortune be hanged! It's your

[52] **atrocious**—exceptionally bad.

[53] unalloyed—pure.

own fault if I can't get your things out of my head."

The immediate tribute to his humor was a long, bewildered moan; after which, for many hours, many days, Dencombe lay motionless and absent. A response so absolute, such a glimpse of a definite result and such a sense of credit worked together in his mind and, producing a strange commotion, slowly altered and transfigured his despair. The sense of cold submersion left him—he seemed to float without an effort. The incident was extraordinary as evidence, and it shed an intenser light. At the last he signed to Doctor Hugh to listen, and, when he was down on his knees by the pillow, brought him very near.

The incident was extraordinary as evidence, and it shed an intenser light.

"You've made me think it all a delusion."

"Not your glory, my friend," stammered the young man.

"Not my glory—what there is of it! It is glory—to have been tested, to have had our little quality and cast our little spell. The thing is to have made somebody care. You happen to be crazy, or course, but that doesn't affect the law."

"You're a great success!" said Doctor Hugh, putting into his young voice the ring of a marriage-bell.

Dencombe lay taking this in; then he gathered strength to speak once more. "A second chance—*that's* the delusion. There never was to be but one. We work in the dark—we do what we can—we give what we have. Our doubt is our passion and our passion is our task. The rest is the madness of art."

"If you've doubted, if you've despaired, you've always 'done' it," his visitor subtly argued.

"We've done something or other," Dencombe conceded.

"Something or other is everything. It's the **feasible**.[54] It's you!"

"Comforter!" poor Dencombe ironically sighed.

"But it's true," insisted his friend.

"It's true. It's frustration that doesn't count."

"Frustration's only life," said Doctor Hugh.

"Yes, it's what passes." Poor Dencombe was barely audible, but he had marked with the words the virtual end of his first and only chance.

---

[54] **feasible**—possible.

QUESTIONS TO CONSIDER

1. Why does Dr. Hugh take such interest in Dencombe?
2. What is Decombe's motive in befriending the doctor?
3. What is your opinion of Dencombe's choice in sending Dr. Hugh away?
4. Dencombe observes, "Our doubt is our passion and our passion is our task. The rest is the madness of art." What does he mean?
5. What is the title of the story intended to mean?
6. What aspects of this story seem modern?

Sherwood Anderson ▶

Sophistication

BY SHERWOOD ANDERSON

Sherwood Anderson (1876–1941) was one of the writers who took Henry James's model of acute analysis and pushed it forward in the first part of the twentieth century. Anderson was born in a small town in Ohio, and received very little formal education. He went to work at fourteen, served in the Spanish-American War, and generally tried his hand at every sort of career. In 1912, Anderson, who was married with three children and trying to juggle a business career with writing at night, had a breakdown. He and his family moved to Chicago, where he was able to devote himself to writing. He published novels in 1916 and 1917, and finally established himself in 1919 with the publication of Winesburg, Ohio. *This book is a series of interconnected stories about a small Midwestern town. Anderson sought to portray the inner lives and motivations of his characters, showing the rapid influence that Sigmund Freud's psychology had gained in America. Freud's theories that there are deep underlying causes for people's behavior quickly became a tool in a writer's hands. Stories could have significance on numerous levels. Anderson also rejected traditional plotting, preferring to focus on key moments in his characters' lives. Anderson's almost plotless stories were revolutionary and introduced a whole new style of writing, one that would be perfected by Ernest Hemingway in the next decade. "Sophistication" is from* Winesburg, Ohio *and displays Anderson's elliptical style and his emphasis on form and meaning over telling a story.*

It was early evening of a day in the late fall and the Winesburg County Fair had brought crowds of country people into town. The day had been clear and the night came on warm and pleasant. On the Trunion Pike, where the road after it left town stretched away between berry fields now covered with dry brown leaves, the dust from passing wagons arose in clouds. Children, curled into little balls, slept on the straw scattered on wagon beds. Their hair was full of dust and their fingers black and sticky. The dust rolled away over the fields and the departing sun set it ablaze with colors.

In the main street of Winesburg crowds filled the stores and the sidewalks. Night came on, horses whinnied, the clerks in the stores ran madly about, children became lost and cried lustily—an American town worked terribly at the task of amusing itself.

Pushing his way through the crowds in Main Street, young George Willard concealed himself in the stairway leading to

Doctor Reefy's office and looked at the people. With feverish eyes he watched the faces drifting past under the store lights. Thoughts kept coming into his head and he did not want to think. He stamped impatiently on the wooden steps and looked sharply about. "Well, is she going to stay with him all day? Have I done all this waiting for nothing?" he muttered.

The sadness of sophistication has come to the boy.

George Willard, the Ohio village boy, was fast growing into manhood and new thoughts had been coming into his mind. All that day, amid the jam of people at the fair, he had gone about feeling lonely. He was about to leave Winesburg to go away to some city where he hoped to get work on a city newspaper and he felt grown up. The mood that had taken possession of him was a thing known to men and unknown to boys. He felt old and a little tired. Memories awoke in him. To his mind his new sense of maturity set him apart, made of him a half tragic figure. He wanted someone to understand the feeling that had taken possession of him after his mother's death.

There is a time in the life of every boy when he for the first time takes the backward view of life. Perhaps that is the moment when he crosses the line into manhood. The boy is walking through the streets of his town. He is thinking of the future and of the figure he will cut in the world. Ambitions and regrets awake within him. Suddenly something happens; he stops under a tree and waits as for a voice calling his name. Ghosts of old things creep into his consciousness; the voices outside of himself whisper a message concerning the limitations of life. From being quite sure of himself and his future he becomes not at all sure. If he be an imaginative boy a door is torn open and for the first time he looks out upon the world, seeing, as though they marched in procession before him, the countless figures of men who before his time have come out of nothingness into the world, lived their lives and again disappeared into nothingness. The sadness of sophistication has come to the boy. With a little gasp he sees himself as merely a leaf blown by the wind through the streets of his village. He knows that in spite of all the stout talk of his fellows he must live and die in uncertainty, a thing blown by the winds, a thing destined like corn to wilt in the sun. He shivers and looks eagerly about. The eighteen years he has lived seem but a moment, a breathing space in the long march of humanity. Already he hears death calling. With all his heart he wants to come close to some other human, touch someone with his hands, be touched by the hand of another. If he prefers that the other be a woman, that is because he believes that a woman will be gentle, that she will understand. He wants, most of all, understanding.

When the moment of sophistication came to George Willard his mind turned to Helen White, the Winesburg banker's daughter. Always he had been conscious of the girl growing into womanhood as he grew into manhood. Once, on a summer night when he was eighteen, he had walked with her on a country road and in her presence had given way to an impulse to boast, to make himself appear big and significant in her eyes. Now he wanted to see her for another purpose. He wanted to tell her of the new impulses that had come to him. He had tried to make her think of him as a man when he knew nothing of manhood and now he wanted to be with her and to try to make her feel the change he believed had taken place in his nature.

As for Helen White, she also had come to a period of change. What George felt, she in her young woman's way felt also. She was no longer a girl and hungered to reach into the grace and beauty of womanhood. She had come home from Cleveland, where she was attending college, to spend a day at the fair. She also had begun to have memories. During the day she sat in the grand-stand with a young man, one of the instructors from the college, who was a guest of her mother's. The young man was of a **pedantic**[1] turn of mind and she felt at once he would not do for her purpose. At the fair she was glad to be seen in his company as he was well dressed and a stranger. She knew that the fact of his presence would create an impression. During the day she was happy, but when night came on she began to grow restless. She wanted to drive the instructor away, to get out of his presence. While they sat together in the grand-stand and while the eyes of former school mates were upon them, she paid so much attention to her escort that he grew interested. "A scholar needs money. I should marry a woman with money," he mused.

Helen White was thinking of George Willard even as he wandered gloomily through the crowds thinking of her. She remembered the summer evening when they had walked together and wanted to walk with him again. She thought that the months she had spent in the city, the going to theaters and the seeing of great crowds wandering in lighted thoroughfares, had changed her profoundly. She wanted him to feel and be conscious of the change in her nature.

The summer evening together that had left its mark on the memory of both the young man and woman had, when looked at quite sensibly, been rather stupidly spent. They had walked out of town along a country road. Then they had stopped by a fence near a field of young corn and George had taken off his coat and let it hang on his arm. "Well, I've stayed here in Winesburg—yes. I've not yet gone away but I'm growing up," he had said. "I've been reading books and I've been thinking. I'm going to try to amount to something in life.

"Well," he explained, "that isn't the point. Perhaps I'd better quit talking."

The confused boy put his hand on the girl's arm. His voice trembled. The two started to walk back along the road toward town. In his desperation George boasted. "I'm going to be a big man, the biggest that ever lived here in Winesburg," he declared. "I want you to do something, I don't know what. Perhaps it is none of my business. I want you to try to be different from other women. You see the point. It's none of my

[1] **pedantic**—characterized by a narrow, often showy, concern with scholarship.

business I tell you. I want you to be a beautiful woman. You see what I want."

The boy's voice failed and in silence the two came back into town and went along the street to Helen White's house. At the gate he tried to say something impressive. Speeches he had thought out came into his head, but they seemed utterly pointless. "I thought—I used to think—I had it in my mind you would marry Seth Richmond. Now I know you won't," was all he could find to say as she went through the gate and toward the door of her house.

On the warm fall evening as he stood in the stairway and looked at the crowd drifting through Main Street, George thought of the talk beside the field of young corn and was ashamed of the figure he had made of himself. In the street the people surged up and down like cattle confined in a pen. Buggies[2] and wagons almost filled the narrow thoroughfare. A band played and small boys raced along the sidewalk, diving between the legs of men. Young men with shining red faces walked awkwardly about with girls on their arms. In a room above one of the stores, where a dance was to be held, the fiddlers tuned their instruments. The broken sounds floated down through an open window and out across the murmur of voices and the loud blare of the horns of the band. The medley of sounds got on young Willard's nerves. Everywhere, on all sides, the sense of crowding, moving life closed in about him. He wanted to run away by himself and think. "If she wants to stay with that fellow she may. Why should I care? What difference does it make to me?" he growled and went along Main Street and through Hern's Grocery into a side street.

George felt so utterly lonely and dejected that he wanted to weep but pride made him walk rapidly along, swinging his arms. He came to Wesley Moyer's Livery[3] and stopped in the shadows to listen to a group of men who talked of a race Wesley's stallion, Tony Tip, had won at the fair during the afternoon. A crowd had gathered in front of the barn and before the crowd walked Wesley, prancing up and down and boasting. He held a whip in his hand and kept tapping the ground. Little puffs of dust arose in the lamp light. "Hell, quit your talking," Wesley exclaimed. "I wasn't afraid, I knew I had 'em beat all the time. I wasn't afraid."

Ordinarily George Willard would have been intensely interested in the boasting of Moyer, the horse man. Now it made him angry. He turned and hurried away along the street. "Old Windbag," he sputtered. "Why does he want to be bragging? Why don't he shut up?"

George went into a vacant lot and, as he hurried along, fell over a pile of rubbish. A nail protruding from an empty barrel tore his trousers. He sat down on the ground and swore. With a pin he mended the torn place and then arose and went on. "I'll go to Helen White's house, that's what I'll do. I'll walk right in. I'll say that I want to see her. I'll walk right in and sit down,

[2] Buggies—small, light, one-horse carriages.

[3] Livery—business that offers vehicles for hire.

that's what I'll do," he declared, climbing over a fence and beginning to run.

On the veranda of Banker White's house Helen was restless and **distraught**.[4] The instructor sat between the mother and daughter. His talk wearied the girl. Although he had also been raised in an Ohio town, the instructor began to put on the airs of the city. He wanted to appear cosmopolitan. "I like the chance you have given me to study the background out of which most of our girls come," he declared. "It was good of you, Mrs. White, to have me down for the day." He turned to Helen and laughed. "Your life is still bound up with the life of this town?" he asked. "There are people here in whom you are interested?" To the girl his voice sounded **pompous**[5] and heavy.

Helen arose and went into the house. At the door leading to a garden at the back she stopped and stood listening. Her mother began to talk. "There is no one here fit to associate with a girl of Helen's breeding," she said.

Helen ran down a flight of stairs at the back of the house and into the garden. In the darkness she stopped and stood trembling. It seemed to her that the world was full of meaningless people saying words. Afire with eagerness she ran through a garden gate and, turning a corner by the banker's barn, went into a little side street. "George! Where are you, George?" she cried, filled with nervous excitement. She stopped running, and leaned against a tree to laugh hysterically. Along the dark little street came George Willard, still saying words. "I'm going to walk right into her house. I'll go right in and sit down," he declared as he came up to her. He stopped and stared stupidly. "Come on," he said and took hold of her hand. With hanging heads they walked away along the street under the trees. Dry leaves rustled underfoot. Now that he had found her George wondered what he had better do and say.

At the upper end of the fair grounds, in Winesburg, there is a half decayed old grand-stand. It has never been painted and the boards are all warped out of shape. The fair grounds stands on top of a low hill rising out of the valley of Wine Creek and from the grand-stand one can see at night, over a corn field, the lights of the town reflected against the sky.

George and Helen climbed the hill to the fair grounds, coming by the path past Waterworks Pond. The feeling of loneliness and isolation that had come to the young man in the crowded streets of his town was both broken and intensified by the presence of Helen. What he felt was reflected in her.

In youth there are always two forces fighting in people. The warm unthinking little animal struggles against the thing that reflects and remembers, and the older, the more sophisticated thing had possession of George Willard. Sensing his mood, Helen walked beside him filled with respect. When they got to the grand-stand they climbed up under the roof and sat down on one of the long bench-like seats.

---

[4] **distraught**—upset.

[5] **pompous**—arrogant, prideful.

There is something memorable in the experience to be had by going into a fair grounds that stands at the edge of a Middle Western town on a night after the annual fair has been held. The sensation is one never to be forgotten. On all sides are ghosts, not of the dead, but of living people. Here, during the day just passed, have come the people pouring in from the town and the country around. Farmers with their wives and children and all the people from the hundreds of little frame houses have gathered within these board walls. Young girls have laughed and men with beards have talked of the affairs of their lives. The place has been filled to overflowing with life. It has itched and squirmed with life and now it is night and the life has all gone away. The silence is almost terrifying. One conceals oneself standing silently beside the trunk of a tree and what there is of a reflective tendency in his nature is intensified. One shudders at the thought of the meaninglessness of life while at the same instant, and if the people of the town are his people, one loves life so intensely that tears come into the eyes.

In that high place in the darkness the two oddly sensitive human atoms held each other tightly and waited.

In the darkness under the roof of the grand-stand, George Willard sat beside Helen White and felt very keenly his own insignificance in the scheme of existence. Now that he had come out of town where the presence of the people stirring about, busy with a multitude of affairs, had been so irritating the irritation was all gone. The presence of Helen renewed and refreshed him. It was as though her woman's hand was assisting him to make some minute re-adjustment of the machinery of his life. He began to think of the people in the town where he had always lived with something like reverence. He had reverence for Helen. He wanted to love and to be loved by her, but he did not want at the moment to be confused by her womanhood. In the darkness he took hold of her hand and when she crept close put a hand on her shoulder. A wind began to blow and he shivered. With all his strength he tried to hold and to understand the mood that had come upon him. In that high place in the darkness the two oddly sensitive human atoms held each other tightly and waited. In the mind of each was the same thought. "I have come to this lonely place and here is this other," was the substance of the thing felt.

In Winesburg the crowded day had run itself out into the long night of the late fall. Farm horses jogged away along lonely country roads pulling their portion of weary people. Clerks began to bring samples of goods in off the sidewalks and lock the doors of stores. In the Opera House a crowd had gathered to see a show and farther down Main Street the fiddlers, their instruments tuned, sweated and worked to keep the feet of youth flying over a dance floor.

In the darkness in the grand-stand Helen White and George Willard remained silent. Now and then the spell that held them was broken and they turned and tried in the dim light to see into each other's eyes. They kissed but that impulse did not last. At the upper end of the fair grounds a half dozen men worked over horses that had raced during the afternoon. The men had built a fire and were heating kettles of water. Only their legs could be seen as they passed back and forth in the light. When the wind blew the little flames of the fire danced crazily about.

George and Helen arose and walked away into the darkness. They went along a path past a field of corn that had not yet been cut. The wind whispered among the dry corn blades. For a moment during the walk back into town the spell that held them was broken. When they had come to the crest of Waterworks Hill they stopped by a tree and George again put his hands on the girl's shoulders. She embraced him eagerly and then again they drew quickly back from that impulse. They stopped kissing and stood a little apart. Mutual respect grew big in them. They were both embarrassed and to relieve their embarrassment dropped into the animalism of youth. They laughed and began to pull and haul at each other. In some way chastened[6] and purified by the mood they had been in they became not man and woman, not boy and girl, but excited little animals.

It was so they went down the hill. In the darkness they played like two splendid young things in a young world. Once, running swiftly forward, Helen tripped George and he fell. He squirmed and shouted. Shaking with laughter, he rolled down the hill. Helen ran after him. For just a moment she stopped in the darkness. There is no way of knowing what woman's thoughts went through her mind but, when the bottom of the hill was reached and she came up to the boy, she took his arm and walked beside him in dignified silence. For some reason they could not have explained they had both got from their silent evening together the thing needed. Man or boy, woman or girl, they had for a moment taken hold of the thing that makes the mature life of men and women in the modern world possible.

[6] chastened—corrected.

QUESTIONS TO CONSIDER

1. Why does George feel so different on this day? How does Helen respond to this change?
2. Which of George's actions reflect his new-found maturity?
3. What are the various possible meanings of the title? What do you think it means?
4. What do you think happens between Helen and George in the future? Explain your answer.
5. How does Anderson's method of presenting George and Helen differ from traditional narratives?

Willa Cather ▶

The Sculptor's Funeral

BY WILLA CATHER

Willa Cather (1876–1947) was born in Virginia, but when she was eight, her family moved to Nebraska, the area with which she is always associated. In the 1870s and 1880s, pioneers were settling the prairie states of Kansas, Nebraska, Montana, North Dakota, and South Dakota. The railroads had opened up these areas, and, in the 1880s alone, more than a million people resettled in the Midwest, looking for land and opportunity. After a short stint on a farm, the Cather family settled in Red Cloud, Nebraska, a town filled with settlers of all nationalities. Cather was an extraordinarily precocious child, developing early and overwhelming interests in reading, music, and art. After attending the University of Nebraska, she worked as a journalist in Pittsburgh from 1896 until 1906, and began writing poems and stories. In 1906, she became the editor of the important McClure's Magazine *in New York, a job she only gave up in 1913 after she had found success with her second novel,* O Pioneers! *(1913). Over the next thirty years she would write ten more novels, dozens of stories, and a wide array of journalism. Cather's fiction documents a certain moment in American history when the country and culture were expanding. Many of her stories are set in the West, in her native Nebraska or in the Southwest, and they show life away from the cities of the East with their sophisticated literary culture. Because of her subject matter, Cather was at first considered a local colorist, but over time her readers and critics realized that she had produced one of the great bodies of modernist fiction, as inventive and acute as any of her contemporaries. Cather's prose is beautiful and her understanding of human motivation profound. A story like "The Sculptor's Funeral" depicts the divide between the East and the Midwest at the turn of the century, yet it also expresses human emotions and motivations in a way that is still powerful and understandable today.*

A group of the townspeople stood on the station siding of a little Kansas town, awaiting the coming of the night train, which was already twenty minutes overdue. The snow had fallen thick over everything; in the pale starlight the line of bluffs across the wide, white meadows south of the town made soft, smoke-colored curves against the clear sky. The men on the siding stood first on one foot and then on the other, their hands thrust deep into their trousers pockets, their overcoats open, their shoulders screwed up with the cold; and they glanced from time to time toward the southeast, where the railroad track wound along the river shore. They conversed in low tones and moved about restlessly, seeming uncertain as to what was expected of them. There was but one of the company who looked as though he knew exactly why he was there, and he kept conspicuously apart; walking to the far end of the platform, returning to the station door, then pacing up the track again, his chin sunk in the high collar of his overcoat, his burly shoulders drooping forward, his **gait**[1] heavy and dogged. Presently he was approached by a tall, spare, grizzled man clad in a faded Grand Army[2] suit, who shuffled out from the group and advanced with a certain deference, craning his neck forward until his back made the angle of a jacknife three-quarters open.

"I reckon she's a-goin to be pretty late again tonight, Jim," he remarked in a squeaky falsetto.[3] "S'pose it's the snow?"

"I don't know," responded the other man with a shade of annoyance, speaking from out an astonishing cataract[4] of red beard that grew fiercely and thickly in all directions.

The spare man shifted the quill toothpick he was chewing to the other side of his mouth. "It ain't likely that anybody from the East will come with the corpse, I s'pose," he went on reflectively.

"I don't know," responded the other, more curtly than before.

"It's too bad he didn't belong to some lodge or other. I like an order funeral myself. They seem more appropriate for people of some reputation," the spare man continued, with an ingratiating[5] concession in his shrill voice, as he carefully placed his toothpick in his vest pocket. He always carried the flag at the G.A.R.[6] funerals in the town.

The heavy man turned on his heel without replying and walked up the siding. The spare man shuffled back to the uneasy group. "Jim's ez full ez a tick, ez ushel," he commented commiseratingly.

Just then a distant whistle sounded, and there was a shuffling of feet on the platform. A number of lanky[7] boys, of all ages, appeared as suddenly and slimily as eels wakened by the crack of thunder; some came from the waiting room, where they had been warming themselves by the red stove, or half asleep on the slat benches; others uncoiled themselves from baggage trucks or slid out of express wagons. Two clambered down from the driver's seat of a hearse that stood backed up against the siding. They straightened their stooping shoulders and lifted their heads, and a flash of momentary animation kindled their dull eyes at that cold, vibrant scream, the worldwide call for men. It stirred them like the note of a trumpet; just as it had often stirred the man who was coming home tonight, in his boyhood.

The night express shot, red as a rocket, from out the eastward marshlands and wound along the river shore under the long lines of shivering poplars that sentineled the meadows, the escaping steam hanging in gray masses against the pale sky and blotting out the Milky Way. In a

---

[1] **gait**—way of moving on foot; stride.

[2] Grand Army—army of the Union, or Northern, side during the Civil War (1861–1865).

[3] falsetto—high-pitched voice.

[4] cataract—flow.

[5] ingratiating—calculated to win favor.

[6] G.A.R.—Grand Army of the Republic, an organization of veterans who fought on the Union side in the Civil War.

[7] lanky—tall, thin.

moment the red glare from the headlight streamed up the snow-covered track before the siding and glittered on the wet, black rails. The burly man with the **disheveled**[8] red beard walked swiftly up the platform toward the approaching train, uncovering his head as he went. The group of men behind him hesitated, glanced questioningly at one another, and awkwardly followed his example. The train stopped, and the crowd shuffled up to the express car just as the door was thrown open, the spare man in the G.A.R. suit thrusting his head forward with curiosity. The express messenger appeared in the doorway, accompanied by a young man in a long ulster[9] and a traveling cap.

"Are Mr. Merrick's friends here?" inquired the young man.

The group on the platform swayed and shuffled uneasily. Philip Phelps, the banker, responded with dignity: "We have come to take charge of the body. Mr. Merrick's father is very feeble and can't be about."

"Send the agent out here," growled the express messenger, "and tell the operator to lend a hand."

The coffin was got out of its rough box and down on the snowy platform. The townspeople drew back enough to make room for it and then formed a close semicircle about it, looking curiously at the palm leaf[10] which lay across the black cover. No one said anything. The baggage-man stood by his truck, waiting to get at the trunks. The engine panted heavily, and the fireman dodged in and out among the wheels with his yellow torch and long oil-can, snapping the spindle boxes.[11] The young Bostonian, one of the dead sculptor's pupils who had come with the body, looked about him helplessly. He turned to the banker, the only one of that black, uneasy, stoop-shouldered group who seemed enough of an individual to be addressed.

"None of Mr. Merrick's brothers are here?" he asked, uncertainly.

The man with the red beard for the first time stepped up and joined the group. "No, they have not come yet; the family is scattered. The body will be taken directly to the house." He stooped and took hold of one of the handles of the coffin.

"Take the long hill road up, Thompson; it will be easier on the horses," called the liveryman as the undertaker snapped the door of the hearse and prepared to mount to the driver's seat.

Laird, the red-bearded lawyer, turned again to the stranger. "We didn't know whether there would be anyone with him or not," he explained. "It's a long walk, so you'd better go up in the hack." He pointed to a single battered conveyance, but the young man replied stiffly: "Thank you, but I think I will go up with the hearse. If you don't object," turning to the undertaker, "I'll ride with you."

They clambered up over the wheels and drove off in the starlight up the long, white hill toward the town. The lamps in the still village were shining from under

---

[8] **disheveled**—untidy.

[9] ulster—long, loose overcoat.

[10] palm leaf—traditional symbol of victory or achievement, which indicates that Harvey Merrick had won considerable renown as a sculptor.

[11] spindle boxes—axles that connect the wheels on a rail engine and on which the wheels revolve.

the low, snow-burdened roofs; and beyond, on every side, the plains reached out into emptiness, peaceful and wide as the soft sky itself, and wrapped in a tangible, white silence.

When the hearse backed up to a wooden sidewalk before a naked, weather-beaten frame house, the same composite, ill-defined group that had stood upon the station siding was huddled about the gate. The front yard was an icy swamp, and a couple of warped planks, extending from the sidewalk to the door, made a sort of rickety footbridge. The gate hung on one hinge, and was opened wide with difficulty. Steavens, the young stranger, noticed that something black was tied to the knob of the front door.

The grating sound made by the casket, as it was drawn from the hearse, was answered by a scream from the house; the front door was wrenched open, and a tall, **corpulent**[12] woman rushed out bareheaded into the snow and flung herself upon the coffin, shrieking: "My boy, my boy! And this is how you've come home to me!"

As Steavens turned away and closed his eyes with a shudder of unutterable repulsion, another woman, also tall, but flat and angular, darted out of the house and caught Mrs. Merrick by the shoulders, crying sharply: "Come, come, Mother; you mustn't go on like this!" Her tone changed to one of **obsequious**[13] solemnity as she turned to the banker. "The parlor is ready, Mr. Phelps."

The bearers carried the coffin along the narrow boards, while the undertaker ran ahead with the coffin-rests. They bore it into a large unheated room that smelled of dampness and disuse and furniture polish, and set it down under a hanging lamp ornamented with jingling glass prisms and before a Rogers group of John Alden and Priscilla,[14] wreathed with smilax. Henry Steavens stared about him with the sickening conviction that there had been some horrible mistake and that he had somehow arrived at the wrong destination. He looked at the clover-green Brussels,[15] the fat plush upholstery, among the hand-painted china plaques and panels and vases, for some mark of identification—for something that might once conceivably have belonged to Harvey Merrick. It was not until he recognized his friend in the crayon portrait of a little boy in kilts and curls, hanging above the piano, that he felt willing to let any of these people approach the coffin.

"Take the lid off, Mr. Thompson. Let me see my boy's face," wailed the elder woman between her sobs. This time Steavens looked fearfully, almost beseechingly into her face, red and swollen under its masses of strong, black, shiny hair. He flushed, dropped his eyes, and then, almost incredulously, looked again. There was a kind of power about her face—a kind of brutal handsomeness, even; but it was scarred and furrowed by violence, and so colored and coarsened by fiercer passions

---

[12] **corpulent**—excessively fat.

[13] **obsequious**—full of servile compliance.

[14] Rogers group . . . Priscilla—sentimental sculpture of two characters from Longfellow's poem "The Courtship of Miles Standish" by the American sculptor John Rogers (1829–1904).

[15] Brussels—carpet made of small loops of yarn.

that grief seemed never to have laid a gentle finger there. The long nose was **distended**[16] and knobbed at the end, and there were deep lines on either side of it; her heavy black brows almost met across her forehead, her teeth were large and square and set far apart—teeth that could tear. She filled the room; the men were obliterated, seemed tossed about like twigs in an angry water, even Steavens felt himself being drawn into the whirlpool.

The daughter—tall, raw-boned woman in crepe,[17] with a mourning comb in her hair which curiously lengthened her long face—sat stiffly upon the sofa, her hands, conspicuous for their large knuckles folded in her lap, her mouth and eyes drawn down, solemnly awaiting the opening of the coffin. Near the door stood a mulatto[18] woman, evidently a servant in the house, with a timid bearing and an **emaciated**[19] face pitifully sad and gentle. She was weeping silently, the corner of her calico apron lifted to her eyes, occasionally suppressing a long quivering sob. Steavens walked over and stood beside her.

Feeble steps were heard on the stairs, and an old man, tall and frail, odorous of pipe smoke, with shaggy, unkempt gray hair and a dingy beard, tobacco-stained about the mouth, entered uncertainly. He went slowly up to the coffin and stood rolling a blue cotton handkerchief between his hands, seeming so pained and embarrassed by his wife's orgy of grief that he had no consciousness of anything else.

"There, there, Annie, dear, don't take on so," he **quavered**[20] timidly, putting out a shaking hand and awkwardly patting her elbow. She turned with a cry and sank upon his shoulder with such violence that he tottered a little. He did not even glance toward the coffin, but continued to look at her with a dull, frightened, appealing expression, as a spaniel looks at the whip. His sunken cheeks slowly reddened and burned with miserable shame. When his wife rushed from the room, her daughter strode after with set lips. The servant stole up to the coffin, bent over it for a moment, and then slipped away to the kitchen, leaving Steavens, the lawyer, and the father to themselves. The old man stood trembling and looking down at his dead son's face. The sculptor's splendid head seemed even more noble in its rigid stillness than in life. The dark hair had crept down upon the wide forehead; the face seemed strangely long, but in it there was not that repose we expect to find in the faces of the dead. The brows were so drawn that there were two deep lines above the beaked nose, and the chin was thrust forward defiantly. It was as though the strain of life had been so sharp and bitter that death could not at once wholly relax the tension and smooth the countenance into perfect peace—as though he were still guarding something precious and holy, which might even yet be wrested from him.

The old man's lips were working under his stained beard. He turned to the

[16] **distended**—swollen.

[17] crepe—light, thin, soft fabric.

[18] mulatto—person having one white parent and one black parent.

[19] **emaciated**—extremely thin.

[20] **quavered**—spoke in a thin, trembling voice.

lawyer with timid deference: "Phelps and the rest are comin' back to set up with Harve, ain't they?" he asked. "Thank 'ee, Jim, thank 'ee." He brushed the hair back gently from his son's forehead. "He was a good boy, Jim; always a good boy. He was ez gentle ez a child and kindest of 'em all—only we didn't none of us ever onderstand him." The tears trickled slowly down his beard and dropped upon the sculptor's coat.

"Martin! Martin! Oh, Martin! come here," his wife wailed from the top of the stairs. The old man started **timorously**:[21] "Yes, Annie, I'm coming." He turned away, hesitated, stood for a moment in miserable indecision; then reached back and patted the dead man's hair softly, and stumbled from the room.

"Poor old man, I didn't think he had any tears left. Seems as if his eyes would have gone dry long ago. At his age nothing cuts very deep," remarked the lawyer.

Something in his tone made Steavens glance up. While the mother had been in the room, the young man had scarcely seen anyone else; but now, from the moment he first glanced into Jim Laird's florid face and bloodshot eyes, he knew that he had found what he had been heartsick at not finding before—the feeling, the understanding that must exist in someone, even here.

The man was red as his beard, with features swollen and blurred by dissipation,[22] and a hot, blazing blue eye. His face was strained—that of a man who is controlling himself with difficulty—and he kept plucking at his beard with a sort of fierce resentment. Steavens, sitting by the window, watched him turn down the glaring lamp, still its jangling pendants with an angry gesture, and then stand with his hands locked behind him, staring down into the master's face. He could not help wondering what link there could have been between the porcelain vessel and so sooty a lump of potter's clay.

From the kitchen an uproar was sounding; when the dining-room door opened, the import of it was clear. The mother was abusing the maid for having forgotten to make the dressing for the chicken salad which had been prepared for the watchers. Steavens had never heard anything in the least like it; it was injured, emotional, dramatic abuse, unique and masterly in its excruciating[23] cruelty, as violent and unrestrained as had been her grief of twenty minutes before. With a shudder of disgust the lawyer went into the dining room and closed the door into the kitchen.

"Poor Roxy's getting it now," he remarked when he came back. "The Merricks took her out of the poorhouse years ago; and if her loyalty would let her, I guess the poor old thing could tell tales that would curdle your blood. She's the mulatto woman who was standing in here a while ago, with her apron to her eyes. The old woman is a fury; there never was anybody like her for demonstrative piety and ingenious cruelty. She made Harvey's

---

[21] **timorously**—fearfully.

[22] dissipation—excessive indulgence in sensual pleasures; intemperance.

[23] excruciating—immensely painful; agonizing.

life a hell for him when he lived at home; he was so sick ashamed of it. I never could see how he kept himself sweet."

"He was wonderful," said Steavens slowly, "wonderful; but until tonight I have never known how wonderful."

"He was wonderful," said Steavens slowly, "wonderful; but until tonight I have never known how wonderful."

"That is the true and eternal wonder of it, anyway; that it can come even from such a dung heap as this," the lawyer cried, with a sweeping gesture which seemed to indicate much more than the four walls within which they stood.

"I think I'll see whether I can get a little air. The room is so close I am beginning to feel rather faint," murmured Steavens, struggling with one of the windows. The sash was stuck, however, and would not yield, so he sat down dejectedly and began pulling at his collar. The lawyer came over, loosened the sash with one blow of his red fist and sent the window up a few inches. Steavens thanked him, but the nausea which had been gradually climbing into his throat for the last half-hour left him with one desire—a desperate feeling that he must get away from this place with what was left of Harvey Merrick. Oh, he comprehended well enough now the quiet bitterness of the smile that he had seen so often on his master's lips!

He remembered that once, when Merrick returned from a visit home, he brought with him a singularly feeling and suggestive bas-relief[24] of a thin, faded old woman, sitting and sewing something pinned to her knee; while a full-lipped, full-blooded little urchin, his trousers held up by a single gallows,[25] stood beside her, impatiently twitching her gown to call her attention to a butterfly he had caught. Steavens, impressed by the tender and delicate modeling of the thin, tired face, had asked him if it were his mother. He remembered the dull flush that had burned up in the sculptor's face.

The lawyer was sitting in a rocking chair beside the coffin, his head thrown back and his eyes closed. Steavens looked at him earnestly, puzzled at the line of the chin, and wondering why a man should conceal a feature of such distinction under that disfiguring shock of beard. Suddenly, as though he felt the young sculptor's keen glance, Jim Laird opened his eyes.

"Was he always a good deal of an oyster?" he asked abruptly. "He was terribly shy as a boy."

"Yes, he was an oyster, since you put it so," rejoined Steavens. "Although he could be very fond of people, he always gave one the impression of being detached. He disliked violent emotion; he was reflective, and rather distrustful of himself—except, of course, as regarded his work. He was sure enough there. He distrusted men pretty thoroughly and women even more, yet somehow without believing ill of them. He was determined, indeed, to believe the best; but he seemed afraid to investigate."

24 bas-relief—sculptural relief that projects very little from the background.

25 gallows—slang word for a pair of suspenders.

"A burnt dog dreads the fire," said the lawyer grimly, and closed his eyes.

Steavens went on and on, reconstructing that whole miserable boyhood. All this raw, biting ugliness had been the portion of the man whose mind was to become an exhaustless gallery of beautiful impressions—so sensitive that the mere shadow of a poplar leaf flickering against a sunny wall would be etched and held there forever. Surely, if ever a man had the magic word in his finger tips, it was Merrick. Whatever he touched, he revealed its holiest secret; liberated it from enchantment and restored it to its **pristine**[26] loveliness. Upon whatever he had come in contact with, he had left a beautiful record of the experience—a sort of **ethereal**[27] signature; a scent, a sound, a color that was his own.

Steavens understood now the real tragedy of his master's life; neither love nor wine, as many had conjectured, but a blow which had fallen earlier and cut deeper than anything else could have done—a shame not his, and yet so unescapably his, to bide in his heart from his very boyhood. And without—the frontier warfare; the yearning of a boy, cast ashore upon a desert of newness and ugliness and sordidness,[28] for all that is chastened and old, and noble with traditions.

At eleven o'clock the tall, flat woman in black crepe announced that the watchers were arriving, and asked them to "step into the dining room." As Steavens rose, the lawyer said dryly: "You go on—it'll be a good experience for you, doubtless; as for me, I'm not equal to that crowd tonight; I've had twenty years of them."

As Steavens closed the door after him he glanced back at the lawyer, sitting by the coffin in the dim light, with his chin resting on his hand.

The same misty group that had stood before the door of the express car shuffled into the dining room. In the light of the kerosene lamp they separated and became individuals. The minister, a pale, feeble-looking man with white hair and blond chin whiskers, took his seat beside a small side table and placed his Bible upon it. The Grand Army man sat down behind the stove and tilted his chair back comfortably against the wall, fishing his quill toothpick from his waistcoat pocket. The two bankers, Phelps and Elder, sat off in a corner behind the dinner table, where they could finish their discussion of the new usury law and its effect on chattel security loans. The real-estate agent, an old man with a smiling, hypocritical face, soon joined them. The coal and lumber dealer and the cattle shipper sat on opposite sides of the hard-coal burner, their feet on the nickelwork. Steavens took a book from his pocket and began to read. The talk around him ranged through various topics of local interest while the house was quieting down. When it was clear that the members of the family were in bed, the Grand Army man hitched his shoulders and, untangling his long legs, caught his heels on the rounds of his chair.

---

26 **pristine**—pure; uncontaminated.

27 **ethereal**—highly refined; delicate.

28 sordidness—filthiness; dirtiness.

"S'pose there'll be a will, Phelps" he queried in his weak falsetto.

The banker laughed disagreeably, and began trimming his nails with a pearl-handled pocketknife.

"There'll scarcely be any need for one, will there?" he queried in his turn.

The restless Grand Army man shifted his position again, getting his knees still nearer his chin. "Why, the ole man says Harve's done right well lately," he chirped.

The other banker spoke up. "I reckon he means by that Harve ain't asked him to mortgage any more farms lately, so as he could go on with his education."

"Seems like my mind don't reach back to a time when Harve wasn't bein' educated," tittered the Grand Army man.

There was a general chuckle. The minister took out his handkerchief and blew his nose sonorously. Banker Phelps closed his knife with a snap. "It's too bad the old man's sons didn't turn out better," he remarked with reflective authority. "They never hung together. He spent money enough on Harve to stock a dozen cattle farms, and he might as well have poured it into Sand Creek. If Harve had stayed at home and helped nurse what little they had, and gone into stock on the old man's bottom farm, they might all have been well fixed. But the old man had to trust everything to tenants and was cheated right and left."

"Harve never could have handled stock none," interposed the cattleman. "He hadn't it in him to be sharp. Do you remember when he bought Sander's mules for eight-year-olds, when everybody in town knew that Sander's father-in-law give 'em to his wife for a wedding present eighteen years before, an' they was full-grown mules then?"

Everyone chuckled, and the Grand Army man rubbed his knees with a spasm of childish delight.

"Harve never was much account for anything practical, and he shore was never fond of work," began the coal and lumber dealer. "I mind the last time he was home; the day he left, when the old man was out to the barn helpin' his hand hitch up to take Harve to the train, and Cal Moots was patchin' up the fence; Harve, he come out on the step and sings out, in his ladylike voice, 'Cal Moots! Cal Moots! please come cord my trunk.'"

"That's Harve for you," approved the Grand Army man. "I kin hear him howlin' yet, when he was a big feller in long pants and his mother used to whale him with a rawhide in the barn for lettin' the cows get foundered[29] in the cornfield when he was drivin' 'em home from pasture. He killed a cow of mine that-a-way once—a pure Jersey and the best milker I had, an' the old man had to put up for her. Harve, he was watchin' the sun set acrost the marshes when the anamile got away; he argued that sunset was oncommon fine."

"Where the old man made his mistake was sending the boy East to school," said Phelps, stroking his goatee[30] and speaking in a deliberate, judicial tone. "There was where he got his head full of trapseing to Paris and all such folly. What Harve

[29] foundered—ill from overeating.

[30] goatee—small chin beard trimmed into a point.

needed, of all people, was a course in some first-class Kansas City business college."

The letters were swimming before Steavens' eyes. Was it possible that these men did not understand, that the palm on the coffin meant nothing to them? The very name of their town would have remained forever buried in the postal guide had it not been now and again mentioned in the world in connection with Harvey Merrick's. He remembered what his master had said to him on the day of his death, after the congestion of both lungs had shut off any probability of recovery, and the sculptor had asked his pupil to send his body home. "It's not a pleasant place to be lying while the world is moving and doing and bettering," he had said with a feeble smile, "but it rather seems as though we ought to go back to the place we came from, in the end. The townspeople will come in for a look at me; and after they have had their say, I shan't have much to fear from the judgment of God!"

The cattleman took up the comment. "Forty's young for a Merrick to cash in; they usually hang on pretty well. Probably he helped it along with whiskey."

"His mother's people were not long-lived, and Harvey never had a robust constitution," said the minister mildly. He would have liked to say more. He had been the boy's Sunday-school teacher and had been fond of him; but he felt that he was not in a position to speak. His own sons had turned out badly, and it was not a year since one of them had made his last trip home in the express car, shot in a gambling house in the Black Hills.

"Nevertheless, there is no disputin' that Harve frequently looked upon the wine when it was red, also variegated, and it shore made an oncommon fool of him," moralized the cattleman.

"Why is it that reputable young men are as scarce as millionaires in Sand City?"

Just then the door leading into the parlor rattled loudly and everyone started involuntarily, looking relieved when only Jim Laird came out. His red face was convulsed with anger, and the Grand Army man ducked his head when he saw the spark in his blue, bloodshot eye. They were all afraid of Jim; he was a drunkard but he could twist the law to suit his client's needs as no other man in all western Kansas could do, and there were many who tried. The lawyer closed the door gently behind him, leaned back against it, and folded his arms cocking his head a little to one side. When he assumed this attitude in the courtroom, ears were always pricked up, as it usually foretold a flood of withering sarcasm.

"I've been with you gentlemen before," he began in a dry, even tone, "when you've sat by the coffins of boys born and raised in this town; and, if I remember rightly, you were never any too well satisfied when you checked them up. What's the matter, anyhow? Why is it that reputable young men are as scarce as millionaires in Sand City? It might almost seem to a stranger that there was, some way, something the matter with your progressive town. Why did Reuben Sayer, the brightest young lawyer you ever turned out, after he had come home from the university as straight as a die, take to drinking and forge a check and shoot himself? Why did Bill Merrit's son die of the shakes in a saloon in Omaha? Why was Mr. Thomas' son, here, shot in a gambling house? Why did young Adams burn his mill to beat the insurance companies and go to the pen?"

The lawyer paused and unfolded his arms, laying one clenched fist quietly on the table. "I'll tell you why. Because you drummed nothing but money and knavery[31] into their ears from the time they wore knickerbockers; because you carped[32] away at them as you've been carping here tonight, holding our friends Phelps and Elder up to them for their models, as our grandfathers held up George Washington and John Adams. But the boys, worse luck, were young, and raw at the business you put them to; and how could they match coppers with such artists as Phelps and Elder? You wanted them to be successful rascals; they were only unsuccessful ones—that's all the difference. There was only one boy ever raised in this borderland between ruffianism and civilization who didn't come to grief, and you hated Harvey Merrick more for winning out than you hated all the other boys who got under the wheels. Lord! Lord, how you did hate him! Phelps, here, is fond of saying that he could buy and sell us all out any time he's a mind to; but he knew Harve wouldn't have given a tinker's damn for his bank and all his cattle farms put together; and a lack of appreciation, that way, goes hard with Phelps.

"Old Nimrod, here, thinks Harve drank too much; and this from such as Nimrod and me!

"Brother Elder says Harve was too free with the old man's money—fell short in filial consideration, maybe. Well, we can all remember the very tone in which brother Elder swore his own father was a liar, in the county court; and we all know that the old man came out of that partnership with his son as bare as a sheared lamb. But maybe I'm getting personal, and I'd better be driving ahead at what I want to say."

The lawyer paused a moment, squared his heavy shoulders, and went on: "Harvey Merrick and I went to school together, back East. We were dead in earnest, and we wanted you all to be proud of us someday. We meant to be great men. Even I, and I haven't lost my sense of humor, gentlemen, I meant to be a great man. I came back here to practice, and I found you didn't in the least want me to be a great man. You wanted me to be a shrewd lawyer—oh, yes! Our veteran here wanted me to get him an increase of pension, because he had dyspepsia;[33] Phelps wanted a new county survey that would put the widow Wilson's little bottom farm inside his south line; Elder wanted to lend money at five per cent a month, and get it collected; old Stark here wanted to wheedle old women up in Vermont into investing their annuities in real-estate mortgages that are not worth the paper

[31] knavery—dishonest or crafty dealing.

[32] carped—criticized.

[33] dyspepsia—indigestion.

they are written on. Oh, you needed me hard enough, and you'll go on needing me!

"Well, I came back here and became the damned shyster[34] you wanted me to be. You pretend to have some sort of respect for me; and yet you'll stand up and throw mud at Harvey Merrick, whose soul you couldn't dirty and whose hands you couldn't tie. Oh, you're a discriminating lot of Christians! There have been times when the sight of Harvey's name in some Eastern paper has made me hang my head like a whipped dog; and again, times when I liked to think of him off there in the world, away from all this hog wallow, climbing the big, clean upgrade he'd set for himself.

"And we? Now that we've fought and lied and sweated and stolen, and hated as only the disappointed strugglers in a bitter, dead little Western town know how to do, what have we got to show for it? Harvey Merrick wouldn't have given one sunset over your marshes for all you've got put together, and you know it. It's not for me to say why in the **inscrutable**[35] wisdom of God, a genius should ever have been called from this place of hatred and bitter waters; but I want this Boston man to know that the drivel he's been hearing here tonight is the only tribute any truly great man could have from such a lot of sick, side-tracked, burnt-dog, land-poor sharks as the here-present financiers of Sand City—upon which town may God have mercy!"

The lawyer thrust out his hand to Steavens as he passed him, caught up his overcoat in the hall, and had left the house before the Grand Army man had had time to lift his ducked head and crane his long neck about at his fellows.

Next day Jim Laird was drunk and unable to attend the funeral services. Steavens called twice at his office, but was compelled to start East without seeing him. He had a presentiment[36] that he would hear from him again, and left his address on the lawyer's table; but if Laird found it, he never acknowledged it. The thing in him that Harvey Merrick had loved must have gone underground with Harvey Merrick's coffin; for it never spoke again, and Jim got the cold he died of driving across the Colorado mountains to defend one of Phelps' sons who had got into trouble out there by cutting government timber.

---

[34] shyster—unethical lawyer.

[35] **inscrutable**—difficult to understand.

[36] presentiment—sense that something is about to occur; premonition.

QUESTIONS TO CONSIDER

1. What caused the death of Harvey Merrick?
2. What does Steavens learn about his teacher by accompanying his corpse home?
3. How does this affect his appreciation of Merrick?
4. What is Jim Laird condemning in his attack on Sand City?
5. What function does the final paragraph serve in the story? Do you think this improves or weakens the story?
   humanizes the hero?
6. What do you think distinguishes Cather's story from earlier local-color writing?

Zora Neale Hurston ▶

Drenched in Light

BY ZORA NEALE HURSTON

Zora Neale Hurston (1891–1960) was one of the most important writers of the Harlem Renaissance, an African-American literary and artistic movement that began in the 1920s in New York City's Harlem district. Hurston was born in Eatonville, Florida, the first self-governing African-American town in the country. She left school at thirteen to work, but a white woman for whom she worked as a maid arranged for Hurston to attend high school, and she was able to go on to college and graduate school at Columbia and Barnard in New York. Hurston studied anthropology and became the first serious collector of Florida's African-American folklore. The stories she heard heavily influenced the fiction she would write, as well as being published as two books, Mules and Men *(1935) and* Tell My Horse *(1938). Once in New York, Hurston became acquainted with many of the leading figures of the Harlem Renaissance. She published stories in the major magazines, collaborated with Langston Hughes, and had a series of plays produced. Almost all of Hurston's work is set in and around Eatonville, and she showed an absolute mastery of Southern dialect and the oral tradition that was a large part of African-American storytelling. In the 1930s, with the Depression putting an end to Harlem's success as an intellectual center, Hurston turned to writing novels.* Their Eyes Were Watching God *(1937) is now considered her masterpiece, but none of Hurston's novels were commercially successful, and she found herself out of fashion. She died in poverty in Florida, and her work was all but forgotten until the 1970s. Like "Drenched in Light," much of Hurston's fiction has an irresistible brightness and humor.*

"You Isie Watts! Git 'own offen dat gate post an' rake up dis yahd!"

The little brown figure perched upon the gate post looked yearningly up the gleaming shell road that led to Orlando, and down the road that led to Sanford and shrugged her thin shoulders. This heaped kindling on Grandma Potts' already burning ire.

"Lawd a-mussy!" she screamed, enraged—"Heah Joel, gimme dat wash stick. Ah'll show dat limb of Satan she kain't shake huhseff at *me.* If she ain't down by de time Ah gets dere, Ah'll break huh down in de lines."[1]

"Aw Gran'ma, Ah see Mist' George and Jim Robinson comin' and Ah wanted to wave at 'em," the child said **petulantly**.[2]

"You jes wave dat rake at dis heah yahd, madame, else Ah'll take you down a button hole lower. You'se too 'oomanish jumpin' up in everybody's face dat pass."

---

[1] lines—loins, area between the ribs and the hips.

[2] **petulantly**—irritably.

This struck the child in a very sore spot for nothing pleased her so much as to sit atop of the gate post and hail the passing vehicles on their way South to Orlando, or North to Sanford. That white shell road was her great attraction. She raced up and down the stretch of it that lay before her gate like a round eyed puppy hailing gleefully all travelers. Everybody in the country, white and colored, knew little Isis Watts, the joyful. The Robinson brothers, white cattlemen, were particularly fond of her and always extended a stirrup for her to climb up behind one of them for a short ride, or let her try to crack the long bull whips and yee whoo at the cows.

Grandma Potts went inside and Isis literally waved the rake at the "chaws" of ribbon cane[3] that lay so bountifully about the yard in company with the knots and peelings,[4] with a thick sprinkling of peanut hulls.[5]

The herd of cattle in their envelope of gray dust came alongside and Isis dashed out to the nearest stirrup and was lifted up.

"Hello theah Snidlits, I was wonderin' wheah you was," said Jim Robinson as she snuggled down behind him in the saddle. They were almost out of the danger zone when Grandma emerged.

"You Isie-s!" she bawled.

The child slid down on the opposite side from the house and executed a flank[6] movement through the corn patch that brought her into the yard from behind the privy.

"You lil' hasion you! Wheah you been?"

"Out in de back yahd" Isis lied and did a cart wheel and a few fancy steps on her way to the front again.

"If you doan git tuh dat yahd, Ah make a mommuk[7] of you!" Isis observed that Grandma was cutting a fancy assortment of switches from peach, guana,[8] and cherry trees.

She finished the yard by raking everything under the edge of the porch and began a romp with the dogs, those lean, floppy eared 'coon hounds that all country folks keep. But Grandma vetoed this also.

"Isie, you set 'own on dat porch! Uh great big 'leben yeah ole gal racin' an' rompin' lak dat—set 'own!"

Isis impatiently flung herself upon the steps.

"Git up offa dem steps, you aggravatin' limb, 'fore Ah git dem hick'ries tuh you, an' set yo' seff on a cheah."

Isis petulantly arose and sat down as violently as possible in a chair, but slid down until she all but sat upon her shoulder blades.

"Now look atcher," Grandma screamed, "Put yo' knees together, an' git up offen yo' backbone! Lawd, you know dis hellion is gwine make me stomp huh insides out."

---

[3] "chaws" of ribbon cane—strips of sugar cane used for chewing.

[4] peelings—thin strips or pieces.

[5] hulls—shells.

[6] flank—side.

[7] mommuk—dialect word meaning "scrap" or "piece."

[8] guana—small tropical tree yielding a durable fiber.

Isis sat bolt upright as if she wore a ramrod[9] down her back and began to whistle. Now there are certain things that Grandma Potts felt no one of this female persuasion should do—one was to sit with the knees separated, "settin' brazen"[10] she called it; another was whistling, another playing with boys, neither must a lady cross her legs.

She was lying on her back imagining herself various personages.

Up she jumped from her seat to get the switches.

"So youse whistlin' in mah face, huh!" She glared till her eyes were beady[11] and Isis bolted for safety. But the noon hour brought John Watts, the widowed father, and this excused the child from sitting for criticism.

Being the only girl in the family, of course she must wash the dishes, which she did in intervals between frolics[12] with the dogs. She even gave Jake, the puppy, a swim in the dishpan by holding him suspended above the water that reeked of "pot likker"—just high enough so that his feet would be immersed. The **deluded**[13] puppy swam and swam without ever crossing the pan, much to his annoyance. Hearing Grandma she hurriedly dropped him on the floor, which he tracked up with feet wet with dishwater.

Grandma took her patching and settled down in the front room to sew. She did this every afternoon, and invariably slept in the big red rocker with her head lolled back over the back, the sewing falling from her hand.

Isis had crawled under the center table with its red plush cover with little round balls for fringe. She was lying on her back imagining herself various personages. She wore trailing robes, golden slippers with blue bottoms. She rode white horses with flaring pink nostrils to the horizon, for she still believed that to be land's end. She was picturing herself gazing over the edge of the world into the abyss when the spool of cotton fell from Grandma's lap and rolled away under the whatnot. Isis drew back from her contemplation of the nothingness at the horizon and glanced up at the sleeping woman. Her head had fallen far back. She breathed with a regular "snark" intake and soft "poosah" exhaust. But Isis was a visual minded child. She heard the snores only subconsciously but she saw straggling beard on Grandma's chin, trembling a little with every "snark" and "poosah." They were long gray hairs curled here and there against the dark brown skin. Isis was moved with pity for her mother's mother.

"Poah Gran'ma needs a shave," she murmured, and set about it. Just then Joel, next older than Isis, entered with a can of bait.

"Come on Isie, les' we all go fishin'. The perch is bitin' fine in Blue Sink."

"Sh-sh—" cautioned his sister, "Ah got to shave Gran'ma."

"Who say so?" Joel asked, surprised.

---

[9] ramrod—rod for cleaning firearms, a reference to very straight posture.

[10] brazen—very bold.

[11] beady—small, round, and shiny.

[12] frolics—playing, merriment.

[13] **deluded**—deceived.

"Nobody doan hafta tell me. Look at her chin. No ladies don't weah no whiskers if they kin help it. But Gran'ma gittin' ole an' she doan know how to shave like me."

The conference adjourned to the back porch lest Grandma wake.

"Aw, Isie, you doan know nothin' 'bout shavin' a-tall—but a *man* lak *me*—"

"Ah do so know."

"You don't not. Ah'm goin' shave her mahseff."

"Naw, you won't neither, Smarty. Ah saw her first an' thought it all up first," Isis declared, and ran to the calico covered box on the wall above the wash basin and seized her father's razor. Joel was quick and seized the mug and brush.

"Now!" Isis cried defiantly, "Ah got the razor."

"Goody, goody, goody, pussy cat, Ah got th' brush an' you can't shave 'thout lather—see! Ah know mo' than you," Joel retorted.

"Aw, who don't know dat?" Isis pretended to scorn. But seeing her progress blocked for lack of lather she compromised.

"Ah know! Les' we all shave her. You lather an' Ah shave."

This was agreeable to Joel. He made mountains of lather and anointed his own chin, and the chin of Isis and the dogs, splashed the walls and at last was persuaded to lather Grandma's chin. Not that he was loath[14] but he wanted his new plaything to last as long as possible.

Isis stood on one side of the chair with the razor clutched cleaver fashion. The niceties of razor-handling had passed over her head. The thing with her was to *hold* the razor—sufficient in itself.

Joel splashed on the lather in great gobs and Grandma awoke.

For one bewildered moment she stared at the grinning boy with the brush and mug but sensing another presence, she turned to behold the business face of Isis and the razor-clutching hand. Her jaw dropped and Grandma, forgetting years and rheumatism,[15] bolted from the chair and fled the house, screaming.

"She's gone to tell papa, Isie. You didn't have no business wid his razor and he's gonna lick yo hide," Joel cried, running to replace mug and brush.

"You too, chuckle-head, you, too," retorted Isis. "You was playin' wid his brush and put it all over the dogs—Ah seen you put it on Ned an' Beulah." Isis shaved some slivers from the door jamb with the razor and replaced it in the box. Joel took his bait and pole and hurried to Blue Sink. Isis crawled under the house to brood over the whipping she knew would come. She had meant well.

But sounding brass and tinkling cymbal[16] drew her forth. The local lodge of the Grand United Order of Odd Fellows led by a braying,[17] thudding band, was marching in full regalia down the road. She had forgotten the barbecue and

---

[14] loath—reluctant, unwilling.

[15] rheumatism—a disease characterized by inflammation, swelling, and stiffness of the joints.

[16] sounding brass and tinkling cymbal—an allusion to Paul's First Letter to the Corinthians in the New Testament.

[17] braying—sounding loudly and harshly.

log-rolling to be held today for the benefit of the new hall.

Music to Isis meant motion. In a minute razor and whipping forgotten, she was doing a fair imitation of the Spanish dancer she had seen in a medicine show some time before. Isis' feet were gifted—she could dance most anything she saw.

No one listened to the Exalted one, for little by little the multitude had surrounded the brown dancer.

Up, up went her spirits, her brown little feet doing all sorts of intricate things and her body in rhythm, hand curving above her head. But the music was growing faint. Grandma nowhere in sight. She stole out of the gate, running and dancing after the band.

Then she stopped. She couldn't dance at the carnival. Her dress was torn and dirty. She picked a long stemmed daisy and, thrust it behind her ear. But the dress, no better. Oh, an idea! In the battered round topped trunk in the bedroom!

She raced back to the house, then, happier, raced down the white dusty road to the picnic grove, gorgeously clad. People laughed good naturedly at her, the band played and Isis danced because she couldn't help it. A crowd of children gather admiringly about her as she wheeled lightly about, hand on hip, flower between her teeth with the red and white fringe of the table-cloth—Grandma's new red table-cloth that she wore in lieu of a Spanish shawl—trailing in the dust. It was too ample for her meager form, but she wore it like a gipsy. Her brown feet twinkled in and out of the fringe. Some grown people joined the children about her. The Grand Exalted Ruler rose to speak; the band was hushed, but Isis danced on, the crowd clapping their hands for her. No one listened to the Exalted one, for little by little the multitude had surrounded the brown dancer.

An automobile drove up to the Crown and halted. Two white men and a lady got out and pushed into the crowd, suppressing mirth discreetly behind gloved hands. Isis looked up and waved them a magnificent hail and went on dancing until—

Grandma had returned to the house and missed Isis and straightway sought her at the festivities expecting to find her in her soiled dress, shoeless, gaping at the crowd, but what she saw drove her frantic. Here was her granddaughter dancing before a gaping crowd in her brand new red tablecloth, and reeking of lemon extract, for Isis had added the final touch to her costume. She *must* have perfume.

Isis saw Grandma and bolted. She heard her cry: "Mah Gawd, mah brand new table cloth Ah jus' bought f'um O'landah!" as she fled through the crowd and on into the woods.

She followed the little creek until she came to the ford in a rutty[18] wagon road that led to Apopka and laid down on the cool grass at the roadside. The April sun was quite hot.

Misery, misery and woe settled down upon her and the child wept. She knew another whipping was in store for her.

---

[18] rutty—full of ruts, holes.

"Oh, Ah wish Ah could die, then Gran'ma an' papa would be sorry they beat me so much. Ah b'leeve Ah'll run away an' never go home no mo'. Ah'm goin' drown mahseff in th' creek!" Her woe grew attractive.

Isis got up and waded into the water. She routed out a tiny 'gator and a huge bull frog. She splashed and sang, enjoying herself immensely. The purr of a motor struck her ear and she saw a large, powerful car jolting along the rutty road toward her. It stopped at the water's edge.

"Well, I declare, it's our little gypsy," exclaimed the man at the wheel. "What are you doing here, now?"

"Ah'm killin' mahseff," Isis declared dramatically. "Cause Gran'ma beats me too much."

There was a hearty burst of laughter from the machine.

"You'll last sometime the way you are going about it. Is this the way to Maitland? We want to go to the Park Hotel."

Isis saw no longer any reason to die. She came up out of the water, holding up the dripping fringe of the tablecloth.

"Naw, indeedy. You go to Maitlan' by the shell road—it goes by mah house—an' turn off at Lake Sebelia to the clay road that takes you right to the do'."

"Well," went on the driver, smiling furtively. "Could you quit dying long enough to go with us?"

"Yessuh," she said thoughtfully, "Ah wanta go wid you."

The door of the car swung open. She was invited to a seat beside the driver. She had often dreamed of riding in one of these heavenly chariots but never thought she would, actually.

"Jump in then, Madame Tragedy, and show us. We lost ourselves after we left your barbecue."

During the drive Isis explained to the kind lady who smelt faintly of violets and to the **indifferent**[19] men that she was really a princess. She told them about her trips to the horizon, about the trailing gowns, the gold shoes with blue bottoms—she insisted on the blue bottoms—the white charger, the time when she was Hercules and had slain numerous dragons and sundry[20] giants. At last the car approached her gate over which stood the umbrella Chinaberry tree. The car was abreast of the gate and had all but passed when Grandma spied her glorious tablecloth lying back against the upholstery of the Packard.

"You Isie-e!" she bawled, "You lil' wretch you! Come heah *dis instunt*."

"That's me," the child confessed, **mortified**,[21] to the lady on the rear seat.

"Oh, Sewell, stop the car. This is where the child lives. I hate to give her up though."

"Do you wanta keep me?" Isis brightened.

"Oh, I wish I could, you shining little morsel. Wait, I'll try to save you a whipping this time."

She dismounted with the **gaudy**[22] lemon flavored **culprit**[23] and advanced to the gate where Grandma stood glowering, switches in hand.

---

[19] **indifferent**—disinterested.

[20] sundry—various.

[21] **mortified**—ashamed.

[22] **gaudy**—showy in a tasteless or vulgar way.

[23] **culprit**—one guilty of a crime.

"You're gointuh ketchit f'um yo' haid to yo' heels m'lady. Jes' come in heah."

"Why, good afternoon," she accosted the furious grandparent. "You're not going to whip this poor little thing, are you?" the lady asked in conciliatory tones.

"Yes, Ma'am. She's de wustest lil' limb dat ever drawed bref. Jes' look at mah new table cloth, dat ain't never been washed. She done traipsed all over de woods, uh dancin' an' uh prancin' in it. She done took a razor to me t'day an' Lawd knows whut mo'."

Isis clung to the white hand fearfully.

"Ah wuzn't gointer hurt Gran'ma, miss—Ah wuz jus' gointer shave her whiskers fuh huh 'cause she's old an' can't."

The white hand closed tightly over the little brown one that was quite soiled. She could understand a voluntary act of love even though it miscarried.

"Now, Mrs. er—er—I didn't get the name—how much did your tablecloth cost?"

"One whole big silvah dollar down at O'landah—ain't had it a week yit."

"Now here's five dollars to get another one. The little thing loves laughter. I want her to go on to the hotel and dance in that tablecloth for me. I can stand a little light today—"

"Oh, yessum, yessum." Grandma cut in, "Everything's alright, sho' she kin go, yessum."

The lady went on: "I want brightness and this Isis is joy itself, why she's drenched in light!"

Isis for the first time in her life, felt herself appreciated and danced up and down in an ecstasy of joy for a minute.

"Now, behave yo'seff, Isie, ovah at de hotel wid de white folks," Grandma cautioned, pride in her voice, though she strove to hide it. "Lawd, ma'am, dat gal keeps me so frackshus, Ah doan know mah haid f'um mah feet. Ah orter comb huh haid, too, befo' she go wid you all."

"No, no, don't bother. I like her as she is. I don't think she'd like it either, being combed and scrubbed. Come on, Isis."

Feeling that Grandma had been somewhat **squelched**[24] did not detract from Isis' spirit at all. She pranced over to the waiting motor and this time seated herself on the rear seat between the sweet, smiling lady and the rather aloof man in gray.

"Ah'm gointer stay wid you all," she said with a great deal of warmth, and snuggled up to her benefactress. "Want me tuh sing a song fuh you?"

"There, Helen, you've been adopted," said the man with a short, harsh laugh.

"Oh, I hope so, Harry." She put her arm about the red draped figure at her side and drew it close until she felt the warm puffs of the child's breath against her side. She looked hungrily ahead of her and spoke into space rather than to anyone in the car. "I want a little of her sunshine to soak into my soul. I need it."

---

[24] **squelched**—crushed, put down, or silenced.

QUESTIONS TO CONSIDER

1. Why does Isis get into so much trouble?
2. Why does Helen want Isis to come with them? What does Isis represent to her?

Ernest Hemingway ▶

Soldier's Home

BY ERNEST HEMINGWAY

Ernest Hemingway (1898–1961) was deeply influenced by Sherwood Anderson's stories (page 201), but took Anderson's methods a step further. Hemingway developed an entirely new narrative technique: a style that was clipped, vivid, and muscular, evolving out of Hemingway's early work as a journalist. He was born near Chicago, but began his career as a newspaperman in Kansas City. He went off to fight in World War I, where he was seriously wounded, and he got his first taste of Europe, and experienced the tragedy that affected his whole generation. The war was one of the worst slaughters in history, decimating the young men of Europe and America. Those who survived no longer felt the same way about society, country, and the tight moral framework in which they grew up. They were called the "Lost Generation," young men and women more interested in pleasure and innovation than work and propriety. Many young Americans went abroad—it was very cheap for Americans to live overseas in the 1920s—and lived in the older, wearier, but more artistically innovative cultures of Europe. Hemingway went to Paris, where he wrote and did some freelance journalism. By the early 1920s, he was making a name for himself with his stories. The publication in 1926 of his novel The Sun Also Rises *pushed Hemingway to the forefront of American letters, a place he has never relinquished. Over the next 35 years, Hemingway produced a major body of work—novels, travel books, short stories, war reporting. He won the Nobel Prize for Literature in 1954. "Soldier's Home" is from Hemingway's first collection,* In Our Time *(1925). It displays Hemingway's powerful style and also the usual near-plotless narratives of his early stories. Hemingway believed that in his best stories he left out a crucial detail or idea, but that the audience implicitly understood it anyway. Hemingway's modern style and plotting were among the most influential literary innovations of the twentieth century.*

Krebs went to the war from a Methodist[1] college in Kansas. There is a picture which shows him among his fraternity brothers, all of them wearing exactly the same height and style collar. He enlisted in the Marines in 1917 and did not return to the United States until the second division returned from the Rhine in the summer of 1919.

There is a picture which shows him on the Rhine[2] with two German girls and another corporal. Krebs and the corporal look too big for their uniforms. The German girls are not beautiful. The Rhine does not show in the picture.

---

[1] Methodist—member of the Protestant denomination founded in the 1700s upon the teachings of John Wesley, which protested against the dominance over worship in the Anglican Church.

[2] Rhine—river flowing from central Switzerland through Germany to the North Sea.

By the time Krebs returned to his home town in Oklahoma the greeting of heroes was over. He came back much too late. The men from the town who had been drafted had all been welcomed elaborately on their return. There had been a great deal of hysteria. Now the reaction had set in. People seemed to think it was rather ridiculous for Krebs to be getting back so late, years after the war was over.

A distaste for everything that had happened to him in the war set in because of the lies he had told.

At first Krebs, who had been at Belleau Wood, Soissons, the Champagne, St. Mihiel, and in the Argonne[3] did not want to talk about the war at all. Later he felt the need to talk but no one wanted to hear about it. His town had heard too many **atrocity**[4] stories to be thrilled by actualities. Krebs found that to be listened to at all he had to lie, and after he had done this twice he, too, had a reaction against the war and against talking about it. A distaste for everything that had happened to him in the war set in because of the lies he had told. All of the times that had been able to make him feel cool and clear inside himself when he thought of them; the times so long back when he had done the one thing, the only thing for a man to do, easily and naturally, when he might have done something else, now lost their cool, valuable quality and then were lost themselves.

His lies were quite unimportant lies and consisted in attributing to himself things other men had seen, done, or heard of, and stating as facts certain apocryphal[5] incidents familiar to all soldiers. Even his lies were not sensational at the pool room. His acquaintances, who had heard detailed accounts of German women found chained to machine guns in the Argonne forest and who could not comprehend, or were barred by their patriotism from interest in, any German machine gunners who were not chained, were not thrilled by his stories.

Krebs acquired the nausea in regard to experience that is the result of untruth or exaggeration, and when he occasionally met another man who had really been a soldier and they talked a few minutes in the dressing room at a dance he fell into the easy pose of the old soldier among other soldiers: that he had been badly, sickeningly frightened all the time. In this way he lost everything.

During this time, it was late summer, he was sleeping late in bed, getting up to walk down town to the library to get a book, eating lunch at home, reading on the front porch until he became bored, and then walking down through the town to spend the hottest hours of the day in the cool dark of the pool room. He loved to play pool.

In the evening he practiced on his clarinet, strolled down town, read, and went to bed. He was still a hero to his two young sisters. His mother would have given him breakfast in bed if he had wanted it. She

[3] Belleau Wood . . . Argonne—places in northern France where the U.S. Army had fought bloody battles during the war.

[4] **atrocity**—relating to an act of violence by an enemy armed force on civilians or prisoners.

[5] apocryphal—fictitious.

often came in when he was in bed and asked him to tell her about the war, but her attention always wandered. His father was noncommittal.[6]

Before Krebs went away to the war he had never been allowed to drive the family motor car. His father was in the real estate business and always wanted the car to be at his command when he required it to take clients out into the country to show them a piece of farm property. The car always stood outside the First National Bank building where his father had an office on the second floor. Now, after the war, it was still the same car.

Nothing was changed in the town except that the young girls had grown up. But they lived in such a complicated world of already defined alliances and shifting feuds that Krebs did not feel the energy or the courage to break into it. He liked to look at them, though. There were so many good-looking young girls. Most of them had their hair cut short. When he went away only little girls wore their hair like that or girls that were fast. They all wore sweaters and shirt waists with round Dutch collars. It was a pattern. He liked to look at them from the front porch as they walked on the other side of the street. He liked to watch them walking under the shade of the trees. He liked the round Dutch collars above their sweaters. He liked their silk stockings and flat shoes. He liked their bobbed[7] hair and the way they walked.

When he was in town their appeal to him was not very strong. He did not like them when he saw them in the Greek's ice cream parlor. He did not want them themselves really. They were too complicated. There was something else. Vaguely he wanted a girl but he did not want to have to work to get her. He would have liked to have a girl but he did not want to have to spend a long time getting her. He did not want to get into the intrigue and the politics. He did not want to have to do any courting. He did not want to tell any more lies. It wasn't worth it.

He did not want any consequences. He did not want any consequences ever again. He wanted to live along without consequences. Besides he did not really need a girl. The army had taught him that. It was all right to pose as though you had to have a girl. Nearly everybody did that. But it wasn't true. You did not need a girl. That was the funny thing. First a fellow boasted how girls mean nothing to him, that he never thought of them, that they could not touch him. Then a fellow boasted that he could not get along without girls, that he had to have them all the time, that he could not go to sleep without them.

That was all a lie. It was all a lie both ways. You did not need a girl unless you thought about them. He learned that in the army. Then sooner or later you always got one. When you were really ripe for a girl you always got one. You did not have to think about it. Sooner or later it would come. He had learned that in the army.

Now he would have liked a girl if she had come to him and not wanted to talk.

---

[6] noncommittal—not revealing thoughts or feelings.

[7] bobbed—cut short.

But here at home it was all too complicated. He knew he could never get through it all again. It was not worth the trouble. That was the thing about French girls and German girls. There was not all this talking. You couldn't talk much and you did not need to talk. It was simple and you were friends. He thought about France and then he began to think about Germany. On the whole he had liked Germany better. He did not want to leave Germany. He did not want to come home. Still, he had come home. He sat on the front porch.

He liked the girls that were walking along the other side of the street. He liked the look of them much better than the French girls or the German girls. But the world they were in was not the world he was in. He would like to have one of them. But it was not worth it. They were such a nice pattern. He liked the pattern. It was exciting. But he would not go through all the talking. He did not want one badly enough. He liked to look at them all, though. It was not worth it. Not now when things were getting good again.

He sat there on the porch reading a book on the war. It was a history and he was reading about all the engagements he had been in. It was the most interesting reading he had ever done. He wished there were more maps. He looked forward with a good feeling to reading all the really good histories when they would come out with good detail maps. Now he was really learning about the war. He had been a good soldier. That made a difference.

One morning after he had been home about a month his mother came into his bedroom and sat on the bed. She smoothed her apron.

"I had a talk with your father last night, Harold," she said, "and he is willing for you to take the car out in the evenings."

"Yeah?" said Krebs, who was not fully awake. "Take the car out? Yeah?"

"Yes. Your father has felt for some time that you should be able to take the car out in the evenings whenever you wished but we only talked it over last night."

"I'll bet you made him," Krebs said.

"No. It was your father's suggestion that we talk the matter over."

"Yeah. I'll bet you made him," Krebs sat up in bed.

"Will you come down to breakfast, Harold?" his mother said.

"As soon as I get my clothes on," Krebs said.

His mother went out of the room and he could hear her frying something downstairs while he washed, shaved, and dressed to go down into the dining-room for breakfast. While he was eating breakfast his sister brought in the mail.

"Well, Hare," she said. "You old sleepyhead. What do you ever get up for?"

Krebs looked at her. He liked her. She was his best sister.

"Have you got the paper?" he asked.

She handed him the Kansas City Star and he shucked off its brown wrapper and opened it to the sporting page. He folded the Star open and propped it against the water pitcher with his cereal dish to steady it, so he could read while he ate.

"Harold," his mother stood in the kitchen doorway, "Harold, please don't muss up the paper. Your father can't read his *Star* if it's been mussed."

"I won't muss it," Krebs said.

His sister sat down at the table and watched him while he read.

"We're playing indoor over at school this afternoon," she said. "I'm going to pitch."

"Good," said Krebs. "How's the old wing?"[8]

"I can pitch better than lots of the boys. I tell them all you taught me. The other girls aren't much good."

"Yeah?" said Krebs.

"I tell them all you're my beau.[9] Aren't you my beau, Hare?"

"You bet."

"Couldn't your brother really be your beau just because he's your brother?"

"I don't know."

"Sure you know. Couldn't you be my beau, Hare, if I was old enough and if you wanted to?"

"Sure. You're my girl now."

"Am I really your girl?"

"Sure."

"Do you love me?"

"Uh, huh."

"Will you love me always?"

"Sure."

"Will you come over and watch me play indoor?"

"Maybe."

"Aw, Hare, you don't love me. If you loved me, you'd want to come over and watch me play indoor."

Krebs's mother came into the dining-room from the kitchen. She carried a plate with two fried eggs and some crisp bacon on it and a plate of buckwheat cakes.

"You run along, Helen," she said. "I want to talk to Harold."

She put the eggs and bacon down in front of him and brought in a jug of maple syrup for the buckwheat cakes. Then she sat down across the table from Krebs.

"I wish you'd put down the paper a minute, Harold," she said.

Krebs took down the paper and folded it.

"Have you decided what you are going to do yet, Harold?" his mother said, taking off her glasses.

"No," said Krebs.

"Don't you think it's about time?" His mother did not say this in a mean way. She seemed worried.

"I hadn't thought about it," Krebs said.

"God has some work for everyone to do," his mother said. "There can be no idle hands in His Kingdom."

"I'm not in His Kingdom," Krebs said.

"We are all of us in His Kingdom."

Krebs felt embarrassed and resentful as always.

"I've worried about you so much, Harold," his mother went on. "I know the temptations you must have been exposed to. I know how weak men are. I know what your own dear grandfather, my own father, told us about the Civil War and I have prayed for you. I pray for you all day long, Harold."

Krebs looked at the bacon fat hardening on his plate.

"Your father is worried, too," his mother went on. "He thinks you have lost

---

8 wing—baseball slang, meaning "pitching arm."

9 beau—boyfriend.

your ambition, that you haven't got a definite aim in life. Charley Simmons, who is just your age, has a good job and is going to be married. The boys are all settling down; they're all determined to get somewhere; you can see that boys like Charley Simmons are on their way to being really a credit to the community."

Krebs said nothing.

"Don't look that way, Harold," his mother said. "You know we love you and I want to tell you for your own good how matters stand. Your father does not want to hamper your freedom. He thinks you should be allowed to drive the car. If you want to take some of the nice girls out riding with you, we are only too pleased. We want you to enjoy yourself. But you are going to have to settle down to work, Harold. Your father doesn't care what you start in at. All work is honorable as he says. But you've got to make a start at something. He asked me to speak to you this morning and then you can stop in and see him at his office."

"Is that all?" Krebs said.

"Yes. Don't you love your mother, dear boy?"

"No," Krebs said.

His mother looked at him across the table. Her eyes were shiny. She started crying.

"I don't love anybody," Krebs said.

It wasn't any good. He couldn't tell her, he couldn't make her see it. It was silly to have said it. He had only hurt her. He went over and took hold of her arm. She was crying with her head in her hands.

"I didn't mean it," he said. "I was just angry at something. I didn't mean I didn't love you."

His mother went on crying. Krebs put his arm on her shoulder.

"Can't you believe me, mother?"

His mother shook her head.

"Please, please, mother. Please believe me."

"All right," his mother said chokily. She looked up at him. "I believe you, Harold."

Krebs kissed her hair. She put her face up to him.

"I'm your mother," she said. "I held you next to my heart when you were a tiny baby."

Krebs felt sick and vaguely nauseated.

"I know, Mummy," he said. "I'll try and be a good boy for you."

"Would you kneel and pray with me, Harold?" his mother asked.

They knelt down beside the dining-room table and Krebs's mother prayed.

"Now, you pray, Harold," she said.

"I can't," Krebs said.

"Try, Harold."

"I can't."

"Do you want me to pray for you?"

"Yes."

So his mother prayed for him and then they stood up and Krebs kissed his mother and went out of the house. He had tried so to keep his life from being complicated. Still, none of it had touched him. He had felt sorry for his mother and she had made him lie. He would go to Kansas City and get a job and she would feel all right about it. There would be one more scene maybe before he got away. He would not go down to his father's office. He would miss that one. He wanted his life to go smoothly. It had just gotten going that way. Well, that was all over now, anyway. He would go over to the schoolyard and watch Helen play indoor baseball.

QUESTIONS TO CONSIDER

1. Why does Hemingway begin the story by describing the picture of Krebs and his fraternity brothers?
2. Why does Krebs not like to talk about the war?
3. How has the war changed him and his view of his town, family, and women?
4. Does his mother understand Krebs? Does she sympathize with what he did during the war? Explain your answers.
5. From reading the story, how would you describe the typical member of the "Lost Generation" that returned from World War I?

Dorothy Parker ▶

Glory in the Daytime

BY DOROTHY PARKER

Dorothy Parker (1893–1967) is most famous as a wit, the creator of some of the most barbed lines in American cultural history. (She once began a book review: "This is not a novel to be tossed aside lightly. It should be thrown with great force.") Parker was raised in New York City and after college began working at magazines. She joined The New Yorker *when it was founded in 1925 and was always associated with its sophisticated circle of writers. This weekly magazine was famed for its mix of short stories, poems, criticism, cartoons, and articles, all written with its trademark sophistication and wit, and Parker was one of the magazine's signature contributors, along with James Thurber, the cartoonist Charles Addams, E. B. White, Ogden Nash, Edmund Wilson, and a long list of America's most prominent writers. Parker's first book of poems,* Enough Rope *(1926), was a bestseller, and allowed her to write full-time. She was already one of the best-known personalities of New York's literary set, many of whom gathered each day at the Algonquin Hotel to lunch and trade quips. With the Depression, Parker went to Hollywood as a screenwriter, where she would spend much of the rest of her life. She continued to turn out impressive stories, but her work will always be associated with the boom times of the 1920s. The high living of that era had taken its toll. Many of Parker's closest friends died young, and she herself battled alcoholism and had two failed marriages. Her writings exhibit her deep pessimism about life, success, and particularly love.*

Mr. Murdock was one who carried no enthusiasm whatever for plays and their players, and that was too bad, for they meant so much to little Mrs. Murdock. Always she had been in a state of devout[1] excitement over the luminous, free, passionate elect who serve the theater. And always she had done her wistful[2] worshiping, along with the multitudes, at the great public altars. It is true that once, when she was a particularly little girl, love had impelled her to write Miss Maude Adams[3] a letter beginning "Dearest Peter," and she had received from Miss Adams a miniature thimble inscribed "A kiss from Peter Pan." (That was a day!) And once, when her mother had taken her holiday shopping, a limousine door was held open and there had passed her, as close as *that*, a wonder of sable[4] and violets and round red curls that seemed to tinkle on the air; so, forever after, she was as good as certain

[1] devout—devoted, earnest.

[2] wistful—yearning, longing.

[3] Maude Adams—delicate American actress (1872–1953) best known for her portrayal of Peter Pan.

[4] sable—fur.

that she had been not a foot away from Miss Billie Burke.[5] But until some three years after her marriage, these had remained her only personal experiences with the people of the lights and the glory.

Then it turned out that Miss Noyes, new come to little Mrs. Murdock's own bridge club, knew an actress. She actually knew an actress; the way you and I know collectors of recipes and members of garden clubs and amateurs of needlepoint.

The name of the actress was Lily Wynton, and it was famous. She was tall and slow and silvery; often she appeared in the role of a duchess, or of a Lady Pam or an Honorable Moira. Critics **recurrently**[6] referred to her as "that great lady of our stage." Mrs. Murdock had attended, over years, matinee performances of the Wynton successes. And she had no more thought that she would one day have opportunity to meet Lily Wynton face to face than she had thought—well, than she had thought of flying!

Yet it was not astounding that Miss Noyes should walk at ease among the glamorous. Miss Noyes was full of depths and mystery, and she could talk with a cigarette still between her lips. She was always doing something difficult, like designing her own pajamas, or reading Proust,[7] or modeling torsos in plasticine.[8] She played excellent bridge. She liked little Mrs. Murdock. "Tiny one," she called her.

"How's for coming to tea tomorrow, tiny one? Lily Wynton's going to drop up," she said, at a therefore memorable meeting of the bridge club. "You might like to meet her."

The words fell so easily that she could not have realized their weight. Lily Wynton was coming to tea. Mrs. Murdock might like to meet her. Little Mrs. Murdock walked home through the early dark, and stars sang in the sky above her.

Little Mrs. Murdock walked home through the early dark, and stars sang in the sky above her.

Mr. Murdock was already at home when she arrived. It required but a glance to tell that for him there had been no singing stars that evening in the heavens. He sat with his newspaper opened at the financial page, and bitterness had its way with his soul. It was not the time to cry happily to him of the impending hospitalities of Miss Noyes; not the time, that is, if one anticipated exclamatory sympathy. Mr. Murdock did not like Miss Noyes. When pressed for a reason, he replied that he just plain didn't like her. Occasionally he added, with a sweep that might have commanded a certain admiration, that all those women made him sick. Usually, when she told him of the **temperate**[9] activities of the bridge club meetings, Mrs. Murdock kept any mention of Miss Noyes's name from the accounts. She had found that this omission

---

[5] Billie Burke (1885–1970)—star of the New York stage in the early 20th century. She was married to the renowned impresario Florenz Ziegfeld in 1914.

[6] **recurrently**—repeatedly.

[7] Proust—Marcel Proust (1871–1922), French novelist famous for the modern classic *Remembrance of Things Past.*

[8] plasticine—synthetic substitute for clay or wax.

[9] **temperate**—moderated, restrained.

made for a more agreeable evening. But now she was caught in such a sparkling swirl of excitement that she had scarcely kissed him before she was off on her story.

"Oh, Jim," she cried. "Oh, what do you think! Hallie Noyes asked me to tea tomorrow to meet Lily Wynton!"

"Who's Lily Wynton?" he said.

"Ah, Jim," she said. "Ah, really, Jim. Who's Lily Wynton! Who's Greta Garbo,[10] I suppose!"

"She some actress or something?" he said.

Mrs. Murdock's shoulders sagged. "Yes, Jim," she said. "Yes. Lily Wynton's an actress."

She picked up her purse and started slowly toward the door. But before she had taken three steps, she was again caught up in her sparkling swirl. She turned to him, and her eyes were shining.

"Honestly," she said, "it was the funniest thing you ever heard in your life. We'd just finished the last rubber—oh, I forgot to tell you, I won three dollars, isn't that pretty good for me?—and Hallie Noyes said to me, 'Come on in to tea tomorrow. Lily Wynton's going to drop up,' she said. Just like that, she said it. Just as if it was anybody."

"Drop up?" he said. "How can you drop up?"

"Honestly, I don't know what I said when she asked me," Mrs. Murdock said. "I suppose I said I'd love to—I guess I must have. But I was so simply—Well, you know how I've always felt about Lily Wynton. Why, when I was a little girl, I used to collect her pictures. And I've seen her in, oh, everything she's ever been in, I should think, and I've read every word about her, and interviews and all. Really and truly, when I think of meeting her—Oh, I'll simply die. What on earth shall I say to her?"

"You might ask her how she'd like to try dropping down, for a change," Mr. Murdock said.

"All right, Jim," Mrs. Murdock said. "If that's the way you want to be."

Wearily she went toward the door, and this time she reached it before she turned to him. There were no lights in her eyes.

"It—it isn't so awfully nice," she said, "to spoil somebody's pleasure in something. I was so thrilled about this. You don't see what it is to me, to meet Lily Wynton. To meet somebody like that, and see what they're like, and hear what they say, and maybe get to know them. People like that mean—well, they mean something different to me. They're not like this. They're not like me. Who do I ever see? What do I ever hear? All my whole life, I've wanted to know—I've almost prayed that someday I could meet— Well. All right, Jim."

She went out, and on to her bedroom.

Mr. Murdock was left with only his newspaper and his bitterness for company. But he spoke aloud.

"'Drop up!'" he said. " 'Drop up,' for God's sake!"

The Murdocks dined, not in silence, but in pronounced quiet. There was something

[10] Greta Garbo (1905–1990)—Swedish-born American movie star.

straitened[11] about Mr. Murdock's stillness; but little Mrs. Murdock's was the sweet, far quiet of one given over to dreams. She had forgotten her weary words to her husband, she had passed through her excitement and her disappointment. Luxuriously she floated on innocent visions of days after the morrow. She heard her own voice in future conversations. . . .

I saw Lily Wynton at Hallie's the other day, and she was telling me all about her new play—no, I'm, terribly sorry, but it's a secret, I promised her I wouldn't tell anyone the name of it . . . Lily Wynton dropped up to tea yesterday, and we just got to talking, and she told me the most interesting things about her life; she said she'd never dreamed of telling them to anyone else. . . . Why, I'd love to come, but I promised to have lunch with Lily Wynton. . . . I had a long, long letter from Lily Wynton. . . . Lily Wynton called me up this morning. . . . Whenever I feel blue, I just go and have a talk with Lily Wynton, and then I'm all right again. . . . Lily Wynton told me . . . Lily Wynton and I . . . "Lily," I said to her . . .

The next morning, Mr. Murdock had left for his office before Mrs. Murdock rose. This had happened several times before, but not often. Mrs. Murdock felt a little queer about it. Then she told herself that it was probably just as well. Then she forgot all about it, and gave her mind to the selection of a costume suitable to the afternoon's event. Deeply she felt that her small wardrobe included no dress adequate to the occasion; for, of course, such an occasion had never before arisen. She finally decided upon a frock of dark blue serge[12] with fluted white muslin[13] about the neck and wrists. It was her style, that was the most she could say for it. And that was all she could say for herself. Blue serge and little white ruffles—that was she.

The very becomingness of the dress lowered her spirits. A nobody's frock, worn by a nobody. She blushed and went hot when she recalled the dreams she had woven the night before, the mad visions of intimacy, of equality with Lily Wynton. **Timidity**[14] turned her heart liquid, and she thought of telephoning Miss Noyes and saying she had a bad cold and could not come. She steadied, when she planned a course of conduct to pursue at teatime. She would not try to say anything; if she stayed silent, she could not sound foolish. She would listen and watch and worship and then come home, stronger, braver, better for an hour she would remember proudly all her life.

Miss Noyes's living-room was done in the early modern period. There were a great many **oblique**[15] lines and acute angles, zigzags of aluminum and horizontal stretches of mirror. The color scheme was sawdust and steel. No seat was more than twelve inches above the floor, no table was made of wood. It was, as has been said of larger places, all right for a visit.

Little Mrs. Murdock was the first arrival. She was glad of that; no, maybe it

---

[11] straitened—stiff.

[12] serge—kind of fabric with diagonal lines or ridges on its surface.

[13] muslin—thin, fine cotton cloth.

[14] **Timidity**—shyness, hesitance.

[15] **oblique**—having a slanting direction.

would have been better to have come after Lily Wynton; no, maybe this was right. The maid motioned her toward the living-room, and Miss Noyes greeted her in the cool voice and the warm words that were her special combination. She wore black velvet trousers, a red cummerbund, and a white silk shirt, opened at the throat. A cigarette clung to her lower lip, and her eyes, as was her habit, were held narrow against its near smoke.

Lily Wynton was a great actress. A great actress meant romance.

"Come in, come in, tiny one," she said. "Bless its little heart. Take off its little coat. Good Lord, you look easily eleven years old in that dress. Sit ye doon, here beside of me. There'll be a spot of tea in a jiff."

Mrs. Murdock sat down on the vast, perilously low divan, and, because she was never good at reclining among cushions, held her back straight. There was room for six like her, between herself and her hostess. Miss Noyes lay back with one ankle flung upon the other knee, and looked at her.

"I'm a wreck," Miss Noyes announced. "I was modeling like a mad thing, all night long. It's taken everything out of me. I was like a thing bewitched."

"Oh, what were you making?" cried Mrs. Murdock.

"Oh, Eve,"[16] Miss Noyes said. "I always do Eve. What else is there to do? You must come pose for me some time, tiny one. You'd be nice to do. Ye-es, you'd be very nice to do. My tiny one."

"Why, I—" Mrs. Murdock said, and stopped. "Thank you very much, though," she said.

"I wonder where Lily is," Miss Noyes said. "She said she'd be here early—well, she always says that. You'll adore her, tiny one. She's really rare. She's a real person. And she's been through perfect hell. God, what a time she's had!"

"Ah, what's been the matter?" said Mrs. Murdock.

"Men," Miss Noyes said. "Men. She never had a man that wasn't a louse." Gloomily she stared at the toe of her flat-heeled patent leather pump. "A pack of lice, always. All of them. Leave her for the first little floozie[17] that comes along."

"But—" Mrs. Murdock began. No, she couldn't have heard right. How could it be right? Lily Wynton was a great actress. A great actress meant romance. Romance meant Grand Dukes and Crown Princes and diplomats touched with gray at the temples and lean, bronzed, reckless Younger Sons. It meant pearls and emeralds and chinchilla[18] and rubies red as the blood that was shed for them. It meant a grim-faced boy sitting in the fearful Indian midnight, beneath the dreary whirring of the *punkahs*,[19] writing a letter to the lady he had seen but once; writing his poor heart out, before he turned to the service revolver

[16] Eve—in the Bible, the first woman.

[17] floozie—woman regarded as cheap and gaudy.

[18] chinchilla—South American rodent that has prized bluish-gray fur.

[19] *punkahs*—in India, large swinging overhead fans that are kept in motion by servants.

that lay beside him on the table. It meant a golden-locked poet, floating face downward in the sea, and in his pocket his last great sonnet to the lady of ivory. It meant brave, beautiful men, living and dying for the lady who was the pale bride of art, whose eyes and heart were soft with only compassion for them.

A pack of lice. Crawling after little floozies; whom Mrs. Murdock swiftly and hazily pictured as rather like ants.

"But—" said little Mrs. Murdock.

"She gave them all her money," Miss Noyes said. "She always did. Or if she didn't, they took it anyway. Took every cent she had, and then spat in her face. Well, maybe I'm teaching her a little bit of sense now. Oh, there's the bell—that'll be Lily. No, sit ye doon, tiny one. You belong there."

Miss Noyes rose and made for the archway that separated the living-room from the hall. As she passed Mrs. Murdock, she stooped suddenly, cupped her guest's round chin, and quickly, lightly kissed her mouth.

"Don't tell Lily," she murmured, very low.

Mrs. Murdock puzzled. Don't tell Lily what? Could Hallie Noyes think that she might babble to the Lily Wynton of these strange confidences about the actress's life? Or did she mean—But she had no more time for puzzling. Lily Wynton stood in the archway. There she stood, one hand resting on the wooden molding and her body swayed toward it, exactly as she stood for her third-act entrance of her latest play, and for a like half-minute.

You would have known her anywhere, Mrs. Murdock thought. Oh, yes, anywhere. Or at least you would have exclaimed, "That woman looks something like Lily Wynton." For she was somehow different in the daylight. Her figure looked heavier, thicker, and her face—there was so much of her face that the surplus sagged from the strong, fine bones. And her eyes, those famous dark, liquid eyes. They were dark, yes, and certainly liquid, but they were set in little hammocks of folded flesh, and seemed to be set but loosely, so readily did they roll. Their whites, that were visible all around the irises, were threaded with tiny scarlet veins.

"I suppose footlights are an awful strain on their eyes," thought little Mrs. Murdock.

Lily Wynton wore, just as she should have, black satin and sables, and long white gloves were wrinkled luxuriously about her wrists. But there were delicate streaks of grime in the folds of her gloves, and down the shining length of her gown there were small, irregularly shaped dull patches; bits of food or drops of drink, or perhaps both, sometime must have slipped their carriers and found brief sanctuary there. Her hat—oh, her hat. It was romance, it was mystery, it was strange, sweet sorrow; it was Lily Wynton's hat, of all the world, and no other could dare it. Black it was, and tilted, and a great, soft plume drooped from it to follow her cheek and curl across her throat. Beneath it, her hair had the various **hues**[20] of neglected brass. But, oh, her hat.

[20] **hues**—colors, shades.

"Darling!" cried Miss Noyes.

"Angel," said Lily Wynton. "My sweet."

It was that voice. It was that deep, soft, glowing voice. "Like purple velvet," someone had written. Mrs. Murdock's heart beat visibly.

"She's a museum piece. She's a devoted wife."

Lily Wynton cast herself upon the steep bosom of her hostess, and murmured there. Across Miss Noyes's shoulder she caught sight of little Mrs. Murdock.

"And who is this?" she said. She disengaged herself.

"That's my tiny one," Miss Noyes said. "Mrs. Murdock."

"What a clever little face," said Lily Wynton. "Clever, clever little face. What does she do, sweet Hallie? I'm sure she writes, doesn't she? Yes, I can feel it. She writes beautiful, beautiful words. Don't you, child?"

"Oh, no, really I—" Mrs. Murdock said.

"And you must write me a play," said Lily Wynton. "A beautiful, beautiful play. And I will play in it, over and over the world, until I am a very, very old lady. And then I will die. But I will never be forgotten, because of the years I played in your beautiful, beautiful play."

She moved across the room. There was a slight hesitancy, a seeming insecurity, in her step, and when she would have sunk into a chair, she began to sink two inches, perhaps, to its right. But she swayed just in time in her descent, and was safe.

"To write," she said, smiling sadly at Mrs. Murdock, "to write. And such a little thing, for such a big gift. Oh, the privilege of it. But the anguish of it, too. The agony."

"But, you see, I—" said little Mrs. Murdock.

"Tiny one doesn't write, Lily," Miss Noyes said. She threw herself back upon the divan. "She's a museum piece. She's a devoted wife."

"A wife!" Lily Wynton said. "A wife. Your first marriage, child?"

"Oh, yes," said Mrs. Murdock.

"How sweet," Lily Wynton said. "How sweet, sweet, sweet. Tell me, child, do you love him very, very much?"

"Why, I—" said little Mrs. Murdock, and blushed. "I've been married for ages," she said.

"You love him," Lily Wynton said. "You love him. And is it sweet to go to bed with him?"

"Oh—" said Mrs. Murdock, and blushed till it hurt.

"The first marriage," Lily Wynton said. "Youth, youth. Yes, when I was your age I used to marry, too. Oh, treasure your love, child, guard it, live in it. Laugh and dance in the love of your man. Until you find out what he's really like."

There came a sudden visitation upon her. Her shoulders jerked upward, her cheeks puffed, her eyes sought to start from their hammocks. For a moment she sat thus, then slowly all subsided into place. She lay back in her chair, tenderly patting her chest. She shook her head sadly, and there was grieved wonder in the look with which she held Mrs. Murdock.

"Gas," said Lily Wynton, in the famous voice. "Gas. Nobody knows what I suffer from it."

"Oh, I'm so sorry," Mrs. Murdock said. "Is there anything—"

"Nothing," Lily Wynton said. "There is nothing. There is nothing that can be done for it. I've been everywhere."

"How's for a spot of tea, perhaps?" Miss Noyes said. "It might help." She turned her face toward the archway and lifted up her voice. "Mary! Where the hell's the tea?"

"You don't know," Lily Wynton said, with her grieved eyes fixed on Mrs. Murdock, "you don't know what stomach distress is. You can never, never know, unless you're a stomach sufferer yourself. I've been one for years. Years and years and years."

"I'm terribly sorry," Mrs. Murdock said.

"Nobody knows the anguish," Lily Wynton said. "The agony."

The maid appeared, bearing a triangular tray upon which was set an heroic-sized tea service of bright white china, each piece a hectagon.[21] She set it down on a table within the long reach of Miss Noyes and retired, as she had come, bashfully.

"Sweet Hallie," Lily Wynton said, "my sweet. Tea—I adore it. I worship it. But my distress turns it to gall and wormwood[22] in me. Gall and wormwood. For hours, I should have no peace. Let me have a little, tiny bit of your beautiful, beautiful brandy, instead."

"You really think you should, darling?" Miss Noyes said. "You know—"

"My angel," said Lily Wynton, "it's the only thing for acidity."

"Well," Miss Noyes said. "But do remember you've got a performance tonight." Again she hurled her voice at the archway. "Mary! Bring the brandy and a lot of soda and ice and things."

"Oh, no, my saint," Lily Wynton said. "No, no, sweet Hallie. Soda and ice are rank poison to me. Do you want to freeze my poor, weak stomach? Do you want to kill poor, poor Lily?"

"Mary!" roared Miss Noyes. "Just bring the brandy and a glass." She turned to little Mrs. Murdock. "How's for your tea, tiny one? Cream? Lemon?"

"Cream, if I may, please," Mrs. Murdock said. "And two lumps of sugar, please, if I may."

"Oh, youth, youth," Lily Wynton said. "Youth and love."

The maid returned with an octagonal tray supporting a decanter of brandy and a wide, squat, heavy glass. Her head twisted on her neck in a spasm of **diffidence**.[23]

"Just pour it for me, will you, my dear?" said Lily Wynton. "Thank you. And leave the pretty, pretty decanter here, on this enchanting little table. Thank you. You're so good to me."

The maid vanished, fluttering. Lily Wynton lay back in her chair, holding in her gloved hand the wide, squat glass, colored brown to the brim. Little Mrs. Murdock lowered her eyes to her teacup, carefully

---

[21] hectagon—hundred-sided figure (presumably an error for hexagon, a six-sided figure).

[22] gall and wormwood—words used to indicate something bitter tasting.

[23] **diffidence**—shyness.

carried it to her lips, sipped, and replaced it on its saucer. When she raised her eyes, Lily Wynton lay back in her chair, holding in her gloved hand the wide, squat, colorless glass.

"My life," Lily Wynton said, slowly, "is a mess. A stinking mess. It always has been, and it always will be. Until I am a very, very old lady. Ah, little Clever-Face, you writers don't know what struggle is."

"But really I'm not—" said Mrs. Murdock.

"To write," Lily Wynton said. "To write. To set one word beautifully beside another word. The privilege of it. The blessed, blessed peace of it. Oh, for quiet, for rest. But do you think those cheap bastards would close that play while it's doing a nickel's worth of business? Oh, no. Tired as I am, sick as I am, I must drag along. Oh, child, child, guard your precious gift. Give thanks for it. It is the greatest thing of all. It is the only thing. To write."

"Darling, I told you tiny one doesn't write," said Miss Noyes. "How's for making more sense? She's a wife."

"Ah, yes, she told me. She told me she had perfect, passionate love," Lily Wynton said. "Young love. It is the greatest thing. It is the only thing." She grasped the decanter; and again the squat glass was brown to the brim.

"What time did you start today, darling?" said Miss Noyes.

"Oh, don't scold me, sweet love," Lily Wynton said. "Lily hasn't been naughty. Her wuzzunt naughty dirl 't all. I didn't get up until late, late, late. And though I parched,[24] though I burned, I didn't have a drink until after my breakfast. 'It is for Hallie,' I said." She raised the glass to her mouth, tilted it, and brought it away, colorless.

"Good Lord, Lily," Miss Noyes said. "Watch yourself. You've got to walk on that stage tonight, my girl."

"All the world's a stage,[25]" said Lily Wynton. "And all the men and women merely players. They have their entrance and their exitses and each man in his time plays many parts, his act being seven ages. At first, the infant, mewling[26] and puking—"

"How's the play doing?" Miss Noyes said.

"Oh, lousily," Lily Wynton said. "Lousily, lousily, lousily. But what isn't? What isn't, in this terrible, terrible world? Answer me that." She reached for the decanter.

"Lily, listen," said Miss Noyes. "Stop that. Do you hear?"

"Please, sweet Hallie," Lily Wynton said. "Pretty please. Poor, poor Lily."

"Do you want me to do what I had to do last time?" Miss Noyes said. "Do you want me to strike you, in front of tiny one, here?"

Lily Wynton drew herself high. "You do not realize," she said, icily, "what acidity is." She filled the glass and held it, regarding it as though through a lorgnon.[27] Suddenly her manner changed, and she looked up and smiled at little Mrs. Murdock.

---

[24] parched—became thirsty.

[25] "All the world's a stage"—quote from Shakespeare's *As You Like It* (Act Two, Scene 7).

[26] mewling—whimpering.

[27] lorgnon—eyeglasses.

"You must let me read it," she said. "You mustn't be so modest."

"Read—?" said little Mrs. Murdock.

"Your play," Lily Wynton said. "Your beautiful, beautiful play. Don't think I am too busy. I always have time. I have time for everything. Oh, my God, I have to go to the dentist tomorrow. Oh, the suffering I have gone through with my teeth. Look!" She set down her glass, inserted a gloved forefinger in the corner of her mouth, and dragged it to the side. "Oogh!" she insisted. "Oogh!"

Mrs. Murdock craned her neck shyly, and caught a glimpse of shining gold.

"Oh, I'm so sorry," she said.

"As wah ee id a me ass ime," Lily Wynton said. She took away her forefinger and let her mouth resume its shape. "That's what he did to me last time," she repeated. "The anguish of it. The agony. Do you suffer with your teeth, little Clever-Face?"

"Why, I'm afraid I've been awfully lucky," Mrs. Murdock said. "I—"

"You don't know," Lily Wynton said. "Nobody knows what it is. You writers—you don't know." She took up her glass, sighed over it, and drained it.

"Well," Miss Noyes said. "Go ahead and pass out, then, darling. You'll have time for a sleep before the theater."

"To sleep," Lily Wynton said. "To sleep, perchance to dream.[28] The privilege of it. Oh, Hallie, sweet, sweet Hallie, poor Lily feels so terrible. Rub my head for me, angel. Help me."

"I'll go get the Eau de Cologne," Miss Noyes said. She left the room, lightly patting Mrs. Murdock's knee as she passed her. Lily Wynton sat in her chair and closed her famous eyes.

"To sleep," she said. "To sleep, perchance to dream."

"I'm afraid," little Mrs. Murdock began. "I'm afraid," she said, "I really must be going home. I'm afraid I didn't realize how awfully late it was."

"Yes, go, child," Lily Wynton said. She did not open her eyes. "Go to him. Go to him, live in him, love him. Stay with him always. But when he starts bringing them into the house—get out."

"I'm afraid—I'm afraid I didn't quite understand," Mrs. Murdock said.

"When he starts bringing his fancy women into the house," Lily Wynton said. "You must have pride, then. You must go. I always did. But it was always too late then. They'd got all my money. That's all they want, marry them or not. They say it's love, but it isn't. Love is the only thing. Treasure your love, child. Go back to him. Go to bed with him. It's the only thing. And your beautiful, beautiful play."

"Oh, dear," said little Mrs. Murdock. "I—I'm afraid it's really terribly late."

There was only the sound of rhythmic breathing from the chair where Lily Wynton lay. The purple voice rolled along the air no longer.

Little Mrs. Murdock stole to the chair upon which she had left her coat. Carefully she smoothed her white muslin frills, so that they would be fresh beneath the jacket.

---

[28] "To sleep, perchance to dream"—quote from the famous "To be or not to be" soliloquy in Shakespeare's *Hamlet* (Act Three, Scene 1).

She felt a tenderness for her frock; she wanted to protect it. Blue serge and little ruffles—they were her own.

When she reached the outer door of Miss Noyes's apartment, she stopped a moment and her manners conquered her. Bravely she called in the direction of Miss Noyes's bedroom.

"Good-by, Miss Noyes," she said. "I've simply got to run. I didn't realize it was so late. I had a lovely time—thank you ever so much."

"Oh, good-by, tiny one," Miss Noyes called. "Sorry Lily went by-by. Don't mind her—she's really a real person. I'll call you up, tiny one. I want to see you. Now where's that damned Cologne?"

"Thank you ever so much," Mrs. Murdock said. She let herself out of the apartment.

Little Mrs. Murdock walked homeward, through the clustering dark. Her mind was busy, but not with memories of Lily Wynton. She thought of Jim; Jim, who had left for his office before she had arisen that morning, Jim, whom she had not kissed good-by. Darling Jim. There were no others born like him. Funny Jim, stiff and cross and silent; but only because he knew so much. Only because he knew the silliness of seeking afar for the glamour and beauty and romance of living. When they were right at home all the time, she thought. Like the Blue Bird,[29] thought little Mrs. Murdock.

Darling Jim. Mrs. Murdock turned in her course, and entered an enormous shop where the most delicate and esoteric of foods were sold for heavy sums. Jim liked red caviar. Mrs. Murdock bought a jar of the shiny, glutinous eggs. They would have cocktails that night, though they had no guests, and the red caviar would be served with them for a surprise, and it would be a little, secret party to celebrate her return to contentment with her Jim, a party to mark her happy **renunciation**[30] of all the glory of the world. She bought, too, a large, foreign cheese. It would give a needed touch to dinner. Mrs. Murdock had not given much attention to ordering dinner, that morning. "Oh, anything you want, Signe," she had said to the maid. She did not want to think of that. She went on home with her packages.

Mr. Murdock was already there when she arrived. He was sitting with his newspaper opened to the financial page. Little Mrs. Murdock ran into him with her eyes a-light. It is too bad that the light in a person's eyes is only the light in a person's eyes, and you cannot tell at a look what causes it. You do not know if it is excitement about you, or something else. The evening before, Mrs. Murdock had run to Mr. Murdock with her eyes a-light.

"Oh, hello," he said to her. He looked back at this paper, and kept his eyes there. "What did you do? Did you drop up to Hank Noyes's?"

Little Mrs. Murdock stopped right where she was.

"You know now perfectly well, Jim," she said, "that Hallie Noyes's first name is Hallie."

---

[29] Blue Bird—symbol of happiness in a 1909 play by Maurice Maeterlinck (1862–1949).

[30] **renunciation**—rejection.

"It's Hank to me," he said. "Hank or Bill. Did what's-her-name show up? I mean drop up. Pardon me."

"To whom are you referring?" said Mrs. Murdock, perfectly.

"What's-her-name," Mr. Murdock said. "The movie star."

"If you mean Lily Wynton," Mrs. Murdock said, "she is not a movie star. She is an actress. She is a great actress."

"Well, did she drop up?" he said.

Mrs. Murdock's shoulders sagged. "Yes," she said. "Yes, she was there, Jim."

"I suppose you're going on the stage now," he said.

"Ah, Jim," Mrs. Murdock said. "Ah, Jim, please. I'm not sorry at all I went to Hallie Noyes's today. It was—it was a real experience to meet Lily Wynton. Something I'll remember all my life."

"What did she do?" Mr. Murdock said. "Hang by her feet?"

"She did no such thing!" Mrs. Murdock said. "She recited Shakespeare, if you want to know."

"Oh, my God," Mr. Murdock said. "That must have been great."

"All right, Jim," Mrs. Murdock said. "If that's the way you want to be."

Wearily she left the room and went down the hall. She stopped at the pantry door, pushed it open, and spoke to the pleasant little maid.

"Oh, Signe," she said. "Oh, good evening, Signe. Put these things somewhere, will you? I got them on the way home. I thought we might have them some time."

Wearily little Mrs. Murdock went on down the hall to her bedroom.

QUESTIONS TO CONSIDER

1. How would you describe Mr. and Mrs. Murdock? Are they compatible?
2. How does Mrs. Murdock's idea of an actress compare with the reality of Lily Wynton?
3. In response to hearing about Lily Wynton's problems with men, Mrs. Murdock fantasizes for a short time about "romance." What does romance mean to her? Where do you think she has derived her ideas about romance?
4. Why does Mrs. Murdock stop to shop on her way home after meeting Lily Wynton? Why is this ironic?
5. The tone of a piece of writing is the writer's attitude toward the subject or the audience. What is distinctly modern about the tone of Parker's story?

F. Scott Fitzgerald ▶

Babylon Revisited

BY F. SCOTT FITZGERALD

F. Scott Fitzgerald (1896–1940) coined the term "The Jazz Age" for the 1920s, and his novels and stories shaped America's ideas about the "new generation grown up to find all Gods dead, all wars fought, all faiths in man shaken." Born in Minnesota to well-to-do parents, Fitzgerald attended Princeton where he devoted himself to writing and to theatrical productions. He flunked out in his junior year and went into the army, but saw no action in World War I. After the armistice, Fitzgerald went to New York, where he worked in an advertising agency while writing at night. The publication of his first novel, The Far Side of Paradise, *in 1920, made him famous. With success, he was able to marry the socialite Zelda Sayre with whom he had been in love for years. They were the glamour couple of the 1920s, spending their time at fashionable places and parties, living the life documented in Fitzgerald's fiction. They spent time in Europe, where Fitzgerald helped Hemingway find a publisher, but their lifestyle took its toll. His masterpiece,* The Great Gatsby, *was published in 1925, but increasingly all his energies were devoted to writing less serious stories for money. With the crash of 1929, the party was over. Zelda began to suffer from a serious mental illness that would see her institutionalized. Fitzgerald himself had a nervous breakdown. He published another novel,* Tender Is the Night, *in 1934, but in the midst of the Depression, it made little impact. Fitzgerald pulled himself together and spent the last seven years of his life writing seriously, but died tragically young, his body worn out by excess. He is remembered as one of America's finest writers. His novels are widely read and admired, communicating the deepest sense of post-World War I depression—that something had gone wrong, that all was a waste. As he wrote in* Tender Is the Night, *"See that little stream—we could walk to it in two minutes. It took the British a month to walk to it—a whole empire walking very slowly, dying in front and pushing forward behind. And another empire walked very slowly backward a few inches a day, leaving the dead like a million bloody rugs. No Europeans will ever do that again in this generation. . . . This took religion and years of plenty and tremendous sureties and the exact relation that existed between the classes." Despite his mode of living, Fitzgerald wrote quickly and well, and his best short stories are among the genre's classics. "Babylon Revisited" presents all the themes of Fitzgerald's work and mirrors many of his own difficulties in the 1930s.*

I

"And where's Mr. Campbell?" Charlie asked.

"Gone to Switzerland. Mr. Campbell's a pretty sick man, Mr. Wales."

"I'm sorry to hear that. And George Hardt?" Charlie inquired.

"Back in America, gone to work."

"And where is the Snow Bird?"[1]

title Babylon—refers to any great and wicked city, an allusion to an ancient city in the Middle East.

1 Snow Bird—slang for cocaine addict.

"He was in here last week. Anyway, his friend, Mr. Schaeffer, is in Paris."

Two familiar names from the long list of a year and a half ago. Charlie scribbled an address in his notebook and tore out the page.

"If you see Mr. Schaeffer, give him this," he said. "It's my brother-in-law's address. I haven't settled on a hotel yet."

He was not really disappointed to find Paris was so empty. But the stillness in the Ritz bar was strange and portentous.[2] It was not an American bar any more—he felt polite in it, and not as if he owned it. It had gone back into France. He felt the stillness from the moment he got out of the taxi and saw the doorman, usually in a frenzy of activity at this hour, gossiping with a *chasseur*[3] by the servants' entrance.

Passing through the corridor, he heard only a single, bored voice in the once-clamorous women's room. When he turned into the bar he traveled the twenty feet of green carpet with his eyes fixed straight ahead by old habit; and then, with his foot firmly on the rail, he turned and surveyed the room, encountering only a single pair of eyes that fluttered up from a newspaper in the corner. Charlie asked for the head barman, Paul, who in the latter days of the bull market[4] had come to work in his own custom-built car—disembarking, however, with due nicety at the nearest corner. But Paul was at his country house today and Alix giving him information.

"No, no more," Charlie said. "I'm going slow these days."

Alix congratulated him: "You were going pretty strong a couple of years ago."

"I'll stick to it all right," Charlie assured him. "I've stuck to it for over a year and a half now."

"How do you find conditions in America?"

"I haven't been to America for months. I'm in business in Prague, representing a couple of concerns there. They don't know about me down there."

Alix smiled.

"Remember the night of George Hardt's bachelor dinner here?" said Charlie. "By the way, what's become of Claude Fessenden?"

Alix lowered his voice confidentially: "He's in Paris, but he doesn't come here any more. Paul doesn't allow it. He ran up a bill of thirty thousand francs, charging all his drinks and his lunches, and usually his dinner, for more than a year. And when Paul finally told him he had to pay, he gave him a bad check."

Alix shook his head sadly.

"I don't understand it, such a dandy[5] fellow. Now he's all bloated up—" he made a plump apple of his hands.

Charlie watched a group of strident queens[6] installing themselves in a corner.

"Nothing affects them," he thought. "Stocks rise and fall, people loaf or work, but they go on forever." The place oppressed him. He called for the dice and shook with Alix for the drink.

---

[2] portentous—foreboding.

[3] *chasseur*—French for "porter."

[4] latter . . . bull market—period just before the Stock Market Crash of 1929. A bull market is characterized by rising stock prices.

[5] dandy—elegant.

[6] queens—disparaging term for homosexuals.

"Here for long, Mr. Wales?"

"I'm here for four or five days to see my little girl."

"Oh-h! You have a little girl?"

He had never eaten at a really cheap restaurant in Paris.

Outside, the fire-red, gas-blue, ghost-green signs shone smokily through the tranquil rain. It was late afternoon and the streets were in movement; the *bistros*[7] gleamed. At the corner of the Boulevard des Capucines he took a taxi. The Place de la Concorde moved by in pink majesty; they crossed the logical Seine, and Charlie felt the sudden provincial quality of the Left Bank.[8]

Charlie directed his taxi to the Avenue de l'Opéra, which was out of his way. But he wanted to see the blue hour[9] spread over the magnificent façade, and imagine that the cab horns, playing endlessly the first few bars of *Le Plus que Lente*,[10] were the trumpets of the Second Empire.[11] They were closing the iron grill in front of Brentano's Bookstore, and people were already at dinner behind the trim little bourgeois hedge of Duval's. He had never eaten at a really cheap restaurant in Paris. Five-course dinner, four francs fifty, eighteen cents, wine included. For some odd reason he wished that he had.

As they rolled on to the Left Bank and he felt its sudden provincialism, he thought, "I spoiled this city for myself. I didn't realize it, but the days came along one after another, and then two years were gone, and everything was gone, and I was gone."

He was thirty-five, and good to look at. The Irish mobility of his face was sobered by a deep wrinkle between his eyes. As he rang his brother-in-law's bell in the Rue Palatine, the wrinkle deepened till it pulled down his brows; he felt a cramping sensation in his belly. From behind the maid who opened the door darted a lovely little girl of nine, who shrieked "Daddy!" and flew up, struggling like a fish, into his arms. She pulled his head around by one ear and set her cheek against his.

"My old pie," he said.

"Oh, daddy, daddy, daddy, daddy, dads, dads, dads!"

She drew him into the salon, where the family waited, a boy and girl his daughter's age, his sister-in-law and her husband. He greeted Marion with his voice pitched carefully to avoid either **feigned**[12] enthusiasm or dislike, but her response was more frankly **tepid**,[13] though she minimized her expression of unalterable distrust by directing her regard toward his child. The two men clasped hands in a friendly way and Lincoln Peters rested his for a moment on Charlie's shoulder.

The room was warm and comfortably American. The three children moved intimately about, playing through the yellow

---

[7] *bistros*—taverns.

[8] Left Bank—section of Paris south of the Seine River. Always thought of as less fancy than the Right Bank.

[9] blue hour—twilight.

[10] *Le Plus que Lente*—slow waltz by Claude Debussy. French taxicabs often had horns playing bits of familiar tunes.

[11] Second Empire—gaudy reign of Napoleon III (1852–1870).

[12] **feigned**—pretended.

[13] **tepid**—lukewarm.

oblongs[14] that led to other rooms; the cheer of six o'clock spoke in the eager smacks of the fire and the sounds of French activity in the kitchen. But Charlie did not relax; his heart sat up rigidly in his body and he drew confidence from his daughter, who from time to time came close to him, holding in her arms the doll he had brought.

"Really extremely well," he declared in answer to Lincoln's question. "There's a lot of business there that isn't moving at all, but we're doing even better than ever. In fact, damn well. I'm bringing my sister over from America next month to keep house for me. My income last year was bigger than it was when I had money. You see, the Czechs—"

His boasting was for a specific purpose; but after a moment, seeing a faint restiveness[15] in Lincoln's eye, he changed the subject:

"Those are fine children of yours, well brought up, good manners."

"We think Honoria's a great little girl too."

Marion Peters came back from the kitchen. She was a tall woman with worried eyes, who had once possessed a fresh American loveliness. Charlie had never been sensitive to it and was always surprised when people spoke of how pretty she had been. From the first there had been an instinctive **antipathy**[16] between them.

"Well, how do you find Honoria?" she asked.

"Wonderful. I was astonished how much she's grown in ten months. All the children are looking well."

"We haven't had a doctor for a year. How do you like being back in Paris?"

"It seems very funny to see so few Americans around."

"I'm delighted," Marion said vehemently. "Now at least you can go into a store without their assuming you're a millionaire. We've suffered like everybody, but on the whole it's a good deal pleasanter."

"But it was nice while it lasted," said Charlie. "We were a sort of royalty, almost **infallible**,[17] with a sort of magic around us. In the bar this afternoon"—he stumbled, seeing his mistake—"there wasn't a man I knew."

She looked at him keenly. "I should think you'd have had enough of bars."

"I only stayed a minute. I take one drink every afternoon, and no more."

"Don't you want a cocktail before dinner?" Lincoln asked.

"I take only one drink every afternoon, and I've had that."

"I hope you keep to it," said Marion.

Her dislike was evident in the coldness with which she spoke, but Charlie only smiled; he had larger plans. Her very aggressiveness gave him an advantage, and he knew enough to wait. He wanted them to initiate the discussion of what they knew had brought him to Paris.

At dinner he couldn't decide whether Honoria was most like him or her mother. Fortunate if she didn't combine the traits of both that had brought them to disaster. A

---

[14] oblongs—doorways.
[15] restiveness—impatience.
[16] **antipathy**—dislike.
[17] **infallible**—perfect.

great wave of protectiveness went over him. He thought he knew what to do for her. He believed in character; he wanted to jump back a whole generation and trust in character again as the eternally valuable element. Everything else wore out.

He left soon after dinner, but not to go home. He was curious to see Paris by night with clearer and more judicious eyes than those of other days. He bought a *strapontin*[18] for the Casino and watched Josephine Baker[19] go through her chocolate arabesques.[20]

After an hour he left and strolled toward Montmartre,[21] up the Rue Pigalle into the Place Blanche. The rain had stopped and there were a few people in evening clothes disembarking from taxis in front of cabarets, and *cocottes*[22] prowling singly or in pairs, and many Negroes. He passed a lighted door from which issued music, and stopped with the sense of familiarity; it was Bricktop's,[23] where he had parted with so many hours and so much money. A few doors farther on he found another ancient rendezvous and incautiously put his head inside. Immediately an eager orchestra burst into sound, a pair of professional dancers leaped to their feet and a maître d'hôtel[24] swooped toward him, crying, "Crowd just arriving, sir!" But he withdrew quickly.

"You have to be damn drunk," he thought.

Zelli's was closed, the bleak and sinister cheap hotels surrounding it were dark; up in the Rue Blanche there was more light and a local, colloquial French crowd. The Poet's Cave had disappeared, but the two great mouths of the Café of Heaven and the Café of Hell still yawned—even devoured, as he watched, the meager contents of a tourist bus—a German, a Japanese, and an American couple who glanced at him with frightened eyes.

So much for the effort and ingenuity of Montmartre. All the catering to vice and waste was on an utterly childish scale, and he suddenly realized the meaning of the word "**dissipate**"[25]—to dissipate into thin air; to make nothing out of something. In the little hours of the night every move from place to place was an enormous human jump, an increase of paying for the privilege of slower and slower motion.

He remembered thousand-franc notes given to an orchestra for playing a single number, hundred-franc notes tossed to a doorman for calling a cab.

But it hadn't been given for nothing.

It had been given, even the most wildly squandered sum, as an offering to destiny that he might not remember the things most worth remembering, the things that now he would always remember—his child taken from his control, his wife escaped to a grave in Vermont.

---

[18] *strapontin*—cheap seat.

[19] Josephine Baker—African-American dancer (1906–1975) who was the rage of Parisian nightlife in the 1920s.

[20] arabesques—dance movements.

[21] Montmartre—quarter in Paris, which had been long famous for its late night cafés and clubs.

[22] *cocottes*—prostitutes.

[23] Bricktop's—fashionable nightclub owned by African American Ada Smith (died 1984), a redhead known as "Bricktop."

[24] maître d'hôtel—headwaiter.

[25] **dissipate**—disperse, drive away.

In the glare of a *brasserie*[26] a woman spoke to him. He bought her some eggs and coffee, and then, eluding her encouraging stare, gave her a twenty-franc note and took a taxi to his hotel.

II

He woke up on a fine fall day—football weather. The depression of yesterday was gone and he liked the people on the streets. At noon he sat opposite Honoria at Le Grand Vatel, the only restaurant he could think of not reminiscent of champagne dinners and long luncheons that began at two and ended in a blurred and vague twilight.

"Now, how about vegetables? Oughtn't you to have some vegetables?"

"Well, yes."

"Here's *épinards* and *chou-fleur* and carrots and *haricots*."[27]

"I'd like chou-fleur."

"Wouldn't you like to have two vegetables?"

"I usually have only one at lunch."

The waiter was pretending to be inordinately fond of children. *"Qu'elle est mignonne, la petite! Elle parle exactement comme une française."*[28]

"How about dessert? Shall we wait and see?"

The waiter disappeared. Honoria looked at her father expectantly.

"What are we going to do?"

"First, we're going to that toy store in the Rue Saint-Honoré and buy you anything you like. And then we're going to the vaudeville at the Empire."

She hesitated. "I like it about the vaudeville, but not the toy store."

"Why not?"

"Well, you brought me this doll." She had it with her. "And I've got lots of things. And we're not rich any more, are we?"

"We never were. But today you are to have anything you want."

"All right," she agreed resignedly.

When there had been her mother and a French nurse he had been inclined to be strict; now he extended himself, reached out for a new tolerance; he must be both parents to her and not shut any of her out of communication.

"I want to get to know you," he said gravely. "First let me introduce myself. My name is Charles J. Wales, of Prague."

"Oh, daddy!" her voice cracked with laughter.

"And who are you, please?" he persisted, and she accepted a rôle immediately: "Honoria Wales, Rue Palatine, Paris."

"Married or single?"

"No, not married. Single."

He indicated the doll. "But I see you have a child, madame."

Unwilling to disinherit it, she took it to her heart and thought quickly: "Yes, I've been married, but I'm not married now. My husband is dead."

He went on quickly, "And the child's name?"

"Simone. That's after my best friend at school."

---

[26] *brasserie*—brewery that also serves as a restaurant in France.

[27] *épinards . . . chou-fleur . . . haricots*—French for "spinach," "cauliflower," and "green beans."

[28] *Qu'elle . . . française,"*—French for "She is charming, the little one. She speaks exactly like a French girl."

"I'm very pleased that you're doing so well at school."

"I'm third this month," she boasted. "Elsie"—that was her cousin—"is only about eighteenth, and Richard is about at the bottom."

"You like Richard and Elsie, don't you?"

"Oh, yes. I like them all right."

Cautiously and casually be asked: "And Aunt Marion and Uncle Lincoln—which do you like best?"

"Oh, Uncle Lincoln, I guess."

He was increasingly aware of her presence. As they came in, a murmur of ". . . adorable" followed them, and now the people at the next table bent all their silences upon her, staring as if she were something no more conscious than a flower.

"Why don't I live with you?" she asked suddenly. "Because mamma's dead?"

"You must stay here and learn more French. It would have been hard for daddy to take care of you so well."

"I don't really need much taking care of any more. I do everything for myself."

Going out of the restaurant, a man and a woman unexpectedly hailed him.

"Well, the old Wales!"

"Hello there, Lorraine . . . Dunc."

Sudden ghosts out of the past: Duncan Schaeffer, a friend from college. Lorraine Quarles, a lovely, pale blonde of thirty; one of a crowd who had helped them make months into days in the lavish times of three years ago.

"My husband couldn't come this year," she said, in answer to his question. "We're poor as hell. So he gave me two hundred a month, and told me I could do my worst on that. . . . This your little girl?"

"What about coming back and sitting down?" Duncan asked.

"Can't do it." He was glad for an excuse. As always, he felt Lorraine's passionate, provocative attraction, but his own rhythm was different now.

"Well, how about dinner?" she asked.

"I'm not free. Give me your address and let me call you."

"Charlie, I believe you're sober," she said judicially. "I honestly believe he's sober, Dunc. Pinch him and see if he's sober."

Charlie indicated Honoria with his head. They both laughed.

"What's your address?" said Duncan skeptically.

He hesitated, unwilling to give the name of his hotel.

"I'm not settled yet. I'd better call you. We're going to see the vaudeville at the Empire."

"There! That's what I want to do," Lorraine said. "I want to see some clowns and acrobats and jugglers. That's just what we'll do, Dunc."

"We've got to do an errand first," said Charlie. "Perhaps we'll see you there."

"All right, you snob. . . . Good-by, beautiful little girl."

"Good-by."

Honoria bobbed politely.

Somehow, an unwelcome encounter. They liked him because he was functioning, because he was serious; they wanted to see him, because he was stronger than they were now, because they wanted to draw a certain **sustenance**[29] from his strength.

At the Empire, Honoria proudly refused to sit upon her father's folded coat. She was already an individual with a code of her own, and Charlie was more and more absorbed by the desire of putting a little of himself into her before she crystallized utterly. It was hopeless to try to know her in so short a time.

Between the acts they came upon Duncan and Lorraine in the lobby where the band was playing.

"Have a drink?"

"All right; but not up at the bar. We'll take a table."

"The perfect father."

Listening abstractedly to Lorraine, Charlie watched Honoria's eyes leave their table, and he followed them wistfully about the room, wondering what they saw. He met her glance and she smiled.

"I liked that lemonade," she said.

What had she said? What had he expected? Going home in a taxi afterward, he pulled her over until her head rested against his chest.

"Darling, do you ever think about your mother?"

"Yes, sometimes," she answered vaguely.

"I don't want you to forget her. Have you got a picture of her?"

"Yes, I think so. Anyhow, Aunt Marion has. Why don't you want me to forget her?"

"She loved you very much."

"I loved her too."

They were silent for a moment.

"Daddy, I want to come and live with you," she said suddenly.

His heart leaped; he had wanted it to come like this.

"Aren't you perfectly happy?"

"Yes, but I love you better than anybody. And you love me better than anybody, don't you, now that mummy's dead?"

"Of course I do. But you won't always like me best, honey. You'll grow up and meet somebody your own age and go marry him and forget you ever had a daddy."

"Yes, that's true," she agreed tranquilly.

He didn't go in. He was coming back at nine o'clock and he wanted to keep himself fresh and new for the thing he must say then.

"When you're safe inside, just show yourself in that window."

"All right. Good-by, dads, dads, dads, dads."

He waited in the dark street until she appeared, all warm and glowing, in the window above and kissed her fingers out into the night.

III

They were waiting. Marion sat behind the coffee service in a dignified black dinner dress that just faintly suggested mourning. Lincoln was walking up and down with the animation of one who had already been talking. They were as anxious as he was to get into the question. He opened it almost immediately:

"I suppose you know what I want to see you about—why I really came to Paris."

---

[29] **sustenance**—supporting of life or health.

Marion played with the black stars on her necklace and frowned.

"I'm awfully anxious to have a home," he continued. "And I'm awfully anxious to have Honoria in it. I appreciate your taking in Honoria for her mother's sake, but things have changed now"—he hesitated and then continued more forcibly—"changed radically with me, and I want to ask you to reconsider the matter. It would be silly for me to deny that about three years ago I was acting badly—"

"I'm awfully anxious to have a home," he continued. "And I'm awfully anxious to have Honoria in it."

Marion looked up at him with hard eyes.

"—But all that's over. As I told you, I haven't had more than a drink a day for over a year, and I take that drink deliberately, so that the idea of alcohol won't get too big in my imagination. You see the idea?"

"No," said Marion **succinctly**.[30]

"It's a sort of stunt I set myself. It keeps the matter in proportion."

"I get you," said Lincoln. "You don't want to admit it's got any attraction for you."

"Something like that. Sometimes I forget and don't take it. But I try to take it. Anyhow, I couldn't afford to drink in my position. The people I represent are more than satisfied with what I've done, and I'm bringing my sister over from Burlington to keep house for me, and I want awfully to have Honoria too. You know that even when her mother and I weren't getting along well we never let anything that happened touch Honoria. I know she's fond of me and I know I'm able to take care of her—well, there you are. How do you feel about it?"

He knew that now he would have to take a beating. It would last an hour or two hours, and it would be difficult, but if he modulated his inevitable resentment to the chastened attitude of the reformed sinner, he might win his point in the end.

Keep your temper, he told himself. You don't want to be justified. You want Honoria.

Lincoln spoke first: "We've been talking it over ever since we got your letter last month. We're happy to have Honoria here. She's a dear little thing, and we're glad to be able to help her, but of course that isn't the question—"

Marion interrupted suddenly. "How long are you going to stay sober, Charlie?" she asked.

"Permanently, I hope."

"How can anybody count on that?"

"You know I never did drink heavily until I gave up business and came over here with nothing to do. Then Helen and I began to run around with—"

"Please leave Helen out of it. I can't bear to hear you talk about her like that."

He stared at her grimly; he had never been certain how fond of each other the sisters were in life.

"My drinking only lasted about a year and a half—from the time we came over until I—collapsed."

---

[30] **succinctly**—briefly.

"It was time enough—"

"It was time enough," he agreed.

"My duty is entirely to Helen," she said. "I try to think what she would have wanted me to do. Frankly, from the night you did that terrible thing you haven't really existed for me. I can't help that. She was my sister."

"Yes."

"When she was dying she asked me to look out for Honoria. If you hadn't been in a sanitarium then, it might have helped matters."

He had no answer.

"I'll never in my life be able to forget the morning when Helen knocked at my door, soaked to the skin and shivering, and said you'd locked her out."

Charlie gripped the sides of the chair. This was more difficult than he expected: he wanted to launch out into a long expostulation[31] and explanation, but he only said: "The night I locked her out—" and she interrupted, "I don't feel up to going over that again."

After a moment's silence Lincoln said: "We're getting off the subject. You want Marion to set aside her legal guardianship and give you Honoria. I think the main point for her is whether she has confidence in you or not."

"I don't blame Marion," Charlie said slowly, "but I think she can have entire confidence in me. I had a good record up to three years ago. Of course, it's within human possibilities I may go wrong again. But if we wait much longer I'll lose Honoria's childhood and my chance for a home." He shook his head. "I'll simply lose her, don't you see?"

"Yes, I see," said Lincoln.

"Why didn't you think of all this before?" Marion asked.

"I suppose I did, from time to time, but Helen and I were getting along badly. When I consented to the guardianship, I was flat on my back in a sanitarium, and the market had cleaned me out. I knew I'd acted badly, and I thought if it would bring any peace to Helen, I'd agree to anything. But now it's different. I'm functioning, I'm behaving damn well, so far as—"

"Please don't swear at me," Marion said.

He looked at her, startled. With each remark the force of her dislike became more and more apparent. She had built up all her fear of life into one wall and faced it toward him. This trivial **reproof**[32] was possibly the result of some trouble with the cook several hours before. Charlie became increasingly alarmed at leaving Honoria in this atmosphere of hostility against himself; sooner or later it would come out, in a word here, a shake of the head there, and some of that distrust would be irrevocably implanted in Honoria. But he pulled his temper down out of his face and shut it up inside him; he had won a point, for Lincoln realized the absurdity of Marion's remark, and asked her lightly since when she had objected to the word "damn."

"Another thing," Charlie said: "I'm able to give her certain advantages now. I'm going to take a French governess to

---

[31] expostulation—effort to dissuade or correct.

[32] **reproof**—rebuke.

Prague with me. I've got a lease on a new apartment—"

He stopped, realizing that he was blundering. They couldn't be expected to accept with **equanimity**[33] the fact that his income was again twice as large as their own.

"I suppose you can give her more luxuries than we can," said Marion. "When you were throwing away money we were living along watching every ten francs. . . . I suppose you'll start doing it again."

"Oh, no," he said. "I've learned. I worked hard for ten years, you know—until I got lucky in the market, like so many people. Terribly lucky. It didn't seem any use working any more, so I quit. It won't happen again."

There was a long silence. All of them felt their nerves straining, and for the first time in a year Charlie wanted a drink. He was sure now that Lincoln Peters wanted him to have his child.

Marion shuddered suddenly; part of her saw that Charlie's feet were planted on the earth now, and her own maternal feeling recognized the naturalness of his desire; but she had lived for a long time with a prejudice—a prejudice founded on a curious disbelief in her sister's happiness, which, in the shock of one terrible night, had turned to hatred for him. It had all happened at a point in her life where the discouragement of ill health and adverse circumstances made it necessary for her to believe in **tangible**[34] villainy and a tangible villain.

"I can't help what I think!" she cried out suddenly. "How much you were responsible for Helen's death, I don't know. It's something you'll have to square with your own conscience."

An electric current of agony surged through him; for a moment he was almost on his feet, an unuttered sound echoing in his throat.

He hung on to himself for a moment, another moment.

"Hold on there," said Lincoln uncomfortably. "I never thought you were responsible for that."

"Helen died of heart trouble," Charlie said dully.

"Yes, heart trouble." Marion spoke as if the phrase had another meaning for her.

Then, in the flatness that followed her outburst, she saw him plainly and she knew he had somehow arrived at control over the situation. Glancing at her husband, she found no help from him, and as abruptly as if it were a matter of no importance, she threw up the sponge.

"Do what you like!" she cried, springing up from her chair. "She's your child. I'm not the person to stand in your way. I think if it were my child I'd rather see her—" She managed to check herself. "You two decide it. I can't stand this. I'm sick. I'm going to bed."

She hurried from the room; after a moment Lincoln said:

"This has been a hard day for her. You know how strongly she feels—" His voice was almost apologetic: "When a woman gets an idea in her head."

---

[33] **equanimity**—calm; composure.

[34] **tangible**—real or concrete.

"Of course."

"It's going to be all right. I think she sees now that you—can provide for the child, and so we can't very well stand in your way or Honoria's way."

"Thank you, Lincoln."

"I'd better go along and see how she is."

"I'm going."

He was still trembling when he reached the street, but a walk down the Rue Bonaparte to the quais[35] set him up, and as he crossed the Seine, fresh and new by the quai lamps, he felt **exultant**.[36] But back in his room he couldn't sleep. The image of Helen haunted him. Helen whom he had loved so until they had senselessly begun to abuse each other's love, tear it into shreds. On that terrible February night that Marion remembered so vividly, a slow quarrel had gone on for hours. There was a scene at the Florida, and then he attempted to take her home, and then she kissed young Webb at a table; after that there was what she had hysterically said. When he arrived home alone he turned the key in the lock in wild anger. How could he know she would arrive an hour later alone, that there would be a snowstorm in which she wandered about in slippers, too confused to find a taxi? Then the aftermath, her escaping pneumonia by a miracle, and all the attendant horror. They were "reconciled," but that was the beginning of the end, and Marion, who had seen with her own eyes and who imagined it to be one of many scenes from her sister's martyrdom, never forgot.

Going over it again brought Helen nearer, and in the white, soft light that steals upon half sleep near morning he found himself talking to her again. She said that he was perfectly right about Honoria and that she wanted Honoria to be with him. She said she was glad he was being good and doing better. She said a lot of other things—very friendly things—but she was in a swing in a white dress, and swinging faster and faster all the time, so that at the end he could not hear clearly all that she said.

IV

He woke up feeling happy. The door of the world was open again. He made plans, vistas, futures for Honoria and himself, but suddenly he grew sad, remembering all the plans he and Helen had made. She had not planned to die. The present was the thing—work to do, and some one to love. But not to love too much, for he knew the injury that a father can do to a daughter or a mother to a son by attaching them too closely; afterward, out in the world, the child would seek in the marriage partner the same blind tenderness and, failing probably to find it, turn against love and life.

It was another bright, crisp day. He called Lincoln Peters at the bank where he worked and asked if he could count on taking Honoria when he left for Prague. Lincoln agreed that there was no reason for delay. One thing—the legal guardianship. Marion wanted to retain that a while longer. She was upset by the whole matter, and it

[35] quais—banks of the Seine.

[36] **exultant**—triumphant.

would oil things if she felt that the situation was still in her control for another year. Charlie agreed, wanting only the tangible; visible child.

Then the question of a governess. Charlie sat in a gloomy agency and talked to a cross Bernaise and to a buxom Breton peasant[37] neither of whom he could have endured. There were others whom he would see tomorrow.

He lunched with Lincoln Peters at Griffons, trying to keep down his exultation.

"There's nothing quite like your own child," Lincoln said. "But you understand how Marion feels too."

"She's forgotten how hard I worked for seven years there," Charlie said. "She just remembers one night."

"There's another thing," Lincoln hesitated. "While you and Helen were tearing around Europe throwing money away, we were just getting along. I didn't touch any of the prosperity because I never got ahead enough to carry anything but my insurance. I think Marion felt there was some kind of injustice in it—you not even working toward the end, and getting richer and richer."

"It went just as quick as it came," said Charlie.

"Yes, a lot of it stayed in the hands of chasseurs and saxophone players and maîtres d'hôtel—well, the big party's over now. I just said that to explain Marion's feeling about those crazy years. If you drop in about six o'clock tonight before Marion's too tired, we'll settle the details on the spot."

Back at his hotel, Charlie found a *pneumatique*[38] that had been redirected from the Ritz bar where Charlie had left his address for the purpose of finding a certain man.

DEAR CHARLIE: You were so strange when we saw you the other day that I wondered if I did something to offend you. If so, I'm not conscious of it. In fact, I have thought about you too much for the last year, and it's always been in the back of my mind that I might see you if I came over here. We *did* have such good times that crazy spring, like the night you and I stole the butcher's tricycle, and the time we tried to call on the president and you had the old derby rim and the wire cane. Everybody seems so old lately, but I don't feel old a bit. Couldn't we get together some time today for old time's sake? I've got a vile hang-over for the moment, but will be feeling better this afternoon and will look for you about five in the sweet-shop at the Ritz.

Always devotedly,
LORRAINE.

His first feeling was one of awe that he had actually, in his mature years, stolen a tricycle and pedaled Lorraine all over the Étoile[39] between the small hours and dawn. In retrospect it was a nightmare. Locking out Helen didn't fit in with any other act of his life, but the tricycle incident

[37] Bernaise . . . Breton peasant—French person from Bearn in the southwest and Brittany in the northwest, respectively.

[38] *pneumatique*—message, originally delivered through a pneumatic tube.

[39] Étoile—open square in Paris where the Arc de Triomphe is located.

did—it was one of many. How many weeks or months of dissipation to arrive at that condition of utter irresponsibility?

He tried to picture how Lorraine had appeared to him then—very attractive; Helen was unhappy about it, though she said nothing. Yesterday, in the restaurant, Lorraine had seemed **trite**,[40] blurred, worn away. He emphatically did not want to see her, and he was glad Alix had not given away his hotel address. It was a relief to think, instead, of Honoria, to think of Sundays spent with her and of saying good morning to her and of knowing she was there in his house at night, drawing her breath in the darkness.

At five he took a taxi and bought presents for all the Peters—a piquant cloth doll, a box of Roman soldiers, flowers for Marion, big linen handkerchiefs for Lincoln.

He saw, when he arrived in the apartment, that Marion had accepted the inevitable. She greeted him now as though he were a **recalcitrant**[41] member of the family, rather than a menacing outsider. Honoria had been told she was going; Charlie was glad to see that her tact made her conceal her excessive happiness. Only on his lap did she whisper her delight and the question "When?" before she slipped away with the other children.

He and Marion were alone for a minute in the room, and on an impulse he spoke out boldly:

"Family quarrels are bitter things. They don't go according to any rules. They're not like aches or wounds; they're more like splits in the skin that won't heal because there's not enough material. I wish you and I could be on better terms."

"Some things are hard to forget," she answered. "It's a question of confidence." There was no answer to this and presently she asked, "When do you propose to take her?"

"As soon as I can get a governess. I hoped the day after tomorrow."

"That's impossible. I've got to get her things in shape. Not before Saturday."

He yielded. Coming back into the room, Lincoln offered him a drink.

"I'll take my daily whisky," he said.

It was warm here, it was a home, people together by a fire. The children felt very safe and important; the mother and father were serious, watchful. They had things to do for the children more important than his visit here. A spoonful of medicine was, after all, more important than the strained relations between Marion and himself. They were not dull people, but they were very much in the grip of life and circumstances. He wondered if he couldn't do something to get Lincoln out of his rut at the bank.

A long peal at the door-bell; the *bonne à tout faire*[42] passed through and went down the corridor. The door opened upon another long ring, and then voices, and the three in the salon looked up expectantly; Richard moved to bring the corridor within his range of vision, and Marion rose. Then the maid came back along the corridor, closely followed by the voices,

---

[40] **trite**—lacking power to provoke interest.

[41] **recalcitrant**—defiant.

[42] *bonne à tout faire*—French for "maid."

which developed under the light into Duncan Schaeffer and Lorraine Quarles.

They were gay, they were hilarious, they were roaring with laughter. For a moment Charlie was astounded; unable to understand how they had ferreted out the Peters' address.

"Ah-h-h!" Duncan wagged his finger roguishly at Charlie. "Ah-h-h!"

They both slid down another cascade[43] of laughter. Anxious and at a loss, Charlie shook hands with them quickly and presented them to Lincoln and Marion. Marion nodded, scarcely speaking. She had drawn back a step toward the fire; her little girl stood beside her, and Marion put an arm about her shoulder.

With growing annoyance at the intrusion, Charlie waited for them to explain themselves After some concentration Duncan said:

"We came to invite you out to dinner. Lorraine and I insist that all this shishi[44] business 'bout your address got to stop."

Charlie came closer to them, as if to force them backward down the corridor.

"Sorry, but I can't. Tell me where you'll be and I'll phone you in half an hour."

This made no impression. Lorraine sat down suddenly on the side of a chair, and focussing her eyes on Richard, cried, "Oh, what a nice little boy! Come here, little boy." Richard glanced at his mother, but did not move. With a perceptible shrug of her shoulders, Lorraine turned back to Charlie:

"Come and dine. Sure your cousins won' mine. See you so sel'om. Or solemn."

"I can't," said Charlie sharply. "You two have dinner and I'll phone you."

Her voice became suddenly unpleasant. "All right, we'll go. But I remember once when you hammered on my door at four A.M. I was enough of a good sport to give you a drink. Come on, Dunc." Still in slow motion, with blurred, angry faces, with uncertain feet, they retired along the corridor.

"Good night," Charlie said.

"Good night!" responded Lorraine emphatically.

When he went back into the salon Marion had not moved, only now her son was standing in the circle of her other arm. Lincoln was still swinging Honoria back and forth like a pendulum from side to side.

"What an outrage!" Charlie broke out. "What an absolute outrage!"

Neither of them answered. Charlie dropped into an armchair, picked up his drink, set it down again and said:

"People I haven't seen for two years having the colossal nerve—" He broke off. Marion had made the sound "Oh!" in one swift, furious breath, turned her body from him with a jerk and left the room.

Lincoln set down Honoria carefully.

"You children go in and start your soup," he said, and when they obeyed, he said to Charlie:

"Marion's not well and she can't stand shocks. That kind of people make her really physically sick."

---

43 cascade—shower.

44 shishi—overly refined; also spelled *chichi.*

"I didn't tell them to come here. They wormed your name out of somebody. They deliberately—"

"Well, it's too bad. It doesn't help matters. Excuse me a minute."

Left alone, Charlie sat tense in his chair. In the next room he could hear the children eating, talking in monosyllables, already oblivious to the scene between their elders. He heard a murmur of conversation from a farther room and then the ticking bell of a telephone receiver picked up, and in a panic he moved to the other side of the room and out of earshot.

In a minute Lincoln came back. "Look here, Charlie. I think we'd better call off dinner for tonight. Marion's in bad shape."

"Is she angry with me?"

"Sort of," he said, almost roughly. "She's not strong and—"

"You mean she's changed her mind about Honoria."

"She's pretty bitter right now. I don't know. You phone me at the bank tomorrow."

"I wish you'd explain to her I never dreamed these people would come here. I'm just as sore as you are."

"I couldn't explain anything to her now."

Charlie got up. He took his coat and hat and started down the corridor. Then he opened the door of the dining room and said in a strange voice, "Good night, children."

Honoria rose and ran around the table to hug him.

"Good night, sweetheart," he said vaguely, and then trying to make his voice more tender, trying to conciliate something, "Good night, dear children."

V

Charlie went directly to the Ritz bar with the furious idea of finding Lorraine and Duncan, but they were not there, and he realized that in any case there was nothing he could do. He had not touched his drink at the Peters', and now he ordered a whisky-and-soda. Paul came over to say hello.

"It's a great change," he said sadly. "We do about half the business we did. So many fellows I hear about back in the States lost everything, maybe not in the first crash, but then in the second. Your friend George Hardt lost every cent, I hear. Are you back in the States?"

"No. I'm in business in Prague."

"I heard that you lost a lot in the crash."

"I did," and he added grimly, "but I lost everything I wanted in the boom."

"Selling short?"[45]

"Something like that."

Again the memory of those days swept over him like a nightmare—the people they had met travelling; the people who couldn't add a row of figures or speak a coherent sentence. The little man Helen had consented to dance with at the ship's party, who had insulted her ten feet from the table, the women and girls carried screaming with drink or drugs out of public places . . . the men who locked their wives

[45] Selling short—stock exchange term referring to contracting to sell a stock that you do not own in hopes that you may acquire it before the date of delivery at a lower price than the one you sold it for.

out in the snow, because the snow of '29 wasn't real snow. If you didn't want it to be snow, you just paid some money.

He went to the phone and called the Peters apartment; Lincoln answered.

"I called up because this thing is on my mind. Has Marion said anything definite?"

"Marion's sick," Lincoln answered shortly. "I know this thing isn't altogether your fault, but I can't have her go to pieces about it. I'm afraid we'll have to let it slide for six months; I can't take the chance of working her up to this state again."

"I see."

"I'm sorry, Charlie."

He went back to his table. His whisky glass was empty, but he shook his head when Alix looked at it questioningly. There wasn't much he could do now except send Honoria some things; he would send her a lot of things tomorrow. He thought rather angrily that this was just money—he had given so many people money. . . .

"No, no more," he said to another waiter. "What do I owe you?"

He would come back some day; they couldn't make him pay forever. But he wanted his child, and nothing was much good now, beside that fact. He wasn't young any more, with a lot of nice thoughts and dreams to have by himself. He was absolutely sure Helen wouldn't have wanted him to be so alone.

QUESTIONS TO CONSIDER

1. Why has Charlie come to Paris? Why did he leave in the first place?
2. Why does Marion hate Charlie so much?
3. What are Lorraine and Duncan looking for from Charlie?
4. Why does Charlie not get to take his daughter at the end of the story?
5. What is Charlie's mood at the end of the story? What does his mood suggest about his future?
6. What is Fitzgerald comparing and contrasting in this story?
7. What contributes to the effectiveness of this comparison?

James Thurber ▶

The Greatest Man in the World

BY JAMES THURBER

James Thurber (1894–1961) was, like Dorothy Parker (page 234), a satirist, well at home in cosmopolitan New York. Thurber is one of the writers who set the tone for The New Yorker, *one of the most influential magazines of the twentieth century. He was born in Ohio and began working for newspapers right out of college. He joined* The New Yorker *in 1927, just after the magazine's founding. His humorous stories, deadpan prose, and minimalist cartoons were an important component of the magazine until his death. Thurber applied his talents to satirizing American attitudes and habits with deadly accuracy. For Thurber, the whole world was ironic and his stories expose his view. "The Greatest Man in the World" humorously attacks the extravagant media hype surrounding successful adventurers such as Charles Lindbergh in the 1920s.*

Looking back on it now, from the vantage point of 1950,[1] one can only marvel that it hadn't happened long before it did. The United States of America had been, ever since Kitty Hawk,[2] blindly constructing the elaborate petard by which, sooner or later, it must be hoist.[3] It was inevitable that some day there would come roaring out of the skies a national hero of insufficient intelligence, background, and character successfully to endure the mounting orgies of glory prepared for aviators who stayed up a long time or flew a great distance. Both Lindbergh[4] and Byrd,[5] fortunately for national decorum and international amity,[6] had been gentlemen; so had our other famous aviators. They wore their laurels[7] gracefully, withstood the awful weather of publicity, married excellent women, usually of fine family, and quietly retired to private life and the enjoyment of their varying fortunes. No untoward[8] incidents, on a

---

[1] 1950—This story was actually written in the early 1930s; Thurber places his narrator in what was then the future.

[2] Kitty Hawk—place in North Carolina where the Wright brothers made the first airplane flight in 1903.

[3] petard . . . hoist—The expression "hoist by one's own petard" means "blown up by one's own bomb."

[4] Lindbergh—Charles Lindbergh (1902–1974), American aviator who in 1927 became the first to fly solo across the Atlantic.

[5] Byrd—Richard Byrd (1888–1957), American aviator and polar explorer who was the first to fly over each of the Poles.

[6] amity—friendship.

[7] laurels—symbolic emblem of victory.

[8] untoward—troublesome.

worldwide scale, marred the perfection of their conduct on the perilous heights of fame. The exception to the rule was, however, bound to occur and it did, in July, 1937, when Jack ("Pal") Smurch, erstwhile[9] mechanic's helper in a small garage in Westfield, Iowa, flew a second-hand, single-motored Bresthaven Dragon-Fly III monoplane all the way around the world, without stopping.

Never before in the history of aviation had such a flight as Smurch's ever been dreamed of.

Never before in the history of aviation had such a flight as Smurch's ever been dreamed of. No one had even taken seriously the weird floating **auxiliary**[10] gas tanks, invention of the mad New Hampshire professor of astronomy, Dr. Charles Lewis Gresham, upon which Smurch placed full reliance. When the garage worker, a slightly built, surly, unprepossessing[11] young man of twenty-two, appeared at Roosevelt Field in early July, 1937, slowly chewing a great quid[12] of scrap tobacco, and announced, "Nobody ain't seen no flyin' yet," the newspapers touched briefly and satirically upon his projected twenty-five-thousand-mile flight. Aëronautical and automotive experts dismissed the idea curtly, implying that it was a hoax, a publicity stunt. The rusty, battered, second-hand plane wouldn't go. The Gresham auxiliary tanks wouldn't work. It was simply a cheap joke.

Smurch, however, after calling on a girl in Brooklyn who worked in the flap-folding department of a large paper-box factory, a girl whom he later described as his "sweet patootie," climbed **nonchalantly**[13] into his ridiculous plane at dawn of the memorable seventh of July, 1937, spit a curve of tobacco juice into the still air, and took off, carrying with him only a gallon of bootleg gin and six pounds of salami.

When the garage boy thundered out over the ocean the papers were forced to record, in all seriousness, that a mad, unknown young man—his name was variously misspelled—had actually set out upon a preposterous attempt to span the world in a rickety, one-engined contraption, trusting to the long-distance refueling device of a crazy schoolmaster. When, nine days later, without having stopped once, the tiny plane appeared above San Francisco Bay, headed for New York, spluttering and choking, to be sure, but still magnificently and miraculously aloft, the headlines, which long since had crowded everything else off the front page—even the shooting of the Governor of Illinois by the Vileti gang—swelled to unprecedented size, and the news stories began to run to twenty-five and thirty columns. It was noticeable, however, that the accounts of the epoch-making flight touched rather lightly upon the aviator himself. This was not because facts about the hero

[9] erstwhile—in the past.

[10] **auxiliary**—reserve.

[11] unprepossessing—unappealing.

[12] quid—cut or piece of chewing tobacco.

[13] **nonchalantly**—with a casual lack of concern.

as a man were too **meager,**[14] but because they were too complete.

Reporters, who had been rushed out to Iowa when Smurch's plane was first sighted over the little French coast town of Serly-le-Mer, to dig up the story of the great man's life, had promptly discovered that the story of his life could not be printed. His mother, a **sullen**[15] short-order cook in a shack restaurant on the edge of a tourists' camping ground near Westfield, met all inquiries as to her son with an angry "Ah, the hell with him; I hope he drowns." His father appeared to be in jail somewhere for stealing spotlights and lap robes[16] from tourists' automobiles; his young brother, a weak-minded lad, had but recently escaped from the Preston, Iowa, Reformatory and was already wanted in several Western towns for the theft of money-order blanks from post offices. These alarming discoveries were still piling up at the very time that Pal Smurch, the greatest hero of the twentieth century, blear-eyed, dead for sleep, half-starved, was piloting his crazy junk-heap high above the region in which the lamentable story of his private life was being unearthed, headed for New York and a greater glory than any man of his time had ever known.

The necessity for printing some account in the papers of the young man's career and personality had led to a remarkable predicament. It was of course impossible to reveal the facts, for a tremendous popular feeling in favor of the young hero had sprung up, like a grass fire, when he was halfway across Europe on his flight around the globe. He was, therefore, described as a modest chap, **taciturn,**[17] blond, popular with his friends, popular with girls. The only available snapshot of Smurch, taken at the wheel of a phony automobile in a cheap photo studio at an amusement park, was touched up so that the little vulgarian looked quite handsome. His twisted leer[18] was smoothed into a pleasant smile. The truth was, in this way, kept from the youth's ecstatic compatriots;[19] they did not dream that the Smurch family was despised and feared by its neighbors in the obscure Iowa town, nor that the hero himself, because of numerous unsavory exploits, had come to be regarded in Westfield as a nuisance and a menace. He had, the reporters discovered, once knifed the principal of his high school—not mortally, to be sure, but he had knifed him; and on another occasion, surprised in the act of stealing an altar-cloth from a church, he had bashed the sacristan[20] over the head with a pot of Easter lilies; for each of these offenses he had served a sentence in the reformatory.

Inwardly, the authorities, both in New York and in Washington, prayed that an understanding Providence might, however awful such a thing seemed, bring disaster to the rusty, battered plane and its illustrious pilot, whose unheard-of flight had aroused

---

14 **meager**—scanty.
15 **sullen**—silently resentful, sulky.
16 lap robes—blankets to spread over the lap.
17 **taciturn**—habitually not talkative.
18 leer—look indicative of slyness or sexual desire.
19 ecstatic compatriots—overjoyed fellow countrymen.
20 sacristan—church official in charge of the sacred objects.

the civilized world to hosannas of hysterical praise. The authorities were convinced that the character of the renowned aviator was such that the limelight of adulation[21] was bound to reveal him to all the world as a congenital[22] hooligan mentally and morally unequipped to cope with his own prodigious fame. "I trust," said the Secretary of State, at one of many secret Cabinet meetings called to consider the national dilemma, "I trust that his mother's prayer will be answered," by which he referred to Mrs. Emma Smurch's wish that her son might be drowned. It was, however, too late for that—Smurch had leaped the Atlantic and then the Pacific as if they were millponds. At three minutes after two o'clock on the afternoon of July 17, 1937, the garage boy brought his idiotic plane into Roosevelt Field for a perfect three-point landing.

It had, of course, been out of the question to arrange a modest little reception for the greatest flier in the history of the world. He was received at Roosevelt Field with such elaborate and **pretentious**[23] ceremonies as rocked the world. Fortunately, however, the worn and spent hero promptly swooned, had to be removed bodily from his plane, and was spirited from the field without having opened his mouth once. Thus he did not jeopardize the dignity of this first reception, a reception illumined by the presence of the Secretaries of War and the Navy, Mayor Michael J. Moriarity of New York, the Premier of Canada, Governors Fanniman, Groves, McFeely, and Critchfield, and a brilliant array of European diplomats. Smurch did not, in fact, come to in time to take part in the gigantic hullabaloo arranged at City Hall for the next day. He was rushed to a secluded nursing home and confined to bed. It was nine days before he was able to get up, or to be more exact, before he was permitted to get up. Meanwhile the greatest minds in the country, in solemn assembly, had arranged a secret conference of city, state, and government officials, which Smurch was to attend for the purpose of being instructed in the ethics and behavior of heroism.

On the day that the little mechanic was finally allowed to get up and dress and, for the first time in two weeks, took a great chew of tobacco, he was permitted to receive the newspapermen—this by way of testing him out. Smurch did not wait for questions. "Youse guys," he said—and the Times man winced—"youse guys can tell the cock-eyed world dat I put it over on Lindbergh, see? Yeh—an' made an ass o' them two frogs." The "two frogs" was a reference to a pair of gallant French fliers who, in attempting a flight only halfway round the world, had, two weeks before, unhappily been lost at sea. The Times man was bold enough, at this point, to sketch out for Smurch the accepted formula for interviews in cases of this kind; he explained that there should be no arrogant statements belittling the achievements of other heroes, particularly heroes of foreign nations. "Ah,

---

[21] limelight of adulation—focus of praise.

[22] congenital—being such as if by nature.

[23] **pretentious**—outwardly extravagant.

the hell with that," said Smurch. "I did it, see? I did it, an' I'm talkin' about it." And he did talk about it.

None of this extraordinary interview was, of course, printed. On the contrary, the newspapers, already under the disciplined direction of a secret directorate[24] created for the occasion and composed of statesmen and editors, gave out to a panting and restless world that "Jacky," as he had been arbitrarily nicknamed, would consent to say only that he was very happy and that anyone could have done what he did. "My achievement has been, I fear, slightly exaggerated," the Times man's article had him protest, with a modest smile. These newspaper stories were kept from the hero, a restriction which did not serve to **abate**[25] the rising **malevolence**[26] of his temper. The situation was, indeed, extremely grave, for Pal Smurch was, as he kept insisting, "rarin' to go." He could not much longer be kept from a nation clamorous to lionize[27] him. It was the most desperate crisis the United States of America had faced since the sinking of the *Lusitania*.[28]

On the afternoon of the twenty-seventh of July, Smurch was spirited away to a conference-room in which were gathered mayors, governors, government officials, behaviorist psychologists, and editors. He gave them each a limp, moist paw and a brief unlovely grin. "Hah ya?" he said. When Smurch was seated, the Mayor of New York arose and, with obvious pessimism, attempted to explain what he must say and how he must act when presented to the world, ending his talk with a high tribute to the hero's courage and integrity. The Mayor was followed by Governor Fanniman of New York, who, after a touching declaration of faith, introduced Cameron Spottiswood, Second Secretary of the American Embassy in Paris, the gentleman selected to coach Smurch in the **amenities**[29] of public ceremonies. Sitting in a chair, with a soiled yellow tie in his hand and his shirt open at the throat, unshaved, smoking a rolled cigarette, Jack Smurch listened with a leer on his lips. "I get ya, I get ya," he cut in, nastily. "Ya want me to ack like a softy, huh? Ya want me to ack like that ——— ——— baby-faced Lindbergh, huh? Well, nuts to that, see?" Everyone took in his breath sharply; it was a sigh and a hiss. "Mr. Lindbergh," began a United States Senator, purple with rage, "and Mr. Byrd—" Smurch, who was paring his nails with a jackknife, cut in again. "Byrd!" he exclaimed. "Aw fa God's sake, dat big—" Somebody shut off his blasphemies with a sharp word. A newcomer had entered the room. Everyone stood up, except Smurch, who, still busy with his nails, did not even glance up. "Mr. Smurch," said someone sternly, "the President of the United States!" It had been thought that the presence of the Chief Executive might have a chastening[30] effect upon the young hero,

---

[24] directorate—group of directors.

[25] **abate**—reduce.

[26] **malevolence**—harmfulness.

[27] lionize—treat a person as a celebrity.

[28] *Lusitania*—ocean liner sunk by a German U-boat in 1915. The loss of 128 Americans did much to bring the U.S. into World War I on the Allied side.

[29] **amenities**—social pleasantries.

[30] chastening—restraining.

and the former had been, thanks to the remarkable cooperation of the press, secretly brought to the obscure conference-room.

"My God, he's fallen out the window!" cried a quick-witted editor.

A great, painful silence fell. Smurch looked up, waved a hand at the President. "How ya comin'?" he asked, and began rolling a fresh cigarette. The silence deepened. Someone coughed in a strained way. "Geez, it's hot, ain't it?" said Smurch. He loosened two more shirt buttons, revealing a hairy chest and the tattooed word "Sadie" enclosed in a stenciled heart. The great and important men in the room, faced by the most serious crisis in recent American history, exchanged worried frowns. Nobody seemed to know how to proceed. "Come awn, come awn," said Smurch. "Let's get the hell out of here! When do I start cuttin' in on de parties, huh? And what's they goin' to be *in* it?" He rubbed a thumb and forefinger together meaningly. "Money!" exclaimed a state senator, shocked, pale. "Yeh, money," said Pal, flipping his cigarette out of a window. "An' big money." He began roiling a fresh cigarette. "Big money," he repeated, frowning over the rice paper. He tilted back in his chair, and leered at each gentleman, separately, the leer of an animal that knows its power, the leer of a leopard loose in a bird-and-dog shop. "Aw fa God's sake, let's get some place where it's cooler," he said. "I been cooped up plenty for three weeks!"

Smurch stood up and walked over to an open window, where he stood staring down into the street, nine floors below. The faint shouting of newsboys floated up to him. He made out his name. "Hot dog!" he cried, grinning, ecstatic. He leaned out over the sill. "You tell 'em, babies!" he shouted down. "Hot diggity dog!" In the tense little knot of men standing behind him, a quick, mad impulse flared up. An unspoken word of appeal, of command, seemed to ring through the room. Yet it was deadly silent. Charles K. L. Brand, secretary to the Mayor of New York City, happened to be standing nearest Smurch; he looked inquiringly at the President of the United States. The President, pale, grim, nodded shortly. Brand, a tall, powerfully built man, once a tackle at Rutgers, stepped forward, seized the greatest man in the world by his left shoulder and the seat of his pants, and pushed him out the window.

"My God, he's fallen out the window!" cried a quick-witted editor.

"Get me out of here!" cried the President. Several men sprang to his side and he was hurriedly escorted out of a door toward a side-entrance of the building. The editor of the Associated Press took charge, being used to such things. Crisply he ordered certain men to leave, others to stay; quickly he outlined a story which all the papers were to agree on, sent two men to the street to handle that end of the tragedy, commanded a Senator to sob and two Congressmen to go to pieces nervously. In a word, he skillfully set the stage for the gigantic task that was to follow, the task of breaking to a grief-stricken world the sad story of the untimely, accidental death of its most illustrious and spectacular figure.

The funeral was, as you know, the most elaborate, the finest, the solemnest, and the saddest ever held in the United States of America. The monument in Arlington Cemetery, with its clean white shaft of marble and the simple device of a tiny plane carved on its base, is a place for pilgrims, in deep reverence, to visit. The nations of the world paid lofty tributes to little Jacky Smurch, America's greatest hero. At a given hour there were two minutes of silence throughout the nation. Even the inhabitants of the small, bewildered town of Westfield, Iowa, observed this touching ceremony; agents of the Department of Justice saw to that. One of them was especially assigned to stand grimly in the doorway of a little shack restaurant on the edge of the tourists' camping ground just outside the town. There, under his stern scrutiny, Mrs. Emma Smurch bowed her head above two hamburger steaks sizzling on her grill—bowed her head and turned away, so that the Secret Service man could not see the twisted, strangely familiar, leer on her lips.

QUESTIONS TO CONSIDER

1. Why do you think Thurber had his narrator looking back from the future?
2. Why is Smurch not allowed to celebrate his achievements? What makes him different from Lindbergh and Byrd?
3. What is Thurber making fun of in this story?
4. What is characteristically modern about Thurber's satirical targets?
5. Do you think that most successful people today are more like Smurch or like Lindbergh and Byrd? Explain your answer.

Katherine Anne Porter ▶

Rope

BY KATHERINE ANNE PORTER

Katherine Anne Porter (1890–1980) was one of the writers of the New South that sprang up in the twentieth century when memories and resentments over the Civil War and Reconstruction were beginning to fade. Born and raised in Texas, she eloped at the age of sixteen, but was divorced by nineteen and working as an actress on stage and in bit parts in film. She nearly died from tuberculosis, and her health turned her from acting to writing. In 1919 she went to New York and began writing stories. Her 1930 collection, Flowering Judas, *brought her recognition as an important stylist: a writer of terse, poignant stories full of irony and symbolic meaning. Many of Porter's stories are set in the South and show both the changes in Southern society and the influence of the ever-present past. Porter's only novel,* Ship of Fools, *was published in 1962 and became a bestseller. Still it is for her stories that she is most praised. These suggestive and symbolic works influenced a whole generation of Southern writers, including William Faulkner, Eudora Welty, and Flannery O'Connor. Porter's ability to succinctly suggest the inherent conflicts between men and women, past and present, and ideal and reality make her stories one of the real achievements of American fiction. "Rope" is one of Porter's lighter pieces, yet her mastery of form and language is obvious, as is her understanding of how men and women relate.*

On the third day after they moved to the country he came walking back from the village carrying a basket of groceries and a twenty-four-yard coil of rope. She came out to meet him, wiping her hands on her green smock. Her hair was tumbled, her nose was scarlet with sunburn; he told her that already she looked like a born country woman. His gray flannel shirt stuck to him, his heavy shoes were dusty. She assured him he looked like a rural character in a play.

Had he brought the coffee? She had been waiting all day long for coffee. They had forgot it when they ordered at the store the first day.

Gosh, no, he hadn't. Lord, now he'd have to go back. Yes, he would if it killed him. He thought, though, he had everything else. She reminded him it was only because he didn't drink coffee himself. If he did he would remember it quick enough. Suppose they ran out of cigarettes? Then she saw the rope. What was that for? Well, he thought it might do to hang clothes on, or something. Naturally she asked him if he thought they were going to run a laundry? They already had a fifty-foot line hanging right before his eyes? Why, hadn't he noticed it, really? It was a blot[1] on the landscape to her.

He thought there were a lot of things a rope might come in handy for. She wanted to know what, for instance. He thought a few seconds, but nothing occurred. They could wait and see, couldn't they? You need all sorts of strange odds and ends around a place in the country. She said, yes, that was so; but she thought just at that time when every penny counted, it seemed funny to buy more rope. That was all. She hadn't meant anything else. She hadn't just seen, not at first, why he felt it was necessary.

Well, thunder, he had bought it because he wanted to, and that was all there was to it. She thought that was reason enough, and couldn't understand why he hadn't said so, at first. Undoubtedly it would be useful, twenty-four yards of rope, there were hundreds of things, she couldn't think of any at the moment, but it would come in. Of course. As he had said, things always did in the country.

But she was a little disappointed about the coffee, and oh, look, look, look at the eggs! Oh, my, they're all running! What had he put on top of them? Hadn't he known eggs mustn't be squeezed? Squeezed, who had squeezed them, he wanted to know. What a silly thing to say. He had simply brought them along in the basket with the other things. If they got broke it was the grocer's fault. He should know better than to put heavy things on top of eggs.

She believed it was the rope. That was the heaviest thing in the pack, she saw him plainly when he came in from the road, the rope was a big package on top of everything. He desired the whole wide world to witness that this was not a fact. He had carried the rope in one hand and the basket in the other, and what was the use of her having eyes if that was the best they could do for her?

Well, anyhow, she could see one thing plain: no eggs for breakfast. They'd have to scramble them now, for supper. It was too damned bad. She had planned to have steak for supper. No ice, meat wouldn't keep. He wanted to know why she couldn't finish breaking the eggs in a bowl and set them in a cool place.

Cool place! if he could find one for her, she'd be glad to set them there. Well, then, it seemed to him they might very well cook the meat at the same time they cooked the eggs and then warm up the meat for tomorrow. The idea simply choked her. Warmed-over meat, when they might as well have had it fresh. Second best and scraps and makeshifts,[2] even to the meat! He rubbed her shoulder a little. It doesn't really matter so much, does it, darling? Sometimes when they were playful, he would rub her shoulder and she would arch and purr. This time she hissed and almost clawed. He was getting ready to say that they could surely manage somehow when she turned on him and said, if he told her they could manage somehow she would certainly slap his face.

---

[1] blot—disfiguring mark.

[2] makeshifts—temporary or expedient substitutes.

He swallowed the words red hot, his face burned. He picked up the rope and started to put it on the top shelf. She would not have it on the top shelf, the jars and tin belonged there; positively she would not have the top shelf cluttered up with a lot of rope. She had borne all the clutter she meant to bear in the flat in town, there was space here at least and she meant to keep things in order.

Oh, would he please hush and go away, and stay away, if he could, for five minutes?

Well, in that case, he wanted to know what the hammer and nails were doing up there? And why had she put them there when she knew very well he needed that hammer and those nails upstairs to fix the window sashes? She simply slowed down everything and made double work on the place with her insane habit of changing things around and hiding them.

She was sure she begged his pardon, and if she had had any reason to believe he was going to fix the sashes this summer she would have left the hammer and nails right where he put them; in the middle of the bedroom floor where they could step on them in the dark. And now if he didn't clear the whole mess out of there she would throw them down the well.

Oh, all right, all right—could he put them in the closet? Naturally not, there were brooms and mops and dustpans in the closet, and why couldn't he find a place for his rope outside her kitchen? Had he stopped to consider there were seven God-forsaken rooms in the house, and only one kitchen?

He wanted to know what of it? And did she realize she was making a complete fool of herself? And what did she take him for, a three-year-old idiot? The whole trouble with her was she needed something weaker than she was to heckle and tyrannize over. He wished to God now they had a couple of children she could take it out on. Maybe he'd get some rest.

Her face changed at this, she reminded him he had forgot the coffee and had bought a worthless piece of rope. And when she thought of all the things they actually needed to make the place even decently fit to live in, well, she could cry, that was all. She looked so **forlorn**,[3] so lost and despairing he couldn't believe it was only a piece of rope that was causing all the racket. What was the matter, for God's sake?

Oh, would he please hush and go away, and stay away, if he could, for five minutes? By all means, yes, he would. He'd stay away indefinitely if she wished. Lord, yes, there was nothing he'd like better than to clear out and never come back. She couldn't for the life of her see what was holding him, then. It was a swell time. Here she was, stuck, miles from a railroad, with a half-empty house on her hands, and not a penny in her pocket, and everything on earth to do; it seemed the God-sent moment for him to get out from under. She was surprised he hadn't stayed in town as it was until she had come out and done the work and got things straightened out. It was his usual trick.

---

[3] **forlorn**—appearing sad or lonely.

It appeared to him that this was going a little far. Just a touch out of bounds, if she didn't mind his saying so. Why the hell had he stayed in town the summer before? To do a half-dozen extra jobs to get the money he had sent her. That was it. She knew perfectly well they couldn't have done it otherwise. She had agreed with him at the time. And that was the only time so help him he had ever left her to do anything by herself.

Oh, he could tell that to his great-grandmother. She had her notion of what had kept him in town. Considerably more than a notion, if he wanted to know. So, she was going to bring all that up again, was she? Well, she could just think what she pleased. He was tired of explaining. It may have looked funny but he had simply got hooked in, and what could he do? It was impossible to believe that she was going to take it seriously. Yes, yes, she knew how it was with a man: if he was left by himself a minute, some woman was certain to kidnap him. And naturally he couldn't hurt her feelings by refusing!

Well, what was she raving about? Did she forget she had told him those two weeks alone in the country were the happiest she had known for four years? And how long had they been married when she said that? All right, shut up! If she thought that hadn't stuck in his craw.[4]

She hadn't meant she was happy because she was away from him. She meant she was happy getting the devilish house nice and ready for him. That was what she had meant, and now look! Bringing up something she had said a year ago simply to justify himself for forgetting her coffee and breaking the eggs and buying a wretched piece of rope they couldn't afford. She really thought it was time to drop the subject, and now she wanted only two things in the world. She wanted him to get that rope from underfoot, and go back to the village and get her coffee, and if he could remember it, he might bring a metal mitt for the skillets, and two more curtain rods, and if there were any rubber gloves in the village, her hands were simply raw, and a bottle of milk of magnesia from the drug-store.

He looked out at the dark blue afternoon sweltering on the slopes, and mopped his forehead and sighed heavily and said, if only she could wait a minute for *anything*, he was going back. He had said so, hadn't he, the very instant they found he had overlooked it?

Oh, yes, well . . . run along. She was going to wash windows. The country was so beautiful! She doubted they'd have a moment to enjoy it. He meant to go, but he could not until he had said that if she wasn't such a hopeless melancholiac[5] she might see that this was only for a few days. Couldn't she remember anything pleasant about the other summers? Hadn't they ever had any fun? She hadn't time to talk about it, and now would he please not leave that rope lying around for her to trip on? He picked it up, somehow it had toppled off the table, and walked out with it under his arm.

---

[4] stuck . . . craw—caused resentment.

[5] melancholiac—person who is sad, depressed.

Was he going this minute? He certainly was. She thought so. Sometimes it seemed to her he had second sight about the precisely perfect moment to leave her ditched.[6] She had meant to put the mattresses out to sun, if they put them out this minute they would get at least three hours, he must have heard her say that morning she meant to put them out. So of course he would walk off and leave her to it. She supposed he thought the exercise would do her good.

Well, he was merely going to get her coffee. A four-mile walk for two pounds of coffee was ridiculous, but he was perfectly willing to do it. The habit was making a wreck of her, but if she wanted to wreck herself there was nothing he could do about it. If he thought it was coffee that was making a wreck of her, she congratulated him: he must have a damned easy conscience.

Conscience or no conscience, he didn't see why the mattresses couldn't very well wait until tomorrow. And anyhow, for God's sake, were they living in the house, or were they going to let the house ride them to death? She paled at this, her face grew **livid**[7] about the mouth, she looked quite dangerous, and reminded him that housekeeping was no more her work than it was his: she had other work to do as well, and when did he think she was going to find time to do it at this rate?

Was she going to start on that again? She knew as well as he did that his work brought in the regular money, hers was only occasional, if they depended on what she made—and she might as well get straight on this question once for all!

That was positively not the point. The question was, when both of them were working on their own time, was there going to be a division of the housework, or wasn't there? She merely wanted to know, she had to make her plans. Why, he thought that was all arranged. It was understood that he was to help. Hadn't he always, in summers?

Hadn't he, though? Oh, just hadn't he? And when, and where, and doing what? Lord, what an **uproarious**[8] joke!

It was such a very uproarious joke that her face turned slightly purple, and she screamed with laughter. She laughed so hard she had to sit down, and finally a rush of tears spurted from her eyes and poured down into the lifted corners of her mouth. He dashed towards her and dragged her up to her feet and tried to pour water on her head. The dipper hung by a string on a nail and he broke it loose. Then he tried to pump water with one hand while she struggled in the other. So he gave it up and shook her instead.

She wrenched away, crying out for him to take his rope and go to hell, she had simply given him up: and ran. He heard her high-heeled bedroom slippers clattering and stumbling on the stairs.

He went out around the house and into the lane; he suddenly realized he had a blister on his heel and his shirt felt as if it were on fire. Things broke so suddenly you didn't know where you were. She could work herself into a fury about simply nothing.

---

[6] **ditched**—stranded.

[7] **livid**—ashen, pallid.

[8] **uproarious**—hilarious.

She was terrible, damn it: not an ounce of reason. You might as well talk to a sieve[9] as that woman when she got going. Damned if he'd spend his life humoring her! Well, what to do now? He would take back the rope and exchange it for something else. Things accumulated, things were mountainous, you couldn't move them or sort them out or get rid of them. They just lay and rotted around. He'd take it back. Hell, why should be? He wanted it. What was it anyhow? A piece of rope. Imagine anybody caring more about a piece of rope than about a man's feelings. What earthly right had she to say a word about it? He remembered all the useless, meaningless things she bought for herself: Why? because I wanted it, that's why! He stopped and selected a large stone by the road. He would put the rope behind it. He would put it in the toolbox when he got back. He'd heard enough about it to last him a life-time.

When he came back she was leaning against the post box beside the road waiting. It was pretty late, the smell of broiled steak floated nose high in the cooling air. Her face was young and smooth and fresh-looking. Her unmanageable funny black hair was all on end. She waved to him from a distance, and he speeded up. She called out that supper was ready and waiting, was he starved?

You bet he was starved. Here was the coffee. He waved it at her. She looked at his other hand. What was that he had there?

Well, it was the rope again. He stopped short. He had meant to exchange it but forgot. She wanted to know why he should exchange it, if it was something he really wanted. Wasn't the air sweet now, and wasn't it fine to be here?

She walked beside him with one hand hooked into his leather belt. She pulled and jostled him a little as he walked, and leaned against him. He put his arm clear around her and patted her stomach. They exchanged wary smiles. Coffee, coffee for the Ootsum-Wootsums! He felt as if he were bringing her a beautiful present.

He was a love, she firmly believed, and if she had had her coffee in the morning, she wouldn't have behaved so funny . . . There was a whippoorwill[10] still coming back, imagine, clear out of season, sitting in the crab-apple tree calling all by himself. Maybe his girl stood him up. Maybe she did. She hoped to hear him once more, she loved whippoorwills . . . He knew how she was, didn't he?

Sure, he knew how she was.

---

[9] **sieve—utensil of wire mesh used to strain and sift.**

[10] **whippoorwill—spotted brown and black bird that is active at night. Its long, monotonous cry gave it its name.**

QUESTIONS TO CONSIDER

1. **Why are the couple out in the country? What do you think they both do for a living?**
2. **What starts their argument? What causes it to end?** coffee
3. **What are the couple really arguing about?**
4. **What is the tone of the story? Do you think Porter wants her readers to laugh? Explain your answer.**
5. **What elements of this story seem distinctly modern?**

Thomas Wolfe ▶

The Far and the Near

BY THOMAS WOLFE

Thomas Wolfe (1900–1938) is a writer who worked on a large scale. He was a hulking six-and-a-half feet tall and his four novels are also big—at his death his editor was left with an eight-foot-high stack of manuscript. Wolfe was born in Asheville, North Carolina, into a family torn by strife. He escaped into books, and entered the University of North Carolina at age fifteen. Wolfe's desire was to be a playwright and he successfully produced a series of works. After graduation he went to Harvard to study drama and became convinced there that his future was not in the theater. He moved to New York, taught English, and devoted his evenings to writing a novel. Wolfe's massive manuscript caught the eye of the famous editor Maxwell Perkins—Hemingway's and Fitzgerald's editor—who pruned it into publishable form. This book, Look Homeward, Angel *(1929), is an autobiographical portrait of Wolfe and his hometown, Asheville. The book was enough of a success to allow Wolfe to give up teaching and to do some traveling. He wrote a short novel next, but then created* Of Time and the River *(1935), the equally epic sequel to* Look Homeward, Angel. *After his death, the stack of manuscript became two more autobiographical novels. Wolfe's short stories were in some ways more successful than his novels; he was able to use his immense talents for creating characters and description in a disciplined, tight form. He himself said that his book of short stories contained his finest writing. Wolfe was an immense writing talent who died tragically young, before he could develop the critical facilities for controlling his ideas and the desire to get everything on paper. "The Far and the Near" is classic Wolfe in that it quickly moves from the everyday existence of his characters to the grander meaning of life.*

On the outskirts of a little town upon a rise of land that swept back from the railway there was a tidy little cottage of white boards, trimmed vividly with green blinds. To one side of the house there was a garden neatly patterned with plots of growing vegetables, and an arbor[1] for the grapes which ripened late in August. Before the house there were three mighty oaks which sheltered it in their clean and massive shade in summer, and to the other side there was a border of gay flowers. The whole place had an air of tidiness, thrift, and modest comfort.

Every day, a few minutes after two o'clock in the afternoon, the limited express between two cities passed this spot. At that moment the great train, having halted for a breathing-space at the town near by, was beginning to lengthen evenly into its stroke,[2] but it had not yet reached

[1] arbor—latticework on which plants are grown.

[2] stroke—movement.

the full drive of its terrific speed. It swung into view deliberately, swept past with a powerful swaying motion of the engine, a low smooth rumble of its heavy cars upon pressed steel, and then it vanished in the cut.[3] For a moment the progress of the engine could be marked by heavy bellowing puffs of smoke that burst at spaced intervals above the edges of the meadow grass, and finally nothing could be heard but the solid clacking tempo of the wheels receding into the drowsy stillness of the afternoon.

Every day for more than twenty years, as the train had approached this house, the engineer had blown on the whistle, and every day, as soon as she heard this signal, a woman had appeared on the back porch of the little house and waved to him. At first she had a small child clinging to her skirts, and now this child had grown to full womanhood, and every day she, too, came with her mother to the porch and waved.

The engineer had grown old and gray in service. He had driven his great train, loaded with its weight of lives, across the land ten thousand times. His own children had grown up and married, and four times he had seen before him on the tracks the ghastly dot of tragedy converging[4] like a cannon ball to its eclipse of horror at the boiler head[5]—a light spring wagon filled with children, with its clustered row of small stunned faces; a cheap automobile stalled upon the tracks, set with the wooden figures of people paralyzed with fear; a battered hobo walking by the rail, too deaf and old to hear the whistle's warning; and a form flung past his window with a scream—all this the man had seen and known. He had known all the grief, the joy, the peril and the labor such a man could know; he had grown seamed and weathered in his loyal service, and now, schooled by the qualities of faith and courage and humbleness that attended his labor, he had grown old, and had the grandeur and the wisdom these men have.

The sight of the little house and of these two women gave him the most extraordinary happiness he had ever known.

But no matter what peril or tragedy he had known, the vision of the little house and the women waving to him with a brave free motion of the arm had become fixed in the mind of the engineer as something beautiful and enduring, something beyond all change and ruin, and something that would always be the same, no matter what mishap, grief or error might break the iron schedule of his days.

The sight of the little house and of these two women gave him the most extraordinary happiness he had ever known. He had seen them in a thousand lights, a hundred weathers. He had seen them through the harsh bare light of wintry gray across the brown and frosted stubble of the earth, and he had seen them again in the green luring sorcery of April.

---

[3] cut—excavated passage through which a railroad train moves.

[4] converging—approaching.

[5] boiler head—front of a locomotive.

He felt for them and for the little house in which they lived such tenderness as a man might feel for his own children, and at length the picture of their lives was carved so sharply in his heart that he felt that he knew their lives completely, to every hour and moment of the day, and he resolved that one day, when his years of service should be ended, he would go and find these people and speak at last with them whose lives had been so wrought into his own.

That day came. At last the engineer stepped from a train onto the station platform of the town where these two women lived. His years upon the rail had ended. He was a pensioned[6] servant of his company, with no more work to do. The engineer walked slowly through the station and out into the streets of the town. Everything was as strange to him as if he had never seen this town before. As he walked on, his sense of bewilderment and confusion grew. Could this be the town he had passed ten thousand times? Were these the same houses he had seen so often from the high windows of his cab? It was all as unfamiliar, as disquieting as a city in a dream, and the **perplexity**[7] of his spirit increased as he went on.

Presently the houses thinned into the straggling outposts of the town, and the street faded into a country road—the one on which the women lived. And the man plodded on slowly in the heat and dust. At length he stood before the house he sought. He knew at once that he had found the proper place. He saw the lordly oaks before the house, the flower beds, the garden and the arbor, and farther off, the glint of rails.

Yes, this was the house he sought, the place he had passed so many times, the destination he had longed for with such happiness. But now that he had found it, now that he was here, why did his hand falter on the gate; why had the town, the road, the earth, the very entrance to this place he loved turned unfamiliar as the landscape of some ugly dream? Why did he now feel this sense of confusion, doubt and hopelessness?

At length he entered by the gate, walked slowly up the path and in a moment more had mounted three short steps that led up to the porch, and was knocking at the door. Presently he heard steps in the hall, the door was opened, and a woman stood facing him.

And instantly, with a sense of bitter loss and grief, he was sorry he had come. He knew at once that the woman who stood there looking at him with a mistrustful eye was the same woman who had waved to him so many thousand times. But her face was harsh and pinched and **meager**;[8] the flesh sagged wearily in sallow[9] folds, and the small eyes peered at him with timid suspicion and uneasy doubt. All the brave freedom, the warmth and the affection that he had read into her gesture, vanished in the moment that he saw her and heard her unfriendly tongue.

And now his own voice sounded unreal and ghastly to him as he tried to

---

[6] pensioned—retired on an income provided by an employer.

[7] **perplexity**—confusion.

[8] **meager**—lean.

[9] sallow—of a sickly yellowish hue or complexion.

explain his presence, to tell her who he was and the reason he had come. But he faltered on, fighting stubbornly against the horror of regret, confusion, disbelief that surged up in his spirit, drowning all his former joy and making his act of hope and tenderness seem shameful to him.

At length the woman invited him almost unwillingly into the house, and called her daughter in a harsh shrill voice. Then, for a brief agony of time, the man sat in an ugly little parlor, and he tried to talk while the two women stared at him with a dull, bewildered hostility, a sullen, **timorous**[10] restraint.

And finally, stammering a crude farewell, he departed. He walked away down the path and then along the road toward town, and suddenly he knew that he was an old man. His heart, which had been brave and confident when it looked along the familiar vista of the rails, was now sick with doubt and horror as it saw the strange and unsuspected **visage**[11] of an earth which had always been within a stone's throw of him, and which he had never seen or known. And he knew that all the magic of that bright lost way, the vista of that shining line, the imagined corner of that small good universe of hope's desire, was gone forever, could never be got back again.

[10] **timorous**—full of apprehension; timid.

[11] **visage**—face.

QUESTIONS TO CONSIDER

1. What do the house and the two women represent to the engineer?
2. Why does the engineer want to visit the house and the women when he retires?
3. What has the engineer grown to understand from his visit? Why had he not realized this before?
4. How might Wolfe's story be described as a modern fable?

Writers as Celebrities

Some American writers, such as Mark Twain and Ernest Hemingway, achieved a fame in their lifetimes that has endured. Others, such as Herman Melville and Zora Neale Hurston, had been largely forgotten by the time they died and were rediscovered after their deaths. The following images reflect different aspects of writers as celebrities.

▲

America's first true literary celebrity was Washington Irving, shown here (seventh from right) at his home, surrounded by other well-known writers and scholars of the day.

▲ Places associated with famous writers often become literary shrines, such as "Arrowhead," Herman Melville's home while he was writing *Moby Dick*.

▲ Twain's appearance on this cigar box reflects the extraordinary degree of his popularity in his time.

◀ Mark Twain's abilities as a public speaker on the lecture circuit increased the fame he had won with his books.

One of the ironies of literary celebrity is that well-known writers are sometimes given awards for their less successful works, such as Willa Cather's 1923 Pulitzer Prize for her novel *One of Ours.* ▶

Ernest Hemingway's public image as an outdoorsman added to the fame he had acquired as a novelist.
▼

▲
In her lifetime, Dorothy Parker was at least as famous for her venomously witty remarks as she was for her poems and short stories. For example, on learning that President "Silent Cal" Coolidge had died, she remarked, "How could they tell?"

◀ Buried in an unmarked grave when she died in 1960, Zora Neale Hurston was rediscovered in the 1970s and is far more famous today than in her lifetime.

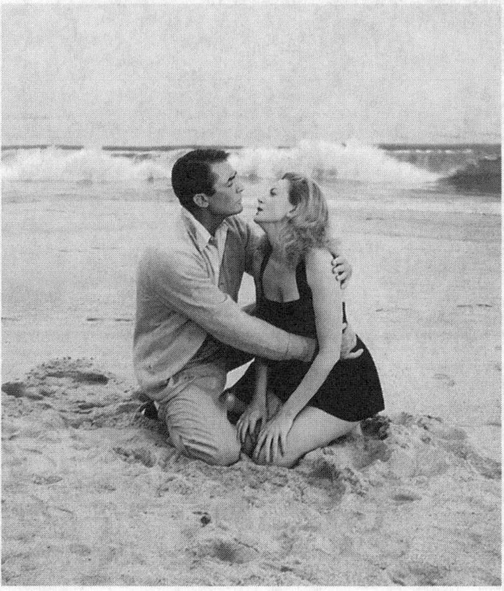

▲ F. Scott Fitzgerald and his wife Zelda were among the most notorious examples of "flaming youth" in the 1920s.

◀ Even after his death, Fitzgerald retained sufficient notoriety to be the subject of a 1959 movie, *Beloved Infidel,* in which he is played by Gregory Peck, shown here with Deborah Kerr as gossip columnist Sheilah Graham, with whom Fitzgerald lived during his final years.

◀ Martha Gellhorn, who wrote 13 novels of her own, resented being most famous as the third wife of Ernest Hemingway.

▲
James Thurber is at least as famous for his whimsical drawings as for his writing.

◀ Richard Wright became suddenly famous in 1940 with the success of his novel *Native Son,* which was both the most militant protest novel about American race relations of its time and a huge bestseller.

◀ Eudora Welty has received many awards for her writing throughout her career, including a Pulitzer Prize, several O. Henry Prizes for short fiction, the National Book Award, and Welty's own favorite, the Chevalier de l'Ordre des Artes et Lettres, France's highest honor for a writer.

◀ One of the best ways for a writer to become famous is to win the Nobel Prize for Literature, as William Faulkner did in 1950.

Beginning with the success of her book *The House on Mango Street* (1985), Sandra Cisneros has become one of the best-known Latino writers. ▶

◀ Alice Walker reached a wider audience when her Pulitzer Prize-winning novel *The Color Purple* (1982) was made into a successful movie.

In 1993, Toni Morrison became the first African-American writer to win the Nobel Prize for Literature.

▼

◀ The many facets of Native-American writer Sherman Alexie's career are indicated by the items on the poster behind him.

Jhumpa Lahiri's first collection of short stories, *The Interpreter of Maladies*, won the 2000 Pulitzer Prize for Fiction. ▶

Part Three

Building a Tradition

The rapid pace of social and cultural change in the United States during the decades following World War I prompted many Americans to reassess the importance of traditional ways of life.

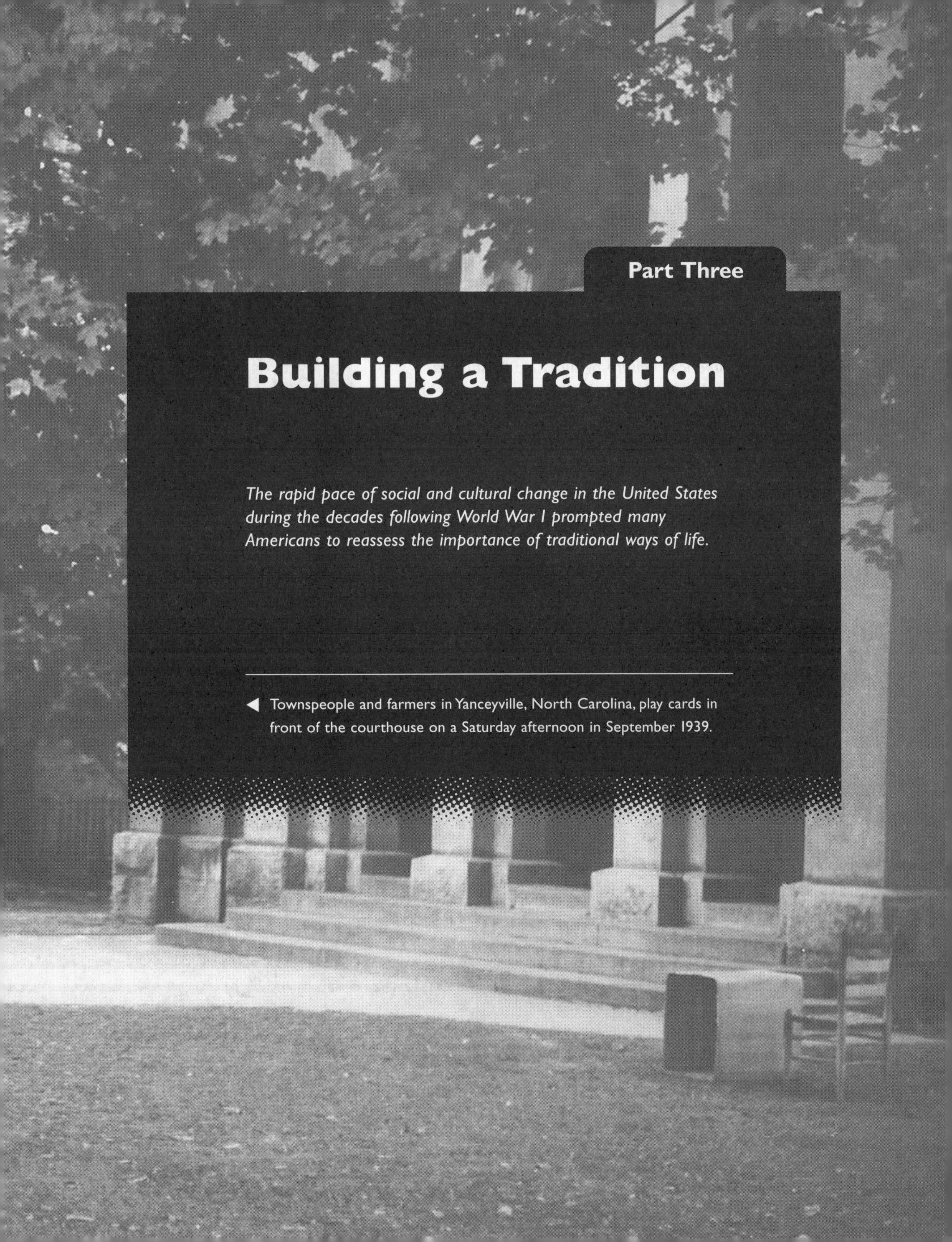

◀ Townspeople and farmers in Yanceyville, North Carolina, play cards in front of the courthouse on a Saturday afternoon in September 1939.

1940–1970

Building a Tradition

Regionalism *Beginning in the 1920s and '30s, some American writers became concerned with what they saw as the increasing homogenization of American culture by mass media such as advertising, movies, and radio. As a result, there was a revival of interest in regional writing, particularly in the South, that examined the effect of local setting on character and the survival of traditional values in a modernized world.*

▲ One of William Faulkner's central themes is the conflict between traditional Southern values and the modern world.

◀ With his powerful protests against race prejudice in both the South and the North, Richard Wright changed the direction of the African-American literary tradition.

Pearl Harbor attacked by the Japanese; U.S. enters World War II.

Jackie Robinson integrates baseball.

Korean War begins; McCarthy era begins.

Brown v. Board of Education decided.

1940 | 1945 | 1950

Atomic bombs dropped on Japan; World War II ends.

Truman wins presidential election.

Eisenhower elected; Ellison's *Invisible Man* published.

▲ Eudora Welty's fiction focused on traditional ways of life in the Mississippi Delta country.

◀ In his novel *Invisible Man*, Ralph Ellison sought to fully express the complexities of contemporary African-American life.

Working within the tradition of Southern regionalism, Flannery O'Connor still created a uniquely personal literary vision in her fiction. ▶

Montgomery bus boycott takes place.

Civil rights march on Washington held; JFK assassinated.

Martin Luther King assassinated; Tet Offensive fought.

1955 **1960** **1965** **1970**

Kerouac's *On the Road* published; *Sputnik* launched.

Civil Rights Act passed; Gulf of Tonkin incident occurs.

Moon landing takes place; Woodstock festival held.

Richard Wright ▶

The Man Who Saw the Flood

RICHARD WRIGHT

Richard Wright (1908–1960) was born in Mississippi to a very poor family of sharecroppers. After the Civil War (1861–1865) this system of agriculture had developed in the South. African Americans did not want to work for whites, but there was a taboo against renting or selling land to former slaves. Poor whites began to let African Americans work the land for a percentage of the crops raised. This system quickly replaced slavery as the way to keep African Americans at the lowest rung of society. To run a farm and buy the necessary goods, they would have to borrow against the future crop. One or two bad harvests put a sharecropper into permanent debt and perpetual servitude. This pattern was not really broken until World War I when huge numbers of African Americans migrated north to take up work in the booming factories of Northern cities. Wright himself was part of this migration, leaving the South and the family he hated in 1923 for a job in Memphis where he devoted himself to reading to get the education he had been denied. In 1932, Wright moved to Chicago, where he began writing and took up political activism by joining the Communist Party. In 1938, his first book, Uncle Tom's Children, *was published, and its stories of the oppression of poor African Americans in the South were hugely acclaimed. Then in 1940, his novel* Native Son *became a bestseller and an important moment in the history of African-American literature. Wright's protagonist, Bigger Thomas, is a vengeful African-American youth who commits two murders because violence is the only way he can respond to American society's widespread racism. Almost all of Wright's fiction has the theme that society is victimizing African Americans, a view that is a product of his Communism as well as his race. In 1946, Wright settled in France, fed up with the persecution that his race and political views brought on. "The Man Who Saw the Flood" presents the tragedy of the poor farmers in the South with an understanding only someone who grew up there could have.*

When the flood waters **recede,**[1] the poor folk along the river start from scratch.

At last the flood waters had receded. A black father, a black mother, and a black child tramped through muddy fields, leading a tired cow by a thin bit of rope. They stopped on a hilltop and shifted the bundles on their shoulders. As far as they could see the ground was covered with

[1] **recede**—move back or away from a limit or point.

flood silt.[2] The little girl lifted a skinny finger and pointed to a mud-caked cabin.

"Look, Pa! Ain tha our home?"

The man, round-shouldered, clad in blue, ragged overalls, looked with bewildered eyes. Without moving a muscle, scarcely moving his lips, he said: "Yeah."

For five minutes they did not speak or move. The flood waters had been more than eight feet high here. Every tree, blade of grass, and stray stick had its flood mark; caky, yellow mud. It clung to the ground, cracking thinly here and there in spider web fashion. Over the stark fields came a gusty spring wind. The sky was high, blue, full of white clouds and sunshine. Over all hung a first-day[3] strangeness.

"The henhouse is gone," sighed the woman.

"N the pigpen," sighed the man.

They spoke without bitterness.

"Ah reckon them chickens is all done drowned."

"Yeah."

"Miz Flora's house is gone, too," said the little girl.

They looked at a clump of trees where their neighbor's house had stood.

"Lawd!"

"Yuh reckon anybody knows where they is?"

"Hard t tell."

The man walked down the slope and stood uncertainly.

"There wuz a road erlong here somewheres," he said.

But there was no road now. Just a wide sweep of yellow, scalloped[4] silt.

"Look, Tom!" called the woman. "Here's a piece of our gate!"

The gatepost was half buried in the ground. A rusty hinge stood stiff, like a lonely finger. Tom pried it loose and caught it firmly in his hand. There was nothing particular he wanted to do with it; he just stood holding it firmly. Finally he dropped it, looked up, and said:

"C mon. Les go down n see whut we kin do."

Because it sat in a slight depression, the ground about the cabin was soft and slimy.

"Gimme tha bag o lime,[5] May," he said.

With his shoes sucking in mud, he went slowly around the cabin, spreading the white lime with thick fingers. When he reached the front again he had a little left; he shook the bag out on the porch. The fine grains of floating lime flickered in the sunlight.

"Tha oughta hep some," he said.

"Now, yuh be careful, Sal!" said May. "Don yuh go n fall down in all this mud, yuh hear?"

"Yessum."

The steps were gone. Tom lifted May and Sally to the porch. They stood a moment looking at the half-opened door. He had shut it when he left, but somehow it seemed natural that he should find it open. The planks in the porch floor were swollen and warped. The cabin had two

---

2 silt—very fine particles of earth and sand carried by water and left behind.

3 first-day—suggesting the dawn of creation.

4 scalloped—patterned with curved markings.

5 lime—solid, white compound of oxygen and calcium. It can be used to kill bacteria.

colors; near the bottom it was a solid yellow; at the top it was the familiar gray. It looked weird, as though its ghost were standing beside it.

The cow lowed.[6]

"Tie Pat t the pos on the en of the porch, May."

May tied the rope slowly, **listlessly**.[7] When they attempted to open the front door, it would not budge. It was not until Tom placed his shoulder against it and gave it a **stout**[8] shove that it scraped back jerkily. The front room was dark and silent. The damp smell of flood silt came fresh and sharp to their nostrils. Only one-half of the upper window was clear, and through it fell a rectangle of dingy light. The floors swam in ooze. Like a mute warning, a wavering flood mark went high around the walls of the room. A dresser sat cater-cornered,[9] its drawers and sides bulging like a bloated corpse. The bed, with the mattress still on it, was like a giant casket forged of mud. Two smashed chairs lay in a corner, as though huddled together for protection.

"Les see the kitchen," said Tom.

The stovepipe was gone. But the stove stood in the same place.

"The stove's still good. We kin clean it."

"Yeah."

"But where's the table?"

"Lawd knows."

"It must've washed erway wid the rest of the stuff, Ah reckon."

They opened the back door and looked out. They missed the barn, the henhouse, and the pigpen.

"Tom, yuh bettah try tha ol pump n see ef eny watah's there."

The pump was stiff. Tom threw his weight on the handle and carried it up and down. No water came. He pumped on. There was a dry hollow cough. Then yellow water trickled. He caught his breath and kept pumping. The water flowed white.

"Thank Gawd! We's got some watah."

"Yuh bettah boil it fo yuh use it," he said.

"Yeah. Ah know."

"Look, Pa! Here's yo ax," called Sally.

Tom took the ax from her. "Yeah. Ah'll need this."

"N here's somethin else," called Sally, digging spoons out of the mud.

"Waal, Ahma git a bucket n start cleanin," said May. "Ain no use in waitin, cause we's gotta sleep on them floors tonight."

When she was filling the bucket from the pump, Tom called from around the cabin. "May, look! Ah done foun mah plow!" Proudly he dragged the silt-caked plow to the pump. "Ah'll wash it n it'll be awright."

"Ahm hongry," said Sally.

"Now, yuh jus wait! Yuh et this mawnin," said May. She turned to Tom. "Now, whutcha gonna do, Tom?"

He stood looking at the mud-filled fields.

"Yuh goin back t Burgess?"

"Ah reckon Ah have to."

"Whut else kin yuh do?

---

6 lowed—mooed.

7 **listlessly**—without energy.

8 **stout**—powerful, forceful.

9 cater-cornered—diagonally.

"Nothin," he said. "Lawd, but Ah sho hate t start all over wid tha white man. Ah'd leave here ef Ah could. Ah owes im nigh eight hundred dollahs. N we needs a hoss, grub, seed, n a lot mo other things. Ef we keeps on like this tha white man'll own us body n soul."

"But, Tom, there ain nothin else t do," she said.

"Ef we try t run erway they'll put us in jail."

"It coulda been worse," she said.

Sally came running from the kitchen. "Pa!"

"Hunh?"

"There's a shelf in the kitchen the flood didn git!"

"Where?"

"Right up over the stove."

"But, chile, ain nothin up there," said May.

"But there's somethin on it," said Sally.

"C mon. Les see."

High and dry, untouched by the floodwater, was a box of matches. And beside it a half-full sack of Bull Durham tobacco. He took a match from the box and scratched it on his overalls. It burned to his fingers before he dropped it.

"May!"

"Hunh?"

"Look! Here's ma bacco n some matches!"

She stared unbelievingly. "Lawd!" she breathed.

Tom rolled a cigarette clumsily.

May washed the stove, gathered some sticks, and after some difficulty, made a fire. The kitchen stove smoked, and their eyes smarted. May put water on to heat and went into the front room. It was getting dark. From the bundles they took a kerosene lamp and lit it. Outside Pat lowed longingly into the thickening gloam and tinkled her cowbell.

"Lawd, but Ah sho hate t start all over wid tha white man. Ah'd leave here ef Ah could."

"Tha old cow's hongry," said May.

"Ah reckon Ah'll have t be gittin erlong t Burgess."

They stood on the front porch.

"Yuh bettah git on, Tom, fo it gits too dark."

"Yeah."

The wind had stopped blowing. In the east a cluster of stars hung.

"Yuh goin, Tom?"

"Ah reckon Ah have t."

"Ma, Ah'm hongry," said Sally.

"Wait erwhile, honey. Ma knows yuh's hongry."

Tom threw his cigarette away and sighed.

"Look! Here comes somebody!"

"Thas Mistah Burgess now!"

A mud-caked buggy rolled up. The shaggy horse was splattered all over. Burgess leaned his white face out of the buggy and spat.

"Well, I see you're back."

"Yessuh."

"How things look?"

"They don look so good, Mistah."

"What seems to be the trouble?"

"Waal. Ah ain got no hoss, no grub, nothin. The only thing Ah got is tha ol cow there. . . ."

"You owe eight hundred dollahs down at the store, Tom."

"Yessuh, Ah know. But, Mistah Burgess, can't yuh knock somethin off tha, seein as how Ahm down n out now?"

"You ate that grub, and I got to pay for it, Tom."

"Yessuh, Ah know."

"It's going to be a little tough, Tom. But you got to go through with it. Two of the boys tried to run away this morning and dodge their debts, and I had to have the sheriff pick em up. I wasn't looking for no trouble out of you, Tom . . . The rest of the families are going back."

Leaning out of the buggy, Burgess waited. In the surrounding stillness the cowbell tinkled again. Tom stood with his back against a post.

"Yuh got t go on, Tom. We ain't got nothin here," said May.

Tom looked at Burgess.

"Mistah Burgess, Ah don wanna make no trouble. But this is jus *too* hard. Ahm worse off now than befo. Ah got to start from scratch."

"Get in the buggy and come with me. I'll stake you with grub. We can talk over how you can pay it back." Tom said nothing. He rested his back against the post and looked at the mud-filled fields.

"Well," asked Burgess. "You coming?" Tom said nothing. He got slowly to the ground and pulled himself into the buggy. May watched them drive off.

"Hurry back, Tom!"

"Awright."

"Ma, tell Pa t bring me some 'lasses,"[10] begged Sally.

"Oh, Tom!"

Tom's head came out of the side of the buggy.

"Hunh?"

"Bring some 'lasses!"

"Hunh?"

"Bring some 'lasses for Sal!"

"Awright!"

She watched the buggy disappear over the crest of the muddy hill. Then she sighed, caught Sally's hand, and turned back into the cabin.

---

[10] 'lasses—molasses, sugar syrup.

QUESTIONS TO CONSIDER

1. What has happened to Tom's farm?
2. Why can't the family just abandon the destroyed farm?
3. How does each family member's attitude about the farm and the flood differ?
4. How do you feel about Mr. Burgess? Is he a sympathetic character?
5. What is Wright condemning in this story?

William Faulkner ▶

The Tall Men

BY WILLIAM FAULKNER

*William Faulkner (1897–1962) won the Nobel Prize in 1950 and is generally regarded as one of the century's outstanding literary figures, but his career as a writer did not have a promising start. Faulkner was a terrible student and tried his hand at innumerable jobs—some of which he lost due to an overfondness for drinking. He published a book of poems in 1924, but it was when Sherwood Anderson suggested Faulkner write a novel that he found his calling. In 1926 his first novel was published, and over the next six years he turned out some of his most important fiction—*The Sound and The Fury *(1929),* As I Lay Dying *(1930), and* Light in August *(1932). These works made the author little money, and in 1932 he became a Hollywood screenwriter, work he would continue to do for more than two decades. By the mid-1940s, Faulkner's serious writing was receiving respectful critical notice, and when he won the Nobel Prize, he was finally established as a major voice. Faulkner's novels and stories seem to crystallize all the themes found throughout Southern literature. He was a local colorist, in that his work is set in the fictional Yoknapatawpha County, which is very much a portrait of Lafayette County, Mississippi, where Faulkner lived most of his life. The grotesqueness and violence that are the marks of the Southern Gothic style are apparent in his work. Faulkner's themes are also typically Southern: the end of the old ways of life, the conflict between traditional and modern values, and the racial and class antagonisms left from the Old South. At the same time, Faulkner was the most modern writer of the South, the psychology and plotting of his stories is closely akin to that of Sherwood Anderson, Ernest Hemingway, and F. Scott Fitzgerald. Faulkner was a technical innovator of great range, whose stories are often related in experimental styles and methods. "The Tall Men" deals with one of Faulkner's central themes—the conflict between Southern tradition and the modern world.*

They passed the dark bulk of the cotton gin.[1] Then they saw the lamplit house and the other car, the doctor's coupé,[2] just stopping at the gate, and they could hear the hound baying.

"Here we are," the old deputy marshal said.

"What's that other car?" the younger man said, the stranger, the state draft investigator.[3]

"Doctor Schofield's," the marshal said. "Lee McCallum asked me to send him out when I telephoned we were coming."

"You mean you warned them?" the investigator said. "You telephoned ahead

---

[1] cotton gin—machine that separates seeds, seed hulls, and other small objects from the fibers of cotton.

[2] coupé—closed two-door automobile.

[3] state draft investigator—official who enforced regulations relating to the military draft.

that I was coming out with a warrant for these two evaders?[4] Is this how you carry out the orders of the United States Government?"

The marshal was a lean, clean old man who chewed tobacco, who had been born and lived in the county all his life.

"I understood all you wanted was to arrest these two McCallum boys and bring them back to town," he said.

"It was!" the investigator said. "And now you have warned them, given them a chance to run. Possibly put the Government to the expense of hunting them down with troops. Have you forgotten that you are under a bond yourself?"

"I ain't forgot it," the marshal said. "And ever since we left Jefferson[5] I been trying to tell you something for you not to forget. But I reckon it will take these McCallums to impress that on you. . . . Pull in behind the other car. We'll try to find out first just how sick whoever it is that is sick is."

The investigator drew up behind the other car and switched off and blacked out his lights. "These people," he said. Then he thought, *But this doddering,*[6] *tobacco-chewing old man is one of them, too, despite the honor and pride of his office, which should have made him different.* So he didn't speak it aloud, removing the keys and getting out of the car, and then locking the car itself, rolling the windows up first, thinking, *These people who lie about and conceal the ownership of land and property in order to hold relief jobs which they have no intention of performing, standing on their constitutional rights, against having to work, who* ***jeopardize***[7] *the very job itself through petty and transparent* ***subterfuge***[8] *to acquire a free mattress which they intend to attempt to sell; who would relinquish even the job, if by so doing they could receive free food and a place, any rathole, in town to sleep in; who, as farmers, make false statements to get seed loans which they will later misuse, and then react in loud vituperative*[9] *outrage and astonishment when caught at it. And then, when at long last a suffering and threatened Government asks one thing of them in return, one thing simply, which is to put their names down on a selective-service list, they refuse to do it.*

The old marshal had gone on. The investigator followed, through a stout paintless gate in a picket fence, up a broad brick walk between two rows of old shabby cedars, toward the rambling and likewise paintless sprawl of the two-story house in the open hall of which the soft lamplight glowed and the lower story of which, as the investigator now perceived, was of logs.

He saw a hall full of soft lamplight beyond a stout paintless gallery running across the log front, from beneath which the same dog which they had heard, a big hound, came booming again, to stand foursquare[10] facing them in the walk, bellowing, until a man's voice spoke to it from the house. He followed the marshal

---

[4] evaders—those who avoid performing some responsibility; here, the duty of registering for the draft.

[5] Jefferson—county seat of Faulkner's fictional Yoknapatawpha County, modeled on his hometown of Oxford, Mississippi.

[6] *doddering*—infirm, feeble.

[7] ***jeopardize***—endanger.

[8] ***subterfuge***—deceptive stratagem or device.

[9] *vituperative*—harshly abusive.

[10] foursquare—firm.

up the steps onto the gallery. Then he saw the man standing in the door, waiting for them to approach—a man of about forty-five, not tall, but blocky, with a brown, still face and horseman's hands, who looked at him once, brief and hard, and then no more, speaking to the marshal, "Howdy, Mr. Gombault. Come in."

"Howdy, Rafe," the marshal said. "Who's sick?"

"Buddy," the other said. "Slipped and caught his leg in the hammer mill this afternoon."

"Is it bad?" the marshal said.

"It looks bad to me," the other said. "That's why we sent for the doctor instead of bringing him in to town. We couldn't get the bleeding stopped."

"I'm sorry to hear that," the marshal said. "This is Mr. Pearson." Once more the investigator found the other looking at him, the brown eyes still, courteous enough in the brown face, the hand he offered hard enough, but the clasp quite limp, quite cold. The marshal was still speaking. "From Jackson. From the draft board." Then he said, and the investigator could **discern**[11] no change whatever in his tone: "He's got a warrant for the boys."

The investigator could discern no change whatever anywhere. The limp hard hand merely withdrew from his, the still face now looking at the marshal. "You mean we have declared war?"

"No," the marshal said.

"That's not the question, Mr. McCallum," the investigator said. "All required of them was to register. Their numbers might not even be drawn this time; under the law of averages, they probably would not be. But they refused—failed, anyway—to register."

"I see," the other said. He was not looking at the investigator. The investigator couldn't tell certainly if he was even looking at the marshal, although he spoke to him, "You want to see Buddy? The doctor's with him now."

"Wait," the investigator said. "I'm sorry about your brother's accident, but I—" The marshal glanced back at him for a moment, his shaggy gray brows beetling,[12] with something at once courteous yet a little impatient about the glance, so that during the instant the investigator sensed from the old marshal the same quality which had been in the other's brief look. The investigator was a man of better than average intelligence; he was already becoming aware of something a little different here from what he had expected. But he had been in relief work in the state several years, dealing almost exclusively with country people, so he still believed he knew them. So he looked at the old marshal, thinking, *Yes. The same sort of people, despite the office, the authority and responsibility which should have changed him.* Thinking again, *These people. These people.* "I intend to take the night train back to Jackson," he said. "My reservation is already made. Serve the warrant and we will—"

"Come along," the old marshal said. "We are going to have plenty of time."

So he followed—there was nothing else to do—fuming and seething, attempting in

---

[11] **discern**—detect.

[12] beetling—jutting.

the short length of the hall to regain control of himself in order to control the situation, because he realized now that if the situation were controlled, it would devolve upon[13] him to control it; that if their departure with their prisoners were **expedited**,[14] it must be himself and not the old marshal who would expedite it. He had been right. The doddering old officer was not only at bottom one of these people, he had apparently been corrupted anew to his old, **inherent**,[15] shiftless sloth and unreliability merely by entering the house. So he followed in turn, down the hall and into a bedroom; whereupon he looked about him not only with amazement but with something very like terror. The room was a big room, with a bare unpainted floor, and besides the bed, it contained only a chair or two and one other piece of old-fashioned furniture. Yet to the investigator it seemed so filled with tremendous men cast in the same mold as the man who had met them that the very walls themselves must bulge. Yet they were not big, not tall, and it was not vitality, exuberance, because they made no sound, merely looking quietly at him where he stood in the door, with faces bearing an almost identical stamp of kinship—a thin, almost frail old man of about seventy, slightly taller than the others; a second one, whitehaired, too, but otherwise identical with the man who had met them at the door; a third one about the same age as the man who had met them, but with something delicate in his face and something tragic and dark and wild in the same dark eyes; the two absolutely identical blue-eyed youths; and lastly the blue-eyed man on the bed over which the doctor, who might have been any city doctor, in his neat city suit, leaned—all of them turning to look quietly at him and the marshal as they entered. And he saw, past the doctor, the slit trousers of the man on the bed and the exposed, bloody, mangled leg, and he turned sick, stopping just inside the door under that quiet, steady regard while the marshal went up to the man who lay on the bed, smoking a cob pipe, a big, old-fashioned, wicker-covered demijohn,[16] such as the investigator's grandfather had kept his whisky in, on the table beside him.

"Well, Buddy," the marshal said, "this is bad."

"Ah, it was my own damn fault," the man on the bed said. "Stuart kept warning me about that frame I was using."

"That's correct," the second old one said.

Still the others said nothing. They just looked steadily and quietly at the investigator until the marshal turned slightly and said, "This is Mr. Pearson. From Jackson. He's got a warrant for the boys."

Then the man on the bed said, "What for?"

"That draft business, Buddy," the marshal said.

"We're not at war now," the man on the bed said.

"No," the marshal said. "It's that new law. They didn't register."

[13] devolve upon—be passed on to.

[14] **expedited**—made easier.

[15] **inherent**—natural.

[16] demijohn—large, narrow-necked bottle made of glass or earthenware, usually encased in wickerwork.

"What are you going to do with them?"

"It's a warrant, Buddy. Swore out."

"That means jail."

"It's a warrant," the old marshal said. Then the investigator saw that the man on the bed was watching him, puffing steadily at the pipe.

"Pour me some whisky, Jackson," he said.

"No," the doctor said. "He's had too much already."

"Pour me some whisky, Jackson," the man on the bed said. He puffed steadily at the pipe, looking at the investigator. "You come from the Government?" he said.

"Yes," the investigator said. "They should have registered. That's all required of them yet. They did not —" His voice ceased, while the seven pairs of eyes contemplated him, and the man on the bed puffed steadily.

"We would have still been here," the man on the bed said. "We wasn't going to run." He turned his head. The two youths were standing side by side at the foot of the bed. "Anse, Lucius," he said.

To the investigator it sounded as if they answered as one, "Yes, father."

"This gentleman has come all the way from Jackson to say the Government is ready for you. I reckon the quickest place to enlist will be Memphis. Go upstairs and pack."

The investigator started, moved forward. "Wait!" he cried.

But Jackson, the eldest, had forestalled[17] him. He said, "Wait," also, and now they were not looking at the investigator. They were looking at the doctor.

"What about his leg?" Jackson said.

"Look at it," the doctor said. "He almost amputated it himself. It won't wait. And he can't be moved now. I'll need my nurse to help me, and some ether, provided he hasn't had too much whisky to stand the anesthetic too. One of you can drive to town in my car. I'll telephone—"

"Ether?" the man on the bed said. "What for? You just said yourself it's pretty near off now. I could whet up one of Jackson's butcher knives and finish it myself, with another drink or two. Go on. Finish it."

"We would have still been here," the man on the bed said. "We wasn't going to run."

"You couldn't stand any more shock," the doctor said. "This is whisky talking now."

"Shucks," the other said. "One day in France[18] we was running through a wheat field and I saw the machine gun, coming across the wheat, and I tried to jump it like you would jump a fence rail somebody was swinging at your middle, only I never made it. And I was on the ground then, and along toward dark that begun to hurt, only about that time something went whang on the back of my helmet, like when you hit a anvil, so I never knowed nothing else until I woke up. There was a heap of us racked up along a bank outside a field dressing station,[19] only it took a long time for the doctor to get around to all of us, and by

[17] forestalled—anticipated.

[18] One day in France—during World War I (1914–1918).

[19] field dressing station—battlefield hospital.

that time it was hurting bad. This here ain't hurt none to speak of since I got a-holt of this johnny-jug. You go on and finish it. If it's help you need, Stuart and Rafe will help you. . . . Pour me a drink, Jackson."

This time the doctor raised the demijohn and examined the level of the liquor. "There's a good quart gone," he said. "If you've drunk a quart of whisky since four o'clock, I doubt if you could stand the anesthetic. Do you think you could stand it if I finished it now?"

"Yes, finish it. I've ruined it; I want to get shut of it."

The doctor looked about at the others, at the still, identical faces watching him. "If I had him in town, in the hospital, with a nurse to watch him, I'd probably wait until he got over this first shock and got the whisky out of his system. But he can't be moved now, and I can't stop the bleeding like this, and even if I had ether or a local anesthetic—"

"Shucks," the man on the bed said. "God never made no better local nor general comfort or anesthetic neither than what's in this johnny-jug. And this ain't Jackson's leg nor Stuart's nor Rafe's nor Lee's. It's mine. I done started it; I reckon I can finish cutting it off any way I want to."

But the doctor was still looking at Jackson. "Well, Mr. McCallum?" he said. "You're the oldest."

But it was Stuart who answered. "Yes," he said. "Finish it. What do you want? Hot water, I reckon."

"Yes," the doctor said. "Some clean sheets. Have you got a big table you can move in here?"

"The kitchen table," the man who had met them at the door said. "Me and the boys—"

"Wait," the man on the bed said. "The boys won't have time to help you." He looked at them again. "Anse, Lucius," he said.

Again it seemed to the investigator that they answered as one, "Yes, father."

"This gentleman yonder is beginning to look impatient. You better start. Come to think of it, you won't need to pack. You will have uniforms in a day or two. Take the truck. There won't be nobody to drive you to Memphis and bring the truck back, so you can leave it at the Gayoso Feed Company until we can send for it. I'd like for you to enlist into the old Sixth Infantry, where I used to be. But I reckon that's too much to hope, and you'll just have to chance where they send you. But it likely won't matter, once you are in. The Government done right by me in my day, and it will do right by you. You just enlist wherever they want to send you, need you, and obey your sergeants and officers until you find out how to be soldiers. Obey them, but remember your name and don't take nothing from no man. You can go now."

"Wait!" the investigator cried again; again he started, moved forward into the center of the room. "I protest this! I'm sorry about Mr. McCallum's accident. I'm sorry about the whole business. But it's out of my hands and out of his hands now. This charge, failure to register according to law, has been made and the warrant issued. It cannot be evaded this way. The course of the action must be completed before any other step can be taken. They should have thought of this when these boys failed to register. If Mr. Gombault refuses to serve this warrant, I will serve it myself and take these men back to Jefferson with me to answer this charge as made. And I must warn Mr. Gombault that he will be cited for contempt!"

The old marshal turned, his shaggy eyebrows beetling again, speaking down to the investigator as if he were a child, "Ain't you found out yet that me or you neither ain't going nowhere for a while?"

"What?" the investigator cried. He looked about at the grave faces once more contemplating him with that remote and speculative regard. "Am I being threatened?" he cried.

"Ain't anybody paying any attention to you at all," the marshal said. "Now you just be quiet for a while, and you will be all right, and after a while we can go back to town."

So he stopped again and stood while the grave, contemplative faces freed him once more of that impersonal and unbearable regard, and saw the two youths approach the bed and bend down in turn and kiss their father on the mouth, and then turn as one and leave the room, passing him without even looking at him. And sitting in the lamplit hall beside the old marshal, the bedroom door closed now, he heard the truck start up and back and turn and go down the road, the sound of it dying away, ceasing, leaving the still, hot night—the Mississippi Indian summer, which had already outlasted half of November—filled with the loud last shrilling of the summer's cicadas, as though they, too, were aware of the imminent season of cold weather and of death.

"I remember old Anse," the marshal said pleasantly, chattily, in that tone in which an adult addresses a strange child. "He's been dead fifteen-sixteen years now. He was about sixteen when the old war[20] broke out, and he walked all the way to Virginia to get into it. He could have enlisted and fought right here at home, but his ma was a Carter, so wouldn't nothing do him but to go all the way back to Virginia to do his fighting, even though he hadn't never seen Virginia before himself; walked all the way back to a land he hadn't never even seen before and enlisted in Stonewall Jackson's army and stayed in it all through the Valley, and right up to Chancellorsville,[21] where them Carolina boys shot Jackson by mistake, and right on up to that morning in 'Sixty-five when Sheridan's cavalry blocked the road from Appomattox[22] to the Valley, where they might have got away again. And he walked back to Mississippi with just about what he had carried away with him when he left, and he got married and built the first story of this house—this here log story we're in right now—and started getting them boys—Jackson and Stuart and Raphael and Lee and Buddy.

---

[20] old war—Civil War (1861–1865).

[21] through the Valley . . . Chancellorsville—from the time of Confederate General Thomas J. "Stonewall" Jackson's campaign in the Shenandoah Valley (March 23–June 9, 1862) to the battle of Chancellorsville (May 2–4, 1863), where Jackson was mistakenly shot by Confederate troops.

[22] Appomattox—site of Confederate surrender in April 1865.

"Buddy come along late, late enough to be in the other war, in France in it. You heard him in there. He brought back two medals, an American medal and a French one, and no man knows till yet how he got them, just what he done. I don't believe he even told Jackson and Stuart and them. He hadn't hardly got back home, with them numbers on his uniform and the wound stripes and them two medals, before he had found him a girl, found her right off, and a year later them twin boys was born, the livin', spittin' image of old Anse McCallum. If old Anse had just been about seventy-five years younger, the three of them might have been thriblets. I remember them—two little critters exactly alike, and wild as spikehorn bucks, running around here day and night both with a pack of coon dogs until they got big enough to help Buddy and Stuart and Lee with the farm and the gin, and Rafe with the horses and mules, when he would breed and raise and train them and take them to Memphis to sell, right on up to three, four years back, when they went to the agricultural college for a year to learn more about whiteface cattle.

"That was after Buddy and them had quit raising cotton. I remember that too. It was when the Government first begun to interfere with how a man farmed his own land, raised his cotton. Stabilizing the price, using up the surplus, they called it, giving a man advice and help, whether he wanted it or not. You may have noticed them boys in yonder tonight; curious folks almost, you might call them. That first year, when county agents was trying to explain the new system to farmers, the agent come out here and tried to explain it to Buddy and Lee and Stuart, explaining how they would cut down the crop, but that the Government would pay farmers the difference, and so they would actually be better off than trying to farm by themselves.

"'Why, we're much obliged,' Buddy says. 'But we don't need no help. We'll just make the cotton like we always done; if we can't make a crop of it, that will just be our lookout and our loss, and we'll try again.'

"So they wouldn't sign no papers nor no cards nor nothing. They just went on and made the cotton like old Anse had taught them to; it was like they just couldn't believe that the Government aimed to help a man whether he wanted help or not, aimed to interfere with how much of anything he could make by hard work on his own land, making the crop and ginning it right here in their own gin, like they had always done, and hauling it to town to sell, hauling it all the way into Jefferson before they found out they couldn't sell it because, in the first place, they had made too much of it and, in the second place, they never had no card to sell what they would have been allowed. So they hauled it back. The gin wouldn't hold all of it, so they put some of it under Rafe's mule shed and they put the rest of it right here in the hall where we are setting now, where they would have to walk around it all winter and keep themselves reminded to be sho and fill out that card next time.

"Only next year they didn't fill out no papers neither. It was like they still couldn't believe it, still believed in the freedom and liberty to make or break according to a man's fitness and will to work, guaranteed by the Government that old Anse had tried to tear in two once and failed, and admitted in good faith he had failed and taken the consequences, and that had give Buddy a medal and taken care of him when he was far away from home in a strange land and hurt.

"So they made that second crop. And they couldn't sell it to nobody neither because they never had no cards. This time they built a special shed to put it under, and I remember how in that second winter Buddy come to town one day to see Lawyer Gavin Stevens. Not for legal advice how to sue the Government or somebody into buying the cotton, even if they never had no card for it, but just to find out why. 'I was for going ahead and signing up for it,' Buddy says. 'If that's going to be the new rule. But we talked it over, and Jackson ain't no farmer, but he knowed father longer than the rest of us, and he said father would have said no, and I reckon now he would have been right.'

"So they didn't raise any more cotton; they had a plenty of it to last a while—twenty-two bales, I think it was. That was when they went into whiteface cattle, putting old Anse's cotton land into pasture, because that's what he would have wanted them to do if the only way they could raise cotton was by the Government telling them how much they could raise and how much they could sell it for, and where, and when, and then pay them for not doing the work they didn't do. Only even when they didn't raise cotton, every year the county agent's young fellow would come out to measure the pasture crops they planted so he could pay them for that, even if they never had no not-cotton to be paid for. Except that he never measured no crop on this place. 'You're welcome to look at what we are doing,' Buddy says. 'But don't draw it down on your map.'

"'But you can get money for this,' the young fellow says. 'The Government wants to pay you for planting all this.'

"'We are aiming to get money for it,' Buddy says. 'When we can't, we will try something else. But not from the Government. Give that to them that want to take it. We can make out.'

"And that's about all. Them twenty-two bales of orphan cotton are down yonder in the gin right now, because there's room for it in the gin now because they ain't using the gin no more. And them boys grew up and went off a year to the agricultural college to learn right about whiteface cattle, and then come back to the rest of them—these here curious folks living off here to themselves, with the rest of the world all full of pretty neon lights burning night and day both, and easy, quick money scattering itself around everywhere for any man to grab a little, and every man with a shiny new automobile already wore out and throwed away and the new one delivered before the first one was even paid for, and everywhere a fine loud grabble and snatch of AAA and WPA[23] and a dozen other three-letter reasons for a man not to work.

---

[23] AAA and WPA—two Depression-era government programs, the Agricultural Adjustment Act, which paid farmers to reduce their crops in an effort to raise farm prices, and the Works Progress Administration, which used public-service projects to create jobs.

Then this here draft comes along, and these curious folks ain't got around to signing that neither, and you come all the way up from Jackson with your paper all signed and regular, and we come out here, and after a while we can go back to town. A man gets around, don't he?"

"Yes," the investigator said. "Do you suppose we can go back to town now?"

"No," the marshal told him in that same kindly tone, "not just yet. But we can leave after a while. Of course you will miss your train. But there will be another one tomorrow."

He rose, though the investigator had heard nothing. The investigator watched him go down the hall and open the bedroom door and enter and close it behind him. The investigator sat quietly, listening to the night sounds and looking at the closed door until it opened presently and the marshal came back, carrying something in a bloody sheet, carrying it gingerly.

"Here," he said. "Hold it a minute."

"It's bloody," the investigator said.

"That's all right," the marshal said. "We can wash when we get through." So the investigator took the bundle and stood holding it while be watched the old marshal go back down the hall and on through it and vanish and return presently with a lighted lantern and a shovel. "Come along," he said. "We're pretty near through now."

The investigator followed him out of the house and across the yard, carrying gingerly the bloody, shattered, heavy bundle in which it still seemed to him he could feel some warmth of life, the marshal striding on ahead, the lantern swinging against his leg, the shadow of his striding scissoring and enormous along the earth, his voice still coming back over his shoulder, chatty and cheerful, "Yes, sir. A man gets around and he sees a heap; a heap of folks in a heap of situations. The trouble is, we done got into the habit of confusing the situations with the folks. Take yourself, now," he said in that same kindly tone, chatty and easy; "you mean all right. You just went and got yourself all fogged up with rules and regulations. That's our trouble. We done invented ourselves so many alphabets and rules and recipes that we can't see anything else; if what we see can't be fitted to an alphabet or a rule, we are lost. We have come to be like critters doctor folks might have created in laboratories, that have learned how to slip off their bones and guts and still live, still be kept alive indefinite and forever maybe even without even knowing the bones and the guts are gone. We have slipped our backbone; we have about decided a man don't need a backbone any more; to have one is old-fashioned. But the groove where the backbone used to be is still there, and the backbone has been kept alive, too, and someday we're going to slip back onto it. I don't know just when nor just how much of a wrench it will take to teach us, but someday."

They had left the yard now. They were mounting a slope; ahead of them the investigator could see another clump of cedars, a small clump, somehow shaggily formal against the starred sky. The marshal entered it and stopped and set the lantern down and, following with the bundle, the investigator saw a small rectangle of earth enclosed by a low brick coping. Then he saw the two graves, or the headstones—two plain granite slabs set upright in the earth.

"Old Anse and Mrs. Anse," the marshal said. "Buddy's wife wanted to be buried with her folks. I reckon she would have been right lonesome up here with just McCallums. Now, let's see." He stood for a moment, his chin in his hand; to the investigator he looked exactly like an old lady trying to decide where to set out a shrub. "They was to run from left to right, beginning with Jackson. But after the boys was born, Jackson and Stuart was to come up here by their pa and ma, so Buddy could move up some and make room. So he will be about here." He moved the lantern nearer and took up the shovel. Then he saw the investigator still holding the bundle. "Set it down," he said. "I got to dig first."

"I'll hold it," the investigator said.

"Nonsense, put it down," the marshal said. "Buddy won't mind."

So the investigator put the bundle down on the brick coping and the marshal began to dig, skillfully and rapidly, still talking in that cheerful, interminable voice, "Yes, sir. We done forgot about folks. Life has done got cheap, and life ain't cheap. Life's a pretty durn valuable thing. I don't mean just getting along from one WPA relief check to the next one, but honor and pride and discipline that make a man worth preserving, make him of any value. That's what we got to learn again. Maybe it takes trouble, bad trouble, to reach it back to us; maybe it was the walking to Virginia because that's where his ma come from, and losing a war and then walking back, that taught it to old Anse. Anyway, he seems to learned it, and to learned it good enough to bequeath it to his boys. Did you notice how all Buddy had to do was to tell them boys of his it was time to go, because the Government had sent them word? And how they told him good-by? Growned men kissing one another without hiding and without shame. Maybe that's what I am trying to say. . . . There." he said. "That's big enough."

He moved quickly, easily; before the investigator could stir, he had lifted the bundle into the narrow trench and was covering it, covering it as rapidly as he had dug, smoothing the earth over it with the shovel. Then he stood up and raised the lantern—a tall, lean old man, breathing easily and lightly.

"I reckon we can go back to town now," he said.

QUESTIONS TO CONSIDER

1. What is the draft investigator's opinion of the marshal?
2. What impression do the McCallum men in the bedroom make on the investigator?
3. Why do you think the marshal lets the McCallum twins drive off and enlist in Memphis?
4. What is the point of the marshal's anecdotes about Anse and Buddy McCallum?
5. Why do you think the McCallums refused to take any type of government assistance?

Eudora Welty ▶

A Visit of Charity

BY EUDORA WELTY

Eudora Welty (1909–2001) was one of the many American writers—including Sarah Orne Jewett, Kate Chopin, Sherwood Anderson, William Faulkner, and William Maxwell—to have devoted their writing to a single place. For Welty it was Jackson, Mississippi, where she was born and where she lived almost her whole life in the same house. The twentieth-century variant of the local-color writers have been less interested in describing the places and the ways of life than in actually preserving what America was once like. The changes in this century have been staggering, and a writer like Welty has, besides creating a beautifully crafted body of literature, actually helped to document the changes. The theme for Welty, as for all of the modern local colorists, was how people can maintain their values and traditions as the world grows smaller. Welty was educated at Mississippi State College and then went to the University of Wisconsin and Columbia University. She worked in New York for a few years—including a stint at The New York Times Book Review*—before returning to Mississippi to work for the Works Progress Administration, a Depression-era agency that employed artists and writers to record the effects of the Depression. Welty traveled through the South taking photographs. She regularly published stories in the 1930s and in 1941 her first collection,* A Curtain of Green, *was published. The following year came her novel* The Robber Bridegroom, *a story full of the folk motifs of old Mississippi. She would write two more novels, but her most characteristic work has been short stories, which she wrote regularly for almost sixty years, until her death from pneumonia. They were a witness to her love of the South and her immense sympathy for the downtrodden and oppressed. "A Visit of Charity" shows Welty at her descriptive best, bringing the shades of people's characters and actions to light.*

It was mid-morning—a very cold, bright day. Holding a potted plant before her, a girl of fourteen jumped off the bus in front of the Old Ladies' Home, on the outskirts of town. She wore a red coat, and her straight yellow hair was hanging down loose from the pointed white cap all the little girls were wearing that year. She stopped for a moment beside one of the prickly dark shrubs with which the city had beautified the Home, and then proceeded slowly toward the building, which was of whitewashed brick and reflected the winter sunlight like a block of ice. As she walked vaguely up the steps she shifted the small pot from hand to hand; then she had to set it down and remove her mittens before she could open the heavy door.

"I'm a Campfire Girl. . . . I have to pay a visit to some old lady," she told the nurse at the desk. This was a woman in a white uniform who looked as if she were cold; she had close-cut hair which stood up on the very top of her head exactly like a sea wave. Marian, the little girl, did not tell her that this visit would give her a minimum of only three points in her score.

"Acquainted with any of our residents?" asked the nurse. She lifted one eyebrow and spoke like a man.

"With any old ladies? No—but—that is, any of them will do," Marian **stammered**.[1] With her free hand she pushed her hair behind her ears, as she did when it was time to study Science.

The nurse shrugged and rose. "You have a nice *multiflora cineraria*[2] there," she remarked as she walked ahead down the hall of closed doors to pick out an old lady.

There was loose, bulging linoleum on the floor. Marian felt as if she were walking on the waves, but the nurse paid no attention to it. There was a smell in the hall like the interior of a clock. Everything was silent until, behind one of the doors, an old lady of some kind cleared her throat like a sheep bleating. This decided the nurse. Stopping in her tracks, she first extended her arm, bent her elbow, and leaned forward from the hips—all to examine the watch strapped to her wrist; then she gave a loud double-rap on the door.

"There are two in each room," the nurse remarked over her shoulder.

"Two what?" asked Marian without thinking. The sound like a sheep's bleating almost made her turn around and run back.

One old woman was pulling the door open in short, gradual jerks, and when she saw the nurse a strange smile forced her old face dangerously **awry**.[3] Marian, suddenly propelled by the strong, impatient arm of the nurse, saw next the side-face of another old woman, even older, who was lying flat in bed with a cap on and a counterpane[4] drawn up to her chin.

"Visitor," said the nurse, and after one more shove she was off up the hall.

Marian stood tongue-tied; both hands held the potted plant. The old woman, still with that terrible, square smile (which was a smile of welcome) stamped on her bony face, was waiting. . . . Perhaps she said something. The old woman in bed said nothing at all, and she did not look around.

Suddenly Marian saw a hand, quick as a bird claw, reach up in the air and pluck the white cap off her head. At the same time, another claw to match drew her all the way into the room, and the next moment the door closed behind her.

"My, my, my," said the old lady at her side.

Marian stood enclosed by a bed, a washstand and a chair; the tiny room had

[1] **stammered**—spoke with involuntary pauses or repetitions.

[2] *multiflora cineraria*—small plant with large heart-shaped leaves and clusters of white, red, or purple flowers.

[3] **awry**—twisted toward one side.

[4] counterpane—bedspread.

altogether too much furniture. Everything smelled wet—even the bare floor. She held on to the back of the chair, which was wicker and felt soft and damp. Her heart beat more and more slowly, her hands got colder and colder, and she could not hear whether the old women were saying anything or not. She could not see them very clearly. How dark it was! The window shade was down, and the only door was shut. Marian looked at the ceiling. . . . It was like being caught in a robbers' cave, just before one was murdered.

"I can't stay but a minute—really, I can't," said Marian suddenly.

"Did you come to be our little girl for a while?" the first robber asked.

Then something was snatched from Marian's hand—the little potted plant.

"Flowers!" screamed the old woman. She stood holding the pot in an undecided way. "Pretty flowers," she added.

Then the old woman in bed cleared her throat and spoke. "They are not pretty," she said, still without looking around, but very distinctly.

Marian suddenly pitched against the chair and sat down in it.

"Pretty flowers," the first old woman insisted. "Pretty—pretty . . ."

Marian wished she had the little pot back for just a moment—she had forgotten to look at the plant herself before giving it away. What did it look like?

"Stinkweeds," said the other old woman sharply. She had a bunchy white forehead and red eyes like a sheep. Now she turned them toward Marian. The fogginess seemed to rise in her throat again, and she bleated, "Who—are—you?"

To her surprise, Marian could not remember her name. "I'm a Campfire Girl," she said finally.

"Watch out for the germs," said the old woman like a sheep, not addressing anyone.

"One came out last month to see us," said the first old woman.

A sheep or a germ? wondered Marian dreamily, holding on to the chair.

"Did not!" cried the other old woman.

"Did so! Read to us out of the Bible, and we enjoyed it!" screamed the first.

"Who enjoyed it!" said the woman in bed. Her mouth was unexpectedly small and sorrowful, like a pet's.

"We enjoyed it," insisted the other. "You enjoyed it—I enjoyed it."

"We all enjoyed it," said Marian, without realizing that she had said a word.

The first old woman had just finished putting the potted plant high, high on the top of the wardrobe, where it could hardly be seen from below. Marian wondered how she had ever succeeded in placing it there, how she could ever have reached so high.

"You mustn't pay any attention to old Addie," she now said to the little girl. "She's ailing today."

"Will you shut your mouth?" said the woman in bed. "I am not."

"You're a story."

"I can't stay but a minute—really, I can't," said Marian suddenly. She looked down at the wet floor and thought that if she were sick in here they would have to let her go.

With much to-do the first old woman sat down in a rocking chair—still another piece of furniture!—and began to rock. With the fingers of one hand she touched a very dirty cameo pin on her chest. "What do you do at school?" she asked.

"I don't know . . ." said Marian. She tried to think but she could not.

"Oh, but the flowers are beautiful," the old woman whispered. She seemed to rock faster and faster; Marian did not see how anyone could rock so fast.

"Ugly," said the woman in bed.

"If we bring flowers—" Marian began, and then fell silent. She had almost said that if Campfire Girls brought flowers to the Old Ladies' Home, the visit would count one extra point, and if they took a Bible with them on the bus and read it to the old ladies, it counted double. But the old woman had not listened, anyway; she was rocking and watching the other one, who watched back from the bed.

"Poor Addie is ailing. She has to take medicine—see?" she said, pointing a horny finger at a row of bottles on the table, and rocking so high that her black comfort shoes lifted off the floor like a little child's.

"I am no more sick than you are," said the woman in bed.

"Oh, yes you are!"

"I just got more sense than you have, that's all," said the other old woman, nodding her head.

"That's only the contrary way she talks when *you all* come," said the first old lady with sudden intimacy. She stopped the rocker with a neat pat of her feet and leaned toward Marian. Her hand reached over—it felt like a petunia leaf, clinging and just a little sticky.

"Will you hush! Will you hush!" cried the other one.

Marian leaned back rigidly in her chair.

"When I was a little girl like you, I went to school and all," said the old woman in the same intimate, menacing voice. "Not here—another town . . ."

"Hush!" said the sick woman. "You never went to school. You never came and you never went. You never were anything—only here. You never were born! You don't know anything. Your head is empty, your heart and hands and your old black purse are all empty, even that little old box that you brought with you you brought empty—you showed it to me. And yet you talk, talk, talk, talk, talk all the time until I think I'm losing my mind! Who are you? You're a stranger—a perfect stranger! Don't you know you're a stranger? Is it possible that they have actually done a thing like this to anyone—sent them in a stranger to talk, and rock, and tell away her whole long **rigmarole**?[5] Do they seriously suppose that I'll be able to keep it up, day in, day out, night in, night out, living in the same room with a terrible old woman—forever?"

Marian saw the old woman's eyes grow bright and turn toward her. This old woman was looking at her with despair and calculation[6] in her face. Her small lips

[5] **rigmarole**—confused, rambling talk.

[6] calculation—cunning.

suddenly dropped apart, and exposed a half circle of false teeth with tan gums.

"Come here, I want to tell you something," she whispered. "Come here!"

Marian was trembling, and her heart nearly stopped beating altogether for a moment.

Marian was trembling, and her heart nearly stopped beating altogether for a moment.

"Now, now, Addie," said the first old woman. "That's not polite. Do you know what's really the matter with old Addie today?" She, too, looked at Marian; one of her eyelids dropped low.

"The matter?" the child repeated stupidly. "What's the matter with her?"

"Why, she's mad because it's her birthday!" said the first old woman, beginning to rock again and giving a little crow[7] as though she had answered her own riddle.

"It is not, it is not!" screamed the old woman in bed. "It is not my birthday, no one knows when that is but myself, and will you please be quiet and say nothing more, or I'll go straight out of my mind!" She turned her eyes toward Marian again, and presently she said in the soft, foggy voice, "When the worst comes to the worst, I ring this bell, and the nurse comes." One of her hands was drawn out from under the patched counterpane—a thin little hand with enormous black freckles. With a finger which would not hold still she pointed to a little bell on the table among the bottles.

"How old are you?" Marian breathed. Now she could see the old woman in bed very closely and plainly, and very abruptly, from all sides, as in dreams. She wondered about her—she wondered for a moment as though there was nothing else in the world to wonder about. It was the first time such a thing had happened to Marian.

"I won't tell!"

The old face on the pillow, where Marian was bending over it, slowly gathered and collapsed. Soft whimpers came out of the small open mouth. It was a sheep that she sounded like—a little lamb. Marian's face drew very close, the yellow hair hung forward.

"She's crying!" She turned a bright, burning face up to the first old woman.

"That's Addie for you," the old woman said spitefully.

Marian jumped up and moved toward the door. For the second time, the claw almost touched her hair, but it was not quick enough. The little girl put her cap on.

"Well, it was a real visit," said the old woman, following Marian through the doorway and all the way out into the hall. Then from behind she suddenly clutched the child with her sharp little fingers. In an affected, high-pitched whine she cried, "Oh, little girl, have you a penny to spare for a poor old woman that's not got anything of her own? We don't have a thing in the world—not a penny for candy—not a thing! Little girl, just a nickel—a penny—"

Marian pulled violently against the old hands for a moment before she was free.

---

7 crow—exultant sound.

Then she ran down the hall, without looking behind her and without looking at the nurse, who was reading *Field & Stream* at her desk. The nurse, after another triple motion to consult her wrist watch, asked automatically the question put to visitors in all institutions: "Won't you stay and have dinner with *us*?"

Marian never replied. She pushed the heavy door open into the cold air and ran down the steps.

Under the prickly shrub she stooped and quickly, without being seen, retrieved a red apple she had hidden there.

Her yellow hair under the white cap, her scarlet coat, her bare knees all flashed in the sunlight as she ran to meet the big bus rocketing through the street.

"Wait for me!" she shouted. As though at an imperial command, the bus ground to a stop.

She jumped on and took a big bite out of the apple.

QUESTIONS TO CONSIDER

1. What is Marian's reason for visiting the old people's home?
2. What does Marian represent to each of the old women?
3. Is Marian's charity well-received?
4. Is Marian's visit really charity? What is your opinion?
5. From whose perspective is the story being told? How does this affect who you have sympathy for?

William Maxwell ▶

The Patterns of Love

BY WILLIAM MAXWELL

William Maxwell (1908–2000) was the fiction editor of The New Yorker *magazine for forty years and, as such, wielded a large influence on American fiction. Since its founding in 1925,* The New Yorker *has been the premier place to publish serious fiction in the United States. The house style of the magazine, which has always favored artful, indirect stories that subtly probe human emotions and avoid topicality and bravado, has been well described by John Updike: "A short story, like the flare of a match, brings human faces out of darkness, and reveals depths beyond statistics." The magazine's roster of regular contributors includes many of America's most important writers: John Cheever, John O'Hara, Truman Capote, J. D. Salinger, Isaac Bashevis Singer, John Updike, and on and on. Maxwell himself belongs on that list. He was principally a writer of short stories, and the settings of his fiction are divided between the two locales he knew well—the small Illinois town he was raised in and New York City, where he spent his career. Maxwell was an extremely subtle writer, such that very little seems to happen in his stories, but his sweet, wistful view of life is evident. "The Patterns of Love" is about a New Yorker spending the weekend in the Connecticut countryside.*

Kate Talbot's bantam rooster,[1] awakened by the sudden appearance of the moon from behind a cloud on a white June night, began to crow. There were three bantams—a cock and two hens—and their roost was in a tree just outside the guest-room windows. The guest room was on the first floor and the Talbots' guest that weekend was a young man by the name of Arnold, a rather light sleeper. He got up and closed the windows and went back to bed. In the sealed room he slept, but was awakened at frequent intervals until daylight Saturday morning.

Arnold had been coming to the Talbots' place in Wilton sometime during the spring or early summer for a number of years. His visits were, for the children, one of a thousand seasonal events that could be counted on, less exciting than the appearance of the first robin or the arrival of violets in the marsh at the foot of the Talbots' hill but akin to them. Sometimes Duncan, the Talbots' older boy, who for a long time was under the impression that Arnold came to see *him*, slept in the guest room when Arnold was there. Last year,

---

[1] bantam rooster—very small type of domestic fowl.

George, Duncan's younger brother, had been given that privilege. This time, Mrs. Talbot, knowing how talkative the boys were when they awoke in the morning, had left Arnold to himself.

When he came out of his room, Mrs. Talbot and George, the apple of her eye, were still at breakfast. George was six, small and delicate and very blond, not really interested in food at any time, and certainly not now, when there was a guest in the house. He was in his pyjamas and a pink quilted bathrobe. He smiled at Arnold with his large and very gentle eyes and said, "Did you miss me?"

"Yes, of course," Arnold said. "I woke up and there was the other bed, flat and empty. Nobody to talk to while I looked at the ceiling. Nobody to watch me shave."

George was very pleased that his absence had been felt. "What is your favorite color?" he asked.

"Red," Arnold said, without having to consider.

"Mine, too," George said, and his face became so illuminated with pleasure at this coincidence that for a moment he looked angelic.

"No matter how much we disagree about other things," Arnold said, "we'll always have that in common, won't we?"

"Yes," George said.

"You'd both better eat your cereal," Mrs. Talbot said.

Arnold looked at her while she was pouring his coffee and wondered if there wasn't something back of her remark—jealousy, perhaps. Mrs. Talbot was a very soft-hearted woman, but for some reason she seemed to be ashamed—or perhaps afraid—to let other people know it. She took refuge continually behind a dry humor. There was probably very little likelihood that George would be as fond of anyone else as he was of his mother for many years to come. There was no real reason for her to be jealous.

"Did the bantams keep you awake?" she asked.

Arnold shook his head.

"Something tells me you're lying," Mrs. Talbot said. "John didn't wake up, but he felt his responsibilities as a host even so. He cried 'Oh!' in his sleep every time a bantam crowed. You'll have to put up with them on Kate's account. She loves them more than her life."

Excluded from the conversation of the grownups, George finished his cereal and ate part of a soft-boiled egg. Then he asked to be excused and, with pillows and pads which had been brought in from the garden furniture the night before, he made a train right across the dining-room floor. The cook had to step over it when she brought a fresh pot of coffee, and Mrs. Talbot and Arnold had to do likewise when they went out through the dining-room door to look at the bantams. There were only two—the cock and one hen—walking around under the Japanese cherry tree on the terrace. Kate was leaning out of an upstairs window, watching them fondly.

"Have you made your bed?" Mrs. Talbot asked.

The head withdrew.

"Kate is going to a houseparty," Mrs. Talbot said, looking at the bantams. "A sort of houseparty. She's going to stay all night at Mary Sherman's house and there are going to be some boys and they're going to dance to the victrola."[2]

"How old is she, for heaven's sake?" Arnold asked.

"Thirteen," Mrs. Talbot said. "She had her hair cut yesterday and it's too short. It doesn't look right, so I have to do something about it."

"White of egg?"[3] Arnold asked.

"How did you know that?" Mrs. Talbot asked in surprise.

"I remembered it from the last time," Arnold said. "I remembered it because it sounded so **drastic**."[4]

"It only works with blonds," Mrs. Talbot said. "Will you be able to entertain yourself for a while?"

"Easily," Arnold said. "I saw *Anna Karenina*[5] in the library and I think I'll take that and go up to the little house."

"Maybe I'd better come with you," Mrs. Talbot said.

The little house was a one-room studio halfway up the hill, about a hundred feet from the big house, with casement windows on two sides and a Franklin stove.[6] It had been built several years before, after Mrs. Talbot had read "A Room of One's Own,"[7] and by now it had a slightly **musty**[8] odor which included lingering traces of wood smoke.

"Hear the wood thrush?" Arnold asked, as Mrs. Talbot threw open the windows for him. They both listened.

"No," she said. "All birds sound alike to me."

"Listen," he said.

This time there was no mistaking it—the liquid notes up and then down the same scale.

"Oh, that," she said. "Yes, I love that," and went off to wash Kate's hair.

From time to time Arnold raised his head from the book he was reading and heard not only the wood thrush but also Duncan and George, quarrelling in the meadow. George's voice was shrill and unhappy and sounded as if he were on the **verge**[9] of tears. Both boys appeared at the window eventually and asked for permission to come in. The little house was out of bounds to them. Arnold nodded. Duncan, who was nine, crawled in without much difficulty, but George had to be hoisted. No sooner were they inside than they began to fight over a wooden gun which had been broken and mended and was rightly George's, it seemed, though Duncan had it and refused to give it up. He refused to give it up one moment, and the next moment, after a sudden change of heart, pressed it upon George—*forced* George to take it, actually, for by that time George

---

[2] victrola—type of record player.

[3] White of egg—way of giving body to hair, akin to using modern hair gel.

[4] **drastic**—serious or radical in nature, extreme.

[5] *Anna Karenina*—novel by Leo Tolstoy. It is the story of a tragic love affair and the novel has many plots contrasting types of love.

[6] Franklin stove—stove used to heat a room. It is connected to the chimney by a funnel.

[7] "A Room of One's Own"—essay by Virginia Woolf that discusses the difficulties of women writers and suggests their need for their own space.

[8] **musty**—stale or moldy in odor.

[9] **verge**—edge.

was more concerned about the Talbots' dog, who also wanted to come in.

The dog was a Great Dane, very mild but also very enormous. He answered to the name of Satan. Once Satan was admitted to the little house, it became quite full and rather noisy, but John Talbot appeared and sent the dog out and made the children leave Arnold in peace. They left as they had come, by the window. Arnold watched them and was touched by the way Duncan turned and helped George, who was too small to jump. Also by the way George accepted this help. It was as if their hostility had two faces and one of them was the face of love. Cain and Abel,[10] Arnold thought, and the wood thrush. All immortal.

John Talbot lingered outside the little house. Something had been burrowing in the lily-of-the-valley bed, he said, and had also uprooted several lady's slippers.[11] Arnold suggested that it might be moles.

"More likely a rat," John Talbot said, and his eyes wandered to a two-foot espaliered[12] pear tree. "That pear tree," he said, "we put in over a year ago."

Mrs. Talbot joined them. She had shampooed not only Kate's hair but her own as well.

"It's still alive," John Talbot said, staring at the pear tree, "but it doesn't put out any leaves."

"I should think it would be a shock to a pear tree to be espaliered," Mrs. Talbot said. "Kate's ready to go."

They all piled into the station wagon and took Kate to her party. Her too short blond hair looked quite satisfactory after the egg shampoo, and Mrs. Talbot had made a boutonnière[13] out of a pink geranium and some little blue and white flowers for Kate to wear on her coat. She got out of the car with her suitcase and waved at them from the front steps of the house.

It was as if their hostility had two faces and one of them was the face of love.

"I hope she has a good time," John Talbot said uneasily as he shifted gears. "It's her first dance with boys. It would be terrible if she didn't have any partners." In his eyes there was a vague threat toward the boys who, in their young **callowness**,[14] might not appreciate his daughter.

"Kate always has a good time," Mrs. Talbot said. "By the way, have you seen both of the bantam hens today?"

"No," John Talbot said.

"One of them is missing," Mrs. Talbot said.

One of the things that impressed Arnold whenever he stayed with the Talbots was the number and variety of animals they had. Their place was not a farm, after all, but merely a big white brick house in the country, and yet they usually had a

10 Cain and Abel—in the Bible, the sons of Adam and Eve. Cain murders Abel.

11 lady's slippers—wild orchids whose flowers look like slippers.

12 espaliered—trained to grow in a flat plane against a wall.

13 boutonnière—flower worn in a buttonhole.

14 **callowness**—immaturity.

dog and a cat, kittens, rabbits, and chickens, all actively involved in the family life. This summer the Talbots weren't able to go in and out by the front door, because a phoebe[15] had built a nest in the porch light. They used the dining-room door instead, and were careful not to leave the porch light on more than a minute or two, lest the eggs be cooked. Arnold came upon some turtle food in his room, and when he asked about it, Mrs. Talbot informed him that there were turtles in the guest room, too. He never came upon the turtles.

The bantams were new this year, and so were the two very small ducklings that at night were put in a paper carton in the sewing room, with an electric-light bulb to keep them warm. In the daytime they hopped in and out of a saucer of milk on the terrace. One of them was called Mr. Rochester[16] because of his distinguished air. The other had no name.

All the while that Mrs. Talbot was making conversation with Arnold, after lunch, she kept her eyes on the dog, who, she explained, was jealous of the ducklings. Once his great head swooped down and he pretended to take a nip at them. A nip would have been enough. Mrs. Talbot spoke to him sharply and he turned his head away in shame.

"They probably smell the way George did when he first came home from the hospital," she said.

"What did George smell like?" Arnold asked.

"Sweetish, actually. Actually awful."

"Was Satan jealous of George when he was a baby?"

"Frightfully," Mrs. Talbot said. "Call Satan!" she shouted to her husband, who was up by the little house. He had found a rat hole near the ravaged lady's slippers and was setting a trap. He called the dog, and the dog went bounding off, devotion in every leap.

While Mrs. Talbot was telling Arnold how they found Satan at the baby's crib one night, Duncan, who was playing only a few yards away with George, suddenly, and for no apparent reason, made his younger brother cry. Mrs. Talbot got up and separated them.

"I wouldn't be surprised if it wasn't time for your nap, George," she said, but he was not willing to let go of even a small part of the day. He wiped his tears away with his fist and ran from her. She ran after him, laughing, and caught him at the foot of the terrace.

Duncan wandered off into a solitary world of his own, and Arnold, after yawning twice, got up and went into the house. Stretched out on the bed in his room, with the Venetian blinds closed, he began to compare the life of the Talbots with his own well-ordered but childless and animalless life in town. Everywhere they go, he thought, they leave tracks behind them, like people walking in the snow. Paths crisscrossing, lines that are perpetually meeting: the mother's loving pursuit of her youngest, the man's love for his daughter, the dog's love for the man, the two boys' preoccupation with each other. Wheels and

[15] phoebe—small, fly-catching bird.

[16] Mr. Rochester—reference to the male hero in Charlotte Brontë's *Jane Eyre*.

diagrams, Arnold said to himself. The patterns of love.

That night Arnold was much less bothered by the crowing, which came to him dimly, through dreams. When he awoke finally and was fully awake, he was conscious of the silence and the sun shining in his eyes. His watch had stopped and it was later than he thought. The Talbots had finished breakfast and the Sunday *Times* was waiting beside his place at the table. While he was eating, John Talbot came in and sat down for a minute, across the table. He had been out early that morning, he said, and had found a chipmunk in the rat trap and also a nest with three bantam eggs in it. The eggs were cold.

He was usually a very quiet, self-contained man. This was the first time Arnold had ever seen him disturbed about anything. "I don't know how we're going to tell Kate," he said. "She'll be very upset."

Kate came home sooner than they expected her, on the bus. She came up the driveway, lugging her suitcase.

"Did you have a good time?" Mrs. Talbot called to her from the terrace.

"Yes," she said, "I had a beautiful time."

Arnold looked at the two boys, expecting them to blurt out the tragedy as soon as Kate put down her suitcase, but they didn't. It was her father who told her, in such a roundabout[17] way that she didn't seem to understand at all what he was saying. Mrs. Talbot interrupted him with the flat facts; the bantam hen was not on her nest and therefore, in all probability, had been killed, maybe by the rat.

Kate went into the house. The others remained on the terrace. The dog didn't snap at the ducklings, though his mind was on them still, and the two boys didn't quarrel. In spite of the patterns on which they seem so intent, Arnold thought, what happens to one of them happens to all. They are helplessly involved in Kate's loss.

At noon other guests arrived, two families with children. There was a picnic, with hot dogs and bowls of salad, cake, and wine, out under the grape arbor.[18] When the guests departed, toward the end of the afternoon, the family came together again on the terrace. Kate was lying on the ground, on her stomach, with her face resting on her arms, her head practically in the ducklings' saucer of milk. Mrs. Talbot, who had stretched out on the garden chaise longue, discovered suddenly that Mr. Rochester was missing. She sat up in alarm and cried, "Where is he?"

"Down my neck," Kate said.

The duck emerged from her crossed arms. He crawled around them and climbed up on the back of her neck. Kate smiled. The sight of the duck's tiny downy head among her pale ash-blond curls made them all burst out laughing. The cloud that had been hanging over the household evaporated into bright sunshine, and Arnold seized that moment to glance at his watch.

They all went to the train with him, including the dog. At the last moment

---

[17] roundabout—indirect.

[18] arbor—latticework on which plants are grown.

Mrs. Talbot, out of a sudden perception of his lonely life, tried to give him some radishes, but he refused them. When he stepped out of the car at the station, the boys were arguing and were with difficulty persuaded to say good-bye to him. He watched the station wagon drive away and then stood listening for the sound of the wood thrush. But, of course, in the center of South Norwalk there was no such sound.

QUESTIONS TO CONSIDER

1. What kind of life does Arnold lead? How is he different from the Talbots?
2. How many types of love can you define in the story?
3. What do the radishes at the end of the story represent? Why does Arnold reject them?
4. What are the "patterns of love"? Do you think Maxwell approves or disapproves of them? Explain your answer.

Martha Gellhorn ▶

The German

BY MARTHA GELLHORN

Martha Gellhorn (1908–1998) is unfairly known more for having been married to Ernest Hemingway than for her own writing. Born in St. Louis, Gellhorn went east to attend Bryn Mawr College, but dropped out after a year to begin writing for newspapers and magazines. She went to Paris as correspondent for The New Republic *in 1930, and in 1934, she returned to America to report on the effects of the Depression. Out of her work as a journalist came Gellhorn's fiction. Her first novel,* What Mad Pursuits *(1934), is based on her experiences in Paris, and her 1936 book of novellas comes from her reporting on poverty and the Depression. This was Gellhorn's lifelong method of working: to go any place there was a story and write a clear, powerful nonfiction report, which over time would be reshaped into fiction. Gellhorn met Ernest Hemingway in Florida in 1936, and they became friends while reporting on the Spanish Civil War the next year. Gellhorn herself would spend the next decade as a war correspondent—in China, Finland, Java, and throughout Europe in World War II. She and Hemingway married in 1940, but when the war wound down, they found that they couldn't really settle down together into peacetime life. They divorced in 1946. Gellhorn published regularly for the rest of her life: six more novels, three collections of stories, travel books, and a great deal of journalism. She was a success in every field and prospered at a time when most journalists were men. Her accomplishments should never be reduced to the fact that she was married to one of America's most important writers.*

The German had lived in Havana[1] for eleven years and no one liked him even before there were political or patriotic reasons not to. He was well known in the cafés around the water front, in the night clubs and at the Jai-Alai;[2] and everywhere he gave offense. He spoke with sneering **condescension**[3] to waiters and shouted insults at the Jai-Alai players if he had bet money on them and they were losing. When he tried to be friendly he was even more **deplorable**,[4] and there was something very wrong about his eyes. He was simply a man of no value and the fact that he was rich and owned a successful business, dealing in cameras and photographic

---

[1] Havana—capital of Cuba.

[2] Jai-Alai—game similar to handball played with a curved basket fastened to the arm for catching and throwing the ball. It is also known as *pelota*.

[3] **condescension**—superior manner.

[4] **deplorable**—wretched, bad.

equipment, did not improve his standing. There were other Germans but he was always known as "The German."

When the German Army entered Paris[5] there was stillness and sorrow in the cafés along the Havana water front. No one had ever been to Paris, but you could imagine it to be a larger, grander Havana, and the people there seemed lost now and hurt beyond healing. One could not feel that the French, any more than the Cubans, would be people to start a war.

There was a little group, drinking in the Bar Nueva York; three Jai-Alai players and a fisherman and two waiters off duty from a café up the street. They were drinking sadly and from time to time one of them would say, "It is not possible," or "What a **barbarity**!"[6]

This was the day after the German Army paraded down the Champs Elysées.

The German, seeing these men from the street, came in noisily as was his habit. The Basque[7] Jai-Alai players turned their backs to him. He circled the table so he could see their faces. They were nothing but exiles from a war they had lost, and they gave themselves an air of pride as if they were the true conquerors. Also they spoke freely and on all occasions against the Nazis, which would not be forgotten when the time came.

"Hola, Jaime!" said the German.

The youngest, tallest, handsomest of the Basques, the best of them and the finest delantero[8] now playing anywhere, looked at the German and did not speak.

"I'll buy you a drink, Jaime," the German said. "We will drink to our victory."

"Tu madre," Jaime said, quietly. The German had lived long enough in Havana to feel the weight of the heaviest Spanish insult, but foreign insults are never entirely serious and he wished to enjoy himself.

"Oh, come, man, do not talk in this childish way," the German said. "When we have won the war, you will be very happy to play pelota in Berlin. There will be a lot of money in it. You will see how glad you are."

Jaime walked around the table and hit the German, across the mouth, with the back of his open hand, in the way that one touches something too indecent to be honored by a clean blow.

The German spoke quickly in his own language, and left the bar. Then the waiter brought fresh drinks and no one mentioned the German or what had happened.

Three nights later, Jaime, going home gay and a little drunk from the Palmas night club, was waylaid by four men who wore handkerchiefs over their faces. His right arm was broken in two places, which meant he would play no more that season and maybe never. Jaime could not identify the four men and the German had a sound alibi for the evening and night; there was

---

[5] German Army entered Paris—reference to Germany's defeat of France in 1940 during World War II.

[6] **barbarity**—uncivilized action, brutality.

[7] Basque—of a people native to the Pyrenees region of northern Spain.

[8] delantero—player of Jai-Alai.

nothing to do about it, in law. The Basques could not bring themselves to the idea of murdering a man, in an unlit alley, many against one, so that plan was discarded though only murder was suitable in return for Jaime's arm and his youth and his talent. They would, instead, find the German one night and smash him up too. For the moment he was being careful but there was plenty of time. The hopeless thing was that no one could see where this would end.

Meanwhile the cruise ships came in, the Mayor got re-elected as arranged, someone started a shark-oil factory, in the pouring sunlight the streets were full of comfortable people, the price of sugar was going up.

QUESTIONS TO CONSIDER

1. Why does no one like the German?
2. Why does Jaime strike the German?
3. Do you think the Basques will take revenge on the German? Explain your answer.
4. What does the last sentence seem to indicate? What is Gellhorn saying about the way people live?

Dawn Powell ▶

Day After Tomorrow

BY DAWN POWELL

Dawn Powell (1896–1965) was born in Mt. Gilead, Ohio, and spent her whole youth itching to get away. In 1918, she arrived in New York, which she would never leave. The journey from country to city became a major theme in her novels and stories. Powell published her first novel in 1928 and over the next thirty years would publish fourteen more, along with plays and numerous stories. Her novels neatly divide into two types: those set in Ohio with characters longing to get to the big city, and those set in New York, full of the people who inhabit the theatrical and fashionable worlds—with both dominated by plots about the trouble of love. Powell was at heart a pessimist, and her fiction takes a dark view of human nature. Although she hated Ohio and loved New York, she does not present the city as the answer to people's dreams. Her New Yorkers are as unhappy and unpleasant as her Ohioans. Powell believed that all relationships were doomed to failure. As she said of her novels, "Fantastic designs made by real human beings earnestly laboring to maladjust themselves to fate. There are no philosophies for them to prove. . . . My characters are not slaves to an author's propaganda. I give them their heads. They furnish their own nooses." This attitude is ever-present, but does not detract from the accomplished comedy of her writing. She was above all an ironist, laughing at all life's little tragedies. Powell herself had a bad marriage, and she spent her adult life caring for her beloved mentally handicapped son. "Day After Tomorrow" is typical Powell, presenting a dark view of married life.

When they found out Lucille was engaged the girls insisted on a celebration. What about tonight?

"But it'll be months!" Lucille protested. "There's no hurry, really. Besides I have Mrs. Brady at five and it'll keep me late."

"I'll do the Brady," said Smitty, the big girl, firmly. "We haven't had a shop party for ages. We'll get Frankie to shut up early."

"Better take your party when you can get it," advised Miss Olsen. "When it gets near the wedding day we may be too busy."

Olsen sat at the cashier's desk, under the drier, which shone like a crown above her radiantly fresh facial. Her eyebrows above the porcelain-tinted face were harried[1] to meager wisps like Smitty's and the other girls'; but where Smitty's mouth was **sullen**,[2] Olsen's was large and good-humored. It was Oley who kept the girls from quarreling and getting on Frankie's

---

[1] harried—attacked; here, plucked.

[2] **sullen**—sulky, showing ill humor; brooding or morose.

nerves. You had to have someone like Oley in a beauty parlor. She made Lucille feel that the party was really a business proposition, something a new girl in the trade had to do. Her reassuring, steady eyes followed Lucille over to the telephone.

Mac was sore when Lucille told him she wouldn't meet him tonight. He was jealous enough of the shop, anyway, especially since she made more money there than he did. He was always saying that she was to stop work when they got married but they both knew she couldn't. Most of the girls in Frankie's were married and had never quit their jobs. Lucille had not set a date for the wedding but once in a long while she and Mac would talk about going down to City Hall day after tomorrow. At the last minute something always stopped them, but that was the way it would happen, they both said, one of these days they'd go through with it.

"OK?" Oley asked when Lucille left the phone, frowning.

The new girl tried to smile.

"Kinda sulky," she confessed. "I told him it was all right, no men going, not even Frankie, but he hung up on me."

"That's my Albert, too," exclaimed Smitty. "Us girls celebrate about one night a year and you'd think it was every night in the week."

"Your four o'clock is here, Miss Schmidt," shouted Miss Olsen, and suddenly the shop was busy again, the way it always was at the last minute, especially if the girls had something planned. It was as if women didn't know they could get three treatments for five dollars at the shop across the street, it was as if they just had to come to Frankie's and pay double, because he was a great artist. Even above the driers roaring and the canaries singing you could hear Frankie telling everybody what a great artist he was. Smitty winked at the new girl but the new girl believed every word he said.

"He really is a genius," she whispered to the customer whose roots she was touching up. "It's a privilege to study hair work under Frankie, I mean that."

"I even made my own toupee,"[3] Frankie was now declaiming, curling iron in hand, in the center of the shop. He had a large pasty pink head adorned by a lavishly curled wig to which he was pointing. "Every place I go people admire that toupee. On the trains, on the street, everywhere. All the time they come up to me, strangers, old, young, everybody. 'Pardon me, sir,' they say, 'that is a beautiful toupee you are wearing. I couldn't help noticing it,' 'Allow me,' they say, 'It's an exquisite piece of work.'"

"Oh it is, Frankie, it is," Lucille eagerly seconded him.

Frankie looked at her approvingly. The new girl was doing all right. Nobody needed to worry about her getting along.

"Frankie thinks you've got a future here," Miss Olsen said to Lucille quietly, when the customer had paid her check. "It's a pity you got other plans."

---

[3] **toupee—partial wig worn to cover a bald spot.**

The new girl was so much younger than the others, so delighted with praise and so eager for advice that you couldn't be jealous of her.

"Oh, but I'll be here a long time anyway," she said happily.

"Oley is the smart one," Smitty sighed to the new girl. "You don't catch her getting married."

She was thrilled that the older girls wanted to celebrate for her but as night approached she worried more and more about Mac. He was low enough lately, anyway, with work so uncertain.

"What does he do, anyway?" Smitty asked, when she explained her qualms. "Or has he got a job?"

"He does special jobs for a radio firm," Lucille evaded. "Naturally high-class technical jobs don't come every day so—But after Election[4] it will be different, of course."

"And why?" inquired Smitty.

"Well," Lucille answered, "because Mac said so."

"Then wait till after Election to get married," counseled Smitty. "Notice if it's different, like he says. Until then pay no attention to what he says about your going on parties."

At six there was a lull in the shop. Mrs. Brady, a weekly problem, all curled, tweezed, tinted and rouged by Smitty, tottered out on high spike heels, balancing a tower of flowers and birds on her new coiffure,[5] her fat little blond chow[6] tucked under her fat little arm. In a twinkling Smitty had jerked down the window shades, barred the door, slammed the appointment book shut. Marie and Freda, the two blondes, whisked bottles and work trays into lockers, the colored boy started sweeping up hair, and old Mrs. Sweeney dragged in her mop and pail. The fresh smell of suds and disinfectant was a pleasure after the clashing perfumes of the day. Under the black coverlets thrown over their cages the canaries twittered sleepily. Frankie did not object to the early closing because it was his night for *Aida*.[7] In pearl-gray topcoat and soft green hat he stood in the salesroom paring his nails and humming lightly, waiting to lock up. Miss Olsen, who was always the first to be ready, passed the time by calling up her friend Helmar to say she would not meet him at the movie tonight, at all. A girl in the shop was going to be married, she said. She did the other girls the favor of calling husbands to say the shop was keeping the staff late tonight.

"Oley is the smart one," Smitty sighed to the new girl. "You don't catch her getting married."

"Listen," answered Miss Olsen complacently adjusting her veil. "If I do all the work why shouldn't I spend the money on my own comfort instead of on some man? I like a twelve-dollar shoe."

---

[4] Election—reference to a forthcoming election when the party in power might change.

[5] coiffure—hairstyle.

[6] chow—medium-sized dog, first bred in China, with a compact body and large head.

[7] *Aida*—Italian opera by Giuseppe Verdi (1813–1901).

"Oley can go out every week like this," grumbled Smitty. "It's only once a year for us married ones, isn't that so, Freda? Well, where do we go first?"

"Have a good time, girls," said Frankie, as they rushed out. "Don't forget tomorrow morning at eight sharp."

They went across the street to the hotel bar first and sat on stools while the bartender kidded them. They were five good-looking, well-dressed girls. They knew what to wear and where to get it cheap. After two old-fashioneds[8] they were comparing complaints about their husbands. The three married ones had all rowed[9] with their husbands about going out tonight, but they didn't care, they had a right to go out with girls for some fun once a year. A person got tired of going out with a husband every minute, you wanted a good time for a change. Marie and Freda stuck together, whispering secrets, so Lucille stuck to Smitty and Oley.

"Listen, you're a darn fool for getting married," Miss Olsen advised the new girl. "The way I look at it is this. Wouldn't you rather buy one good ticket to Radio City than two to some lousy neighborhood movie? That's the question a girl should ask herself before she takes on a husband."

"It's the truth," said Smitty. "You know how it is. Either a man can't get a job or if he can it don't suit him and he don't make much. You're better off like Oley here, giving the boyfriend a nice present at Christmas, say a good watch or a swell dressing gown. That's the way I see it."

Two traveling men[10] were trying to horn in on the party so they decided to get going.

"We always end up in Greenwich Village,"[11] said Smitty. "Boy, oh boy. But don't tell your boyfriend. Come on, kids, here's a taxi."

They stopped at three other bars on the way down, whenever they saw a place that looked gay.[12] Smitty could drink like a trooper but after a few drinks Miss Olsen got her sentences mixed up and finally stopped saying anything but "Hooray for me!" Lucille got the giggles and swore she never had so much fun in her life. She felt guilty having so much fun without Mac and suggested calling him up. He might come down.

"Not a chance," said Smitty. "We don't want any men along."

By the time they got down to Sheridan Square they had had about five old-fashioneds apiece and no dinner. No matter where they went they took a taxi, even if they were only going a block. Marie got to crying because she said before she was married she used to take taxis every day and now it was about twice a year. The mascara kept running down her cheeks and Freda kept swabbing[13] off her friend's face and trying to make her up again, but Marie

[8] old-fashioneds—cocktails.

[9] rowed—argued.

[10] traveling men—salesmen.

[11] Greenwich Village—section of New York known for night life.

[12] gay—lively.

[13] swabbing—using a small piece of absorbent material to clean off makeup.

would cry it right off again. Everyone was borrowing from Oley by this time, because she always carried money, and besides she could take it right out of their envelopes on Saturday.

"Albert will just have to wait another week for his suit," said Smitty, two dollars in the red. "We were to make a last payment on it this payday. He'll be raving. You know. A man has to look just so when he's not working or he gets low in his mind."

"Wait till he's working!" Marie sniveled. "Then all the money goes for cleaning and pressing and shoeshines. The wife has to pay the rent and gas and bread and cook the beefsteak for his boss."

"I guess it depends a lot on the fella," said Lucille.

"Hooray for me," said Miss Olsen, and then they were at the Joint. The Joint was a long barroom lit up with blue lights, crowded with shouting drinkers and funny-looking Villagers. A juke box was blaring out "I'm in Love With a Wonderful Guy" so Smitty grabbed Lucille and they danced, falling into the booth at last over Oley's knees and screaming with laughter.

"Dancing," said Marie, "that's another thing I miss."

A boy with a drawing pad came up and wanted to do their portraits for a dollar and Oley consented. She took off her glasses and held her square handsome **ruddy**[14] face turned to the right for twenty minutes while the waiter brought their hamburgers and beer. The girls wanted to kid the artist because he was a good-looking lad. They could hardly eat for staring at him.

"Look at the complexion on him!" marveled Marie. "Mrs. Brady would give a million dollars for a skin like that."

"It's just the shade of our *rose foncé*,"[15] murmured Smitty. "And look at how he wears his clothes. Boy, it would be a pleasure to dress a fella like that, you could dress him straight from Student Wear and he'd look custom-made."

"He could walk right out of the store without an alteration," said Freda.

"It's when they got a pot like Bill that clothes cost so much," said Marie. "It's a case of skimping over the stomach or else the behind. His new forty-dollar gabardine cuts him right through the middle."

"Tell him to lay off the starches,"[16] said Freda.

Oley gave the boy a dollar for her portrait. There was real talent there, she said, and it made her look like Ingrid Bergman,[17] some. But the other girls just kept staring at the artist, as he walked away.

"The way he walks, even," said Smitty dreamily. "You could take a fella like that anywhere and have people take notice. Look at the wave. Frankie ought to see that. The manicure, even. I could look at a fella like that all day and never get tired. If he was mine I'd get him evening clothes, top hat, the whole works."

"And those eyelashes!" said Marie. "Still and all he looks kinda weak."

[14] **ruddy**—having a healthy, reddish color.

[15] *rose foncé*—French name for the color mauve, a pale reddish purple.

[16] starches—white, odorless, tasteless food substances found in foods such as potatoes and rice.

[17] Ingrid Bergman—Swedish actress (1915–1982) who starred in American films.

"I suppose you prefer a prizefighter type," sneered Smitty. "Listen, if you got to have a husband, give me one that shows off what I put into 'em, that's all I say. All Albert can do with his clothes is to look warm."

Lucille was beginning to get serious. She thought of Mac and how the girls would kid about a heavy, solid baldish fellow like that with no steady job, no sex appeal, just a fellow you liked. She was worried too, as it got toward eleven, because Mac might take it into his head to drop by her place, checking up on her. She timidly reminded Smitty that it took nearly an hour to get up to 181st Street.

"Listen to the sissy," jeered Marie. "Afraid of the boyfriend, eh? Let him beef. You'll get used to it, honey. Ask him who it is that pays the bills, that's what to say when they get to beefing."

"I got nothing on my mind," boasted Oley. "If Helmar don't like what I do he can take a powder.[18] I got other men friends."

She rolled up her portrait carefully.

"You don't know how smart you are, Oley," said Marie.

"Hooray," said Oley. "Hooray for me."

"That boy!" Smitty said. "Did you see his teeth? I'll bet his dentist bill don't run five dollars a year."

"Forget it!" said Oley. "This party's for Lucille, here, not for that Village sheik."[19]

"That's right," said Smitty, and raised her glass. "To the bride!"

They finished off their glasses but Lucille didn't drink because you didn't drink when it was a toast to you and besides she was getting a queer feeling.

"What say we go?" said Oley. "You kids pay me Saturday."

The juke box played "Anniversary Waltz" and Freda and Lucille started dancing their way out. The girls were calling Lucille "Baby" now because they said she didn't know the first thing. Outside the air was chilly for June and everyone envied Oley her foxes, even though she said they were only half paid for. They took the subway up to Times Square where Oley and the two blondes changed to East Side and Smitty and Lucille took the Broadway Express. On the way up Smitty got to telling off-color[20] jokes till they thought they'd die laughing. At 181st Smitty went west and Lucille hurried east. She was still laughing when she saw Mac in front of her rooming house. He was walking up and down smoking his pipe and she knew he was sore but she was too happy to care. It was like the girls said, you had a right to a good time once a year.

"Afraid of the boyfriend, eh? Let him beef. You'll get used to it, honey."

"There was some man," he said, grabbing her arm. He wouldn't let her go inside the vestibule[21] without an argument. "You can't kid me, there was some other man in it. It was Frankie."

---

[18] take a powder—slang meaning "make a quick departure."

[19] sheik—attractive male.

[20] off-color—in bad taste, improper.

[21] vestibule—entrance hall.

"There wasn't any man in it, dopey," she said irritably. "This was just pleasure."

She went in, letting the door slam, not giving him a chance to ask how much of her salary she'd spent, money that should have been saved toward the apartment. While she undressed she got to thinking of Smitty and her husband having that same argument that very minute, probably, and the other girls the same, and she thought only Oley was having a good night's sleep without a care. So far as that went it wasn't too late for her to change her own mind. The wedding date wasn't really set. There was still time to decide on one ticket to Radio City instead of two to a neighborhood movie. When Mac started bawling her out tomorrow she'd have something to say right back.

She climbed into bed with her night-gown on wrong side out. She lay there in the dark watching the blue garage lights go on and off across the street, thinking what a wonderful evening they had had. She thought about Oley's silver foxes and twelve-dollar shoes and the boy with the *rose foncé* complexion.

"Hooray for me!" she shouted suddenly. She must have been a little tight.[22]

[22] tight—slang word for "drunk."

QUESTIONS TO CONSIDER

1. How are Oley and Smitty alike? How are they different?
2. What is it that the characters in "Day After Tomorrow" seem to value the most?
3. What does Powell seem to think of marriage? What is her reasoning?

Maeve Brennan ▶

The Bride

BY MAEVE BRENNAN

Maeve Brennan (1916–1981) was born and raised in Dublin, Ireland. In 1934, her father became Ireland's ambassador to the United States, and the family moved to Washington. She went to college at Georgetown University, and when her family returned to Dublin, Brennan stayed behind. She moved to New York and went to work for The New Yorker. *She published occasional stories, but the majority of her work was for the magazine's famed "Talk of the Town" section, in which the celebrated and odd events of the city are recorded with irony and wit. Brennan was a master of this section's wry style and became one of the sharpest chroniclers of New York's ironies. However, her own life had a great share of tragedies. She married another* New Yorker *writer, St. Clair McKelway, in 1954, but the marriage collapsed five years later because of McKelway's alcoholism and manic depression. Then in the 1970s, Brennan herself had a mental breakdown, and spent the rest of her life suffering periodic bouts of mental illness. Much of her fiction documents the loneliness of women, particularly those trapped in bad marriages. Brennan's body of fiction is quite small; she published thirty-nine stories. Of these, two-thirds are set in Dublin, in a house and community almost exactly like where she grew up. The rest of her fiction is set in the New York environment Brennan knew so well: the city itself and the suburbs where the well-to-do resided. "The Bride" is typical of Brennan's work: a short and acute portrait of one woman's situation in life.*

At seven o'clock on the evening before her wedding day, Margaret Casey finished her packing, locked her suitcase, and sat down on the edge of her bed to catch her breath. Her room was on the top floor of the house in Scarsdale[1] where she had worked as a maid for ten years. She was alone in the house. The phone was shut off, the refrigerator was disconnected, the windows all were locked, and all the beds, except hers, stripped for the summer. The family had early that morning driven off to their cottage in the Berkshires,[2] where they would remain until October. Margaret had dreaded the moment of their departure, fearing her own tears, which fell easily, but at the last minute she smiled brilliantly, and waved, and saw the car disappear out onto the road calmly enough, although for

[1] Scarsdale—northern suburb of New York City, where many well-to-do families live.

[2] Berkshires—range of hills in western Massachusetts where many New Yorkers go in the summer to escape the heat.

a moment there she felt she must cry after them to come back, come back, if only for an hour, and not leave her by herself at a time like this.

Of course, it was her own idea in the first place to get married the day after they left for the summer. Summer had seemed a comfortable, indefinite time away the night last February that she had given in to Carl's persistence and given him her promise. She liked Carl, but she wasn't much inclined to marry him. All that night, she lay awake in a panic, thinking of ways to break with him. It would be heartless to tell him straight out that she had no use for him. Crafty, she decided to do one thing at a time. First she would give Mrs. Smith her notice, and then she would just steal away to another town and find a new job and not let Carl know anything about it. But when she went in, when they were having breakfast, and gave her notice, the sight of Mrs. Smith's stricken face was too much for her, and to ease her guilt she blurted out that she was going to marry Carl, and settle down, and stop working, and have a home of her own. Mr. and Mrs. Smith were astonished and delighted at her good fortune, and their pleasure made her so generous that she embroidered the case a little, describing the house (not yet built) that Carl hoped to buy, and telling about his plan to go into business with his brother someday, not right away. Mrs. Smith said she hoped Margaret would let her give a little wedding breakfast here in the house after the ceremony, but Margaret quickly said no, that her plans were made to be married the day after they left for the summer. After some argument, Mrs. Smith gave in to her, and laughed, and said that after all Margaret was the bride and it was only right she should have things her way. Back in the kitchen, Margaret sat as astonished as though they had ordered her out of the house. All I wanted to do was give notice; she thought; and here I've gone and committed myself.

All I wanted to do was give notice; she thought; and here I've gone and committed myself.

Still, July seemed a long time off. There would surely be some way to free herself. She could pick a fight with Carl, or she might confide in Mrs. Smith and ask her advice. But it grew harder and harder to speak up. Anyway, she found herself growing fond of Carl. It was the first time in her life she had ever had anyone of her own, and he was very considerate of her. He was coming along now in a few minutes to take her out to dinner.

She contrasted this evening with the evening, twelve years ago in Ireland, before her sister Madge was married. That evening, Madge never stopped posturing around in her wedding dress of blue silk, showing off before the neighbors while her mother sat in the middle of the room crying because she was losing her big girl and the family would soon be all scattered. "Next thing little Margaret will be leaving me," cried the mother, and Margaret had darted to her mother's side and protested that no, no, she would never leave, and the neighbors nodded approvingly and said that was a good daughter, that one. Still, good daughter and all, it was Madge who was the favorite, and when, after a year, Madge decided to economize by moving back into her old home, Margaret felt very out of place with the perpetual fuss over Madge's baby and Madge's husband and Madge's aches and pains. Margaret was already out working by then, and when her uncle in New York wrote offering to lend her the passage over, she accepted at once, believing up to the last minute before she left that the mother would come to her senses and forbid her to go. But the mother appeared delighted to see Margaret get her "chance," and there were fewer tears shed over Margaret's departure for a foreign land than over Madge's decision to marry a boy she had known all her life.

Margaret had found great satisfaction in the money orders she sent home weekly, knowing the power they gave her mother over the household. After the debt to her uncle was paid off, she sent more and more money home, stinting[3] herself to send as much as she could. She always meant to start saving her fare home, but she really believed that when the time came for her to see her mother again, the money would turn up somehow. She wanted to go back there and best[4] Madge, once and for all. She had a dream of saving up enough to go back and start a little business, enough to support her mother and herself, or to go back with a comfortable nest egg and find some good man to marry. None of her hopes had come true. All of her hopes had turned into regrets; only the hurt, strained feeling in her heart was the same. Everything had turned out wrong. The mother was five months dead now, and there no longer seemed any way to get back at Madge, sitting triumphant there in possession of all the old bits of ornaments and furniture and everything that remained of the old home. Not that Madge had offered to send her anything—not even a few of the old photographs—and it would be too bitter to reveal her jealousy and longing by asking for them. Madge had known what she was doing, all right.

If only God had given Margaret the strength to wait a while longer, something might have turned up. She might have won the Sweep,[5] or some old lady might have turned up who wanted a companion to travel to Ireland with her, or somebody—her uncle, maybe—might have died and left her a legacy. There was no limit to the things that might have happened, if she'd only had patience. But the night she heard her mother was dead, Carl was so sympathetic that she committed herself further than she had ever meant to. It was the way he put his arm around her that undid her, the closeness of his body giving her a warmth she had forgotten since her mother's lap. How well he knew the time to take advantage of me, she thought angrily. His persistence had put her off the first time she met him. She should have

[3] stinting—being sparing with.

[4] best—defeat.

[5] Sweep—Irish Sweepstakes, a national lottery.

been firm then, and got rid of him for good. That was the German in him, enabling him to hang on until he got what he was after. He would never fit in with the crowd at home. They would laugh at him behind his back and say he was thick. Madge's cruel eyes would cut clear through the smart American clothes to see the soft, good-natured, easily hurt fellow underneath. Madge would laugh to hear Mr. Smith say that Carl was a fine, steady fellow who would always be a credit to the community. Mr. and Mrs. Smith had been very nice about the whole thing. Mr. Smith had given Margaret three months' salary as a wedding present, and Mrs. Smith gave her her wedding outfit. Her dress, a jacket and skirt of navy-blue shantung,[6] hung now in the closet, with the new shoes in a box on the floor underneath and the new hat in a box on the shelf above. Except for her rosary beads, she had nothing old and familiar from Ireland to bring with her into her new home. Madge had stolen everything, and without even lifting a finger.

One time, when Margaret was a little girl, before her father died, her mother and father had gone for a ride in a charabanc,[7] out into the country. When they came back, they talked about the hotel where they'd had tea, and about the woods and rivers they had seen. They promised that Margaret would have a charabanc ride one Sunday, and she believed them and began to go every Sunday to watch the buses fill up with passengers. A lot of young people used to go, laughing and pushing and jostling each other to see who would get the best seat. Margaret had her seat all picked out—the one up in front near the driver—but she never had the chance to ride in it. There was always some excuse to keep her from going. Sometimes one of the charabancs went on a mystery tour. The driver of the charabanc knew where he was going, but the passengers had to guess, and never could be sure of their destination until they arrived there. The people going off on the mystery tours seemed even gayer than the usual charabanc crowds. Margaret longed to go with them, although she had a half fear that the mystery charabancs never came back at all. She might just as well have gone on one and not come back, for all the good she had made of her life.

A joyful shouting came from downstairs, and Margaret ran out onto the landing. It was Carl. He had let himself in by the back door. He was accustomed to back doors, being a plumber. When he reached the second-floor landing, he looked up and saw her.

"How's my girl?" he shouted, as though they were miles apart. His voice was hard in the emptiness of the house. He had been drinking, she could hear it in his voice, but she would say nothing about it this time. He threw his head back and stretched his arms wide, clowning in his unaccustomed happiness, but she was not touched by his emotion. She stared down at him in astonishment and fear.

---

[6] shantung—heavy, uneven silk fabric.

[7] charabanc—large motorbus in Britain.

"What's the matter?" he shouted, throwing himself down on his arms on the banisters. "Were you afraid I wasn't going to come? Were you afraid I might leave you at the church? You can get *that* idea out of your head. You're not getting away from me *that* easy."

She wanted to scream at him that he was beneath her, and that she despised him, and that she was not bound to him yet and never would be bound to him, but instead she spoke civilly,[8] saying that she would be ready in a minute, and warning him not to come up into the room, because her wedding dress was hanging there and she didn't want him to see it ahead of time, for fear of bringing bad luck on the two of them.

---

[8] civilly—politely.

QUESTIONS TO CONSIDER

1. Why did Margaret not simply leave her job and Carl as she had planned?
2. How does she view her relationship with her family in Ireland?
3. What does the charabanc represent to Margaret?
4. Why does Margaret judge Carl so sharply? Do you think she will grow to love him? Explain your answer.

Isaac Bashevis Singer ▶

Gimpel the Fool

BY ISAAC BASHEVIS SINGER

Isaac Bashevis Singer (1904–1991) was born in Poland and did not come to the United States until 1935. Singer had studied to be a rabbi, but decided in his twenties to be a writer and part of the thriving Jewish intellectual world of Poland. The language of this world was Yiddish, a mixture of German and Hebrew that rose up in Eastern Europe and over time became a universal language for Eastern European Jews. Even in the United States, Singer continued to write in Yiddish, collaborating on the translation of his stories into English. Singer lived in New York, where he went to work for the Daily Forward, *a newspaper published in Yiddish for the large Jewish community of the city. In his career, Singer published more than forty books. He concentrated on documenting the Jews of New York and on recalling the traditional ways of life in Eastern Europe. Singer was very fond of Jewish folklore, and magic and folk motifs appear regularly in his stories. The great shadow on his life, and that of everyone he knew, was the Holocaust, which destroyed everything that Singer had known in his youth. Sadness and guilt about survival are part of many of Singer's stories about New York's Jewish community. Singer was also a key figure in the postwar rise of Jewish-American literature. "Gimpel the Fool" was translated by the future Nobel laureate Saul Bellow, and its publication in* Partisan Review *in 1953 is often cited as the moment Jewish-American fiction came of age. Over the next decade, Singer's fiction appeared in English translation with increasing regularity, and he had no problems placing his new stories. In 1978, Singer was awarded the Nobel Prize, and cited for his preservation of Yiddish culture and his great gifts as a storyteller. "The storyteller and poet of our time," he wrote, "as in any other time, must be an entertainer of the spirit in the full sense of the word, not just a preacher of social and political ideals. There is no paradise for bored readers and no excuse for tedious literature that does not intrigue the reader, uplift his spirit, give him joy and escape that true art always grants." There is no better description of what Singer's own writing is like.*

I

I am Gimpel the fool. I don't think myself a fool. On the contrary. But that's what folks call me. They gave me the name while I was still in school. I had seven names in all: **imbecile**,[1] donkey, flax-head,[2] dope, glump, ninny, and fool. The last name stuck. What did my foolishness consist of? I was easy to take in. They said, "Gimpel, you know the rabbi's wife has been brought to childbed?" So I skipped school. Well, it turned out to be a lie. How was I supposed to know? She

---

[1] **imbecile**—feeble-minded, stupid person.

[2] flax-head—Flax is a plant whose fibers are used to make linen cloth.

hadn't had a big belly. But I never looked at her belly. Was that really so foolish? The gang laughed and hee-hawed, stomped and danced and chanted a good-night prayer. And instead of the raisins they give when a woman's lying in, they stuffed my hand full of goat turds. I was no weakling. If I slapped someone he'd see all the way to Cracow.[3] But I'm really not a slugger by nature. I think to myself, Let it pass. So they take advantage of me.

I was coming home from school and heard a dog barking. I'm not afraid of dogs, but of course I never want to start up with them. One of them may be mad, and if he bites there's not a Tartar[4] in the world who can help you. So I made tracks. Then I looked around and saw the whole market place wild with laughter. It was no dog at all but Wolf-Leib the thief. How was I supposed to know it was he? It sounded like a howling bitch.

When the pranksters and leg-pullers found that I was easy to fool, every one of them tried his luck with me. "Gimpel, the Czar[5] is coming to Frampol; Gimpel, the moon fell down in Turbeen; Gimpel, little Hodel Furpiece found a treasure behind the bathhouse." And I like a *golem*[6] believed everyone. In the first place, everything is possible, as it is written in the Wisdom of the Fathers, I've forgotten just how. Second, I had to believe when the whole town came down on me! If I ever dared to say, "Ah, you're kidding!" there was trouble. People got angry. "What do you mean! You want to call everyone a liar?" What was I to do? I believed them, and I hope at least that did them some good.

I was an orphan. My grandfather who brought me up was already bent toward the grave. So they turned me over to a baker, and what a time they gave me there! Every woman or girl who came to bake a pan of cookies or dry a batch of noodles had to fool me at least once. "Gimpel, there's a fair in heaven; Gimpel, the rabbi gave birth to a calf in the seventh month; Gimpel, a cow flew over the roof and laid brass eggs." A student from the *yeshiva*[7] came once to buy a roll, and he said, "You, Gimpel, while you stand here scraping with your baker's shovel the Messiah has come. The dead have arisen." "What do you mean?" I said. "I heard no one blowing the ram's horn!" He said, "Are you deaf?" And all began to cry, "We heard it, we heard!" Then in came Reitze the candle-dipper and called out in her hoarse voice, "Gimpel, your father and mother have stood up from the grave. They're looking for you."

To tell the truth, I knew very well that nothing of the sort had happened, but all the same, as folks were talking, I threw on my wool vest and went out. Maybe something had happened. What did I stand to lose by looking? Well, what a cat music[8] went up! And then I took a vow to believe nothing more. But that was no go either.

---

[3] Cracow—city in Poland.

[4] Tartar—member of one of the Mongol tribes who invaded Russia and Europe in the Middle Ages.

[5] Czar—ruler of imperial Russia, who would have been the sovereign over this part of Poland.

[6] *golem*—in Hebrew mythology, an artificial human being, endowed with life, but lacking intelligence.

[7] *yeshiva*—Jewish seminary.

[8] cat music—sound of people laughing.

They confused me so that I didn't know the big end from the small.

I went to the rabbi to get some advice. He said, "It is written, better to be a fool all your days than for one hour to be evil. You are not a fool. They are the fools. For he who causes his neighbor to feel shame loses Paradise himself." Nevertheless the rabbi's daughter took me in. As I left the rabbinical court she said, "Have you kissed the wall yet?" I said, "No; what for?" She answered, "It's a law; you've got to do it after every visit." Well, there didn't seem to be any harm in it. And she burst out laughing. It was a fine trick. She put one over on me, all right.

"You are not a fool. They are the fools. For he who causes his neighbor to feel shame loses Paradise himself."

I wanted to go off to another town, but then everyone got busy matchmaking, and they were after me so they nearly tore my coat tails off. They talked at me and talked until I got water on the ear. She was no **chaste**[9] maiden, but they told me she was virgin pure. She had a limp, and they said it was deliberate, from **coyness**.[10] She had a bastard, and they told me the child was her little brother. I cried, "You're wasting your time. I'll never marry that whore." But they said indignantly, "What a way to talk! Aren't you ashamed of yourself? We can take you to the rabbi and have you fined for giving her a bad name." I saw then that I wouldn't escape them so easily and I thought, They're set on making me their butt. But when you're married the husband's the master, and if that's all right with her it's agreeable to me too. Besides, you can't pass through life **unscathed**,[11] nor expect to.

I went to her clay house, which was built on the sand, and the whole gang, hollering and chorusing, came after me. They acted like bearbaiters.[12] When we came to the well they stopped all the same. They were afraid to start anything with Elka. Her mouth would open as if it were on a hinge, and she had a fierce tongue. I entered the house. Lines were strung from wall to wall and clothes were drying. Barefoot she stood by the tub, doing the wash. She was dressed in a worn hand-me-down gown of plush. She had her hair put up in braids and pinned across her head. It took my breath away, almost, the reek of it all.

Evidently she knew who I was. She took a took at me and said, "Look who's here! He's come, the drip. Grab a seat."

I told her all; I denied nothing. "Tell me the truth," I said, "are you really a virgin, and is that mischievous Yechiel actually your little brother? Don't be deceitful with me, for I'm an orphan."

"I'm an orphan myself," she answered, "and whoever tries to twist you up, may the end of his nose take a twist. But don't let them think they can take advantage of me. I want a dowry of fifty guilders,[13] and

[9] **chaste**—morally pure in thought and conduct.

[10] **coyness**—shyness, acting falsely demure.

[11] **unscathed**—unharmed, uninjured.

[12] bearbaiters—people engaged in bearbaiting, the pastime of setting dogs on a chained bear.

[13] guilders—type of coin.

let them take up a collection besides. Otherwise they can kiss my you-know-what." She was very plain-spoken. I said, "Don't bargain with me. Either a flat 'yes' or a flat 'no'—go back where you came from."

I thought, No bread will ever be baked from *this* dough. But ours is not a poor town. They consented to everything and proceeded with the wedding. It so happened that there was a dysentery[14] epidemic at the time. The ceremony was held at the cemetery gates, near the little corpse-washing hut. The fellows got drunk. While the marriage contract was being drawn up I heard the most pious high rabbi ask, "Is the bride a widow or a divorced woman?" And the sexton's[15] wife answered for her, "Both a widow and divorced." It was a black moment for me. But what was I to do, run away from under the marriage canopy?[16]

There was singing and dancing. An old granny danced opposite me, hugging a braided white *chalah*.[17] The master of revels made a "God 'a mercy" in memory of the bride's parents. The schoolboys threw burrs, as on *Tishe b'Av*[18] fast day. There were a lot of gifts after the sermon: a noodle board, a kneading trough, a bucket, brooms, ladles, household articles galore. Then I took a look and saw two strapping young men carrying a crib. "What do we need this for?" I asked.

So they said, "Don't rack your brains about it. It's all right, it'll come in handy." I realized I was going to be rooked. Take it another way though, what did I stand to lose? I reflected, I'll see what comes of it. A whole town can't go altogether crazy.

II

At night I came where my wife lay, but she wouldn't let me in. "Say, look here, is this what they married us for?" I said. And she said, "My monthly has come." "But yesterday they took you to the ritual bath,[19] and that's afterward, isn't it supposed to be?" "Today isn't yesterday," said she, "and yesterday's not today. You can beat it if you don't like it." In short, I waited.

Not four months later she was in childbed. The townsfolk hid their laughter with their knuckles. But what could I do? She suffered intolerable pains and clawed at the walls. "Gimpel," she cried, "I'm going. Forgive me!" The house filled with women. They were boiling pans of water. The screams rose to the welkin.[20]

The thing to do was to go to the House of Prayer to repeat Psalms, and that was what I did.

The townsfolk liked that, all right. I stood in a corner saying Psalms and prayers, and they shook their heads at me. "Pray, pray!" they told me. "Prayer never made any woman pregnant." One of the congregation put a straw to my mouth and

---

[14] dysentery—disease of the intestines, producing diarrhea with blood and mucus.

[15] sexton—employee of a religious community in charge of caring for the building and property.

[16] marriage canopy—In a Jewish wedding, the bride and groom stand under a canopy called a *huppah*.

[17] *chalah*—type of bread which is served on Jewish holidays.

[18] *Tishe b'Av*—day of mourning that commemorates the disasters and persecutions that have overtaken Jews.

[19] ritual bath—Orthodox Jewish women go to the *mikvah*, a ritual bath after menstruation.

[20] welkin—sky.

said, "Hay for the cows." There was something to that too, by God!

She gave birth to a boy. Friday at the synagogue[21] the sexton stood up before the Ark, pounded on the reading table, and announced, "The wealthy Reb[22] Gimpel invites the congregation to a feast in honor of the birth of a son." The whole House of Prayer rang with laughter. My face was flaming. But there was nothing I could do. After all, I *was* the one responsible for the circumcision honors and rituals.

Half the town came running. You couldn't wedge another soul in. Women brought peppered chick-peas, and there was a keg of beer from the tavern. I ate and drank as much as anyone, and they all congratulated me. Then there was a circumcision, and I named the boy after my father, may he rest in peace. When all were gone and I was left with my wife alone, she thrust her head through the bed-curtain and called me to her.

"Gimpel," said she, "why are you silent? Has your ship gone and sunk?"

"What shall I say?" I answered. "A fine thing you've done to me! If my mother had known of it she'd have died a second time."

She said, "Are you crazy, or what?"

"How can you make such a fool," I said, "of one who should be the lord and master?"

"What's the matter with you?" she said. "What have you taken it into your head to imagine?"

I saw that I must speak bluntly and openly. "Do you think this is the way to use an orphan?" I said. "You have borne a bastard."

She answered, "Drive this foolishness out of your head. The child is yours."

"How can he be mine?" I argued. "He was born seventeen weeks after the wedding."

She told me then that he was premature. I said, "Isn't he a little too premature?" She said she had had a grandmother who carried just as short a time and she resembled this grandmother of hers as one drop of water does another. She swore to it with such oaths that you would have believed a peasant at the fair if he had used them. To tell the plain truth, I didn't believe her; but when I talked it over the next day with the schoolmaster he told me that the very same thing had happened to Adam and Eve. Two they went up to bed, and four they descended.

"There isn't a woman in the world who is not the granddaughter of Eve," he said.

That was how it was—they argued me dumb. But then, who really knows how such things happen?

I began to forget my sorrow. I loved the child madly, and he loved me too. As soon as he saw me he'd wave his little hands and want me to pick him up, and when he was colicky I was the only one who could pacify him. I bought him a little bone teething ring and a little gilded cap. He was forever catching the evil eye[23] from someone, and then I had to run to get one of those abracadabras for him that would

---

[21] synagogue—Jewish house of worship.

[22] Reb—Jewish title of respect for a man.

[23] evil eye—look or stare believed to harm others.

get him out of it. I worked like an ox. You know how expenses go up when there's an infant in the house. I don't want to lie about it; I didn't dislike Elka either, for that matter. She swore at me and cursed, and I couldn't get enough of her. What strength she had! One of her looks could rob you of the power of speech. And her orations! Pitch and sulphur, that's what they were full of, and yet somehow also full of charm. I adored her every word. She gave me bloody wounds though.

In the evening I brought her a white loaf as well as a dark one, and also poppyseed rolls I baked myself. I thieved because of her and swiped everything I could lay hands on, macaroons, raisins, almonds, cakes. I hope I may be forgiven for stealing from the Saturday pots the women left to warm in the baker's oven. I would take out scraps of meat, a chunk of pudding, a chicken leg or head, a piece of tripe, whatever I could nip quickly. She ate and became fat and handsome.

I had to sleep away from home all during the week, at the bakery. On Friday nights when I got home she always made an excuse of some sort. Either she had heartburn, or a stitch in the side, or hiccups, or headaches. You know what women's excuses are. I had a bitter time of it. It was rough. To add to it, this little brother of hers, the bastard, was growing bigger. He'd put lumps on me, and when I wanted to hit back she'd open her mouth and curse so powerfully I saw a green haze floating before my eyes. Ten times a day she threatened to divorce me. Another man in my place would have taken French leave[24] and disappeared. But I'm the type that bears it and says nothing. What's one to do? Shoulders are from God, and burdens too.

One night there was a calamity in the bakery; the oven burst, and we almost had a fire. There was nothing to do but go home, so I went home. Let me, I thought, also taste the joy of sleeping in bed in midweek. I didn't want to wake the sleeping mite[25] and tiptoed into the house. Coming in, it seemed to me that I heard not the snoring of one but, as it were, a double snore, one a thin enough snore and the other like the snoring of a slaughtered ox. Oh, I didn't like that! I didn't like it at all. I went up to the bed, and things suddenly turned black. Next to Elka lay a man's form. Another in my place would have made an uproar, and enough noise to rouse the whole town, but the thought occurred to me that I might wake the child. A little thing like that—why frighten a little swallow like that, I thought. All right then, I went back to the bakery and stretched out on a sack of flour, and till morning I never shut an eye. I shivered as if I had had malaria. "Enough of being a donkey," I said to myself. "Gimpel isn't going to be a sucker all his life. There's a limit even to the foolishness of a fool like Gimpel."

Shoulders are from God, and burdens too.

In the morning I went to the rabbi to get advice, and it made a great commotion

[24] French leave—leave without permission or telling anyone.

[25] mite—little thing; here, baby.

in the town. They sent the beadle[26] for Elka right away. She came, carrying the child. And what do you think she did? She denied it, denied everything, bone and stone! "He's out of his head," she said. "I know nothing of dreams or divinations." They yelled at her, warned her, hammered on the table, but she stuck to her guns: it was a false accusation, she said.

The butchers and the horse-traders took her part. One of the lads from the slaughterhouse came by and said to me, "We've got our eye on you, you're a marked man." Meanwhile the child started to bear down and soiled itself. In the rabbinical court there was an Ark of the Covenant, and they couldn't allow that, so they sent Elka away.

I said to the rabbi, "What shall I do?"

"You must divorce her at once," said he.

"And what if she refuses?" I asked.

He said, "You must serve the divorce, that's all you'll have to do."

I said, "Well, all right, Rabbi. Let me think about it."

"There's nothing to think about," said he. "You mustn't remain under the same roof with her."

"And if I want to see the child?" I asked.

"Let her go, the harlot,"[27] said he, "and her brood of bastards with her."

The verdict he gave was that I mustn't even cross her threshold—never again, as long as I should live.

During the day it didn't bother me so much. I thought, It was bound to happen, the **abscess**[28] had to burst. But at night when I stretched out upon the sacks I felt it all very bitterly. A longing took me, for her and for the child. I wanted to be angry, but that's my misfortune exactly, I don't have it in me to be really angry. In the first place—this was how my thoughts went—there's bound to be a slip sometimes. You can't live without errors. Probably that lad who was with her led her on and gave her presents and what not, and women are often long on hair and short on sense, and so he got around her. And then since she denies it so, maybe I was only seeing things? Hallucinations do happen. You see a figure or a mannikin[29] or something, but when you come up closer it's nothing, there's not a thing there. And if that's so, I'm doing her an injustice. And when I got so far in my thoughts I started to weep. I sobbed so that I wet the flour where I lay. In the morning I went to the rabbi and told him that I had made a mistake. The rabbi wrote on with his quill, and he said that if that were so he would have to reconsider the whole case. Until he had finished I wasn't to go near my wife, but I might send her bread and money by messenger.

III

Nine months passed before all the rabbis could come to an agreement. Letters went back and forth. I hadn't realized that there could be so much **erudition**[30] about a matter like this.

Meantime Elka gave birth to still another child, a girl this time. On the Sabbath

---

[26] beadle—official employed to keep order.

[27] harlot—prostitute.

[28] **abscess**—collection of pus in any part of the body.

[29] mannikin—life-size reproduction of the human body; a mannequin.

[30] **erudition**—deep and extensive learning.

I went to the synagogue and invoked a blessing on her. They called me up to the Torah,[31] and I named the child for my mother-in-law, may she rest in peace. The louts and loudmouths of the town who came into the bakery gave me a going over. All Frampol refreshed its spirits because of my trouble and grief. However, I resolved that I would always believe what I was told. What's the good of *not* believing? Today it's your wife you don't believe; tomorrow it's God Himself you won't take stock in.

By an apprentice who was her neighbor I sent her daily a corn or a wheat loaf, or a piece of pastry, rolls or bagels, or, when I got the chance, a slab of pudding, a slice of honeycake, or wedding strudel—whatever came my way. The apprentice was a good-hearted lad, and more than once he added something on his own. He had formerly annoyed me a lot, plucking my nose and digging me in the ribs, but when he started to be a visitor to my house he became kind and friendly. "Hey, you, Gimpel," he said to me, "you have a very decent little wife and two fine kids. You don't deserve them."

"But the things people say about her," I said.

"Well, they have long tongues," he said, "and nothing to do with them but babble. Ignore it as you ignore the cold of last winter."

One day the rabbi sent for me and said, "Are you certain, Gimpel, that you were wrong about your wife?"

I said, "I'm certain."

"Why, but look here! You yourself saw it."

"It must have been a shadow," I said.

"The shadow of what?"

"Just of one of the beams, I think."

"You can go home then. You owe thanks to the Yanover rabbi. He found an obscure reference in Maimonides[32] that favored you.

I seized the rabbi's hand and kissed it.

I wanted to run home immediately. It's no small thing to be separated for so long a time from wife and child. Then I reflected, I'd better go back to work now, and go home in the evening. I said nothing to anyone, although as far as my heart was concerned it was like one of the Holy Days. The women teased and twitted me as they did every day, but my thought was, Go on, with your loose talk. The truth is out, like the oil upon the water. Maimonides says it's right, and therefore it is right!

At night, when I had covered the dough to let it rise, I took my share of bread and a little sack of flour and started homeward. The moon was full and the stars were glistening, something to terrify the soul. I hurried onward, and before me darted a long shadow. It was winter, and a fresh snow had fallen. I had a mind to sing, but it was growing late and I didn't want to wake the householders. Then I felt like whistling, but remembered that you don't whistle at night because it brings the demons out. So I was silent and walked as fast as I could.

---

[31] Torah—scroll containing the first five books of the Hebrew Bible.

[32] Maimonides—Moses Maimonides (1135–1204), Jewish philosopher.

Dogs in the Christian yards barked at me when I passed, but I thought, Bark your teeth out! What are you but mere dogs? Whereas I am a man, the husband of a fine wife, the father of promising children.

As I approached the house my heart started to pound as though it were the heart of a criminal. I felt no fear, but my heart went thump! thump! Well, no drawing back. I quietly lifted the latch and went in. Elka was asleep. I looked at the infant's cradle. The shutter was closed, but the moon forced its way through the cracks. I saw the newborn child's face and loved it as soon as I saw it immediately—each tiny bone.

Then I came nearer to the bed. And what did I see but the apprentice lying there beside Elka. The moon went out all at once. It was utterly black, and I trembled. My teeth chattered. The bread fell from my hands and my wife waked and said, "Who is that, ah?"

I muttered, "It's me."

"Gimpel?" she asked. "How come you're here? I thought it was forbidden."

"The rabbi said," I answered and shook as with a fever.

"Listen to me, Gimpel," she said, "go out to the shed and see if the goat's all right. It seems she's been sick." I have forgotten to say that we had a goat. When I heard she was unwell I went into the yard. The nannygoat was a good little creature. I had a nearly human feeling for her.

With hesitant steps I went up to the shed and opened the door. The goat stood there on her four feet. I felt her everywhere, drew her by the arms, examined her udders, and found nothing wrong. She had probably eaten too much bark. "Good night, little goat," I said. "Keep well." And the little beast answered with a "Maa" as though to thank me for the good will.

I went back. The apprentice had vanished.

"Where," I asked, "is the lad?"

"What lad?" my wife answered.

"What do you mean?" I said. "The apprentice. You were sleeping with him."

"The things I have dreamed this night and the night before," she said, "may they come true and lay you low, body and soul! An evil spirit has taken root in you and dazzles your sight." She screamed out, "You hateful creature! You moon calf! You spook! You uncouth man! Get out, or I'll scream all Frampol out of bed!"

Before I could move, her brother sprang out from behind the oven and struck me a blow on the back of the head. I thought he had broken my neck. I felt that something about me was deeply wrong, and I said, "Don't make a scandal. All that's needed now is that people should accuse me of raising spooks and *dybbuks*."[33] For that was what she had meant. "No one will touch bread of my baking."

In short, I somehow calmed her.

"Well," she said, "that's enough. Lie down, and be shattered by wheels."

Next morning I called the apprentice aside. "Listen here, brother!" I said. And so on and so forth. "What do you say?" He stared at me as though I had dropped from the roof or something.

---

[33] *dybbuks*—demons in Jewish theology.

"I swear," he said, "you'd better go to an herb doctor or some healer. I'm afraid you have a screw loose, but I'll hush it up for you." And that's how the thing stood.

To make a long story short, I lived twenty years with my wife. She bore me six children, four daughters and two sons. All kinds of things happened, but I neither saw nor heard. I believed, and that's all. The rabbi recently said to me, "Belief in itself is beneficial. It is written that a good man lives by his faith."

Suddenly my wife took sick. It began with a trifle, a little growth upon the breast. But she evidently was not destined to live long; she had no years. I spent a fortune on her. I have forgotten to say that by this time I had a bakery of my own and in Frampol was considered to be something of a rich man. Daily the healer came, and every witch doctor in the neighborhood was brought. They decided to use leeches, and after that to try cupping.[34] They even called a doctor from Lublin, but it was too late. Before she died she called me to her bed and said, "Forgive me, Gimpel."

I said, "What is there to forgive? You have been a good and faithful wife."

"Woe, Gimpel!" she said. "It was ugly how I deceived you all these years. I want to go clean to my Maker, and so I have to tell you that the children are not yours."

If I had been clouted on the head with a piece of wood it couldn't have bewildered me more.

"Whose are they?" I asked.

"I don't know," she said, "there were a lot. . . . But they're not yours." And as she spoke she tossed her head to the side, her eyes turned glassy, and it was all up with Elka. On her whitened lips there remained a smile.

I imagined that, dead as she was, she was saying, "I deceived Gimpel. That was the meaning of my brief life."

IV

One night, when the period of mourning was done, as I lay dreaming on the flour sacks, there came the Spirit of Evil himself and said to me, "Gimpel, why do you sleep?"

"The whole world deceives you," he said, "and you ought to deceive the world in your turn."

I said, "What should I be doing? Eating *kreplach*?"[35]

"The whole world deceives you," he said, "and you ought to deceive the world in your turn."

"How can I deceive all the world?" I asked him.

He answered, "You might accumulate a bucket of urine every day and at night pour it into the dough. Let the sages of Frampol eat filth."

"What about judgment in the world to come?" I said.

"There is no world to come," he said. "They've sold you a bill of goods and talked you into believing you carried a cat in your belly. What nonsense!"

"Well then," I said, "and is there a God?"

[34] leeches . . . cupping—archaic medical treatments which involved drawing blood to cure a patient.

[35] *kreplach*—dumplings.

He answered, "There *is* no God either."

"What," I said, "*is* there, then?"

"A thick mire."

He stood before my eyes with a goatish beard and horns, longtoothed, and with a tail. Hearing such words, I wanted to snatch him by the tail, but I tumbled from the flour sacks and nearly broke a rib. Then it happened that I had to answer the call of nature, and, passing, I saw the risen bread, which seemed to say to me, "Do it!" In brief, I let myself be persuaded.

At dawn the apprentice came. We kneaded the dough, scattered caraway seeds on it, and set it to bake. Then the apprentice went away, and I was left sitting in the little trench by the oven, on a pile of rags. Well, Gimpel, I thought, you've revenged yourself on them for all the shame they've put on you. Outside the frost glittered, but it was warm beside the oven. The flames heated my face. I bent my head and fell into a doze.

I saw in a dream, at once, Elka in her shroud. She called to me, "What have you done, Gimpel?"

I said to her, "It's all your fault," and started to cry.

"You fool!" she said. "You fool! Because I was false is everything false too? I never deceived anyone but myself. I'm paying for it all, Gimpel. They spare you nothing here."

I looked at her face. It was black. I was startled and waked, and remained sitting dumb. I sensed that everything hung in the balance. A false step now and I'd lose Eternal Life. But God gave me His help. I seized the long shovel and took out the loaves, carried them into the yard, and started to dig a hole in the frozen earth.

My apprentice came back as I was doing it. "What are you doing, boss?" he said, and grew pale as a corpse.

"I know what I'm doing," I said, and I buried it all before his very eyes.

Then I went home, took my hoard from its hiding place, and divided it among the children. "I saw your mother tonight," I said. "She's turning black, poor thing."

They were so astounded they couldn't speak a word.

"Be well," I said, "and forget that such a one as Gimpel ever existed." I put on my short coat, a pair of boots, took the bag that held my prayer shawl in one hand, my stick in the other, and kissed the *mezzuzah*.[36] When people saw me in the street they were greatly surprised.

"Where are you going?" they said.

I answered, "Into the world." And so I departed from Frampol.

I wandered over the land, and good people did not neglect me. After many years I became old and white; I heard a great deal, many lies and falsehoods, but the longer I lived the more I understood that there were really no lies. Whatever doesn't really happen is dreamed at night. It happens to one if it doesn't happen to another, tomorrow if not today, or a century hence if not next year. What difference can it make? Often I heard tales of which I said,

---

36 *mezzuzah*—small oblong container at the front door of a Jewish house. It contains a passage from the Bible as a reminder to obey God's laws when leaving the house.

"Now this is a thing that cannot happen." But before a year had elapsed I heard that it actually had come to pass somewhere.

Going from place to place, eating at strange tables, it often happens that I spin yarns—improbable things that could never have happened—about devils, magicians, windmills, and the like. The children run after me, calling, "Grandfather, tell us a story." Sometimes they ask for particular stories, and I try to please them. A fat young boy once said to me, "Grandfather, it's the same story you told us before." The little rogue, he was right.

So it is with dreams too. It is many years since I left Frampol, but as soon as I shut my eyes I am there again. And whom do you think I see? Elka. She is standing by the washtub, as at our first encounter, but her face is shining and her eyes as radiant as the eyes of a saint, and she speaks outlandish words to me, strange things. When I wake I have forgotten it all. But while the dream lasts I am comforted. She answers all my queries, and what comes out is that all is right. I weep and implore, "Let me be with you." And she consoles me and tells me to be patient. The time is nearer than it is far. Sometimes she strokes and kisses me and weeps upon my face. When I awaken I feel her lips and taste the salt of her tears.

No doubt the world is entirely an imaginary world, but it is only once removed from the true world. At the door of the **hovel**[37] where I lie, there stands the plank on which the dead are taken away. The gravedigger Jew has his spade ready. The grave waits and the worms are hungry; the **shrouds**[38] are prepared—I carry them in my beggar's sack. Another *shnorrer*[39] *is* waiting to inherit my bed of straw. When the time comes I will go joyfully. Whatever may be there, it will be real, without complication, without **ridicule**,[40] without deception. God be praised: there even Gimpel cannot be deceived.

---

[37] **hovel**—small, miserable dwelling.

[38] **shrouds**—cloths used to wrap a body for burial.

[39] *shnorrer*—beggar.

[40] **ridicule**—words or actions intended to make fun of someone.

QUESTIONS TO CONSIDER

1. In what ways does Gimpel deserve his reputation as a fool? In what ways does he show himself to be intelligent?
2. What is the rabbi's advice to Gimpel about being taken for a fool? Does Gimpel take this advice to heart? Explain your answer.
3. What does Gimpel mean when he says at the end, "the longer I lived the more I understood that there were really no lies."
4. Do you think Gimpel lived his life well? Why or why not?

Bernard Malamud ▶

The Magic Barrel

BY BERNARD MALAMUD

Bernard Malamud (1914–1986) came of age as a writer in the postwar era when the American literary world expanded to include many hitherto forgotten minorities and ethnicities. In the 1950s, Malamud, along with Isaac Bashevis Singer (page 340) and writers like Saul Bellow and Philip Roth, pushed Jewish-American fiction to the forefront of American literature. As one critic observed of the 1950s and early 1960s, "If one did not live in the United States, but knew it only through the fiction published and critically discussed in the country's serious journals, one might have concluded that America was predominantly a nation of Jews." Malamud was born and educated in New York. After college he held varied jobs, and in the 1940s began to write regularly. His first novel, The Natural, *was published in 1952, followed by* The Assistant *in 1957. These two novels present the poles of Malamud's fiction, the first a parody and satire, the second a serious moral commentary. Throughout his career, Malamud alternated between these styles, in both his stories and his novels, but the basic theme of his writing was suffering. As one of the characters in* The Assistant *remarks, "If you live, you suffer." To Malamud, the examination of Jewish lives was a study in suffering and catastrophe, both self-inflicted and as part of a tragic history. From the 1950s onward, Malamud taught in universities while continuing to produce award-winning fiction. "The Magic Barrel" is from a book of stories that won the National Book Award in 1958 and shows Malamud's great gift for characterization and dialogue.*

Not long ago there lived in uptown New York, in a small, almost meager room, though crowded with books, Leo Finkle, a rabbinical student at the Yeshiva University.[1] Finkle, after six years of study, was to be **ordained**[2] in June and had been advised by an acquaintance that he might find it easier to win himself a congregation if he were married. Since he had no present prospects of marriage, after two tormented days of turning it over in his mind, he called in Pinye Salzman, a marriage broker whose two-line advertisement he had read in the *Forward*.[3]

The matchmaker appeared one night out of the dark fourth-floor hallway of the graystone rooming house where Finkle lived, grasping a black, strapped portfolio that had been worn thin with use. Salzman, who had been long in the business, was of slight but dignified build, wearing an old hat, and an overcoat too short and tight for him. He smelled frankly of fish, which he

[1] Yeshiva University—Jewish seminary in New York.

[2] **ordained**—authorized as a rabbi.

[3] *Forward*—*Jewish Daily Forward*, a Yiddish-language newspaper published in New York City.

loved to eat, and although he was missing a few teeth, his presence was not displeasing, because of an **amiable**[4] manner curiously contrasted with mournful eyes. His voice, his lips, his wisp of beard, his bony fingers were animated, but give him a moment of repose and his mild blue eyes revealed a depth of sadness, a characteristic that put Leo a little at ease although the situation, for him, was **inherently**[5] tense.

He at once informed Salzman why he had asked him to come, explaining that his home was in Cleveland, and that but for his parents, who had married comparatively late in life, he was alone in the world. He had for six years devoted himself almost entirely to his studies, as a result of which, understandably, he had found himself without time for a social life and the company of young women. Therefore he thought it the better part of trial and error—of embarrassing fumbling—to call in an experienced person to advise him on these matters. He remarked in passing that the function of the marriage broker was ancient and honorable, highly approved in the Jewish community, because it made practical the necessary without hindering joy. Moreover, his own parents had been brought together by a matchmaker. They had made, if not a financially profitable marriage—since neither had possessed any worldly goods to speak of—at least a successful one in the sense of their everlasting devotion to each other. Salzman listened in embarrassed surprise, sensing a sort of apology. Later, however, he experienced a glow of pride in his work, an emotion that had left him years ago, and he heartily approved of Finkle.

The two went to their business. Leo had led Salzman to the only clear place in the room, a table near a window that overlooked the lamp-lit city. He seated himself at the matchmaker's side but facing him, attempting by an act of will to suppress the unpleasant tickle in his throat. Salzman eagerly unstrapped his portfolio and removed a loose rubber band from a thin packet of much-handled cards. As he flipped through them, a gesture and sound that physically hurt Leo, the student pretended not to see and gazed **steadfastly**[6] out the window. Although it was still February, winter was on its last legs, signs of which he had for the first time in years begun to notice. He now observed the round white moon, moving high in the sky through a cloud **menagerie**,[7] and watched with half-open mouth as it penetrated a huge hen, and dropped out of her like an egg laying itself. Salzman, though pretending through eyeglasses he had just slipped on, to be engaged in scanning the writing on the cards, stole occasional glances at the young man's distinguished face, noting with pleasure the long, severe scholar's nose, brown eyes heavy with learning, sensitive yet ascetic[8] lips, and a certain, almost hollow quality of the dark cheeks. He gazed around at shelves upon shelves of books and let out a soft, contented sigh.

When Leo's eyes fell upon the cards, he counted six spread out in Salzman's hand.

---

[4] **amiable**—good-natured, having a pleasant disposition.

[5] **inherently**—essentially or necessarily.

[6] **steadfastly**—fixedly, in an unchanging manner.

[7] **menagerie**—group of different types of animals.

[8] ascetic—severe, stern.

"So few?" he asked in disappointment.

"You wouldn't believe me how much cards I got in my office," Salzman replied. "The drawers are already filled to the top, so I keep them now in a barrel, but is every girl good for a new rabbi?"

Leo blushed at this, regretting all he had revealed of himself in a curriculum vitae[9] he had sent to Salzman. He had thought it best to acquaint him with his strict standards and specifications, but in having done so, he felt he had told the marriage broker more than was absolutely necessary.

He hesitantly inquired, "Do you keep photographs of your clients on file?"

"First comes family, amount of dowry, also what kind promises," Salzman replied, unbuttoning his tight coat and settling himself in the chair. "After come pictures, rabbi."

"Call me Mr. Finkle. I'm not yet a rabbi."

Salzman said he would, but instead called him doctor, which he changed to rabbi when Leo was not listening too attentively.

Salzman adjusted his horn-rimmed spectacles, gently cleared his throat and read in an eager voice the contents of the top card:

"Sophie P. Twenty four years. Widow one year. No children. Educated high school and two years college. Father promises eight thousand dollars. Has wonderful wholesale business. Also real estate. On the mother's side comes teachers, also one actor. Well known on Second Avenue."

Leo gazed up in surprise. "Did you say a widow?"

"A widow don't mean spoiled, rabbi. She lived with her husband maybe four months. He was a sick boy she made a mistake to marry him."

"Marrying a widow has never entered my mind."

"This is because you have no experience. A widow, especially if she is young and healthy like this girl, is a wonderful person to marry. She will be thankful to you the rest of her life. Believe me, if I was looking now for a bride, I would marry a widow."

Leo reflected, then shook his head.

Salzman hunched his shoulders in an almost **imperceptible**[10] gesture of disappointment. He placed the card down on the wooden table and began to read another:

"Lily H. High school teacher. Regular. Not a substitute. Has savings and new Dodge car. Lived in Paris one year. Father is successful dentist thirty-five years. Interested in professional man. Well Americanized family. Wonderful opportunity."

"I knew her personally," said Salzman. "I wish you could see this girl. She is a doll. Also very intelligent. All day you could talk to her about books and theater and what not. She also knows current events."

"I don't believe you mentioned her age?"

"Her age?" Salzman said, raising his brows. "Her age is thirty-two years."

Leo said after a while, "I'm afraid that seems a little too old."

Salzman let out a laugh. "So how old are you, rabbi?"

---

[9] curriculum vitae—summary of personal background.

[10] **imperceptible**—so slight or subtle as to be nearly invisible.

"Twenty-seven."

"So what is the difference, tell me, between twenty-seven and thirty-two? My own wife is seven years older than me. So what did I suffer?—Nothing. If Rothschild's daughter[11] wants to marry you, would you say on account her age, no?"

"Yes," Leo said dryly.

Salzman shook off the no in the yes. "Five years don't mean a thing. I give you my word that when you will live with her for one week you will forget her age. What does it mean five years—that she lived more and knows more than somebody who is younger? On this girl, God bless her, years are not wasted. Each one that it comes makes better the bargain."

"What subjects does she teach in high school?"

"Languages. If you heard the way she speaks French, you will think it is music. I am in the business twenty-five years, and I recommend her with my whole heart. Believe me, I know what I'm talking, rabbi."

"What's on the next card?" Leo said abruptly.

Salzman reluctantly turned up the third card:

"Ruth K. Nineteen years. Honor student. Father offers thirteen thousand cash to the right bridegroom. He is a medical doctor. Stomach specialist with marvelous practice. Brother in law owns own garment business. Particular people."

Salzman looked as if he had read his trump card.

"Did you say nineteen?" Leo asked with interest.

"On the dot."

"Is she attractive?" He blushed. "Pretty?"

Salzman kissed his finger tips. "A little doll. On this I give you my word. Let me call the father tonight and you will see what means pretty."

But Leo was troubled. "You're sure she's that young?"

"This I am positive. The father will show you the birth certificate."

"Are you positive there isn't something wrong with her?" Leo insisted.

"Who says there is wrong?"

"I don't understand why an American girl her age should go to a marriage broker."

A smile spread over Salzman's face.

"So for the same reason you went, she comes."

Leo flushed. "I am pressed for time."

Salzman, realizing he had been **tactless**,[12] quickly explained. "The father came, not her. He wants she should have the best, so he looks around himself. When we will locate the right boy he will introduce him and encourage. This makes a better marriage than if a young girl without experience takes for herself. I don't have to tell you this."

"But don't you think this young girl believes in love?" Leo spoke uneasily.

Salzman was about to **guffaw**[13] but caught himself and said soberly, "Love comes with the right person, not before."

Leo parted dry lips but did not speak. Noticing that Salzman had snatched a

---

[11] Rothschild's daughter—reference to the Rothschilds, a famously wealthy Jewish family in Europe.

[12] **tactless**—blunt, inconsiderate.

[13] **guffaw**—laugh heartily.

glance at the next card, he cleverly asked, "How is her health?"

"Perfect," Salzman said, breathing with difficulty. "Of course, she is a little lame on her right foot from an auto accident that it happened to her when she was twelve years, but nobody notices on account she is so brilliant and also beautiful."

"Your worries are finished. I have for you a first-class bride."

Leo got up heavily and went to the window. He felt curiously bitter and **upbraided**[14] himself for having called in the marriage broker. Finally, he shook his head.

"Why not?" Salzman persisted, the pitch of his voice rising.

"Because I detest stomach specialists."

"So what do you care what is his business? After you marry her do you need him? Who says he must come every Friday night in your house?"

Ashamed of the way the talk was going, Leo dismissed Salzman, who went home with heavy, melancholy eyes.

Though he had felt only relief at the marriage broker's departure, Leo was in low spirits the next day. He explained it as arising from Salzman's failure to produce a suitable bride for him. He did not care for his type of clientele.[15] But when Leo found himself hesitating whether to seek out another matchmaker, one more polished than Pinye, he wondered if it could be—his protestations to the contrary, and although he honored his father and mother—that he did not, in essence, care for the matchmaking institution? This thought he quickly put out of mind yet found himself still upset. All day he ran around in the woods—missed an important appointment, forgot to give out his laundry, walked out of a Broadway cafeteria without paying and had to run back with the ticket in his hand; had even not recognized his landlady in the street when she passed with a friend and courteously called out, "A good evening to you, Doctor Finkle." By nightfall, however, he had regained sufficient calm to sink his nose into a book and there found peace from his thoughts.

Almost at once there came a knock on the door. Before Leo could say enter, Salzman, commercial cupid,[16] was standing in the room. His face was gray and meager, his expression hungry, and he looked as if he would expire on his feet. Yet the marriage broker managed, by some trick of the muscles, to display a broad smile.

"So good evening. I am invited?"

Leo nodded, disturbed to see him again, yet unwilling to ask the man to leave.

Beaming still, Salzman laid his portfolio on the table. "Rabbi, I got for you tonight good news."

"I've asked you not to call me rabbi. I'm still a student."

"Your worries are finished. I have for you a first-class bride."

"Leave me in peace concerning this subject," Leo pretended lack of interest.

"The world will dance at your wedding."

"Please, Mr. Salzman, no more."

---

[14] **upbraided**—reproached or criticized sharply.

[15] clientele—customers.

[16] cupid—in Roman mythology, the god of love.

"But first must come back my strength," Salzman said weakly. He fumbled with the portfolio straps and took out of the leather case an oily paper bag, from which he extracted a hard, seeded roll and a small, smoked white fish. With a quick motion of his hand he stripped the fish out of its skin and began ravenously to chew. "All day in a rush," he muttered.

Leo watched him eat.

"A sliced tomato you have maybe?" Salzman hesitantly inquired.

"No."

The marriage broker shut his eyes and ate. When he had finished he carefully cleaned up the crumbs and rolled up the remains of the fish, in the paper bag. His spectacled eyes roamed the room until he discovered, amid some piles of books, a one-burner gas stove. Lifting his hat he humbly asked, "A glass tea you got, rabbi?"

Conscience-stricken, Leo rose and brewed the tea. He served it with a chunk of lemon and two cubes of lump sugar, delighting Salzman.

After he had drunk his tea, Salzman's strength and good spirits were restored.

"So tell me, rabbi," he said amiably, "you considered some more the three clients I mentioned yesterday?"

"There was no need to consider."

"Why not?"

"None of them suits me."

"What then suits you?"

Leo let it pass because he could give only a confused answer.

Without waiting for a reply, Salzman asked, "You remember this girl I talked to you—the high school teacher?"

"Age thirty-two?"

But, surprisingly, Salzman's face lit in a smile. "Age twenty-nine."

Leo shot him a look. "Reduced from thirty-two?"

"A mistake," Salzman avowed. "I talked today with the dentist. He took me to his safety deposit box and showed me the birth certificate. She was twenty-nine years last August. They made her a party in the mountains where she went for her vacation. When her father spoke to me the first time I forgot to write the age and I told you thirty-two, but now I remember this was a different client, a widow."

"The same one you told me about? I thought she was twenty-four?"

"A different. Am I responsible that the world is filled with widows?"

"No, but I'm not interested in them, nor for that matter, in school teachers."

Salzman pulled his clasped hands to his breast. Looking at the ceiling he devoutly exclaimed, "Yiddishe kinder,[17] what can I say to somebody that he is not interested in high school teachers? So what then you are interested?"

Leo flushed but controlled himself.

"In what else will you be interested," Salzman went on, "if you not interested in this fine girl that she speaks four languages and has personally in the bank ten thousand dollars? Also her father guarantees further twelve thousand. Also she has a new car, wonderful clothes, talks on all subjects, and she will give you a first-class

[17] Yiddishe kinder—Yiddish for "Jewish children," the sense of the phrase is that the young know nothing.

home and children. How near do we come in our life to paradise?"

"If she's so wonderful, why wasn't she married ten years ago?"

"Why?" said Salzman with a heavy laugh. "—Why? Because she is *partikiler*.[18] This is why. She wants the *best*."

Leo was silent, amused at how he had entangled himself. But Salzman had aroused his interest in Lily H., and he began seriously to consider calling on her. When the marriage broker observed how intently Leo's mind was at work on the facts he had supplied, he felt certain they would soon come to an agreement.

Late Saturday afternoon, conscious of Salzman, Leo Finkle walked with Lily Hirschorn along Riverside Drive. He walked briskly and erectly, wearing with distinction the black fedora he had that morning taken with **trepidation**[19] out of the dusty hat box on his closet shelf, and the heavy black Saturday coat he had thoroughly whisked clean. Leo also owned a walking stick, a present from a distant relative, but quickly put temptation aside and did not use it. Lily, petite and not unpretty, had on something signifying the approach of spring. She was au courant,[20] animatedly, with all sorts of subjects, and he weighed her words and found her surprisingly sound—score another for Salzman, whom he uneasily sensed to be somewhere around, hiding perhaps high in a tree along the street, flashing the lady signals with a pocket mirror; or perhaps a cloven-hoofed Pan,[21] piping nuptial ditties[22] as he danced his invisible way before them, strewing wild buds on the walk and purple grapes in their path, symbolizing fruit of a union, though there was of course still none.

Lily startled Leo by remarking, "I was thinking of Mr. Salzman, a curious figure, wouldn't you say?"

Not certain what to answer, he nodded.

She bravely went on, blushing, "I for one am grateful for his introducing us. Aren't you?"

He courteously replied, "I am."

"I mean," she said with a little laugh—and it was all in good taste, or at least gave the effect of being not in bad—"do you mind that we came together so?"

He was not displeased with her honesty, recognizing that she meant to set the relationship **aright**,[23] and understanding that it took a certain amount of experience in life, and courage, to want to do it quite that way. One had to have some sort of past to make that kind of beginning.

He said that he did not mind. Salzman's function was traditional and honorable—valuable for what it might achieve, which, he pointed out, was frequently nothing.

Lily agreed with a sigh. They walked on for a while and she said after a long silence, again with a nervous laugh, "Would you mind if I asked you something a little

---

18 *partikiler*—Yiddish corruption of *particular*.

19 **trepidation**—apprehension or dread.

20 au courant—French for "knowledgeable" or "well-informed."

21 Pan—in Greek mythology, the god of the woods who had the legs of a goat, hence cloven-hoofed.

22 nuptial ditties—wedding songs.

23 **aright**—proper, correct.

bit personal? Frankly, I find the subject fascinating." Although Leo shrugged, she went on half embarrassedly, "How was it that you came to your calling? I mean was it a sudden passionate inspiration?"

Leo, after a time, slowly replied, "I was always interested in the Law."[24]

"You saw revealed in it the presence of the Highest?"

He nodded and changed the subject. "I understand that you spent a little time in Paris, Miss Hirschorn?"

"Oh, did Mr. Salzman tell you, Rabbi Finkle?" Leo winced but she went on, "It was ages ago and almost forgotten. I remember I had to return for my sister's wedding."

And Lily would not be put off. "When," she asked in a trembly voice, "did you become **enamored**[25] of God?"

He stared at her. Then it came to him that she was talking not about Leo Finkle, but of a total stranger, some mystical figure, perhaps even passionate prophet that Salzman had dreamed up for her—no relation to the living or dead. Leo trembled with rage and weakness. The trickster had obviously sold her a bill of goods, just as he had him, who'd expected to become acquainted with a young lady of twenty-nine, only to behold, the moment he laid eyes upon her strained and anxious face, a woman past thirty-five and aging rapidly. Only his self control had kept him this long in her presence.

"I am not," he said gravely, "a talented religious person," and in seeking words to go on, found himself possessed by shame and fear. "I think," he said in a strained manner, "that I came to God not because I loved Him, but because I did not."

This confession he spoke harshly because its unexpectedness shook him.

"I think," he said in a strained manner, "that I came to God not because I loved Him, but because I did not."

Lily wilted. Leo saw a profusion of loaves of bread go flying like ducks high over his head, not unlike the winged loaves by which he had counted himself to sleep last night. Mercifully, then, it snowed, which he would not put past Salzman's **machinations**.[26]

He was infuriated with the marriage broker and swore he would throw him out of the room the minute he reappeared. But Salzman did not come that night, and when Leo's anger had subsided, an unaccountable despair grew in its place.

At first he thought this was caused by his disappointment in Lily, but before long it became evident that he had involved himself with Salzman without a true knowledge of his own intent. He gradually realized—with an emptiness that seized him with six hands—that he had called in the broker to find him a bride because he was incapable of doing it himself. This terrifying insight he had derived as a result of his meeting and conversation with Lily

---

24 Law—reference to the Torah, the body of Jewish religious law.

25 **enamored**—captivated by, in love with.

26 **machinations**—schemes.

Hirschorn. Her probing questions had somehow irritated him into revealing—to himself more than her—the true nature of his relationship to God, and from that it had come upon him, with shocking force, that apart from his parents, he had never loved anyone. Or perhaps it went the other way, that he did not love God so well as he might, because he had not loved man. It seemed to Leo that his whole life stood starkly revealed and he saw himself for the first time as he truly was—unloved and loveless. This bitter but somehow not fully unexpected revelation brought him to a point of panic, controlled only by extraordinary effort. He covered his face with his hands and cried.

The week that followed was the worst of his life. He did not eat and lost weight. His beard darkened and grew ragged. He stopped attending seminars and almost never opened a book. He seriously considering leaving the Yeshiva, although he was deeply troubled at the thought of the loss of all his years of study—saw them like pages torn from a book, strewn over the city—and at the devastating effect of this decision upon his parents. But he had lived without knowledge of himself, and never in the Five Books and all the Commentaries[27] —mea culpa[28]—had the truth been revealed to him. He did not know where to turn, and in all this **desolating**[29] loneliness there was no *to whom*, although he often thought of Lily but not once could bring himself to go downstairs and make the call. He became touchy and irritable, especially with his landlady, who asked him all manner of personal questions; on the other hand, sensing his own disagreeableness, he waylaid her on the stairs and apologized abjectly, until mortified, she ran from him. Out of this, however, he drew the consolation that he was a Jew and that a Jew suffered. But gradually, as the long and terrible week drew to a close, he regained his composure and some idea of purpose in life: to go on as planned. Although he was imperfect, the ideal was not. As for his quest of a bride, the thought of continuing afflicted him with anxiety and heartburn, yet perhaps with this new knowledge of himself he would be more successful than in the past. Perhaps love would now come to him and a bride to that love. And for this **sanctified**[30] seeking who needed a Salzman?

The marriage broker, a skeleton with haunted eyes, returned that very night. He looked, withal, the picture of frustrated expectancy—as if he had steadfastly waited the week at Miss Lily Hirschorn's side for a telephone call that never came.

Casually coughing, Salzman came immediately to the point: "So how did you like her?"

Leo's anger rose and he could not refrain from chiding the matchmaker: "Why did you lie to me, Salzman?"

Salzman's pale face went dead white, the world had snowed on him.

"Did you not state that she was twenty-nine?" Leo insisted.

---

[27] Five Books . . . Commentaries—that part of the old Testament in the Bible that forms the Torah.

[28] mea culpa—Latin phrase meaning "through my fault," an expression of penitence.

[29] **desolating**—making lonely, forlorn, or wretched.

[30] **sanctified**—holy, pure.

"I gave you my word—"

"She was thirty-five, if a day. At *least* thirty-five."

"Of this don't be too sure. Her father told me—"

"Never mind. The worst of it was that you lied to her."

"How did I lie to her, tell me?"

"You told her things about me that weren't true. You made me out to be more, consequently less than I am. She had in mind a totally different person, a sort of semimystical Wonder Rabbi."

"All I said, you was a religious man."

"I can imagine."

Salzman sighed. "This is my weakness that I have," he confessed. "My wife says to me I shouldn't be a salesman, but when I have two fine people that they would be wonderful to be married, I am so happy that I talk too much." He smiled wanly. "This is why Salzman is a poor man."

Leo's anger left him. "Well, Salzman, I'm afraid that's all."

The marriage broker fastened hungry eyes on him.

"You don't want any more a bride?"

"I do," said Leo, "but I have decided to seek her in a different way. I am no longer interested in an arranged marriage. To be frank, I now admit the necessity of premarital love. That is, I want to be in love with the one I marry."

"Love?" said Salzman, astounded. After a moment he remarked, "For us, our love is our life, not for the ladies. In the **ghetto**[31] they—"

"I know, I know," said Leo. "I've thought of it often. Love, I have said to myself, should be a by-product of living and worship rather than its own end. Yet for myself I find it necessary to establish the level of my need and fulfill it."

Salzman shrugged but answered, "Listen, rabbi, if you want love, this I can find for you also. I have such beautiful clients that you will love them the minute your eyes will see them."

Leo smiled unhappily. "I'm afraid you don't understand."

But Salzman hastily unstrapped his portfolio and withdrew a manila packet from it.

"Pictures," he said, quickly laying the envelope on the table.

Leo called after him to take the pictures away, but as if on the wings of the wind, Salzman had disappeared.

March came. Leo had returned to his regular routine. Although he felt not quite himself yet—lacked energy—he was making plans for a more active social life. Of course it would cost something, but he was an expert in cutting corners; and when there were no corners left he would make circles rounder. All the while Salzman's pictures had lain on the table, gathering dust. Occasionally as Leo sat studying, or enjoying a cup of tea, his eyes fell on the manila envelope, but he never opened it.

The days went by and no social life to speak of developed with a member of the opposite sex—it was difficult, given the circumstances of his situation. One morning Leo toiled up the stairs to his room and stared out the window at the city. Although

[31] **ghetto**—ethnic district in a city.

the day was bright his view of it was dark. For some time he watched people in the street below hurrying along and then turned with a heavy heart to his little room. On the table was the packet. With a sudden relentless gesture he tore it open. For a half-hour he stood by the table in a state of excitement, examining the photographs of the ladies Salzman had included. Finally, with a deep sigh he put them down. There were six, of varying degrees of attractiveness, but look at them long enough and they all became Lily Hirschorn: all past their prime, all starved behind bright smiles, not a true personality in the lot. Life, despite their frantic yoohooings, had passed them by; they were pictures in a brief case that stank of fish. After a while, however, as Leo attempted to return the photographs into the envelope, he found in it another, a snapshot of the type taken by a machine for a quarter. He gazed at it a moment and let out a cry.

Her face deeply moved him. Why, he could at first not say.

Her face deeply moved him. Why, he could at first not say. It gave him the impression of youth—spring flowers, yet age—a sense of having been used to the bone, wasted; this came from the eyes, which were hauntingly familiar, yet absolutely strange. He had a vivid impression that he had met her before, but try as he might he could not place her although he could almost recall her name, as if he had read it in her own handwriting. No, this couldn't be; he would have remembered her. It was not, he affirmed, that she had an extraordinary beauty—no, though her face was attractive enough; it was that *something* about her moved him. Feature for feature, even some of the ladies of the photographs could do better; but she leaped forth to his heart—had *lived,* or wanted to—more than just wanted, perhaps regretted how she had lived—had somehow deeply suffered: it could be seen in the depths of those reluctant eyes, and from the way the light enclosed and shone from her, and within her, opening realms of possibility: this was her own. Her he desired. His head ached and eyes narrowed with the intensity of his gazing, then as if an obscure fog had blown up in the mind, he experienced fear of her and was aware that he had received an impression, somehow, of evil. He shuddered, saying softly, it is thus with us all. Leo brewed some tea in a small pot and sat sipping it without sugar, to calm himself. But before he had finished drinking, again with excitement he examined the face and found it good: good for Leo Finkle. Only such a one could understand him and help him seek whatever he was seeking. She might, perhaps, love him. How she had happened to be among the discards in Salzman's barrel he could never guess, but he knew he must urgently go find her.

Leo rushed downstairs, grabbed up the Bronx telephone book, and searched for Salzman's home address. He was not listed, nor was his office. Neither was he in the Manhattan book. But Leo remembered having written down the address on a slip of paper after he had read Salzman's advertisement in the "personals" column of the *Forward*. He ran up to his room and tore through his papers, without luck. It was exasperating. Just when he needed the matchmaker he was nowhere to be found. Fortunately Leo remembered to look in his wallet. There on a card he found his name written and a Bronx address. No phone number was listed, the reason—Leo now recalled—he had originally communicated with Salzman by letter. He got on his coat, put a hat on over his skull cap and hurried to the subway station. All the way to the far end of the Bronx he sat on the edge of his seat. He was more than once tempted to take out the picture and see if the girl's face was as he remembered it, but he refrained, allowing the snapshot to remain in his inside coat pocket, content to have her so close. When the train pulled into the station he was waiting at the door and bolted out. He quickly located the street Salzman had advertised.

The building be sought was less than a block from the subway, but it was not an office building, nor even a loft, nor a store in which one could rent office space. It was a very old tenement house. Leo found Salzman's name in pencil on a soiled tag under the bell and climbed three dark flights to his apartment. When he knocked, the door was opened by a thin, asthmatic, gray-haired woman, in felt slippers.

"Yes?" she said, expecting nothing. She listened without listening. He could have sworn he had seen her, too, before but knew it was an illusion.

"Salzman—does he live here? Pinye Salzman," he said, "the matchmaker?"

She stared at him a long minute. "Of course."

He felt embarrassed. "Is he in?"

"No." Her mouth, though left open, offered nothing more.

"The matter is urgent. Can you tell me where his office is?"

"In the air." She pointed upward.

"You mean he has no office?" Leo asked.

"In his socks."

He peered into the apartment. It was sunless and dingy, one large room divided by a half-open curtain, beyond which he could see a sagging metal bed. The near side of a room was crowded with rickety chairs, old bureaus, a three-legged table, racks of cooking utensils, and all the apparatus of a kitchen. But there was no sign of Salzman or his magic barrel, probably also a figment of the imagination. An odor of frying fish made Leo weak to the knees.

"Where is he?" he insisted. "I've got to see your husband."

At length she answered, "So who knows where he is? Every time he thinks a new thought he runs to a different place. Go home, he will find you."

"Tell him Leo Finkle."

She gave no sign she had heard.

He walked downstairs, depressed.

But Salzman, breathless, stood waiting at his door.

Leo was astounded and overjoyed. "How did you get here before me?"

"I rushed."

"Come inside."

They entered. Leo fixed tea, and a sardine sandwich for Salzman. As they were drinking he reached behind him for the packet of pictures and handed them to the marriage broker.

Salzman put down his glass and said expectantly, "You found somebody you like?"

"Not among these."

The marriage broker turned away.

"Here is the one I want." Leo held forth the snapshot.

Salzman slipped on his glasses and took the picture into his trembling hand. He turned ghastly and let out a groan.

"What's the matter?" cried Leo.

"Excuse me. Was an accident this picture. She isn't for you."

Salzman frantically shoved the manila packet into his portfolio. He thrust the snapshot into his pocket and fled down the stairs.

Leo, after momentary paralysis, gave chase and cornered the marriage broker in the **vestibule**.[32] The landlady made hysterical outcries but neither of them listened.

"Give me back the picture, Salzman."

"No." The pain in his eyes was terrible.

"Tell me who she is then."

"This I can't tell you. Excuse me."

He made to depart, but Leo, forgetting himself, seized the matchmaker by his tight coat and shook him frenziedly.

"Please," sighed Salzman. "*Please*."

Leo ashamedly let him go. "Tell me who she is," he begged. "It's very important for me to know."

"She is a wild one—wild, without shame. This is not a bride for a rabbi."

"She is not for you. She is a wild one—wild, without shame. This is not a bride for a rabbi."

"What do you mean wild?"

"Like an animal. Like a dog. For her to be poor was a sin. This is why to me she is dead now."

"In God's name, what do you mean?"

"Her I can't introduce to you," Salzman said.

"Why are you so excited?"

"Why, he asks," Salzman said, bursting into tears. "This is my baby, my Stella, she should burn in hell."

Leo hurried up to bed and hid under the covers. Under the covers he thought his life through. Although he soon fell asleep he could not sleep her out of his mind. He woke, beating his breast. Though he prayed to be rid of her, his prayers went unanswered. Through days of torment he endlessly struggled not to love her; fearing success, he escaped it. He then concluded to convert her to goodness, himself to God. The idea alternately nauseated and exalted him.

He perhaps did not know that he had come to a final decision until he encountered Salzman in a Broadway cafeteria. He was sitting alone at a rear table, sucking the bony remains of a fish. The marriage broker appeared haggard, and transparent to the point of vanishing.

Salzman looked up at first without recognizing him. Leo had grown a pointed beard and his eyes were weighted with wisdom.

---

[32] **vestibule**—small entrance hall.

"Salzman," he said, "love has at last come to my heart."

"Who can love from a picture?" mocked the marriage broker.

"It is not impossible."

"If you can love her, then you can love anybody. Let me show you some new clients that they just sent me their photographs. One is a little doll."

"Just her I want," Leo murmured.

"Don't be a fool, doctor. Don't bother with her."

"Put me in touch with her, Salzman," Leo said humbly. "Perhaps I can be of service."

Salzman had stopped eating and Leo understood with emotion that it was now arranged.

Leaving the cafeteria, he was, however, afflicted by a tormenting suspicion that Salzman had planned it all to happen this way.

Leo was informed by letter that she would meet him on a certain corner, and she was there one spring night, waiting under a street lamp. He appeared, carrying a small bouquet of violets and rosebuds. Stella stood by the lamp post, smoking. She wore white with red shoes, which fitted his expectations, although in a troubled moment he had imagined the dress red, and only the shoes white. She waited uneasily and shyly. From afar he saw that her eyes—clearly her father's—were filled with desperate innocence. He pictured, in her, his own redemption. Violins and lit candles revolved in the sky. Leo ran forward with flowers outthrust.

Around the corner, Salzman, leaning against a wall, chanted prayers for the dead.

QUESTIONS TO CONSIDER

1. Why does Leo go to a marriage broker?
2. What does he learn about himself from meeting Lily?
3. Do you think Salzman is good at his job? Why or why not?
4. What does Stella represent for Leo?
5. What evidence is there that Salzman set the whole thing up?

Flannery O'Connor ▶

Everything That Rises Must Converge

BY FLANNERY O'CONNOR

Flannery O'Connor (1925–1964) was born in Georgia into a devout Catholic family. She began writing at an early age, and after college in Georgia attended the Writers Workshop at the University of Iowa. After graduating, she was diagnosed with lupus, an incurable blood disease with many debilitating symptoms—O'Connor's father had died of lupus at a young age. After the diagnosis, O'Connor returned home to Georgia to write and undergo treatment. She lived with her mother, who cared for her after the serious attacks began in 1950. O'Connor's first novel, Wise Blood, *was published in 1952 and was critically acclaimed. Like much of her fiction, it deals with a young Southerner in the midst of a religious crisis—in this case trying to found a new church. Her only other novel,* The Violent Bear It Away, *had a similar plot, and such themes are repeatedly found in O'Connor's stories. Her use of grotesque and macabre images put O'Connor firmly in the tradition of the Southern Gothic. "Everything That Rises Must Converge" has fewer gothic elements than most of O'Connor's stories, but they are still there in the sometimes bizarre descriptions and darkly comic tone. Her story is a psychological portrait of a mother and son, but it also exposes the latent racism of much of the South's white community in the years after World War II, racism that would be battled by the Civil Rights movement.*

Her doctor had told Julian's mother that she must lose twenty pounds on account of her blood pressure, so on Wednesday nights Julian had to take her downtown on the bus for a reducing class at the Y.[1] The reducing class was designed for working girls over fifty, who weighed from 165 to 200 pounds. His mother was one of the slimmer ones, but she said ladies did not tell their age or weight. She would not ride the buses by herself at night since they had been **integrated**,[2] and because the reducing class was one of her few pleasures, necessary for her health, and *free,* she said Julian could at least put himself out to take her, considering all she did for him. Julian did

[1] Y—short for the Young Men's Christian Association (YMCA), or the Young Women's Christian Association (YWCA).

[2] **integrated**—opened to people of all races and ethnic groups without restriction.

not like to consider all she did for him, but every Wednesday night he braced himself and took her.

She was almost ready to go, standing before the hall mirror, putting on her hat, while he, his hands behind him, appeared pinned to the door frame, waiting like Saint Sebastian[3] for the arrows to begin piercing him. The hat was new and had cost her seven dollars and a half. She kept saying, "Maybe I shouldn't have paid that for it. No, I shouldn't have. I'll take it off and return it tomorrow. I shouldn't have bought it."

Julian raised his eyes to heaven. "Yes, you should have bought it," he said. "Put it on and let's go." It was a hideous hat. A purple velvet flap came down on one side of it and stood up on the other; the rest of it was green and looked like a cushion with the stuffing out. He decided it was less comical than **jaunty**[4] and pathetic. Everything that gave her pleasure was small and depressed him.

She lifted the hat one more time and set it down slowly on top of her head. Two wings of gray hair protruded on either side of her florid face, but her eyes, sky-blue, were as innocent and untouched by experience as they must have been when she was ten. Were it not that she was a widow who had struggled fiercely to feed and clothe and put him through school and who was supporting him still, "until he got on his feet," she might have been a little girl that he had to take to town.

"It's all right, it's all right," he said. "Let's go." He opened the door himself and started down the walk to get her going. The sky was a dying violet and the houses stood out darkly against it, bulbous[5] liver-colored monstrosities of a uniform ugliness though no two were alike. Since this had been a fashionable neighborhood forty years ago, his mother persisted in thinking they did well to have an apartment in it. Each house had a narrow collar of dirt around it in which sat, usually, a grubby child. Julian walked with his hands in his pockets, his head down and thrust forward and his eyes glazed with the determination to make himself completely numb during the time he would be sacrificed to her pleasure.

The door closed and he turned to find the dumpy figure, surmounted by the **atrocious**[6] hat, coming toward him. "Well," she said, "you only live once and paying a little more for it, I at least won't meet myself coming and going."

"Some day I'll start making money," Julian said gloomily—he knew he never would—"and you can have one of those jokes whenever you take the fit." But first they would move. He visualized a place where the nearest neighbors would be three miles away on either side.

"I think you're doing fine," she said, drawing on her gloves. "You've only been out of school a year. Rome wasn't built in a day."

She was one of the few members of the Y reducing class who arrived in hat

---

[3] Saint Sebastian—Christian martyr who died from being shot by arrows. The scene was often produced in Renaissance art.

[4] **jaunty**—crisp and dapper in appearance.

[5] bulbous—rounded or swollen.

[6] **atrocious**—exceptionally bad, distasteful.

and gloves and who had a son who had been to college. "It takes time," she said, "and the world is in such a mess. This hat looked better on me than any of the others, though when she brought it out I said, 'Take that thing back. I wouldn't have it on my head,' and she said, 'Now wait till you see it on,' and when she put it on me, I said, 'We-ull,' and she said, 'If you ask me, that hat does something for you and you do something for the hat, and besides,' she said, 'with that hat, you won't meet yourself coming and going.'"

"Of course," she said, "if you know who you are, you can go anywhere."

Julian thought he could have stood his lot better if she had been selfish, if she had been an old hag who drank and screamed at him. He walked along, **saturated**[7] in depression, as if in the midst of his martyrdom he had lost his faith. Catching sight of his long, hopeless, irritated face, she stopped suddenly with a grief-stricken look, and pulled back on his arm. "Wait on me," she said. "I'm going back to the house and take this thing off and tomorrow I'm going to return it. I was out of my head. I can pay the gas bill with that seven-fifty."

He caught her arm in a vicious grip. "You are not going to take it back," he said. "I like it."

"Well," she said, "I don't think I ought . . ."

"Shut up and enjoy it," he muttered, more depressed than ever.

"With the world in the mess it's in," she said, "it's a wonder we can enjoy anything. I tell you, the bottom rail is on the top."[8]

Julian sighed.

"Of course," she said, "if you know who you are, you can go anywhere." She said this every time he took her to the reducing class. "Most of them in it are not our kind of people," she said, "but I can be gracious to anybody. I know who I am."

"They don't give a damn for your graciousness," Julian said savagely. "Knowing who you are is good for one generation only. You haven't the foggiest idea where you stand now or who you are."

She stopped and allowed her eyes to flash at him. "I most certainly do know who I am," she said, "and if you don't know who you are, I'm ashamed of you."

"Oh hell," Julian said.

"Your great-grandfather was a former governor of this state," she said. "Your grandfather was a prosperous landowner. Your grandmother was a Godhigh."

"Will you look around you," he said tensely, "and see where you are now?" and he swept his arm jerkily out to indicate the neighborhood, which the growing darkness at least made less dingy.

"You remain what you are," she said. "Your great-grandfather had a plantation and two hundred slaves."

"There are no more slaves," he said irritably.

"They were better off when they were," she said. He groaned to see that she

[7] **saturated**—completely full of.

[8] the bottom . . . the top—expression meaning the natural order has been reversed.

was off on that topic. She rolled onto it every few days like a train on an open track. He knew every stop, every junction, every swamp along the way, and knew the exact point at which her conclusion would roll majestically into the station: "It's ridiculous. It's simply not realistic. They should rise, yes, but on their own side of the fence."

"Let's skip it," Julian said.

"The ones I feel sorry for," she said, "are the ones that are half white. They're tragic."

"Will you skip it?"

"Suppose we were half white. We would certainly have mixed feelings."

"I have mixed feelings now," he groaned.

"Well let's talk about something pleasant," she said. "I remember going to Grandpa's when I was a little girl. Then the house had double stairways that went up to what was really the second floor—all the cooking was done on the first. I used to like to stay down in the kitchen on account of the way the walls smelled. I would sit with my nose pressed against the plaster and take deep breaths. Actually the place belonged to the Godhighs but your grandfather Chestny paid the mortgage and saved it for them. They were in reduced circumstances," she said, "but reduced or not, they never forgot who they were."

"Doubtless that decayed mansion reminded them," Julian muttered. He never spoke of it without contempt or thought of it without longing. He had seen it once when he was a child before it had been sold. The double stairways had rotted and been torn down. Negroes were living in it. But it remained in his mind as his mother had known it. It appeared in his dreams regularly. He would stand on the wide porch, listening to the rustle of oak leaves, then wander through the high-ceilinged hall into the parlor that opened onto it and gaze at the worn rugs and faded draperies. It occurred to him that it was he, not she, who could have appreciated it. He preferred its threadbare elegance to anything he could name and it was because of it that all the neighborhoods they had lived in had been a torment to him—whereas she had hardly known the difference. She called her insensitivity "being adjustable."

"And I remember the old darky who was my nurse, Caroline. There was no better person in the world. I've always had a great respect for my colored friends," she said. "I'd do anything in the world for them and they'd . . ."

"Will you for God's sake get off that subject?" Julian said. When he got on a bus by himself, he made it a point to sit down beside a Negro, in reparation as it were for his mother's sins.

"You're mighty touchy tonight," she said. "Do you feel all right?"

"Yes I feet all right," he said. "Now lay off."

She pursed her lips. "Well, you certainly are in a vile humor," she observed. "I just won't speak to you at all."

They had reached the bus stop. There was no bus in sight and Julian, his hands still jammed in his pockets and his head thrust forward, scowled down the empty street. The frustration of having to wait on the bus as well as ride on it began to creep up his neck like a hot hand. The presence of his mother was borne in upon him as she gave a pained sigh. He looked at her bleakly. She was holding herself very erect under the preposterous hat, wearing it like a banner of her imaginary dignity. There was in him an evil urge to break her spirit. He suddenly unloosened his tie and pulled it off and put it in his pocket.

His mother immediately began a general conversation meant to attract anyone who felt like talking.

She stiffened. "Why must you look like *that* when you take me to town?" she said. "Why must you deliberately embarrass me?"

"If you'll never learn where you are," he said, "you can at least learn where I am."

"You look like a—thug," she said.

"Then I must be one," he murmured.

"I'll just go home," she said. "I will not bother you. If you can't do a little thing like that for me . . ."

Rolling his eyes upward, he put his tie back on. "Restored to my class," he muttered. He thrust his face toward her and hissed, "True culture is in the mind, the *mind*," he said, and tapped his head, "the mind."

"It's in the heart," she said, "and in how you do things and how you do things is because of who you *are*."

"Nobody in the damn bus cares who you are."

"I care who I am," she said icily.

The lighted bus appeared on top of the next hill and as it approached, they moved out into the street to meet it. He put his hand under her elbow and hoisted her up on the creaking step. She entered with a little smile, as if she were going into a drawing room where everyone had been waiting for her. While he put in the tokens, she sat down on one of the broad front seats for three which faced the aisle. A thin woman with protruding teeth and long yellow hair was sitting on the end of it. His mother moved up beside her and left room for Julian beside herself. He sat down and looked at the floor across the aisle where a pair of thin feet in red and white canvas sandals were planted.

His mother immediately began a general conversation meant to attract anyone who felt like talking. "Can it get any hotter?" she said and removed from her purse a folding fan, black with a Japanese scene on it, which she began to flutter before her.

"I reckon it might could," the woman with the protruding teeth said, "but I know for a fact my apartment couldn't get no hotter."

"It must get the afternoon sun," his mother said. She sat forward and looked up and down the bus. It was half filled. Everybody was white. "I see we have the bus to ourselves," she said. Julian cringed.[9]

"For a change," said the woman across the aisle, the owner of the red and white canvas sandals. "I come on one the other day and they were thick as fleas—up front and all through."

[9] cringed—shrank back, as if in fear.

"The world is in a mess everywhere," his mother said. "I don't know how we've let it get in this fix."

"What gets my goat is all those boys from good families stealing automobile tires," the woman with the protruding teeth said. "I told my boy, I said you may not be rich but you been raised right and if I ever catch you in any such mess, they can send you on to the reformatory. Be exactly where you belong."

"Training tells," his mother said. "Is your boy in high school?"

"Ninth grade," the woman said.

"My son just finished college last year. He wants to write but he's selling typewriters until he gets started," his mother said.

The woman leaned forward and peered at Julian. He threw her such a **malevolent**[10] look that she **subsided**[11] against the seat. On the floor across the aisle there was an abandoned newspaper. He got up and got it and opened it out in front of him. His mother discreetly continued the conversation in a lower tone but the woman across the aisle said in a loud voice, "Well that's nice. Selling typewriters is close to writing. He can go right from one to the other."

"I tell him," his mother said, "that Rome wasn't built in a day."

Behind the newspaper Julian was withdrawing into the inner compartment of his mind where he spent most of his time. This was a kind of mental bubble in which he established himself when he could not bear to be a part of what was going on around him. From it he could see out and judge but in it he was safe from any kind of penetration from without. It was the only place where he felt free of the general idiocy of his fellows. His mother had never entered it but from it he could see her with absolute clarity.

The old lady was clever enough and he thought that if she had started from any of the right **premises**,[12] more might have been expected of her. She lived according to the laws of her own fantasy world, outside of which he had never seen her set foot. The law of it was to sacrifice herself for him after she had first created the necessity to do so by making a mess of things. If he had permitted her sacrifices, it was only because her lack of foresight had made them necessary. All of her life had been a struggle to act like a Chestny without the Chestny goods, and to give him everything she thought a Chestny ought to have; but since, said she, it was fun to struggle, why complain? And when you had won, as she had won, what fun to took back on the hard times! He could not forgive her that she had enjoyed the struggle and that she thought *she* had won.

What she meant when she said she had won was that she had brought him up successfully and had sent him to college and that he had turned out so well—good looking (her teeth had gone unfilled so that his could be straightened), intelligent (he realized he was too intelligent to be a success), and with a future ahead of him (there was of course no future ahead of him). She

---

[10] **malevolent**—malicious, exhibiting ill will.

[11] **subsided**—sank down.

[12] **premises**—propositions on which an argument is based or from which a conclusion is drawn.

excused his gloominess on the grounds that he was still growing up and his radical ideas on his lack of practical experience. She said he didn't yet know a thing about "life," that he hadn't even entered the real world—when already he was as disenchanted with it as a man of fifty.

The further irony of all this was that in spite of her, he had turned out so well. In spite of going to only a third-rate college, he had, on his own initiative, come out with a first-rate education; in spite of growing up dominated by a small mind, he had ended up with a large one; in spite of all her foolish views, he was free of prejudice and unafraid to face facts. Most miraculous of all, instead of being blinded by love for her as she was for him, he had cut himself emotionally free of her and could see her with complete objectivity. He was not dominated by his mother.

The bus stopped with a sudden jerk and shook him from his meditation. A woman from the back lurched forward with little steps and barely escaped falling in his newspaper as she righted herself. She got off and a large Negro got on. Julian kept his paper lowered to watch. It gave him a certain satisfaction to see injustice in daily operation. It confirmed his view that with a few exceptions there was no one worth knowing within a radius of three hundred miles. The Negro was well dressed and carried a briefcase. He looked around and then sat down on the other end of the seat where the woman with the red and white canvas sandals was sitting. He immediately unfolded a newspaper and obscured himself behind it. Julian's mother's elbow at once prodded insistently into his ribs. "Now you see why I won't ride on these buses by myself," she whispered.

The woman with the red and white canvas sandals had risen at the same time the Negro sat down and had gone further back in the bus and taken the seat of the woman who had got off. His mother leaned forward and cast her an approving look.

Julian rose, crossed the aisle, and sat down in the place of the woman with the canvas sandals. From this position, he looked serenely across at his mother. Her face had turned an angry red. He stared at her, making his eyes the eyes of a stranger. He felt his tension suddenly lift as if he had openly declared war on her.

He would have liked to get in conversation with the Negro and to talk with him about art or politics or any subject that would be above the comprehension of those around them, but the man remained entrenched behind his paper. He was either ignoring the change of seating or had never noticed it. There was no way for Julian to convey his sympathy.

His mother kept her eyes fixed reproachfully on his face. The woman with the protruding teeth was looking at him **avidly**[13] as if he were a type of monster new to her.

"Do you have a light?" he asked the Negro.

Without looking away from his paper, the man reached in his pocket and handed him a packet of matches.

---

[13] **avidly**—enthusiastically or greedily.

"Thanks," Julian said. For a moment he held the matches foolishly. A NO SMOKING sign looked down upon him from over the door. This alone would not have deterred him; he had no cigarettes. He had quit smoking some months before because he could not afford it. "Sorry," he muttered and handed back the matches. The Negro lowered the paper and gave him an annoyed look. He took the matches and raised the paper again.

His mother continued to gaze at him but she did not take advantage of his momentary discomfort. Her eyes retained their battered look. Her face seemed to be unnaturally red, as if her blood pressure had risen. Julian allowed no glimmer of sympathy to show on his face. Having got the advantage, he wanted desperately to keep it and carry it through. He would have liked to teach her a lesson that would last her a while, but there seemed no way to continue the point. The Negro refused to come out from behind his paper.

Julian folded his arms and looked **stolidly**[14] before him, facing her but as if he did not see her, as if he had ceased to recognize her existence. He visualized a scene in which, the bus having reached their stop, he would remain in his seat and when she said, "Aren't you going to get off?" he would look at her as at a stranger who had rashly addressed him. The corner they got off on was usually deserted, but it was well lighted and it would not hurt her to walk by herself the four blocks to the Y. He decided to wait until the time came and then decide whether or not he would let her get off by herself. He would have to be at the Y at ten to bring her back, but he could leave her wondering if he was going to show up. There was no reason for her to think she could always depend on him.

He retired again into the high-ceilinged room sparsely settled with large pieces of antique furniture. His soul expanded momentarily but then he became aware of his mother across from him and the vision shriveled. He studied her coldly. Her feet in little pumps dangled like a child's and did not quite reach the floor. She was training on him an exaggerated look of reproach. He felt completely detached from her. At that moment he could with pleasure have slapped her as he would have slapped a particularly obnoxious child in his charge.

He began to imagine various unlikely ways by which he could teach her a lesson. He might make friends with some distinguished Negro professor or lawyer and bring him home to spend the evening. He would be entirely justified but her blood pressure would rise to 300. He could not push her to the extent of making her have a stroke, and moreover, he had never been successful at making any Negro friends. He had tried to strike up an acquaintance on the bus with some of the better types, with ones that looked like professors or ministers or lawyers. One morning he had sat down next to a distinguished-looking dark brown man who had answered his questions with a **sonorous**[15] solemnity but who had turned out to be an undertaker. Another day he had sat down beside a cigar-smoking Negro

[14] **stolidly**—impassively, showing little emotion.

[15] **sonorous**—impressive style of speech.

with a diamond ring on his finger, but after a few stilted[16] pleasantries, the Negro had rung the buzzer and risen, slipping two lottery tickets into Julian's hand as he climbed over him to leave.

He imagined his mother lying desperately ill and his being able to secure only a Negro doctor for her. He toyed with that idea for a few minutes and then dropped it for a momentary vision of himself participating as a sympathizer in a sit-in demonstration. This was possible but he did not linger with it. Instead, he approached the ultimate horror. He brought home a beautiful suspiciously Negroid woman. Prepare yourself, he said. There is nothing you can do about it. This is the woman I've chosen. She's intelligent, dignified, even good, and she's suffered and she hasn't thought it *fun*. Now persecute us, go ahead and persecute us. Drive her out of here, but remember, you're driving me too. His eyes were narrowed and through the **indignation**[17] he had generated, he saw his mother across the aisle, purple-faced, shrunken to the dwarf-like proportions of her moral nature, sitting like a mummy beneath the ridiculous banner of her hat.

He was tilted out of his fantasy again as the bus stopped. The door opened with a sucking hiss and out of the dark a large, gaily dressed, sullen-looking colored woman got on with a little boy. The child, who might have been four, had on a short plaid suit and a Tyrolean hat with a blue feather in it. Julian hoped that he would sit down beside him and that the woman would push in beside his mother. He could think of no better arrangement.

As she waited for her tokens, the woman was surveying the seating possibilities—he hoped with the idea of sitting where she was least wanted. There was something familiar-looking about her but Julian could not place what it was. She was a giant of a woman. Her face was set not only to meet opposition but to seek it out. The downward tilt of her large lower lip was like a warning sign: DON'T TAMPER WITH ME. Her bulging figure was encased in a green crepe dress and her feet overflowed in red shoes. She had on a hideous hat. A purple velvet flap came down on one side of it and stood up on the other; the rest of it was green and looked like a cushion with the stuffing out. She carried a mammoth red pocketbook that bulged throughout as if it were stuffed with rocks.

To Julian's disappointment, the little boy climbed up on the empty seat beside his mother. His mother lumped all children, black and white, into the common category, "cute," and she thought little Negroes were on the whole cuter than little white children. She smiled at the little boy as he climbed on the seat.

Meanwhile the woman was bearing down upon the empty seat beside Julian. To his annoyance, she squeezed herself into it. He saw his mother's face change as the woman settled herself next to him and he realized with satisfaction that this was more objectionable to her than it was to him. Her face seemed almost gray and there was a look of dull recognition in her

[16] stilted—stiff, awkward.

[17] **indignation**—anger aroused by something unjust or mean.

eyes, as if suddenly she had sickened at some awful confrontation. Julian saw that it was because she and the woman had, in a sense, swapped sons. Though his mother would not realize the symbolic significance of this, she would feel it. His amusement showed plainly on his face.

The woman next to him muttered something unintelligible to herself. He was conscious of a kind of bristling next to him, a muted growling like that of an angry cat. He could not see anything but the red pocketbook upright on the bulging green thighs. He visualized the woman as she had stood waiting for her tokens—the ponderous figure, rising from the red shoes upward over the solid hips, the mammoth bosom, the haughty face, to the green and purple hat.

His eyes widened.

The vision of the two hats, identical, broke upon him with the radiance of a brilliant sunrise. His face was suddenly lit with joy. He could not believe that Fate had thrust upon his mother such a lesson. He gave a loud chuckle so that she would look at him and see that he saw. She turned her eyes on him slowly. The blue in them seemed to have turned a bruised purple. For a moment he had an uncomfortable sense of her innocence, but it lasted only a second before principle rescued him. Justice entitled him to laugh. His grin hardened until it said to her as plainly as if he were saying aloud: Your punishment exactly fits your pettiness. This should teach you a permanent lesson.

Her eyes shifted to the woman. She seemed unable to bear looking at him and to find the woman preferable. He became conscious again of the bristling presence at his side. The woman was rumbling like a volcano about to become active. His mother's mouth began to twitch slightly at one corner. With a sinking heart, he saw incipient[18] signs of recovery on her face and realized that this was going to strike her suddenly as funny and was going to be no lesson at all. She kept her eyes on the woman and an amused smile came over her face as if the woman were a monkey that had stolen her hat. The little Negro was looking up at her with large fascinated eyes. He had been trying to attract her attention for some time.

His face was suddenly lit with joy. He could not believe that Fate had thrust upon his mother such a lesson.

"Carver!" the woman said suddenly. "Come heah!"

When he saw that the spotlight was on him at last, Carver drew his feet up and turned himself toward Julian's mother and giggled.

"Carver!" the woman said. "You heah me? Come heah!"

Carver slid down from the seat but remained squatting with his back against the base of it, his head turned slyly around toward Julian's mother, who was smiling at him. The woman reached a hand across the aisle and snatched him to her. He righted himself and hung backwards on her knees, grinning at Julian's mother.

---

[18] **incipient**—beginning to appear.

"Isn't he cute?" Julian's mother said to the woman with the protruding teeth.

"I reckon he is," the woman said without conviction.

The Negress yanked him upright but he eased out of her grip and shot across the aisle and scrambled, giggling wildly, onto the seat beside his love.

"I think he likes me," Julian's mother said, and smiled at the woman. It was the smile she used when she was being particularly gracious to an inferior. Julian saw everything lost. The lesson had rolled off her like rain on a roof.

The woman stood up and yanked the little boy off the seat as if she were snatching him from **contagion**.[19] Julian could feel the rage in her at having no weapon like his mother's smile. She gave the child a sharp slap across his leg. He howled once and then thrust his head into her stomach and kicked his feet against her shins. "Be-have," she said vehemently.

The bus stopped and the Negro who had been reading the newspaper got off. The woman moved over and set the little boy down with a thump between herself and Julian. She held him firmly by the knee. In a moment he put his hands in front of his face and peeped at Julian's mother through his fingers.

"I see yoooooooo!" she said and put her hand in front of her face and peeped at him.

The woman slapped his hand down. "Quit yo' foolishness," she said, "before I knock the living Jesus out of you!"

Julian was thankful that the next stop was theirs. He reached up and pulled the cord. The woman reached up and pulled it at the same time. Oh my God, he thought. He had the terrible intuition that when they got off the bus together, his mother would open her purse and give the little boy a nickel. The gesture would be as natural to her as breathing. The bus stopped and the woman got up and lunged to the front, dragging the child, who wished to stay on, after her. Julian and his mother got up and followed. As they neared the door, Julian tried to relieve her of her pocketbook.

"No," she murmured. "I want to give the little boy a nickel."

"No!" Julian hissed. "No!"

She smiled down at the child and opened her bag. The bus door opened and the woman picked him up by the arm and descended with him, hanging at her hip. Once in the street she set him down and shook him.

Julian's mother had to close her purse while she got down the bus step but as soon as her feet were on the ground, she opened it again and began to rummage inside. "I can't find but a penny," she whispered, "but it looks like a new one."

"Don't do it!" Julian said fiercely between his teeth. There was a streetlight on the corner and she hurried to get under it so that she could better see into her pocketbook. The woman was heading off rapidly down the street with the child still hanging backward on her hand.

"Oh little boy!" Julian's mother called and took a few quick steps and caught up with them just beyond the lamppost. "Here's a bright new penny for you," and

[19] **contagion**—harmful or corrupting influence, or a disease transmitted by contact.

she held out the coin, which shone bronze in the dim light.

The huge woman turned and for a moment stood, her shoulders lifted and her face frozen with frustrated rage, and stared at Julian's mother. Then all at once she seemed to explode like a piece of machinery that had been given one ounce of pressure too much. Julian saw the black fist swing out with the red pocketbook. He shut his eyes and cringed as he heard the woman shout, "He don't take nobody's pennies!" When he opened his eyes, the woman was disappearing down the street with the little boy staring wide-eyed over her shoulder. Julian's mother was sitting on the sidewalk.

"I told you not to do that," Julian said angrily. "I told you not to do that!"

He stood over her for a minute, gritting his teeth. Her legs were stretched out in front of her and her hat was on her lap. He squatted down and looked her in the face. It was totally expressionless. "You got exactly what you deserved," he said. "Now get up."

He picked up her pocketbook and put what had fallen out back in it. He picked the hat up off her lap. The penny caught his eye on the sidewalk and he picked that up and let it drop before her eyes into the purse. Then he stood up and leaned over and held his hands out to pull her up. She remained immobile. He sighed. Rising above them on either side were black apartment buildings, marked with irregular rectangles of light. At the end of the block a man came out of a door and walked off in the opposite direction. "All right," he said, "suppose somebody happens by and wants to know why you're sitting on the sidewalk?"

She took the hand and, breathing hard, pulled heavily up on it and then stood for a moment, swaying slightly as if the spots of light in the darkness were circling around her. Her eyes, shadowed and confused, finally settled on his face.

He shut his eyes and cringed as he heard the woman shout, "He don't take nobody's pennies!"

He did not try to conceal his irritation. "I hope this teaches you a lesson," he said. She leaned forward and her eyes raked his face. She seemed trying to determine his identity. Then, as if she found nothing familiar about him, she started off with a headlong movement in the wrong direction.

"Aren't you going on to the Y?" he asked.

"Home," she muttered.

"Well, are we walking?"

For answer she kept going. Julian followed along, his hands behind him. He saw no reason to let the lesson she had had go without backing it up with an explanation of its meaning. She might as well be made to understand what had happened to her. "Don't think that was just an uppity Negro woman," he said. "That was the whole colored race which will no longer take your condescending pennies. That was your black double. She can wear the same hat as you, and to be sure," he added **gratuitously**[20] (because he thought it was

[20] **gratuitously**—unnecessarily.

funny), "it looked better on her than it did on you. What all this means," he said, "is that the old world is gone. The old manners are **obsolete**[21] and your graciousness is not worth a damn." He thought bitterly of the house that had been lost for him. "You aren't who you think you are," he said.

She continued to plow ahead, paying no attention to him. Her hair had come undone on one side. She dropped her pocketbook and took no notice. He stooped and picked it up and handed it to her but she did not take it.

"You needn't act as if the world had come to an end," he said, "because it hasn't. From now on you've got to live in a new world and face a few realities for a change. Buck up," he said, "it won't kill you."

She was breathing fast.

"Let's wait on the bus," he said.

"Home," she said thickly.

"I hate to see you behave like this," he said. "Just like a child. I should be able to expect more of you." He decided to stop where he was and make her stop and wait for a bus. "I'm not going any farther," he said, stopping. "We're going on the bus."

She continued to go on as if she had not heard him. He took a few steps and caught her arm and stopped her. He looked into her face and caught his breath. He was looking into a face he had never seen before. "Tell Grandpa to come get me," she said.

He stared, **stricken**.[22]

"Tell Caroline to come get me," she said.

Stunned, he let her go and she lurched forward again, walking as if one leg were shorter than the other. A tide of darkness seemed to be sweeping her from him. "Mother!" he cried. "Darling, sweetheart, wait!" Crumpling, she fell to the pavement. He dashed forward and felt at her side, crying, "Mamma, Mamma!" He turned her over. Her face was fiercely distorted. One eye, large and staring, moved slightly to the left as if it had become unmoored. The other remained fixed on him, raked his face again, found nothing and closed.

"Wait here, wait here!" he cried and jumped up and began to run for help toward a cluster of lights he saw in the distance ahead of him. "Help, help!" he shouted, but his voice was thin, scarcely a thread of sound. The lights drifted farther away the faster he ran and his feet moved numbly as if they carried him no where. The tide of darkness seemed to sweep him back to her, postponing from moment to moment his entry into the world of guilt and sorrow.

---

[21] **obsolete**—no longer in use; old-fashioned and outmoded.

[22] **stricken**—affected by strong emotion or trouble.

QUESTIONS TO CONSIDER

1. How does Julian's mother's attitude about race relate to her general view of her position in the world?
2. What is Julian's attitude toward his mother?
3. What does Julian think the coincidence of the hats will teach his mother?
4. In the end what is it that does teach her the lesson?
5. What is the meaning of the title of the story?

Regionalism

Regionalism, an emphasis on the characteristic landscapes, speech, customs, and traditions of particular areas, has been part of American literature since colonial times. The local colorists of the late 1800s and the regionalists of the 1920s and 1930s are notable examples of this persistent emphasis. The following photographs (primarily from the 1930s and early 1940s) show some of the characteristic landscapes of different sections of the United States.

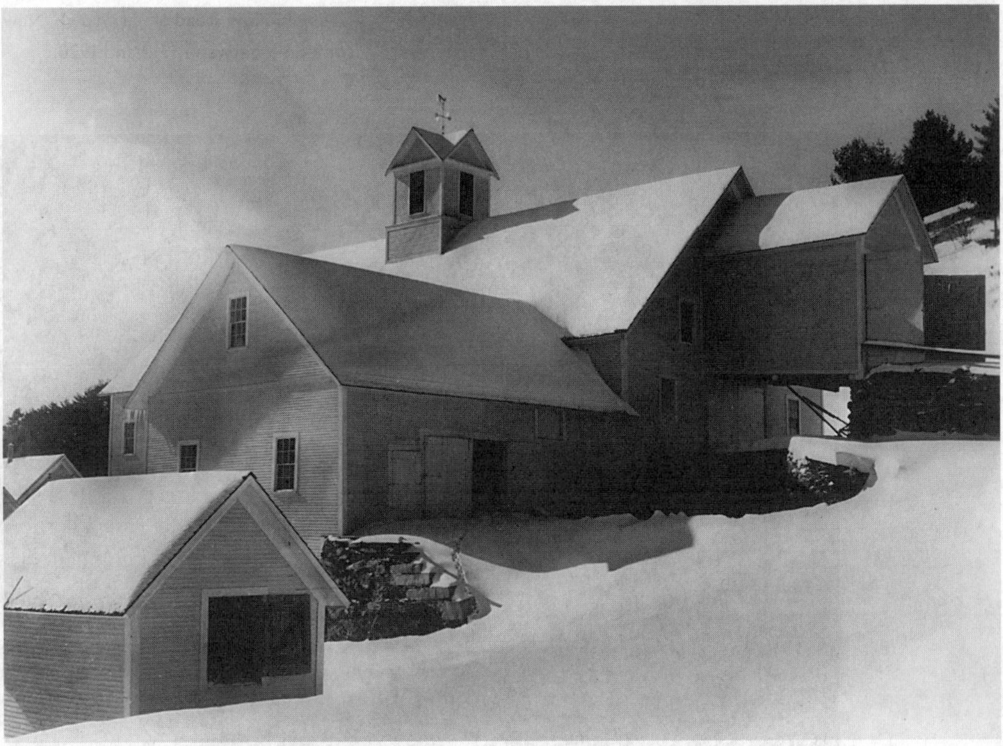

▲
A barn on a New Hampshire dairy farm in February 1936.

The shore at Cromwell Harbor, Mount Desert Island, Maine.

Sleepy Hollow Road in Tarrytown, New York, sometime between 1910 and 1920.

▲
First Congregational Church in Southington, Connecticut, in May 1942.

▲
New York City at night in 1937.

Times Square in New York City in March 1943. ▶

Bathgate Avenue in the Bronx in December 1936. ▶

▲
The balcony and veranda of an old plantation house in New Orleans in September 1938.

▲
Townspeople in front of the old Talbott Tavern in Bardstown, Kentucky, on a Saturday afternoon in July 1940.

A street in Camden, Tennessee, in October 1935.
▼

◀ A house in Nicholson Hollow, Shenandoah National Park, Virginia, in October 1935.

◀ A cotton patch in the Mississippi Delta in July 1937.

The main street in Childersberg, Alabama, in May 1941.
▼

▲
A residential street in Waupon, Wisconsin, in July 1941.

▲
A residential street in Elgin, Illinois, in August 1941.

DRUG STORE
Coca-Cola
HARRIS
Coca-Cola
Coca-Cola

▲
A corn farm in Grundy County, Iowa, in April 1940.

◀ A street in Hettinger, North Dakota, in February 1942.

▲
A cowboy with his pony near Pie Town, New Mexico, in June 1940.

A foreclosed tenant farm "tractored off" in the Texas Panhandle in June 1938.

▼

▲
Main street of Jackson, Montana, in April 1942.

Hamilton, Montana, in April 1942. ▶

▲
Glacier National Park in August 1941.

▲
Fisherman's Wharf, San Francisco.

Pacific Coast near Monterey, California, around 1927. ▶

NK
HE
ST
廣
生
天仁茗
萬壽宮
Kodak
VC
-220V
藥材
SANG LUNG
HERBS

Part Four

New Voices and Identities

Energized by the struggle for civil rights that began in the 1950s, a cultural awakening also commenced among various groups, including African Americans, Hispanic Americans, Native Americans, and Asian Americans. One result of this was the inclusion of many new voices in American literature.

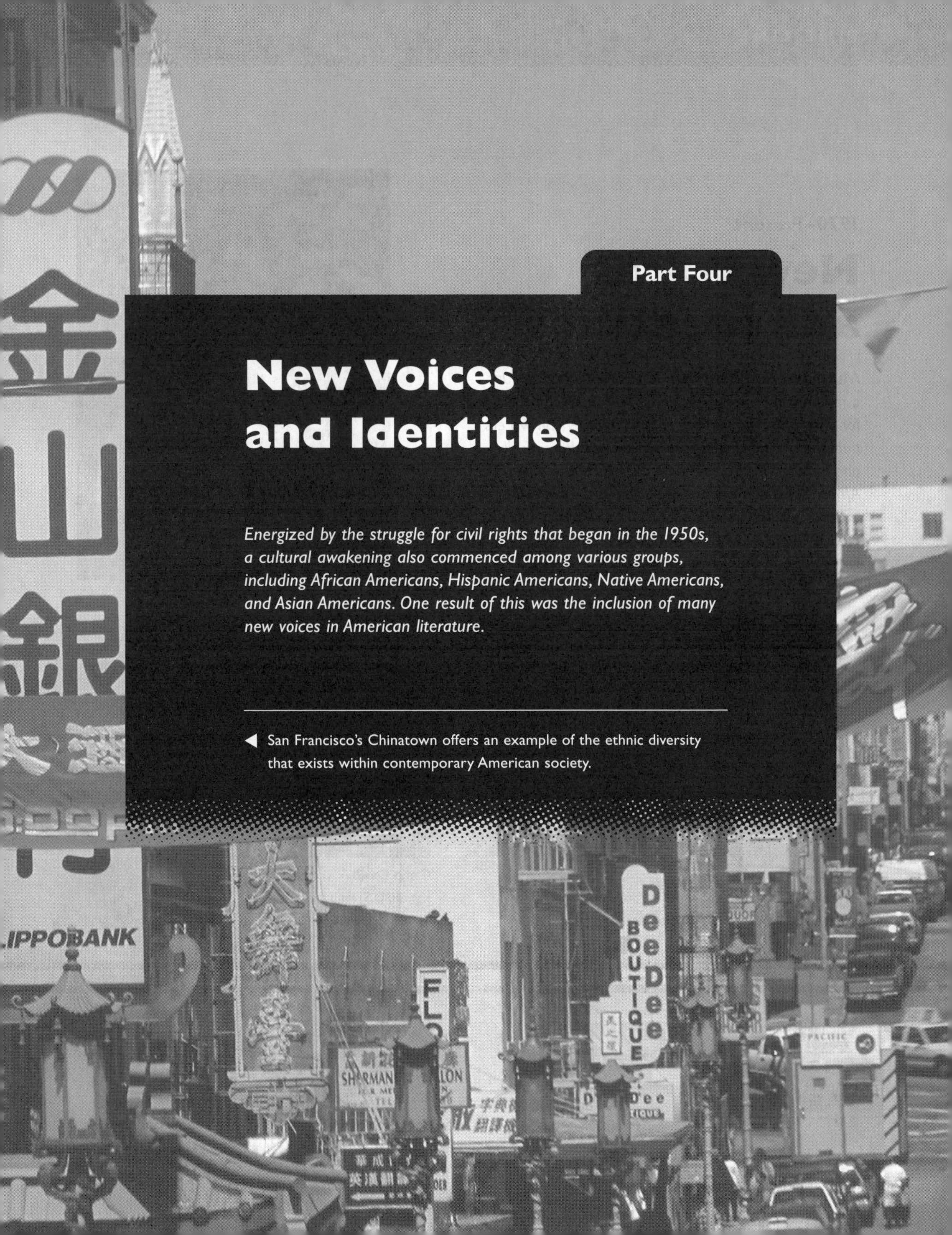

◀ San Francisco's Chinatown offers an example of the ethnic diversity that exists within contemporary American society.

1970–Present

New Voices and Identities

Multicultural Literature *In the 1960s and 1970s, a minority arts movement developed out of the struggle for civil rights. The number of African-American writers published in the United States increased dramatically and included for the first time a significant number of African-American women. Beginning in the 1970s, increasing numbers of Hispanic, Asian-American, and Native-American writers joined African Americans in giving voice to their cultural identities.*

▲ Gish Jen's fiction often deals with problems experienced by Chinese Americans in adjusting to American society.

Invasion of Cambodia begins; National Guard kills students at Kent State.

1970

Watergate scandal begins.

U.S. pulls out of Vietnam.

Nixon resigns as president.

Saigon falls to Communist forces.

1975

Star Wars released.

Camp David Accords signed; U.S. embassy in Tehran taken over.

1980

Ronald Reagan elected.

AIDS identified by scientists.

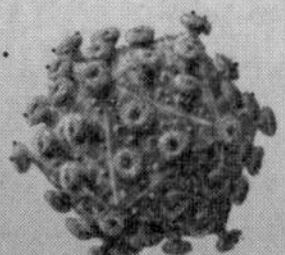

Sandra Day O'Connor appointed to Supreme Court; Vietnam Veterans Memorial dedicated.

◀ In his mid-twenties, African-American writer James Baldwin left the United States for Europe, seeking an environment where he could feel like an individual, rather than a racial abstraction.

Born in the Dominican Republic, Julia Alvarez used the experience of adapting to American culture as the basis for her first book, *How the Garcia Girls Lost Their Accents.* ▼

Space shuttle *Challenger* explodes.

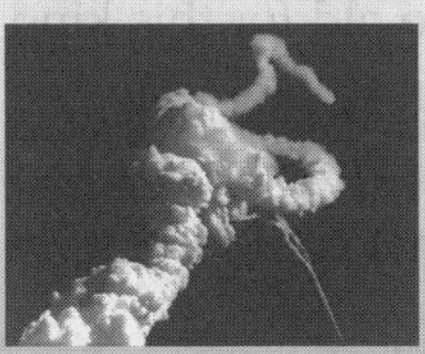

Gulf War fought.

Toni Morrison wins Nobel Prize.

George W. Bush elected.

1985 1990 1995 2000

Berlin Wall falls.

Rodney King riots occur in LA; Bill Clinton elected.

Tillie Olsen ▶

Tell Me a Riddle

BY TILLIE OLSEN

Tillie Olsen (1913–   ) has not been a very prolific writer. Instead, her life has been devoted to radical politics and raising a large family. She was born in Nebraska, where her father was head of the Communist Party. From an early age, Olsen was involved with the party, beginning by writing sketches and articles for the Young People's Socialist League. She was also writing essays and began a novel (which was not published until 1974). Olsen married in 1943 and had four daughters. The pressures of family life caused her to give up writing until the late 1950s, when she began to publish essays and stories again. Her 1961 collection, Tell Me A Riddle, *won the O. Henry Award, and by the end of the decade, Olsen was not only a highly regarded writer, but also teaching at various universities. Her writing tends to focus on the divisions of society between race, class, and gender. She has fought these things all her life, and her fiction is merely one more weapon in the battle. "Tell Me a Riddle" is the story of a long quarrel in a marriage and of facing the inevitable.*

I

For forty-seven years they had been married. How deep back the stubborn, **gnarled**[1] roots of the quarrel reached, no one could say—but only now, when tending to the needs of others no longer **shackled**[2] them together, the roots swelled up visible, split the earth between them, and the tearing shook even to the children, long since grown.

Why now, why now? wailed Hannah.

As if when we grew up weren't enough, said Paul.

Poor Ma. Poor Dad. It hurts so for both of them, said Vivi. They never had very much; at least in old age they should be happy.

Knock their heads together, insisted Sammy; tell 'em: you're too old for this kind of thing; no reason not to get along now.

Lennie wrote to Clara: They've lived over so much together; what could possibly tear them apart?

Something **tangible**[3] enough.

Arthritic hands, and such work as he got, occasional. Poverty all his life, and

---

[1] **gnarled**—knotty or misshapen.

[2] **shackled**—chained.

[3] **tangible**—real, concrete.

there was little breath left for running. He could not, could not turn away from this desire: to have the troubling of responsibility, the fretting with money, over and done with; to be free, to be *care*-free where success was not measured by accumulation, and there was use for the vitality still in him.

There was a way. They could sell the house, and with the money join his lodge's Haven, cooperative for the aged. Happy **communal**[4] life, and was he not already an official; had he not helped organize it, raise funds, served as a trustee?

But she—would not consider it.

"What do we need all this for?" he would ask loudly, for her hearing aid was turned down and the vacuum was shrilling. "Five rooms" (pushing the sofa so she could get into the corner) "furniture" (smoothing down the rug) "floors and surfaces to make work. Tell me, why do we need it?" And he was glad he could ask in a scream.

"Because I'm use't."

"Because you're use't. This is a reason, Mrs. Word Miser? Used to can get unused!"

"Enough unused I have to get used to already. . . . Not enough words?" turning off the vacuum a moment to hear herself answer. "Because soon enough we'll need only a little closet, no windows, no furniture, nothing to make work, but for worms. Because now I want room. . . . Screech and blow like you're doing, you'll need that closet even sooner. . . . Ha, again!" for the vacuum bag wailed, puffed half up, hung stubbornly limp. "This time fix it so it stays; quick before the phone rings and you get too important-busy."

But while he struggled with the motor, it **seethed**[5] in him. Why fix it? Why have to bother? And if it can't be fixed, have to wring the mind with how to pay the repair? At the Haven they come in with their own machines to clean your room or your cottage; you fish, or play cards, or make jokes in the sun, not with knotty fingers fight to mend vacuums.

Over the dishes, coaxingly: "For once in your life, to be free, to have everything done for you, like a queen."

"I never liked queens."

"No dishes, no garbage, no towel to sop, no worry what to buy, what to eat."

"And what else would I do with my empty hands? Better to eat at my own table when I want, and to cook and eat how I want."

"In the cottages they buy what you ask, and cook it how you like. *You* are the one who always used to say: better mankind born without mouths and stomachs than always to worry for money to buy, to shop, to fix, to cook, to wash, to clean."

"How cleverly you hid that you heard. I said it then because eighteen hours a day I ran. And you never scraped a carrot or knew a dish towel sops. Now—for you and me—who cares? A herring out of a jar is enough. But when *I* want, and nobody to bother." And she turned off her ear button, so she would not have to hear.

---

[4] **communal**—shared by the people of a community.

[5] **seethed**—boiled, was in a state of turmoil.

But as *he* had no peace, juggling and rejuggling the money to figure: how will I pay for this now?; prying out the storm windows (there they take care of this); jolting in the streetcar on errands (there I would not have to ride to take care of this or that); fending the patronizing[6] relatives just back from Florida (at the Haven it matters what one is, not what one can afford), he gave *her* no peace.

"Look! In their bulletin. A reading circle. Twice a week it meets."

"Haumm," her answer of not listening.

"A reading circle. Chekhov they read that you like, and Peretz.[7] Cultured people at the Haven that you would enjoy."

"Enjoy!" She tasted the word. "Now, when it pleases you, you find a reading circle for me. And forty years ago when the children were morsels and there was a Circle, did you stay home with them once so I could go? Even once? You trained me well. I do not need others to enjoy. Others!" Her voice trembled. "Because *you* want to be there with others. Already it makes me sick to think of you always around others. Clown, grimacer,[8] floormat, yesman, entertainer, whatever they want of you."

And now it was he who turned on the television loud so he need not hear.

Old scar tissue ruptured and the wounds festered anew. Chekhov indeed. She thought without softness of that young wife, who in the deep night hours while she nursed the current baby, and perhaps held another in her lap, would try to stay awake for the only time there was to read. She would feel again the weather of the outside on his cheek when, coming late from a meeting, he would find her so, and stimulated and **ardent**,[9] sniffing her skin, coax: "I'll put the baby to bed, and you—put the book away, don't read, don't read."

That had been the most **beguiling**[10] of all the "don't read, put your book away" her life had been. Chekhov indeed!

"Money?" She shrugged him off. "Could we get poorer than once we were? And in America, who starves?"

But as still he pressed:

"Let me alone about money. Was there ever enough? Seven little ones—for every penny I had to ask—and sometimes, remember, there was nothing. But always *I* had to manage. Now *you* manage. Rub your nose in it good."

But from those years she had had to manage, old humiliations and terrors rose up, lived again, and forced her to relive them. The children's needings; that grocer's face or this merchant's wife she had had to beg credit from when credit was a disgrace; the scenery of the long blocks walked around when she could not pay; school coming, and the desperate going over the old to see what could yet be remade; the soups of meat bones begged "for-the-dog" one winter. . . .

---

6 patronizing—treating as an inferior.

7 Chekhov . . . Peretz—Anton Chekhov (1860–1904), Russian playwright and short story writer; Isaac Peretz (1852–1915), Jewish poet and novelist born in a part of Poland that was then ruled by Russia.

8 grimacer—one who makes exaggerated faces.

9 **ardent**—passionate.

10 **beguiling**—deceiving.

Enough. Now they had no children. Let *him* wrack his head for how they would live. She would not exchange her solitude for anything. *Never again to be forced to move to the rhythms of others.*

For in this solitude she had won to a reconciled peace.

Tranquillity from having the empty house no longer an enemy, for it stayed clean—not as in the days when it was her family, the life in it, that had seemed the enemy: tracking, smudging, littering, dirtying, engaging her in endless defeating battle—and on whom her endless defeat had been spewed.

The few old books, memorized from rereading; the pictures to ponder (the magnifying glass superimposed on her heavy eyeglasses). Or if she wishes, when he is gone, the phonograph, that if she turns up very loud and strains, she can hear: the ordered sounds and the struggling.

Out in the garden, growing things to nurture. Birds to be kept out of the pear tree, and when the pears are heavy and ripe, the old fury of work, for all must be canned, nothing wasted.

And her one social duty (for she will not go to luncheons or meetings) the boxes of old clothes left with her, as with a life-practiced eye for finding what is still wearable within the worn (again the magnifying glass superimposed on the heavy glasses) she scans and sorts—this for rag or rummage, that for mending and cleaning, and this for sending away.

Being able at last to live within, and not move to the rhythms of others, as life had helped her to: denying; removing; isolating; taking the children one by one; then deafening, half-blinding—and at last, presenting her solitude.

And in it she had won to a reconciled peace.

Now he was violating it with his constant campaigning: *Sell the house and move to the Haven.* (You sit, you sit—there too you could sit like a stone.) He was making of her a battleground where old grievances tore. (Turn on your ear button—I am talking.) And stubbornly she resisted—so that from wheedling, reasoning, manipulation, it was bitterness he now started with.

And it came to where every happening lashed up a quarrel.

"I will sell the house anyway," he flung at her one night. "I am putting it up for sale. There will be a way to make you sign."

The television blared, as always it did on the evenings he stayed home, and as always it reached her only as noise. She did not know if the tumult was in her or outside. Snap! she turned the sound off. "Shadows," she whispered to him, pointing to the screen, "look, it is only shadows." And in a scream: "Did you say that you will sell the house? Look at me, not at that. I am no shadow. You cannot sell without me."

"Leave on the television. I am watching."

"Like Paulie, like Jenny, a four-year-old. Staring at shadows. *You cannot sell the house.*"

"I will. We are going to the Haven. There you would not hear the television when you do not want it. I could sit in the social room and watch. You could lock yourself up to smell your unpleasantness in a room by yourself—for who would want to come near you?"

"No, no selling." A whisper now.

"The television is shadows. Mrs. Enlightened! Mrs. Cultured! A world comes into your house—and it is shadows. People you would never meet in a thousand lifetimes. Wonders. When you were four years old, yes, like Paulie, like Jenny, did you know of Indian dances, alligators, how they use bamboo in Malaya? No, you scratched in your dirt with the chickens and thought Olshana[11] was the world. Yes, Mrs. Unpleasant, I will sell the house, for there better can we be rid of each other than here."

"Yes, Mrs. Unpleasant, I will sell the house, for there better can we be rid of each other than here."

She did not know if the tumult was outside, or in her. Always a ravening[12] inside, a pull to the bed, to lie down, to **succumb**.[13]

"Have you thought maybe Ma should let a doctor have a look at her?" asked their son Paul after Sunday dinner, regarding his mother crumpled on the couch, instead of, as was her custom, busying herself in Nancy's kitchen.

"Why not the President too?"

"Seriously, Dad. This is the third Sunday she's lain down like that after dinner. Is she that way at home?"

"A regular love affair with the bed. Every time I start to talk to her."

Good protective reaction, observed Nancy to herself. The workings of hos-til-ity.

"Nancy could take her. I just don't like how she looks. Let's have Nancy arrange an appointment."

"You think she'll go?" regarding his wife gloomily. "All right, we have to have doctor bills, we have to have doctor bills." Loudly: "Something hurts you?"

She startled, looked to his lips. He repeated: "Mrs. Take It Easy, something hurts?"

"Nothing. . . . Only you."

"A woman of honey. That's why you're lying down?"

"Soon I'll get up to do the dishes, Nancy."

"Leave them, Mother, I like it better this way."

"Mrs. Take It Easy, Paul says you should start ballet. You should go to see a doctor and ask: how soon can you start ballet?"

"A doctor?" she begged. "Ballet?"

"We were talking, Ma," explained Paul, "you don't seem any too well. It would be a good idea for you to see a doctor for a checkup."

"I get up now to do the kitchen. Doctors are bills and foolishness, my son. I need no doctors."

---

[11] Olshana—town in Russia.

[12] ravening—hunger.

[13] **succumb**—submit.

"At the Haven," he could not resist pointing out, "a doctor is *not* bills. He lives beside you. You start to sneeze, he is there before you open up a Kleenex. You can be sick there for free, all you want."

"Diarrhea of the mouth, is there a doctor to make you dumb?"

"Ma. Promise me you'll go. Nancy will arrange it."

"It's all of a piece when you think of it," said Nancy, "the way she attacks my kitchen, scrubbing under every cup hook, doing the inside of the oven so I can't enjoy Sunday dinner, knowing that half-blind or not, she's going to find every speck of dirt. . . ."

"Don't, Nancy, I've told you—it's the only way she knows to be useful. What did the *doctor* say?"

"A real fatherly lecture. Sixty-nine is young these days. Go out, enjoy life, find interests. Get a new hearing aid, this one is antiquated. Old age is sickness only if one makes it so. Geriatrics,[14] Inc."

"So there was nothing physical."

"Of course there was. How can you live to yourself like she does without there being? Evidence of a kidney disorder, and her blood count is low. He gave her a diet, and she's to come back for follow-up and lab work. . . . But he was clear enough: Number One prescription—start living like a human being. . . . When I think of your dad, who could really play the invalid with that arthritis of his, as active as a teenager, and twice as much fun. . . ."

"You didn't tell me the doctor says your sickness is in you, how you live." He pushed his advantage. "Life and enjoyments you need better than medicine. And this diet, how can you keep it? To weigh each morsel and scrape away each bit of fat, to make this soup, that pudding. There, at the Haven, they have a dietician, they would do it for you."

She is silent.

"You would feel better there, I know it," he says gently. "There there is life and enjoyments all around."

"What is the matter, Mr. Importantbusy, you have no card game or meeting you can go to?"—turning her face to the pillow.

For a while he cut his meetings and going out, fussed over her diet, tried to wheedle her into leaving the house, brought in visitors:

"I should come to a fashion tea. I should sit and look at pretty babies in clothes I cannot buy. This is pleasure?"

"Always you are better than everyone else. The doctor said you should go out. Mrs. Brem comes to you with goodness and you turn her away."

"Because *you* asked her to, she asked me."

"They won't come back. People you need, the doctor said. Your own cousins I asked; they were willing to come and make peace as if nothing had happened. . . ."

[14] Geriatrics—branch of medicine dealing with the health problems of the aged.

"No more crushers of people, pushers, hypocrites, around me. No more in *my* house. You go to them if you like."

"Kind he is to visit. And you, like ice."

"A babbler. All my life around babblers. Enough!"

"She's even worse, Dad? Then let her stew a while," advised Nancy. "You can't let it destroy you; it's a psychological thing, maybe too far gone for any of us to help."

After him she sobbed curses he had not heard in years, old-country curses from their childhood.

So he let her stew. More and more she lay silent in bed, and sometimes did not even get up to make the meals. No longer was the tongue-lashing **inevitable**[15] if he left the coffee cup where it did not belong, or forgot to take out the garbage or mislaid the broom. The birds grew bold that summer and for once pocked the pears, undisturbed.

A bellyful of bitterness and every day the same quarrel in a new way and a different old grievance the quarrel forced her to enter and relive. And the new torment: I am not really sick, the doctor said it, then why do I feel so sick?

One night she asked him: "You have a meeting tonight? Do not go. Stay . . . with me."

He had planned to watch "This Is Your Life," but half sick himself from the heavy heat, and sickening therefore the more after the brooks and woods of the Haven, with satisfaction he grated:

"Hah, Mrs. Live Alone And Like It wants company all of a sudden. It doesn't seem so good the time of solitary when she was a girl exile in Siberia.[16] 'Do not go. Stay with me.' A new song for Mrs. Free As A Bird. Yes, I am going out, and while I am gone chew this aloneness good, and think how you keep us both from where if you want people, you do not need to be alone."

"Go, go. All your life you have gone without me."

After him she sobbed curses he had not heard in years, old-country curses from their childhood: Grow, oh shall you grow like an onion, with your head in the ground. Like the hide of a drum shall you be, beaten in life, beaten in death. Oh shall you be like a chandelier, to hang, and to burn. . . .

She was not in their bed when he came back. She lay on the cot on the sun porch. All week she did not speak or come near him; nor did he try to make peace or care for her.

He slept badly, so used to her next to him. After all the years, old harmonies and dependencies deep in their bodies; she curled to him, or he coiled to her, each warmed, warming, turning as the other turned, the nights a long embrace.

It was not the empty bed or the storm that woke him, but a faint singing. *She* was singing. Shaking off the drops of rain, the

---

[15] **inevitable**—unavoidable.

[16] Siberia—region of Russia that stretches from the Ural Mountains to the Pacific Ocean. It is where the Russian government sent prisoners.

lightning riving[17] her lifted face, he saw her so; the cot covers on the floor.

"This is a private concert?" he asked. "Come in, you are wet."

"I can breathe now," she answered; "my lungs are rich." Though indeed the sound was hardly a breath.

"Come in, come in." Loosing the bamboo shades. "Look how wet you are." Half helping, half carrying her, still faint-breathing her song.

A Russian love song of fifty years ago.

He had found a buyer, but before he told her, he called together those children who were close enough to come. Paul, of course, Sammy from New Jersey, Hannah from Connecticut, Vivi from Ohio.

With a kindling of energy for her beloved visitors, she arrayed the house, cooked and baked. She was not prepared for the solemn after-dinner **conclave**,[18] they too probing in and tearing. Her frightened eyes watched from mouth to mouth as each spoke.

His stories were eloquent and funny of her refusal to go back to the doctor; of the scorned invitations; of her stubborn silence or the **bile**[19] "like a Niagara"; of her contrariness: "If I clean it's no good how I cleaned; if I don't clean, I'm still a master who thinks he has a slave."

(Vinegar he poured on me all his life; I am well marinated; how can I be honey now?)

Deftly he marched in the rightness for moving to the Haven; their money from social security free for visiting the children, not sucked into daily needs and into the house; the activities in the Haven for him; but mostly the Haven for *her:* her health, her need of care, distraction, amusement, friends who shared her interests.

"This does offer an outlet for Dad," said Paul; "he's always been an active person. And economic peace of mind isn't to be sneezed at, either. I could use a little of that myself."

But when they asked: "And you, Ma, how do you feel about it?" could only whisper:

"For him it is good. It is not for me. I can no longer live between people."

"You lived all your life *for* people," Vivi cried.

"Not with." Suffering doubly for the unhappiness on her children's faces.

"You have to find some compromise," Sammy insisted. "Maybe sell the house and buy a trailer. After forty-seven years there's surely some way you can find to live in peace."

"There is no help, my children. Different things we need."

"Then live alone!" he could control himself no longer. "I have a buyer for the house. Half the money for you, half for me. Either alone or with me to the Haven. You think I can live any longer as we are doing now?"

"Ma doesn't have to make a decision this minute, however you feel, Dad," Paul said quickly, "and you wouldn't want her to. Let's let it lay a few months, and then talk some more."

---

17 riving—splitting.

18 **conclave**—meeting.

19 **bile**—bitterness.

"I think I can work it out to take Mother home with me for a while," Hannah said. "You both look terrible, but especially you, Mother. I'm going to ask Phil to have a look at you."

"Sure," cracked Sammy. "What's the use of a doctor husband if you can't get free service out of him once in a while for the family? And absence might make the heart . . . you know."

"There was something after all," Paul told Nancy in a colorless voice. "That was Hannah's Phil calling. Her gall bladder. . . . Surgery."

"Her *gall* bladder. If that isn't classic. 'Bitter as gall'—talk of psychosom[20]——"

He stepped closer, put his hand over her mouth, and said in the same colorless, plodding voice. "We have to get Dad. They operated at once. The cancer was everywhere, surrounding the liver, everywhere. They did what they could . . . at best she has a year. Dad . . . we have to tell him."

II

Honest in his weakness when they told him, and that she was not to know. "I'm not an actor. She'll know right away by how I am. Oh that poor woman. I am old too, it will break me into pieces. Oh that poor woman. She will spit on me: 'So my sickness was how I live.' Oh Paulie, how she will be, that poor woman. Only she should not suffer. . . . I can't stand sickness, Paulie, I can't go with you."

But went. And play-acted.

"A grand opening and you did not even wait for me. . . . A good thing Hannah took you with her."

"Fashion teas I needed. They cut out what tore in me; just in my throat something hurts yet. . . . Look! so many flowers, like a funeral. Vivi called, did Hannah tell you? And Lennie from San Francisco, and Clara; and Sammy is coming." Her gnome's[21] face pressed happily into the flowers.

It is impossible to predict in these cases, but once over the immediate effects of the operation, she should have several months of comparative well-being.

The money, where will come the money?

Travel with her, Dad. Don't take her home to the old associations. The other children will want to see her.

The money, where will I wring the money?

Whatever happens, she is not to know. No, you can't ask her to sign papers to sell the house; nothing to upset her. Borrow instead, then after. . . .

I had wanted to leave you each a few dollars to make life easier, as other fathers do. There will be nothing left now. (Failure! you and your "business is exploitation." Why didn't you make it when it could be made?—Is that what you're thinking, Sammy?)

Sure she's unreasonable, Dad—but you have to stay with her; if there's to be any happiness in what's left of her life, it depends on you.

---

[20] psychosom—psychosomatic, relating to a physical disorder with a mental or emotional cause.

[21] gnome's—dwarflike.

Prop me up, children, think of me, too.
Shuffled, chained with her, bitter woman.
No Haven, and the little money going. . . .
How happy she looks, poor creature.

The look of excitement. The straining to hear everything (the new hearing aid turned full). Why are you so happy, dying woman?

How the petals are, fold on fold, and the gladioli color. The autumn air.

Stranger grandsons, tall above the little gnome grandmother, the little spry grandfather. Paul in a frenzy of picture-taking before going.

She, wandering the great house. Feeling the books; laughing at the maple shoemaker's bench of a hundred years ago used as a table. The ear turned to music.

"Let us go home. See how good I walk now." "One step from the hospital," he answers, "and she wants to fly. Wait till Doctor Phil says."

"Look—the birds too are flying home. Very good Phil is and will not show it, but he is sick of sickness by the time he comes home."

"Mrs. Telepathy, to read minds," he answers; "read mine what it says: when the trunks of medicines become a suitcase, then we will go."

The grandboys, they do not know what to say to us. . . . Hannah, she runs around here, there, when is there time for herself?

Let us go home. Let us go home.

Musing; gentleness—*but for the incidents of the rabbi*[22] *in the hospital, and of the candles of benediction.*

Of the rabbi in the hospital:

Now tell me what happened, Mother.

From the sleep I awoke, Hannah's Phil, and he stands there like a devil in a dream and calls me by name. I cannot hear. I think he prays. Go away, please, I tell him, I am not a believer. Still he stands, while my heart knocks with fright.

You scared *him,* Mother. He thought you were delirious.

Who sent him? Why did he come to me?

It is a custom. The men of God come to visit those of their religion they might help. The hospital makes up the list for them—race, religion—and you are on the Jewish list.

Not for rabbis. At once go and make them change. Tell them to write: Race, human; Religion, none.

And of the candles of benediction:

Look how you have upset yourself, Mrs. Excited Over Nothing. Pleasant memories you should leave.

Go in, go back to Hannah and the lights. Two weeks I saw candles and said nothing. But she asked me.

So what was so terrible? She forgets you never did, she asks you to light the Friday candles and say the benediction like Phil's mother when she visits. If the candles give her pleasure, why shouldn't she have the pleasure?

Not for pleasure she does it. For emptiness. Because his family does. Because all around her do.

---

[22] *rabbi*—ordained preacher and teacher of Jewish law and tradition.

That is not a good reason too? But you did not hear her. For heritage, she told you. For the boys, from the past they should have tradition.

Superstition! From the savages, afraid of the dark, of themselves: mumbo words and magic lights to scare away ghosts.

She told you: how it started does not take away the goodness. For centuries, peace in the house it means.

Swindler! does she look back on the dark centuries? Candles bought instead of bread and stuck into a potato for a candlestick? Religion that stifled and said: in Paradise, woman, you will be the footstool of your husband, and in life—poor chosen Jew—ground under, despised, trembling in cellars. And cremated. And cremated.

This is religion's fault? You think you are still an orator of the 1905 revolution?[23] Where are the pills for quieting? Which are they?

Heritage. How have we come from the savages, how no longer to be savages—this to teach. To look back and learn what humanizes man—this to teach. To smash all ghettos[24] that divide us—not to go back, not to go back—this to teach. Learned books in the house, will humankind live or die, and she gives to her boys—superstition.

Hannah that is so good to you. Take your pill, Mrs. Excited For Nothing, swallow.

Heritage! But when did I have time to teach? Of Hannah I asked only hands to help.

Swallow.

Otherwise—musing; gentleness.

Not to travel. To go home.

The children want to see you. We have to show them you are as thorny a flower as ever.

Not to travel.

Vivi wants you should see her new baby. She sent the tickets—airplane tickets—a Mrs. Roosevelt she wants to make of you. To Vivi's we have to go.

A new baby. How many warm, seductive babies. She holds him stiffly, *away* from her, so that he wails. And a long shudder begins, and the sweat beads on her forehead.

"Hush, shush," croons the grandfather, lifting him back. "You should forgive your grandmamma, little prince, she has never held a baby before, only seen them in glass cases. Hush, shush."

"You're tired, Ma," says Vivi. "The travel and the noisy dinner. I'll take you to lie down."

(A long travel from, to, what the feel of a baby evokes.)

In the airplane, cunningly designed to encase from motion (no wind, no feel of flight), she had sat severely and still, her face turned to the sky through which they **cleaved**[25] and left no scar.

So this was how it looked, the determining, the crucial sky, and this was how

---

[23] 1905 revolution—popular revolution in Russia that forced the repressive monarchy to make some concessions, but also led to a ruthless crackdown on revolutionary elements in Russia.

[24] ghettos—parts of European cities where Jews were required to live.

[25] **cleaved**—cut.

man moved through it, remote above the dwindled earth, the concealed human life. Vulnerable life, that could scar.

There was a steerage ship[26] of memory that shook across a great, circular sea: clustered, ill human beings; and through the thick-stained air, tiny fretting waters in a window round like the airplane's—sun round, moon round. (The round thatched roofs of Olshana.) Eye round—like the smaller window that framed distance the solitary year of exile when only her eyes could travel, and no voice spoke. And the polar winds hurled themselves across snows trackless and endless and white—like the clouds which had closed together below and hidden the earth.

Now they put a baby in her lap. Do not ask me, she would have liked to beg. Enough the worn face of Vivi, the remembered grandchildren. I cannot, cannot. . . .

Cannot what? Unnatural grandmother, not able to make herself embrace a baby.

She lay there in the bed of the two little girls, her new hearing aid turned full, listening to the sound of the children going to sleep, the baby's fretful crying and hushing, the clatter of dishes being washed and put away. They thought she slept. Still she rode on.

It was not that she had not loved her babies, her children. The love—the passion of tending—had risen with the need like a torrent; and like a torrent drowned and **immolated**[27] all else. But when the need was done—oh the power that was lost in the painful damming back and drying up of what still surged, but had nowhere to go. Only the thin pulsing left that could not quiet, suffering over lives one felt, but could no longer hold nor help.

On that torrent she had borne them to their own lives, and the riverbed was desert long years now. Not there would she dwell, a memoried wraith.[28] Surely that was not all, surely there was more. Still the springs, the springs were in her seeking. Somewhere an older power that beat for life. Somewhere coherence, transport, meaning. If they would but leave her in the air now stilled of clamor, in the reconciled solitude, to journey to her self.

And they put a baby in her lap. Immediacy to embrace, and the breath of *that* past: warm flesh like this that had claims and nuzzled away all else and with lovely mouths devoured; hot-living like an animal—intensely and now; the turning maze; the long drunkenness; the drowning into needing and being needed. Severely she looked back—and the shudder seized her again, and the sweat. Not that way. Not there, not now could she, not yet. . . .

And all that visit, she could not touch the baby.

"Daddy, is it the . . . sickness she's like that?" asked Vivi. "I was so glad to be having the baby—for her. I told Tim, it'll give her more happiness than anything, being around a baby again. And she hasn't played with him once."

He was not listening, "Aahh little seed of life, little charmer," he crooned,

[26] steerage ship—passenger ship offering very cheap accommodations.

[27] **immolated**—destroyed.

[28] wraith—ghost.

"Hollywood should see you. A heart of ice you would melt. Kick, kick. The future you'll have for a ball. In 2050 still kick. Kick for your grandaddy then."

Attentive with the older children; sat through their performances (command performance; we command you to be the audience); helped Ann sort autumn leaves to find the best for a school program; listened gravely to Richard tell about his rock collection, while her lips mutely formed the words to remember: *igneous, sedimentary, metamorphic;* looked for missing socks, books, and bus tickets; watched the children whoop after their grandfather who knew how to tickle, chuck, lift, toss, do tricks, tell secrets, make jokes, match riddle for riddle. (Tell me a riddle, Grammy. I know no riddles, child.) Scrubbed sills and woodwork and furniture in every room; folded the laundry; straightened drawers, emptied the heaped baskets waiting for ironing (while he or Vivi or Tim nagged: You're supposed to rest here, you've been sick) but to none tended or gave food—and could not touch the baby.

Tell me a riddle, Grammy. I know no riddles, child.

After a week she said: "Let us go home. Today call about the tickets."

"You have important business, Mrs. Inahurry? The President waits to consult with you?" He shouted, for the fear of the future raced in him. "The clothes are still warm from the suitcase, your children cannot show enough how glad they are to see you, and you want home. There is plenty of time for home. We cannot be with the children at home."

"Blind to around you as always: the little ones sleep four in a room because we take their bed. We are two more people in a house with a new baby, and no help."

"Vivi is happy so. The children should have their grandparents a while, she told to me. I should have my mommy and daddy. . . ."

"Babbler and blind. Do you look at her so tired? How she starts to talk and she cries? I am not strong enough yet to help. Let us go home."

(To reconciled solitude.)

For it seemed to her the crowded noisy house was listening to her, listening for *her. She could feel it like a great ear pressed under her heart. And everything knocked: quick constant raps: let me in, let me in.*

How was it that soft reaching tendrils also became blows that knocked?

C'mon, Grandma, I want to show you. . . .

Tell me a riddle, Grandma. *(I know no riddles.)*

Look, Grammy, he's so dumb he can't even find his hands. (Dody and the baby on a blanket over the fermenting autumn mould.)

I made them—for you. (Ann) (Flat paper dolls with aprons that lifted on scalloped skirts that lifted on flowered pants; hair of yarn and great ringed questioning eyes.)

Watch me, Grandma. (Richard snaking

up the tree, hanging exultant, free, with one hand at the top. Below Dody hunching over in pretend-cooking.) *(Climb too, Dody, climb and look.)*

Be my nap bed, Grammy. (The "No!" too late.) Morty's abandoned heaviness, while his fingers ladder up and down her hearing-aid cord to his drowsy chant: eentsiebeentsiespider. *(Children trust.)*

It's to start off your own rock collection, Grandma. That's a trilobite fossil, 200 million years old (millions of years on a boy's mouth) and that one's obsidian, black glass.

Knocked and knocked.

Mother, I *told* you the teacher said we had to bring it back all filled out this morning. Didn't you even ask Daddy? Then tell *me* which plan and I'll check it: evacuate or stay in the city or wait for you to come and take me away. (Seeing the look of straining to hear.) It's for Disaster, Grandma. *(Children trust.)*

Vivi in the maze of the long, the lovely drunkenness. The old old noises: baby sounds; screaming of a mother flayed to exasperation; children quarreling; children playing, singing; laughter.

And Vivi's tears and memories, spilling so fast, half the words not understood.

She had started remembering out loud deliberately, so her mother would know the past was cherished, still lived in her.

Nursing the baby: My friends marvel, and I tell them, oh it's easy to be such a cow. I remember how beautiful my mother seemed nursing my brother, and the milk just flows . . . . Was that Davy? It must have been Davy . . . .

Lowering a hem: How did you ever . . . when I think how you made everything we wore . . . Tim, just think, seven kids and Mommy sewed everything . . . do I remember you sang while you sewed? That white dress with the red apples on the skirt you fixed over for me, was it Hannah's or Clara's before it was mine?

Washing sweaters: Ma, I'll never forget, one of those days so nice you washed clothes outside; one of the first spring days it must have been. The bubbles just danced while you scrubbed, and we chased after, and you stopped to show us how to blow our own bubbles with green onion stalks . . . you always. . . .

"Strong onion, to still make you cry after so many years," her father said, to turn the tears into laughter.

While Richard bent over his homework: Where is it now, do we still have it, the Book of the Martyrs? It always seemed so, well—exalted, when you'd put it on the round table and we'd all look at it together; there was even a halo from the lamp. The lamp with the beaded fringe you could move up and down; they're in style again, pulley lamps like that, but without the fringe. You know the book I'm talking about, Daddy, the Book of the Martyrs, the first picture was a bust of Socrates?[29] I wish there was something like that for the children, Mommy, to give them what you. . . . (And the tears splashed again.)

(What I intended and did not? Stop it,

[29] Socrates—Greek philosopher (470?–399 B.C.), executed for his teachings.

(What I intended and did not? Stop it, daughter, stop it, leave that time. And he, the hyprocrite, sitting there with tears in his eyes—it was nothing to you then, nothing.)

. . . The time you came to school and I almost died of shame because of your accent and because I knew you knew I was ashamed; how could I? . . . Sammy's harmonica and you danced to it once, yes you did, you and Davy squealing in your arms. . . . That time you bundled us up and walked us down to the railway station to stay the night 'cause it was heated and we didn't have any coal, that winter of the strike, you didn't think I remembered that, did you, Mommy? . . . How you'd call us out to see the sunsets. . . .

Day after day, the spilling memories. Worse now, questions, too. Even the grandchildren: Grandma, in the olden days, when you were little. . . .

It was the afternoons that saved.

While they thought she napped, she would leave the mosaic on the wall (of children's drawings, maps, calendars, pictures, Ann's cardboard dolls with their great ringed questioning eyes) and hunch in the girls' closet on the low shelf where the shoes stood, and the girls' dresses covered.

For that while she would painfully sheathe against the listening house, the tendrils and noises that knocked, and Vivi's spilling memories. Sometimes it helped to braid and unbraid the sashes that dangled, or to trace the pattern on the hoop slips.

Today she had jacks and children under jet trails to forget. Last night, Ann and Dody silhouetted in the window against a sunset of flaming man-made clouds of jet trail, their jacks ball accenting the peaceful noise of dinner being made. Had she told them, yes she had told them of how they played jacks in her village though there was no ball, no jacks. Six stones, round and flat, toss them out, the seventh on the back of the hand, toss, catch and swoop up as many as possible, toss again. . . .

Of stones (repeating Richard) there are three kinds: earth's fire jetting; rock of layered centuries; crucibled[30] new out of the old *(igneous, sedimentary, metamorphic)*. But there was that other—frozen to black glass, never to transform or hold the fossil memory . . . (let not my seed fall on stone). There was an ancient man who fought to heights a great rock that crashed back down eternally—eternal labor, freedom, labor . . . (stone will perish, but the word remain). And you, David, who with a stone slew,[31] screaming: Lord, take my heart of stone and give me flesh.

Who was screaming? Why was she back in the common room of the prison, the sun motes dancing in the shafts of light, and the informer being brought in, a prisoner now, like themselves. And Lisa leaping, yes, Lisa, the gentle and tender, biting at the betrayer's jugular.[32] Screaming and screaming.

No, it is the children screaming. Another of Paul and Sammy's terrible fights?

In Vivi's house. Severely: you are in Vivi's house.

---

[30] crucibled—melted.

[31] David . . . slew—David, Israelite in the Bible who killed the giant Philistine warrior Goliath with a single stone.

[32] jugular—vein in the neck.

Blows, screams, a call: "Grandma!" For her? Oh please not for her. Hide, hunch behind the dresses deeper. But a trembling little body hurls itself beside her—surprised, smothered laughter, arms surround her neck, tears rub dry on her cheek, and words too soft to understand whisper into her ear (Is this where you hide too, Grammy? It's my secret place, we have a secret now).

And the sweat beads, and the long shudder seizes.

It seemed the great ear pressed inside now, and the knocking. "We have to go home," she told him, "I grow ill here."

"It's your own fault, Mrs. Bodybusy, you do not rest, you do too much." He raged, but the fear was in his eyes. "It was a serious operation, they told you to take care. . . . All right, we will go to where you can rest."

But where? Not home to death, not yet. He had thought to Lennie's, to Clara's; beautiful visits with each of the children. She would have to rest first, be stronger. If they could but go to Florida—it glittered before him, the never-realized promise of Florida. California: of course. (The money, the money, dwindling!) Los Angeles first for sun and rest, then to Lennie's in San Francisco.

He told her the next day. "You saw what Nancy wrote: snow and wind back home, a terrible winter. And look at you—all bones and a swollen belly. I called Phil: he said: 'A prescription, Los Angeles sun and rest.'"

She watched the words on his lips. "You have sold the house," she cried, "that is why we do not go home. That is why you talk no more of the Haven, why there is money for travel. After the children you will drag me to the Haven."

"The Haven! Who thinks of the Haven any more? Tell her, Vivi, tell Mrs. Suspicious: a prescription, sun and rest, to make you healthy. . . . And how could I sell the house without *you?*"

At the place of farewells and greetings, of winds of coming and winds of going, they say their good-byes.

They look back at her with the eyes of others before them: Richard with her own blue blaze; Ann with the nordic eyes of Tim; Morty's dreaming brown of a great-grandmother he will never know; Dody with the laughing eyes of him who had been her springtide love (who stands beside her now); Vivi's, all tears.

The baby's eyes are closed in sleep.

Good-bye, my children.

III

It is to the back of the great city he brought her, to the dwelling places of the cast-off old. Bounded by two lines of amusement piers to the north and to the south, and between a long straight paving rimmed with black benches facing the sand—sands so wide the ocean is only a far fluting.[33]

In the brief vacation season, some of the boarded stores fronting the sands open,

[33] fluting—architectural ornament consisting of a series of uniform lines.

and families, young people and children, may be seen. A little tasseled tram shuttles between the piers, and the lights of roller coasters prink[34] and tweak over those who come to have sensation made in them.

The rest of the year it is abandoned to the old, all else boarded up and still; seemingly empty, except the occasional days and hours when the sun, like a tide, sucks them out of the low rooming houses, casts them onto the benches and sandy rim of the walk—and sweeps them into decaying enclosures once again.

A few newer apartments glint among the low bleached squares. It is in one of these Lennie's Jeannie has arranged their rooms. "Only a few miles north and south people pay hundreds of dollars a month for just this gorgeous air, Grandaddy, just this ocean closeness."

She had been ill on the plane, lay ill for days in the unfamiliar room. Several times the doctor came by—left medicine she would not take. Several times Jeannie drove in the twenty miles from work, still in her Visiting Nurse uniform, the lightness and brightness of her like a healing.

"Who can believe it is winter?" he asked one morning. "Beautiful it is outside like an ad. Come, Mrs. Invalid, come to taste it. You are well enough to sit in here, you are well enough to sit outside. The doctor said it too."

But the benches were encrusted with people, and the sands at the sidewalk's edge. Besides, she had seen the far ruffle of the sea: "there take me," and though she leaned against him, it was she who led.

Plodding and plodding, sitting often to rest, he grumbling. Patting the sand so warm. Once she scooped up a handful, cradling it close to her better eye; peered, and flung it back. And as they came almost to the brink and she could see the glistening wet, she sat down, pulled off her shoes and stockings, left him and began to run. "You'll catch cold," he screamed, but the sand in his shoes weighed him down—he who had always been the agile one—and already the white spray creamed her feet.

He pulled her back, took a handkerchief to wipe off the wet and the sand. "Oh no," she said, "the sun will dry," seized the square and smoothed it flat, dropped on it a mound of sand, knotted the kerchief corners and tied it to a bag—"to look at with the strong glass" (for the first time in years explaining an action of hers)—and lay down with the little bag against her cheek, looking toward the shore that nurtured life as it first crawled toward consciousness the millions of years ago.

He took her one Sunday in the evil-smelling bus, past flat miles of blister houses, to the home of relatives. Oh what is this? she cried as the light began to smoke and the houses to dim and recede. Smog, he said, everyone knows but you. . . . Outside he kept his arms about her, but she walked with hands pushing the heavy air as if to open it, whispered: who has done this? sat down suddenly to vomit at the curb and for a long while refused to rise.

---

[34] prink—adorn in a showy manner.

One's age as seen on the altered face of those known in youth. Is this they he has come to visit? This Max and Rose, smooth and pleasant, introducing them to polite children, disinterested grandchildren, "the whole family, once a month on Sundays. And why not? We have the room, the help, the food."

Talk of cars, of houses, of success: this son that, that daughter this. And *your* children? Hastily skimped over, the intermarriages, the obscure work—"my doctor son-in-law, Phil"—all he has to offer. She silent in a corner. (Car-sick like a baby, he explains.) Years since he has taken her to visit anyone but the children, and old apprehensions prickle: "no incidents," he silently begs, "no incidents." He itched to tell them. "A very sick woman," significantly, indicating her with his eyes, "a very sick woman." Their restricted faces did not react. "Have you thought maybe she'd do better at Palm Springs?" Rose asked. "Or at least a nicer section of the beach, nicer people, a pool." Not to have to say "money" he said instead: "would she have sand to look at through a magnifying glass?" and went on, detail after detail, the old habit betraying of parading the queerness of her for laughter.

After dinner—the others into the living room in men- or women-clusters, or into the den to watch TV—the four of them alone. She sat close to him, and did not speak. Jokes, stories, people they had known, beginning of reminiscence, Russia fifty-sixty years ago. Strange words across the Duncan Phyfe[35] table: *hunger; secret meetings; human rights; spies; betrayals; prison; escape*—interrupted by one of the grandchildren: "Commercial's on; any Coke left? Gee, you're missing a real hair-raiser." And then a granddaughter (Max proudly: "look at her, an American queen") drove them home on her way back to U.C.L.A. No incident—except that there had been no incidents.

The first few mornings she had taken with her the magnifying glass, but he would sit only on the benches, so she rested at the foot, where slatted bench shadows fell, and unless she turned her hearing aid down, other voices invaded.

Now on the days when the sun shone and she felt well enough, he took her on the tram to where the benches ranged in oblongs, some with tables for checkers or cards. Again the blanket on the sand in the striped shadows, but she no longer brought the magnifying glass. He played cards, and she lay in the sun and looked towards the waters; or they walked—two blocks down to the scaling hotel, two blocks back—past chili-hamburger stands, open-doored bars, Next-to-New and Perpetual Rummage Sale stores.

Once, out of the aimless walkers, slow and shuffling like themselves, someone ran unevenly towards them, embraced, kissed, wept: "dear friends, old friends." A friend of *hers,* not his: Mrs. Mays who had lived next door to them in Denver when the children were small.

Thirty years are compressed into a dozen sentences; and the present, not even

[35] Duncan Phyfe—Scottish-born American cabinet maker (1768–1854), whose furniture designs were very influential.

in three. All is told: the children scattered; the husband dead; she lives in a room two blocks up from the sing hall—and points to the domed auditorium jutting before the pier. The leg? phlebitis;[36] the heavy breathing? that, one does not ask. She, too, comes to the benches each day to sit. And tomorrow, tomorrow, are they going to the community sing? Of course he would have heard of it, everybody goes—the big doings they wait for all week. They have never been? She will come to them for dinner tomorrow and they will all go together.

So it is that she sits in the wind of the singing, among the thousand various faces of age.

She had turned off her hearing aid at once they came into the auditorium—as she would have wished to turn off sight.

One by one they streamed by and imprinted on her—and though the savage zest of their singing came voicelessly soft and distant, the faces still roared—the faces densened the air—chorded into children-chants, mother-croons, singing of the chained love serenades, Beethoven[37] storms, mad Lucia's scream[38] drunken joy-songs, keens for the dead, work-singing

while from floor to balcony to dome a
bare-footed sore-covered little girl
threaded the sound-thronged tumult,
danced her ecstasy of grimace to flutes
that scratched at a cross-roads
village wedding

Yes, faces became sound, and the sound became faces; and faces and sound became weight—pushed, pressed

"Air" —her hands claw his.

"Whenever I enjoy myself. . . ." Then he saw the gray sweat on her face. "Here. Up. Help me, Mrs. Mays," and they support her out to where she can gulp the air in sob after sob.

"A doctor, we should get for her a doctor."

"Tch, it's nothing," says Ellen Mays, "I get it all the time. You've missed the tram; come to my place. Fix your hearing aid, honey . . . close . . . tea. My view. See, she *wants* to come. Steady now, that's how." Adding mysteriously: "Remember your advice, easy to keep your head above water, empty things float. Float."

The singing a fading march for them, tall woman with a swollen leg, weaving little man, and the swollen thinness they help between.

The stench in the hall: mildew? decay? "We sit and rest then climb. My gorgeous view. We help each other and here we are."

The stench along into the slab of room. A washstand for a sink, a box with oilcloth tacked around for a cupboard, a three-burner gas plate. Artificial flowers, colorless with dust. Everywhere pictures foaming: wedding, baby, party, vacation, graduation, family pictures. From the narrow couch under a slit of window, sure enough the view: lurching rooftops

---

36 phlebitis—inflammation of a vein.

37 Beethoven—Ludwig van Beethoven (1770–1827), German composer.

38 Lucia's scream—reference to the opera *Lucia di Lammermoor* by Italian composer Gaetano Donizetti (1797–1848). In the last act, Lucia has gone mad and delivers a terrifying scream.

and a scallop of ocean heaving, preening, twitching under the moon.

"While the water heats. Excuse me . . . down the hall." Ellen Mays has gone.

"You'll live?" he asks mechanically, sat down to feel his fright; tried to pull her alongside.

She pushed him away. "For air," she said; stood clinging to the dresser. Then, in a terrible voice:

After a lifetime of room: Of many rooms.

Shhh.

You remember how she lived. Eight children. And now one room like a coffin.

She pays rent!

Shrinking the life of her into one room like a coffin Rooms and rooms like this I lie on the quilt and hear them talk

Please, Mrs. Orator-without-Breath.

Once you went for coffee I walked I saw A Balzac[39] a Chekhov to write it Rummage Alone On scraps

Better old here than in the old country!

On scraps Yet they sang like like Wondrous! *Humankind one has to believe* So strong for what? To rot not grow?

Your poor lungs beg you. They sob between each word.

Singing. Unused the life in them. She in this poor room with her pictures Max You The children Everywhere unused the life And who has meaning? Century after century still all in us not to grow?

Coffins, rummage, plants: sick woman. Oh lay down. We will get for you the doctor.

"And when will it end. Oh, *the end.*" *That* nightmare thought, and this time she writhed, crumpled against him, seized his hand (for a moment again the weight, the soft distant roaring of humanity) and on the strangled-for breath, begged: "Man . . . we'll destroy ourselves?"

You remember how she lived. Eight children. And now one room like a coffin.

And looking for answer—in the helpless pity and fear for her (for *her*) that distorted his face—she understood the last months, and knew that she was dying.

IV

"Let us go home," she said after several days.

"You are in training for a cross-country trip? That is why you do not even walk across the room? Here, like a prescription Phil said, till you are stronger from the operation. You want to break doctor's orders?"

She saw the fiction was necessary to him, was silent; then: "At home I will get better. If the doctor here says?"

"And winter? And the visits to Lennie and to Clara? All right," for he saw the tears in her eyes, "I will write Phil, and talk to the doctor."

Days passed. He reported nothing. Jeannie came and took her out for air, past the boarded concessions, the hooded and tented amusement rides, to the end of the pier. They watched the spent waves feeding the new, the gulls in the clouded

[39] Balzac—Honoré de Balzac (1799–1850), French novelist.

sky; even up where they sat, the wind-blown sand stung.

She did not ask to go down the crooked steps to the sea.

Back in her bed, while he was gone to the store, she said: "Jeannie, this doctor, he is not one I can ask questions. Ask him for me, can I go home?"

Jeannie looked at her, said quickly: "Of course, poor Granny. You want your own things around you, don't you? I'll call him tonight. . . . Look, I've something to show you," and from her purse unwrapped a large cookie, intricately shaped like a little girl. "Look at the curls—can you hear me well, Granny?—and the darling eyelashes. I just came from a house where they were baking them."

"The dimples, there in the knees," she marveled, holding it to the better light, turning, studying, "like art. Each singly they cut, or a mold?"

"Singly," said Jeannie, "and if it is a child only the mother can make them. Oh Granny, it's the likeness of a real little girl who died yesterday—Rosita. She was three years old. *Pan del Muerto,* the Bread of the Dead. It was the custom in the part of Mexico they came from."

Still she turned and inspected. "Look, the hollow in the throat, the little cross necklace. . . . I think for the mother it is a good thing to be busy with such bread. You know the family?"

Jeannie nodded. "On my rounds. I nursed. . . . Oh Granny, it is like a party; they play songs she liked to dance to. The coffin is lined with pink velvet and she wears a white dress. There are candles. . . ."

"In the house?" Surprised, "They keep her in the house?"

"Yes," said Jeannie, "and it is against the health law. I think she is . . . prepared there. The father said it will be sad to bury her in this country; in Oaxaca[40] they have a feast night with candles each year; everyone picnics on the graves of those they loved until dawn."

"Yes, Jeannie, the living must comfort themselves." And closed her eyes.

"You want to sleep, Granny?"

"Yes, tired from the pleasure of you. I may keep the Rosita? There stand it, on the dresser, where I can see; something of my own around me."

In the kitchenette, helping her grandfather unpack the groceries, Jeannie said in her light voice:

"I'm resigning my job, Grandaddy."

"Ah, the lucky young man. Which one is he?"

"Too late. You're spoken for." She made a pyramid of cans, unstacked, and built again.

"Something is wrong with the job?"

"With me. I can't be—" she searched for the word— "What they call professional enough. I let myself feel things. And tomorrow I have to report a family. . . ." The cans clicked again. "It's not that, either. I just don't know what I want to do, maybe go back to school, maybe go to art school. I thought if you went to San Francisco I'd come along and talk it over

---

[40] Oaxaca—city in southeast Mexico.

with Momma and Daddy. But I don't see how you can go. She wants to go home. She asked me to ask the doctor."

The doctor told her himself. "Next week you may travel, when you are a little stronger." But next week there was the fever of an infection, and by the time that was over, she could not leave the bed—a rented hospital bed that stood beside the double bed he slept in alone now.

Outwardly the days repeated themselves. Every other afternoon and evening he went out to his newfound cronies, to talk and play cards. Twice a week, Mrs. Mays came. And the rest of the time, Jeannie was there.

By the sickbed stood Jeannie's FM radio. Often into the room the shapes of music came. She would lie curled on her side, her knees drawn up, intense in listening (Jeannie sketched her so, coiled, convoluted like an ear), then thresh her hand out and abruptly snap the radio mute—still to lie in her attitude of listening, concealing tears.

Once Jeannie brought in a young Marine to visit, a friend from high-school days she had found wandering near the empty pier. Because Jeannie asked him to, gravely, without self-consciousness, he sat himself cross-legged on the floor and performed for them a dance of his native Samoa.

Long after they left, a tiny thrumming sound could be heard where, in her bed, she strove to repeat the beckon, flight, surrender of his hands, the fluttering footbeats, and his low plaintive[41] calls.

Hannah and Phil sent flowers. To deepen her pleasure, he placed one in her hair. "Like a girl," he said, and brought the hand mirror so she could see. She looked at the pulsing red flower, the yellow skull face; a desolate, excited laugh shuddered from her, and she pushed the mirror away—but let the flower burn.

The week Lennie and Helen came, the fever returned. With it the excited laugh, and incessant words. She, who in her life had spoken but seldom and then only when necessary (never having learned the easy, social uses of words), now in dying, spoke incessantly.

In a half-whisper: "Like Lisa she is, your Jeannie. Have I told you of Lisa who taught me to read? Of the highborn she was, but noble in herself. I was sixteen; they beat me; my father beat me so I would not go to her. It was forbidden, she was a Tolstoyan.[42] At night, past dogs that howled, terrible dogs, my son, in the snows of winter to the road, I to ride in her carriage like a lady, to books. To her, life was holy, knowledge was holy, and she taught me to read. They hung her. Everything that happens one must try to understand why. She killed one who betrayed many. Because of betrayal, betrayed all she lived and believed. In one minute she killed, before my eyes (there is so much blood in a human being, my son), in prison with me. All that happens, one must try to understand.

[41] plaintive—mournful.

[42] Tolstoyan—follower of the ideas of Russian writer Leo Tolstoy (1828–1910), who believed in equality, non-violence, simplicity of life, and universal education.

"The name?" Her lips would work. "The name that was their pole star; the doors of the death houses fixed to open on it; I read of it my year of penal servitude. Thuban!"[43] very excited, "Thuban, in ancient Egypt the pole star. Can you see, look out to see it, Jeannie, if it swings around *our* pole star that seems to *us* not to move.

"Yes, Jeannie, at your age my mother and grandmother had already buried children . . . yes, Jeannie, it is more than oceans between Olshana and you . . . yes, Jeannie, they danced, and for all the bodies they had they might as well be chickens, and indeed, they scratched and flapped their arms and hopped.

"And Andrei Yefimitch, who for twenty years had never known of it and never wanted to know, said as if he wanted to cry: but why my dear friend this malicious laughter?" Telling to herself half-memorized phrases from her few books. "Pain I answer with tears and cries, baseness with indignation, meanness with repulsion . . . for life may be hated or wearied of, but never despised."

Delirious: "Tell me, my neighbor, Mrs. Mays, the pictures never lived, but what of the flowers? Tell them who ask: no rabbis, no ministers, no priests, no speeches, no ceremonies: ah, false—let the living comfort themselves. Tell Sammy's boy, he who flies, tell him to go to Stuttgart[44] and see where Davy has no grave. And what?" A conspirator's laugh. "And what? where millions have no graves—save air."

In delirium or not, wanting the radio on; not seeming to listen, the words still jetting, wanting the music on. Once, silencing it abruptly as of old, she began to cry, unconcealed tears this time. "You have pain, Granny?" Jeannie asked.

"The music," she said, "still it is there and we do not hear; knocks, and our poor human ears too weak. What else, what else we do not hear?"

Once she knocked his hand aside as he gave her a pill, swept the bottles from her bedside table: "no pills, let me feel what I feel," and laughed as on his hands and knees he groped to pick them up.

Nighttimes her hand reached across the bed to hold his.

A constant retching began. Her breath was too faint for sustained speech now, but still the lips moved:

When no longer necessary to injure others
Pick pick pick Blind chicken
As a human being responsibility

"David!" imperious, "Basin!" and she would vomit, rinse her mouth, the wasted throat working to swallow, and begin the chant again.

She will be better off in the hospital now, the doctor said.

He sent the telegrams to the children, was packing her suitcase, when her hoarse voice startled. She had roused, was pulling herself to sitting.

"Where now?" she asked. "Where now do you drag me?"

---

[43] Thuban—constellation of stars more commonly known as Draconis.

[44] Stuttgart—city in southwest Germany.

You do not even have to have a baby to go this time," he soothed, looking for the brush to pack. "Remember, after Davy you told me—worthy to have a baby for the pleasure of the hospital?"

"Where now? Not home yet?" Her voice mourned. "Where *is* my home?"

He rose to ease her back. "The doctor, the hospital," he started to explain, but deftly, like a snake, she had slithered out of bed and stood swaying, propped behind the night table.

"Coward," she hissed, "runner."

"You stand," he said senselessly.

"To take me there and run. Afraid of a little vomit."

He reached her as she fell. She struggled against him, half slipped from his arms, pulled herself up again.

"Weakling," she taunted, "to leave me there and run. Betrayer. All your life you have run."

He sobbed, telling Jeannie. "A Marilyn Monroe to run for her virtue. Fifty-nine pounds she weighs, the doctor said, and she beats at me like a Dempsey.[45] Betrayer, she cries, and I running like a dog when she calls; day and night, running to her, her vomit, the bedpan. . . ."

"She needs you, Grandaddy," said Jeannie. "Isn't that what they call love? I'll see if she sleeps, and if she does, poor worn-out darling, we'll have a party, you and I: I brought us rum babas."

They did not move her. By her bed now stood the tall hooked pillar that held the solutions—blood and dextrose—to feed her veins. Jeannie moved down the hall to take over the sickroom, her face so radiant, her grandfather asked her once: "you are in love?" (Shameful the joy, the pure overwhelming joy from being with her grandmother; the peace, the serenity that breathed.) "My darling escape," she answered incoherently, "my darling Granny"—as if that explained.

Now one by one the children came, those that were able. Hannah, Paul, Sammy. Too late to ask: and what did you learn with your living, Mother, and what do we need to know?

Clara, the eldest, clenched:

Pay me back, Mother, pay me back for all you took from me. Those others you crowded into your heart. The hands I needed to be for you, the heaviness, the responsibility.

Is this she? Noises the dying make, the crablike hands crawling over the covers. The ethereal singing.

She hears that music, that singing from childhood; forgotten sound—not heard since, since. . . . And the hardness breaks like a cry: Where did we lose each other, first mother, singing mother?

Annulled: the quarrels, the gibing, the harshness between; the fall into silence and the withdrawal.

I do not know you, Mother. Mother, I never knew you.

Lennie, suffering not alone for her who was dying, but for that in her which never

[45] Dempsey—Jack Dempsey (1895–1983), heavyweight boxing champion from 1919 to 1926.

lived (for that which in him might never live). From him too, unspoken words: *good-bye Mother who taught me to mother myself.*

Not Vivi, who must stay with her children; not Davy, but he is already here, having to die again with *her* this time, for the living take their dead with them when they die.

Light she grew, like a bird, and, like a bird, sound bubbled in her throat while the body fluttered in agony. Night and day, asleep or awake (though indeed there was no difference now) the songs and the phrases leaping.

And he, who had once dreaded a long dying (from fear of himself, from horror of the dwindling money) now desired her quick death profoundly, for *her* sake. He no longer went out, except when Jeannie forced him; no longer laughed, except when, in the bright kitchenette, Jeannie coaxed his laughter (and she, who seemed to hear nothing else, would laugh too, conspiratorial wisps of laughter).

Light, like a bird, the fluttering body, the little claw hands, the beaked shadow on her face; and the throat, bubbling, straining.

He tried not to listen, as he tried not to look on the face in which only the forehead remained familiar, but trapped with her the long nights in that little room, the sounds worked themselves into his consciousness, with their punctuation of death swallows, whimpers, gurglings.

Even in reality (swallow) *life's lack of it*

Slaveships deathtrains clubs eeenough

The bell summons what enables

78,000 in one minute (whisper of a scream) *78,000 human beings we'll destroy ourselves?*

"Aah, Mrs. Miserable," he said, as if she could hear, "all your life working, and now in bed you lie, servants to tend, you do not even need to call to be tended, and still you work. Such hard work it is to die? Such hard work?"

The body threshed, her hand clung in his. A melody, ghost-thin, hovered on her lips, and like a guilty ghost, the vision of her bent in listening to it, silencing the record instantly he was near. Now, heedless of his presence, she floated the melody on and on.

"Hid it from me," he complained, "how many times you listened to remember it so?" And tried to think when she had first played it, or first begun to silence her few records when he came near—but could reconstruct nothing. There was only this room with its tall hooked pillar and its swarm of sounds.

No man one except through others

Strong with the not yet in the now

Dogma dead war dead one country

"It helps, Mrs. Philosopher, words from books? It helps?" And it seemed to him that for seventy years she had hidden a tape recorder, infinitely microscopic, within her, that it had coiled infinite mile on mile, trapping every song, every melody, every word read, heard, and spoken—and that maliciously she was playing back only what said nothing of him, of the children, of their intimate life together.

"Left us indeed, Mrs. Babbler," he reproached, "you who called others babbler and cunningly saved your words. A lifetime you tended and loved, and now not a word of us, for us. Left us indeed? Left me."

And he took out his solitaire deck, shuffled the cards loudly, slapped them down.

Lift high banner of reason (tatter of an orator's voice) *justice freedom light*
Humankind life worthy capacities
Seeks (blur of shudder) *belong*
human being

"Words, words," he accused, "and what human beings did you seek around you, Mrs. Live Alone, and what humankind think worthy?"

Though even as he spoke, he remembered she had not always been isolated, had not always wanted to be alone (as he knew there had been a voice before this **gossamer**[46] one; before the hoarse voice that broke from silence to lash, make incidents, shame him—a girl's voice of eloquence that spoke their holiest dreams). But again he could reconstruct, image, nothing of what had been before, or when, or how, it had changed.

Ace, queen, jack. The pillar shadow fell, so, in two tracks; in the mirror depths glistened a moonlike blob, the empty solution bottle. And it worked in him: *of reason and justice and freedom . . . Dogma dead:* he remembered the full quotation, laughed bitterly. "Hah, good you do not know what you say; good Victor Hugo[47] died and did not see it, his twentieth century."

Deuce, ten, five. Dauntlessly she began a song of their youth of belief:

These things shall be, a loftier race
than e'er the world hath known shall rise
with flame of freedom in their souls
and light of knowledge in their eyes

King, four, jack "In the twentieth century, hah!"

They shall be gentle, brave and strong
to spill no drop of blood, but dare
earth and fire and sea and air

"To spill no drop of blood, hah! So, cadaver,[48] and you too, cadaver Hugo, 'in the twentieth century ignorance will be dead, dogma will be dead, war will be dead, and for all mankind one country—of fulfilment?' Hah!"

And every life (long strangling cough)
shall
be a song

The cards fell from his fingers. Without warning, the bereavement and betrayal he had sheltered—compounded through the years—hidden even from himself—revealed itself,
uncoiled,
released,
sprung

and with it the monstrous shapes of what had actually happened in the century.

---

[46] **gossamer**—delicate, light, flimsy.

[47] Victor Hugo—French writer (1802–1885).

[48] cadaver—corpse.

A ravening hunger or thirst seized him. He groped into the kitchenette, switched on all three lights, piled a tray—"you have finished your night snack, Mrs. Cadaver, now I will have mine." And he was shocked at the tears that splashed on the tray.

"Salt tears. For free. I forgot to shake on salt?"

Whispered: "Lost, how much I lost."

Escaped to the grandchildren whose childhoods were childish, who had never hungered, who lived unravaged by disease in warm houses of many rooms, had all the school for which they cared, could walk on any street, stood a head taller than their grandparents, towered above—beautiful skins, straight backs, clear straightforward eyes. "Yes, you in Olshana," he said to the town of sixty years ago, "they would be nobility to you."

And was this not the dream then, come true in ways undreamed? he asked.

And are there no other children in the world? he answered, as if in her harsh voice.

And the flame of freedom, the light of knowledge?

And the drop, to spill no drop of blood?

And he thought that at six Jeannie would get up and it would be his turn to go to her room and sleep, that he could press the buzzer and she would come now; that in the afternoon Ellen Mays was coming, and this time they would play cards and he could marvel at how rouge can stand half an inch on the cheek; that in the evening the doctor would come, and he could beg him to be merciful, to stop the feeding solutions, to let her die.

To let her die, and with her their youth of belief out of which her bright, betrayed words foamed; stained words, that on her working lips came stainless.

Hours yet before Jeannie's turn. He could press the buzzer and wake her to come now; he could take a pill, and with it sleep; he could pour more brandy into his milk glass, though what he had poured was not yet touched.

Instead he went back, checked her pulse, gently tended with his knotty fingers as Jeannie had taught.

She was whimpering; her hand crawled across the covers for his. Compassionately he enfolded it, and with his free hand gathered up the cards again. Still was there thirst or hunger ravening in him.

That world of their youth—dark ignorant, terrible with hate and disease—how was it that living in it, in the midst of corruption, filth, treachery, degradation, they had not mistrusted man nor themselves; had believed so beautifully, so . . . falsely?

"Aaah, children," he said out loud, "how we believed, how we belonged." And he yearned to package for each of the children, the grandchildren, for everyone, *that joyous certainty, that sense of mattering, of moving and being moved, of being one and indivisible with the great of the past, with all that freed, ennobled man.* Package it, stand on corners, in front of stadiums and on crowded beaches, knock on doors, give it as a fabled gift.

"And why not in cereal boxes, in soap packages?" he mocked himself. "Aah. You have taken my senses, cadaver. "

Words foamed, died unsounded. Her body writhed; she made kissing motions with her mouth. (Her lips moving as she read, poring over the Book of the Martyrs, the magnifying glass superimposed over the heavy eyeglasses.) *Still she believed?* "Eva!" he whispered. "Still you believed? You lived by it? These Things Shall Be?"

"One pound soup meat," she answered distinctly, "one soup bone."

"My ears heard you. Ellen Mays was witness: 'Humankind . . . one has to believe.'" Imploringly: "Eva!"

"Bread, day-old." She was mumbling. "Please, in a wooden box . . . for kindling. The thread, hah, the thread breaks. Cheap thread"—and a gurgling, enormously loud, began in her throat.

"I ask for stone; she gives me bread—day-old." He pulled his hand away, shouted: "Who wanted questions? Everything you have to wake?" Then dully, "Ah, let me help you turn, poor creature."

Words jumbled, cleared. In a voice of crowded terror:

"Paul, Sammy, don't fight.

"Hannah, have I ten hands?

"How can I give it, Clara, how can I give it if I don't have?"

"You lie," he said sturdily, "there was joy too." Bitterly: "Ah how cheap you speak of us at the last."

As if to rebuke him, as if her voice had no relationship with her flailing body, she sang clearly, beautifully, a school song the children had taught her when they were little; begged:

"Not look my hair where they cut. . . ."

(The crown of braids shorn.) And instantly he left the mute old woman poring over the Book of the Martyrs; went past the mother treading at the sewing machine, singing with the children; past the girl in her wrinkled prison dress, hiding her hair with scarred hands, lifting to him her awkward, shamed, imploring eyes of love; and took her in his arms, dear, personal, fleshed, in all the heavy passion he had loved to rouse from her.

"Eva!"

Her little claw hand beat the covers. How much, how much can a man stand? He took up the cards, put them down, circled the beds, walked to the dresser, opened, shut drawers, brushed his hair, moved his hand bit by bit over the mirror to see what of the reflection he could blot out with each move, and felt that at any moment he would die of what was unendurable. Went to press the buzzer to wake Jeannie, looked down, saw on Jeannie's sketch pad the hospital bed, with *her;* the double bed alongside, with him; the tall pillar feeding into her veins, and their hands, his and hers, clasped, feeding each other. And as if he had been instructed he went to his bed, lay down, holding the sketch (as if it could shield against the monstrous shapes of loss, of betrayal, of death) and with his free hand took hers back into his.

So Jeannie found them in the morning.

That last day the agony was perpetual. Time after time it lifted her almost off the bed, so they had to fight to hold her down. He could not endure and left the room; wept as if there never would be tears enough.

Jeannie came to comfort him. In her light voice she said: Grandaddy, Grandaddy don't cry. She is not there, she promised me. On the last day, she said she would go back to when she first heard music, a little girl on the road of the village where she was born. She promised me. It is a wedding and they dance, while the flutes so joyous and vibrant tremble in the air. Leave her there, Grandaddy, it is all right. She promised me. Come back, come back and help her poor body to die.

For two of that generation
Seevya and Genya

Death deepens the wonder

QUESTIONS TO CONSIDER

1. Why does the husband want to move to the Haven?
2. Why does the wife refuse to go? What do you think is her unstated reason for refusing to leave her house?
3. For what reasons do the children take one or the other parent's side?
4. What happened to the wife in Russia? How does this still affect her?
5. How are the characters of the husband and wife alike? How are they different?
6. Which of the two do you admire more? Why?
7. How does the title come up in the story? What do you think it means?
8. What do you think Tillie Olsen is trying to document in this story?

James Baldwin ▶

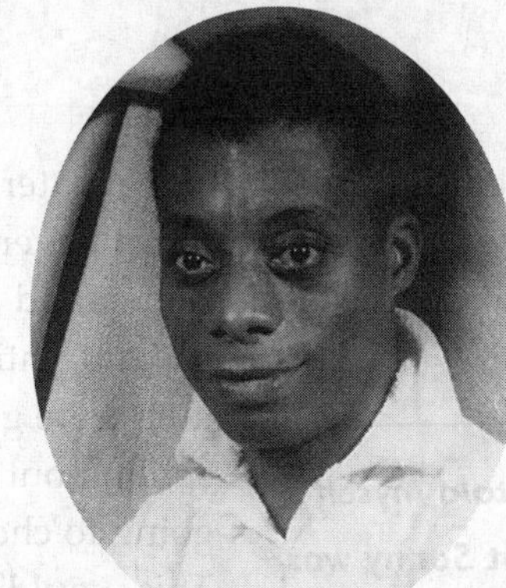

Sonny's Blues

BY JAMES BALDWIN

James Baldwin (1924–1987) was one of the most eloquent and powerful critics of postwar America. His principal subject was race and what he saw as the institutionalization of racial discrimination in America. Baldwin was born in Harlem, New York City's African-American neighborhood. His father was a storefront preacher whose brutality and inability to keep his family above the poverty line left an indelible mark on his son's view of the world. While attending high school, Baldwin also worked as an evangelical preacher, an experience recreated in his first novel, Go Tell It on the Mountain *(1953). Richard Wright was the key influence in Baldwin's life. He encouraged the young writer and secured him a grant that enabled Baldwin to settle into serious writing, out of which came that first autobiographical novel. The book was widely acclaimed, and Baldwin's essays began to appear with regularity in the serious press. His second novel,* Giovanni's Room *(1956), is the story of a tragic homosexual love affair, which treated homosexuality in an open way. Baldwin was already spending portions of each year in France, and the controversy over the novel inspired him to stay out of the United States even more. Baldwin continued to produce fiction regularly, but his influence was much larger with his essays. These brilliant pieces were passionate accounts of race relations, but made enemies on both sides of every question. Baldwin's clarity as a thinker and oratorical skills still shine through these essays decades after they were written as topical pieces. Despite Baldwin's fame, the audience for his novels dwindled. Younger and more radical African-American writers appeared and dismissed Baldwin. After the 1960s, he found himself in the precarious position of being considered out of date. Baldwin's last years were full of disappointment, but in the years since his death he has claimed his rightful place in American literature.*

I read about it in the paper, in the subway, on my way to work. I read it, and I couldn't believe it, and I read it again. Then perhaps I just stared at it, at the newsprint spelling out his name, spelling out the story. I stared at it in the swinging lights of the subway car, and in the faces and bodies of the people, and in my own face, trapped in the darkness which roared outside.

It was not to be believed and I kept telling myself that, as I walked from the subway station to the high school. And at the same time I couldn't doubt it. I was scared, scared for Sonny. He became real to me again. A great block of ice got settled in my belly and kept melting there slowly all day long, while I taught my classes algebra. It was a special kind of ice. It kept melting, sending trickles of ice water all up and down my veins, but it never got less. Sometimes it hardened and seemed to expand until I felt my guts were going to come spilling out or that I was going to choke or scream. This would always be at a moment when I was remembering some specific thing Sonny had once said or done.

I told myself that Sonny was wild, but he wasn't crazy.

When he was about as old as the boys in my classes his face had been bright and open, there was a lot of copper in it; and he'd had wonderfully direct brown eyes, and great gentleness and privacy. I wondered what he looked like now. He had been picked up, the evening before, in a raid on an apartment downtown, for peddling and using heroin.

I couldn't believe it: but what I mean by that is that I couldn't find any room for it anywhere inside me. I had kept it outside me for a long time. I hadn't wanted to know. I had had suspicions, but I didn't name them, I kept putting them away. I told myself that Sonny was wild, but he wasn't crazy. And he'd always been a good boy, he hadn't ever turned hard or evil or disrespectful, the way kids can, so quick, so quick, especially in Harlem. I didn't want to believe that I'd ever see my brother going down, coming to nothing, all that light in his face gone out, in the condition I'd already seen so many others. Yet it had happened and here I was, talking about algebra to a lot of boys who might, every one of them for all I knew, be popping off needles every time they went to the head.[1] Maybe it did more for them than algebra could.

I was sure that the first time Sonny had ever had horse,[2] he couldn't have been much older than these boys were now. These boys, now, were living as we'd been living then, they were growing up with a rush and their heads bumped abruptly against the low ceiling of their actual possibilities. They were filled with rage. All they really knew were two darknesses, the darkness of their lives, which was now closing in on them, and the darkness of the movies, which had blinded them to that other darkness, and in which they now, **vindictively**,[3] dreamed, at once more together than they were at any other time, and more alone.

When the last bell rang, the last class ended, I let out my breath. It seemed I'd been holding it for all that time. My clothes were wet—I may have looked as though I'd been sitting in a steam bath, all dressed up, all afternoon. I sat alone in the classroom a long time. I listened to the boys outside, downstairs, shouting and cursing and laughing. Their laughter struck me for perhaps the first time. It was not the joyous laughter which—God knows why—one associates with children. It was mocking and insular,[4] its intent was to **denigrate**.[5] It was disenchanted, and in this, also, lay the authority of their curses. Perhaps I was

[1] head—slang for toilet (on a ship).

[2] horse—slang for the drug heroin.

[3] **vindictively**—spitefully, maliciously.

[4] insular—detached.

[5] **denigrate**—belittle, deny the importance of another.

listening to them because I was thinking about my brother and in them I heard my brother. And myself.

One boy was whistling a tune, at once very complicated and very simple, it seemed to be pouring out of him as though he were a bird, and it sounded very cool and moving through all that harsh, bright air, only just holding its own through all those other sounds.

I stood up and walked over to the window and looked down into the courtyard. It was the beginning of the spring and the **sap**[6] was rising in the boys. A teacher passed through them every now and again, quickly, as though he or she couldn't wait to get out of that courtyard, to get those boys out of their sight and off their minds. I started collecting my stuff. I thought I'd better get home and talk to Isabel.

The courtyard was almost deserted by the time I got downstairs. I saw this boy standing in the shadow of a doorway, looking just like Sonny. I almost called his name. Then I saw that it wasn't Sonny, but somebody we used to know, a boy from around our block. He'd been Sonny's friend. He'd never been mine, having been too young for me, and, anyway, I'd never liked him. And now, even though he was a grown-up man, he still hung around that block, still spent hours on the street corners, was always high and raggy. I used to run into him from time to time and he'd often work around to asking me for a quarter or fifty cents. He always had some real good excuse, too, and I always gave it to him. I don't know why.

But now, abruptly, I hated him. I couldn't stand the way he looked at me, partly like a dog, partly like a cunning child. I wanted to ask him what the hell he was doing in the school courtyard.

He sort of shuffled over to me, and he said, "I see you got the papers. So you already know about it."

"You mean about Sonny? Yes, I already know about it. How come they didn't get you?"

He grinned. It made him repulsive and it also brought to mind what he'd looked like as a kid. "I wasn't there. I stay away from them people."

"Good for you." I offered him a cigarette and I watched him through the smoke. "You come all the way down here just to tell me about Sonny?"

"That's right." He was sort of shaking his head and his eyes looked strange, as though they were about to cross. The bright sun deadened his damp dark brown skin and it made his eyes look yellow and showed up the dirt in his kinked hair. He smelled funky. I moved a little away from him and I said, "Well, thanks. But I already know about it and I got to get home."

"I'll walk you a little ways," he said. We started walking. There were a couple of kids still **loitering**[7] in the courtyard and one of them said goodnight to me and looked strangely at the boy beside me.

"What're you going to do?" he asked me. "I mean, about Sonny?"

---

[6] **sap**—energy, vitality.

[7] **loitering**—standing around aimlessly.

"Look. I haven't seen Sonny for over a year, I'm not sure I'm going to do anything. Anyway, what the hell *can* I do?"

"That's right," he said quickly, "ain't nothing you can do. Can't much help old Sonny no more, I guess."

It was what I was thinking and so it seemed to me he had no right to say it.

"I'm surprised at Sonny, though," he went on—he had a funny way of talking, he looked straight ahead as though he were talking to himself—"I thought Sonny was a smart boy, I thought he was too smart to get hung."

"I guess he thought so too," I said sharply, "and that's how he got hung. And how about you? You're pretty damn smart, I bet."

Then he looked directly at me, just for a minute. "I ain't smart," he said. "If I was smart, I'd have reached for a pistol a long time ago."

"Look. Don't tell *me* your sad story, if it was up to me, I'd give you one." Then I felt guilty—guilty, probably, for never having supposed that the poor bastard *had* a story of his own, much less a sad one, and I asked, quickly, "What's going to happen to him now?"

He didn't answer this. He was off by himself some place.

"Funny thing," he said, and from his tone we might have been discussing the quickest way to get to Brooklyn, "when I saw the papers this morning, the first thing I asked myself was if I had anything to do with it. I felt sort of responsible."

I began to listen more carefully. The subway station was on the corner, just before us, and I stopped. He stopped, too. We were in front of a bar and he ducked slightly, peering in, but whoever he was looking for didn't seem to be there. The juke box was blasting away with something black and bouncy and I half watched the barmaid as she danced her way from the juke box to her place behind the bar. And I watched her face as she laughingly responded to something someone said to her, still keeping time to the music. When she smiled one saw the little girl, one sensed the doomed, still-struggling woman beneath the battered face of the semi-whore.

"I never *give* Sonny nothing," the boy said finally, "but a long time ago I come to school high and Sonny asked me how it felt." He paused, I couldn't bear to watch him, I watched the barmaid, and I listened to the music which seemed to be causing the pavement to shake. "I told him it felt great." The music stopped, the barmaid paused and watched the juke box until the music began again. "It did."

All this was carrying me some place I didn't want to go. I certainly didn't want to know how it felt. It filled everything, the people, the houses, the music, the dark, quicksilver barmaid, with menace; and this menace was their reality.

"What's going to happen to him now?" I asked again.

"They'll send him away some place and they'll try to cure him." He shook his head. "Maybe he'll even think he's kicked the habit. Then they'll let him loose"—he gestured, throwing his cigarette into the gutter. "That's all."

"What do you mean, that's *all*?"

But I knew what he meant.

"I *mean*, that's *all*." He turned his head and looked at me, pulling down the corners of his mouth. "Don't you know what I mean?" he asked, softly.

"How the hell *would* I know what you mean?" I almost whispered it, I don't know why.

"That's right," he said to the air, "how would *he* know what I mean?" He turned toward me again, patient and calm, and yet I somehow felt him shaking, shaking as though he were going to fall apart. I felt that ice in my guts again, the dread I'd felt all afternoon; and again I watched the barmaid, moving about the bar, washing glasses, and singing. "Listen. They'll let him out and then it'll just start all over again. That's what I mean."

"You mean—they'll let him out. And then he'll just start working his way back in again. You mean he'll never kick the habit. Is that what you mean?"

"That's right," he said, cheerfully. "*You* see what I mean."

"Tell me," I said at last, "why does he want to die? He must want to die, he's killing himself, why does he want to die?"

He looked at me in surprise. He licked his lips. "He don't want to die. He wants to live. Don't nobody want to die, ever."

Then I wanted to ask him—too many things. He could not have answered, or if he had, I could not have borne the answers. I started walking. "Well, I guess it's none of my business."

"It's going to be rough on old Sonny," he said. We reached the subway station. "This is your station?" he asked. I nodded. I took one step down. "Damn!" he said, suddenly. I looked up at him. He grinned again. "Damn it if I didn't leave all my money home. You ain't got a dollar on you, have you? Just for a couple of days, is all."

"He don't want to die. He wants to live. Don't nobody want to die, ever."

All at once something inside gave and threatened to come pouring out of me. I didn't hate him any more. I felt that in another moment I'd start crying like a child.

"Sure," I said. "Don't sweat." I looked in my wallet and didn't have a dollar, I only had five. "Here," I said. "That hold you?"

He didn't look at it—he didn't want to look at it. A terrible, closed look came over his face, as though he were keeping the number on the bill a secret from him and me. "Thanks," he said, and now he was dying to see me go. "Don't worry about Sonny. Maybe I'll write him or something."

"Sure," I said. "You do that. So long."

"Be seeing you," he said. I went on down the steps.

And I didn't write Sonny or send him anything for a long time. When I finally did, it was just after my little girl died, and he wrote me back a letter which made me feel like a bastard.

Here's what he said:

Dear brother,

You don't know how much I needed to hear from you. I wanted to write you many a time but I dug how much I must have hurt you and so I didn't write. But now I feel like a man who's been trying to climb up out of some deep, real deep and funky hole and just saw the sun up there, outside. I got to get outside.

I can't tell you much about how I got here. I mean I don't know how to tell you. I guess I was afraid of something or I was trying to escape from something and you know I have never been very strong in the head (smile). I'm glad Mama and Daddy are dead and can't see what's happened to their son and I swear if I'd known what I was doing I would never have hurt you so, you and a lot of other fine people who were nice to me and who believed in me.

I don't want you to think it had anything to do with me being a musician. It's more than that. Or maybe less than that. I can't get anything straight in my head down here and I try not to think about what's going to happen to me when I get outside again. Sometime I think I'm going to flip and *never* get outside and sometime I think I'll come straight back. I tell you one thing, though, I'd rather blow my brains out than go through this again. But that's what they all say, so they tell me. If I tell you when I'm coming to New York and if you could meet me, I sure would appreciate it. Give my love to Isabel and the kids and I was sure sorry to hear about little Gracie. I wish I could be like Mama and say the Lord's will be done, but I don't know it seems to me that trouble is the one thing that never does get stopped and I don't know what good it does to blame it on the Lord. But maybe it does some good if you believe it.

Your brother,

Sonny

Then I kept in constant touch with him and I sent him whatever I could and I went to meet him when he came back to New York. When I saw him many things I thought I had forgotten came flooding back to me. This was because I had begun, finally, to wonder about Sonny, about the life that Sonny lived inside. This life, whatever it was, had made him older and thinner and it had deepened the distant stillness in which he had always moved. He looked very unlike my baby brother. Yet, when he smiled, when we shook hands, the baby brother I'd never known looked out from the depths of his private life, like an animal waiting to be **coaxed**[8] into the light.

"How you been keeping?" he asked me.

"All right. And you?"

"Just fine." He was smiling all over his face. "It's good to see you again."

"It's good to see you."

The seven years' difference in our ages lay between us like a **chasm**:[9] I wondered if these years would ever operate between us as a bridge. I was remembering, and it made it hard to catch my breath, that I had been there when he was born; and I had heard the first words he had ever spoken.

---

[8] **coaxed**—persuaded.

[9] **chasm**—deep, steep-sided opening in the earth's surface; abyss or gorge.

When he started to walk, he walked from our mother straight to me. I caught him just before he fell when he took the first steps he ever took in this world.

"How's Isabel?"

"Just fine. She's dying to see you."

"And the boys?"

"They're fine, too. They're anxious to see their uncle."

"Oh, come on. You know they don't remember me."

"Are you kidding? Of course they remember you."

He grinned again. We got into a taxi. We had a lot to say to each other, far too much to know how to begin.

As the taxi began to move, I asked, "You still want to go to India?"

He laughed. "You still remember that. Hell, no. This place is Indian enough for me."

"It used to belong to them," I said.

And he laughed again. "They damn sure knew what they were doing when they got rid of it."

Years ago, when he was around fourteen, he'd been all hipped on the idea of going to India. He read books about people sitting on rocks, naked, in all kinds of weather, but mostly bad, naturally, and walking barefoot through hot coals and arriving at wisdom. I used to say that it sounded to me as though they were getting away from wisdom as fast is they could. I think he sort of looked down on me for that.

"Do you mind," he asked, "if we have the driver drive alongside the park? On the west side—I haven't seen the city in so long."

"Of course not," I said. I was afraid that I might sound as though I were humoring him, but I hoped he wouldn't take it that way.

So we drove along, between the green of the park and the stony, lifeless elegance of hotels and apartment buildings, toward the vivid, killing streets of our childhood. These streets hadn't changed, though housing projects jutted up out of them now like rocks in the middle of a boiling sea. Most of the houses in which we had grown up had vanished, as had the stores from which we had stolen, the basements in which we had first tried sex, the rooftops from which we had hurled tin cans and bricks. But houses exactly like the houses of our past yet dominated the landscape, boys exactly like the boys we once had been found themselves smothering in these houses, came down into the streets for light and air and found themselves encircled by disaster. Some escaped the trap, most didn't. Those who got out always left something of themselves behind, as some animals amputate a leg and leave it in the trap. It might be said, perhaps, that I had escaped, after all, I was a school teacher; or that Sonny had, he hadn't lived in Harlem for years. Yet, as the cab moved uptown through streets which seemed, with a rush, to darken with dark people, and as I **covertly**[10] studied Sonny's face, it came to me that what we both were seeking through our separate cab windows was that part of ourselves which had been left behind. It's always at the hour of trouble

[10] **covertly**—not openly done.

and confrontation that the missing member[11] aches.

We hit 110th Street and started rolling up Lenox Avenue. And I'd known this avenue all my life, but it seemed to me again, as it had seemed on the day I'd first heard about Sonny's trouble, filled with a hidden menace which was its very breath of life.

"We almost there," said Sonny.

"Almost." We were both too nervous to say anything more.

We live in a housing project. It hasn't been up long. A few days after it was up it seemed uninhabitably new, now, of course, it's already rundown. It looks like a **parody**[12] of the good, clean, faceless life—God knows the people who live in it do their best to make it a parody. The beat-looking grass lying around isn't enough to make their lives green, the hedges will never hold out the streets, and they know it. The big windows fool no one, they aren't big enough to make space out of no space. They don't bother with the windows, they watch the TV screen instead. The playground is most popular with the children who don't play at jacks, or skip rope, or roller skate, or swing, and they can be found in it after dark. We moved in partly because it's not too far from where I teach, and partly for the kids; but it's really just like the houses in which Sonny and I grew up. The same things happen, they'll have the same things to remember. The moment Sonny and I started into the house I had the feeling that I was simply bringing him back into the danger he had almost died trying to escape.

Sonny has never been talkative. So I don't know why I was sure he'd be dying to talk to me when supper was over the first night. Everything went fine, the oldest boy remembered him, and the youngest boy liked him, and Sonny had remembered to bring something for each of them; and Isabel, who is really much nicer than I am, more open and giving, had gone to a lot of trouble about dinner and was genuinely glad to see him. And she's always been able to tease Sonny in a way that I haven't. It was nice to see her face so vivid again and to hear her laugh and watch her make Sonny laugh. She wasn't, or, anyway, she didn't seem to be, at all uneasy or embarrassed. She chatted as though there were no subject which had to be avoided and she got Sonny past his first, faint stiffness. And thank God she was there, for I was filled with that icy dread again. Everything I did seemed awkward to me, and everything I said sounded **freighted**[13] with hidden meaning. I was trying to remember everything I'd heard about dope addiction and I couldn't help watching Sonny for signs. I wasn't doing it out of malice. I was trying to find out something about my brother. I was dying to hear him tell me he was safe.

"Safe!" my father grunted, whenever Mama suggested trying to move to a neighborhood which might be safer for children. "Safe, hell! Ain't no place safe for kids, nor nobody."

[11] **member**—limb, such as an arm or a leg.

[12] **parody**—loose imitation of something that intentionally mocks or ridicules the original.

[13] **freighted**—loaded down with, burdened.

He always went on like this, but he wasn't, ever, really as bad as he sounded, not even on weekends, when he got drunk. As a matter of fact, he was always on the lookout for "something a little better," but he died before he found it. He died suddenly, during a drunken weekend in the middle of the war, when Sonny was fifteen. He and Sonny hadn't ever got on too well. And this was partly because Sonny was the apple of his father's eye. It was because he loved Sonny so much and was frightened for him, that he was always fighting with him. It doesn't do any good to fight with Sonny. Sonny just moves back, inside himself, where he can't be reached. But the principal reason that they never hit it off is that they were so much alike. Daddy was big and rough and loud-talking, just the opposite of Sonny, but they both had—that same privacy.

Mama tried to tell me something about this, just after Daddy died. I was home on leave from the army.

This was the last time I ever saw my mother alive. Just the same, this picture gets all mixed up in my mind with pictures I had of her when she was younger. The way I always see her is the way she used to be on a Sunday afternoon, say, when the old folks were talking after the big Sunday dinner. I always see her wearing pale blue. She'd be sitting on the sofa. And my father would be sitting in the easy chair, not far from her. And the living room would be full of church folks and relatives. There they sit, in chairs all around the living room, and the night is creeping up outside, but nobody knows it yet. You can see the darkness growing against the windowpanes and you hear the street noises every now and again, or maybe the jangling beat of a tambourine from one of the churches close by, but it's real quiet in the room. For a moment nobody's talking, but every face looks darkening, like the sky outside. And my mother rocks a little from the waist, and my father's eyes are closed. Everyone is looking at something a child can't see. For a minute they've forgotten the children. Maybe a kid is lying on the rug, half asleep. Maybe somebody's got a kid in his lap and is absent-mindedly stroking the kid's head. Maybe there's a kid, quiet and big-eyed, curled up in a big chair in the corner. The silence, the darkness coming, and the darkness in the faces frighten the child obscurely. He hopes that the hand which strokes his forehead will never stop—will never die. He hopes that there will never come a time when the old folks won't be sitting around the living room, talking about where they've come from, and what they've seen, and what's happened to them and their kinfolk.

It doesn't do any good to fight with Sonny. Sonny just moves back, inside himself, where he can't be reached.

But something deep and watchful in the child knows that this is bound to end, is already ending. In a moment someone will get up and turn on the light. Then the old folks will remember the children and they won't talk any more that day. And when light fills the room, the child is filled with darkness. He knows that every time this happens he's moved just a little closer to that darkness outside. The darkness outside is what the old folks have been talking about. It's what they've come from. It's what they endure. The child knows that they won't talk any more because if he knows too much about what's happened to *them*, he'll know too much too soon, about what's going to happen to *him*.

The last time I talked to my mother, I remember I was restless. I wanted to get out and see Isabel. We weren't married then and we had a lot to straighten out between us.

There Mama sat, in black, by the window. She was humming an old church song, *Lord, you brought me from a long ways off*. Sonny was out somewhere. Mama kept watching the streets.

"I don't know," she said, "if I'll ever see you again, after you go off from here. But I hope you'll remember the things I tried to teach you."

"Don't talk like that," I said, and smiled. "You'll be here a long time yet."

She smiled, too, but she said nothing. She was quiet for a long time. And I said, "Mama, don't you worry about nothing. I'll be writing all the time, and you be getting the checks. . . ."

"I want to talk to you about your brother," she said, suddenly. "If anything happens to me he ain't going to have nobody to look out for him."

"Mama," I said, "ain't nothing going to happen to you or Sonny. Sonny's all right. He's a good boy and he's got good sense."

"It ain't a question of his being a good boy," Mama said, "nor of his having good sense. It ain't only the bad ones, nor yet the dumb ones that gets sucked under." She stopped, looking at me. "Your Daddy once had a brother," she said, and she smiled in a way that made me feel she was in pain. "You didn't never know that, did you?"

"No," I said, "I never knew that," and I watched her face.

"Oh, yes," she said, "your Daddy had a brother." She looked out of the window again. "I know you never saw your Daddy cry. But *I* did—many a time, through all these years."

I asked her, "What happened to his brother? How come nobody's ever talked about him?"

This was the first time I ever saw my mother look old.

"His brother got killed," she said, "when he was just a little younger than you are now. I knew him. He was a fine boy. He was maybe a little full of the devil, but he didn't mean nobody no harm."

Then she stopped and the room was silent, exactly as it had sometimes been on those Sunday afternoons. Mama kept looking out into the streets.

"He used to have a job in the mill," she said, "and, like all young folks, he just liked to perform on Saturday nights. Saturday nights, him and your father would drift around to different places, go to dances and things like that, or just sit around with people they knew, and your father's brother would sing, he had a fine voice, and play along with himself on his guitar. Well, this particular Saturday night, him and your father was coming home from some place, and they were both a little drunk and there was a moon that night, it was bright like day. Your father's brother was feeling kind of good, and he was whistling to himself, and he had his guitar slung over his shoulder. They was coming down a hill and beneath them was a road that turned off from the highway. Well, your father's brother, being always kind of frisky, decided to run down this hill, and he did, with that guitar banging and clanging behind him, and he ran across the road, and he was making water behind a tree. And your father was sort of amused at him and he was still coming down the hill, kind of slow. Then he heard a car motor and that same minute his brother stepped from behind the tree, into the road, in the moonlight. And he started to cross the road. And your father started to run down the hill, he says he don't know why. This car was full of white men. They was all drunk, and when they seen your father's brother they let out a great whoop and holler and they aimed the car straight at him. They was having fun, they just wanted to scare him, the way they do sometimes, you know. But they was drunk. And I guess the boy, being drunk, too, and scared, kind of lost his head. By the time he jumped it was too late. Your father says he heard his brother scream when the car rolled over him, and he heard the wood of that guitar when it give, and he heard them strings go flying, and he heard them white men shouting, and the car kept on a-going and it ain't stopped till this day. And, time your father got down the hill, his brother weren't nothing but blood and pulp."

Tears were gleaming on my mother's face. There wasn't anything I could say.

"He never mentioned it," she said, "because I never let him mention it before you children. Your Daddy was like a crazy man that night and for many a night thereafter. He says he never in his life seen anything as dark as that road after the lights of that car had gone away. Weren't nothing, weren't nobody on that road, just your Daddy and his brother and that busted guitar. Oh, yes. Your daddy never did really get right again. Till the day he died he weren't sure but that every white man he saw was the man that killed his brother."

She stopped and took out her handkerchief and dried her eyes and looked at me.

"I ain't telling you all this," she said, "to make you scared or bitter or to make you hate nobody. I'm telling you this because you got a brother. And the world ain't changed."

I guess I didn't want to believe this. I guess she saw this in my face. She turned away from me, toward the window again, searching those streets.

"But I praise my Redeemer," she said at last, "that He called your Daddy home before me. I ain't saying it to throw no flowers at myself, but, I declare, it keeps me from feeling too cast down to know I helped your father get safely through this world. Your father always acted like he was the roughest, strongest man on earth. And everybody took him to be like that. But if he hadn't had me there—to see his tears!"

She was crying again. Still, I couldn't move. I said, "Lord, Lord, Mama, I didn't know it was like that."

"Oh, honey," she said, "there's a lot that you don't know. But you are going to find out." She stood up from the window and came over to me. "You got to hold on to your brother," she said, "and don't let him fall, no matter what it looks like is happening to him and no matter how evil you gets with him. You going to be evil with him many a time. But don't you forget what I told you, you hear?"

I sensed myself in the presence of something I didn't really know how to handle, didn't understand.

"I won't forget," I said. "Don't you worry, I won't forget. I won't let nothing happen to Sonny."

My mother smiled as though she were amused at something she saw in my face. Then, "You may not be able to stop nothing from happening. But you got to let him know you's *there.*"

Two days later I was married, and then I was gone. And I had a lot of things on my mind and I pretty well forgot my promise to Mama until I got shipped home on a special furlough[14] for her funeral.

And, after the funeral, with just Sonny and me alone in the empty kitchen, I tried to find out something about him.

"What do you want to do?" I asked him.

"I'm going to be a musician," he said.

For he had graduated, in the time I had been away, from dancing to the juke box to finding out who was playing what, and what they were doing with it, and he had bought himself a set of drums.

"You mean, you want to be a drummer?" I somehow had the feeling that being a drummer might be all right for other people but not for my brother Sonny.

"I don't think," he said, looking at me very gravely, "that I'll ever be a good drummer. But I think I can play a piano."

I frowned. I'd never played the role of the older brother quite so seriously before, had scarcely ever, in fact, *asked* Sonny a damn thing. I sensed myself in the presence of something I didn't really know how to handle, didn't understand. So I made my frown a little deeper as I asked: "What kind of musician do you want to be?"

He grinned. "How many kinds do you think there are?"

"Be *serious,*" I said.

He laughed, throwing his head back, and then looked at me. "I *am* serious."

"Well, then, for Christ's sake, stop kidding around and answer a serious question. I mean, do you want to be a concert pianist, you want to play classical music and all that, or—or what?" Long before I finished he was laughing again. "For Christ's *sake,* Sonny!"

He sobered, but with difficulty. "I'm sorry. But you sound so—*scared!*" and he was off again.

"Well, you may think it's funny now, baby, but it's not going to be so funny when you have to make your living at it, let me tell you *that*." I was furious because I

[14] furlough—military leave of absence.

knew he was laughing at me and I didn't know why.

"No," he said, very sober now, and afraid, perhaps, that he'd hurt me, "I don't want to be a classical pianist. That isn't what interests me. I mean"—he paused, looking hard at me, as though his eyes would help me to understand, and then gestured helplessly, as though perhaps his hand would help—"I mean, I'll have a lot of studying to do, and I'll have to study *everything*, but, I mean, I want to play *with*—jazz musicians." He stopped. "I want to play jazz," he said.

Well, the word had never before sounded as heavy, as real, as it sounded that afternoon in Sonny's mouth. I just looked at him and I was probably frowning a real frown by this time. I simply couldn't see why on earth he'd want to spend his time hanging around nightclubs, clowning around on bandstands, while people pushed each other around a dance floor. It seemed—beneath him, somehow. I had never thought about it before, had never been forced to, but I suppose I had always put jazz musicians in a class with what Daddy called "good-time people."

"Are you *serious*?"

"Hell, *yes*, I'm serious."

He looked more helpless than ever, and annoyed, and deeply hurt.

I suggested, helpfully: "You mean—like Louis Armstrong?"[15]

His face closed as though I'd struck him. "No. I'm not talking about none of that old-time, down home crap."

"Well, look, Sonny, I'm sorry, don't get mad. I just don't altogether get it, that's all. Name somebody—you know, a jazz musician you admire."

"Bird."[16]

"Who?"

"Bird! Charlie Parker! Don't they teach you nothing in the damn army?"

I lit a cigarette. I was surprised and then a little amused to discover that I was trembling. "I've been out of touch," I said. "You'll have to be patient with me. Now. Who's this Parker character?"

"He's just one of the greatest jazz musicians alive," said Sonny, **sullenly**,[17] his hands in his pockets, his back to me. "Maybe *the* greatest," he added, bitterly, "that's probably why *you* never heard of him."

"All right," I said, "I'm ignorant. I'm sorry. I'll go out and buy all the cat's records right away, all right?"

"It don't," said Sonny, with dignity, "make any difference to me. I don't care what you listen to. Don't do me no favors."

I was beginning to realize that I'd never seen him so upset before. With another part of my mind I was thinking that this would probably turn out to be one of those things kids go through and that I shouldn't make it seem important by pushing it too hard. Still, I didn't think it would do any harm to ask: "Doesn't all this take a lot of time? Can you make a living at it?"

---

[15] Louis Armstrong—American trumpeter (1900–1971) who greatly influenced the development of jazz.

[16] Bird—nickname for Charlie Parker (1920–1955), a jazz saxophonist, one of the founders of the bop style of jazz after World War II. Commonly considered one of jazz's finest musicians.

[17] **sullenly**—sulkily, gloomily.

He turned back to me and half leaned, half sat, on the kitchen table. "Everything takes time," he said, "and—well, yes, sure, I can make a living at it. But what I don't seem to be able to make you understand is that it's the only thing I want to do."

"Well, Sonny," I said, gently, "you know people can't always do exactly what they *want* to do—"

"*No*, I don't know that," said Sonny, surprising me. "I think people *ought* to do what they want to do, what else are they alive for?"

"You getting to be a big boy," I said desperately, "it's time you started thinking about your future."

"I'm thinking about my future," said Sonny, grimly. "I think about it all the time."

I gave up. I decided, if he didn't change his mind, that we could always talk about it later. "In the meantime," I said, "you got to finish school." We had already decided that he'd have to move in with Isabel and her folks. I knew this wasn't the ideal arrangement because Isabel's folks are inclined to be dicty[18] and they hadn't especially wanted Isabel to marry me. But I didn't know what else to do. "And we have to get you fixed up at Isabel's."

There was a long silence. He moved from the kitchen table to the window. "That's a terrible idea. You know it yourself."

"Do you have a *better* idea?"

He just walked up and down the kitchen for a minute. He was as tall as I was. He had started to shave. I suddenly had the feeling that I didn't know him at all.

He stopped at the kitchen table and picked up my cigarettes. Looking at me with a kind of mocking, amused defiance, be put one between his lips. "You mind?"

"You smoking already?"

He lit the cigarette and nodded, watching me through the smoke. "I just wanted to see if I'd have the courage to smoke in front of you." He grinned and blew a great cloud of smoke to the ceiling. "It was easy." He looked at my face. "Come on, now. I bet you was smoking at my age, tell the truth."

I didn't say anything but the truth was on my face, and he laughed. But now there was something very strained in his laugh. "Sure. And I bet that ain't all you was doing."

He was frightening me a little. "Cut the crap," I said. "We already decided that you was going to go and live at Isabel's. Now what's got into you all of a sudden?"

"*You* decided it," he pointed out. "*I* didn't decide nothing." He stopped in front of me, leaning against the stove, arms loosely folded. "Look, brother. I don't want to stay in Harlem no more, I really don't." He was very earnest. He looked at me, then over toward the kitchen window. There was something in his eyes I'd never seen before, some thoughtfulness, some worry all his own. He rubbed the muscle of one arm. "It's time I was getting out of here."

"Where do you want to *go*, Sonny?"

"I want to join the army. Or the navy, I don't care. If I say I'm old enough, they'll believe me."

[18] dicty—slang for "dictatorial."

Then I got mad. It was because I was so scared. "You must be crazy. You damn fool, what the hell do you want to go and join the *army* for?"

"I just told you. To get out of Harlem."

"Sonny, you haven't even finished *school*. And if you really want to be a musician, how do you expect to study if you're in the *army?*"

He looked at me, trapped, and in anguish. "There's ways. I might be able to work out some kind of deal. Anyway, I'll have the G.I. Bill[19] when I come out."

"*If* you come out." We stared at each other. "Sonny, please. Be reasonable. I know the setup is far from perfect. But we got to do the best we can."

"I ain't learning nothing in school," he said. "Even when I go." He turned away from me and opened the window and threw his cigarette out into the narrow alley. I watched his back. "At least, I ain't learning nothing you'd want me to learn." He slammed the window so hard I thought the glass would fly out, and turned back to me. "And I'm sick of the stink of these garbage cans!"

"Sonny," I said, "I know how you feel. But if you don't finish school now, you're going to be sorry later that you didn't." I grabbed him by the shoulders. "And you only got another year. It ain't so bad. And I'll come back and I swear I'll help you do *whatever* you want to do. Just try to put up with it till I come back. Will you please do that? For me?"

He didn't answer and he wouldn't look at me.

"Sonny. You hear me?"

He pulled away. "I hear you. But you never hear anything *I* say."

I didn't know what to say to that. He looked out of the window and then back at me. "OK," he said, and sighed. "I'll try."

"I ain't learning nothing in school," he said. "Even when I go."

Then I said, trying to cheer him up a little, "They got a piano at Isabel's. You can practice on it."

And as a matter of fact, it did cheer him up for a minute. "That's right," he said to himself. "I forgot that." His face relaxed a little. But the worry, the thoughtfulness, played on it still, the way shadows play on a face which is staring into the fire.

But I thought I'd never hear the end of that piano. At first, Isabel would write me, saying how nice it was that Sonny was so serious about his music and how, as soon as he came in from school, or wherever he had been when he was supposed to be at school, he went straight to that piano and stayed there until suppertime. And, after supper, he went back to that piano and stayed there until everybody went to bed. He was at the piano all day Saturday and all day Sunday. Then he bought a record player and started playing records. He'd play one record over and over again, all day long sometimes, and he'd improvise along with it on the piano. Or he'd play

[19] G.I. Bill—government aid for the education of veterans.

one section of the record, one chord,[20] one change, one progression,[21] then he'd do it on the piano. Then back to the record. Then back to the piano.

Well, I really don't know how they stood it. Isabel finally confessed that it wasn't like living with a person at all, it was like living with sound. And the sound didn't make any sense to her, didn't make any sense to any of them—naturally. They began, in a way, to be afflicted by this presence that was living in their home. It was as though Sonny were some sort of god, or monster. He moved in an atmosphere which wasn't like theirs at all. They fed him and he ate, he washed himself, he walked in and out of their door; he certainly wasn't nasty or unpleasant or rude, Sonny isn't any of those things; but it was as though he were all wrapped up in some cloud, some fire, some vision all his own; and there wasn't any way to reach him.

At the same time, he wasn't really a man yet, he was still a child, and they had to watch out for him in all kinds of ways. They certainly couldn't throw him out. Neither did they dare to make a great scene about that piano because even they dimly sensed, as I sensed, from so many thousands of miles away, that Sonny was at that piano playing for his life.

But he hadn't been going to school. One day a letter came from the school board and Isabel's mother got it—there had, apparently, been other letters but Sonny had torn them up. This day, when Sonny came in, Isabel's mother showed him the letter and asked where he'd been spending his time. And she finally got it out of him that he'd been down in Greenwich Village,[22] with musicians and other characters, in a white girl's apartment. And this scared her and she started to scream at him and what came up, once she began—though she denies it to this day—was what sacrifices they were making to give Sonny a decent home and how little he appreciated it.

Sonny didn't play the piano that day. By evening, Isabel's mother had calmed down but then there was the old man to deal with, and Isabel herself. Isabel says she did her best to be calm but she broke down and started crying. She says she just watched Sonny's face. She could tell, by watching him, what was happening with him. And what was happening was that they penetrated his cloud, they had reached him. Even if their fingers had been a thousand times more gentle than human fingers ever are, he could hardly help feeling that they had stripped him naked and were spitting on that nakedness. For he also had to see that his presence, that music, which was life or death to him, had been torture for them and that they had endured it, not at all for his sake, but only for mine. And Sonny couldn't take that. He can take it a little better today than he could then but he's still not very good at it and, frankly, I don't know anybody who is.

The silence of the next few days must have been louder than the sound of all the

---

[20] chord—combination of two or more musical notes sounded together in harmony.

[21] progression—sequence of tones or chords.

[22] Greenwich Village—section of New York long associated with artists and writers.

music ever played since time began. One morning, before she went to work, Isabel was in his room for something and she suddenly realized that all of his records were gone. And she knew for certain that he was gone. And he was. He went as far as the navy would carry him. He finally sent me a postcard from some place in Greece and that was the first I knew that Sonny was still alive. I didn't see him any more until we were both back in New York and the war had been long over.

He was a man by then, of course, but I wasn't willing to see it. He came by the house from time to time, but we fought almost every time we met. I didn't like the way he carried himself, loose and dream-like all the time, and I didn't like his friends, and his music seemed to be merely an excuse for the life he led. It sounded just that weird and disordered.

Then we had a fight, a pretty awful fight, and I didn't see him for months. By and by I looked him up, where he was living, in a furnished room in the Village, and I tried to make it up. But there were lots of other people in the room and Sonny just lay on his bed, and he wouldn't come downstairs with me, and he treated these other people as though they were his family and I weren't. So I got mad and then he got mad, and then I told him that he might just as well be dead as live the way he was living. Then he stood up and he told me not to worry about him any more in life, that he *was* dead as far as I was concerned. Then he pushed me to the door and the other people looked on as though nothing were happening, and he slammed the door behind me. I stood in the hallway, staring at the door. I heard somebody laugh in the room and then the tears came to my eyes. I started down the steps, whistling to keep from crying, I kept whistling to myself, *You going to need me, baby, one of these cold, rainy days.*

I read about Sonny's trouble in the spring. Little Grace died in the fall. She was a beautiful little girl. But she only lived a little over two years. She died of polio[23] and she suffered. She had a slight fever for a couple of days, but it didn't seem like anything and we just kept her in bed. And we would certainly have called the doctor, but the fever dropped, she seemed to be all right. So we thought it had just been a cold. Then, one day, she was up, playing, Isabel was in the kitchen fixing lunch for the two boys when they'd come in from school, and she heard Grace fall down in the living room. When you have a lot of children you don't always start running when one of them falls, unless they start screaming or something. And, this time, Gracie was quiet. Yet, Isabel says that when she heard that *thump* and then that silence, something happened to her to make her afraid. And she ran to the living room and there was little Grace on the floor, all twisted up, and the reason she hadn't screamed was that she couldn't get her breath. And when she did scream, it was the worst sound, Isabel says, that she'd ever heard in all her life, and she still hears it sometimes in her dreams. Isabel

[23] polio—infectious disease that destroys the nervous tissue, causing infantile paralysis.

will sometimes wake me up with a low, moaning, strangling sound and I have to be quick to awaken her and hold her to me and where Isabel is weeping against me seems a mortal wound.

I think I may have written Sonny the very day that little Grace was buried. I was sitting in the living room in the dark, by myself, and I suddenly thought of Sonny. My trouble made his real.

One Saturday afternoon, when Sonny had been living with us, or anyway, been in our house, for nearly two weeks, I found myself wandering aimlessly about the living room, drinking from a can of beer, and trying to work up courage to search Sonny's room. He was out, he was usually out whenever I was home, and Isabel had taken the children to see their grandparents. Suddenly I was standing still in front of the living room window, watching Seventh Avenue. The idea of searching Sonny's room made me still. I scarcely dared to admit to myself what I'd be searching for. I didn't know what I'd do if I found it. Or if I didn't.

On the sidewalk across from me, near the entrance to a barbecue joint, some people were holding an old-fashioned revival meeting. The barbecue cook, wearing a dirty white apron, his conked[24] hair reddish and metallic in the pale sun, and a cigarette between his lips, stood in the doorway, watching them. Kids and older people paused in their errands and stood there, along with some older men and a couple of very tough-looking women who watched everything that happened on the avenue, as though they owned it, or were maybe owned by it. Well, they were watching this, too. The revival was being carried on by three sisters in black, and a brother. All they had were their voices and their Bibles and a tambourine. The brother was testifying and while he testified two of the sisters stood together, seeming to say, amen, and the third sister walked around with the tambourine outstretched and a couple of people dropped coins into it. Then the brother's testimony ended and the sister who had been taking up the collection dumped the coins into her palm and transferred them to the pocket of her long black robe. Then she raised both hands, striking the tambourine against the air, and then against one hand, and she started to sing. And the two other sisters and the brother joined in.

It was strange, suddenly, to watch, though I had been seeing these meetings all my life. So, of course, had everybody else down there. Yet, they paused and watched and listened and I stood still at the window. *"'Tis the old ship of Zion,"* they sang, and the sister with the tambourine kept a steady, jangling beat, *"it has rescued many a thousand!"* Not a soul under the sound of their voices was hearing this song for the first time, not one of them had been rescued. Nor had they seen much in the way of rescue work being done around them. Neither did they especially believe in the holiness of the three sisters and the brother, they knew too much about them, knew where they lived, and how. The woman with the tambourine, whose voice

24 conked—chemically straightened and greased down.

dominated the air, whose face was bright with joy, was divided by very little from the woman who stood watching her, a cigarette between her heavy, chapped lips, her hair a cuckoo's nest, her face scarred and swollen from many beatings, and her black eyes glittering like coal. Perhaps they both knew this, which was why, when, as rarely, they addressed each other, they addressed each other as Sister. As the singing filled the air the watching, listening faces underwent a change, the eyes focusing on something within; the music seemed to soothe a poison out of them; and time seemed, nearly, to fall away from the sullen, **belligerent**,[25] battered faces, as though they were fleeing back to their first condition, while dreaming of their last. The barbecue cook half shook his head and smiled, and dropped his cigarette and disappeared into his joint. A man fumbled in his pockets for change and stood holding it in his hand impatiently, as though he had just remembered a pressing appointment further up the avenue. He looked furious. Then I saw Sonny, standing on the edge of the crowd. He was carrying a wide, flat notebook with a green cover, and it made him look, from where I was standing, almost like a schoolboy. The coppery sun brought out the copper in his skin, he was very faintly smiling, standing very still. Then the singing stopped, the tambourine turned into a collection plate again. The furious man dropped in his coins and vanished, so did a couple of the women, and Sonny dropped some change in the plate, looking directly at the woman with a little smile. He started across the avenue, toward the house. He has a slow, loping walk, something like the way Harlem hipsters walk, only he's imposed on this his own half-beat. I had never really noticed it before.

I stayed at the window, both relieved and apprehensive. As Sonny disappeared from my sight, they began singing again. And they were still singing when his key turned in the lock.

"Hey," he said.

"Hey, yourself. You want some beer?"

"No. Well, maybe." But he came up to the window and stood beside me, looking out. "What a warm voice," he said.

They were singing. *If I could only hear my mother pray again!*

"Yes," I said, "and she can sure beat that tambourine."

"But what a terrible song," he said, and laughed. He dropped his notebook on the sofa and disappeared into the kitchen. "Where's Isabel and the kids?"

"I think they went to see their grandparents. You hungry?"

"No." He came back into the living room with his can of beer. "You want to come some place with me tonight?"

I sensed, I don't know how, that I couldn't possibly say no. "Sure. Where?"

He sat down on the sofa and picked up his notebook and started leafing through it. "I'm going to sit in with some fellows in a joint in the Village."

"You mean, you're going to play, tonight?"

---

[25] **belligerent**—hostile, aggressive, inclined toward fighting.

"That's right." He took a swallow of his beer and moved back to the window. He gave me a sidelong look. "If you can stand it."

"I'll try," I said.

He smiled to himself and we both watched as the meeting across the way broke up. The three sisters and the brother, heads bowed, were singing *God be with you till we meet again.* The faces around them were very quiet. Then the song ended. The small crowd dispersed. We watched the three women and the lone man walk slowly up the avenue.

"When she was singing before," said Sonny, abruptly, "her voice reminded me for a minute of what heroin feels like sometimes—when it's in your veins. It makes you feel sort of warm and cool at the same time. And distant. And—and sure." He sipped his beer, very deliberately not looking at me. I watched his face. "It makes you feel—in control. Sometimes you've got to have that feeling."

"Do you?" I sat down slowly in the easy chair.

"Sometimes." He went to the sofa and picked up his notebook again. "Some people do."

"In order," I asked, "to play?" And my voice was very ugly, full of **contempt**[26] and anger.

"Well"—he looked at me with great, troubled eyes, as though, in fact, he hoped his eyes would tell me things he could never otherwise say—"they *think* so. And *if* they think so—!"

"And what do *you* think?" I asked.

He sat on the sofa and put his can of beer on the floor. "I don't know," he said, and I couldn't be sure if he were answering my question or pursuing his thoughts. His face didn't tell me. "It's not so much to *play*. It's to *stand* it, to be able to make it at all. On any level." He frowned and smiled: "In order to keep from shaking to pieces."

"But these friends of yours," I said, "they seem to shake themselves to pieces pretty fast."

"Maybe." He played with the notebook. And something told me that I should curb my tongue, that Sonny was doing his best to talk, that I should listen. "But of course you only know the ones that've gone to pieces. Some don't—or at least they haven't *yet* and that's just about all *any* of us can say." He paused. "And then there are some who just live, really, in hell, and they know it and they see what's happening and they go right on. I don't know." He sighed, dropped the notebook, folded his arms. "Some guys, you can tell from the way they play, they on something *all* the time. And you can see that, well, it makes something real for them. But of course," he picked up his beer from the floor and sipped it and put the can down again, "they *want* to, too, you've got to see that. Even some of them that say they don't—*some*, not all."

"And what about you?" I asked—I couldn't help it. "What about you? Do *you* want to?"

He stood up and walked to the window and I remained silent for a long time. Then

[26] **contempt**—disdain, scorn, disgust.

he sighed. "Me," he said. Then: "While I was downstairs before, on my way here, listening to that woman sing, it struck me all of a sudden how much suffering she must have had to go through—to sing like that. It's *repulsive* to think you have to suffer that much."

I said: "But there's no way not to suffer—is there, Sonny?"

"I believe not," he said and smiled, "but that's never stopped anyone from trying." He looked at me. "Has it?" I realized, with this mocking look, that there stood between us, forever, beyond the power of time or forgiveness, the fact that I had held silence—so long!—when he had needed human speech to help him. He turned back to the window. "No, there's no way not to suffer. But you try all kinds of ways to keep from drowning in it, to keep on top of it, and to make it seem—well, like *you*. Like you did something, all right, and now you're suffering for it. You know?" I said nothing. "Well you know," he said, impatiently, "why *do* people suffer? Maybe it's better to do something to give it a reason, *any* reason."

"But we just agreed," I said, "that there's no way not to suffer. Isn't it better, then, just to—take it?"

"But nobody just takes it," Sonny cried, "that's what I'm telling you! *Everybody* tries not to. You're just hung up on the *way* some people try—it's not *your* way!"

The hair on my face began to itch, my face felt wet. "That's not true," I said, "that's not true. I don't give a damn what other people do, I don't even care how they suffer. I just care how *you* suffer." And he looked at me. "Please believe me," I said, "I don't want to see you—die—trying not to suffer."

"I won't," he said flatly, "die trying not to suffer. At least, not any faster than anybody else."

"But there's no need," I said, trying to laugh, "is there? in killing yourself."

I wanted to say more, but I couldn't. I wanted to talk about will power and how life could be—well, beautiful. I wanted to say that it was all within; but was it? or, rather, wasn't that exactly the trouble? And I wanted to promise that I would never fail him again. But it would all have sounded—empty words and lies.

So I made the promise to myself and prayed that I would keep it.

"It's terrible sometimes, inside," he said, "that's what's the trouble. You walk these streets, black and funky and cold, and there's not really a living ass to talk to, and there's nothing shaking, and there's no way of getting it out—that storm inside. You can't talk it and you can't make love with it, and when you finally try to get with it and play it, you realize *nobody's* listening. So *you've* got to listen. You got to find a way to listen."

And then he walked away from the window and sat on the sofa again, as though all the wind had suddenly been knocked out of him. "Sometimes you'll do *anything* to play, even cut your mother's throat." He laughed and looked at me. "Or your brother's." Then he sobered. "Or your own." Then: "Don't worry. I'm all right now and I think I'll *be* all right.

But I can't forget—where I've been. I don't mean just the physical place I've been, I mean where I've *been.* And *what* I've been."

"What have you been, Sonny?" I asked.

He smiled—but sat sideways on the sofa, his elbow resting on the back, his fingers playing with his mouth and chin, not looking at me. "I've been something I didn't recognize, didn't know I could be. Didn't know anybody could be." He stopped, looking inward, looking helplessly young, looking old. "I'm not talking about it now because I feel *guilty* or anything like that—maybe it would be better if I did, I don't know. Anyway, I can't really talk about it. Not to you, not to anybody," and now he turned and faced me. "Sometimes, you know, and it was actually when I was most *out* of the world, I felt that I was in it, that I was *with* it, really, and I could play or I didn't really have to *play*, it just came out of me, it was there. And I don't know how I played, thinking about it now, but I know I did awful things, those times, sometimes, to people. Or it wasn't that I *did* anything to them—it was that they weren't real." He picked up the beer can; it was empty; he rolled it between his palms: "And other times—well, I needed a fix, I needed to find a place to lean, I needed to clear a space to *listen*—and I couldn't find it, and I—went crazy, I did terrible things to *me*, I was terrible *for* me." He began pressing the beer can between his hands, I watched the metal begin to give. It glittered, as he played with it like a knife, and I was afraid he would cut himself, but I said nothing. "Oh well. I can never tell you. I was all by myself at the bottom of something, stinking and sweating and crying and shaking, and I smelled it, you know? *my* stink, and I thought I'd die if I couldn't get away from it and yet, all the same, I knew that everything I was doing was just locking me in with it. And I didn't know," he paused, still flattening the beer can, "I didn't know, I still *don't* know, something kept telling me that maybe it was good to smell your own stink, but I didn't think that *that* was what I'd been trying to do—and—who can stand it?" and he abruptly dropped the ruined beer can, looking at me with a small, still smile, and then rose, walking to the window as though it were the **lodestone**[27] rock. I watched his face, he watched the avenue. "I couldn't tell you when Mama died—but the reason I wanted to leave Harlem so bad was to get away from drugs. And then, when I ran away, that's what I was running from—really. When I came back, nothing had changed, *I* hadn't changed, I was just—older." And he stopped, drumming with his fingers on the windowpane. The sun had vanished, soon darkness would fall. I watched his face. "It can come again," he said, almost as though speaking to himself. Then he turned to me. "It can come again," he repeated. "I just want you to know that."

"All right," I said, at last. "So it can come again. All right."

He smiled, but the smile was sorrowful. "I had to try to tell you," he said.

---

[27] **lodestone**—like a magnetic ore that attracts iron or steel objects.

"Yes," I said. "I understand that."

"You're my brother," he said, looking straight at me, and not smiling at all.

"Yes," I repeated, "yes. I understand that."

He turned back to the window, looking out. "All that hatred down there," he said, "all that hatred and misery and love. It's a wonder it doesn't blow the avenue apart."

We went to the only nightclub on a short, dark street, downtown. We squeezed through the narrow, chattering, jampacked bar to the entrance of the big room, where the bandstand was. And we stood there for a moment, for the lights were very dim in this room and we couldn't see. Then, "Hello, boy," said the voice and an enormous black man, much older than Sonny or myself, erupted out of all that atmospheric lighting and put an arm around Sonny's shoulder. "I been sitting right here," he said, "waiting for you."

He had a big voice, too, and heads in the darkness turned toward us.

Sonny grinned and pulled a little away, and said, "Creole, this is my brother. I told you about him."

Creole shook my hand. "I'm glad to meet you, son," he said, and it was clear that he was glad to meet me *there*, for Sonny's sake. And he smiled, "You got a real musician in *your* family," and he took his arm from Sonny's shoulder and slapped him, lightly, affectionately, with the back of his hand.

"Well. Now I've heard it all," said a voice behind us. This was another musician, and a friend of Sonny's, a coal-black cheerful-looking man, built close to the ground. He immediately began confiding to me, at the top of his lungs, the most terrible things about Sonny, his teeth gleaming like a lighthouse and his laugh coming up out of him like the beginning of an earthquake. And it turned out that everyone at the bar knew Sonny, or almost everyone; some were musicians, working there, or nearby, or not working, some were simply hangers-on, and some were there to hear Sonny play. I was introduced to all of them and they were all very polite to me. Yet, it was clear that, for them, I was only Sonny's brother. Here, I was in Sonny's world. Or, rather: his kingdom. Here, it was not even a question that his veins bore royal blood.

Here, I was in Sonny's world. Or, rather: his kingdom.

They were going to play soon and Creole installed me, by myself, at a table in a dark corner. Then I watched them, Creole, and the little black man, and Sonny, and the others, while they horsed around, standing just below the bandstand. The light from the bandstand spilled just a little short of them and, watching them laughing and gesturing and moving about, I had the feeling that they, nevertheless, were being most careful not to step into that circle of light too suddenly: that if they moved into the light too suddenly, without thinking, they would perish in flame. Then, while I watched, one of them, the small black man, moved into the light and crossed the bandstand and started fooling around with his drums. Then—being funny and being, also, extremely ceremonious—Creole took Sonny by the arm and led him to the piano. A woman's voice called Sonny's name and a few hands started clapping. And Sonny, also being funny and being ceremonious, and so touched, I think, that he could have cried, but neither hiding it nor showing it, riding it like a man, grinned, and put both hands to his heart and bowed from the waist.

Creole then went to the bass fiddle and a lean, very bright-skinned brown man jumped up on the bandstand and picked up his horn. So there they were, and the atmosphere on the bandstand and in the room began to change and tighten. Someone stepped up to the microphone and announced them. Then there were all kinds of murmurs. Some people at the bar shushed others. The waitress ran around, frantically getting in the last orders, guys and chicks got closer to each other, and the lights on the bandstand, on the quartet, turned to a kind of **indigo**.[28] Then they all looked different there. Creole looked about him for the last time, as though he were making certain that all his chickens were in the coop, and then he—jumped and struck the fiddle. And there they were.

All I know about music is that not many people ever really hear it. And even then, on the rare occasions when something opens within, and the music enters, what we mainly hear, or hear **corroborated**,[29] are personal, private, vanishing **evocations**.[30] But the man who creates the music is hearing something else, is dealing with the roar rising from the void and imposing order on it as it hits the air. What is evoked in him, then, is of another order, more terrible because it has no words, and triumphant, too, for that same reason. And his triumph, when he triumphs, is ours. I just watched Sonny's face. His face was troubled, he was working hard, but he wasn't with it. And I had the feeling that, in a way, everyone on the bandstand was waiting for him, both waiting for him and pushing him along. But as I began to watch Creole, I realized that it was Creole who held them all back. He had them on a short rein. Up there, keeping the beat with his whole body, wailing on the fiddle, with his eyes half closed, he was listening to everything, but he was listening to Sonny. He was having a dialogue with Sonny. He wanted Sonny to leave the shoreline and strike out for the deep water. He was Sonny's witness that deep water and drowning were not the same thing—he had been there, and he knew. And he wanted Sonny to know. He was waiting for Sonny to do the things on the keys which would let Creole know that Sonny was in the water.

And, while Creole listened, Sonny moved, deep within, exactly like someone in torment. I had never before thought of how awful the relationship must be between the musician and his instrument. He has to fill it, this instrument, with the breath of life, his own. He has to make it do what he wants it to do. And a piano is just a piano. It's made out of so much wood and wires and little hammers and

---

[28] **indigo**—dark blue.

[29] **corroborated**—strengthened.

[30] **evocations**—re-creations through imagination.

big ones, and ivory. While there's only so much you can do with it, the only way to find this out is to try; to try and make it do everything.

And Sonny hadn't been near a piano for over a year. And he wasn't on much better terms with his life, not the life that stretched before him now. He and the piano **stammered**,[31] started one way, got scared, stopped; started another way, panicked, marked time, started again; then seemed to have found a direction, panicked again, got stuck. And the face I saw on Sonny I'd never seen before. Everything had been burned out of it, and, at the same time, things usually hidden were being burned in, by the fire and fury of the battle which was occurring in him up there.

Yet, watching Creole's face as they neared the end of the first set,[32] I had the feeling that something had happened, something I hadn't heard. Then they finished, there was scattered applause, and then, without an instant's warning, Creole started into something else, it was almost **sardonic**,[33] it was *Am I Blue*. And, as though he commanded, Sonny began to play. Something began to happen. And Creole let out the reins. The dry, low, black man said something awful on the drums, Creole answered, and the drums talked back. Then the horn insisted, sweet and high, slightly detached perhaps, and Creole listened, commenting now and then, dry, and driving, beautiful and calm and old. Then they all came together again, and Sonny was part of the family again. I could tell this from his face. He seemed to have found, right there beneath his fingers, a brand-new piano. It seemed that he couldn't get over it. Then, for a while, just being happy with Sonny, they seemed to be agreeing with him that brand-new pianos certainly were a gas.

Then Creole stepped forward to remind them that what they were playing was the blues. He hit something in all of them, he hit something in me, myself, and the music tightened and deepened, apprehension began to beat the air. Creole began to tell us what the blues were all about. They were not about anything very new. He and his boys up there were keeping it new, at the risk of ruin, destruction, madness, and death, in order to find new ways to make us listen. For, while the tale of how we suffer, and how we are delighted, and how we may triumph is never new, it always must be heard. There isn't any other tale to tell, it's the only light we've got in all this darkness.

And this tale, according to that face, that body, those strong hands on those strings, has another aspect in every country, and a new depth in every generation. Listen, Creole seemed to be saying, listen. Now these are Sonny's blues. He made the little black man on the drums know it, and the bright, brown man on the horn. Creole wasn't trying any longer to get Sonny in the water. He was wishing him Godspeed. Then he stepped back, very slowly, filling

[31] **stammered**—involuntarily and repetitively paused and stumbled.

[32] set—section of a musical performance.

[33] **sardonic**—scornful, mocking, derisive.

the air with the immense suggestion that Sonny speak for himself.

Then they all gathered around Sonny and Sonny played. Every now and again one of them seemed to say, amen. Sonny's fingers filled the air with life, his life. But that life contained so many others. And Sonny went all the way back, he really began with the spare, flat statement of the opening phrase of the song. Then he began to make it his. It was very beautiful because it wasn't hurried and it was no longer a **lament**.[34] I seemed to hear with what burning he had made it his, with what burning we had yet to make it ours, how we could cease lamenting. Freedom lurked around us and I understood, at last, that he could help us to be free if we would listen, that he would never be free until we did. Yet, there was no battle in his face now, I heard what he had gone through, and would continue to go through until he came to rest in earth. He had made it his: that long line, of which we knew only Mama and Daddy. And he was giving it back, as everything must be given back, so that, passing through death, it can live forever. I saw my mother's face again, and felt, for the first time, how the stones of the road she had walked on must have bruised her feet. I saw the moonlit road where my father's brother died. And it brought something else back to me, and carried me past it, I saw my little girl again and felt Isabel's tears again, and I felt my own tears begin to rise. And I was yet aware that this was only a moment, that the world waited outside, as hungry as a tiger, and that trouble stretched above us, longer than the sky.

Then it was over. Creole and Sonny let out their breath, both soaking wet, and grinning. There was a lot of applause and some of it was real. In the dark, the girl came by and I asked her to take drinks to the bandstand. There was a long pause, while they talked up there in the indigo light and after awhile I saw the girl put a Scotch and milk on top of the piano for Sonny. He didn't seem to notice it, but just before they started playing again, he sipped from it and looked toward me, and nodded. Then he put it back on top of the piano. For me, then, as they began to play again, it glowed and shook above my brother's head like the very cup of trembling.

[34] **lament**—expression of grief, mourning, or regret.

QUESTIONS TO CONSIDER

1. Why does the narrator not write to Sonny in prison at first?
2. What makes him change his mind?
3. What is his mother trying to tell the narrator when she says, "You got to let him know you's there"? Does he follow this advice?
4. What does the narrator learn about Sonny from hearing him play?
5. How does each of the brothers differ in his view of life and how it should be led?
6. How does this story comment on race troubles African Americans faced in Baldwin's day?

Alice Walker ▶

Roselily

BY ALICE WALKER

Alice Walker (1944–   ) was born in Eatonton, Georgia, the last of eight children in a family of sharecroppers. Walker was an excellent student and, thanks to money raised by her community and a scholarship from the state of Georgia, she was able to go to Spelman College. The Civil Rights movement was sweeping through the South, and Walker embraced it. She participated in demonstrations and discovered the power of protest, later describing herself and her fellow protesters as "young and bursting with fear and determination to change our world." After two years at Spelman, Walker transferred to Sarah Lawrence College in New York, where she discovered feminism and the difficult position of African-American women. She came to believe that sexism was as great a problem for African-American women as racism. After graduation in 1965, Walker returned to the South and worked to promote voter registration and African-American rights. She also spent time collecting folklore and stories from African-American women in Mississippi. In 1968 her first book, Once: Poems, *was published. This was followed by her first novel,* The Third Life of Grange Copeland, *in 1970. Walker regularly published stories and poems and began teaching at universities. Published in 1982, her novel* The Color Purple *won both the Pulitzer Prize and the American Book Award. With the film version in 1985, Alice Walker became a household name, and she has used her fame to fight for the causes she believes in. "Every one of these writings represents my struggle not simply to survive the past and remain nurtured by it but to embrace the present and fight for the future." "Roselily," typical of Walker's work, is as much a critique of society as a work of fiction.*

Dearly Beloved,[1]

She dreams; dragging herself across the world. A small girl in her mother's white robe and veil, knee raised waist high through a bowl of quicksand soup. The man who stands beside her is against this standing on the front porch of her house, being married to the sound of cars whizzing by on highway 61.

we are gathered here

Like cotton to be weighed. Her fingers at the last minute busily removing dry leaves and twigs. Aware it is a superficial sweep. She knows he blames Mississippi for the respectful way the men turn their heads up in the yard, the women stand waiting and knowledgeable, their children held from mischief by teachings from the wrong God. He glares beyond them to the

[1] *Dearly Beloved*—The italicized lines are all lines from the traditional Christian wedding ceremony.

occupants of the cars, white faces glued to promises beyond a country wedding, noses thrust forward like dogs on a track. For him they **usurp**[2] the wedding.

in the sight of God

Yes, open house. That is what country black folks like. She dreams she does not already have three children. A squeeze around the flowers in her hands chokes off three and four and five years of breath. Instantly she is ashamed and frightened in her superstition. She looks for the first time at the preacher, forces humility into her eyes, as if she believes he is, in fact, a man of God. She can imagine God, a small black boy, timidly pulling the preacher's coattail.

to join this man and this woman

She thinks of ropes, chains, handcuffs, his religion. His place of worship. Where she will be required to sit apart with covered head. In Chicago, a word she hears when thinking of smoke, from his description of what a **cinder**[3] was, which they never had in Panther Burn. She sees hovering over the heads of the clean neighbors in her front yard black specks falling, clinging, from the sky. But in Chicago. Respect, a chance to build. Her children at last from underneath the **detrimental**[4] wheel. A chance to be on top. What a relief, she thinks. What a vision, a view, from up so high.

in holy matrimony.

Her fourth child she gave away to the child's father who had some money. Certainly a good job. Had gone to Harvard. Was a good man but weak because good language meant so much to him he could not live with Roselily. Could not abide TV in the living room, five beds in three rooms, no Bach[5] except from four to six on Sunday afternoons. No chess at all. She does not forget to worry about her son among his father's people. She wonders if the New England climate will agree with him. If he will ever come down to Mississippi, as his father did,[6] to try to right the country's wrongs. She wonders if he will be stronger than his father. His father cried off and on throughout her pregnancy. Went to skin and bones. Suffered nightmares, retching and falling out of bed. Tried to kill himself. Later told his wife he found the right baby through friends. Vouched for, the sterling qualities that would make up his character.

It is not her nature to blame. Still, she is not entirely thankful. She supposes New England, the North, to be quite different from what she knows. It seems right somehow to her that people who move there to live return home completely changed. She thinks of the air, the smoke,

---

[2] **usurp**—take over; seize another's rights or position.

[3] **cinder**—partly burned substance that will not produce any more flame.

[4] **detrimental**—causing damage, harm, or loss.

[5] Bach—Johann Sebastian Bach (1685–1750), German composer and organist, one of the most significant figures in the history of music.

[6] as his father did—reference to the Civil Rights era when many Northerners, particularly college students, came to the South to participate in sit-ins, voter registration drives, and other forms of protest.

the cinders. Imagines cinders big as hailstones; heavy, weighing on the people. Wonders how this pressure finds its way into the veins, roping the springs of laughter.

If there's anybody here that knows a reason why

But of course they know no reason why beyond what they daily have come to know. She thinks of the man who will be her husband, feels shut away from him because of the stiff severity of his plain black suit. His religion. A lifetime of black and white. Of veils. Covered head. It is as if her children are already gone from her. Not dead, but exalted on a pedestal, a stalk that has no roots. She wonders how to make new roots. It is beyond her. She wonders what one does with memories in a brand-new life. This had seemed easy, until she thought of it. "The reasons why . . . the people who" . . . she thinks, and does not wonder where the thought is from.

these two should not be joined

She thinks of her mother, who is dead. Dead, but still her mother. Joined. This is confusing. Of her father. A gray old man who sold wild mink, rabbit, fox skins to Sears, Roebuck.[7] He stands in the yard, like a man waiting for a train. Her young sisters stand behind her in smooth green dresses, with flowers in their hands and hair. They giggle, she feels, at the absurdity of the wedding. They are ready for something new. She thinks the man beside her should marry one of them. She feels old. **Yoked**.[8] An arm seems to reach out from behind her and snatch her backward. She thinks of cemeteries and the long sleep of grandparents mingling in the dirt. She believes that she believes in ghosts. In the soil giving back what it takes.

together,

In the city. He sees her in a new way. This she knows, and is grateful. But is it new enough? She cannot always be a bride and virgin, wearing robes and veil. Even now her body itches to be free of satin and voile, organdy[9] and lily of the valley. Memories crash against her. Memories of being bare to the sun. She wonders what it will be like. Not to have to go to a job. Not to work in a sewing plant. Not to worry about learning to sew straight seams in workingmen's overalls, jeans and dress pants. Her place will be in the home, he has said, repeatedly, promising her rest she had prayed for. But now she wonders. When she is rested, what will she do? They will make babies—she thinks practically about her fine brown body, his strong black one. They will be **inevitable**.[10] Her hands will be full. Full of what? Babies. She is not comforted.

let him speak

---

[7] Sears, Roebuck—famous mail order department store.

[8] **Yoked**—joined securely.

[9] voile, organdy—Voile is a light, sheer fabric often used for making dresses. Organdy is a stiff, transparent fabric.

[10] **inevitable**—unavoidable.

She wishes she had asked him to explain more of what he meant. But she was impatient. Impatient to be done with sewing. With doing everything for three children, alone. Impatient to leave the girls she had known since childhood, their children growing up, their husbands hanging around her, already old, seedy. Nothing about them that she wanted, or needed. The fathers of her children driving by, waving, not waving; reminders of times she would just as soon forget. Impatient to see the South Side,[11] where they would live and build and be respectable and respected and free. Her husband would free her. A romantic hush. Proposal. Promises. A new life! Respectable, **reclaimed**,[12] renewed. Free! In robe and veil.

or forever hold

She does not even know if she loves him. She loves his **sobriety**.[13] His refusal to sing just because he knows the tune. She loves his pride. His blackness and his gray car. She loves his understanding of her *condition*. She thinks she loves the effort he will make to redo her into what he truly wants. His love of her makes her completely conscious of how unloved she was before. This is something; though it makes her unbearably sad. Melancholy. She blinks her eyes. Remembers she is finally being married, like other girls. Like other girls, women? Something strains upward behind her eyes. She thinks of the something as a rat trapped, cornered, scurrying to and fro in her head, peering through the windows of her eyes. She wants to live for once. But doesn't know quite what that means. Wonders if she has ever done it. If she ever will. The preacher is **odious**[14] to her. She wants to strike him out of the way, out of her light, with the back of her hand. It seems to her he has always been standing in front of her, barring her way.

his peace.

The rest she does not hear. She feels a kiss, passionate, rousing, within the general **pandemonium**.[15] Cars drive up blowing their horns. Firecrackers go off. Dogs come from under the house and begin to yelp and bark. Her husband's hand is like the clasp of an iron gate. People congratulate. Her children press against her. They look with awe and **distaste**[16] mixed with hope at their new father. He stands curiously apart, in spite of the people crowding about to grasp his free hand. He smiles at them all but his eyes are as if turned inward. He knows they cannot understand that he is not a Christian. He will not explain himself. He feels different, he looks it. The old women thought he was like one of their sons except that he had somehow got away from them. Still a son, not a son. Changed.

---

[11] South Side—area of Chicago that has long been mostly African-American.

[12] **reclaimed**—made respectable or reformed; turned from evil.

[13] **sobriety**—seriousness or solemnity.

[14] **odious**—arousing strong dislike.

[15] **pandemonium**—noisy disorder.

[16] **distaste**—dislike or uneasiness.

She thinks how it will be later in the night in the silvery gray car. How they will spin through the darkness of Mississippi and in the morning be in Chicago, Illinois. She thinks of Lincoln,[17] the president. That is all she knows about the place. She feels ignorant, *wrong*, backward. She presses her worried fingers into his palm. He is standing in front of her. In the crush of well-wishing people, he does not look back.

[17] Lincoln—Abraham Lincoln (1809–1865), sixteenth U.S. president. For most of his life, Lincoln made his home in Illinois.

QUESTIONS TO CONSIDER

1. Why is the narrator getting married?
2. How do her motives differ from those of the bridegroom?
3. What is the relation of the italicized lines to the text? How do they add to the meaning of the story?
4. What do you think Alice Walker thinks of marriage?
5. What is Walker saying about the place of women in society?

Raymond Carver ▶

The Student's Wife

BY RAYMOND CARVER

Raymond Carver (1938–1988) was the leader of a new school of realistic fiction that sprang up in the 1960s and focused on the starkest realities of American working-class life. Sometimes called "Dirty Realism," Carver's stories tell of the broken lives of the down and out: drunkenness, depression, bad marriages, dead-end jobs, and violence are the material from which he worked up his stories. Carver was born in Oregon. His father was a heavy drinking blue-collar worker, and his mother a waitress. They separated early in Carver's life. He himself got married right out of high school, and the next decade was spent working menial jobs trying to keep his family afloat. He was always attempting to write and finally was able to go to college in 1959. In the late 1960s, his stories began to catch attention, and in 1974 his first volume was published. The collections that followed gained him critical notice and major awards, but Carver's life was falling apart due to alcoholism and a failed marriage. In the 1980s he pulled himself together, and the stories in his final collections show a more mature and contemplative tone. What was so influential about Carver's work was the flat, plain style and the economy of words and sentences. Carver has often been compared to Hemingway, and his influence on contemporary writers has certainly been as great as Hemingway's was in the 1920s and 1930s.

He had been reading to her from Rilke,[1] a poet he admired, when she fell asleep with her head on his pillow. He liked reading aloud, and he read well—a confident **sonorous**[2] voice, now pitched low and **somber**,[3] now rising, now thrilling. He never looked away from the page when he read and stopped only to reach to the nightstand for a cigaret. It was a rich voice that spilled her into a dream of caravans just setting out from walled cities and bearded men in robes. She had listened to him for a few minutes, then she had closed her eyes and drifted off.

He went on reading aloud. The children had been asleep for hours, and outside a car rubbered by now and then on the wet pavement. After a while he put down the book and turned in the bed to reach for the lamp. She opened her eyes suddenly, as if

---

[1] Rilke—Rainer Maria Rilke (1875–1926), renowned German poet.

[2] **sonorous**—producing a deep, full, or rich sound.

[3] **somber**—gloomy, dark, or melancholy.

frightened, and blinked two or three times. Her eyelids looked oddly dark and fleshy to him as they flicked up and down over her fixed glassy eyes. He stared at her.

"Are you dreaming?" he asked.

She nodded and brought her hand up and touched her fingers to the plastic curlers at each side of her head. Tomorrow would be Friday, her day for all the four-to-seven-year-olds in the Woodlawn Apartments. He kept looking at her, leaning on his elbow, at the same time trying to straighten the spread with his free hand. She had a smooth-skinned face with prominent cheekbones; the cheekbones, she sometimes insisted to friends, were from her father, who had been one-quarter Nez Perce.[4]

Then: "Make me a little sandwich of something, Mike. With butter and lettuce and salt on the bread."

He did nothing and he said nothing because he wanted to go to sleep. But when he opened his eyes she was still awake, watching him.

"Can't you go to sleep, Nan?" he said, very solemnly. "It's late."

"I'd like something to eat first," she said. "My legs and arms hurt for some reason, and I'm hungry."

He groaned extravagantly as he rolled out of bed.

He fixed her the sandwich and brought it in on a saucer. She sat up in bed and smiled when he came into the bedroom, then slipped a pillow behind her back as she took the saucer. He thought she looked like a hospital patient in her white nightgown.

"What a funny little dream I had."

"What were you dreaming?" he said, getting into bed and turning over onto his side away from her. He stared at the nightstand waiting. Then he closed his eyes slowly.

"Do you really want to hear it?" she said.

"Sure," he said.

She settled back comfortably on the pillow and picked a crumb from her lip.

"Well. It seemed like a real long drawn-out kind of dream, you know, with all kinds of relationships going on, but I can't remember everything now. It was all very clear when I woke up, but it's beginning to fade now. How long have I been asleep, Mike? It doesn't really matter, I guess. Anyway, I think it was that we were staying someplace overnight. I don't know where the kids were, but it was just the two of us at some little hotel or something. It was on some lake that wasn't familiar. There was another, older, couple there and they wanted to take us for a ride in their motorboat." She laughed, remembering, and leaned forward off the pillow. "The next thing I recall is we were down at the boat landing. Only the way it turned out, they had just one seat in the boat, a kind of bench up in the front, and it was only big enough for three. You and I started arguing about who was going to sacrifice and sit all cooped up in the back. You said you were, and I said I was. But I finally squeezed in the back of the boat. It was so narrow it

[4] Nez Perce—Native-American tribe that used to live in Idaho, Oregon, and Washington.

hurt my legs, and I was afraid the water was going to come in over the sides. Then I woke up."

"That's some dream," he managed to say and felt drowsily that he should say something more. "You remember Bonnie Travis? Fred Travis' wife? She used to have color dreams, she said."

She looked at the sandwich in her hand and took a bite. When she had swallowed, she ran her tongue in behind her lips and balanced the saucer on her lap as she reached behind and plumped up the pillow. Then she smiled and leaned back against the pillow again.

"Do you remember that time we stayed overnight on the Tilton River, Mike? When you caught that big fish the next morning?" She placed her hand on his shoulder. "Do you remember that?" she said.

She did. After scarcely thinking about it these last years, it had begun coming back to her lately. It was a month or two after they'd married and gone away for a weekend. They had sat by a little campfire that night, a watermelon in the snow-cold river, and she'd fried Spam and eggs and canned beans for supper and pancakes and Spam and eggs in the same blackened pan the next morning. She had burned the pan both times she cooked, and they could never get the coffee to boil, but it was one of the best times they'd ever had. She remembered he had read to her that night as well: Elizabeth Browning[5] and a few poems from the *Rubáiyát*.[6] They had had so many covers over them that she could hardly turn her feet under all the weight. The next morning he had hooked a big trout, and people stopped their cars on the road across the river to watch him play it in.

"Well? Do you remember or not?" she said, patting him on the shoulder. "Mike?"

"I remember," he said. He shifted a little on his side, opened his eyes. He did not remember very well, he thought. What he did remember was very carefully combed hair and loud half-baked ideas about life and art, and he did not want to remember that.

"That was a long time ago, Nan," he said.

"We'd just got out of high school. You hadn't started to college," she said.

He waited, and then he raised up onto his arm and turned his head to look at her over his shoulder. "You about finished with that sandwich, Nan?" She was still sitting up in the bed.

She nodded and gave him the saucer.

"I'll turn off the light," he said.

"If you want," she said.

Then he pulled down into the bed again and extended his foot until it touched against hers. He lay still for a minute and then tried to relax.

"Mike, you're not asleep, are you?"

"No," he said. "Nothing like that."

"Well, don't go to sleep before me," she said. "I don't want to be awake by myself."

---

[5] Elizabeth Browning—English poet (1806–1861) famous for her sonnets.

[6] *Rubáiyát*—poem by Persian poet Omar Khayyam (1050?–1123) that is famous in its English translation by Edward FitzGerald.

He didn't answer, but he inched a little closer to her on his side. When she put her arm over him and planted her hand flat against his chest, he took her fingers and squeezed them lightly. But in moments his hand dropped away to the bed, and he sighed.

"Mike? Honey? I wish you'd rub my legs. My legs hurt," she said.

"God," he said softly. "I was sound asleep."

"Well, I wish you'd rub my legs and talk to me. My shoulders hurt, too. But my legs especially."

He turned over and began rubbing her legs, then fell asleep again with his hand on her hip.

"Mike?"

"What is it, Nan? Tell me what it *is*."

"I wish you'd rub me all over," she said, turning onto her back. "My legs and arms both hurt tonight." She raised her knees to make a tower with the covers.

He opened his eyes briefly in the dark and then shut them. "Growing pains, huh?"

"O God, yes," she said, wiggling her toes, glad she had drawn him out. "When I was ten or eleven years old I was as big then as I am now. You should've seen me! I grew so fast in those days my legs and arms hurt me all the time. Didn't you?"

"Didn't I what?"

"Didn't you ever feel yourself growing?"

"Not that I remember," he said.

At last he raised up on his elbow, struck a match, and looked at the clock. He turned his pillow over to the cooler side and lay down again.

She said, "You're asleep, Mike. I wish you'd want to talk."

"All right," he said, not moving.

"Just hold me and get me off to sleep. I can't go to sleep," she said.

He turned over and put his arm over her shoulder as she turned onto her side to face the wall.

"Why don't you tell me all the things you like and the things you don't like."

"Mike?"

He tapped his toes against her foot.

"Why don't you tell me all the things you like and the things you don't like."

"Don't know any right now," he said. "Tell me if you want," he said.

"If you promise to tell *me*. Is that a promise?"

He tapped her foot again.

"Well . . ." she said and turned onto her back, pleased. "I like good foods, steaks and hash-brown potatoes, things like that. I like good books and magazines, riding on trains at night, and those times I flew in an airplane." She stopped. "Of course none of this is in order of preference. I'd have to think about it if it was in the order of preference. But I like that, flying in airplanes. There's a moment as you leave the ground you feel whatever happens is all right." She put her leg across his ankle. "I like staying up late at night and then staying in bed the next morning. I wish we could do that all the time, not just once in a while. And I like sex. I like to be touched now and then when I'm not expecting it. I like going to movies and drinking beer with friends afterwards. I like to have friends. I like Janice Hendricks very much. I'd like to go dancing at least once a week. I'd like to have nice clothes all the time. I'd like to be able to buy the kids nice clothes every time they need it without having to wait. Laurie needs a new little outfit right now for Easter. And I'd like to get Gary a little suit or something. He's old enough. I'd like you to have a new suit, too. You really need a new suit more than he does. And I'd like us to have a place of our own. I'd like to stop moving around every year, or every other year. Most of all," she said, "I'd like us both just to live a good honest life without having to worry about money and bills and things like that. You're asleep," she said.

"I'm not," he said.

"I can't think of anything else. You go now. Tell me what you'd like."

"I don't know. Lots of things," he mumbled.

"Well, tell me. We're just talking, aren't we?"

"I wish you'd leave me alone, Nan." He turned over to his side of the bed again and let his arm rest off the edge. She turned too and pressed against him.

"Mike?"

"Jesus," he said. Then: "All right. Let me stretch my legs a minute, then I'll wake up."

In a while she said, "Mike? Are you asleep?" She shook his shoulder gently, but there was no response. She lay there for a time huddled against his body, trying to sleep. She lay quietly at first, without moving, crowded against him and taking only very small, very even breaths. But she could not sleep.

She tried not to listen to his breathing, but it began to make her uncomfortable. There was a sound coming from inside his nose when he breathed. She tried to regulate her breathing so that she could breathe in and out at the same rhythm he did. It was no use. The little sound in his nose made everything no use. There was a webby squeak in his chest too. She turned again and nestled her bottom against his, stretched her arm over to the edge and cautiously put her fingertips against the cold wall. The covers had pulled up at the foot of the bed, and she could feel a draft when she moved her legs. She heard two people coming up the stairs to the apartment next door. Someone gave a throaty laugh before opening the door. Then she heard a chair drag on the floor. She turned again. The toilet flushed next door, and then it flushed again. Again she turned, onto her back this time, and tried to relax. She remembered an article she'd once read in a magazine: If all the bones and muscles and joints in the body could join together in perfect relaxation, sleep would almost certainly come. She took a long breath, closed her eyes, and lay perfectly still, arms straight along her sides. She tried to relax. She tried to imagine her legs suspended, bathed in something gauze-like. She turned onto her stomach. She closed her eyes, then she opened them. She thought of the fingers of her hand lying curled on the sheet in front of her lips. She raised a finger and lowered it to the sheet. She touched the wedding band on her ring finger with her thumb. She turned onto her side and then onto her back again. And then she began to feel afraid, and in one unreasoning moment of longing she prayed to go to sleep.

Please, God, let me go to sleep.

She tried to sleep.

"Mike," she whispered.

There was no answer.

She heard one of the children turn over in the bed and bump against the wall in the next room. She listened and listened but there was no other sound. She laid her hand under her left breast and felt the beat of her heart rising into her fingers. She turned onto her stomach and began to cry, her head off the pillow, her mouth against the sheet. She cried. And then she climbed out over the foot of the bed.

She washed her hands and face in the bathroom. She brushed her teeth. She brushed her teeth and watched her face in the mirror. In the living room she turned up the heat. Then she sat down at the kitchen table, drawing her feet up underneath the nightgown. She cried again. She lit a cigaret from the pack on the table. After a time she walked back to the bedroom and got her robe.

She looked in on the children. She pulled the covers up over her son's shoulders. She went back to the living room and sat in the big chair. She paged through a magazine and tried to read. She gazed at the photographs and then she tried to read again. Now and then a car went by on the street outside and she looked up. As each car passed she waited, listening. And then she looked down at the magazine again. There was a stack of magazines in the rack by the big chair. She paged through them all.

When it began to be light outside she got up. She walked to the window. The cloudless sky over the hills was beginning to turn white. The trees and the row of two-story apartment houses across the street were beginning to take shape as she watched. The sky grew whiter, the light expanding rapidly up from behind the hills. Except for the times she had been up with one or another of the children (which she did not count because she had never looked outside, only hurried back to bed or to the kitchen), she had seen few sunrises in her life and those when she was little. She knew that none of them had been like this. Not in pictures she had seen nor in any book she had read had she learned a sunrise was so terrible as this.

She waited and then she moved over to the door and turned the lock and stepped out onto the porch. She closed the robe at her throat. The air was wet and cold. By stages things were becoming very visible. She let her eyes see everything until they fastened on the red winking light atop the radio tower atop the opposite hill.

She went through the dim apartment, back into the bedroom. He was knotted up in the center of the bed, the covers bunched over his shoulders, his head half under the pillow. He looked desperate in his heavy sleep, his arm flung out across her side of the bed, his jaws clenched. As she looked, the room grew very light and the pale sheets whitened grossly before her eyes.

She wet her lips with a sticking sound and got down on her knees. She put her hands out on the bed.

"God," she said. "God, will you help us, God?" she said.

QUESTIONS TO CONSIDER

1. How do Nan's and Mike's personalities differ?
2. What is it that Nan wants out of life?
3. What do you think Nan is so worried about?
4. What can you infer from her desires that their life is like?

Louise Erdrich ▶

Snares

BY LOUISE ERDRICH

Louise Erdrich (1954–) is a woman between two worlds, and her goal as a writer is to bridge the differences she feels as the daughter of a Native-American mother and a German-American father. Erdrich grew up near a Chippewa reservation in North Dakota, where her parents taught at the reservation school. As a youth, she took her heritage for granted, and it was not until college at Dartmouth that she began to be interested in Native-American culture and its survival. When she began to write in the 1970s, this heritage was her main inspiration and subject. Her first novel, Love Medicine *(1984), is the story of two Chippewa families trying to survive. The book brilliantly combined Native-American folklore and modernist storytelling and made her the best known of a new generation of Native-American writers. Over the years the story of* Love Medicine *has grown into a loose tetralogy, as Erdrich has followed her characters through* The Beet Queen *(1986),* Tracks *(1988), and* The Bingo Palace *(1994). Erdrich's style reflects the school of "magic realism" that has flourished in the Americas since the 1960s. Magic realist stories incorporate elements of folklore, magic, and the supernatural in starkly realistic stories: stories which in Erdrich's case are also quite minimalist. "Snares" is a tale of how things change on the reservations, but how they stay the same.*

It began after church with Margaret and her small granddaughter, Lulu, and was not to end until the long days of Lent[1] and a hard-packed snow. There were factions on the reservation, a treaty settlement in the Agent's hands. There were Chippewa who signed their names in the year 1924, and there were Chippewa who saw the cash offered as a flimsy bait. I was one and Fleur Pillager, Lulu's mother, was another who would not lift her hand to sign. It was said that all the power to witch, harm, or cure lay in Fleur, the lone survivor of the old Pillager clan. But as much as people feared Fleur, they listened to Margaret Kashpaw. She was the ringleader of the holdouts, a fierce, one-minded widow with a vinegar tongue.

Margaret Kashpaw had knots of muscles in her arms. Her braids were thin, gray as iron, and usually tied strictly behind her back so they wouldn't swing. She was plump as a basket below and tough as roots on top. Her face was gnarled around a beautiful sharp nose. Two shell earrings caught the light and flashed whenever she turned her head. She

---

[1] Lent—Christian season of penance.

had become increasingly religious in the years after her loss, and finally succeeded in dragging me to the Benediction Mass, where I was greeted by Father Damien, from whom I occasionally won small sums at dice.

"Grandfather Nanapush," he smiled, "at last."

"These benches are a hardship for an old man," I complained. "If you spread them with soft pine-needle cushions I'd have come before."

Father Damien stared thoughtfully at the tough pews, folded his hands inside the sleeves of his robe.

"You must think of their unyielding surfaces as helpful," he offered. "God sometimes enters the soul through the humblest parts of our anatomies,[2] if they are sensitized to suffering."

"A god who enters through the rear door," I countered, "is no better than a thief."

Father Damien was used to me, and smiled as he walked to the altar. I adjusted my old bones, longing for some relief, trying not to rustle for fear of Margaret's jabbing elbow. The time was long. Lulu probed all my pockets with her fingers until she found a piece of hard candy. I felt no great presence in this cold place and decided, as my back end ached and my shoulders stiffened, that our original gods were better, the Chippewa characters who were not exactly perfect but at least did not require sitting on hard boards.

When Mass was over and the smell of incense was thick in all our clothes, Margaret, Lulu, and I went out into the starry cold, the snow and stubble fields, and began the long walk to our homes. It was dusk. On either side of us the heavy trees stood motionless and blue. Our footsteps squeaked against the dry snow, the only sound to hear. We spoke very little, and even Lulu ceased her singing when the moon rose to half, poised like a balanced cup. We knew the very moment someone else stepped upon the road.

We had turned a bend and the footfalls came unevenly, just out of sight. There were two men, one mixed-blood or white, from the drop of his hard boot soles, and the other one quiet, an Indian. Not long and I heard them talking close behind us. From the rough, quick tension of the Indian's language, I recognized Lazarre. And the mixed-blood must be Clarence Morrissey. The two had signed the treaty and spoke in its favor to anyone they could collar at the store. They even came to people's houses to beg and argue that this was our one chance, our good chance, that the government would withdraw the offer. But wherever Margaret was, she slapped down their words like mosquitoes and said the only thing that lasts life to life is land. Money burns like tinder, flows like water. And as for promises, the wind is steadier. It is no wonder that, because she spoke so well, Lazarre and Clarence Morrissey wished to silence her. I sensed their bad intent as they passed us, an unpleasant edge of excitement in their looks and greetings.

They went on, disappeared in the dark brush.

---

2 anatomies—bodies.

"Margaret," I said, "we are going to cut back." My house was close, but Margaret kept walking forward as if she hadn't heard.

I took her arm, caught the little girl close, and started to turn us, but Margaret would have none of this and called me a coward. She grabbed the girl to her. Lulu, who did not mind getting tossed between us, laughed, tucked her hand into her grandma's pocket, and never missed a step. Two years ago she had tired of being carried, got up, walked. She had the balance of a little mink. She was slippery and clever, too, which was good because when the men jumped from the darkest area of brush and grappled with us half a mile on, Lulu slipped free and scrambled into the trees.

They were occupied with Margaret and me, at any rate. We were old enough to snap in two, our limbs dry as dead branches, but we fought as though our enemies were the Nadouissouix kidnappers of our childhood. Margaret uttered a war cry that had not been heard for fifty years, and bit Lazarre's hand to the bone, giving a wound which would later prove the death of him. As for Clarence, he had all he could do to wrestle me to the ground and knock me half unconscious. When he'd accomplished that, he tied me and tossed me into a wheelbarrow, which was hidden near the road for the purpose of lugging us to the Morrissey barn.

I came to my senses **trussed**[3] to a **manger**,[4] sitting on a **bale**.[5] Margaret was roped to another bale across from me, staring straight forward in a rage, a line of froth caught between her lips. On either side of her, shaggy cows chewed and shifted their thumping hooves. I rose and staggered, the weight of the manger on my back. I planned on Margaret biting through my ropes with her strong teeth, but then the two men entered.

I'm a talker, a fast-mouth who can't keep his thoughts straight, but lets fly with words and marvels at what he hears from his own mouth. I'm a smart one. I always was a devil for convincing women. And I wasn't too bad a shot, in other ways, at convincing men. But I had never been tied up before.

"*Booshoo*," I said. "Children, let us loose, your game is too rough!"

They stood between us, puffed with their secrets.

"Empty old windbag," said Clarence.

"I have a bargain for you," I said, looking for an opening. "Let us go and we won't tell Pukwan." Edgar Pukwan was the tribal police. "Boys get drunk sometimes and don't know what they're doing."

Lazarre laughed once, hard and loud. "We're not drunk," he said. "Just wanting what's coming to us, some justice, money out of it."

"Kill us," said Margaret. "We won't sign."

"Wait," I said. "My cousin Pukwan will find you boys, and have no mercy. Let us go. I'll sign and get it over with, and I'll persuade the old widow."

---

[3] **trussed**—tied up or bound tightly.

[4] **manger**—trough in which food for animals is placed.

[5] **bale**—large bound or wrapped package of material.

I signaled Margaret to keep her mouth shut. She blew air into her cheeks. Clarence looked expectantly at Lazarre, as if the show were over, but Lazarre folded his arms and was convinced of nothing.

I saw in his eyes that he intended us great harm. I saw his greed.

"You lie when it suits, skinny old dog," he said, wiping at his lips as if in hunger. "It's her we want, anyway. We'll shame her so she shuts her mouth."

"Easy enough," I said, smooth, "now that you've got her tied. She's plump and good looking. Eyes like a doe! But you forget that we're together, almost man and wife."

This wasn't true at all, and Margaret's face went rigid with tumbling fury and confusion. I kept talking.

"So of course if you do what you're thinking of doing you'll have to kill me afterward, and that will make my cousin Pukwan twice as angry, since I owe him a fat payment for a gun which he lent me and I never returned. All the same," I went on —their heads were spinning —"I'll forget you bad boys ever considered such a crime, something so terrible that Father Damien would nail you on boards just like in the example on the wall in church."

"Quit jabbering." Lazarre stopped me in a deadly voice.

It was throwing pebbles in a dry lake. My words left no ripple. I saw in his eyes that he intended us great harm. I saw his greed. It was like watching an ugly design of bruises come clear for a moment and reconstructing the evil blows that made them.

I played my last card.

"Whatever you do to Margaret you are doing to the Pillager woman!" I dropped my voice. "The witch, Fleur Pillager, is her own son's wife."

Clarence was too young to be frightened, but his mouth hung in interested puzzlement. My words had a different effect on Lazarre, as a sudden light shone, a consequence he hadn't considered.

I cried out, seeing this, "Don't you know she can think about you hard enough to stop your heart?" Lazarre was still deciding. He raised his fist and swung it casually and tapped my face. It was worse not to be hit full on.

"Come near!" **crooned**[6] Margaret in the old language. "Let me teach you how to die."

But she was trapped like a fox. Her earrings glinted and spun as she hissed her death song over and over, which signaled something to Lazarre, for he shook himself angrily and drew a razor from his jacket. He **stropped**[7] it with fast, vicious movements while Margaret sang shriller, so full of hate that the ropes should have burned, shriveled, fallen from her body. My struggle set the manger cracking against the barn walls and further confused the cows, who bumped each other and complained. At a sign from Lazarre, Clarence sighed, rose, and smashed me. The last I saw before I blacked out, through the tiny

[6] **crooned**—sang or hummed softly.

[7] **stropped**—sharpened a razor with a leather band.

closing pinhole of light, was Lazarre approaching Margaret with the blade.

When I woke, minutes later, it was to worse shock. For Lazarre had sliced Margaret's long braids off and was now, carefully, shaving her scalp. He started almost tenderly at the wide part, and then pulled the edge down each side of her skull. He did a clean job. He shed not one drop of her blood.

And I could not even speak to curse them. For pressing my jaw down, thick above my tongue, her braids, never cut in this life till now, were tied to silence me. Powerless, I tasted their flat, animal perfume.

It wasn't much later, or else it was forever, that we walked out into the night again. Speechless, we made our way in fierce pain down the road. I was damaged in spirit, more so than Margaret. For now she tucked her shawl over her naked head and forgot her own bad treatment. She called out in dread each foot of the way, for Lulu. But the smart, bold girl had hidden till all was clear and then run to Margaret's house. We opened the door and found her sitting by the stove in a litter of scorched matches and kindling. She had not the skill to start a fire, but she was dry-eyed. Though very cold, she was alert and then captured with wonder when Margaret slipped off her shawl.

"Where is your hair?" she asked.

I took my hand from my pocket. "Here's what's left of it. I grabbed this when they cut me loose." I was shamed by how pitiful I had been, relieved when Margaret snatched the thin gray braids from me and coiled them round her fist.

"I knew you would save them, clever man!" There was satisfaction in her voice.

I set the fire blazing. It was strange how generous this woman was to me, never blaming me or mentioning my failure. Margaret stowed her braids inside a birch-bark box and merely instructed me to lay it in her grave, when that time occurred. Then she came near the stove with a broken mirror from beside her washstand and looked at her own image.

"My," she pondered, "my." She put the mirror down. "I'll take a knife to them."

And I was thinking too. I was thinking I would have to kill them.

But how does an aching and half-starved grandfather attack a young, well-fed Morrissey and a tall, sly Lazarre? Later, I rolled up in blankets in the corner by Margaret's stove, and I put my mind to this question throughout that night until, exhausted, I slept. And I thought of it first thing next morning, too, and still nothing came. It was only after we had some hot *gaulette*[8] and walked Lulu back to her mother that an idea began to grow.

Fleur let us in, hugged Lulu into her arms, and looked at Margaret, who took off her scarf and stood bald, face burning again with smoldered fire. She told Fleur all of what happened, sparing no detail. The two women's eyes held, but Fleur said nothing. She put Lulu down, smoothed the front of her calico shirt, flipped her heavy braids over her shoulders, tapped one finger

[8] *gaulette*—biscuit.

on her perfect lips. And then, calm, she went to the washstand and scraped the edge of her hunting knife keen as glass. Margaret and Lulu and I watched as Fleur cut her braids off, shaved her own head, and folded the hair into a quilted skin pouch. Then she went out, hunting, and didn't bother to wait for night to cover her tracks.

Snares demand clever fingers and a scheming mind, and snares had never failed me.

I would have to go out hunting too.

I had no gun, but anyway that was a white man's revenge. I knew how to wound with barbs of words, but had never wielded a skinning knife against a human, much less two young men. Whomever I missed would kill me, and I did not want to die by their lowly hands.

In fact, I didn't think that after Margaret's interesting kindness I wanted to leave this life at all. Her head, smooth as an egg, was ridged delicately with bone, and gleamed as if it had been **buffed**[9] with a flannel cloth. Maybe it was the strangeness that attracted me. She looked forbidding, but the absence of hair also set off her eyes, so black and full of lights. She reminded me of that queen from England, of a water snake or a shrewd young bird. The earrings, which seemed part of her, mirrored her moods like water, and when they were still rounds of green lights against her throat I seemed, again, to taste her smooth, smoky braids in my mouth.

I had better things to do than fight. So I decided to accomplish revenge as quickly as possible. I was a talker who used my brains as my weapon. When I hunted, I preferred to let my game catch itself.

Snares demand clever fingers and a scheming mind, and snares had never failed me. Snares are quiet, and best of all snares are slow. I wanted to give Lazarre and Morrissey time to consider why they had to strangle. I thought hard. One- or two-foot deadfalls are required beneath a snare so that a man can't put his hand up and loosen the knot. The snares I had in mind also required something stronger than a cord, which could be broken, and finer than a rope, which even Lazarre might see and avoid. I pondered this closely, yet even so I might never have found the solution had I not gone to Mass with Margaret and grown curious about the workings of Father Damien's pride and joy, the piano in the back of the church, the instrument whose keys he breathed on, polished, then played after services, and sometimes alone. I had noticed that his hands usually stayed near the middle of the keyboard, so I took the wires from either end.

In the meantime, I was not the only one concerned with punishing Lazarre and Clarence Morrissey. Fleur was seen in town. Her thick skirts brushed the snow into clouds behind her. Though it was cold she left her head bare so everyone could see the frigid sun glare off her skull. The light reflected in the eyes of Lazarre and

[9] **buffed**—polished or shined.

Clarence, who were standing at the door of the pool hall. They dropped their cue sticks in the slush and ran back to Morrissey land. Fleur walked the four streets, once in each direction, then followed.

The two men told of her visit, how she passed through the Morrissey house touching here, touching there, sprinkling powders that ignited and stank on the hot stove. How Clarence swayed on his feet, blinked hard, and chewed his fingers. How Fleur stepped up to him, drew her knife. He smiled foolishly and asked her for supper. She reached forward and trimmed off a hank of his hair. Then she stalked from the house, leaving a taste of cold wind, and then chased Lazarre to the barn.

She made a black silhouette against the light from the door. Lazarre pressed against the wood of the walls, watching, hypnotized by the sight of Fleur's head and the quiet blade. He did not defend himself when she approached, reached for him, gently and efficiently cut bits of his hair, held his hands, one at a time, and trimmed the nails. She waved the razor-edged knife before his eyes and swept a few eyelashes into a white square of flour sacking that she then carefully folded into her blouse.

For days after, Lazarre babbled and wept. Fleur was murdering him by use of bad medicine, he said. He showed his hand, the bite that Margaret had dealt him, and the dark streak from the wound, along his wrist and inching up his arm. He even used that bound hand to scratch his name from the treaty, but it did no good.

I figured that the two men were doomed at least three ways now. Margaret won the debate with her Catholic training and decided to damn her soul by taking up the ax, since no one else had destroyed her enemies. I begged her to wait for another week, all during which it snowed and thawed and snowed again. It took me that long to arrange the snare to my satisfaction, near Lazarre's shack, on a path both men took to town.

I set it out one morning before anyone stirred, and watched from an old pine twisted along the ground. I waited while the smoke rose in a silky feather from the tiny tin spout on Lazarre's roof. I had to sit half a day before Lazarre came outside, and even then it was just for wood, nowhere near the path. I had a hard time to keep my blood flowing, my stomach still. I ate a handful of dry berries Margaret had given me, and a bit of pounded meat. I doled it to myself and waited until finally Clarence showed. He walked the trail like a blind ghost and stepped straight into my noose.

It was perfect, or would have been if I had made the deadfall two inches wider, for in falling Clarence somehow managed to spread his legs and straddle the deep hole I'd cut. It had been invisible, covered with snow, and yet in one foot-pedaling instant, the certain knowledge of its construction sprang into Clarence's brain and told his legs to reach for the sides. I don't know how he did it, but there he was poised. I waited, did not show myself. The noose jerked enough to cut slightly into the fool's neck, a too-snug fit. He was spread-eagled and on tiptoe, his arms straight out.

If he twitched a finger, lost the least control, even tried to yell, one foot would go, the noose constrict.

But Clarence did not move. I could see from behind my branches that he didn't even dare to change the expression on his face. His mouth stayed frozen in shock. Only his eyes shifted, darted fiercely and wildly, side to side, showing all the agitation he must not release, searching desperately for a means of escape. They focused only when I finally stepped toward him, quiet, from the pine.

We were in full view of Lazarre's house, face to face. I stood before the boy. Just a touch, a sudden kick, perhaps no more than a word, was all that it would take. But I looked into his eyes and saw the knowledge of his situation. Pity entered me. Even for Margaret's shame, I couldn't do the thing I might have done.

I turned away and left Morrissey still balanced on the ledge of snow.

What money I did have, I took to the trading store next day. I bought the best bonnet on the reservation. It was black as a coal scuttle, large, and shaped the same.

"It sets off my doe eyes," Margaret said and stared me down.

She wore it every day, and always to Mass. Not long before Lent and voices could be heard: "There goes Old Lady Coal bucket." Nonetheless, she was proud, and softening day by day, I could tell. By the time we got our foreheads crossed with ashes,[10] she consented to be married.

"I hear you're thinking of exchanging the vows," said Father Damien as I shook his hand on our way out the door.

"I'm having relations with Margaret already," I told him, "that's the way we do things."

This had happened to him before, so he was not even stumped as to what remedy he should use.

"Make a confession, at any rate," he said, motioning us back into the church.

So I stepped into the little box and knelt. Father Damien slid aside the shadowy door. I told him what I had been doing with Margaret and he stopped me partway through.

"No more details. Pray to Our Lady."

"There is one more thing."

"Yes?"

"Clarence Morrissey, he wears a scarf to church around his neck each week. I snared him like a rabbit."

Father Damien let the silence fill him.

"And the last thing," I went on. "I stole the wire from your piano."

The silence spilled over into my stall, and I was held in its grip until the priest spoke.

"Discord is hateful to God. You have offended his ear." Almost as an afterthought, Damien added, "And his commandment. The violence among you must cease."

"You can have the wire back," I said. I had used only one long strand. I also agreed that I would never use my snares

[10] foreheads . . . ashes—observance performed on Ash Wednesday, first day of Lent.

on humans, an easy promise. Lazarre was already caught.

Just two days later, while Margaret and I stood with Lulu and her mother inside the trading store, Lazarre entered, gesturing, his eyes rolled to the skull. He stretched forth his arm and pointed along its deepest black vein and dropped his jaw wide. Then he stepped backward into a row of traps that the trader had set to show us how they worked. Fleur's eye lit, her white scarf caught the sun as she turned. All the whispers were true. Fleur had scratched Lazarre's figure into a piece of birchbark, drawn his insides, and rubbed a bit of rouge up his arm until the red stain reached his heart. There was no sound as he fell, no cry, no word, and the traps of all types that clattered down around his body jumped and met for a long time, snapping air.

QUESTIONS TO CONSIDER

1. What is dividing the reservation at the beginning of the story? What is each side's point of view?
2. What do Morrissey and Lazarre hope to accomplish by kidnapping Margaret?
3. Why does Fleur cut off her hair?
4. Why does the narrator not kill Morrissey when he has the chance? What is your opinion of his decision?
5. What kills Lazarre? How did you infer this?
6. What is Erdrich trying to say about life on the reservation in "Snares"?

Gish Jen ▶

The Water-Faucet Vision

BY GISH JEN

Gish Jen (1957–   ) is the child of Chinese immigrants. Her parents were studying in the United States when the Communist Revolution occurred in China in 1949, making it impossible to return home. Jen was raised in an affluent suburb, Scarsdale, New York, and attended Harvard University. After a semester of business school, she decided to devote herself to writing. Her first novel, Typical American, *was published in 1991, and her second,* Mona in the Promised Land, *brought her acclaim. Jen's stories have been published in most of America's most famous magazines, and one was included in John Updike's* Best American Short Stories of the Century. *Jen's fiction has explored the world of Chinese Americans from many perspectives.* Typical American *is about an immigrant couple trying to make it in 1950s America, and* Mona in the Promised Land *describes the trials of a Chinese-American teenager who wants to convert to Judaism. Jen is married to an Irish American and some of her stories include the differing perspectives on assimilation.* "The Water-Faucet Vision" *is, like many of Jen's stories, wryly comic, but also acute in describing the difficulties of growing up and of being different in America.*

To protect my sister Mona and me from the pains—or, as they pronounced it, the "pins"—of life, my parents did their fighting in Shanghai[1] **dialect**,[2] which we didn't understand; and when my father one day pitched a brass vase through the kitchen window, my mother told us he had done it by accident.

"By accident?" said Mona.

My mother chopped the foot off a mushroom.

"By accident?" said Mona. "By *accident*?"

Later I tried to explain to her that she shouldn't have persisted like that, but it was hopeless.

"What's the matter with throwing things," she shrugged. "He was mad."

That was the difference between Mona and me: Fighting was just fighting to her. If she worried about anything, it was only that she might turn out too short to become

---

[1] Shanghai—major seaport in eastern China.

[2] **dialect**—variety of a language spoken in a particular geographic region, distinguished by pronunciation, grammar, or vocabulary.

a ballerina, in which case she was going to be a piano player.

I, on the other hand, was going to be a **martyr.**[3] I was in fifth grade then, and the hyperimaginative sort—the kind of girl who grows **morbid**[4] in Catholic school, who longs to be chopped or frozen to death but then has nightmares about it from which she wakes up screaming and clutching a stuffed bear. It was not a bear that I clutched, though, but a string of three malachite[5] beads that I had found in the marsh by the old aqueduct[6] one day. Apparently once part of a necklace, they were each wonderfully striated[7] and swirled, and slightly humped toward the center, like a jellyfish; so that if I squeezed one, it would slip smoothly away, with a grace that altogether enthralled and—on those dream-harrowed nights—soothed me, soothed me as nothing had before or has since. Not that I've lacked occasion for soothing: Though it's been four months since my mother died, there are still nights when sleep stands away from me, stiff as a well-paid sentry. But that is another story. Back then I had my malachite beads, and if I worried them long and patiently enough, I was sure to start feeling better, more awake, even a little special—imagining, as I liked to, that my nightmares were communications from the Almighty Himself, preparation for my painful destiny. Discussing them with Patty Creamer, who had also promised her life to God, I called them "almost visions"; and Patty, her mouth wadded with the three or four sticks of doublemint she always seemed to have going at once, said, "I bet you'll be doin' miracleth by seventh grade."

Miracles. Today Patty laughs to think she ever spent good time stewing on such matters, her attention having long turned to rugs, and artwork, and antique Japanese bureaus—things she believes in.

"A good bureau's more than just a bureau," she explained last time we had lunch. "It's a hedge against life. I tell you, if there's one thing I believe, it's that cheap stuff's just money out the window. Nice stuff, on the other hand—now that you can always cash out, if life gets rough. *That* you can count on."

In fifth grade, though, she counted on different things.

"You'll be doing miracles too," I told her, but she shook her shaggy head and looked **doleful.**[8]

"Na' me," she chomped. "Buzzit's okay. The kin' things I like, prayers work okay on."

"Like?"

"Like you 'member that dreth I liked?"

She meant the yellow one, with the criss-cross straps.

"Well gueth what."

"Your mom got it for you."

She smiled. "And I only jutht prayed for it for a week," she said.

---

[3] **martyr**—one who chooses to suffer death or great sacrifices in order to further a belief, cause, or principle, often religious.

[4] **morbid**—preoccupied with unwholesome thoughts or feelings.

[5] malachite—green mineral that is used for ornaments.

[6] aqueduct—water channel.

[7] striated—striped, grooved, or ridged.

[8] **doleful**—filled with grief or sadness.

As for myself, though, I definitely wanted to be able to perform a wonder or two. Miracle-working! It was the carrot of carrots: It kept me doing my homework, taking the sacraments;[9] it kept me mournfully on key in music hour, while my classmates hiccuped and squealed their carefree hearts away. Yet I couldn't have said what I wanted such powers for, exactly. That is, I thought of them the way one might think of, say, an ornamental sword—as a kind of collectible, which also happened to be a means of defense.

Miracle-working! It was the carrot of carrots: It kept me doing my homework, taking the sacraments.

But then Patty's father walked out on her mother, and for the first time, there was a miracle I wanted to do. I wanted it so much I could see it: Mr. Creamer made into a spitball; Mr. Creamer shot through a straw into the sky; Mr. Creamer unrolled and re-plumped, plop back on Patty's doorstep. I would've cleaned out his mind and given him a shave en route. I would've given him a box of peanut fudge, tied up with a ribbon, to present to Patty with a kiss.

But instead all I could do was try to tell her he'd come back.

"He will not, he will not!" she sobbed. "He went on a boat to Rio Deniro.[10] To Rio Deniro!"

I tried to offer her a stick of gum, but she wouldn't take it.

"He said he would rather look at water than at my mom's fat face. He said he would rather look at water than at me." Now she was really wailing, and holding her ribs so tightly that she almost seemed to be hurting herself—so tightly that just looking at her arms wound around her like snakes made my heart feel squeezed.

I patted her on the arm. A one-winged pigeon waddled by.

"He said I wasn't even his kid, he said I came from Uncle Johnny. He said I was garbage, just like my mom and Uncle Johnny. He said I wasn't even his kid, he said I wasn't his Patty, he said I came from Uncle Johnny!"

"From your Uncle Johnny?" I said stupidly.

"From Uncle Johnny," she cried. "From Uncle Johnny!"

"He said that?" I said. Then, wanting to go on, to say *something*, I said, "Oh Patty, don't cry."

She kept crying.

I tried again. "Oh Patty, don't cry," I said. Then I said, "Your dad was a jerk anyway."

The pigeon produced a large runny dropping.

It was a good twenty minutes before Patty was calm enough for me just to run to the girls' room to get her some toilet paper; and by the time I came back she was sobbing again, saying "To Rio Deniro, to Rio Deniro" over and over again, as though the words had stuck in her and couldn't be gotten out. As we

---

[9] **sacraments—here, the religious practices of confession and communion in the Catholic Church.**

[10] **Rio Deniro—mispronunciation of "Rio de Janeiro," a large city on the southeast coast of Brazil.**

had missed the regular bus home and the late bus too, I had to leave her a second time to go call my mother, who was only mad until she heard what had happened. Then she came and picked us up, and bought us each a Fudgsicle.

Some days later, Patty and I started a program to work on getting her father home. It was a serious business. We said extra prayers, and lit votive[11] candles; I tied my malachite beads to my uniform belt, fondling them as though they were a rosary, I a nun. We even took to walking about the school halls with our hands folded—a sight so **ludicrous**[12] that our wheeze of a principal personally took us aside one day.

"I must tell you," she said, using her nose as a speaking tube, "that there is really no need for such peee-ity."

But we persisted, promising to marry God and praying to every saint we could think of. We gave up gum, then gum and Slim Jims both, then gum and Slim Jims and ice cream—and when even that didn't work, we started on more innovative things. The first was looking at flowers. We held our hands beside our eyes like blinders as we hurried by the violets by the flagpole, the window box full of tulips outside the nurse's office. Next it was looking at boys: Patty gave up angel-eyed Jamie Halloran and I, gymnastic Anthony Rossi. It was hard, but in the end our efforts paid off. Mr. Creamer came back a month later, and though he brought with him nothing but dysentery,[13] he was at least too sick to have all that much to say.

Then, in the course of a fight with my father, my mother somehow fell out of their bedroom window.

Recently—thinking a mountain vacation might cheer me—I sublet my apartment to a handsome but somber newlywed couple, who turned out to be every bit as responsible as I'd hoped. They cleaned out even the eggshell chips I'd sprinkled around the base of my plants as fertilizer, leaving behind only a shiny silverplate cake server and a list of their hopes and goals for the summer. The list, tacked precariously to the back of the kitchen door, began with a **fervent**[14] appeal to God to help them get their wedding thank-yous written in three weeks or less. (You could see they had originally written "two weeks" but scratched it out—no miracles being demanded here.) It went on:

Please help us, Almighty Father in Heaven Above, to get Ann a teaching job within a half-hour drive of here in a nice neighborhood.

Please help us, Almighty Father in Heaven Above, to get John a job doing anything where he won't strain his back and that is within a half-hour drive of here.

Please help us, Almighty Father in Heaven Above, to get us a car.

Please help us, A.F. in H.A., to learn French.

[11] votive—given in fulfillment of a vow or pledge.

[12] **ludicrous**—laughable because of obvious absurdity.

[13] dysentery—disease of the intestines, producing diarrhea with blood and mucus.

[14] **fervent**—heartfelt; expressing great emotion.

Please help us, A.F. in H.A., to find seven dinner recipes that cost less than 60 cents a serving and can be made in a half-hour. And that don't have tomatoes, since You in Your Heavenly Wisdom made John allergic.

Please help us, A.F. in H.A., to avoid books in this apartment such as You in Your Heavenly Wisdom allowed John, for Your Heavenly Reasons, to find three nights ago (June 2nd).

Et cetera. In the left-hand margin they kept score of how they had fared with their requests, and it was heartening to see that nearly all of them were marked "Yes! Praise the Lord!" (sometimes shortened to PTL), with the sole exception of learning French, which was mysteriously marked "No! PTL to the Highest."

That note touched me. Strange and familiar both, it seemed like it had been written by some cousin of mine—some cousin who had stayed home to grow up, say, while I went abroad and learned what I had to, though the learning was painful. This, of course, is just a manner of speaking; in fact, I did my growing up at home, like anybody else.

But the learning was painful: I never knew exactly how it happened that my mother went hurtling through the air that night years ago, only that the wind had been chopping at the house, and that the argument had started about the state of the roof. Someone had been up to fix it the year before, but it wasn't a roofer, it was some man my father had insisted could do just as good a job for a quarter of the price. And maybe he could have, had he not somehow managed to step through a knot in the wood under the shingles and break his uninsured ankle. Now the shingles were coming loose again, and the attic insulation was mildewing besides, and my father was wanting to sell the house altogether, which he said my mother had wanted to buy so she could send pictures of it home to her family in China.

"The Americans have a saying," he said. "They saying, 'You have to keep up with the Jones family.' I'm saying if the Jones family in Shanghai, you can send any picture you want, *an-y* picture. Go take picture of those rich guys' house. You want to act like rich guys, right? Go take picture of those rich guys' house."

At that point my mother sent Mona and me to wash up, and started speaking Shanghaiese. They argued for some time in the kitchen, while we listened from the top of the stairs, our faces wedged between the bumpy Spanish scrolls of the wrought iron railing. First my mother ranted,[15] then my father, then they both ranted at once until finally there was a thump, followed by a long quiet.

"Do you think they're kissing now?" said Mona. "I bet they're kissing, like this." She pursed her lips like a fish and was about to put them to the railing when we heard my mother locking the back door. We hightailed it into bed; my parents creaked up the stairs. Everything at that point seemed fine. Once in their bedroom, though, they started up again, first softly, then louder and louder, until my mother turned on a radio to try to disguise the

---

[15] ranted—spoke violently, loudly; raved.

noise. A door slammed; they began shouting at one another; another door slammed; a shoe or something banged the wall behind Mona's bed.

"How're we supposed to sleep?" said Mona, sitting up.

There was another thud, more yelling in Shanghaiese, and then my mother's voice pierced the wall, in English. "So what you want I should do? Go to work like Theresa Lee?"

My father rumbled something back.

"You think you're big shot because you have job, right? You're big shot, but you never get promotion, you never get raise. All I do is spend money, right? So what do you do, you tell me. So what do you do!"

Something hit the floor so hard that our room shook.

"So kill me," screamed my mother. "You know what you are? You are failure. Failure! You are failure!"

Then there was a sudden, terrific, bursting crash—and after it, as if on a bungled cue, the serene blare of an a cappella[16] soprano, picking her way down a scale.

By the time Mona and I knew to look out the window, a neighbor's pet beagle was already on the scene, sniffing and barking at my mother's body, his tail crazy with excitement; then he was barking at my stunned and trembling father, at the shrieking ambulance, the police, at crying Mona in her bunny-footed pajamas, and at me, barefoot in the cold grass, squeezing her shoulder with one hand and clutching my malachite beads with the other.

My mother wasn't dead, only unconscious, the paramedics figured that out right away, but there was blood everywhere, and though they were reassuring about her head wounds as they strapped her to the stretcher, commenting also on how small she was, how delicate, how light, my father kept saying, "I killed her, I killed her" as the ambulance screeched and screeched headlong, forever, to the hospital. I was afraid to touch her, and glad of the metal rail between us, even though its sturdiness made her seem even frailer than she was; I wished she was bigger, somehow, and noticed, with a pang, that the new red slippers we had given her for Mother's Day had been lost somewhere along the way. How much she seemed to be leaving behind, as we **careened**[17] along—still not there, still not there—Mona and Dad and the medic and I taking up the whole ambulance, all the room, so there was no room for anything else; no room even for my mother's real self, the one who should have been pinching the color back to my father's gray face, the one who should have been calming Mona's cowlick—the one who should have been bending over us, to help us to be strong, to help us get through, even as we bent over her.

Something hit the floor so hard that our room shook.

Then suddenly we were there, the glowing square of the emergency room entrance opening like the gates of heaven; and immediately the talk of miracles

[16] a capella—sung without musical accompaniment.

[17] **careened**—lurched and swerved while in motion.

began. Alive, a miracle. No bones broken, a miracle. A miracle that the hemlocks cushioned her fall, a miracle that they hadn't been trimmed in a year and a half. It was a miracle that all that blood, the blood that had seemed that night to be everywhere, was from one shard of glass, a single shard, can you imagine, and as for the gash in her head, the scar would be covered by hair. The next day my mother cheerfully described just how she would part it so that nothing would show at all.

"You're a lucky duck-duck," agreed Mona, helping herself, with a little *pirouette*,[18] to the cherry atop my mother's chocolate pudding.

That wasn't enough for me, though. I was relieved, yes, but what I wanted by then was a real miracle, not for her simply to have survived but for the whole thing never to have happened—for my mother's head never to had to been shaved and bandaged like that, for her high, proud forehead to never have been swollen down over her eyes, for her face and neck and hands never to have been painted so many shades of blue-black, and violet, and **chartreuse**.[19] I still want those things—for my parents not to have had to live with this affair like a prickle-bush between them, for my father to have been able to look my mother in her swollen eyes and curse the madman, the monster that could have dared done this to the woman he loved. I wanted to be able to touch my mother without shuddering, to be able to console my father, to be able to get that crash out of my head, the sound of that soprano—so many things that I didn't know how to pray for them, that I wouldn't have known where to start even if I had the power to work miracles, right there, right then.

A week later, when my mother was home, and her head beginning to bristle with new hairs, I lost my malachite beads. I had been carrying them in a white cloth pouch that Patty had given me, and was swinging the pouch on my pinky on my way home from school, when I swung just a bit too hard, and it went sailing in a long arc through the air, whooshing like a perfectly thrown basketball through one of those holes of a nearby sewer. There was no chance of fishing it out: I looked and looked, crouching on the sticky pavement until the asphalt had crazed the skin of my hands and knees, but all I could discern was an evil-smelling musk, glassy and smug and impenetrable.

My loss didn't quite hit me until I was home, but then it produced an agony all out of proportion to my string of pretty beads. I hadn't cried at all during my mother's accident, and now I was crying all afternoon, all through dinner, and then after dinner too, crying past the point where I knew what I was crying for, wishing dimly that I had my beads to hold, wishing dimly that I could pray but refusing, refusing, I didn't know why, until I finally fell into an exhausted sleep on the couch, where my parents left me for the night—glad, no doubt, that one of the more tedious of my childhood crises seemed to

---

[18] **pirouette**—turn of the body on the point of the toe or the ball of the foot in ballet.

[19] **chartreuse**—strong greenish yellow.

be finally winding off the reel of life, onto the reel of memory. They covered me, and somehow grew a pillow under my head, and, with uncharacteristic disregard for the living-room rug, left some milk and pecan sandies on the coffee table, in case I woke up hungry. Their thoughtfulness was prescient:[20] I did wake up in the early part of the night; and it was then, amid the unfamiliar sounds and shadows of the living room, that I had what I was sure was a true vision.

Even now what I saw retains an odd clarity: the requisite strange light flooding the room, first orange, and then a bright yellow-green, then a crackling bright burst like a Roman candle going off near the piano. There was a distinct smell of coffee, and a long silence. The room seemed to be getting colder. Nothing. A creak; the light starting to wane,[21] then waxing[22] again, brilliant pink now. Still nothing. Then, as the pink started to go a little purple, a perfectly normal middle-aged man's voice, speaking something very like pig latin, told me quietly not to despair, not to despair, my beads would be returned to me.

That was all. I sat a moment in the dark, then turned on the light, gobbled down the cookies—and in a happy flash understood I was so good, really, so near to being a saint that my malachite beads would come back through the town water system. All I had to do was turn on all the faucets in the house, which I did, one by one, stealing quietly into the bathroom and kitchen and basement. The old **spigot**[23] by the washing machine was too gunked up to be coaxed very far open, but that didn't matter. The water didn't have to be full blast, I understood that. Then I gathered together my pillow and blanket and trundled up to my bed to sleep.

By the time I woke up in the morning I knew that my beads hadn't shown up, but when I knew it for certain, I was still disappointed; and as if that weren't enough, I had to face my parents and sister, who were all abuzz with the mystery of the faucets. Not knowing what else to do, I, like a puddlebrain, told them the truth. The results were predictably painful.

"Callie had a *vision*," Mona told everyone at the bus stop. "A vision with lights, and sinks in it!"

Sinks, visions. I got it all day, from my parents, from my classmates, even some sixth and seventh graders. Someone drew a cartoon of me with a halo over my head in one of the girls' room stalls; Anthony Rossi made gurgling noises as he walked on his hands at recess. Only Patty tried not to laugh, though even she was something less than **unalloyed**[24] understanding.

"I don't think miracles are thupposed to happen in *thewers*," she said.

Such was the end of my saintly ambitions. It wasn't the end of all holiness; the ideas of purity and goodness still tippled[25] my brain, and over the years I came slowly to grasp of what grit true faith was made. Last night, though, when my father called

---

[20] prescient—foreknowing.

[21] wane—diminish.

[22] waxing—becoming gradually larger or more intense.

[23] **spigot**—faucet.

[24] **unalloyed**—pure or complete.

[25] tippled—intoxicated.

to say that he couldn't go on living in our old house, that he was going to move to a smaller place, another place, maybe a condo—he didn't know how, or where—I found myself still wistful for the time religion seemed all I wanted it to be. Back then the world was a place that could be set right: One had only to direct the hand of the Almighty and say, just here, Lord, we hurt here—and here, and here, and here.

QUESTIONS TO CONSIDER

1. How are Callie and Patty's attitudes to religion and prayer alike and different?
2. How would the youthful and the adult Callie differ in their reactions to the note left by the Christian couple who rented the apartment?
3. Why does everyone make fun of Callie's vision?
4. What do you think Jen's attitude is to Callie's vision?
5. What are the differences between the parents, who emigrated from China, and their daughters, who are Chinese-American?

Julia Alvarez ▶

Daughter of Invention

BY JULIA ALVAREZ

Julia Alvarez (1950–) was raised in the Dominican Republic, but moved to the United States when she was ten. Her struggle to adapt to a new country was the direct inspiration for her book How the Garcia Girls Lost Their Accents *(1991). Alvarez made the adjustment and assimilated well enough to become a professor of English at Middlebury College. While pursuing her academic career, she was also writing. The series of interconnected stories that make up* How the Garcia Girls Lost Their Accents *was Alvarez's first published book, and it became a bestseller. Her second novel,* In the Time of Butterflies *(1994), recounts the terrifying experiences of three sisters who opposed a dictatorial regime in the Dominican Republic. Alvarez is one of the leaders, along with Sandra Cisneros (page 498), of a new generation of Hispanic writers, who are at home in the United States but want to celebrate their traditions and culture. The following story is from* How the Garcia Girls Lost Their Accents *and describes the differences often seen between immigrants and their children.*

For a period after they arrived in this country, Laura García tried to invent something. Her ideas always came after the sightseeing visits she took with her daughters to department stores to see the wonders of this new country. On his free Sundays, Carlos carted the girls off to the Statue of Liberty or the Brooklyn Bridge or Rockefeller Center, but as far as Laura was concerned, these were men's wonders. Down in housewares were the true treasures women were after.

Laura and her daughters would take the escalator, marveling at the moving staircase, she teasing them that this might be the ladder Jacob saw with angels moving up and down to heaven.[1] The moment they lingered by a display, a perky saleslady approached, no doubt thinking a young mother with four girls in tow fit the perfect profile for the new refrigerator with automatic defrost or the heavy duty washing machine with the prewash soak cycle. Laura paid close attention during the demonstrations, asking intelligent questions, but at the last minute saying she would talk it over with her husband. On the drive home, try as they might, her daughters could not engage their mother in conversation, for inspired by what she had just seen, Laura had begun inventing.

[1] **the ladder . . . to heaven**—vision seen by the patriarch Jacob in the Bible.

She never put anything actual on paper until she had settled her house down at night. On his side of the bed her husband would be conked out for an hour already, his Spanish newspapers draped over his chest, his glasses propped up on his bedside table, looking out eerily at the darkened room like a disembodied bodyguard. In her lighted corner, pillows propped behind her, Laura sat up inventing. On her lap lay one of those innumerable pads of paper her husband brought home from his office, compliments of some pharmaceutical company, advertising tranquilizers or antibiotics or skin cream. She would be working on a sketch of something familiar but drawn at such close range so she could attach a special nozzle or handier handle, the thing looked peculiar. Her daughters would giggle over the odd doodles they found in kitchen drawers or on the back shelf of the downstairs toilet. Once Yoyo was sure her mother had drawn a picture of a man's you-know-what; she showed her sisters her find, and with coy, posed faces they inquired of their mother what she was up to. Ay, that was one of her failures, she explained to them, a child's double-compartment drinking glass with an outsized, built-in straw.

Her daughters would seek her out at night when she seemed to have a moment to talk to them: they were having trouble at school or they wanted her to persuade their father to give them permission to go into the city or to a shopping mall or a movie—in broad daylight, Mami! Laura would wave them out of her room. "The problem with you girls . . ." The problem boiled down to the fact that they wanted to become Americans and their father—and their mother, too, at first—would have none of it.

"You girls are going to drive me crazy!" she threatened, if they kept nagging. "When I end up in Bellevue,[2] you'll be safely sorry!"

She spoke in English when she argued with them. And her English was a mishmash of mixed-up idioms[3] and sayings that showed she was "green behind the ears," as she called it.

If her husband insisted she speak in Spanish to the girls so they wouldn't forget their native tongue, she'd snap, "When in Rome, do unto the Romans."

Yoyo, the Big Mouth, had become the spokesman for her sisters, and she stood her ground in that bedroom. "We're not going to that school anymore, Mami!"

"You have to." Her eyes would widen with worry. "In this country, it is against the law not to go to school. You want us to get thrown out?"

"You want us to get killed? Those kids were throwing stones today!"

"Sticks and stones don't break bones," she chanted. Yoyo could tell, though, by the look on her face, it was as if one of those stones the kids had aimed at her daughters had hit her. But she always

[2] Bellevue—New York City's public mental hospital.

[3] idioms—expressions in a given language that are peculiar to themselves grammatically or cannot be understood from the individual meanings of the elements.

pretended they were at fault. "What did you do to provoke them? It takes two to tangle, you know."

"Thanks, thanks a lot, Mom!" Yoyo stormed out of that room and into her own. Her daughters never called her Mom except when they wanted her to feel how much she had failed them in this country. She was a good enough Mami, fussing and scolding and giving advice, but a terrible girlfriend parent, a real failure of a Mom.

Back she went to her pencil and pad, scribbling and tsking[4] and tearing off sheets, finally giving up, and taking up her *New York Times*. Some nights, though, if she got a good idea, she rushed into Yoyo's room, a flushed look on her face, her tablet of paper in her hand, a **cursory**[5] knock on the door she'd just thrown open. "Do I have something to show you, Cuquita!"

This was Yoyo's time to herself, after she finished her homework, while her sisters were still downstairs watching TV in the basement. Hunched over her small desk, the overhead light turned off, her desk lamp poignantly[6] lighting only her paper, the rest of the room in warm, soft, uncreated darkness, she wrote her secret poems in her new language.

"You're going to ruin your eyes!" Laura began, snapping on the overly bright overhead light, scaring off whatever shy passion Yoyo, with the blue thread of her writing, had just begun coaxing out of a labyrinth of feelings.

"Oh, Mami!" Yoyo cried out, her eyes blinking up at her mother. "I'm writing."

"Ay, Cuquita." That was her **communal**[7] pet name for whoever was in her favor. "Cuquita, when I make a million, I'll buy you your very own typewriter." (Yoyo had been nagging her mother for one just like the one her father had bought to do his order forms at home.) "Gravy on the turkey" was what she called it when someone was buttering her up. She buttered and poured. "I'll hire you your very own typist."

"What did you do to provoke them? It takes two to tangle, you know."

Down she plopped on the bed and held out her pad. "Take a guess, Cuquita?" Yoyo studied the rough sketch a moment. Soap sprayed from the nozzle head of a shower when you turned the knob a certain way? Instant coffee with creamer already mixed in? Time-released water capsules for your potted plants when you were away? A keychain with a timer that would go off when your parking meter was about to expire? (The ticking would help you find your keys easily if you mislaid them.) The famous one, famous only in hindsight, was the stick person dragging a square by a rope—a suitcase with wheels? "Oh, of course," Yoyo said, humoring her. "What every household needs: a shower like a car wash, keys ticking like a bomb, luggage on a leash!" By now, it had become something

---

[4] **tsking**—expressing disapproval by making a clucking sound with the tongue.

[5] **cursory**—performed with haste and scant attention to detail.

[6] **poignantly**—touchingly.

[7] **communal**—shared by the people of a community.

of a family joke, their Thomas Edison Mami, their Benjamin Franklin Mom.

Her face fell. "Come on now! Use your head." One more wrong guess, and she'd show Yoyo, pointing with her pencil to the different highlights of this incredible new wonder. "Remember that time we took the car to Bear Mountain, and we re-ah-lized that we had forgotten to pack an opener with our pick-a-nick?" (Her daughters kept correcting her, but she insisted this was how it should be said.) "When we were ready to eat we didn't have any way to open the refreshments cans?" (This before fliptop lids, which she claimed had crossed her mind.) "You know what this is now?" Yoyo shook her head. "Is a car bumper, but see this part is a removable can opener. So simple and yet so necessary, eh?"

"Yeah, Mami. You should **patent**[8] it." Yoyo shrugged as her mother tore off the scratch paper and folded it, carefully, corner to corner, as if she were going to save it. But then, she tossed it in the wastebasket on her way out of the room and gave a little laugh like a **disclaimer**.[9] "It's half of one or two dozen of another."

None of her daughters was very encouraging. They resented her spending time on those dumb inventions. Here they were trying to fit in America among Americans; they needed help figuring out who they were, why the Irish kids whose grandparents had been micks were calling them spics. Why had they come to this country in the first place? Important, crucial, final things, and here was their own mother, who didn't have a second to help them puzzle any of this out, inventing gadgets to make life easier for the American Moms.

Sometimes Yoyo challenged her. "Why, Mami? Why do it? You're never going to make money. The Americans have already thought of everything, you know that."

"Maybe not. Maybe, just maybe, there's something they've missed that's important. With patience and calm, even a burro can climb a palm." This last was one of her many Dominican[10] sayings she had imported into her scrambled English.

"But what's the point?" Yoyo persisted.

"Point, point, does everything need a point? Why do you write poems?"

Yoyo had to admit it was her mother who had the point there. Still, in the **hierarchy**[11] of things, a poem seemed much more important than a potty that played music when a toilet-training toddler went in its bowl.

They talked about it among themselves, the four girls, as they often did now about the many puzzling things in this new country.

"Better she reinvents the wheel than be on our cases all the time," the oldest, Carla, observed. In the close quarters of an American nuclear family, their mother's **prodigious**[12] energy was becoming a real

---

8 **patent**—register an invention with the government to gain sole right to make, use, and sell it for a set period of time.

9 **disclaimer**—denial of responsibility or connection.

10 Dominican—of the Dominican Republic, a country in the Caribbean. It is the eastern two-thirds of the island of Hispaniola.

11 **hierarchy**—categorization according to some organizing principle.

12 **prodigious**—extraordinary.

drain on their self-determination. Let her have a project. What harm could she do, and besides, she needed that acknowledgement. It had come to her automatically in the old country from being a de la Torre. "García de la Torre," Laura would enunciate carefully, giving her maiden as well as married name when they first arrived. But the blank smiles had never heard of her name. She would show them. She would prove to these Americans what a smart woman could do with a pencil and pad.

She had a near miss once. Every night, she liked to read *The New York Times* in bed before turning off her light, to see what the Americans were up to. One night, she let out a yelp to wake up her husband beside her. He sat bolt upright, reaching for his glasses which in his haste, he knocked across the room. "*¿Qué pasa? ¿Qué pasa?*" What is wrong? There was terror in his voice, the same fear she'd heard in the Dominican Republic before they left. They had been watched there; he was followed. They could not talk, of course, though they had whispered to each other in fear at night in the dark bed. Now in America, he was safe, a success even; his Centro de Medicina in the Bronx was thronged with the sick and the homesick yearning to go home again. But in dreams, he went back to those awful days and long nights, and his wife's screams confirmed his secret fear: they had not gotten away after all; the SIM[13] had come for them at last.

"*Ay,* Cuco! Remember how I showed you that suitcase with little wheels so we should not have to carry those heavy bags when we traveled? Someone stole my idea and made a million!" She shook the paper in his face. "See, see! This man was no *bobo!*[14] He didn't put all his pokers on a back burner. I kept telling you, one of these days my ship would pass me by in the night!" She wagged her finger at her husband and daughters, laughing all the while, one of those eerie laughs crazy people in movies laugh. The four girls had congregated in her room. They eyed their mother and each other. Perhaps they were all thinking the same thing, wouldn't it be weird and sad if Mami did end up in Bellevue?

"I kept telling you, one of these days my ship would pass me by in the night!"

"*¡Ya, ya!*" She waved them out of her room at last. "There is no use trying to drink spilt milk, that's for sure."

It was the suitcase rollers that stopped Laura's hand; she had weathervaned a minor brainstorm. And yet, this **plagiarist**[15] had gotten all the credit, and the money. What use was it trying to compete with the Americans: they would always have the head start. It was their country, after all. Best stick close to home. She cast her sights about—her daughters ducked—and found her husband's office in need. Several days a week, dressed professionally in a white smock with a little name tag pinned on the

---

[13] SIM—secret police of Dominican dictator Rafael Trujillo Molina (1891–1961), who ruled the Dominican Republic from 1930 to 1961. Trujillo imprisoned or killed his political opponents. Many fled to the United States to escape his repressive regime.

[14] *bobo*—Spanish meaning "fool."

[15] **plagiarist**—copier.

lapel, a shopping bag full of cleaning materials and rags, she rode with her husband in his car to the Bronx. On the way, she organized the glove compartment or took off the address stickers from the magazines for the waiting room because she had read somewhere how by means of these stickers drug addict patients found out where doctors lived and burglarized their homes looking for syringes. At night, she did the books, filling in columns with how much money they had made that day. Who had time to be inventing silly things!

She did take up her pencil and pad one last time. But it was to help one of her daughters out. In ninth grade, Yoyo was chosen by her English teacher, Sister Mary Joseph, to deliver the Teacher's Day address at the school assembly. Back in the Dominican Republic growing up, Yoyo had been a terrible student. No one could ever get her to sit down to a book. But in New York, she needed to settle somewhere, and since the natives were unfriendly, and the country inhospitable, she took root in the language. By high school, the nuns were reading her stories and compositions out loud in English class.

But the **specter**[16] of delivering a speech brown-nosing the teachers jammed her imagination. At first she didn't want to and then she couldn't seem to write that speech. She should have thought of it as "a great honor," as her father called it. But she was **mortified.**[17] She still had a slight accent, and she did not like to speak in public, subjecting herself to her classmates' ridicule. It also took no great figuring to see that to deliver a **eulogy**[18] for a convent full of crazy, old, overweight nuns was no way to endear herself to her peers.

But she didn't know how to get out of it. Night after night, she sat at her desk, hoping to polish off some quick, noncommittal little speech. But she couldn't get anything down.

The weekend before the assembly Monday morning Yoyo went into a panic. Her mother would just have to call in tomorrow and say Yoyo was in the hospital, in a coma.

Laura tried to calm her down. "Just remember how Mister Lincoln couldn't think of anything to say at the Gettysburg, but then, bang! *Four score and once upon a time ago,"* she began reciting. "Something is going to come if you just relax. You'll see, like the Americans say, *Necessity is the daughter of invention.* I'll help you."

That weekend, her mother turned all her energy towards helping Yoyo write her speech. "Please, Mami, just leave me alone, please," Yoyo pleaded with her. But Yoyo would get rid of the goose only to have to contend with the gander.[19] Her father kept poking his head in the door just to see if Yoyo had "fulfilled your obligations," a phrase he had used when the girls were younger and he'd check to see whether they had gone to the bathroom before a car trip. Several times that weekend around the supper table, he recited his own high

---

[16] **specter**—haunting or disturbing image or prospect.

[17] **mortified**—ashamed, humiliated.

[18] **eulogy**—speech of praise.

[19] gander—male goose.

school valedictorian[20] speech. He gave Yoyo pointers on delivery, notes on the great orators and their tricks. (Humbleness and praise and falling silent with great emotion were his favorites.)

Laura sat across the table, the only one who seemed to be listening to him. Yoyo and her sisters were forgetting a lot of their Spanish, and their father's formal, **florid**[21] diction was hard to understand. But Laura smiled softly to herself, and turned the lazy Susan at the center of the table around and around as if it were the prime mover,[22] the first gear of her attention.

That Sunday evening, Yoyo was reading some poetry to get herself inspired: Whitman's[23] poems in an old book with an engraved cover her father had picked up in a thrift shop next to his office. *I celebrate myself and sing myself. . . . He most honors my style who learns under it to destroy the teacher.* The poet's words shocked and thrilled her. She had gotten used to the nuns, a literature of appropriate sentiments, poems with a message, expurgated[24] texts. But here was a flesh and blood man, belching and laughing and sweating in poems. *Who touches this book touches a man.*

That night, at last, she started to write, recklessly, three, five pages, looking up once only to see her father passing by the hall on tiptoe. When Yoyo was done, she read over her words, and her eyes filled. She finally sounded like herself in English!

As soon as she had finished that first draft, she called her mother to her room. Laura listened attentively while Yoyo read the speech out loud, and in the end, her eyes were glistening too. Her face was soft and warm and proud. "*Ay,* Yoyo, you are going to be the one to bring our name to the headlights in this country! That is a beautiful, beautiful speech I want for your father to hear it before he goes to sleep. Then I will type it for you, all right?"

"Ay, Yoyo, you are going to be the one to bring our name to the headlights in this country!"

Down the hall they went, mother and daughter, faces flushed with accomplishment. Into the master bedroom where Carlos was propped up on his pillows, still awake, reading the Dominican papers, already days old. Now that the dictatorship had been toppled, he had become interested in his country's fate again. The **interim**[25] government was going to hold the first free elections in thirty years. History was in the making, freedom and hope were in the air again! There was still some question in his mind whether or not he might move his family back. But Laura had gotten used to the life here. She did not want to go back to the old country where, de la Torre or not, she was only a wife and a mother (and a failed one at that, since she had never provided the required

[20] valedictorian—given by the student with the highest academic rank in a class.

[21] **florid**—very ornate; flowery.

[22] prime mover—initial force that engages or moves a machine.

[23] Whitman—Walt Whitman (1819–1892), American poet.

[24] expurgated—with objectionable material removed before publication.

[25] **interim**—temporary.

son). Better an independent nobody than a high-class houseslave. She did not come straight out and disagree with her husband's plans. Instead, she fussed with him about reading the papers in bed, soiling their sheets with those poorly printed, foreign tabloids. "*The Times* is not that bad!" she'd claim if her husband tried to humor her by saying they shared the same dirty habit.

The minute Carlos saw his wife and daughter filing in, he put his paper down, and his face brightened as if at long last his wife had delivered the son, and that was the news she was bringing him. His teeth were already grinning from the glass of water next to his bedside lamp, so he lisped when he said, "Eh-speech, eh-speech!"

"It is so beautiful, Cuco," Laura coached him, turning the sound on his TV off. She sat down at the foot of the bed. Yoyo stood before both of them, blocking their view of the soldiers in helicopters landing amid silenced gun reports and explosions. A few weeks ago it had been the shores of the Dominican Republic. Now it was the jungles of Southeast Asia they were saving. Her mother gave her the nod to begin reading.

Yoyo didn't need much encouragement. She put her nose to the fire, as her mother would have said, and read from start to finish without looking up. When she concluded, she was a little embarrassed at the pride she took in her own words. She pretended to quibble with a phrase or two, then looked questioningly to her mother. Laura's face was radiant. Yoyo turned to share her pride with her father.

The expression on his face shocked both mother and daughter. Carlos's toothless mouth had collapsed into a dark zero.

His eyes bored into Yoyo, then shifted to Laura. In barely **audible**[26] Spanish, as if secret microphones or informers were all about, he whispered to his wife, "You will permit her to read *that*?"

Laura's eyebrows shot up, her mouth fell open. In the old country, any whisper of a challenge to authority could bring the secret police in their black V.W.'s. But this was America. People could say what they thought. "What is wrong with her speech?" Laura questioned him.

"What ees wrrrong with her eh-speech?" Carlos wagged his head at her. His anger was always more frightening in his broken English. As if he had mutilated the language in his fury and now there was nothing to stand between them and his raw, dumb anger. "What is wrong? I will tell you what is wrong. It show no gratitude. It is boastful. *I celebrate myself? The best student learns to destroy the teacher?"* He mocked Yoyo's plagiarized words. "That is **insubordinate**.[27] It is improper. It is disrespecting of her teachers—" In his anger he had forgotten his fear of lurking spies: each wrong he voiced was a decibel[28] higher than the last outrage. Finally, he shouted at Yoyo, "As your father, I forbid you to make that eh-speech!"

Laura leapt to her feet, a sign that *she* was about to deliver her own speech. She was a small woman, and she spoke all her

[26] **audible**—loud enough to be heard.

[27] **insubordinate**—not submissive to authority.

[28] decibel—unit of loudness.

pronouncements standing up, either for more projection or as a carry-over from her girlhood in convent schools where one asked for, and literally, took the floor in order to speak. She stood by Yoyo's side, shoulder to shoulder. They looked down at Carlos. "That is no tone of voice—" she began.

But now, Carlos was truly furious. It was bad enough that his daughter was rebelling, but here was his own wife joining forces with her. Soon he would be surrounded by a houseful of independent American women. He too leapt from the bed, throwing off his covers. The Spanish newspapers flew across the room. He snatched the speech out of Yoyo's hands, held it before the girl's wide eyes, a vengeful, mad look in his own, and then once, twice, three, four, countless times, he tore the speech into shreds.

"Are you crazy?" Laura lunged at him. "Have you gone mad? That is her speech for tomorrow you have torn up!"

"Have you gone mad?" He shook her away. "You were going to let her read that . . . that insult to her teachers?"

"Insult to her teachers!" Laura's face had crumpled up like a piece of paper. On it was written a love note to her husband, an unhappy, haunted man. "This is America, Papi, America! You are not in a savage country anymore!"

Meanwhile, Yoyo was on her knees, weeping wildly, collecting all the little pieces of her speech, hoping that she could put it back together before the assembly tomorrow morning. But not even a sibyl[29] could have made sense of those tiny scraps of paper. All hope was lost. "He broke it, he broke it," Yoyo moaned as she picked up a handful of pieces.

Probably, if she had thought a moment about it, she would not have done what she did next. She would have realized her father had lost brothers and friends to the dictator Trujillo. For the rest of his life, he would be haunted by blood in the streets and late night disappearances. Even after all these years, he cringed if a black Volkswagen passed him on the street. He feared anyone in uniform: the meter maid giving out parking tickets, a museum guard approaching to tell him not to get too close to his favorite Goya.[30]

"This is America, Papi, America! You are not in a savage country anymore!"

On her knees, Yoyo thought of the worst thing she could say to her father. She gathered a handful of scraps, stood up and hurled them in his face. In a low, ugly whisper, she pronounced Trujillo's hated nickname: "Chapita! You're just another Chapita!"

It took Yoyo's father only a moment to register the **loathsome**[31] nickname before he came after her. Down the halls they raced, but Yoyo was quicker than he and made it into her room just in time to lock the door as her father threw his weight against it. He called down curses on her head, ordered her on his authority as her

[29] sibyl—prophetess.

[30] Goya—Francisco de Goya (1746–1828), Spanish painter and etcher.

[31] **loathsome**—hateful.

father to open that door! He **throttled**[32] that doorknob, but all to no **avail**.[33] Her mother's love of gadgets saved Yoyo's hide that night. Laura had hired a locksmith to install good locks on all the bedroom doors after the house had been broken into once while they were away. Now if burglars broke in again, and the family were at home, there would be a second round of locks for the thieves to contend with.

"Lolo," she said, trying to calm him down. "Don't you ruin my new locks."

Finally he did calm down, his anger spent. Yoyo heard their footsteps retreating down the hall. Their door clicked shut. Then, muffled voices, her mother's rising in anger, in persuasion, her father's deeper murmurs of explanation and self-defense. The house fell silent a moment, before Yoyo heard, far off, the gun blasts and explosions, the serious, self-important voices of newscasters reporting their TV war.

A little while later, there was a quiet knock at Yoyo's door, followed by a **tentative**[34] attempt at the door knob. "Cuquita?" her mother whispered. "Open up, Cuquita."

"Go away," Yoyo wailed, but they both knew she was glad her mother was there, and needed only a moment's protest to save face.

Together they concocted a speech: two brief pages of stale compliments and the polite commonplaces on teachers, a speech wrought by necessity and without much invention by mother and daughter late into the night on one of the pads of paper Laura had once used for her own inventions. After it was drafted, Laura typed it up while Yoyo stood by, correcting her mother's **misnomers**[35] and mis-sayings.

Yoyo came home the next day with the success story of the assembly. The nuns had been flattered, the audience had stood up and given "our devoted teachers a standing **ovation**,"[36] what Laura had suggested they do at the end of the speech.

She clapped her hands together as Yoyo recreated the moment. "I stole that from your father's speech, remember? Remember how he put that in at the end?" She quoted him in Spanish, then translated for Yoyo into English.

That night, Yoyo watched him from the upstairs hall window, where she'd retreated the minute she heard his car pull up in front of the house. Slowly, her father came up the driveway, a grim expression on his face as he grappled with a large, heavy cardboard box. At the front door, he set the package down carefully and patted all his pockets for his house keys. (If only he'd had Laura's ticking key chain!) Yoyo heard the snapping open of locks downstairs. She listened as he struggled to maneuver the box through the narrow doorway. He called her name several times, but she did not answer him.

"My daughter, your father, he love you very much," he explained from the bottom of the stairs. "He just want to protect you." Finally, her mother came up and pleaded

---

[32] **throttled**—twisted (as if strangling).

[33] **avail**—purpose, effect.

[34] **tentative**—uncertain, hesitant.

[35] **misnomers**—errors in meaning.

[36] **ovation**—prolonged enthusiastic applause.

with Yoyo to go down and **reconcile**[37] with him. "Your father did not mean to harm. You must pardon him. Always it is better to let bygones be forgotten, no?"

Downstairs, Yoyo found her father setting up a brand new electric typewriter on the kitchen table. It was even better than her mother's. He had outdone himself with all the extra features: a plastic carrying case with Yoyo's initials decaled below the handle, a brace to lift the paper upright while she typed, an erase cartridge, an automatic margin tab, a plastic hood like a toaster cover to keep the dust away. Not even her mother could have invented such a machine!

But Laura's inventing days were over just as Yoyo's were starting up with her school-wide success. Rather than the rolling suitcase everyone else in the family remembers, Yoyo thinks of the speech her mother wrote as her last invention. It was as if, after that, her mother had passed on to Yoyo her pencil and pad and said, "Okay, Cuquita, here's the buck. You give it a shot."

37 **reconcile**—reestablish a close relationship.

QUESTIONS TO CONSIDER

1. Why do the kids resent Mami's inventing?
2. Why does she eventually give up?
3. Do you think Yoyo is more like her father or her mother? Why do you think this?
4. Why does Yoyo's father dislike her speech? Why does he then grow so angry at her?
5. How do you feel about his reaction to Yoyo's speech?
6. How is the immigrant experience reflected in this story?

Sandra Cisneros ▶

Divine Providence

BY SANDRA CISNEROS

Sandra Cisneros (1954–) is one of the leaders of an emerging school of Latina or Chicana writers: women of Mexican-American heritage. Cisneros was born in Chicago into a large family. Her father was Mexican and her mother was a Mexican American. Cisneros's youth was spent shuttling back and forth between Chicago and Mexico City. Cisneros writes both poetry and fiction, but it was her first novel, The House on Mango Street *(1983), that made her famous. Drawing heavily on her own experiences, Cisneros depicted the life of young women in the Chicano community. Her subsequent books have continued this exploration of ethnic identity in America. Besides writing, Cisneros has devoted herself to teaching and to acting as an advocate for Chicanas. Many of her stories deal with difficulties faced by Mexican-American women in a male-dominated culture. Cisneros is also a colorful stylist, using her heritage of oral poetry and her own talents as a poet to create a luminous style of description and storytelling.*

Why is Alma Alvarado crying? Until today she could wake to her mama calling *Alma, Alma,* very gently, the way her mama does—*so as to give the soul time to fly back from the dreams.* The sky was blue and smelled of fresh bread and oatmeal. The navy–blue uniform with the detachable collar and cuffs waited patiently on its hanger same as always. She would save a spear of the breakfast papaya for the parrot in the garden of la Señora Cuca, walk to school with her leather school satchel[1] on her back, sing the Himno Nacional[2] in a loud patriotic voice, color a map of the república,[3] eat a ham and cheese torta[4] for lunch, and on the way home buy a bag of Japanese peanuts from the man with one fat foot and the other skinny, throw her satchel in the air and catch it, play in the courtyard—*but not beyond!*—climb the spiral staircase to the rooftop—clink, clang, clang—peer into the rooftop room that once belonged to la Luz Maria before the abuela[5] ran her off for stealing a half kilo of butter, tease the mean dog el Lobo who likes to bark from the roof at anyone who walks

---

[1] satchel—small bag, often having a shoulder strap.

[2] Himmo Nacional—National Hymn (or anthem) of Mexico.

[3] república—Republic of Mexico.

[4] torta—sandwich.

[5] abuela—old woman; here, Alma's grandmother.

down their street, eat a tangerine and toss the peels over the wall to the neighbor's chickens, guess how many shards[6] of glass were cemented on the wall ledge to keep out the thieves, stare at the volcanoes that once were people but are now simply volcanoes, read a Familia Burrón[7] comic book and be read to, wash her feet before going to sleep, have her mama sing—*Sleep, my little girl, sleep, rrruuu*–rrruuu, *rrruuu*–rrruuu, *rrruuu*–rrruuu—all in Spanish which sounds sweet.

But this afternoon her mama was busy washing clothes by hand on the scrubboard sink with a tin bowl of water and a coffee can of detergent, wedding ring sitting plainly beside the straw brush, a ring pretty to look through with its rainbow stone and gold band thick and heavy, the kind of ring a girl like Alma likes to wear on her own hand to pretend she is the mother, because today her mama had said yes, finally yes, while wiping a strand of hair from her face, *yes*, without looking up, *just leave me be*, pretending she didn't hear the parrot cries of the papa's mama, *Just go see what it is your abuela wants this time*, the mama will say, and Alma will have to go up to the abuela's room with its scent of candles and mothballs and overripe fruit, because the abuela has fallen into the habit of hiding food under her pillow—*In this house they never feed me!*—forgetting she already ate an hour before, will hide hard knobs of bread, or a half tortilla, or a black banana, or those cookies called fatties that crumble into a paste and taste like smoke, the ones they fry on griddles in front of the church and wrap in papel de china,[8] all under the embroidered pillow thinking no one the wiser when all along a string of brown ants always gives her away, because the mama can no longer climb up and down the stairs anymore in her condition since the baby they will name Reynaldo is asleep inside her mama's belly, the child her mama hopes will anchor her papa home nights and mend the marriage like the neighbor lady Doña Eufemia Delgado Ruiz advised.

But now the ring is gone, gone, *I swear I don't know how, Mama, I swear it was on my hand when I reached to flush the toilet like so*, and if Señor Meléndez the plumber can't bring it back, Mama will have her baby right now from so much nerves and crying, while the abuela is screaming in her mad parrot voice for her supper, the papa on the telephone and the mama lying down with a cold washcloth on her forehead, *and the water swirled, Mama, swirled without a nose or tail* when the mama's ring leapt from her hand and disappeared with two little sausages of caca, and now there is no way to bring the ring back except by pumping furiously this useless plunger,[9] though perhaps the ring is floating through the sewers of Mexico City by now, and into the muddy canals of Xochimilco[10] where a plump woman in a green satin cocktail

---

[6] shards—broken pieces.

[7] Familia Burrón—family in a popular Mexican comic book.

[8] papel de china—tissue paper.

[9] plunger—device used to unclog drains and pipes.

[10] Xochimilco—lake near Mexico City famous for its "floating gardens."

dress is trailing a pink hand from a flowered chalupa[11] named *Perlita*, beyond the floating gardens and beneath the ruins of an abandoned city where an eagle once perched on a cactus and bit a serpent,[12] and has swooped and tumbled and somersaulted into the eddies[13] and spirals of the Gulf of Mexico waters that are as warm and salty as tears, while, no doubt, little and big sharks are nibbling on a ragged piece of seaweed the moment the ring settles finally on the sea bottom with a soundless poof of sand.

And it will be just as his mother predicted long ago for going against her better judgment and marrying a girl beneath his station in life. Unless the ring comes back like the neighbor lady Doña Eufemia Delgado Ruiz advised, the marriage will be finished regardless how many candles are lit, or promises made, or supplications to St. Anthony[14] recited, Ave Maria, Padre Nuestro,[15] world without end, amen. Why is Alma Alvarado crying?

[11] chalupa—small canoe.

[12] abandoned city . . . serpent—According to Aztec legend, their city of Tenochtitlán was founded in fulfilment of a prophecy on the spot where an eagle was seen perching on a cactus and devouring a serpent. Mexico City stands on the ancient site of Tenochtitlán.

[13] eddies—circular currents.

[14] St. Anthony—Christian saint (1195–1231) famed for his preaching, who is venerated for helping the poor and defenseless.

[15] Ave Maria, Padre Nuestro—beginnings of two famous prayers; the Hail Mary and the Lord's Prayer, respectively.

QUESTIONS TO CONSIDER

1. At the point when the story starts, how has Alma Alvarado's life been?
2. What is the situation of each member of Alma's family?
3. Why is Alma crying?
4. What is the meaning of the title "Divine Providence"?

Sherman Alexie ▶

This Is What It Means to Say Phoenix, Arizona

BY SHERMAN ALEXIE

Sherman Alexie (1967–   ) is one of the most acclaimed young Native-American writers. He grew up on the Spokane Indian Reservation in Washington state and from an early age witnessed the disastrous life of Native Americans on the reservations, facing such problems as high unemployment and alcoholism. Alexie was a precocious student and began seriously writing at university. His first book, a collection of poems and stories called The Business of Fancydancing, *was published in 1992. Since then he has published nine more books, including two novels. In 1999,* The New Yorker, *where he regularly publishes, included him in a list of the twenty best young writers in America. "This Is What It Means to Say Phoenix, Arizona" comes from the collection* The Lone Ranger and Tonto Fistfight in Heaven. *In 1997, Alexie turned it into the movie* Smoke Signals, *the first movie to be written, produced, and directed by a Native American.*

Just after Victor lost his job at the Bureau of Indian Affairs,[1] he also found out that his father had died of a heart attack in Phoenix, Arizona. Victor hadn't seen his father in a few years, had only talked to him on the telephone once or twice, but there still was a genetic[2] pain, which was as real and immediate as a broken bone. Victor didn't have any money. Who does have money on a reservation, except the cigarette and fireworks salespeople? His father had a savings account waiting to be claimed, but Victor needed to find a way to get from Spokane to Phoenix. Victor's mother was just as poor as he was, and the rest of his family didn't have any use at all for him. So Victor called the tribal council.

"Listen," Victor said. "My father just died. I need some money to get to Phoenix to make arrangements."

"Now, Victor," the council said, "you know we're having a difficult time financially."

"But I thought the council had special funds set aside for stuff like this."

"Now, Victor, we do have some money available for the proper return of tribal members' bodies. But I don't think we

---

[1] Bureau of Indian Affairs—U.S. government department that oversees Indian reservations.

[2] genetic—of the origin or development of something.

have enough to bring your father all the way back from Phoenix."

"Well," Victor said. "It ain't going to cost all that much. He had to be **cremated**.[3] Things were kind of ugly. He died of a heart attack in his trailer and nobody found him for a week. It was really hot, too. You get the picture."

Thomas was a storyteller whom nobody wanted to listen to.

"Now, Victor, we're sorry for your loss and the circumstances. But we can really only afford to give you one hundred dollars."

"That's not even enough for a plane ticket."

"Well, you might consider driving down to Phoenix."

"I don't have a car. Besides, I was going to drive my father's pickup back up here."

"Now, Victor," the council said, "we're sure there is somebody who could drive you to Phoenix. Or could anybody lend you the rest of the money?"

"You know there ain't nobody around with that kind of money."

"Well, we're sorry, Victor, but that's the best we can do."

Victor accepted the tribal council's offer. What else could he do? So he signed the proper papers, picked up his check, and walked over to the Trading Post to cash it.

While Victor stood in line, he watched Thomas Builds-the-Fire standing near the magazine rack talking to himself. Like he always did. Thomas was a storyteller whom nobody wanted to listen to. That's like being a dentist in a town where everybody has false teeth.

Victor and Thomas Builds-the-Fire were the same age, had grown up and played in the dirt together. Ever since Victor could remember, it was Thomas who had always had something to say.

Once, when they were seven years old, when Victor's father still lived with the family, Thomas closed his eyes and told Victor this story: "Your father's heart is weak. He is afraid of his own family. He is afraid of you. Late at night, he sits in the dark. Watches the television until there's nothing but that white noise. Sometimes he feels like he wants to buy a motorcycle and ride away. He wants to run and hide. He doesn't want to be found."

Thomas Builds-the-Fire had known that Victor's father was going to leave, known it before anyone. Now Victor stood in the Trading Post with a one-hundred-dollar check in his hand, wondering if Thomas knew that Victor's father was dead, if he knew what was going to happen next.

Just then, Thomas looked at Victor, smiled, and walked over to him.

"Victor, I'm sorry about your father," Thomas said.

"How did you know about it?" Victor asked.

"I heard it on the wind. I heard it from the birds. I felt it in the sunlight. Also, your mother was just in here crying."

[3] **cremated**—burned.

"Oh," Victor said and looked around the Trading Post. All the other Indians stared, surprised that Victor was even talking to Thomas. Nobody talked to Thomas anymore because he told the same damn stories over and over again. Victor was embarrassed, but he thought that Thomas might be able to help him. Victor felt a sudden need for tradition.

"I can lend you the money you need," Thomas said suddenly. "But you have to take me with you."

"I can't take your money," Victor said. "I mean, I haven't hardly talked to you in years. We're not really friends anymore."

"I didn't say we were friends. I said you had to take me with you."

"Let me think about it."

Victor went home with his one hundred dollars and sat at the kitchen table. He held his head in his hands and thought about Thomas Builds-the-Fire, remembered little details, tears and scars, the bicycle they shared for a summer, so many stories.

Thomas Builds-the-Fire sat on the bicycle, waiting in Victor's yard. He was ten years old and skinny. His hair was dirty because it was the Fourth of July.

"Victor," Thomas yelled. "Hurry up. We're going to miss the fireworks."

After a few minutes, Victor ran out of his family's house, **vaulted**[4] over the porch railing, and landed gracefully on the sidewalk.

Thomas gave him the bike and they headed for the fireworks. It was nearly dark and the fireworks were about to start.

"You know," Thomas said, "it's strange how us Indians celebrate the Fourth of July. It ain't like it was our independence everybody was fighting for."

"You think about things too much," Victor said. "It's just supposed to be fun. Maybe Junior will be there."

"Which Junior? Everybody on this reservation is named Junior."

The fireworks were small, hardly more than a few bottle rockets and a fountain. But it was enough for two Indian boys. Years later, they would need much more.

Afterward, sitting in the dark, fighting off mosquitoes, Victor turned to Thomas Builds-the-Fire.

"Hey," Victor said. "Tell me a story."

Thomas closed his eyes and told this story: "There were these two Indian boys who wanted to be warriors. But it was too late to be warriors in the old way. All the horses were gone. So the two Indian boys stole a car and drove to the city. They parked the stolen car in the front of the police station and then hitchhiked back home to the reservation. When they got back, all their friends cheered and their parents' eyes shone with pride. 'You were very brave,' everybody said to the two Indian boys. 'Very brave.'"

"Ya-hey," Victor said. "That's a good one. I wish I could be a warrior."

"Me too," Thomas said.

Victor sat at his kitchen table. He counted his one hundred dollars again and again. He knew he needed more to make it

[4] **vaulted**—leaped.

to Phoenix and back. He knew he needed Thomas Builds-the-Fire. So he put his money in his wallet and opened the front door to find Thomas on the porch.

"Ya-hey, Victor," Thomas said. "I knew you'd call me."

Thomas walked into the living room and sat down in Victor's favorite chair.

"I've got some money saved up," Thomas said. "It's enough to get us down there, but you have to get us back."

"I've got this hundred dollars," Victor said. "And my dad had a savings account I'm going to claim."

"How much in your dad's account?"

"Enough. A few hundred."

"Sounds good. When we leaving?"

When they were fifteen and had long since stopped being friends, Victor and Thomas got into a fistfight. That is, Victor was really drunk and beat Thomas up for no reason at all. All the other Indian boys stood around and watched it happen. Junior was there and so were Lester, Seymour, and a lot of others.

The beating might have gone on until Thomas was dead if Norma Many Horses hadn't come along and stopped it.

"Hey, you boys," Norma yelled and jumped out of her car. "Leave him alone."

If it had been someone else, even another man, the Indian boys would've just ignored the warnings. But Norma was a warrior. She was powerful. She could have picked up any two of the boys and smashed their skulls together. But worse than that, she would have dragged them all over to some tepee and made them listen to some elder tell a dusty old story.

The Indian boys scattered, and Norma walked over to Thomas and picked him up.

"Hey, little man, are you O.K?" she asked.

Thomas gave her a thumbs-up.

"Why they always picking on you?"

Thomas shook his head, closed his eyes, but no stories came to him, no words or music. He just wanted to go home, to lie in his bed and let his dreams tell the stories for him.

Thomas Builds-the-Fire and Victor sat next to each other in the airplane, coach section. A tiny white woman had the window seat. She was busy twisting her body into pretzels. She was flexible.

"I have to ask," Thomas said, and Victor closed his eyes in embarrassment.

"Don't," Victor said.

"Excuse me, miss," Thomas asked. "Are you a gymnast or something?"

"There's no something about it," she said. "I was first alternate on the 1980 Olympic team."

"Really?" Thomas asked.

"Really."

"I mean, you used to be a world-class athlete?" Thomas asked.

"My husband thinks I still am."

Thomas Builds-the-Fire smiled. She was a mental gymnast too. She pulled her leg straight up against her body so that she could've kissed her kneecap.

"I wish I could do that," Thomas said.

Victor was ready to jump out of the plane. Thomas, that crazy Indian storyteller with ratty old braids and broken teeth, was flirting with a beautiful Olympic gymnast. Nobody back home on the reservation would ever believe it.

"Well," the gymnast said. "It's easy. Try it."

Thomas grabbed at his leg and tried to pull it up into the same position as the gymnast's. He couldn't even come close, which made Victor and the gymnast laugh.

"Hey," she asked. "You two are Indian, right?"

"Full-blood," Victor said.

"Not me," Thomas said. "I'm half magician on my mother's side and half clown on my father's."

They all laughed.

"What are your names?" she asked.

"Victor and Thomas."

"Mine is Cathy. Pleased to meet you all."

The three of them talked for the duration of the flight. Cathy the gymnast complained about the government, how they screwed the 1980 Olympic team by boycotting the games.[5]

"Sounds like you all got a lot in common with Indians," Thomas said.

Nobody laughed.

After the plane landed in Phoenix and they had all found their way to the terminal, Cathy the gymnast smiled and waved goodbye.

"She was really nice," Thomas said.

"Yeah, but everybody talks to everybody on airplanes," Victor said.

"You always used to tell me I think too much," Thomas said. "Now it sounds like you do."

"Maybe I caught it from you."

"Yeah."

Thomas and Victor rode in a taxi to the trailer where Victor's father had died.

"Listen," Victor said as they stopped in front of the trailer. "I never told you I was sorry for beating you up that time."

"Oh, it was nothing. We were just kids and you were drunk."

"Yeah, but I'm still sorry."

"That's all right."

Victor paid for the taxi, and the two of them stood in the hot Phoenix summer. They could smell the trailer.

"This ain't going to be nice," Victor said. "You don't have to go in."

"You're going to need help."

Victor walked to the front door and opened it. The stink rolled out and made them both gag. Victor's father had lain in that trailer for a week in hundred-degree temperatures before anyone had found him. And the only reason anyone found him was the smell. They needed dental records to identify him. That's exactly what the coroner said. They needed dental records.

"Oh, man," Victor said. "I don't know if I can do this."

"Well, then don't."

"But there might be something valuable in there."

"I thought his money was in the bank."

"It is. I was talking about pictures and letters and stuff like that."

---

[5] **boycotting the games**—After the Soviet invasion of Afghanistan in 1979, U.S. President Jimmy Carter withdrew American athletes from competition in the 1980 Olympic Games in Moscow. Fifty other countries supported the American boycott.

"Oh," Thomas said as he held his breath and followed Victor into the trailer.

When Victor was twelve, he stepped into an underground wasps' nest. His foot was caught in the hole and no matter how hard he struggled, Victor couldn't pull free. He might have died there, stung a thousand times, if Thomas Builds-the-Fire had not come by.

"Take care of each other *is what my dreams were saying.* Take care of each other."

"Run," Thomas yelled and pulled Victor's foot from the hole. They ran then, hard as they ever had, faster than Billy Mills, faster than Jim Thorpe,[6] faster than the wasps could fly.

Victor and Thomas ran until they couldn't breathe, ran until it was cold and dark outside, ran until they were lost and it took hours to find their way home. All the way back, Victor counted his stings.

"Seven," Victor said. "My lucky number."

Victor didn't find much to keep in the trailer. Only a photo album and a stereo. Everything else had that smell stuck in it or was useless anyway. "I guess this is all," Victor said. "It ain't much."

"Better than nothing," Thomas said.

"Yeah, and I do have the pickup."

"Yeah," Thomas said. "It's in good shape."

"Dad was good about that stuff."

"Yeah, I remember your dad."

"Really?" Victor asked. "What do you remember?"

Thomas Builds-the-Fire closed his eyes and told this story: "I remember when I had this dream that told me to go to Spokane,[7] to stand by the falls in the middle of the city and wait for a sign. I knew I had to go there but I didn't have a car. Didn't have a license. I was only thirteen. So I walked all the way, took me all day, and I finally made it to the falls. I stood there for an hour waiting. Then your dad came walking up. 'What the hell are you doing here?' he asked me. I said, 'Waiting for a vision.' Then your father said, 'All you're going to get here is mugged.' So he drove me over to Denny's, bought me dinner, and then drove me home to the reservation. For a long time, I was mad because I thought my dreams had lied to me. But they hadn't. Your dad was my vision. *Take care of each other* is what my dreams were saying. *Take care of each other.*"

Victor was quiet for a long time. He searched his mind for memories of his father, found the good ones, found a few bad ones, added it all up, and smiled.

"My father never told me about finding you in Spokane," Victor said.

"He said he wouldn't tell anybody. Didn't want me to get in trouble. But he said I had to watch out for you as part of the deal."

"Really?"

[6] Billy Mills . . . Jim Thorpe—gold-medal Olympic athletes of Native-American descent. Billy Mills (1938–) participated in the 1964 Tokyo Olympics, Jim Thorpe in the 1912 Games in Stockholm.

[7] Spokane—city in eastern Washington on the falls of the Spokane River.

"Really. Your father said you would need the help. He was right."

"That's why you came down here with me, isn't it?" Victor asked.

"I came because of your father."

Victor and Thomas climbed into the pickup, drove over to the bank, and claimed the three hundred dollars in the savings account.

Thomas Builds-the-Fire could fly.

Once, he jumped off the roof of the tribal school and flapped his arms like a crazy eagle. And he flew. For a second he **hovered**,[8] suspended above all the other Indian boys, who were too smart or too scared to jump too.

"He's flying," Junior yelled, and Seymour was busy looking for the trick wires or mirrors. But it was real. As real as the dirt when Thomas lost altitude and crashed to the ground.

He broke his arm in two places.

"He broke his wing, he broke his wing, he broke his wing," all the Indian boys chanted as they ran off, flapping their wings, wishing they could fly too. They hated Thomas for his courage, his brief moment as a bird. Everybody has dreams about flying. Thomas flew.

One of his dreams came true for just a second, just enough to make it real.

Victor's father, his ashes, fit in one wooden box with enough left over to fill a cardboard box.

"He always was a big man," Thomas said.

Victor carried part of his father out to the pickup, and Thomas carried the rest. They set him down carefully behind the seats, put a cowboy hat on the wooden box and a Dodgers cap on the cardboard box. That was the way it was supposed to be.

"Ready to head back home?" Victor asked.

"It's going to be a long drive."

"Yeah, take a couple days, maybe."

"We can take turns," Thomas said.

"O.K.," Victor said, but they didn't take turns. Victor drove for sixteen hours straight north, made it halfway up Nevada toward home before he finally pulled over.

"Hey, Thomas," Victor said. "You got to drive for a while."

"O.K."

Thomas Builds-the-Fire slid behind the wheel and started off down the road. All through Nevada, Thomas and Victor had been amazed at the lack of animal life, at the absence of water, of movement.

"Where is everything?" Victor had asked more than once.

Now, when Thomas was finally driving, they saw the first animal, maybe the only animal in Nevada. It was a long-eared jackrabbit.

"Look," Victor yelled. "It's alive."

Thomas and Victor were busy congratulating themselves on their discovery when the jackrabbit darted out into the road and under the wheels of the pickup.

"Stop the damn car," Victor yelled, and Thomas did stop and backed the pickup to the dead jackrabbit.

[8] **hovered**—remained suspended in the air.

"Oh, man, he's dead," Victor said as he looked at the squashed animal.

"Really dead."

"The only thing alive in this whole state and we just killed it."

"The only thing alive in this whole state and we just killed it."

"I don't know," Thomas said. "I think it was suicide."

Victor looked around the desert, sniffed the air, felt the emptiness and loneliness, and nodded his head.

"Yeah," Victor said. "It had to be suicide."

"I can't believe this," Thomas said. "You drive for a thousand miles and there ain't even any bugs smashed on the windshield. I drive for ten seconds and kill the only living thing in Nevada."

"Yeah," Victor said. "Maybe I should drive."

"Maybe you should."

Thomas Builds-the-Fire walked through the corridors of the tribal school by himself. Nobody wanted to be anywhere near him because of all those stories. Story after story.

Thomas closed his eyes and this story came to him: "We are all given one thing by which our lives are measured, one determination. Mine are the stories that can change or not change the world. It doesn't matter which, as long as I continue to tell the stories. My father, he died on Okinawa[9] in World War II, died fighting for this country, which had tried to kill him for years. My mother, she died giving birth to me, died while I was still inside her. She pushed me out into the world with her last breath. I have no brothers or sisters. I have only my stories, which came to me before I even had the words to speak. I learned a thousand stories before I took my first thousand steps. They are all I have. It's all I can do."

Thomas Builds-the-Fire told his stories to all those who would stop and listen. He kept telling them long after people had stopped listening.

Victor and Thomas made it back to the reservation just as the sun was rising. It was the beginning of a new day on earth, but the same old stuff on the reservation.

"Good morning," Thomas said.

"Good morning."

The tribe was waking up, ready for work, eating breakfast, reading the newspaper, just like everybody else does. Willene LeBret was out in her garden, wearing a bathrobe. She waved when Thomas and Victor drove by.

"Crazy Indians made it," she said to herself and went back to her roses.

Victor stopped the pickup in front of Thomas Builds-the-Fire's HUD[10] house. They both yawned, stretched a little, shook dust from their bodies.

"I'm tired," Victor said.

"Of everything," Thomas added.

They both searched for words to end the journey. Victor needed to thank

[9] Okinawa—bloody battle between Japanese and American forces in the South Pacific in the spring of 1945.

[10] HUD—Department of Housing and Urban Development.

Thomas for his help and for the money, and to make the promise to pay it all back.

"Don't worry about the money," Thomas said. "It don't make any difference anyhow."

"Probably not, enit?"

"Nope."

Victor knew that Thomas would remain the crazy storyteller who talked to dogs and cars, who listened to the wind and pine trees. Victor knew that he couldn't really be friends with Thomas, even after all that had happened. It was cruel but it was real. As real as the ash, as Victor's father, sitting behind the seats.

"I know how it is," Thomas said. "I know you ain't going to treat me any better than you did before. I know your friends would give you too much stuff about it."

Victor was ashamed of himself. Whatever happened to the tribal ties, the sense of community? The only real thing he shared with anybody was a bottle and broken dreams. He owed Thomas something, anything.

"Listen," Victor said and handed Thomas the cardboard box that contained half of his father. "I want you to have this."

Thomas took the ashes and smiled, closed his eyes, and told this story: "I'm going to travel to Spokane Falls one last time and toss these ashes into the water. And your father will rise like a salmon, leap over the bridge, over me, and find his way home. It will be beautiful. His teeth will shine like silver, like a rainbow. He will rise, Victor, he will rise."

Victor smiled.

"I was planning on doing the same thing with my half," Victor said. "But I didn't imagine my father looking anything like a salmon. I thought it'd be like cleaning the attic or something. Like letting things go after they've stopped having any use."

"Nothing stops, cousin," Thomas said. "Nothing stops."

Thomas Builds-the-Fire got out of the pickup and walked up his driveway. Victor started the pickup and began the drive home.

"Wait," Thomas yelled suddenly from his porch. "I just got to ask one favor."

Victor stopped the pickup, leaned out the window, and shouted back.

"What do you want?" he asked.

"Just one time when I'm telling a story somewhere, why don't you stop and listen?" Thomas asked.

"Just once?"

"Just once."

Victor waved his arms to let Thomas know that the deal was good. It was a fair trade. That's all Thomas had ever wanted from his whole life. So Victor drove his father's pickup toward home while Thomas went into his house, closed the door behind him, and heard a new story come to him in the silence afterward.

QUESTIONS TO CONSIDER

1. What does Victor's conversation with the Tribal Council suggest about reservation policies?
2. How do Victor's and Thomas's characters differ?
3. Why did Victor and Thomas cease to be friends? Why can't they be friends after they return from the trip?
4. How is Thomas different when away from the reservation? What does this indicate about his character?
5. Why does Thomas help Victor out? Is he living up to his vision or is it something else?

Tobias Wolff ▶

The Night in Question

BY TOBIAS WOLFF

Tobias Wolff (1945–   ) is one of the leading writers of a recent school of American writing, known as "Dirty Realism." Like the work of Raymond Carver (page 462), Wolff's stories have focused on the underside of American society. Wolff himself has seen a great variety of American life. Born in Alabama, his parents divorced early, and his mother took him to live in Connecticut, Florida, Utah, and Washington. Wolff was a bit of a juvenile delinquent, and when he attended prep school in Pennsylvania, he was expelled after a year. He drifted into the army and spent four years as a paratrooper, including a tour of duty in Vietnam. Once out of the army, Wolff went back to school and spent three years at Oxford University. He wanted to write, and to support himself taught classes, waited tables, and worked as a journalist. In 1975, he was awarded a fellowship at Stanford University and published his first novel. Since then, Wolff has had a successful career as a university teacher and has published a series of well-regarded books, including a powerful memoir of his youth, This Boy's Life *(1989). Wolff is a taut writer, not wasting space but quickly moving his characterizations forward. "The Night in Question" could easily have been much longer, but Wolff has said all that needs to be said about a pair of siblings and the brother's troubled life.*

Frances had come to her brother's apartment to hold his hand over a disappointment in love, but Frank ate his way through half the cherry pie she'd brought him and barely mentioned the woman. He was in an **exalted**[1] state over a sermon he'd heard that afternoon. Dr. Violet had outdone himself, Frank said. This was his best; this was the gold standard. Frank wanted to repeat it to Frances, the way he used to act out movie scenes for her when they were young.

"Gotta run, Franky."

"It's not that long," Frank said. "Five minutes. Ten—at the outside."

Three years earlier he had driven Frances' car into a highway **abutment**[2] and almost died, then almost died again, in detox,[3] of a *grand mal*[4] seizure. Now he wanted to preach sermons at her. She supposed she was grateful. She said she'd give him ten minutes.

---

[1] **exalted**—elevated in character or purity of emotions; lofty.

[2] **abutment**—structure, often concrete, that borders the edge of a highway.

[3] detox—reference to treatment for drug or alcohol addiction.

[4] *grand mal*—severe form of epileptic seizure.

It was a muggy night, but as always Frank wore a long-sleeved shirt to hide the weird tattoos he woke up with one morning when he was stationed in Manila. The shirt was white, starched and crisply ironed. The tie he'd worn to church was still **cinched**[5] up hard under his prominent Adam's apple. A big man in a small room, he paced in front of the couch as he gathered himself to speak. He favored his left leg, whose knee had been shattered in the crash; every time his right foot came down, the dishes clinked in the cupboards.

Something terrible was going to happen in the story, something Frances would regret having heard.

"Okay, here goes," he said. "I'll have to fill in here and there, but I've got most of it." He continued to walk, slowly, deliberately, hands behind his back, head bent at an angle that suggested meditation. "My dear friends," he said, "you may have read in the paper not long ago of a man of our state, a parent like many of yourselves here today . . . but a parent with a terrible choice to make. His name is Mike Bolling. He's a railroad man, Mike, a switchman, been with the railroad ever since he finished high school, same as his father and grandfather before him. He and Janice've been married ten years now. They were hoping for a whole houseful of kids, but the Lord decided to give them one instead, a very special one. That was nine years ago. Benny, they named him—after Janice's father. He died when she was just a youngster, but she remembered his big lopsided grin and the way he threw back his head when he laughed, and she was hoping some of her dad's spirit would rub off on his name. Well, it turned out she got all the spirit she could handle, and then some.

"Benny. He came out in high gear and never shifted down. Mike liked to say you could run a train off him, the energy he had. Good student, natural athlete, but his big thing was mechanics. One of those boys, you put him in the same room with a clock and he's got it in pieces before you can turn around. By the time he was in second grade he could put the clocks back together, not to mention the vacuum cleaner and the TV and the engine of Mike's old lawn mower."

This didn't sound like Frank. Frank was plain in his speech, neither formal nor folksy, so spare and sometimes harsh that his jokes sounded like challenges, or insults. Frances was about the only one who got them. This tone was putting her on edge. Something terrible was going to happen in the story, something Frances would regret having heard. She knew that. But she didn't stop him. Frank was her little brother, and she would deny him nothing.

When Frank was still a baby, not even walking yet, Frank Senior, their father, had set out to teach his son the meaning of the word no. At dinner he'd dangle his wristwatch before Frank's eyes, then say no! and jerk it back just as Frank grabbed for it. When Frank persisted, Frank Senior would slap his hand until he was howling

---

[5] **cinched**—fastened securely and tightly.

with fury and desire. This happened night after night. Frank would not take the lesson to heart; as soon as the watch was offered, he snatched at it. Frances followed her mother's example and said nothing. She was eight years old, and while she feared her father's attention she also missed it, and resented Frank's **obstinacy**[6] and the disturbance it caused. Why couldn't he learn? Then her father slapped Frank's face. This was on New Year's Eve. Frances still remembered the stupid tasseled hats they were all wearing when her father slapped her baby brother. In the void of time after the slap there was no sound but the long rush of air into Frank's lungs as, red-faced, twisting in his chair, he gathered himself to scream. Frank Senior lowered his head. Frances saw that he'd surprised himself and was afraid of what would follow. She looked at her mother, whose eyes were closed. In later years Frances tried to think of a moment when their lives might have turned by even a degree, turned and gone some other way, and she always came back to this instant when her father knew the wrong he had done, was shaken and open to **rebuke**.[7] What might have happened if her mother had come flying out of her chair and stood over him and told him to stop, now and forever? Or if she had only *looked* at him, confirming his shame? But her eyes were closed, and stayed closed until Frank blasted them with his despair and Frank Senior left the room. As Frances knew even then, her mother could not allow herself to see what she had no strength to oppose. Her heart was bad. Three years later she reached for a bottle of ammonia, said "Oh," sat down on the floor and died.

Frances did oppose her father. In defiance of his orders, she brought food to Frank's room when he was banished, stood up for him and told him he was right to stand up for himself. Frank Senior had decided that his son needed to be broken, and Frank would not break. He went after everything his father said no to, with Frances egging him on and mothering him when he got caught. In time their father ceased to give reasons for his displeasure. As his silence grew heavier, so did his hand. One night Frances grabbed her father's belt as he started after Frank, and when he flung her aside Frank head-rammed him in the stomach. Frances jumped on her father's back and the three of them crashed around the room. When it was over Frances was flat on the floor with a split lip and a ringing sound in her ears, laughing like a madwoman. Frank was crying. That was the first time.

Frank Senior said no to his son in everything, and Frances would say no to him in nothing. Frank was aware of her reluctance and learned to exploit it, most shamelessly in the months before his accident. He'd invaded her home, caused her trouble at work, nearly destroyed her marriage. To this day her husband had not forgiven Frances for what he called her **complicity**[8] in that

---

[6] **obstinacy**—refusal to give up on an attitude or course of action.

[7] **rebuke**—sharp criticism or reprimand.

[8] **complicity**—involvement as an accomplice in a wrongdoing.

nightmare. But her husband had never been thrown across a room, or kicked, or slammed headfirst into a door. No one had ever spoken to him as her father had spoken to Frank. He did not understand what it was to be helpless and alone. No one should be alone in this world. Everyone should have someone who kept faith, no matter what, all the way.

He doesn't know where Benny is, but he has a pretty good idea.

"On the night in question," Frank said, "Mike's foreman called up and asked him to take another fellow's shift at the drawbridge station where he'd been working. A Monday night it was, mid-January, bitter cold. Janice was at a PTA meeting when Mike got the call, so he had no choice but to bring Benny along with him. It was against the rules, strictly speaking, but he needed the overtime and he'd done it before, more than once. Nobody ever said anything. Benny always behaved himself, and it was a good chance for him and Mike to buddy up, batch it[9] a little. They'd talk and kid around, heat up some franks, then Mike would set Benny up with a sleeping bag and air mattress. A regular adventure.

"A bitter night, like I said. There was a furnace at the station, but it wasn't working. The guy Mike relieved had on his parka and a pair of mittens. Mike ribbed him about it, but pretty soon he and Benny put their own hats and gloves back on. Mike brewed up some hot chocolate, and they played gin rummy, or tried to—it's not that easy with gloves on. But they weren't thinking about winning or losing. It was good enough just being together, the two of them, with the cold wind blowing up against the windows. Father and son: what could be better than that? Then Mike had to raise the bridge for a couple of boats, and things got pretty tense because one of them steered too close to the bank and almost ran aground. The skipper had to reverse engines and go back downriver and take another turn at it. The whole business went on a lot longer than it should have, and by the time the second boat got clear Mike was running way behind schedule and under pressure to get the bridge down for the express train out of Portland. That was when he noticed Benny was missing."

Frank stopped by the window and looked out in an unseeing way. He seemed to be contemplating whether to go on. But then he turned away from the window and started in again, and Frances understood that this little moment of reflection was just another part of the sermon.

"Mike calls Benny's name. No answer. He calls him again, and he doesn't spare the volume. You have to understand the position Mike is in. He has to get the bridge down for that train and he's got just about enough time to do it. He doesn't know where Benny is, but he has a pretty good idea. Just where he isn't supposed to be. Down below, in the engine room.

"The engine room. The mill, as Mike and the other operators call it. You can

[9] batch it—live like bachelors.

imagine the kind of power that's needed to raise and lower a drawbridge, aside from the engine itself—all the winches and levers, pulleys and axles and wheels and so on. Massive machinery. Gigantic screws turning everywhere, gears with teeth like file cabinets. They've got catwalks and little crawlways through the works for the mechanics, but nobody goes down there unless they know what they're doing. You have to know what you're doing. You have to know exactly where to put your feet, and you've got to keep your hands in close and wear all the right clothes. And even if you know what you're doing, you never go down there when the bridge is being moved. Never. There's just too much going on, too many ways of getting snagged and pulled into the works. Mike has told Benny a hundred times, stay out of the mill. That's the iron rule when Benny comes out to the station. But Mike made the mistake of taking him down for a quick look one day when the engine was being serviced, and he saw how Benny lit up at the sight of all that steel, all that machinery. Benny was just dying to get his hands on those wheels and gears, see how everything fit together. Mike could feel it pulling at Benny like a big magnet. He always kept a close eye on him after that, until this one night, when he got distracted. And now Benny's down in there. Mike knows it as sure as he knows his own name."

Frances said, "I don't want to hear this story."

Frank gave no sign that he'd heard her. She was going to say something else, but made a sour face and let him go on.

"To get to the engine room, Mike would have to go through the passageway to the back of the station and either wait for the elevator or climb down the emergency ladder. He doesn't have time to do the one or the other. He doesn't have time for anything but lowering the bridge, and just barely enough time for that. He's got to get that bridge down now or the train is going into the river with everyone on board. This is the position he's in; this is the choice he has to make. His son, his Benjamin, or the people on that train.

"Now, let's take a minute to think about the people on that train. Mike's never met any of them, but he's lived long enough to know what they're like. They're like the rest of us. There are some who know the Lord, and love their neighbors, and live in the light. And there are the others. On this train are men who whisper over cunning papers and take from the widow even her **mean**[10] portion. On this train is the man whose factories kill and **maim**[11] his workers. There are thieves on this train, and liars, and hypocrites. There is the man whose wife is not enough for him, who cannot be happy until he possesses every woman who walks the earth. There is the false witness. There is the bribe-taker. There is the woman who abandons her husband and children for her own pleasure. There is the seller of spoiled goods, the coward, and the **usurer**,[12] and

---

[10] **mean**—low in value or amount; paltry.

[11] **maim**—disable or disfigure, usually by the removal of a limb or other body part.

[12] **usurer**—person who lends money at an unfairly high rate of interest.

there is the man who lives for his drug, who will do anything for that false promise—steal from those who give him work, from his friends, his family, yes, even from his own family, scheming for their pity, borrowing in bad faith, breaking into their very homes. All these are on the train, awake and hungry as wolves, and also on the train are the sleepers, the sleepers with open eyes who sleepwalk through their days, neither doing evil nor resisting it, like soldiers who lie down as if dead and will not join the battle, not for their cities and homes, not even for their wives and children. For such people, how can Mike give up his son, his Benjamin, who is guilty of nothing?

"He can't. Of course he can't, not on his own. But Mike isn't on his own. He knows what we all know, even when we try to forget it: We are never alone, ever. We are in our Father's presence in the light of day and in the dark of night, even in that darkness where we run from Him, hiding our faces like fearful children. He will not leave us. No. He will never leave us alone. Though we lock every window and bar every door, still He will enter. Though we empty our hearts and turn them to stone, yet shall He make His home there.

"He will not leave us alone. He is with all of you, as He is with me. He is with Mike, and also with the bribe-taker on the train, and the woman who needs her friend's husband, and the man who needs a drink. He knows their needs better than they do. He knows that what they truly need is Him, and though they flee His voice He never stops telling them that He is there. And at this moment, when Mike has nowhere to hide and nothing left to tell himself, then he can hear, and he knows that he is not alone, and he knows what it is that he must do. It has been done before, even by Him who speaks, the Father of All, who gave His own son, His beloved, that others might be saved."

"No!" Frances said.

Frank stopped and looked at Frances as if he couldn't remember who she was.

"That's it," she said. "That's my **quota**[13] of holiness for the year."

"But there's more."

"I know, I can see it coming. The guy kills his kid, right? I have to tell you, Frank, that's a crummy story. What're we supposed to get from a story like that—we should kill our own kid to save some stranger?"

"There's more to it than that."

"Okay, then, make it a trainload of strangers, make it ten trainloads of strangers. I should do this because the so-called Father of All did it? Is that the point? How do people think up stuff like this, anyway? It's an awful story."

"It's true."

"True? Franky. Please, you're not a moron."

"Dr. Violet knows a man who was on that train."

"I'll just bet he does. Let me guess." Frances screwed her eyes shut, then popped them open. "The drug addict! Yes, and he reformed afterward and worked

[13] **quota**—amount alotted to each person; proportional share.

with street kids in Brazil and showed everybody that Mike's sacrifice was not in vain. Is that how it goes?"

"You're missing the point, Frances. It isn't about that. Let me finish."

"No. It's a terrible story, Frank. People don't act like that. I sure as hell wouldn't."

"You haven't been asked. He doesn't ask us to do what we can't do."

"I don't care what He asks. Where'd you learn to talk like that, anyway? You don't even sound like yourself."

"I had to change. I had to change the way I thought about things. Maybe I sound a little different too."

"Yeah, well you sounded better when you were drunk."

Frank seemed about to say something, but didn't. He backed up a step and lowered himself into a hideous plaid La-Z-Boy left behind by the previous tenant. It was stuck in the upright position.

"I don't care if the Almighty poked a gun in my ear, I would never do that," Frances said. "Not in a million years. Neither would you. Honest, now, little brother, would you grind me up if I was the one down in the mill, would you push the Francesburger button?"

"It isn't a choice I have to make."

"Yeah, yeah, I know. But say you did."

"I don't. He doesn't hold guns to our heads."

"Oh, really? What about hell, huh? What do you call that? But so what. Screw hell, I don't care about hell. Do I get crunched or not?"

"Don't put me to the test, Frances. It's not your place."

"I'm down in the mill, Frank. I'm stuck in the gears and here comes the train with Mother Teresa[14] and five hundred sinners on board, *whoo whoo, whoo whoo.* Who, Frank, who? Who's it going to be?"

"I don't care if the Almighty poked a gun in my ear, I would never do that," Frances said.

Frances wanted to laugh. Glumly erect in the chair, hands gripping the armrests, Frank looked like he was about to take off into a hurricane. But she kept that little reflection to herself. Frank was thinking, and she had to let him. She knew what his answer would be—in the end there could be no other answer—but he couldn't just say *she's my sister* and let it go at that. No, he'd have to noodle up some righteous, high-sounding reasons for choosing her. And maybe he wouldn't, at first, maybe he'd chicken out and come up with the Bible-school answer. Frances was ready for that, she was up for a fight; she could bring him around. Frances didn't mind a fight, and she especially didn't mind fighting for her brother. For her brother she'd fought neighborhood punks, snotty teachers and unappreciative coaches, loan sharks, landlords, bouncers. From the time she was a scabby-kneed girl she'd taken on her own father, and if push came to shove she'd take on the Father of All, that incomprehensible bully. She was ready. It would be like old times, the two of them waiting in her room upstairs while Frank Senior

[14] Mother Teresa—Albanian-born nun (1910–1997) who worked in India and won the 1979 Nobel Peace Prize.

worked himself into a rage below, muttering, slamming doors, stinking up the house with the cigars he puffed when he was on a tear. She remembered it all—the tremor in her legs, the hammering pulse in her neck as the smell of smoke grew stronger. She could still taste that smoke and hear her father's steps on the stairs, Frank panting beside her, moving closer, his voice whispering her name and her own voice answering as fear gave way to ferocity and unaccountable joy, *It's okay, Franky. I'm here.*

QUESTIONS TO CONSIDER

1. What is the form of the story? Do you think it adds to its impact or distracts?
2. What happened to Frances and Franky's mother? Why?
3. What role does Frank Senior exercise in the story?
4. What does the last sentence of the story mean? What does Franky represent to Frances?
5. What do you think is Tobias Wolff's attitude toward religion?

Jhumpa Lahiri ▶

The Third and Final Continent

BY JHUMPA LAHIRI

Jhumpa Lahiri (1966–) was born in London to Indian parents, but she grew up in Rhode Island. She was educated in Boston and went on to graduate school feeling that she could not have a career as a writer. However, she continued to write part-time, and in 1997 became part of a writing workshop that gave her real confidence. Within seven months she had found an agent and been published in The New Yorker, *long the indicator of success for American writers. Lahiri's first collection,* The Interpreter of Maladies, *was published in 1999 and won not only the Pulitzer Prize, but also the O. Henry Award. Lahiri has said that it is often hard to define where she is from, finding "Rhode Island" an unsatisfactory answer considering her name and heritage, and "India" even less so as she has never lived there. The question of assimilation and belonging runs through her stories, which often deal with the experience of the vast numbers of Indians who have moved to Europe and the United States since the 1960s in search of economic opportunity. "The Third and Final Continent" is such a story, describing the journey of a young Indian to security and comfort in the United States.*

I left India in 1964 with a certificate in commerce and the equivalent, in those days, of ten dollars to my name. For three weeks I sailed on the *SS Roma*, an Italian cargo vessel, in a cabin next to the ship's engine, across the Arabian Sea, the Red Sea, the Mediterranean, and finally to England. I lived in London, in Finsbury Park, in a house occupied entirely by penniless Bengali[1] bachelors like myself, at least a dozen and sometimes more, all struggling to educate and establish ourselves abroad.

I attended lectures at LSE[2] and worked at the university library to get by. We lived three or four to a room, shared a single, icy toilet, and took turns cooking pots of egg curry, which we ate with our hands on a table covered with newspapers.

Apart from our jobs we had few responsibilities. On weekends we lounged barefoot in drawstring pajamas, drinking tea and smoking Rothmans, or set out to watch cricket at Lord's. Some weekends the house was crammed with still more Bengalis, to whom we had introduced

---

[1] Bengali—from a region of eastern India.

[2] LSE—London School of Economics.

ourselves at the greengrocer, or on the Tube,[3] and we made yet more egg curry, and played Mukesh[4] on a Grundig reel-to-reel, and soaked our dirty dishes in the bathtub. Every now and then someone in the house moved out, to live with a woman whom his family back in Calcutta had determined he was to wed. In 1969, when I was thirty-six years old, my own marriage was arranged. Around the same time, I was offered a full-time job in America, in the processing department of a library at MIT.[5] The salary was generous enough to support a wife, and I was honored to be hired by a world-famous university, and so I obtained a sixth-preference green card[6] and prepared to travel farther still.

By then I had enough money to go by plane. I flew first to Calcutta, to attend my wedding, and a week later I flew to Boston, to begin my new job. During the flight I read The Student Guide to North America . . . for although I was no longer a student I was on a budget all the same. I learned that Americans drove on the right side of the road, not the left, and that they called a lift an elevator and an engaged phone busy. "The pace of life in North America is different from Britain, as you will soon discover," the guidebook informed me. "Everybody feels he must get to the top. Don't expect an English cup of tea." As the plane began its descent over Boston Harbor, the pilot announced the weather and the time, and that President Nixon had declared a national holiday: two American men had landed on the moon. Several passengers cheered. "God bless America!" one of them hollered. Across the aisle, I saw a woman praying.

I spent my first night at the YMCA in Central Square, Cambridge, an inexpensive accommodation recommended by my guidebook. It was within walking distance of M.I.T. The room contained a cot, a desk, and a small wooden cross on one wall. A sign on the door said that cooking was strictly forbidden. A bare window overlooked Massachusetts Avenue. . . . Car horns, shrill and prolonged, blared one after another. Flashing sirens heralded endless emergencies, and a fleet of buses rumbled past, their doors opening and closing with a powerful hiss, throughout the night. The noise was constantly distracting, at times suffocating. I felt it deep in my ribs, just as I had felt the furious drone of the engine on the *SS Roma*. But there was no ship's deck to escape to, no glittering ocean to thrill my soul, no breeze to cool my face, no one to talk to. I was too tired to pace the gloomy corridors of the YMCA in my pajamas. Instead I sat at the desk and stared out the window. . . . In the morning I reported to my job at the Dewey Library, a beige fortlike building by Memorial Drive. I also opened a bank account, rented a post office box, and bought a plastic bowl and a spoon at Woolworth's. I went to Purity Supreme,

---

[3] Tube—subway system in London.

[4] Mukesh—Mukesh Chand Mathur (1923–1976), a famous Indian singer.

[5] MIT—Massachusetts Institute of Technology, the most important American university for the study of science and engineering.

[6] green card—permit for non-citizens to live and work in the United States.

wandering up and down the aisles, converting ounces to grams and comparing prices to things in England. In the end I bought a carton of milk and a box of cornflakes. This was my first meal in America. . . . Even the simple chore of buying milk was new to me; in London we'd had bottles delivered each morning to our door.

In a week I had adjusted, more or less. I ate cornflakes and milk, morning and night, and bought some bananas for variety, slicing them into the bowl with the edge of my spoon. . . . I bought a larger carton of milk and learned to leave it on the shaded part of the windowsill, as I had seen another resident at the YMCA do. To pass the time in the evenings I read the Boston Globe downstairs, in a spacious room with stained-glass windows. I read every article and advertisement, so that I would grow familiar with things, and when my eyes grew tired I slept. Only I did not sleep well. Each night I had to keep the window wide open; it was the only source of air in the stifling room, and the noise was intolerable. I would lie on the cot with my fingers pressed into my ears, but when I drifted off to sleep my hands fell away, and the noise of the traffic would wake me up again. Pigeon feathers drifted onto the windowsill, and one evening, when I poured milk over my cornflakes, I saw that it had soured. Nevertheless I resolved to stay at the YMCA for six weeks, until my wife's passport and green card were ready. Once she arrived I would have to rent a proper apartment, and from time to time I studied the classified section of the newspaper, or stopped in at the housing office at MIT during my lunch break to see what was available in my price range. It was in this manner that I discovered a room for immediate occupancy, in a house on a quiet street, the listing said, for eight dollars per week. I dialed from a pay telephone, sorting through the coins with which I was still unfamiliar, smaller and lighter than shillings,[7] heavier and brighter than *paisas*.[8]

"Who is speaking?" a woman demanded. Her voice was bold and clamorous.

"Yes, good afternoon, madame. I am calling about the room for rent."

"Harvard or Tech?"

"I beg your pardon?"

"Are you from Harvard or Tech?"

Gathering that Tech referred to the Massachusetts Institute of Technology, I replied, "I work at Dewey Library," adding tentatively, "at Tech."

"I only rent rooms to boys from Harvard or Tech!"

"Yes, madame."

I was given an address and an appointment for seven o'clock that evening. Thirty minutes before the hour I set out, my guidebook in my pocket, my breath fresh with Listerine. I turned down a street shaded with trees, perpendicular to Massachusetts Avenue. . . . In spite of the heat I wore a coat and tie, regarding the event as I would any other interview; I had

---

[7] shillings—former coins in England.

[8] *paisas*—coins of the smallest denomination in India.

never lived in the home of a person who was not Indian. The house, surrounded by a chain-link fence, was off-white with dark-brown trim, . . . with a tangle of forsythia bushes plastered against the front and sides. When I pressed the calling bell, the woman with whom I had spoken on the phone hollered from what seemed to be just the other side of the door, "One minute, please!"

Several minutes later the door was opened by a tiny, extremely old woman. A mass of snowy hair was arranged like a small sack on top of her head. As I stepped into the house she sat down on a wooden bench positioned at the bottom of a narrow carpeted staircase. Once she was settled on the bench, in a small pool of light, she peered up at me, giving me her undivided attention. She wore a long black skirt that spread like a stiff tent to the floor, and a starched white shirt edged with ruffles at the throat and cuffs. Her hands, folded together in her lap, had long **pallid**[9] fingers, with swollen knuckles and tough yellow nails. Age had battered her features so that she almost resembled a man, with sharp, shrunken eyes and prominent creases on either side of her nose. Her lips, chapped and faded, had nearly disappeared, and her eyebrows were missing altogether. Nevertheless she looked fierce.

"Lock up!" she commanded. She shouted even though I stood only a few feet away. "Fasten the chain and firmly press that button on the knob! This is the first thing you shall do when you enter, is that clear?"

I locked the door as directed and examined the house. Next to the bench . . . was a small round table, its legs fully concealed, much like the woman's, by a skirt of lace. The table held a lamp, a transistor radio, a leather change purse with a silver clasp, and a telephone. A thick wooden cane coated with a layer of dust was propped against one side. There was a parlor to my right, lined with bookcases and filled with shabby claw-footed furniture. In the corner of the parlor I saw a grand piano with its top down, piled with papers. The piano's bench was missing; it seemed to be the one on which the woman was sitting. Somewhere in the house a clock chimed seven times.

"You're **punctual**!"[10] the woman proclaimed "I expect you shall be so with the rent!"

"I have a letter, madame." In my jacket pocket was a letter from M.I.T. confirming my employment, which I had brought along to prove that I was indeed from Tech.

She stared at the letter, then handed it back to me carefully, gripping it with her fingers as if it were a dinner plate heaped with food instead of a sheet of paper. She did not wear glasses, and I wondered if she'd read a word of it. "The last boy was always late! Still owes me eight dollars! Harvard boys aren't what they used to be! Only Harvard and Tech in this house! How's Tech, boy?"

"It is very well."

"You checked the lock?"

"Yes, madame."

---

[9] **pallid**—pale and sickly-looking.

[10] **punctual**—on time, neither early nor late.

She slapped the space beside her on the bench with one hand, and told me to sit down. For a moment she was silent. Then she **intoned**,[11] as if she alone possessed this knowledge:

"There is an American flag on the moon!"

"Yes, madame." Until then I had not thought very much about the moon shot. It was in the newspaper, of course, article upon article. The astronauts had landed on the shores of the Sea of Tranquillity, I had read, traveling farther than anyone in the history of civilization. For a few hours they explored the moon's surface. They gathered rocks in their pockets, described their surroundings (a magnificent desolation, according to one astronaut), spoke by phone to the president, and planted a flag in lunar soil. The voyage was hailed as man's most awesome achievement. . . .

The woman **bellowed**,[12] "A flag on the moon, boy! I heard it on the radio! Isn't that splendid?"

"Yes, madame."

But she was not satisfied with my reply. Instead she commanded, "Say 'Splendid'!"

I was both baffled and somewhat insulted by the request. It reminded me of the way I was taught multiplication tables as a child, repeating after the master, sitting cross-legged, without shoes or pencils, on the floor of my one-room Tollygunge school. It also reminded me of my wedding, when I had repeated endless Sanskrit[13] verses after the priest, verses I barely understood, which joined me to my wife. I said nothing.

"Say 'Splendid'!" the woman bellowed once again.

"Splendid," I murmured. I had to repeat the word a second time at the top of my lungs, so she could hear. I was especially reluctant to raise my voice to an elderly woman, but she did not appear to be offended. If anything the reply pleased her because her next command was:

"There is an American flag on the moon!"

"Go see the room!"

I rose from the bench and mounted the narrow staircase. There were five doors, two on either side of an equally narrow hallway, and one at the opposite end. Only one door was open. The room contained a twin bed under a sloping ceiling, a brown oval rug, a basin with an exposed pipe, and a chest of drawers. One door, painted white, led to a closet, another to a toilet and a tub. . . . The window was open; net curtains stirred in the breeze. I lifted them away and inspected the view: a small back yard, with a few fruit trees and an empty clothesline. I was satisfied. . . .

When I returned to the foyer[14] and told her, she picked up the leather change purse on the table, opened the clasp, fished about with her fingers, and produced a key on a thin wire hoop. She informed me that there was a kitchen at the back of the house, accessible through the parlor. I was welcome to use the stove as long as I left it as I

[11] **intoned**—spoke with a particular tone of voice.
[12] **bellowed**—yelled loudly.
[13] Sanskrit—classical language of India.
[14] foyer—entrance hall.

found it. Sheets and towels were provided, but keeping them clean was my own responsibility. The rent was due Friday mornings on the ledge above the piano keys. "And no lady visitors!"

"I am a married man, madame." It was the first time I had announced this fact to anyone.

But she had not heard. "No lady visitors!" she insisted. She introduced herself as Mrs. Croft.

My wife's name was Mala. The marriage had been arranged by my older brother and his wife. I regarded the proposition with neither objection nor enthusiasm. It was a duty expected of me, as it was expected of every man. She was the daughter of a schoolteacher in Beleghata. I was told that she could cook, knit, embroider, sketch landscapes, and recite poems by Tagore,[15] but these talents could not make up for the fact that she did not possess a fair complexion, and so a string of men had rejected her to her face. She was twenty-seven, an age when her parents had begun to fear that she would never marry, and so they were willing to ship their only child halfway across the world in order to save her from **spinsterhood**.[16]

For five nights we shared a bed. Each of those nights, after applying cold cream and braiding her hair, . . . she turned from me and wept; she missed her parents. Although I would be leaving the country in a few days, custom dictated that she was now a part of my household, and for the next six weeks she was to live with my brother and his wife, cooking, cleaning, serving tea and sweets to guests. I did nothing to console her. I lay on my own side of the bed, reading my guidebook by flashlight and anticipating my journey. At times I thought of the tiny room on the other side of the wall which had belonged to my mother. Now the room was practically empty; the wooden **pallet**[17] on which she'd once slept was piled with trunks and old bedding. Nearly six years ago, before leaving for London, I had watched her die on that bed, had found her playing with her excrement in her final days. Before we cremated her I had cleaned each of her fingernails with a hairpin, and then, because my brother could not bear it, I had assumed the role of eldest son, and had touched the flame to her temple, to release her tormented soul to heaven.

The next morning I moved into Mrs. Croft's house. When I unlocked the door I saw that she was sitting on the piano bench, on the same side as the previous evening. She wore the same black skirt, the same starched white blouse, and had her hands folded together the same way in her lap. She looked so much the same that I wondered if she'd spent the whole night on the bench. I put my suitcase upstairs . . . and headed off to work. That evening when I came home from the university, she was still there.

"Sit down, boy!" She slapped the space beside her.

---

[15] Tagore—Rabindranath Tagore (1862–1941), Indian poet and novelist, winner of the Nobel Prize in 1913.

[16] **spinsterhood**—status of being an unmarried woman.

[17] **pallet**—narrow bed.

I perched beside her on the bench. I had a bag of groceries with me—more milk, more cornflakes, and more bananas, for my inspection of the kitchen earlier in the day had revealed no spare pots, pans, or cooking utensils. There were only two saucepans in the refrigerator, both containing some orange broth, and a copper kettle on the stove.

"Good evening, madame."

She asked me if I had checked the lock. I told her I had.

For a moment she was silent. Then suddenly she declared, with the equal measures of disbelief and delight as the night before, "There's an American flag on the moon, boy!"

"Yes, madame."

"A flag on the moon! Isn't that splendid?"

I nodded, dreading what I knew was coming. "Yes, madame."

"Say 'Splendid'!"

This time I paused, looking to either side in case anyone was there to overhear me, though I knew perfectly well that the house was empty. I felt like an idiot. But it was a small enough thing to ask.

"Splendid!" I cried out.

Within days it became our routine. In the mornings when I left for the library Mrs. Croft was either hidden away in her bedroom, on the other side of the staircase, or she was sitting on the bench, **oblivious**[18] of my presence, listening to the news or classical music on the radio. But each evening when I returned the same thing happened: she slapped the bench, ordered me to sit down, declared that there was a flag on the moon, and declared that it was splendid. I said it was splendid, too, and then we sat in silence. As awkward as it was, and as endless as it felt to me then, the nightly encounter lasted only about ten minutes; inevitably she would drift off to sleep, her head falling abruptly toward her chest, leaving me free to retire to my room. By then, of course, there was no flag standing on the moon. The astronauts, I had read in the paper, had seen it fall before they flew back to Earth. But I did not have the heart to tell her.

Friday morning, when I my first week's rent was due, I went to the piano in the parlor to place my money on the ledge. The piano keys were dull and discolored. When I pressed one, it made no sound at all. I had put eight one-dollar bills in an envelope and written Mrs. Croft's name on the front of it. I was not in the habit of leaving money unmarked and unattended. From where I stood I could see the profile of her tent-shaped skirt. She was sitting on the bench, listening to the radio. It seemed unnecessary to make her get up and walk all the way to the piano. I never saw her walking about, and assumed, from the cane always propped against the round table at her side, that she did so with difficulty. When I approached the bench she peered up at me and demanded:

"What is your business?"

"The rent, madame."

"On the ledge above the piano keys!"

---

[18] **oblivious**—completely unaware.

"I have it here." I extended the envelope toward her, but her fingers, folded together in her lap, did not budge. I bowed slightly and lowered the envelope, so that it hovered just above her hands. After a moment she accepted it, and nodded her head.

That night when I came home, she did not slap the bench, but out of habit I sat beside her as usual. She asked me if I had checked the lock, but she mentioned nothing about the flag on the moon. Instead she said:

"It was very kind of you!"

"I beg your pardon, madame?"

"Very kind of you!"

She was still holding the envelope in her hands.

On Sunday there was a knock on my door. An elderly woman introduced herself: she was Mrs. Croft's daughter, Helen. She walked into the room and looked at each of the walls as if for signs of change, glancing at the shirts that hung in the closet, the neckties draped over the doorknob, the box of cornflakes on the chest of drawers, the dirty bowl and spoon in the basin. She was short and thick-waisted, with cropped silver hair and bright pink lipstick. She wore a sleeveless summer dress, a necklace of white plastic beads, and spectacles on a chain that hung like a swing against her chest. The backs of her legs were mapped with dark blue veins, and her upper arms sagged like the flesh of a roasted eggplant. She told me she lived in Arlington, a town farther up Massachusetts Avenue. "I come once a week to bring Mother groceries. Has she sent you packing yet?"

"It is very well, madame."

"Some of the boys run screaming. But I think she likes you. You're the first boarder she's ever referred to as a gentleman."

"Not at all, madame."

She looked at me, noticing my bare feet (I still felt strange wearing shoes indoors, and always removed them before entering my room.) "Are you new to Boston?"

"New to America, madame."

"From?" She raised her eyebrows.

"I am from Calcutta, India."

"Is that right? We had a Brazilian fellow, about a year ago. You'll find Cambridge a very international city."

I nodded, and began to wonder how long our conversation would last. But at that moment we heard Mrs. Croft's electrifying voice rising up the stairs. When we stepped into the hallway we heard her hollering:

"You are to come downstairs immediately!"

"What is it?" Helen hollered back.

"Immediately!"

I put on my shoes. Helen sighed.

We walked down the staircase. I followed Helen, who seemed to be in no hurry, and complained at one point that she had a bad knee. "Have you been walking without your cane?" Helen called out. "You know you're not supposed to walk without that cane." She paused, resting her hand on the banister, and looked back at me. "She slips sometimes."

For the first time Mrs. Croft seemed vulnerable. I pictured her on the floor in front of the bench, flat on her back, staring at the ceiling, her feet pointing in opposite directions. But when we reached the bottom of the staircase she was sitting there as usual, her hands folded together in her lap. Two grocery bags were at her feet. . . . she did not slap the bench, or ask us to sit down. She glared.

"What is it, Mother?"

"It's improper!"

"What's improper?"

"It is improper for a lady and gentleman who are not married to one another to hold a private conversation without a **chaperone**!"[19]

Helen said she was sixty-eight years old, old enough to be my mother, but Mrs. Croft insisted that Helen and I speak to each other downstairs, in the parlor. She added that it was also improper for a lady of Helen's station to reveal her age, and to wear a dress so high above the ankle.

"For your information, Mother, it's 1969. What would you do if you actually left the house one day and saw a girl in a miniskirt?"

Mrs. Croft sniffed. "I'd have her arrested."

Helen shook her head and picked up one of the grocery bags. I picked up the other one, and followed her through the parlor and into the kitchen. The bags were filled with cans of soup, which Helen opened up one by one with a few cranks of a can opener. She tossed the old soup in the saucepans into the sink, rinsed the pans under the tap, filled them with soup from the newly opened cans, and put them back in the refrigerator. "A few years ago she could still open the cans herself," Helen said. "She hates that I do it for her now. But the piano killed her hands." She put on her spectacles, glanced at the cupboards, and spotted my tea bags. "Shall we have a cup?"

I filled the kettle on the stove. "I beg your pardon, madame. The piano?"

"She used to give lessons. For forty years. It was how she raised us after my father died." Helen put her hands on her hips, staring at the open refrigerator. She reached into the back, pulled out a wrapped stick of butter, frowned, and tossed it into the garbage. "That ought to do it," she said, and put the unopened cans of soup in the cupboard. I sat at the table and watched as Helen washed the dirty dishes, tied up the garbage bag, watered a spider plant over the sink, and poured boiling water into two cups. She handed one to me without milk, the string of the tea bag trailing over the side, and sat down at the table.

"Excuse me, madame, but is it enough?"

Helen took a sip of her tea. Her lipstick left a smiling pink stain on the rim of the cup. "Is what enough?"

"The soup in the pans. Is it enough food for Mrs. Croft?"

"She won't eat anything else. She stopped eating solids after she turned one hundred. That was, let's see, three years ago."

I was mortified. I had assumed Mrs. Croft was in her eighties, perhaps as old as ninety. I had never known a person who had lived for over a century. That

---

[19] **chaperone**—person, usually an older woman, who supervises young unmarried women on social occasions.

this person was a widow who lived alone mortified me further still. It was widowhood that had driven my own mother insane. My father, who worked as a clerk at the General Post Office of Calcutta, died of encephalitis[20] when I was sixteen. My mother refused to adjust to life without him; instead she sank deeper into a world of darkness from which neither I, nor my brother, nor concerned relatives, nor psychiatric clinics on Rash Behari Avenue could save her. What pained me most was to see her so unguarded, to hear her burp after meals or expel gas in front of company without the slightest embarrassment. After my father's death my brother abandoned his schooling and began to work in the jute[21] mill he would eventually manage, in order to keep the household running. And so it was my job to sit by my mother's feet and study for my exams as she counted and recounted the bracelets on her arm as if they were the beads of an **abacus**.[22] We tried to keep an eye on her. Once she had wandered half naked to the tram[23] depot before were able to bring her inside again.

I had never known a person who had lived for over a century.

"I am happy to warm Mrs. Croft's soup in the evenings," I suggested. . . . "It is no trouble."

Helen looked at her watch, stood up, and poured the rest of her tea into the sink. "I wouldn't if I were you. That's the sort of thing that would kill her altogether."

That evening, when Helen had gone back to Arlington and Mrs. Croft and I were alone again, I began to worry. Now that I knew how very old she was, I worried that something would happen to her in the middle of the night, or when I was out during the day. As vigorous as her voice was, and **imperious**[24] as she seemed, I knew that even a scratch or a cough could kill a person that old; each day she lived, I knew, was something of a miracle. . . . Helen didn't seem worried. She came and went, bringing soup for Mrs. Croft, one Sunday after the next.

In this manner the six weeks of that summer passed. I came home each evening, after my hours at the library, and spent a few minutes on the piano bench with Mrs. Croft. . . . Some evenings I sat beside her long after she had drifted off to sleep, still in awe of how many years she had spent on this earth. At times I tried to picture the world she had been born into, in 1866—a world, I imagined, filled with women in long black skirts, and chaste conversations in the parlor. Now, when I looked at her hands with their swollen knuckles folded together in her lap, I imagined them smooth and slim, striking the piano keys. At times I came downstairs before going to sleep, to make sure she was sitting upright on the bench, or was safe in her bedroom. On Fridays I made sure to

[20] encephalitis—inflammation of the brain.

[21] jute—rough fiber from the bark of certain East Indian plants, used for making twine, rope, and fabrics.

[22] **abacus**—simple device used for calculating that is made of beads strung on wire.

[23] tram—streetcar.

[24] **imperious**—bullying; overbearing.

put the rent in her hands. There was nothing I could do for her beyond these simple gestures. I was not her son, and apart from those eight dollars, I owed her nothing.

At the end of August, Mala's passport and green card were ready. I received a telegram with her flight information; my brother's house in Calcutta had no telephone. Around that time I also received a letter from her, written only a few days after we had parted. There was no salutation; addressing me by name would have assumed an intimacy we had not yet discovered. It contained only a few lines. "I write in English in preparation for the journey. Here I am very much lonely. Is it very cold there. Is there snow. Yours, Mala."

I was not touched by her words. We had spent only a handful of days in each other's company. And yet we were bound together; for six weeks she had worn an iron bangle on her wrist, and applied vermillion powder to the part in her hair, to signify to the world that she was a bride. In those six weeks I regarded her arrival as I would the arrival of a coming month, or season—something inevitable, but meaningless at the time. So little did I know her that, while details of her face sometimes rose to my memory, I could not **conjure**[25] up the whole of it.

A few days after receiving the letter, as I was walking to work in the morning, I saw an Indian woman on the other side of Massachusetts Avenue, wearing a sari[26] with its free end nearly dragging on the footpath, and pushing a child in a stroller. An American woman with a small black dog on a leash was walking to one side of her. Suddenly the dog began barking. From the other side of the street I watched as the Indian woman, startled, stopped in her path, at which point the dog leaped up and seized the end of the sari between its teeth. The American woman **scolded**[27] the dog, appeared to apologize, and walked quickly away, leaving the Indian woman to fix her sari in the middle of the footpath, and quiet her crying child. She did not see me standing there, and eventually she continued on her way. Such a mishap, I realized that morning, would soon be my concern. It was my duty to take care of Mala, to welcome her and protect her. I would have to buy her her first pair of snow boots, her first winter coat. I would have to tell her which streets to avoid, which way the traffic came, tell her to wear her sari so that the free end did not drag on the footpath. A five-mile separation from her parents, I recalled with some irritation, had caused her to weep.

Unlike Mala, I was used to it all by then: used to cornflakes and milk, used to Helen's visits, used to sitting on the bench with Mrs. Croft. The only thing I was not used to was Mala. Nevertheless I did what I had to do. I went to the housing office at MIT and found a furnished apartment a few blocks away, with a double bed and a private kitchen and bath, for forty dollars a

---

[25] **conjure**—make appear.

[26] sari—principal dress of Indian and Pakistani women, consisting of a long piece of cotton or silk wrapped around the body with one end falling to the feet and the other thrown over the shoulder.

[27] **scolded**—criticized for wrongdoing.

week. One last Friday I handed Mrs. Croft eight one-dollar bills in an envelope, brought my suitcase downstairs, and informed her that I was moving. She put my key into her change purse. The last thing she asked me to do was hand her the cane propped against the table, so that she could walk to the door and lock it behind me. "Goodbye, then," she said, and retreated back into the house. I did not expect any display of emotion, but I was disappointed all the same. I was only a boarder, a man who paid her a bit of money and passed in and out of her home for six weeks. Compared with a century, it was no time at all.

At the airport I recognized Mala immediately. The free end of her sari did not drag on the floor, but was draped in a sign of bridal modesty over her head, just as it had draped my mother until the day my father died. Her thin brown arms were stacked with gold bracelets, a small red circle was painted on her forehead, and the edges of her feet were tinted with a decorative red dye. I did not embrace her, or kiss her, or take her hand. Instead I asked her, speaking Bengali for the first time in America, if she was hungry.

She hesitated, then nodded yes.

I told her I had prepared some egg curry at home. "What did they give you to eat on the plane?"

"I didn't eat."

"All the way from Calcutta?"

"The menu said oxtail soup."

"But surely there were other items."

"The thought of eating an ox's tail made me lose my appetite."

When we arrived home, Mala opened up one of her suitcases, and presented me with two pullover sweaters, both made with bright blue wool, which she had knitted in the course of our separation, one with a V neck, the other covered with cables. I tried them on; both were tight under the arms. She had also brought me two new pairs of drawstring pajamas, a letter from my brother, and a packet of loose Darjeeling tea. I had no present for her apart from the egg curry. We sat at a bare table, staring at our plates. We ate with our hands, another thing I had not yet done in America.

"The house is nice," she said. "Also the egg curry." With her left hand she held the end of her sari to her chest, so it would not slip off her head.

"I don't know many recipes."

She nodded, peeling the skin off each of her potatoes before eating them. At one point the sari slipped to her shoulders. She readjusted it at once.

"There is no need to cover your head," I said. "I don't mind. It doesn't matter here."

She kept it covered anyway.

I waited to get used to her, to her presence at my side, at my table and in my bed, but a week later we were still strangers. I still was not used to coming home to an apartment that smelled of steamed rice, and finding that the basin in the bathroom was always wiped clean, our two toothbrushes lying side by side, a cake of Pears soap resting in the soap dish. I was not used to the fragrance of the coconut oil she rubbed every other night into her scalp, or the delicate sound her bracelets made as she moved about the apartment. In the mornings she was always awake before I was. The first morning when I came into the kitchen she had heated up the leftovers and set a plate with a spoonful of salt on its edge, assuming I would eat rice for breakfast, as most Bengali husbands did. I told her cereal would do, and the next morning when I came into the kitchen she had already poured the cornflakes into my bowl. One morning she walked with me down Massachusetts Avenue to MIT, where I gave her a short tour of the campus. . . . The next morning before I left for work she asked me for a few dollars. I parted with them reluctantly, but I knew that this, too, was now normal. When I came home from work there was a potato peeler in the kitchen drawer, and a tablecloth on the table, and chicken curry made with fresh garlic and ginger on the stove. . . . After dinner I read the newspaper, while Mala sat at the kitchen table, working on a cardigan for herself with more of the blue wool, or writing letters home.

. . . On Friday, I suggested going out. Mala set down her knitting and disappeared into the bathroom. When she emerged I regretted the suggestion; she had put on a silk sari and extra bracelets, and coiled her hair with a flattering side part on top of her head. She was prepared as if for a party, or at the very least for the cinema, but I had no such destination in mind. The evening was balmy. We walked several blocks down Massachusetts Avenue, looking into the windows of restaurants and shops. Then, without thinking, I led her down the quiet street where for so many nights I had walked alone.

"This is where I lived before you came," I said, stopping at Mrs. Croft's chain-link fence.

"In such a big house?"

"I had a small room upstairs. At the back."

"Who else lives there?"

"A very old woman."

"With her family?"

"Alone."

"But who takes care of her?"

I opened the gate. "For the most part she takes care of herself."

I wondered if Mrs. Croft would remember me; I wondered if she had a new boarder to sit with her each evening. When I pressed the bell I expected the same long wait as that day of our first meeting, when I did not have a key. But this time, the door was opened almost immediately, by Helen. Mrs. Croft was not sitting on the bench. The bench was gone.

"Hello there," Helen said, smiling with her bright pink lips at Mala. "Mother's in the parlor. Will you be visiting awhile?"

"As you wish, madame."

"Then I think I'll run to the store, if you don't mind. She had a little accident. We can't leave her alone these days, not even for a minute."

I locked the door after Helen and walked into the parlor. Mrs. Croft was lying flat on her back, her head on a peach-colored cushion, a thin white quilt spread over her body. Her hands were folded together on her chest. When she saw me she pointed at the sofa, and told me to sit down. I took my place as directed, but Mala wandered over to the piano and sat on the bench, which was now positioned where it belonged.

"I broke my hip!" Mrs. Croft announced, as if no time had passed.

"Oh dear, madame."

"I fell off the bench!"

"I am so sorry, madame."

"It was the middle of the night! Do you know what I did, boy?"

I shook my head.

"I called the police!"

She stared up at the ceiling and grinned sedately, exposing a crowded row of long gray teeth. Not one was missing. "What do you say to that, boy?"

As stunned as I was, I knew what I had to say. With no hesitation at all, I cried out, "Splendid!"

Mala laughed then. Her voice was full of kindness, her eyes bright with amusement. I had never heard her laugh before, and it was loud enough so that Mrs. Croft heard, too. She turned to Mala and glared.

"Who is she, boy?"

"She is my wife, madame."

Mrs. Croft pressed her head at an angle against the cushion to get a better look. "Can you play the piano?"

"No, madame," Mala replied.

"Then stand up!"

Mala rose to her feet, adjusting the end of her sari over her head and holding it to her chest, and, for the first time since her arrival, I felt sympathy. I remembered my first days in London, learning how to take the Tube to Russell Square, riding an escalator for the first time, unable to understand that when the man cried "piper" it meant "paper," unable to decipher, for a whole year, that the conductor said "mind the gap" as the train pulled away from each station. Like me, Mala had traveled far from home, not knowing where she was going, or what she would find, for no reason other than to be my wife. As strange as it seemed, I knew in my heart that one day her death would affect me, and stranger still, that mine would affect her. I wanted somehow to explain this to Mrs. Croft, who was still **scrutinizing**[28] Mala from top to toe with what seemed to be placid disdain.[29] I wondered if Mrs. Croft had ever seen a woman in a sari, with a dot painted on her forehead and bracelets stacked on her wrists. I wondered what she would object to. I wondered if she could see the red dye still vivid on Mala's feet, all but obscured by the bottom edge of her sari. At last Mrs. Croft declared, with the equal measures of disbelief and delight I knew well:

"She is a perfect lady!"

Now it was I who laughed. I did so quietly, and Mrs. Croft did not hear me. But Mala had heard, and, for the first time, we looked at each other and smiled.

I like to think of that moment in Mrs. Croft's parlor as the moment when the

[28] **scrutinizing**—carefully or critically examining.

[29] placid disdain—calm contempt.

distance between Mala and me began to lessen. Although we were not yet fully in love, I like to think of the months that followed as a honeymoon of sorts. Together we explored the city and met other Bengalis, some of whom are still friends today. We discovered that a man named Bill sold fresh fish on Prospect Street, and that a shop in Harvard Square called Cardullo's sold bay leaves and cloves. In the evenings we walked to the Charles River to watch sailboats drift across the water, or had ice cream cones in Harvard Yard. We bought an Instamatic camera with which to document our life together, and I took pictures of her posing in front of the Prudential Building, so that she could send them to her parents. At night we kissed, shy at first but quickly bold, and discovered pleasure and solace in each other's arms. I told her about my voyage on the *SS Roma*, and about Finsbury Park and the YMCA, and my evenings on the bench with Mrs. Croft. When I told her stories about my mother, she wept. It was Mala who consoled me when, reading the *Globe* one evening, I came across Mrs. Croft's obituary. I had not thought of her in several months—by then those six weeks of the summer were already a remote interlude in my past—but when I learned of her death I was stricken, so much so that when Mala looked up from her knitting she found me staring at the wall, the newspaper neglected in my lap, unable to speak. Mrs. Croft's was the first death I mourned in America, for hers was the first life I had admired; she had left this world at last, ancient and alone, never to return.

As for me, I have not strayed much farther. Mala and I live in a town about twenty miles from Boston, on a tree-lined street much like Mrs. Croft's, in a house we own, with a garden that saves us from buying tomatoes in summer, and room for guests. We are American citizens now, so that we can collect Social Security when it is time. Though we visit Calcutta every few years, . . . we have decided to grow old here. I work in a small college library. We have a son who attends Harvard University. Mala no longer drapes the end of her sari over her head, or weeps at night for her parents, but occasionally she weeps for our son. So we drive to Cambridge to visit him, or bring him home for a weekend, so that he can eat rice with us with his hands, and speak in Bengali, things we sometimes worry he will no longer do after we die.

It was Mala who consoled me when, reading the Globe one evening, I came across Mrs. Croft's obituary.

Whenever we make that drive, I always make it a point to take Massachusetts Avenue, in spite of the traffic. I barely recognize the buildings now, but each time I am there I return instantly to those six weeks as if they were only the other day, and I slow down and point to Mrs. Croft's street, saying to my son, here was my first home in America, where I lived with a woman who was a hundred and three. "Remember?" Mala says, and smiles, amazed, as I am, that there was ever a time that we were strangers. My son always expresses his astonishment, not at Mrs. Croft's age, but at how little I paid in rent, a fact nearly as inconceivable to him as a flag on the moon was to a woman born in 1866. In my son's eyes I see the ambition that had first hurled me across the world. In a few years he will graduate and pave his own way, alone and unprotected. But I remind myself that he has a father who is still living, a mother who is happy and strong. Whenever he is discouraged, I tell him that if I can survive on three continents, then there is no obstacle he cannot conquer. While the astronauts, heroes forever, spent mere hours on the moon, I have remained in this new world for nearly thirty years. I know that my achievement is quite ordinary. I am not the only man to seek his fortune far from home, and certainly I am not the first. Still, there are times I am bewildered by each mile I have traveled, each meal I have eaten, each person I have known, each room in which I have slept. As ordinary as it all appears, there are times when it is beyond my imagination.

QUESTIONS TO CONSIDER

1. Why has the narrator traveled away from India to England and America?
2. What effect does the visit to Mrs. Croft's by the narrator and Mala produce?
3. How do the worlds of Mrs. Croft, the narrator, and his son differ?

Nathan Englander ▶

The Gilgul of Park Avenue

BY NATHAN ENGLANDER

Nathan Englander (1970–) had his first book published only in 1999, but he is already established as a new voice in American fiction. Considered to be a direct heir of the great postwar generation of Jewish-American writers, The New Yorker *called him one of the twenty best young writers in America in 1999, and his collection* For the Relief of Unbearable Urges *received rave reviews. Englander was raised in an Orthodox Jewish community in Long Island. Orthodox Jews adhere as closely as they can to the religion's ancient rituals and traditions: keeping kosher and the Sabbath, wearing a yarmulke, studying the Torah, attending seminary rather than secular schools. Englander has said that his education was resolutely anti-intellectual, and that it was his interest in books that started him on another path. He persuaded his parents to let him attend the State University of New York, and he spent one of his college years in Jerusalem, discovering a Jewish society that was more open. He knew he wanted to write and attended the famous Writer's Workshop at the University of Iowa and then moved to Jerusalem. Englander's stories are amazingly varied—set in closed Orthodox communities, Stalin's Russia, World War II, New York City, and so on—but they all deal with questions of faith and Jewishness. "The Gilgul of Park Avenue" is a humorous, but acute portrait of a man discovering faith, and the consequences for his marriage.*

The Jewish day begins in the calm of evening, when it won't shock the system with its arrival. It was then, three stars visible in the Manhattan sky and a new day fallen, that Charles Morton Luger understood he was the bearer of a Jewish soul.

Ping! Like that it came. Like a knife against a glass.

Charles Luger knew, as he knew anything at all, that there was a Yiddishe neshama[1] functioning inside.

He was not one to engage taxicab drivers in conversation, but such a thing as this he felt obligated to share. A New York story of the first order, like a woman giving birth in an elevator, or a hot-dog vendor performing open-heart surgery with pocketknife and Bic pen. Was not this a rebirth in itself? It was something, he was sure. So he leaned forward in his seat, raised a fist, and knocked on the Plexiglas divider.

[1] Yiddishe neshama—Hebrew for a "Jewish soul."

The driver looked into his rearview mirror.

"Jewish," Charles said. "Jewish, here in the back."

The driver reached up and slid the partition over so that it hit its groove loudly.

"Oddly, it seems that I'm Jewish. Jewish in your cab."

"No problem here. Meter ticks the same for all **creeds**."[2] He pointed at the digital display.

Charles thought about it. A positive experience or, at least, **benign**.[3] Yes, benign. What had he expected?

He looked out the window at Park Avenue, a Jew looking out at the world. Colors no brighter or darker, though he was, he admitted, already searching for someone with a beanie,[4] a landsman who might look his way, wink, confirm what he already knew.

The cab slowed to a halt outside his building, and Petey the doorman was already on his way to the curb. Charles removed his money clip and peeled off a fifty. He reached over the seat, holding on to the bill.

"Jewish," Charles said, pressing the fifty into the driver's hand. "Jewish right here in your cab."

Charles hung his coat and placed his briefcase next to the stand filled with ornate canes and umbrellas that Sue—carefully scouting them out around the city—did not let him touch. Sue had redone the foyer[5] and the living room and dining room all in chintz fabric, an overwhelming amount of flora and fauna[6] patterns, a vast slippery-looking expanse. Charles rushed through it to the kitchen, where Sue was removing dinner from the refrigerator.

She was reading the note the maid had left, and lit burners and turned dials accordingly. Charles came up behind her. He inhaled the scent of perfume and the faint odor of cigarettes laced underneath. Sue turned and they kissed, more passionate than friendly, which was neither an everyday occurrence nor altogether rare. She was still wearing her contacts; her eyes were a radiant blue.

"You won't believe it," Charles said—surprised to find himself **elated**.[7] He was a levelheaded man, not often victim to extremes of mood.

"What won't I believe?" Sue said. She separated herself from him and slipped a tray into the oven.

Sue was art director at a glossy magazine, her professional life comparatively glamorous. The daily doings of a financial analyst, Charles felt, did not even merit polite attention. He never told her anything she wouldn't believe.

"Well, what is it, Charles?" She held a glass against the recessed ice machine in the refrigerator. "Damn," she said. Charles, at breakfast, had left it set on CRUSHED.

"You wouldn't believe my taxi ride," he said, suddenly aware that a person

---

[2] **creeds**—religions or other systems of belief.

[3] **benign**—not harmful; gentle or mild.

[4] beanie—reference to the yarmulke, the skull cap worn by Jewish men.

[5] foyer—entrance hall.

[6] flora and fauna—plant and animal.

[7] **elated**—exultant, joyful.

disappointed by ice chips wouldn't take well to such a change.

"Your face," she said.

"Nothing, just remembering. A heck of a ride. A maniac. Taxi driver running lights. Up on the sidewalk. Took Third before the bridge traffic cleared."

The maid had prepared creamed chicken. When they sat down to dinner Charles stared at his plate. Half an hour Jewish and already he felt obliged. He knew there were dietary laws, milk and meat forbidden to touch, but he didn't know if chicken was considered meat and didn't dare ask Sue and chance a confrontation, not until he'd formulated a plan. He'd call Dr. Birnbaum, his psychologist, in the morning. Or maybe he'd find a rabbi. Who better to guide him in such matters?

And so, a Marrano[8] in modern times, Charles ate his chicken like a gentile[9]—all the while a Jew in his heart.

At work the next morning, Charles got right on it.

He pulled out the yellow pages, referenced and cross-referenced, following the "see" list throughout the phone book. More than one listing with "Zion" put him in touch with a home for the aged. "Redemption" led him farther off course. Going back to the phone book, he came upon an organization that seemed frighteningly appropriate. For one, it was a Royal Hills number, a neighborhood thick with Jews.

The listing was for the Royal Hills Mystical Jewish Reclamation Center, or, as the recorded voice said, the R-HMJRC—just like that, with a pause after the R. It was a sort of **clearinghouse**[10] for the Judeo-supernatural: press 1 for messianic time clock, press 2 for dream interpretation and counseling, 3 for numerology,[11] and 4 for a retreat schedule. The "and 4" took the wind out of his sails. A bad sign. Recordings never said "and 4" and then "and 5." But the message went on. A small miracle. "For all gilgulim,[12] cases of possible reincarnation or recovered memory, please call Rabbi Zalman Meintz at the following number."

When they sat down to dinner Charles stared at his plate. Half an hour Jewish and already he felt obliged.

Charles took it down, elated. This is exactly why he'd moved to New York from Idaho so many years before. Exactly the reason. Because you could find anything in the Manhattan yellow pages. Anything. A book as thick as a cinder block.

The R-HMJRC was a beautifully renovated brownstone in the heart of Royal Hills. It was Gothic looking. The front

[8] Marrano—In Spain and Portugal when the Inquisition flourished many Jews converted to Christianity to avoid persecution and exile. Those who continued to practice Judaism in secret were known as *Marranos*.

[9] gentile—person who is not Jewish.

[10] **clearinghouse**—here, a place where many different services are available.

[11] numerology—practice of foretelling the future by the study of number combinations.

[12] gilgulim—Hebrew word for "revolving." It refers to the transmigration of souls; that is, that the soul is eternal and passes to another body after death.

steps had been widened to the width of the building, and the whole **façade**[13] of the first two floors had been torn out and replaced with a stone arch, a glass wall behind it. The entry hall was marble, and Charles was impressed. There is money in the God business, he told himself, making a mental note.

Like this it went: standing in the middle of the marble floor, feeling the cold space, the only thing familiar being his unfamiliar self. And then it was back. Ping! Once again, understanding.

Only yesterday his whole life was his life, familiar, totally his own. Something he lived in like an old wool sweater. Today: Brooklyn, an archway, white marble.

"Over here, over here. Follow my voice. Come to the light."

Charles had taken the stairs until they ended, and entered what appeared to be an attic, slanted ceilings and dust, overflowing with attic-like stuff, chairs and a rocking horse, a croquet set and boxes, everywhere boxes—as if all the remnants of the brownstone's former life had been driven upward.

"There is a path on your right. Make your way, it's possible. I got here." The speech was punctuated with something like laughter. It was vocalized joy, a happy stutter.

The path led to the front of the building and a clearing demarcated[14] by an Oriental screen. The rabbi sat in a leather armchair across from a battered couch—both clearly salvaged from the spoils that cluttered the room.

"Zalman," the man said, jumping up, shaking Charles's hand. "Rabbi Zalman Meintz."

"Charles Luger," Charles said, taking off his coat.

The couch, though it had seen brighter days, was clean. Charles had expected dust to rise when he sat. As soon as he touched the fabric, he got depressed. More chintz. The sun-dulled flowers crawling all over it.

"Just moved in," Zalman said. "New space. Much bigger. But haven't, as you see"—he pointed at specific things, a mirror, a china hutch—"please excuse—or forgive—please excuse our appearance. More important matters come first. Very busy lately, very busy." As if to illustrate, a phone perched on a doll-house set to ringing. "You see," Zalman said. He reached over, turned off the ringer. "Like that all day—at night too. Busier even at night."

The surroundings didn't inspire confidence, but Zalman did. He couldn't have been much more than thirty but looked, to Charles, like a real Jew: long black beard, black suit, black hat at his side, and a nice big caricaturish nose, like Fagin's[15] but friendlier.

"Well then, Mr. Luger. What brings you to my lair?"

Charles was still unready to talk. He turned his attention to a painted seascape on the wall. "That the Galilee?"[16]

---

[13] **façade**—front of a building.

[14] demarcated—set off; bounded.

[15] Fagin's—reference to a Jewish character in Charles Dickens's *Oliver Twist*.

[16] Galilee—sea in northern Israel, associated with Jesus Christ, who ministered on its shores.

"Oh, no." Rabbi Meintz laughed and, sitting back, crossed his legs. For the first time Charles noticed that the man was sporting a pair of heavy wool socks and suede sandals. "That's Bolinas. My old stomping grounds."

"Bolinas?" Charles said. "California?"

"I see what's happening here. Very obvious." Zalman uncrossed his legs, reached out, and put a hand on Charles's knee. "Don't be shy," he said. "You've made it this far. Searched me out in a bright corner of a Brooklyn attic. If such a meeting has been ordained, which, by its very nature, it has been, then let's make the most of it."

"I'm Jewish," Charles said. He said it with all the force, excitement, and relief of any of life's great admissions. There was silence. Zalman was smiling, listening intently, and, apparently, waiting.

"Yes," he said, maintaining the smile, barely jarring it to speak. "And?"

"Since yesterday," Charles said. "In a cab."

"Oh," Zalman said. And, "Oh! Now I get it."

"It just came over me."

"Wild," Zalman said. He clapped his hands, looked up at the ceiling, laughed. "Miraculous."

"Unbelievable," Charles added.

"No!" Zalman said, his smile gone, a single finger held up in Charles's face. "No, it's not unbelievable. That it is not. I believe you. Knew before you said—exactly why I didn't respond. A Jew sits in front of me and tells me he's Jewish. This is no surprise. To see a man, so Jewish, a person who could be my brother, who is my brother, tell me he has only now discovered he's Jewish—that, my friend, that is truly miraculous." During his speech he had slowly moved his finger back, and then thrust it into Charles's face anew. "But not unbelievable. I see cases of this all the time."

"Then it's possible? That it's true?"

"Already so Jewish"—Zalman laughed—"asking questions you've already answered. You know the truth better than I do. You're the one who came to the discovery. How do you feel?"

"Fine," Charles said. "Different but fine."

"Well don't you think you'd be upset if it was wrong what you knew? Don't you think you'd be less than fine if this were a nightmare? Somehow suffering if you'd gone crazy?"

"Who said anything about crazy?" Charles asked. Crazy, he was not.

"Did I?" Zalman said. He grabbed at his chest. "An accident, purely. Slip of the tongue. So many who come have trouble with the news at home. Their families doubt."

Charles shifted. "I haven't told her."

Zalman raised an eyebrow, turned his head to favor the accusing eye.

"There is a wife who doesn't know?"

"That's why I'm here. For guidance." Charles put his feet up on the couch, lay down like at Dr. Birnbaum's. "I need to tell her, to figure out how. I need, also, to know what to do. I ate milk and meat last night."

"First history," Zalman said. He slipped off a sandal. "Your mother's not Jewish?"

"No, no one. Ever. Not that I know."

"This is also possible," Rabbi Zalman said. "It may be only that your soul was at Sinai.[17] Maybe an Egyptian slave that came along. But once the soul witnessed the miracles at Sinai, accepted there the word, well, it became a Jewish soul. Do you believe in the soul, Mr. Luger?"

"I'm beginning to."

"All I'm saying is that the soul doesn't live or die. It's not an **organic**[18] thing like the body. It is there. And it has a history."

"And mine belonged to a Jew?"

"No, no. That's exactly the point. Jew, non-Jew, doesn't matter. The body doesn't matter. It is the soul itself that is Jewish."

They talked for over an hour. Zalman gave him books, *The Chosen, A Hedge of Roses*, and a copy of *The Code of Jewish Law*. Charles agreed to cancel his shrink appointment for the next day, and Zalman would come to his office to study with him. There would be payment, of course. A minor fee, expenses, some for charity and ensured good luck. The money was not the important thing, Zalman assured him. The crucial thing was having a guide to help him through his transformation. And who better than Zalman, a man who'd come to the Jewish religion the same way? Miserable in Bolinas, addicted to sorrow and drugs, he was on the brink when he discovered his Jewish soul. "And you never needed a formal conversion?" Charles asked, astounded.

"No," Zalman said. "Such things are for others, for the **litigious**[19] and stiff minded; such rituals are not needed for those who are called by their souls."

"Tell me then," Charles said. He spoke out of the side of his mouth, feeling confident and chummy. "Where'd you get the shtick[20] from? You look Jewish, you talk Jewish—the authentic article. I turn Jewish and get nothing. You come from Bolinas and sound like you've never been out of Brooklyn."

"And if I'd discovered I was Italian, I'd play bocci[21] like a pro. Such is my nature, Mr. Luger. I am most open to letting take form that which is truly inside."

This was, of course, a matter of personal experience. Zalman's own. Charles's would inevitably be different. Unique. If it was slower—the change—then let it be so. After all, Zalman counseled, the laws were not to be devoured like bonbons but to be embraced as he was ready. Hadn't it taken him fifty-five years to learn he was Jewish? Yes, everything in good time.

"Except," Zalman said, standing up. "You must tell your wife first thing. Kosher can wait. Tefillin[22] can wait. But there is

[17] Sinai—mountain where the Bible records the Israelites received the Ten Commandments from God after escaping from Egypt.

[18] **organic**—of the human body; living.

[19] **litigious**—those who are only convinced by the process of legal proceedings.

[20] shtick—Yiddish meaning "characteristic routine."

[21] bocci—popular Italian game played with a ball in an enclosed court.

[22] Tefillin—phylacteries, that is, two cubical black leather boxes worn by Jewish men during morning prayers. They contain scriptural passages.

one thing the tender soul can't bear—the sacrifice of Jewish pride."

Sue had a root canal after work. She came home late, carrying a pint of ice cream. Charles had already set the table and served dinner on the off chance she might be able to eat.

"How was it?" he asked, lighting a candle, pouring the wine.

He did not tease her, did not say a word about her slurred speech or sagging face. He pretended it was a permanent injury, that it was nerve damage, acted as if it were a business dinner and Sue were a client with a crippled lip.

Sue approached the table and lifted the bottle. "Well you're not leaving me, I can tell that much. You'd never have opened your precious Haut-Brion to tell me you were running off to Greece with your secretary."

"True," he said. "I'd have saved it to drink on our veranda in Mykonos."

"Glad to see," she said, standing on her toes and planting a wet and pitifully slack kiss on his cheek, "that the fantasy has already gotten that far."

"The wine's actually a feeble attempt at topic **broaching**."[23]

Sue pried the top off her ice cream and placed the carton in the center of her plate. They both sat down.

"Do tell," she said.

"I'm Jewish." That easy. It was not, after all, the first time.

"Is there a punch line?" she asked. "Or am I supposed to supply that?"

He said nothing.

"OK. Let's try it again. I'll play along. Go, give me your line."

"In the cab yesterday. I just knew. I understood, felt it for real. And—" He looked at her face, contorted, dead with anesthesia.[24] A surreal expression to receive in return for surreal news. "And it hasn't caused me any grief. Except for my fear of telling you. Otherwise, I actually feel sort of good about it. Different. But like things, big things, are finally right."

"Let's get something out of the way first." She made a face, a horrible face. Charles thought maybe she was trying to bite her lip—or scowl. "OK?"

"Shoot."

"What you're really trying to tell me is: Honey, I'm having a nervous breakdown and this is the best way to tell you. Correct?" She plunged a teaspoon into the ice cream and came up with a massive spoonful. "If it's not a nervous breakdown, I want to know if you feel like you're clinically insane."

"I didn't expect this to go smoothly," Charles said.

"You pretend that you knew I'd react badly." Sue spoke quickly and (Charles tried not to notice) drooled. "Really though, with your tireless optimism, you thought I would smile and tell you to be Jewish. That's what you thought, Charles." She jammed her spoon back into the carton, left it buried. "Let me tell you, this time you were way off. Wrong in your heart and right in your head. It couldn't

[23] **broaching**—beginning to talk about; bringing up.

[24] anesthesia—pain medication.

have gone smoothly. Do you know why? Do you know?"

"Why?" he asked.

"Because what you're telling me, out of the blue, out of nowhere, because what you're telling me is, **inherently**,[25] crazy."

Charles nodded repeatedly, as if a bitter truth were confirmed.

"He said you would say that."

"Who said, Charles?"

"The rabbi."

"You've started with rabbis?" She pressed at her sleeping lip.

"Of course, rabbis. Who else gives advice to a Jew?"

Charles read the books at work the next day and filled a legal pad with notes. When the secretary buzzed with Dr. Birnbaum on the line inquiring about the sudden cancelation, Charles, for the first time since he'd begun his treatment fifteen thousand dollars before, did not take the doctor's call. He didn't take any, absorbed in reading *A Hedge of Roses*, the definitive guide to a healthy marriage through ritual purity, and waiting for Rabbi Zalman.

When Charles heard Zalman outside his office, he buzzed his secretary. This was a first, as well. Charles never buzzed the secretary until she had buzzed him first. There was a **protocol**[26] for entry to his office. It's good for a visitor to hear buzz and counterbuzz. It sets a tone.

"So," Zalman said, seating himself. "Did you tell her?'

Charles placed his fountain pen back in its holder. He straightened the base with two hands. "She sort of half believes me. Enough to worry. Not enough to tear my head off. But she knows I'm not kidding. And she does think I'm crazy."

"And how do you feel?"

"Content." Charles leaned back in his swivel chair, his arms dangling over the sides. "Jewish and content. Excited. Still excited. The whole thing's **ludicrous**.[27] I was one thing and now I'm another. But neither holds any real meaning. It's only that when I discovered I was Jewish, I think I also discovered God."

"Like Abraham,"[28] Zalman said, with a worshipful look at the ceiling. "Now it's time to smash some idols." He pulled out a serious-looking book, leather bound and gold embossed. A book full of secrets, Charles was sure. They studied until Charles told Zalman he had to get back to work. "No fifty-minute hour here," Zalman said, taking a swipe at the psychologist. They agreed to meet daily and shook hands twice before Zalman left.

He wasn't gone long enough to have reached the elevators when Walter, the CEO, barged into Charles's office, stopping immediately inside the door.

"Who's the fiddler on the roof?"[29] Walter said.

"Broker."

"Of what?" Walter tapped his wedding band against the nameplate on the door.

---

[25] **inherently**—of a thing's very nature.

[26] **protocol**—established procedure.

[27] **ludicrous**—laughable because of obvious absurdity.

[28] Abraham—in the Bible, the ancestor of the Jews.

[29] fiddler . . . roof—reference to 1964 musical based on Sholem Aleichem's stories of Russian Jews.

"Commodities," Charles said. "Metals."

"Metals." Another tap of the ring. A knowing wink.

"Promise me something, Charley. This guy tries to sell you the steel out of the Brooklyn Bridge, at least bargain with the man."

There had been a few nights of relative quiet and a string of dinners with nonconfrontational foods. Among them: a risotto and then a blackened trout, a spaghetti squash with an eye-watering vegetable marinara, and—in response to a craving of Sue's—a red snapper with tomato and those little bits of caramelized garlic the maid did so well.

Sue had, for all intents and purposes, ignored Charles's admission and, mostly, ignored Charles. Charles spent his time in the study reading the books Zalman had brought him.

This was how the couple functioned until the day the maid left a pot of beef bourguignon.

"The meat isn't kosher[30] and neither is the wine," Charles said, referring to the wine both in and out of his dinner. "There's a pound of bacon fat in this. I'm not complaining, only letting you know. Really. Bread will do me fine." He reached over and took a few slices from the basket, refilled his wineglass with water.

Sue glared at him.

"You're not complaining?"

"No," he said, and reached for the butter.

"Well, I'm complaining! I'm complaining right now!" Sue slammed a fist down so that her glass tipped over, spilling wine onto the tablecloth she loved. They both watched the tablecloth soak up the wine, the lace and the stitching, which fattened and swelled, the color spreading along the workmanship as if through a series of veins. Neither moved.

"Sue, your tablecloth."

"Damn my tablecloth," she said.

"Oh my." He took a sip of water.

"Oh my is right. You bet, mister." She made a noise that Charles considered to be a growl. His wife of twenty-seven years had growled at him.

"If you think I'll ever forgive you for starting this when I was crippled with Novocain. Attacking me when I could hardly talk. If you think," she said, "if you think I'm going to start paying twelve dollars and fifty cents for a roast chicken, you are terribly, terribly wrong."

"What is this about chickens?" Charles did not raise his voice.

"The religious lady at work. She puts in orders on Wednesday. Every week she orders the same goddamn meal. A twelve-dollar-and-fifty-cent roast chicken." Sue shook her head. "You should have married an airline chef if you wanted kosher meals."

"Different fight, Sue. We're due for a fight, but I think you're veering toward the wrong one."

"Why don't you tell me then," she said. "Since all has been revealed to you,

[30] kosher—right or clean according to Jewish law.

why don't you enlighten me as to the nature of the conflict."

"Honestly, I think you're threatened. So I want you to know. I still love you. You're still my wife. This should make you happy for me. I've found God."

"You threw out all the cheese, Charles. How could God hate cheese?"

"Exactly the problem. You didn't find our God. I'd have been good about it if you found our God—or even a less demanding one. A deity less queer."

She scanned the table again, as if to find one of his transgressions left out absentmindedly like house keys. "Today the cheese is gone. You threw out all the cheese, Charles. How could God hate cheese?"

"A woman who thinks peaches are too suggestive for the fruit bowl could give in on a quirk or two."

"You think I don't notice what's going on, that I don't notice you making ablutions[31] in the morning?" Sue dipped her napkin into her water glass. "I've been waiting for your midlife crisis. But I expected something I could handle, a small test. An imposition.[32] Something to rise above and prove my love for you in a grand display of **resilience**.[33] Why couldn't you have turned into a vegan?[34] Or a liberal Democrat? Slept with your secretary for real." Sue dabbed at the wine stain. "Any of those and I would've made do."

Charles scrutinized her.

"So essentially you're saying it would be OK if I changed into a West Side Jew. Like if we suddenly lived in the Apthorp."[35]

Sue thought about it.

"Well, if you have to be Jewish, why so Jewish? Why not like the Browns in six-K? Their kid goes to Haverford. Why," she said, closing her eyes and pressing two fingers to her temple, "why do people who find religion always have to be so damn extreme?"

"Extreme," Charles felt, was too extreme a word considering all there was to know and all the laws he had yet to implement. He hadn't been to synagogue. He hadn't yet observed the Sabbath. He had only changed his diet and said a few prayers.

For this he'd been driven from his own bedroom.

Occasionally Sue sought him out, always with **impeccable**[36] timing. She came into the den the first morning he donned prayer shawl and phylacteries, which even to Charles looked especially strange. The leather box and the strap twirled tightly around his arm, another box planted square in the center of his head. He was in the midst of the Eighteen Benedictions when Sue entered, and was forced to listen to her **tirade**[37] in silence.

"My Charley, always topping them all," she said, watching as he rocked back

[31] ablutions—washing or cleansing according to ritual guidelines.

[32] imposition—burdensome or unfair demand.

[33] **resilience**—ability to recover quickly from change or misfortune.

[34] vegan—strict vegetarian who eats no animal products, including milk and eggs.

[35] Apthorp—famous apartment building on the Upper West Side of Manhattan.

[36] **impeccable**—perfect; without flaw or error.

[37] **tirade**—long, angry, violent speech.

and forth, his lips moving. "I've heard of wolf men and people being possessed. I've even seen modern vampires on TV. Real people who drink blood. But this beats all." She left him and then returned with a mug of coffee in hand.

"I spoke to Dr. Birnbaum. I was going to call him myself, to see how he was dealing with your change." She blew on her coffee. "Guess what, Charley. He calls me first. Apologizes for crossing boundaries, then tells me you've stopped coming, that you won't take his calls. Oh, I say, that's because Charley's Jewish and is very busy meeting with the rabbi. He's good, your shrink. Remains calm. And then, completely deadpan, he asks me—as if it makes any difference—what kind of rabbi. I told him what you told me, word for word. The kind from Bolinas. The kind who doesn't need to be ordained because he's been a rabbi in his past nine lives. And what, I asked him, does one man, one man himself ten generations a rabbi, what does he need with anyone's diploma?" Sue put the mug down on a lamp stand.

"Dr. Birnbaum's coming to dinner next week. On Monday. I even ordered kosher food, paper plates, the whole deal. You'll be able to eat in your own house like a human being. An evening free of antagonism where we can discuss this like adults. His idea. He said to order kosher food once first before leaving you. So I placed an order." She smoothed down her eyebrows, waited for a response. "You can stop your praying, Charles"—she turned to leave—"your chickens are on the way."

Charles had no suits left. Shatnez, the mixing of linen and wool, is strictly forbidden. On Zalman's recommendation, he sent his wardrobe to Royal Hills for testing and was forced to go to work the next day in slacks and suspenders, white shirt, and tie. Walter hadn't left him alone since he'd arrived. "It ain't Friday, Charley," he kept saying. "Casual day is only once a week." This he interchanged with "Why go to so much trouble? A nicely pressed bathrobe would be fine."

Charles had worked himself into a funk by the time Zalman entered his office. He'd accomplished nothing all morning.

"I am weakening," Charles said. "The revelation lasts about a second, comes and goes, a hot flash in the back of a taxi. But the headache it leaves you with—a whopper of a headache—that persists."

Zalman scratched at his nostril with a pinkie, a sort of refined form of picking. "Were you in a fraternity in college?"

"Of course," Charles said.

"Then consider this pledging. You've been tapped, given a bid, and now is the hard part before all the good stuff. Now's when you buy the letters on the sly and try them on at home in front of the mirror."

"Wonderful, Zalman. Well put. But not so simple. I've got to tell my boss something soon. And tensions have risen at home. We're having dinner on Monday. My wife and my shrink versus me. She's even ordered kosher food, trying to be friendly about it."

"Kosher food." A knee-slapper, a big laugh. "The first step. Doesn't sound anything but positive to me. By any chance, has she gone to the ritual bath yet?"

Charles spun his chair around, looked out the window, then, slowly, spun it back. "Zalman," he said, "that's a tough one. And it sort of makes me think you're not following. Sue refuses to go for a couple of reasons. One because she hates me, and our marriage is falling apart. And two, she maintains—and it's a valid point, a fairly good argument—that she's not Jewish."

"I see."

"I want you to come on Monday, Zalman. A voice of reason will come in handy after the weekend. I'm going to keep my first Shabbos.[38] And if Sue remains true to form, I'm in for a doozy."

"Find out where the food is from. If it's really kosher catered, I'll be there."

The clocks had not changed for the season, and Shabbos still came early. Charles put on his suit jacket—deemed kosher—and his coat and went home without explanation. He didn't touch the candlesticks on the mantelpiece, didn't risk raising Sue's ire. Instead he dug a pair, dented and tarnished, from a low cabinet in the overstuffed and unused butler's pantry. The maid passed, said nothing. She took her pocketbook and the day's garbage into the service hall.

In the absence of wife or daughter, the honor of ushering in the Sabbath falls upon the lone man. Charles cleared a space on the windowsill in the study and, covering his eyes before the lit candles, made the blessing. He paused at the place where the woman is permitted to petition the Lord with wishes and private blessings, and stood, palms cool against his eyes, picturing Sue.

The candles flickered next to the window, burning lopsided and fast.

Charles extended the footrest on his recliner. He closed his eyes and thought back to his first night away from home, sleeping on a mattress next to his cousin's bed. He was four or five, and his cousin, older, slept with the bedroom door shut tight, not even a crack of light from the hallway. It was the closest to this experience, the closest he could remember to losing and gaining a world.

The candles were out when Charles heard Sue pass on her way to the bedroom. He tried to come up with a topic of conversation, friendly and day to day. He came up with nothing, couldn't remember what they'd talked about over their life together. What had they said to each other when there was nothing pressing? What had they chatted about for twenty-seven years?

He got up and went to her.

Sue was sitting at the far window on the petite antique chair that was intended only to be admired. She held a cigarette and flicked the ash into a small porcelain dish resting on her knee. In half silhouette against the electric dusk of the city, Sue appeared as relaxed as Charles had seen her since long before his revelation. He could tell, or thought he could, that she was concentrating on ignoring his presence. She would not have her moment of peace compromised.

[38] Shabbos—Hebrew word for the "Sabbath."

This was his wife. A woman who, if she preferred, could pretend he was not there. A woman always able to live two realities at once. She could spend a day at work slamming down phones, storming down hallways with layouts she'd torn in half, then come home to entertain, serve dinner, pass teacups in a way that hushed a room.

How was he to explain his own lack of versatility? Here was a woman who lived in two generations simultaneously. How was he to make clear his struggle living in one? And how to tell the woman of two lives that he had invited over Zalman, who carried in his soul a full ten?

On Sunday Charles was reading a copy of Leon Uris's *QB VII*[39] when Sue ran—truly ran—into the study and grabbed him by the arm. He was shocked and made the awkward movements of someone who is both dumbfounded and manhandled at the very same time, like a tourist mistakenly seized by the police.

"Sue, what are you doing?"

"I could kill you," she said. And though smaller, she had already pulled him to his feet. Charles followed her to the foyer.

"What is this?" she yelled, slamming open the door.

"A mezuzah,"[40] he said. "If you mean that." He pointed at the small metal casing nailed to the doorpost. "I need it," he said. "I have to kiss it."

"Oh my God," she said, slamming the door closed, giving the neighbors no more than a taste. "My God!" She steadied herself, put a hand against the wall. "Well where did it come from? It's got blue paint on it. Where does one buy a used mezuzah?"

"I don't know where to get one. I pried it off eleven-D with a letter opener. They don't even use it. Steve Fraiman had me in to see their Christmas tree last year. Their daughter is dating a black man."

"Are you insane? Five years on the waiting list to get into this building and now you're vandalizing the halls. You think anyone but me will believe your cockamamy story? Oh, I'm not a Nazi, Mrs. Fraiman, just a middle-aged man who woke up a Jew."

"It happened in a cab. I didn't wake up anything."

Sue put her other hand against the wall and let her head hang.

"I've invited the rabbi," Charles said.

"You think that's going to upset me? You think I didn't know you'd drag him into this? Good, bring him. Maybe they have a double open at Bellevue."[41]

"This is very intolerant, Sue." He reached out to touch her.

"Go back to the study," she said. "Go paw one of your books."

They considered the table. Charles and Sue stood at opposite ends, appraising the job the maid had done.

It was admirable.

---

[39] Leon Uris's *QB VII*—novel about the Holocaust.

[40] mezuzah—small oblong container at the front door of a Jewish house. It contains a passage from the Bible as a reminder to obey God's laws when leaving the house.

[41] Bellevue—New York's public mental hospital.

There was a paper tablecloth and paper cups and plastic champagne glasses with snap-on bases. There were patterned paper napkins that matched the pattern on the plates, plastic forks and plastic spoons, and a few other things—cheap but not disposable. Knives, for instance, the knives were real, new, wooden-handled steak knives. Sue had even gone to the trouble of finding a decent bottle of kosher wine. One bottle. The other was a blackberry. Charles wondered if the blackberry was a warning as to what continued religiosity might do to the refined **palate**.[42] Screw-top wine. Sugary plonk.[43] He was going to comment, but looking again at the lavish spread, both leaves inserted into the table, the polished silver on the credenza,[44] he reconsidered. It was more than a truce. It was an attempt to be open—or at least a request that the maid make it resemble as much.

"Mortifying," she said. "Like a child's birthday party. We've got everything except for a paper donkey tacked to the wall."

"I appreciate it, Sue. I really, really do." He had sweetness in his voice, real love for the first time since he'd made his announcement.

"Eighty-eight dollars' worth of the blandest food you've ever had. The soup is inedible, pure salt. I had a spoonful and needed to take an extra high-blood-pressure pill. I'll probably die before dinner's over, and then we'll have no problems."

"More and more," Charles said, taking a yarmulke from his pocket and fastening it to his head, "more and more, you're the one that sounds like a Jew."

When Charles answered the knock on the study door, he was surprised to find Zalman standing there, surprised that Sue hadn't come to get him.

"She is very nice, your wife," Zalman said. "A sensible woman, it appears."

"Appearances are important," Charles said.

Zalman brightened, and **exuded**[45] joy as he did.

"It will be fine," he said. He hooked Charles's arm into his own and led him down the hall.

Sue and Dr. Birnbaum—sporting a yellow sweater—were already seated. Charles sat at the head of the table, and Zalman stood behind his chair.

The most painful silence Charles had ever experienced ensued. He was aware of his breathing, his pulse and temperature. He could feel the contents of his intestines, the blood in his head, the air settling on his eardrums, lake-smooth without sound.

It was Zalman who spoke.

"Is there a place where I can wash?" he asked.

Before eating bread, Charles knew.

"Yes," Charles said. "I'll come too."

He looked at Sue as he got up. Charles knew what she was thinking.

[42] **palate**—sense of taste.

[43] plonk—cheap wine.

[44] credenza—buffet, sideboard.

[45] **exuded**—exhibited a great amount of a quality or emotion.

Say it, he wanted to tell her. Point it out to Dr. Birnbaum. You're right. It's true.

Ablutions.

Ablutions all the time.

Rabbi Zalman made a blessing over the bread, and Dr. Birnbaum muttered, "Amen."

Sue just stared. A man with a beard, a long black beard and sidelocks, was sitting in her house. Charles wanted to tell her she was staring but stopped himself with "Sue."

"What!" she said. 'What, Charles?"

"Shall we eat?"

"Yes," Zalman said, his smile broad, his teeth bright white and Californian. "Let's eat first. We can discuss better on full stomachs." Reaching first one way and then the other, Zalman picked up a bottle and poured himself a brimming glass of blackberry wine.

They ate in a lesser but still oppressive silence. All showed it in their **countenances**,[46] except for Zalman, who was deeply involved in the process of eating and paused only once, to say "Jewish name—Birnbaum," before going back to his food. The other three took turns looking from one to the other and back to their plates. There was a lot of staring at Zalman when there was nowhere to put their eyes.

"The barley is delicious." Dr. Birnbaum smiled as if Sue had cooked any of the food.

"Thank you," she said, snatching the empty container from next to Zalman and heading to the kitchen for another. Dr. Birnbaum took that opportunity to broach the topic with Charles.

"I don't think it's unfair to say I was startled by your news."

"Just your everyday revelation, nothing special."

"Even so, I would have hoped you'd feel comfortable discussing it with me. After all this time."

Sue returned with a quart container of barley, the plastic top in her hand. Charles cleared his throat and then there was quiet. She cocked her head. A slight tilt, an inquisitive look. Had there ever been silence at one of her dinner parties? Had her presence ever brought a conversation to an abrupt end?

She slammed the container onto the table, startling Zalman (he looked up at her and removed a bit of barley from his beard).

"I was about to explain my presence," Dr. Birnbaum said. "Let Charles know that there's no secret agenda. This isn't a competency hearing.[47] And I'm not packing a syringe full of Thorazine."[48]

"That was before," Sue said. "Last week, before your patient started pilfering Judaica.[49] Before he started mortifying me in this building. Do you know that on Friday night he rode the elevator up and down like an idiot waiting for someone to press our floor? Like a retarded child. He gets in the elevator and keeps explaining it to everyone, 'Can't press the button on my

[46] **countenances**—facial expressions.

[47] competency hearing—legal examination to determine sanity.

[48] Thorazine—strong tranquilizing drug.

[49] Judaica—Jewish religious objects.

Sabbath, ha ha.' He can't ask people outright, because you're only allowed to *hint*."

"Very good," Zalman said. "A fine student."

"You," she said to Zalman. "**Interloper**!"[50] And then, turning back to Dr. Birnbaum, "I heard it from old Mrs. Dallal. She's the one who pressed the button. Our poor old next-door neighbor forced to ride the elevator with this maniac. She told me she was talking to Petey the doorman and couldn't figure out why the elevator door kept opening and Charley wouldn't come out. She told me that she actually asked him, 'Do you want to come out?' Now is that insane, Doctor, or is it not? Do sane people need to be invited out of elevators, or do they just get out on their own?"

"You can't give people permission to ignore God. It is not your right."

Charles spoke first:

"She turned the light off in the bathroom on Friday night. She knows I can't touch the lights. I had to go in the dark. It's malicious."

"We are at the table, Charles. Paper plates or not. A man who holds his fork like an animal or not, we shall have some manners."

Zalman laughed out loud at Sue's insult.

"Those are manners, embarrassing a guest?" Now Charles yelled. "And a rabbi, yet."

"He, Charley, is not even Jewish. And neither are you. One need not be polite to the insane. As long as you don't hose them down, all is in good taste."

"She's malicious, Doctor. She brought you here to watch her insult me."

"If I'm supposed to put my two cents in," Dr. Birnbaum said, "I suppose now is the time."

"Two cents?" Zalman said. "What does that come out to for you, a consonant?"

"Thank you," the doctor said. "A perfect example of the **inane**[51] kind of aggression that can turn a conversation into a brawl."

"It's because you're not wearing a tie," Charles said. "How can you control people without a tie?"

"I'm not trying to control anyone."

"It's true," Zalman said. "I went to a shrink for twelve years. Started in seventh grade. They don't control. They **absolve**.[52] Like atheist priests. No responsibility for your actions, no one to answer to. Anarchists with advanced degrees." Zalman spoke right to the doctor. "You can't give people permission to ignore God. It is not your right."

"Sir," Dr. Birnbaum said. "Rabbi. As Charles's spiritual adviser, I invite you to join me in trying to help the situation."

"Exactly why I'm here," Zalman said. He pushed his chair back, rested his elbows on the table. "There is one way to help and that is to give Charles your blessing or whatever you call it. Shrinks always say it's OK, so tell him it's OK, tell her it's OK, and then all will be better."

---

[50] **Interloper**—meddler.

[51] **inane**—senseless.

[52] **absolve**—pronounce clear or free of blame or guilt.

"I can't do that—don't, in fact, do that," the doctor said. He addressed his patient. "Should we go into another room and talk?"

"If I wanted that, I'd have come to our sessions. All the therapy in the world could not bring the simple comfort that I've found in worshiping God."

"Listen to this," Sue said. "Do you hear the kind of thing I have to endure? **Palaver**!"[53] The doctor looked at Sue, raised his hand, and patted the air.

"I'm listening," he said. "I actually do want to hear it. But from him. That Charles has gone from Christian nonbeliever to Orthodox Jew is clear. It is also perplexing." He spoke in sensible rhythms. The others listened, all primed to interrupt. "I came to dinner to hear from Charles why he changed."

"Because of his soul," Zalman said, throwing his arms up in frustration. "He's always had this soul. His way of thinking has always been agreeable, it is only that now God let him know He wasn't pleased with the way Charley was acting."

"It's true," Charles said. "That's how it feels, like it was always in me, but that now it's time for me to do God-pleasing work."

Sue didn't speak but clenched her whole body, fists and shoulders and teeth.

"And God-pleasing work is living the life of the Orthodox Jew?" The doctor was all softness. "Are you sure it might not be something else—like gardening or meditation? Have you considered philanthropy, Charley, I mean, as a for-instance?"

"Do you not see what he is doing?" Zalman said. "The sharp tongue of the philosopher." Zalman jumped to his feet. The table shook under his weight, though silently, devoid of the usual collection of silver and crystal and robbing him of some drama. "Tell him what the King of the Khazars[54] told his own sharp-tongued philosopher five hundred years ago." He pointed an accusing finger. "Thy words are convincing, yet they do not correspond to what I wish to find."

"Just shut up. Would you, please?" Sue said.

"It's all right, Zalman," Charles said. And Zalman sat. "It's not how I would have put it," Charles said, "but it's how I feel. You see, Doctor—with your eyes, I mean. You see how I look, how I'm acting. No different than before. Different rituals, maybe. Different foods. But the same man. Only that I feel peaceful, fulfilled."

As Charles spoke, Sue slipped from her chair, slid to the floor as might a drunk. She did not fall over, but rested on her knees, interlocking fingers and bowing her head.

She rested in the traditional Christian pose of prayer. His wife who was mortified by a white purse after Labor Day was on her knees in front of company.

"Sue, what are you doing? Get up off the floor."

She raised her chin but kept her eyes shut.

---

[53] **Palaver**—idle chatter made in an effort to charm another.

[54] **Khazars**—tribe that dominated the Volga region of Russia from the eighth to the tenth centuries. They had converted to Judaism in the eighth century.

"What?" she said. "Do you have a monopoly on God? Are you the only one who can pray?"

"Point taken. Your point is taken."

"There is no point," she said. "I understand now. You were as desperate as I've become. God is for the desperate. For when there is nothing left to do."

I'm going to hope and pray. I'll even pray to your God, beg Him to make you forget Him.

"There is always something," Zalman said. No one acknowledged him.

"There are options, Sue." Charles was perspiring through his shirt.

Sue opened her eyes and sat on the floor, leaning on an arm, her legs at her side.

"No," she said. She did not cry, but all could tell that if she hit the wrong note, the wrong word, if she was in any way agitated further, she would lose her composure completely. "You don't seem to understand, Charles. Because you don't want to. But I do not have any idea what to do."

If there was one sacrifice Charles thought she would not be able to make it was this, to be open in front of outsiders, to look tired and overworked in front of a table set with paper plates.

"Is that what you want to hear, Charles? I'm not resigned to a damn thing. I'm not going to kill you or have you committed or dragged up to the summer house for deprogramming." Charles was at once relieved and frightened—for she had clearly considered her options. "But I will, Charley, be thinking and waiting. You can't stop me from that. I'm going to hope and pray. I'll even pray to your God, beg Him to make you forget Him. To cast you out."

"That's wrong, Sue." It sounded wrong.

"No, Charles. It's fair. More fair than you've been to me. You have an **epiphany**[55] and want everyone else to have the same one. Well, if we did, even if it was the best, greatest, holiest thing in the world. If every person had the same one, the most you would be left with is a bright idea."

"I don't know if that's theologically sound," Zalman said, twisting the pointed ends of his beard.

"It's wonderful," the doctor said. He had a look on his face full of pride.

Charles got down on the floor and sat cross-legged in front of Sue. "What does that mean, Sue? What does it mean for me?"

"It means that your moment of grace has passed. Real or not. It's gone now. You are left with life—daily life. I'm only letting you know that as much as you worry about staying in God's favor, you should worry about staying in mine. It's like taking a new lover, Charles. You're as dizzy as a schoolgirl. But remember which one of us dropped into your life and which of us has been in for the long haul. I am going to try and stick it out. But let me warn you. As quick as God came into your life, I might one day be gone."

"I can't live that way," Charles said.

---

[55] **epiphany**—sudden realization of the truth, essence, or meaning of something.

"That is what I go to sleep wishing."

Out of the corner of his eye Charles caught Dr. Birnbaum trying to slip out of the room without interrupting the conversation's flow. He watched the doctor recede, backing away with quiet steps, then turned to Sue. He turned to her and let all the resentment he felt come into his face. He let the muscles go, felt his eyelids drop and harden, spoke to her as intimately as if Zalman were not there.

"The biggest thing that ever happened to me, and you make me feel as if I should have kept it to myself."

She considered it. "True. It would have been better. I would much rather have found a box after you were gone: prayer books and skullcaps, used needles and women's underwear. At this point, at my age, it would have been easier to find it all after you were gone."

Charles looked to Zalman, who was, like the doctor, slowly making an exit.

"You're leaving me too?"

"Not as elegant as the doctor, but not so stupid as to miss when it's time to go."

"One minute," Charles said to his wife. "One minute and I'll be back," he pleaded, untucking his legs. "I'll walk him to the door. Our guest."

Charles followed the rabbi down the front hallway. Zalman put on his coat and tilted his hat forward, an extra edge against the city below.

"This is a crucial time," Charles said.

They were by the umbrella stand. Zalman pulled out a cane. He scratched at his nose with a pinkie. "It's an age-old problem. To all the great ones, tests are given. I wouldn't be surprised if the King of the Khazars faced the same one."

"What happened to the king?" Charles asked. "How does it turn out for the great ones?"

Zalman leaned the cane against the wall. "It doesn't matter. The point is they all had God. They knew in their hearts God."

Charles put a hand on Zalman's shoulder. "I'm only asking for you to tell me."

"You already know," he said. The joy drained from his face. "You know but want me to lie."

"Is that so bad?"

The rabbi's face looked long and soft; the rapture did not return. "No hope, Mr. Luger. I tell you this from one Jew to another. There is no hope for the pious."

Charles made his way back to the table only to find Sue gone, the table clean, and the chairs in place. Could it have been more than a minute? He saw the garbage can from the pantry in the middle of the kitchen, the paper tablecloth sticking out the top. A disposable dinner, the dining room as if untouched.

He started toward the bedroom and stopped at the study door. Sue was standing by the windowsill beside the tarnished candlesticks which were fused in place where the wax had run off the bases. She picked at the hardened formations, forcing her nail underneath and lifting them away from the painted wood of the sill.

"It's not sacrilegious, I hope?" She continued picking at the wax that ran over the silver necks in braids.

"No," Charles said. "I don't believe it is."

He crossed the room to stand beside Sue. He reached over for the hand that scratched at the fine layers of wax on the sill. "So it'll stay there," he said. "So what."

"It will ruin the paint," she said.

"It will make the window frame look real. Like someone lives in the apartment and uses this room."

Charles looked around the study, at the lamp and the bookcase, then out the window at the buildings and the sky. He had not read that far into the Bible and still thought God might orchestrate his rescue.

He took hold of Sue's other hand and held them both in place. He wanted her to understand that there had indeed been a change of magnitude, but that the mark it left was not great. The real difference was contained in his soul, after all.

Sue's gaze fell past him before meeting his eyes.

He tried to appear open before her, to allow Sue to observe him with the profound clarity he had only so recently come to know. Charles was desperate with willingness. He struggled to stand without judgment, to be only for Sue, to be wholly seen, wanting her to love him changed.

QUESTIONS TO CONSIDER

1. What is Charles looking for in life?
2. How do you think he finds it in being Jewish?
3. How does Sue handle the change in Charles? What is your opinion of what she does?
4. What is the status of Charles and Sue's relationship at the end of the story?
5. Who do you have more sympathy for—Charles or Sue? Explain your answer.
6. What is the tone of the story? What attitude do you think Englander wants the reader to take toward Charles and his conversion?
7. What do you think Englander is trying to say about religion and modernity?

Lucy Honig ▶

English as a Second Language

BY LUCY HONIG

Lucy Honig (1948–) is a prize-winning writer who has published two novels and a short story collection. She has always held a second job, which has ranged from farming in the Maine woods to running a human rights commission to teaching English to immigrants. Since 1995 she has taught at the School of Public Health at Boston University. "English as a Second Language" was inspired by Honig's time teaching English to immigrants in New York. Her students were from all over the world and "were struggling to live, struggling to be understood. . . . Over the course of the day I'd see things more and more through my students' eyes and finally I'd emerge from the gentle intimacy of this classroom into the tumult of the streets of lower Manhattan where, for a few moments each week, everything was brand new and totally befuddling."

Inside Room 824, Maria parked the vacuum cleaner, fastened all the locks and the safety chain and kicked off her shoes. Carefully she lay a stack of fluffy towels on the bathroom vanity. She turned the air conditioning up high and the lights down low. Then she hoisted up the skirt of her uniform and settled all the way back on the king-sized bed with her legs straight out in front of her. Her feet and ankles were swollen. She wriggled her toes. She threw her arms out in each direction and still her hands did not come near the edges of the bed. From here she could see, out the picture window, the puffs of green treetops in Central Park, the tiny people circling along the paths below. She tore open a small foil bag of cocktail peanuts and ate them very slowly, turning each one over separately with her tongue until the salt dissolved. She snapped on the TV with the remote control and flipped channels.

The big mouth game show host was kissing and hugging a woman playing on the left-hand team. Her husband and children were right there with her, and *still* he encircled her with his arms. Then he sidled up to the daughter, a girl younger than her own Giuliette, and *hugged* her and kept *holding* her, asking questions. None of his business, if this girl had a boyfriend back in Saginaw![1]

[1] Saginaw—city in central Michigan.

"Mama, you just don't understand." That's what Jorge always said when she watched TV at home. He and his teenaged friends would sit around in their torn bluejeans dropping potato chips between the cushions of her couch and laughing, **writhing**[2] with laughter while she sat like a stone.

That man pinched and kissed her, an old woman, in front of the whole world!

Now the team on the right were hugging each other, squealing, jumping up and down. They'd just won a whole new kitchen—refrigerator, dishwasher, clothes washer, microwave, *everything*! Maria could win a whole new kitchen too, someday. You just spun a wheel, picked some words. She could do that.

She saw herself on TV with Carmen and Giuliette and Jorge. Her handsome children were so quick to press the buzzers the other team never had a chance to answer first. And they got every single answer right. Her children shrieked and clapped and jumped up and down each time the board lit up. They kissed and hugged that man whenever they won a prize. That man put his hands on her beautiful young daughters. That man pinched and kissed *her*, an old woman, in front of the whole world! Imagine seeing this back home! Maria frowned, chewing on the foil wrapper. There was nobody left at home in Guatemala,[3] nobody to care if a strange man squeezed her wrinkled flesh on the TV.

"Forget it, Mama. They don't let poor people on these programs," Jorge said one day.

"But poor people need the money, they can win it here!"

Jorge sighed impatiently. "They don't give it away because you *need* it!"

It was true, she had never seen a woman with her kids say on a show: My husband's dead. Jorge knew. They made sure before they invited you that you were the right kind of people and you said the right things. Where would she put a new kitchen in her cramped apartment anyway? No hookups for a washer, no space for a two-door refrigerator. . . .

She slid sideways off the bed, carefully smoothed out the quilted spread, and squeezed her feet into her shoes. Back out in the hall she counted the bath towels in her cart to see if there were enough for the next wing. Then she wheeled the cart down the long corridor, silent on the deep blue rug.

Maria pulled the new pink dress on over her head, eased her arms into the sleeves, then let the skirt slide into place. In the mirror she saw a small dark protrusion from a large pink flower. She struggled to zip up in back, then she fixed the neck, attaching the white collar she had crocheted. She pinned the rhinestone brooch[4] on next. Shaking the pantyhose out of the package, she remembered the phrase: the cow before the horse, wasn't

[2] **writhing**—twisting or squirming; moving around.

[3] Guatemala—country in northwestern Central America.

[4] brooch—decorative pin or clasp.

that it? She should have put these on first. Well, so what. She rolled down the left leg of the nylons, stuck her big toe in, and drew the sheer fabric around her foot, unrolling it up past her knee. Then she did the right foot, careful not to catch the hose on the small flap of scar.

The right foot bled badly when she ran over the broken glass, over what had been the only window of the house. It had shattered from gunshots across the dirt yard. The chickens dashed around frantically, squawking, trying to fly, spraying brown feathers into the air. When she had seen Pedro's head turn to blood and the two oldest boys dragged away, she swallowed every word, every cry, and ran with the two girls. The fragments of glass stayed in her foot for all the days of hiding. They ran and ran and ran and somehow Jorge caught up and they were found by their own side and smuggled out. And still she was silent, until the nurse at the border went after the glass and drained the mess inside her foot. Then she had sobbed and screamed, "Aaiiee!"

"Mama stop thinking and get ready," said Carmen.

"It is too short, your skirt," Maria said in Spanish. "What will they say?"

Carmen laughed. "It's what they all wear, except for you old ladies."

"Not to work! Not to school!"

"Yes, to work, to school! And Mama, you are going for an award for your English, for all you've learned, so please speak English!"

Maria squeezed into the pink high heels and held each foot out, one by one, so she could admire the beautiful slim arch of her own instep, like the feet of the American ladies on Fifth Avenue. Carmen laughed when she saw her mother take the first faltering steps, and Maria laughed too. How much she had already practiced in secret, and still it was so hard! She teetered on them back and forth from the kitchen to the bedroom, trying to feel steady, until Carmen finally sighed and said, "Mama, quick now or you'll be late!"

She didn't know if it was a good omen or a bad one, the two Indian women on the subway. They could have been sitting on the dusty ground at the market in San ______, selling corn or clay pots, with the bright-colored striped shawls and full skirts, the black hair pulled into two braids down each back, the deeply furrowed square faces, set in those impassive expressions, seeing everything, seeing nothing. They were exactly as they must have been back home, but she was seeing them *here*, on the downtown IRT[5] from the Bronx, surrounded by businessmen in suits, kids with big radio boxes, girls in skin-tight jeans and dark purple lipstick. Above them, advertisements for family planning and TWA. They were like stone-age men sitting on the train in loincloths made from animal skins, so out of place, out of time. Yet timeless. Maria thought, they are timeless guardian spirits, here to accompany me to my honors. Did anyone else see

[5] IRT—one of the subway lines in New York City.

them? As strange as they were, nobody looked. Maria's heart pounded faster. The boys with the radios were standing right over them and never saw them. They were invisible to everyone but her. Maria was utterly convinced of it. The spirit world had come back to life, here on the number 4 train! It was a miracle!

"Mama, look, you see the grand-mothers?" said Carmen.

"Of course I see them," Maria replied, trying to hide the disappointment in her voice. So Carmen saw them too. They were not invisible. Carmen rolled her eyes and smirked **derisively**[6] as she nodded in their direction, but before she could put her derision into words, Maria become stern. "Have respect," she said. "They are the same as your father's people." Carmen's face sobered at once.

She panicked when they got to the big school by the river. "Like the United Nations," she said, seeing so much glass and brick, an endless **esplanade**[7] of concrete.

"It's only a college, Mama. People learn English here, too. And more, like nursing, electronics. This is where Anna's brother came for computers."

"Las Naciones Unidas," Maria repeated, and when the guard stopped them to ask where they were going, she answered in Spanish: to the literacy award ceremony.

"English, Mama!" whispered Carmen.

But the guard also spoke in Spanish: take the escalator to the third floor.

"See, he knows," Maria retorted.

"That's not the point," murmured Carmen, taking her mother by the hand.

Every inch of the enormous room was packed with people. She clung to Carmen and stood by the door paralyzed until Cheryl, her teacher, pushed her way to them and greeted Maria with a kiss. Then she led Maria back through the press of people to the small group of award winners from other programs. Maria smiled shakily and nodded hello.

"They're all here now!" Cheryl called out. A photographer rushed over and began to move the students closer together for a picture.

"Hey Bernie, wait for the Mayor!" someone shouted to him. He spun around, called out some words Maria did not understand, and without even turning back to them, he disappeared. But they stayed there, huddled close, not knowing if they could move. The Chinese man kept smiling, the tall black man stayed slightly crouched, the Vietnamese woman squinted, confused, her glasses still hidden in her fist. Maria saw all the cameras along the sides of the crowd, and the lights, and the people from television with video machines, and more lights. Her stomach began to jump up and down. Would she be on television, in the newspapers? Still smiling, holding his pose, the Chinese man next to her asked, "Are you nervous?"

---

[6] **derisively**—done in a way that mocks or acts superior to another.

[7] **esplanade**—flat, open stretch of pavement or grass, often beside a body of water.

"Oh yes," she said. She tried to remember the expression Cheryl had taught them. "I have worms in my stomach," she said.

He was a much bigger man than she had imagined from seeing him on TV. His face was bright red as they ushered him into the room and quickly through the crowd, just as it was his turn to take the **podium**.[8] He said hello to the other speakers and called them by their first names. The crowd drew closer to the little stage, the people standing farthest in the back pushed in. Maria tried hard to listen to the Mayor's words. "Great occasion . . . pride of our city . . . ever since I created the program . . . people who have worked so hard . . . overcoming hardship . . . come so far." Was that them? Was he talking about them already? Why were the people out there all starting to laugh? She strained to understand, but still caught only fragments of his words, "My mother used to say . . . and I said, Look, Mama . . ." He was talking about his mother now; he called her Mama, just like Maria's kids called her. But everyone laughed so hard. At his mother? She forced herself to smile; up front, near the podium, everyone could see her. She should seem to pay attention and understand. Looking out into the crowd she felt dizzy. She tried to find Carmen among all the pretty young women with big eyes and dark hair. There she was! Carmen's eyes met Maria's; Carmen waved. Maria beamed out at her. For a moment she felt like she belonged there, in this crowd. Everyone was smiling, everyone was so happy while the Mayor of New York stood at the podium telling jokes. How happy Maria felt too!

"Maria Perez grew up in the countryside of Guatemala, the oldest daughter in a family of 19 children," read the Mayor as Maria stood quaking by his side. She noticed he made a slight wheezing noise when he breathed between words. She saw the hairs in his nostrils, black and white and wiry. He paused. "Nineteen children!" he exclaimed, looking at the audience. A small gasp was passed along through the crowd. Then the Mayor looked back at the sheet of paper before him. "Maria never had a chance to learn to read and write, and she was already the mother of five children of her own when she fled Guatemala in 1980 and made her way to New York for a new start."

It was her own story, but Maria had a hard time following.

It was her own story, but Maria had a hard time following. She had to stand next to him while he read it, and her feet had started to hurt, crammed into the new shoes. She shifted her weight from one foot to the other.

"At the age of 45, while working as a chambermaid and sending her children through school, Maria herself started school for the first time. In night courses she learned to read and write in her native

[8] **podium**—stand for holding the notes of a public speaker.

Spanish. Later, as she was pursuing her G.E.D. in Spanish, she began studying English as a Second Language. This meant Maria was going to school five nights a week! Still she worked as many as 60 hours cleaning rooms at the Plaza Hotel.[9]

"Maria's ESL teacher, Cheryl Sands, says—and I quote—'Maria works harder than any student I have ever had. She is an inspiration to her classmates. Not only has she learned to read and write in her new language, but she initiated an oral history project in which she taped and transcribed interviews with other students, who have told their stories from around the world.' Maria was also one of the first in New York to apply for amnesty under the 1986 Immigration Act. Meanwhile, she has passed her enthusiasm for education to her children: her son is now a junior in high school, her youngest daughter attends the State University, and her oldest daughter, who we are proud to have with us today, is in her second year of law school on a scholarship."

Two older sons were dragged through the dirt, chickens squawking in mad confusion, feathers flying. She heard more gunshots in the distance, screams, chickens squawking. She heard, she ran. Maria looked down at her bleeding feet. Wedged tightly into the pink high heels, they throbbed.

The Mayor turned toward her. "Maria I think it's wonderful that you have taken the trouble to preserve the folklore of students from so many countries." He paused. Was she supposed to say something? Her heart stopped beating. What was folklore? What was preserved? She smiled up at him, hoping that was all she needed to do.

"Maria, tell us now, if you can, what was one of the stories you collected in your project?"

This was definitely a question, meant to be answered. Maria tried to smile again. She strained on tiptoes to reach the microphone, pinching her toes even more tightly in her shoes.

"Okay," she said, setting off a high-pitched ringing from the microphone.

The Mayor said, "Stand back," and tugged at her collar. She quickly stepped away from the microphone. "Okay," she said again, and this time there was no shrill sound. "One of my stories, from Guatemala. You want to hear?"

The Mayor put his arm around her shoulder and squeezed hard. Her first impulse was to wriggle away, but he held tight. "Isn't she wonderful?" he asked the audience. There was a low ripple of applause. "Yes, we want to hear!"

She turned and looked up at his face. Perspiration was shining on his forehead and she could see by the bright red bulge of his neck that his collar was too tight. "In my village in Guatemala," she began, "the mayor did not go along—get along—with the government so good."

"Hey, Maria," said the Mayor, "I know exactly how he felt!" The people in the audience laughed. Maria waited until they were quiet again.

---

[9] Plaza Hotel—one of New York's oldest and most luxurious hotels.

"One day our mayor met with the people in the village. Like you meet people here. A big crowd in the square."

"The people liked him, your mayor?"

"Oh, yes," said Maria. "Very much. He was very good. He tried for more roads, more doctors, new farms. He cared very much about his people."

The Mayor shook his head up and down. "Of course," he said, and again the audience laughed.

Maria said, "The next day after the meeting, the meeting in the square with all the people, soldiers come and shoot him dead."

For a second there was total silence. Maria realized she had not used the past tense and felt a deep, horrible stab of shame for herself, shame for her teacher. She was a disgrace! But she did not have more than a second of this horror before the whole audience began to laugh. What was happening? They couldn't be laughing at her bad verbs? They couldn't be laughing at her dead mayor! They laughed louder and louder and suddenly flashbulbs were going off around her, the TV cameras swung in close, too close, and the Mayor was grabbing her by the shoulders again, holding her tight, posing for one camera after another as the audience burst into wild applause. But she hadn't even finished! Why were they laughing?

"What timing, huh?" said the Mayor over the uproar. "What d'ya think, the Republicans put her here, or maybe the Board of Estimate?" Everyone laughed even louder and he still clung to her and cameras still moved in close, lights kept going off in her face and she could see nothing but the sharp white poof! of light over and over again. She looked for Carmen and Cheryl, but the white poof! poof! poof! blinded her. She closed her eyes and listened to the uproar, now beginning to subside, and in her mind's eye saw chickens trying to fly, chickens fluttering around the yard littered with broken glass.

He squeezed her shoulders again and leaned into the microphone. "There are ways to get rid of mayors, and ways to get rid of mayors, huh Maria?"

The surge of laughter rose once more, reached a **crescendo**,[10] and then began to subside again. "But wait," said the Mayor. The cameramen stepped back a bit, poising themselves for something new.

"I want to know just one more thing, Maria," said the Mayor, turning to face her directly again. The crowd quieted. He waited a few seconds more, then asked his question. "It says here 19 children. What was it like growing up in a house with 19 children? How many *bathrooms* did you have?"

Her stomach dropped and twisted as the mayor put his hand firmly on the back of her neck and pushed her toward the microphone again. It was absolutely quiet now in the huge room. Everyone was waiting for her to speak. She cleared her throat and made the microphone do the shrill hum. Startled, she jumped back. Then there was silence. She took a big, trembling breath.

[10] **crescendo**—climax of loudness.

"We had no bathrooms there, Mister Mayor," she said. "Only the outdoors."

The clapping started immediately, then the flashbulbs burning up in her face. The Mayor turned to her, put a hand on each of her shoulders, bent lower and kissed her! Kissed her on the cheek!

"Isn't she terrific?" he asked the audience, his hand on the back of her neck again, drawing her closer to him.

"Isn't she terrific?" he asked the audience, his hand on the back of her neck again, drawing her closer to him. The audience clapped louder, faster. "Isn't she just the greatest?"

She tried to smile and open her eyes, but the lights were still going off—poof! poof!—and the noise was deafening.

"Mama, look, your eyes were closed there, too," **chided**[11] Jorge, sitting on the floor in front of the television set.

Maria had watched the camera move from the announcer at the studio desk to her own stout form in bright pink, standing by the Mayor.

"In my village in Guatemala," she heard herself say, and the camera showed her wrinkled face close up, eyes open now but looking nowhere. Then the mayor's face filled the screen, his forehead glistening, and then suddenly all the people in the audience, looking ahead, **enrapt**,[12] took his place. Then there was her wrinkled face again, talking without a smile. ". . . soldiers come and shoot him dead." Maria winced, hearing the wrong tense of her verbs. The camera shifted from her face to the Mayor. In the brief moment of shamed silence after she'd uttered those words, the Mayor drew his finger like a knife across his throat. And—the audience began to laugh.

'Turn it off!" she yelled to Jorge. "Off! this minute!"

Late that night she sat alone in the unlighted room, soaking her feet in Epsom salts. The glow of the television threw shadows across the wall, but the sound was off. The man called Johnny was on the screen, talking. The people in the audience and the men in the band and the movie stars sitting on the couch all had their mouths wide open in what she knew were screams of laughter while Johnny wagged his tongue. Maria heard nothing except brakes squealing below on the street and the lonely clanging of garbage cans in the alley.

She thought about her English class and remembered the pretty woman, Ling, who often fell asleep in the middle of a lesson. The other Chinese students all teased her. Everyone knew that she sewed coats in a sweatshop all day. After the night class she took the subway to the Staten Island Ferry, and after the ferry crossing she had to take a bus home. Her parents were old and sick and she did all their cooking and cleaning late at night. She struggled to keep awake in class; it seemed to take all her energy simply to smile and listen. She said very little and the teacher never forced

[11] **chided**—stated disapproval; scolded.

[12] **enrapt**—spellbound, fascinated.

her, but she fell further and further behind. They called her the Quiet One.

One day just before the course came to an end the Quiet One asked to speak. There was no reason, no **provocation**[13]—they'd been talking informally about their summer plans—but Ling spoke with a sudden urgency. Her English was very slow. Seeing what a terrible effort it was for her, the classmates all tried to help when she searched for words.

"In my China village there was a teacher," Ling began. "Man teacher." She paused. "All children love him. He teach mathematic. He very—" She stopped and looked up toward the ceiling. Then she gestured with her fingers around her face.

"Handsome!" said Charlene, the oldest of the three Haitian sisters in the class.

Ling smiled broadly. "Handsome! Yes, he very handsome. Family very rich before. He have sister go to Hong Kong who have many, many money."

"*Much* money," said Maria,

"Much, much money," repeated Ling thoughtfully. "Teacher live in big house."

"In China? Near you?"

"Yes. Big house with much old picture." She stopped and furrowed her forehead, as if to gather words inside of it.

"Art? Paint? Pictures like that?" asked Xavier.

Ling nodded eagerly. "Yes. In big house. Most big house in village."

"But big house, money, rich like that, bad in China," said Fu Wu. "Those year, Government bad to you. How they let him do?"

"In *my* country," said Carlos, "government bad to you if you got small house, *no* money."

"Me too," said Maria.

"Me too," said Charlene.

The Chinese students laughed.

Ling shrugged and shook her head. "Don't know. He have big house. Money gone, but keep big house. Then I am little girl." She held her hand low to the floor.

"I *was* a little girl," Charlene said gently.

"I *was*," said Ling. "Was, was." She giggled for a moment, then seemed to spend some time in thought. "We love him. All children love—all children did loved him. He giving tea in house. He was—was—so handsome!" She giggled. All the women in the class giggled. "He very nice. He learn music, he go . . . he went to school far away."

"America?"

Ling shook her head. "Oh no, no. You know, another . . . west."

"Europa!" exclaimed Maria proudly. "Espain!"

"No, no, another."

"France!" said Patricia, Charlene's sister. "He went to school in France?"

"Yes, France," said Ling. Then she stopped again, this time for a whole minute. The others waited patiently. No one said a word. Finally she continued, "But big boys in more old school not like him. He too handsome."

"Oooh!" sang out a chorus of women. "Too handsome!"

---

[13] **provocation**—incitement to action.

"The boys were jealous," said Carlos.

Ling seized the word. "Jealous! Jealous! They very jealous. He handsome, he study France, he very nice to children, he give tea and cake in big house, he show picture on wall." Her torrent of words came to an end and she began to think again, visibly, her brow furrowing. "Big school boys, they . . ." She stopped.

"Jealous!" sang out the others.

"Yes," she said, shaking her head "no." "But more. More bad. Hate. They hate him."

"That's bad," said Patricia.

"Yes, very bad," Ling paused, looking at the floor. "And they heat."

"Hate."

"No, they heat."

All the class looked puzzled. Heat? Heat? They turned to Cheryl.

The teacher spoke for the first time. "Hit? Ling, do you mean hit? They hit him?" Cheryl slapped the air with her hand.

Ling nodded, her face somehow serious and smiling at the same time. "Hit many time. And also so." She scooted her feet back and forth along the floor.

"Oooh," exclaimed Charlene, frowning. "They kicked him with the feet."

"Yes," said Ling. "They kicked him with the feet and hit him with the hands, many many time they hit, they kick."

"Where this happened?" asked Xavier.

"In the school. In classroom like . . ." She gestured to mean their room.

"In the school?" asked Xavier. "But other people were they there? They say stop, no?"

"No. Little children in room. They cry, they . . ." She covered her eyes with her hand, then uncovered them. "Big boys kick and hit. No one stop. No one help."

Everyone in class fell silent. Maria remembered: they could not look at one another then. They could not look at their teacher.

Ling continued, "They break him, very hurt much place." She stopped. They all fixed their stares on Ling, they could bear looking only at her. "Many place," she said. Her face had not changed, it was still half smiling. But now there were drops coming from her eyes, a single tear down each side of her now. Maria would never forget it. Ling's face did not move or wrinkle or frown. Her body was absolutely still. Her shoulders did not quake. Nothing in the shape or motion of her eyes or mouth changed. None of the things that Maria had always known happen when you cry happened when Ling shed tears. Just two drops rolled slowly down her two pale cheeks as she smiled.

"He very hurt. He was very hurt. He blood many place. Boys go away. Children cry. Teacher break and hurt. Later he in hospital. I go there visit him." She stopped, looking thoughtful. "I went there." One continuous line of wetness glistened down each cheek. "My mother, my father say don't go, but I see him. I say, 'You be better?' But he hurt. Doctors no did helped. He alone. No doctor. No nurse. No medicine. No family." She stopped. They all stared in silence for several moments.

Finally Carlos said, "Did he went home?"

Ling shook her head. "He go home but no walk." She stopped. Maria could not help watching those single lines of tears moving down the pale round face. "A year, more, no walk. Then go."

"Go where?"

"End."

Again there was a deep silence. Ling looked down, away from them, her head bent low.

"Oh, no," murmured Charlene. "He died."

Maria felt the catch in her throat, the sudden wetness of tears on her own two cheeks, and when she looked up she saw that all the other students, men and women both, were crying too.

Maria wiped her eyes. Suddenly all her limbs ached, her bones felt stiff and old. She took her feet from the basin and dried them with a towel. Then she turned off the television and went to bed.

QUESTIONS TO CONSIDER

1. Why did Maria take her family from Guatemala?
2. What has Maria done to deserve her award?
3. What is your view of the degree of her success?
4. What is being compared and contrasted in the award sequence between the Mayor and Maria?
5. What is the meaning of Ling's story? How does it reflect the difficulty of the immigrant experience?

Magazines in America

Since their beginnings in colonial times, magazines have played a major role in shaping American literature. Magazines have provided a market for the work of both new and established writers. Influential magazine editors have guided both writers and readers.

▲
Edgar Allan Poe edited a number of magazines, expressing his literary theories in influential criticism, such as his review of Nathaniel Hawthorne's *Twice-Told Tales* in *Graham's Magazine*, May 1842.

Founded in 1857 and first edited by James Russell Lowell, the *Atlantic Monthly* confined its pages to well-known New England writers in its early years. ▶

▲
By the late 1850s, with Sarah Josepha Hale as editor, *Godey's Lady's Book* had become the most successful magazine in the country and an important influence on American taste.

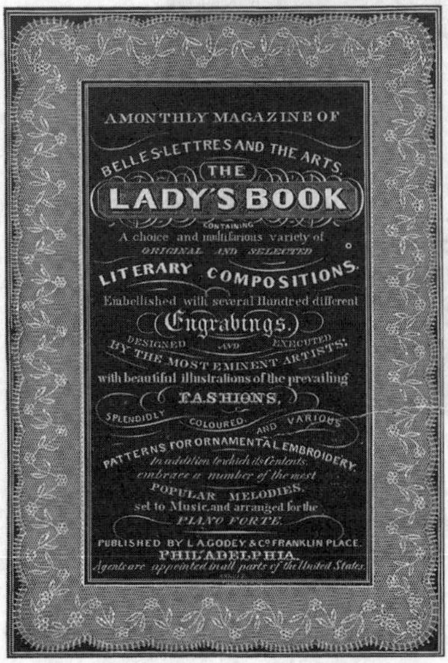

A MONTHLY MAGAZINE OF
BELLES-LETTRES AND THE ARTS.
THE
LADY'S BOOK
CONTAINING
A choice and multifarious variety of
ORIGINAL AND SELECTED
LITERARY COMPOSITIONS.
Embellished with several Hundred different
Engravings.
DESIGNED AND EXECUTED
BY THE MOST EMINENT ARTISTS;
with beautiful illustrations of the prevailing
FASHIONS,
SPLENDIDLY COLOURED. AND VARIOUS
PATTERNS FOR ORNAMENTAL EMBROIDERY.
In addition to which its Contents
embrace a number of the most
POPULAR MELODIES,
set to Music and arranged for the
PIANO FORTE.
PUBLISHED BY L.A.GODEY & Co FRANKLIN PLACE.
PHILADELPHIA.
Agents are appointed in all parts of the United States.

◀ Founded in 1830, *Godey's Lady's Book* published Poe, Hawthorne, and Harriet Beecher Stowe—and a great amount of sentimental fiction.

▲
Under the editorship of William Dean Howells in the 1870s, the *Atlantic Monthly* began to include the work of newer authors from the South, Midwest, and Far West.

Founded in 1850, *Harper's Magazine* in its early years drew heavily on British writers, but later published such Americans as Herman Melville, Henry James, and Sarah Orne Jewett.

SCRIBNER'S
MAGAZINE

PUBLISHED MONTHLY
WITH ILLUSTRATIONS

VOLUME I JANUARY - JUNE

1887

·CHARLES SCRIBNER'S SONS NEW YORK·
·F. WARNE & Cº LONDON·

Known for its openness to new authors, *Scribner's Magazine* (1887–1939) was the first important literary magazine to publish the fiction of Ernest Hemingway and Thomas Wolfe.

▲ In 1893, S. S. McClure (1857–1949) founded *McClure's Magazine,* which soon became the most influential periodical in America. *McClure's* was famous for attacks on corruption in politics and business, but also published fiction by such writers as O. Henry, Jack London, and Willa Cather.

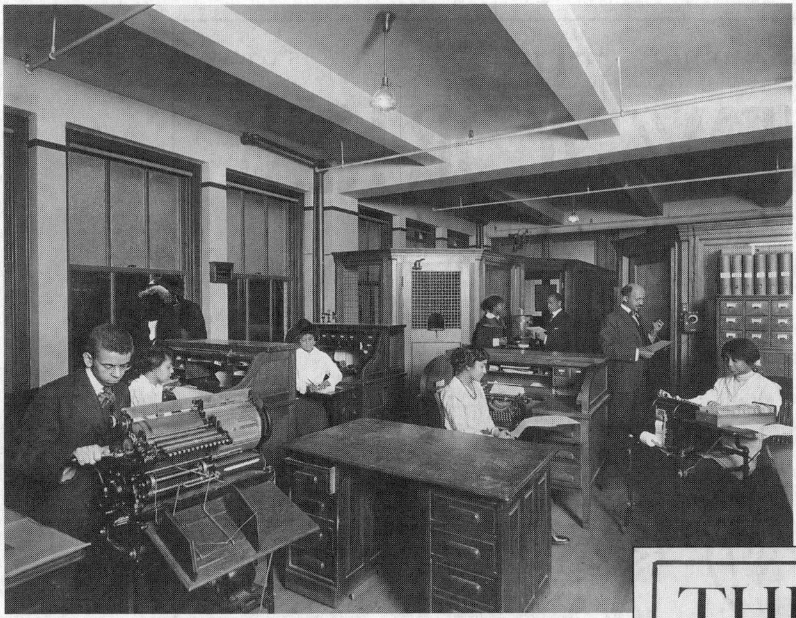

▲
W. E. B. DuBois (second from right) is shown in the editorial offices of *The Crisis* shortly after its founding in 1910.

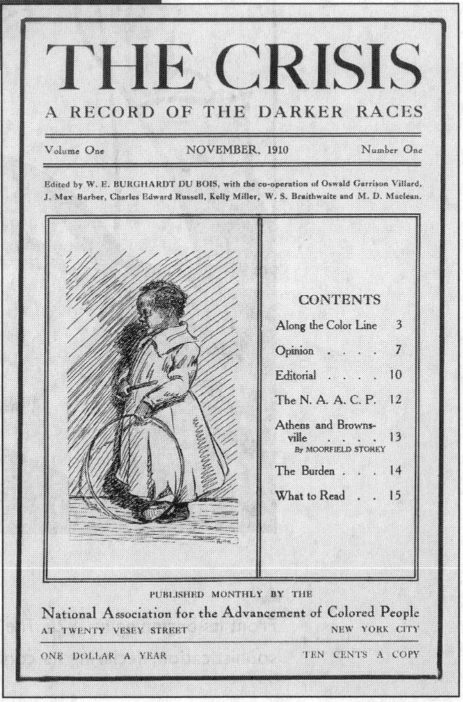

THE CRISIS

A RECORD OF THE DARKER RACES

Volume One NOVEMBER, 1910 Number One

Edited by W. E. BURGHARDT DU BOIS, with the co-operation of Oswald Garrison Villard, J. Max Barber, Charles Edward Russell, Kelly Miller, W. S. Braithwaite and M. D. Maclean.

CONTENTS

PUBLISHED MONTHLY BY THE
National Association for the Advancement of Colored People
AT TWENTY VESEY STREET NEW YORK CITY
ONE DOLLAR A YEAR TEN CENTS A COPY

Edited by W. E. B. DuBois from its founding until 1932, *The Crisis* published important African-American writers of the Harlem Renaissance era. ▶

From its beginning in 1925, *The New Yorker* magazine established a style of urbane sophistication, declaring its contents "not for the old lady in Dubuque."

Harold Ross founded *The New Yorker* and edited it until his death in 1951, assembling an extraordinary group of staff and contributors that included Dorothy Parker, James Thurber, Joseph Mitchell, and William Maxwell. ▶

Under the direction of fiction editors like William Maxwell, *The New Yorker* had a profound influence on the style of the modern American short story.
▼

▲

The Saturday Evening Post became one of the most successful magazines in American history by publishing stories with mass appeal.

This photograph of a newsstand in Omaha in 1938 gives an idea of what the American public's taste in fiction was then. ▶

MORNING
EVENING AND SUNDAY
1939 CARS
IN THE AUTOMOTIVE ISSUE
Collier's
TIME
WESTERN
AMAZING
BETTER ENGLISH
College Humor
SUCCESSFUL FARMING
POULTRY
THE NEW YORKER
ARGOSY
DOUBLE DETECTIVE
ACTION STORIES
NORTHWEST
10 BLACK BOOK DETECTIVE
Lariat
ASTOUNDING SCIENCE-FICTION
McCALL'S
SCREENLAND
Silver Screen
True Story
REDBOOK
LIFE
Look
Companion
The Billboard
SEE THE 1939 CARS
PIC
PHOTOPLAY
Your Life
Reader's Digest

Magazines still serve a significant role in publishing and reviewing American fiction, as this sampling of present-day publications indicates.

July/August 2000
$4.95 USA/$5.95 CAN
BOOK
The Magazine for the Reading Life
Toni Morrison's
The Bluest Eye
and nine other
first novels you
shouldn't have missed
Stephen Ambrose
on the railroad that joined America
Sherman Alexie
the toughest Indian writer
Larry McMurtry
books his Texas hometown
plus reviews of Michael Ondaatje, Jane Austen, Mario Puzo and more
Spring 2000 $7.95
Prairie Schooner
Writing from Alaska
3 2000
$6.00
DORIS LESSING
Ben, in the World
Partisan Review
GOING TO THE MOVIES
Morris Dickstein
REVIEWS
AT THE GALLERIES
Karen Wilkin
POETRY
Millicent Bell
Kay Ryan
WILLIAM PHILLIPS
Comment
ADAM MICHNIK
Jan Kott's Venom
RICHARD MOORE
On Gogol's "Overcoat"
ADAM ZAGAJEWSKI
Another Beauty
THOMAS NOWOTNY
Austria—A Pariah Country
STEPHEN SCHWARTZ
Rebuilding the Balkans?
DOMINIQUE SCHNAPPER
Memory in Politics
ELIZABETH DALTON
Sex and Race in Wide Sargasso Sea
TRACY SALVAGE
Jean Hélion's Lasting Judgment
MAXIM D. SHRAYER
On Russian Village Prose
The Iowa Review
VOLUME THIRTY
NUMBER ONE
2000
Jay Hopler, Josie Kearns, Paul Epstein, Joanna Klink, Nachoem Wijnberg, Arpine Konyalian Grenier, Alissa Leigh, Laurence Goldstein, Sarah Manguso, Andrew Osborn, Gary Fincke, Angela Pneuman, Dawn Diez Willis, Michael Theune, Shyam Oberoi, Ricardo Pau-Llosa, Angela Regas, Lia Purpura, Dara Wier, Dan Pope, Brad Richard, Alyce Miller, Terry Evans, Richard Siken, Carl Phillips, Mark Axelrod, Diane Furtney, Jack Shadoian, Jenny Hamilton, Natalia Rachel Singer, Tom Whalen, John Beer
$6.95 U.S.
$9.95 Can.

Texts

201 "Sophistication" from *Sherwood Anderson's Winesburg, Ohio* edited by Ray Lewis White, 1997. Reprinted with the permission of Ohio University Press/Swallow Press, Athens, Ohio.

220 "Drenched in Light" as taken from *The Complete Stories* by Zora Neale Hurston. Introduction copyright © 1995 by Henry Louis Gates, Jr., and Sieglinde Lemke. Compilation copyright © 1995 by Vivian Bowden, Lois J. Hurston Gaston, Clifford Hurston, Lucy Ann Hurston, Winifred Hurston Clark, Zora Mack Goins, Edgar Hurston, Sr., and Barbara Hurston Lewis. Afterword and Bibliography copyright © 1995 by Henry Louis Gates. Reprinted by permission of HarperCollins Publishers, Inc. "Drenched in Light" was originally published in *Opportunity,* December 1924.

227 "Soldier's Home." Reprinted with permission of Scribner, a Division of Simon & Schuster, from *In Our Time* by Ernest Hemingway. Copyright 1925 by Charles Scribner's Sons. Copyright renewed 1953 by Ernest Hemingway.

234 "Glory in the Daytime", copyright 1933, renewed © 1961 by Dorothy Parker, from *The Portable Dorothy Parker* by Dorothy Parker. Used by permission of Viking Penguin, a division of Penguin Putnam Inc.

246 From "Babylon Revisited." Reprinted with permission of Scribner, a Division of Simon & Schuster, from *The Short Stories of F. Scott Fitzgerald,* edited by Matthew J. Bruccoli. Copyright 1931 by The Curtis Publishing Company. Copyright renewed © 1959 by Francis Scott Fitzgerald Lanahan.

263 "The Greatest Man in the World" from *The Middle-Aged Man on the Flying Trapeze,* copyright © 1935 by James Thurber. Copyright © renewed 1963 by Helen Thurber and Rosemary A. Thurber. Reprinted by arrangement with Rosemary A. Thurber and Barbara Hogenson Agency. All rights reserved.

270 "Rope" from *Flowering Judas and Other Stories,* copyright 1930 and renewed 1958 by Katherine Anne Porter, reprinted by permission of Harcourt, Inc.

276 "The Far and the Near." Reprinted with the permission of Scribner, a Division of Simon & Schuster, from *From Death to Morning* by Thomas Wolfe. Copyright 1935 by Charles Scribner's Sons; copyright renewed © 1963 by Paul Gitlin, Administrator C.T.A. of the Estate of Thomas Wolfe.

296 "The Man Who Saw the Flood" from *Eight Men* by Richard Wright. Copyright 1940 ©1961 by Richard Wright. Copyright renewed 1989 by Ellen Wright. Reprinted by permission of HarperCollins Publishers, Inc.

301 "The Tall Men" from *Collected Stories of William Faulkner* by William Faulkner. Copyright © 1941 & renewed 1969 Estelle Faulkner & Jill Faulkner Summers. Reprinted by permission of Random House, Inc.

312 "A Visit of Charity" from *A Curtain of Green and Other Stories,* copyright 1941 and renewed 1969 by Eudora Welty, reprinted by permission of Harcourt, Inc.

318 "The Patterns of Love" from *Over By the River and Other Stories* by William Maxwell. Copyright 1945 by William Maxwell. Reprinted by permission of Alfred A. Knopf, a Division of Random House, Inc.

325 "The German" from *The Honeyed Peace* by Martha Gellhorn, 1953. Reprinted by permission of the Martha Gellhorn Estate.

328 "Day After Tomorrow" an excerpt from *Dawn Powell at Her Best* by Dawn Powell published by Steerforth Press of South Royalton, Vermont, 802-763-2808. Copyright © 1994 by the Estate of Dawn Powell. Reprinted by permission.

335 "The Bride" from *The Rose Garden* by Maeve Brennan. Copyright © 1999 by Maeve Brennan. Reprinted by permission of Counterpoint Press, a member of Perseus Books, L.L.C.

340 "Gimpel the Fool" by Isaac Bashevis Singer, translated by Saul Bellow, copyright 1953, 1954 by The Viking Press, Inc. renewed © 1981, 1982 by Viking Penguin, Inc., from *A Treasury of Yiddish Stories* by Irving Howe and Eliezer Greenberg. Used by permission of Viking Penguin, a division of Penguin Putnam, Inc.

352 "The Magic Barrel" from *The Magic Barrel* by Bernard Malamud. Reprinted by permission of Russell & Volkening as agents for the author. Copyright © 1954, 1958 by Bernard Malamud, renewed 1986 by Bernard Malamud.

366 "Everything That Rises Must Converge" from *The Complete Stories* by Flannery O'Connor. Copyright © 1971 by the Estate of Mary Flannery O'Connor. Reprinted by permission of Farrar, Straus and Giroux, LLC.

402 "Tell Me A Riddle" from *Tell Me A Riddle* by Tillie Olsen. Introduction by John Leonard, copyright © 1956, 1957, 1960, 1961 by Tillie Olsen. Introduction © 1994, by Dell Publishing. Used by permission of Dell Publishing, a division of Random House, Inc.

431 "Sonny's Blues" © 1965 by James Baldwin was originally published in *Partisan Review.* Copyright renewed. Collected in *Going to Meet the Man,* published by Vintage Books. Reprinted by arrangement with The James Baldwin Estate.

457 "Roselily" from *In Love & Trouble: Stories of Black Women,* copyright © 1972 by Alice Walker, reprinted by permission of Harcourt, Inc.

462 "The Student's Wife" from *Will You Please Be Quiet, Please?* by Raymond Carver. Reprinted by permission of International Creative Management, Inc. Copyright © 1991 by Tess Gallagher.

469 "Snares" by Louise Erdrich. Copyright © 1987 by Louise Erdrich, reprinted with the permission of The Wylie Agency, Inc.

478 "The Water Faucet Vision" by Gish Jen. Copyright © 1987 by Gish Jen. First published in *Nimrod*. Reprinted by permission of the author.
487 "Daughter of Invention" from *How the Garcia Girls Lost Their Accents.* Copyright © 1991 by Julia Alvarez. Published by Plume, an imprint of Dutton Signet, a division of Penguin USA, Inc., and originally in hardcover by Algonquin Books of Chapel Hill. Reprinted by permission of Susan Bergholz Literary Services, New York. All rights reserved.
498 "Divine Providence" by Sandra Cisneros. Copyright © 1992 by Sandra Cisneros. First published in *New Chicana/Chicano Writing*, ed. Charles Tatum, University of Arizona, 1992. Reprinted by permission of Susan Bergholz Literary Services, New York. All rights reserved.
501 "This Is What It Means to Say Phoenix, Arizona" from *The Lone Ranger and Tonto Fistfight in Heaven* by Sherman Alexie. Copyright © 1993 by Sherman Alexie. Used by permission of Grove/Atlantic, Inc.
511 "The Night in Question" from *The Night in Question* by Tobias Wolff. Copyright © 1996 by Tobias Wolff. Reprinted by permission of Alfred A. Knopf, a Division of Random House, Inc.
519 "The Third and Final Continent" from *Interpreter of Maladies* by Jhumpa Lahiri. Copyright © 1999 by Jhumpa Lahiri. Reprinted by permission of Houghton Mifflin Company. All rights reserved.
535 "The Gilgul of Park Avenue" from *For the Relief of Unbearable Urges* by Nathan Englander. Copyright © 1999 by Nathan Englander. Reprinted by permission of Alfred A. Knopf, a Division of Random House, Inc.
555 "English as a Second Language" is from The *Truly Needy and Other Stories* by Lucy Honig, © 1999 by University of Pittsburgh Press. Reprinted by permission of the University of Pittsburgh Press.

Images

Illustration credits: (T) top, (C) center, (B) bottom, (L) left, (R)right.

cover Fairfield Porter (American, 1907–1975), *Untitled (First Avenue)*, c. 1945. Oil on canvas, 32 x 26 1/4 in., The Parrish Art Museum, Southampton, N.Y., Gift of the Estate of Fairfield Porter (1980.10.16). Photo: Gary Mamay. **x, 1, 2 TL** Courtesy Library of Congress. **2 TR** © Denver Public Library. **2BL, 2BR, 3TL** Courtesy Library of Congress. **3TR** © The Granger Collection. **3BL, 3BR, 4** Courtesy Library of Congress. **5TL** © The Granger Collection. **5TR, 5BL, 5BR, 6, 21, 36, 41, 71** Courtesy Library of Congress. **80** © University of Virginia Library. **94** Courtesy Library of Congress. **107** © The Newberry Library/Stock Montage. **111** Courtesy Library of Congress. **121** Courtesy National Archives. **131, 167–171** Courtesy Library of Congress. **172** Nebraska State Historical Society. **173** © Archive Photos. **174T** Courtesy Library of Congress. **174B** © JFK Library. **175T** Bettman/Corbis. **175B** Courtesy Library of Congress. **176** © Flannery O'Connor Collection, Ina Dillard Russell Library, Georgia College & State University. **177** Courtesy Library of Congress. **178, 179** © Theo Westenberger/Liaison Agency. **180–182, 183TL, 183TR, 183BL** Courtesy Library of Congress. **183BR** Corbis/Bettman. **184, 201, 208, 220, 227, 234, 246, 263, 270, 276** Courtesy Library of Congress. **280** © The Granger Collection. **281** Courtesy Library of Congress. **282T** © The Granger Collection. **282B** Courtesy Library of Congress. **283L** © SuperStock International. **283R** © Bettman/Corbis. **284T, B** Courtesy Library of Congress. **285T** © Timepix. **285B, 286T, 286B** Bettman/Corbis. **287** ©Timepix. **288T** Courtesy National Archives. **288** Book Cover from *The Collected Stories of Eudora Welty*, copyright © 1980 by Eudora Welty, reprinted by permission of Harcourt, Inc. **289T** © Random House. **289B** Archive Photos/SAGA/Frank Capri. **290** Liaison Agency. **291T** © AP/World Wide. **292–295, 301, 312, 318, 325, 328** Courtesy Library of Congress. **335** © Karl Bissinger. **340** Courtesy National Archives. **352** Courtesy Library of Congress. **366** © Georgia College. **379–395** Courtesy Library of Congress. **396** © Archive Photos. **397** Courtesy Library of Congress. **398–399** © Corbis. **400T** © Jerry Bauer Photography. **400B:TL** Courtesy Library of Congress. **TR** © Russell Kightley Media. **BL, R** Courtesy Library of Congress. **401TL** © Archive Photos. **401TR** © Jerry Bauer Photography. **401B:TL** © NASA. **TR** © Robin Adshead/Corbis. **BL** ©Reuters/David Brauchli/ Archive Photos. **BR** © Jacques Chenet/Corbis. **402** © Jerry Bauer Photography. **431** Courtesy Library of Congress. **457** © Archive Photos/SAGA/Frank Capri. **462** © Chester Higgins, JR/New York Times. **469, 478, 487** © Jerry Bauer Photography. **498** © Random House. **501, 511, 519** © Jerry Bauer Photography. **535** © Lawrence Schwartzwald/Liaison Agency. **555** © Joe Anzalone/University of Pittsburgh Press. **566L** Courtesy Library of Congress. **566R** © Courtesy of the *Atlantic Monthly.* **567T** © Archive Photos. **567B** © The Granger Collection. **568** © Corbis. **569T** © Hulton Getty Picture Library. **569B** Courtesy Library of Congress. **570** © The Granger Collection. **571** © Corbis. **572** © 1925, 1962 The New Yorker. **573T** © Archive Photos. **573B** Courtesy Library of Congress. **574, 575** Courtesy Library of Congress. **576C** *The Kenyon Review*, New Series, Spring 2000, Vol. XXII, No. 2, photo by Mary Black Kinsman. **576R** © *Ploughshares*, published by Emerson College, Spring 2000 Vol. 26/No. 1. **577T** © *Book* 2000. **557B** Photograph by Terry Evans for *The Iowa Review.* **577L** *Prairie Schooner*: © University of Nebraska Press, Cover photo by John Creed. **577R** © *The Partisan Review*, March 2000.

Index of Themes

Many selections appear under more than one theme.

Small Towns and the Countryside

The Idea of Tradition

The Artist

Index of Authors and Titles